HUMAN GEOGRAPHY

I A SPATIAL PERSPECTIVE I

NATIONAL GEOGRAPHIC

Bednarz   I   Bockenhauer   I   Hiebert

Acknowledgments

Grateful acknowledgment is given to the authors, artists, photographers, museums, publishers, and agents for permission to reprint copyrighted material. Every effort has been made to secure the appropriate permission. If any omissions have been made or if corrections are required, please contact the Publisher.

AP® is a trademark registered by the College Board, which is not affiliated with, and does not endorse, this product.

Acknowledgments and credits continue on page R26.

For product information and technology assistance, contact us at Customer & Sales Support, **888-915-3276**

For permission to use material from this text or product, submit all requests online at **www.cengage.com/permissions**

Further permissions questions can be emailed to **permissionrequest@cengage.com**

National Geographic Learning | Cengage
1 N. State Street, Suite 900
Chicago, IL 60602

National Geographic Learning, a Cengage company, is a provider of quality core and supplemental educational materials for the PreK-12, adult education, and ELT markets. Cengage is a leading provider of customized learning solutions with employees residing in nearly 40 different countries and sales in more than 125 countries around the world. Find your local representative at **NGL.Cengage.com/RepFinder.**

Visit National Geographic Learning online at **NGL.Cengage.com.**

ISBN: 978-0-357-11908-2

Printed in the United States of America

Print Number: 01
Print Year: 2020

NATIONAL GEOGRAPHIC EXPLORERS, PHOTOGRAPHERS, AND AFFILIATES

LYNSEY ADDARIO
Photographer

WILLIAM ALLARD
Photographer

ANNA ANTONIOU
Explorer

SHABANA BASIJ-RASIKH
Explorer

JENNIFER BURNEY
Explorer

ADJANY COSTA
Explorer

T. H. CULHANE
Explorer

ZACHARY DAMATO
Explorer

WADE DAVIS
Explorer

GUILLERMO DE ANDA
Explorer

JASON DE LEÓN
Explorer

MEGHAN DHALIWAL
Explorer

AARON VINCENT ELKAIM
Photographer

MARIA SILVINA FENOGLIO
Explorer

CHARLES FITZPATRICK
Esri

MICHAEL FRACHETTI
Explorer

CAROLINE GERDES
Explorer

JERRY GLOVER
Explorer

DAVID GUTTENFELDER
Photographer

FRED HIEBERT
Archaeologist-in-Residence

HINDOU OUMAROU IBRAHIM
Explorer

SANDHYA NARAYANAN
Explorer

SARAH PARCAK
Explorer

BILL PARKINSON
Explorer

DANIEL RAVEN-ELLISON
Explorer

ANDRÉS RUZO
Explorer

PARDIS SABETI
Explorer

ENRIC SALA
Explorer-in-Residence

PAUL SALOPEK
Explorer

AZIZ ABU SARAH
Explorer

LILLYGOL SEDAGHAT
Explorer

SHAH SELBE
Explorer

NORA SHAWKI
Explorer

JOHN STANMEYER
Photographer

GEORGE STEINMETZ
Photographer

TRISTRAM STUART
Explorer

AMY TOENSING
Photographer

MICHAEL WESCH
Explorer

Cape Town, South Africa

WORLD POLITICAL MAP xviii
WORLD PHYSICAL MAP xx
FOREWORD 1

| UNIT 1 |

THINKING GEOGRAPHICALLY

.... 2

NATIONAL GEOGRAPHIC EXPLORER ENRIC SALA: Safeguarding Pristine Seas 4

CHAPTER 1
THE POWER OF GEOGRAPHY: GEOGRAPHIC THINKING   6

1.1 WHAT IS HUMAN GEOGRAPHY? 7
  Case Study: New Orleans—Site vs. Situation 12
  National Geographic Explorer Adjany Costa: Conserving the Delta 14

1.2 SPATIAL PATTERNS: SCALE AND REGION 15
  Case Study: India—Regional Differences in Scale 19

1.3 GLOBALIZATION AND SUSTAINABILITY 20

CHAPTER 1 SUMMARY & REVIEW 24

CHAPTER 2
GEOGRAPHIC INQUIRY: DATA, TOOLS, AND TECHNOLOGY   26

2.1 THINKING LIKE A GEOGRAPHER: THE GEO-INQUIRY PROCESS 27

2.2 GEOGRAPHIC DATA AND TOOLS 29
  Case Study: Detroit—GIS Helps Find Safer Routes 33
  National Geographic Explorer Sarah Parcak: Protecting Archaeological Sites 35

2.3 UNDERSTANDING MAPS 36

2.4 THE POWER OF DATA 44
  National Geographic Explorer Shah Selbe: Deploying Technology for Conservation Purposes .. 47

CHAPTER 2 SUMMARY & REVIEW 48

UNIT 1

WRITING ACROSS UNITS, REGIONS & SCALES 50

MAPS & MODELS ARCHIVE 52

Shenzhen, China

UNIT 2

POPULATION AND MIGRATION
PATTERNS AND PROCESSES 50

NATIONAL GEOGRAPHIC EXPLORER PAUL SALOPEK: Out of Eden, A Walk Through Time 60

CHAPTER 3
PATTERNS OF POPULATION   62

3.1 WHERE PEOPLE LIVE 63
    National Geographic Explorer Lillygol Sedaghat:
    Transforming Trash 69

3.2 CONSEQUENCES OF POPULATION
    DISTRIBUTION 70
    Case Study: Population Distribution at the
    Country Scale 72

3.3 POPULATION COMPOSITION 74

3.4 MEASURING GROWTH AND DECLINE 77
    Feature: Examining Population Pyramids at
    Different Scales 83

CHAPTER 3 SUMMARY & REVIEW 84

CHAPTER 4
POPULATION GROWTH
AND DECLINE   86

4.1 WHY POPULATIONS GROW AND DECLINE 87

4.2 THEORIES OF POPULATION CHANGE 92
    National Geographic Explorer Pardis Sabeti:
    Cracking the Genetic Code 97
    Case Study: Zika Virus in South and North America ... 98

4.3 POPULATION POLICIES 99
    Case Study: China's Population Policies 100

4.4 CONSEQUENCES OF
    DEMOGRAPHIC CHANGE 103

CHAPTER 4 SUMMARY & REVIEW 108

CHAPTER 5
MIGRATION   110

5.1 WHY DO PEOPLE MIGRATE? 111

5.2 TYPES OF MIGRATION 115
    National Geographic Explorer Jason De León:
    Documenting the Stories of Migrants 119
    Case Study: Migration from Central America 121

5.3 REFUGEES AND INTERNALLY
    DISPLACED PERSONS 122
    Case Study: Surviving War in Syria 125
    National Geographic Photographer Lynsey Addario:
    Documenting Journeys 126

5.4 MIGRATION AND POLICY 128
    Feature: Walls That Divide Us 131

5.5 EFFECTS OF MIGRATION 133

CHAPTER 5 SUMMARY & REVIEW 138

UNIT 2

WRITING ACROSS UNITS, REGIONS & SCALES 140

MAPS & MODELS ARCHIVE 142

La Paz, Bolivia

UNIT 3

CULTURAL PATTERNS AND PROCESSES 148

NATIONAL GEOGRAPHIC EXPLORER FRED HIEBERT: Discovery and Preservation 150

CHAPTER 6
CONCEPTS OF CULTURE 152

6.1 AN INTRODUCTION TO CULTURE 153
Case Study: Wisconsin's American Indian Nations 156

6.2 CULTURAL LANDSCAPES 157
Case Study: Tehrangeles 160

6.3 IDENTITY AND SPACE 163

6.4 CULTURAL PATTERNS 168
National Geographic Explorer Sandhya Narayanan:
Studying Indigenous Languages 172

CHAPTER 6 SUMMARY & REVIEW 176

CHAPTER 7
CULTURAL CHANGE 178

7.1 CULTURAL DIFFUSION 179
Feature: A Portrait of Relocation Diffusion 180
Case Study: African Culture in Brazil 184

7.2 PROCESSES OF CULTURAL CHANGE 185
Case Study: Fútbol—A Globalizing Force 191
National Geographic Photographer William Allard:
Introducing People Across Cultures 192

7.3 CONSEQUENCES OF CULTURAL CHANGE 194

CHAPTER 7 SUMMARY & REVIEW 198

CHAPTER 8
SPATIAL PATTERNS OF
LANGUAGE AND RELIGION 200

8.1 PATTERNS OF LANGUAGE 201

8.2 THE DIFFUSION OF LANGUAGE 206
Case Study: French or English in Quebec? 213

8.3 PATTERNS OF RELIGION 214
National Geographic Explorer Wade Davis:
Preserving the Ethnosphere 217
Case Study: Shared Sacred Sites 218

8.4 UNIVERSALIZING AND ETHNIC RELIGIONS 219

CHAPTER 8 SUMMARY & REVIEW 226

UNIT 3

WRITING ACROSS UNITS, REGIONS & SCALES 228
MAPS & MODELS ARCHIVE 230

Panmunjom, South Korea

| UNIT 4 |

POLITICAL PATTERNS AND PROCESSES 236

NATIONAL GEOGRAPHIC EXPLORER AZIZ ABU SARAH: Reconciliation Through Narrative 238

CHAPTER 9
THE CONTEMPORARY POLITICAL MAP
240

9.1 THE COMPLEX WORLD POLITICAL MAP 241

9.2 POLITICAL POWER AND GEOGRAPHY 244

9.3 POLITICAL PROCESSES OVER TIME 247

Case Study: The Kurds 248

9.4 THE NATURE AND FUNCTION OF BOUNDARIES 249

Case Study: The DMZ in Korea 251

National Geographic Photographer David Guttenfelder: Revealing Mysteries 252

CHAPTER 9 SUMMARY & REVIEW 258

CHAPTER 10
SPATIAL PATTERNS OF POLITICAL POWER
260

10.1 ORGANIZATION OF STATES 261

National Geographic Explorer Anna Antoniou: Understanding a Divided Cyprus 262

Case Study: Political Control and Nunavut 268

10.2 ELECTORAL GEOGRAPHY 269

Case Study: Gerrymandering and Race 272

CHAPTER 10 SUMMARY & REVIEW 274

CHAPTER 11
POLITICAL CHALLENGES AND CHANGES
276

11.1 DEVOLUTION: CHALLENGES TO STATE SOVEREIGNTY 277

Case Study: Irredentism in Ukraine 279

National Geographic Explorer Michael Wesch: Technology's Impact on Society 282

11.2 SUPRANATIONALISM: TRANSCENDING STATE BOUNDARIES 283

Case Study: Brexit 287

11.3 FORCES THAT UNIFY AND FORCES THAT DIVIDE 288

CHAPTER 11 SUMMARY & REVIEW 292

UNIT 4

WRITING ACROSS UNITS, REGIONS & SCALES 294

MAPS & MODELS ARCHIVE 296

Buck Island Ranch, Florida

UNIT 5

AGRICULTURE AND RURAL LAND-USE
PATTERNS AND PROCESSES

.... 302

NATIONAL GEOGRAPHIC EXPLORER **JERRY GLOVER:** Agriculture for a Hungry Future 304

CHAPTER 12
AGRICULTURE: HUMAN-
ENVIRONMENT INTERACTION   306

12.1 AGRICULTURE AND THE ENVIRONMENT 307

12.2 AGRICULTURAL PRACTICES 312
   Feature: Rural Survey Methods 313
   Feature: Rural Settlement Patterns 315
     National Geographic Photographer George Steinmetz:
     Viewing the World from Above 322

12.3 AGRICULTURAL ORIGINS AND DIFFUSIONS....324

12.4 ADVANCES IN AGRICULTURE........................... 329
   Case Study: Women and Africa's Green Revolution.. 335

CHAPTER 12 SUMMARY & REVIEW 336

CHAPTER 13
PATTERNS AND PRACTICES OF
AGRICULTURAL PRODUCTION   338

13.1 AGRICULTURE PRODUCTION REGIONS 339
   Feature: The Changing Dairying and
   Ranching Industries 342

13.2 THE SPATIAL ORGANIZATION
   OF AGRICULTURE... 343
     National Geographic Explorer Tristram Stuart:
     Eating Ugly 347

13.3 THE VON THÜNEN MODEL 348

13.4 AGRICULTURE AS A GLOBAL SYSTEM............. 350
   Case Study: Coffee Production and Consumption .. 355

CHAPTER 13 SUMMARY & REVIEW 356

CHAPTER 14
AGRICULTURAL SUSTAINABILITY
IN A GLOBAL MARKET   358

14.1 CONSEQUENCES OF AGRICULTURAL
   PRACTICES...359
     National Geographic Explorer
     Hindou Oumarou Ibrahim: Mapping
     Indigenous Climate Knowledge...........................367
   Case Study: Building Africa's Great Green Wall 369

14.2 CHALLENGES OF CONTEMPORARY
   AGRICULTURE.. 370
   Feature: Precision Agriculture................................ 373

14.3 FEEDING THE WORLD 377
   Case Study: Food Deserts..................................... 380
     National Geographic Explorer Jennifer Burney:
     Local Changes, Global Consequences.................. 383

14.4 WOMEN IN AGRICULTURE 384

CHAPTER 14 SUMMARY & REVIEW 388

UNIT 5

WRITING ACROSS UNITS, REGIONS & SCALES........ 390

MAPS & MODELS ARCHIVE 392

Delhi, India

UNIT 6

CITIES AND URBAN LAND-USE
PATTERNS AND PROCESSES 398

NATIONAL GEOGRAPHIC EXPLORER DANIEL RAVEN-ELLISON: Geography for the People   400

CHAPTER 15
URBAN SETTLEMENTS   402

15.1 THE ORIGIN AND INFLUENCES
OF URBANIZATION 403

   National Geographic Explorer Michael Frachetti:
   Unearthing Secrets of a Silk Road City 406

15.2 FACTORS THAT INFLUENCE
URBAN GROWTH 407

   Case Study: Re-Urbanizing Liverpool 411

15.3 THE SIZE AND DISTRIBUTION OF CITIES 412

   National Geographic Feature:
   City of the Future 416

15.4 CITIES AND GLOBALIZATION 420

   Case Study: How Shanghai Grew 423

   National Geographic Feature:
   The Shape of Cities 424

CHAPTER 15 SUMMARY & REVIEW 428

CHAPTER 16
THE URBAN LANDSCAPE   430

16.1 THE INTERNAL STRUCTURE OF CITIES 431

   Case Study: Informal Housing in Cape Town 438

16.2 URBAN HOUSING 439

   Case Study: Land-Use Change in Beijing 441

16.3 URBAN INFRASTRUCTURE 444

   National Geographic Explorer T. H. Culhane:
   Empowering People with Clean Energy 445

CHAPTER 16 SUMMARY & REVIEW 450

CHAPTER 17
URBAN LIVING   452

17.1 DESIGNING FOR URBAN LIFE 453

17.2 CAUSES AND IMPACTS OF
URBAN CHANGES 460

   Case Study: The Effects of Redlining in Cleveland 462

   Feature: New York City's High Line 471

17.3 CREATING SUSTAINABLE URBAN PLACES 472

   National Geographic Explorer Zachary Damato:
   A Wild Mile in the City 473

   National Geographic Explorer Maria Silvina Fenoglio:
   Transforming Urban Rooftops 475

   National Geographic Feature:
   Designing to Scale Smart Buildings 478

   Case Study: Milan and Urban Sustainability 479

CHAPTER 17 SUMMARY & REVIEW 480

UNIT 6

WRITING ACROSS UNITS, REGIONS & SCALES 482

MAPS & MODELS ARCHIVE 484

Cowley, Oxford, England

UNIT 7

INDUSTRIAL AND ECONOMIC DEVELOPMENT PATTERNS AND PROCESSES .. 490

NATIONAL GEOGRAPHIC EXPLORER SHABANA BASIJ-RASIKH: Educating Afghan Girls 492

CHAPTER 18
THE GROWTH AND DIFFUSION OF INDUSTRIALIZATION   494

18.1 PROCESSES OF INDUSTRIALIZATION 495
Case Study: The Fourth Industrial Revolution 503

18.2 HOW ECONOMIES ARE STRUCTURED 504
Case Study: Damming the Xingu River 509
National Geographic Photographer Aaron Vincent Elkaim: Documenting Impacts of the Belo Monte Dam 510

18.3 PATTERNS OF INDUSTRIAL LOCATION 512

CHAPTER 18 SUMMARY & REVIEW 518

CHAPTER 19
MEASURING HUMAN DEVELOPMENT   520

19.1 HOW IS DEVELOPMENT MEASURED? 521

19.2 MEASURING GENDER INEQUALITY 527
Case Study: "Women-Only" Cities 531
National Geographic Photographer Amy Toensing: Widow Warriors 532

19.3 CHANGING ROLES OF WOMEN 534
Case Study: The Development of the Grameen Bank 539

19.4 THEORIES OF DEVELOPMENT 540

CHAPTER 19 SUMMARY & REVIEW 544

CHAPTER 20
GLOBALIZATION, INTERDEPENDENCE, AND SUSTAINABILITY   546

20.1 TRADE RELATIONS AND GLOBAL CORPORATIONS 547

20.2 CONNECTED ECONOMIES 552
Case Study: The Financial Crisis of 2007–2008 553

20.3 DEVELOPING A SUSTAINABLE WORLD 560
Case Study: Reducing Waste in Fisheries 561
National Geographic Explorer Andrés Ruzo: Sustainable Ecotourism 565

CHAPTER 20 SUMMARY & REVIEW 566

UNIT 7

WRITING ACROSS UNITS, REGIONS & SCALES 568

MAPS & MODELS ARCHIVE 570

COVID-19: A Global Pandemic R1

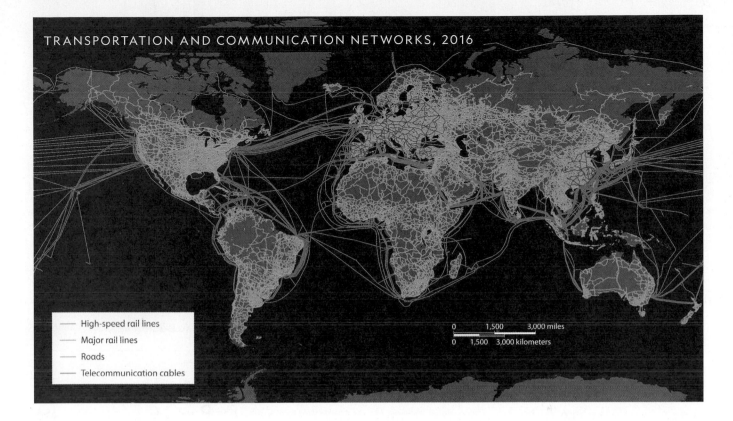

TRANSPORTATION AND COMMUNICATION NETWORKS, 2016

— High-speed rail lines
— Major rail lines
— Roads
— Telecommunication cables

0   1,500   3,000 miles
0   1,500   3,000 kilometers

VISUALS AND FEATURES

MAPS

Pristine Seas Expeditions & Protected Areas 5

Downtown Denver 9

London City Center 9

Transatlantic Travel Times 10

New Orleans's Situation 13

New Orleans's Site 13

Scales of Analysis: Food Insecurity in the United States 15

Food Insecurity: Mississippi 15

Formal Region: The Pampas 16

Functional Region: Airline Flight Routes 17

Functional Region: D.C. Metro System 17

Perceptual Region: The Midwest 18

Transportation and Communication Networks, 2016 20

World System Theory 22

New York and Philadelphia Media Markets 25

GIS-Created Map of Traffic in Toronto 31

Map Scales 37

Robinson Projection 38

Mercator Projection 38, 55

Gall-Peters Projection 39

Azimuthal Projection 39

Surface Temperatures of the Contiguous
United States, July 25, 2019 40

Gasoline Consumption by State, 2018 41

Contiguous United States Population, 2018 41

Milk Cow Inventory of the United States, 2017 42

2016 U.S. Presidential Election 43

Influenza Activity in the United States, Week 48, 2019 44

Earthquakes in South Central Europe, 2010–2018 45

Risk of Homelessness in Los Angeles County, 2017 46

Destinations of International Tourists, 2015 49

Asia, 2018 54

Pakistan, 2017 54

225 Baker St NW, Atlanta, Georgia 55

Dot Map of Precipitation in the Contiguous US, 2019 56

Isoline Map of Precipitation in the Contiguous US, 2019 56

Amazon Wildfires in South America, 2019 57

World Population Distribution, 2016 64

Population Density: Chile and Sweden 67

Population Density: Egypt (2018) and Canada (2014) 73

World Dependency Ratios, 2019 74

World Sex Ratios, 2019 76

Total Fertility Rate, 2019 77

Infant Mortality Rate, 2018 79

Average Annual Rate of Population Change, 2017 89

Average Annual Population Growth Rate, 1997–2015 90

Transmission of Zika Virus in Brazil, 2014–2016 98

Elderly Dependency Ratio, 2018 106

World Life Expectancy, 2015 107

Migration Between Pakistan and India, 1947 113

Immigrants by Host Country, 2017 116

Rohingya Refugee Camps, 2018 120

Total Refugees by Country of Origin, 2017 123

The Great Migration, 1910–1929 128

Relocation Diffusion: The Blues, c. 1850–1950 137

Internet Freedom Around the World, 2018 155

Property Rights in Law and Practice for Women, 2017 165

Protection Against Discrimination Based on Sexual
Orientation, 2019 167

Somali Refugee Arrivals, 2010–2016 173

Religious Affiliation in Northern Ireland, 2011 175

Cultural Diffusion: Colonial Languages in Africa 186

The Silk Road 187

20th Century Dialects of American English 203

Language Families 207

Kurgan Hearth Theory 208

Anatolian Hearth Theory 208

Diffusion of the English Language 209

Diffusion of the Austronesian Language Family 210

Endangered Languages, 2010 212

Estimated Majority Religions, 2020 215

Majority Religious Adherents by U.S. County, 2010 216

Diffusion of Christianity and Islam 220

Diffusion of Buddhism 221

Distribution of Hindus, 2010 223

Diffusion of Judaism, 300 C.E 225

San Francisco, 2019 230

LGBTQIA+ Student Anti-bullying Laws, 2019 231

Commitment to Religion, 2018 234

Countries That Recognize Palestine as a State, 2019 242

Europe, 1914 243

Europe, 2020 243

Global Oil Choke Points, 2016 246

Kurdistan Region 248

Africa: Political Boundaries and Cultural Groups, 2019 254

World Maritime Boundaries, 2019 256

Disputed Territory in the South China Sea 257

South America, 2020 259

The United Kingdom of Great Britain and
Northern Ireland, 2020 261

Unitary and Federal States, 2020 263

Mexico's State Boundaries, 2020 264

Projected Congressional Reapportionment, 2020 269

Maryland's 3rd Congressional District 271

North Carolina Congressional Districts, 2012–2014 273

North Carolina Congressional Districts, 2016–2018 273

Pennsylvania's 15th Congressional District (2011) 275

Pennsylvania's 7th Congressional District (2019) 275

Ukraine: Disputed Territories 279

The Soviet Union 280

After the Soviet Union's Collapse 281

NATO Members and Partners, 2019 284

The German Confederation, 1815 288

Crimea (Ukraine Perspective) 296

Crimea (Russia Perspective) 296

Ethnic Distribution in the Former Yugoslavia, 2015 296

Canada, 2020 296

Global Oil Choke Points 297

India's Disputed Borders, 2019 298

Catalonia, 2019 298

Region Where Catalan is Spoken 298

Groups Responsible for Drawing
U.S. Congressional Districts 299

Brexit Vote, June 2016 300

Philippines, 2020 300

The Fragile States Index, 2019 301

Global Cropland, 2015 307

Köppen Climate Classifications, 2016 310

U.S. Corn Production, 2018 316

U.S. Soybean Production, 2018 316

Agricultural Regions Around the World 320

Topography of the World 320

Agricultural Hearths 326

Diffusion of Agriculture and Domesticated Animals 327

The Columbian Exchange 328

Food Exports and Imports 352

Top Coffee-Producing Countries, 2019 355

Percentage of U.S. Agricultural Income Derived
from Crops Grown for Animal Feed, 2012 357

Ogallala Aquifer, 1955–2015 360

The Great Green Wall Initiative 369

Global Crop Diversity, 2016 371

Estimated Percentage of Undernourished Population,
2015–2017 378

Houston Food Desert 380

Female Agriculture Workers in Selected
Countries, 2010 384

USDA Plant Hardiness Zones, Contiguous US, 2012 392

USDA Plant Hardiness Zones, Arizona, 2012 392

Kidman Cattle Ranches, Australia, 2016 393

Global Banana Trade, 2017 395

Agriculture's Footprint, 2014 396

Atlantic Fall Line 404

Toronto's Suburban Growth 410

Megacities, 2018 and 2030 420

Chicago's Railroads, 1955 429

Land Use in Boston, 2017 440

London's Green Belt, 2019 456

Historic Redlining Map, 1936 463

Cleveland Neighborhood Grading, 2015 463

Urbanization of Delhi, 1989–2018 464

Temperatures in Washington, D.C., August 28, 2018 481

Southwestern Kenya 485

Seattle Zoning Map, 2019 489

World Industrial Output and Coal Deposits, 2016 497

Industrialization in Great Britain, c. 1850 499

Spread of the Industrial Revolution in Europe,
1840–1890 500

Share of the Labor Force Working in Agriculture, 2017 506

Major U.S. Manufacturing Region, 20th Century 513

Industrialization in Europe, c. 1850 519
World Literacy Rates, 2015 525
Human Development Index, 2017 526
Ratio of Women to Men in the Labor Market, 2017...........530
WTO, OPEC, EU Countries, 2020 549
The Great Recession, 2007–2009 554
International Division of Labor 557
Africa, Europe, and Asia, 2020 572
Commodity-Dependent Countries 2013–2017................ 573
Active Regional Trade Agreements, 2019 575

MODELS AND THEORIES

Distance Decay and Space-Time Compression 10
World System Theory...22, 53, 572
Malthus's Theory of Population Growth........................92, 144
Demographic Transition 94, 143
Epidemiological Transition 95, 144
Ravenstein's Laws of Migration...............................111, 145
Distance Decay 118
Gravity Model.. 146, 412, 484
Bid-Rent Theory 312, 431, 485
The von Thünen Model 348
Central Place Theory 414, 485
Burgess Concentric-Zone............................... 432, 486
Hoyt Sector 432, 486
Harris and Ullman Multiple-Nuclei....................... 432, 486
Galactic City 434, 487
Latin American City 436, 487
African City 436, 488
Southeast Asian City 436, 488
Least-Cost Theory...514, 571
Rostow's Stages of Economic Growth......................541, 572
Core-Periphery 542

CASE STUDIES

New Orleans—Site vs. Situation 11
India—Regional Differences in Scale 19
Detroit—GIS Helps Find Safer Routes............................ 33
Population Distribution at the Country Scale 72
Zika Virus in South and North America 98
China's Population Policies 100
Migration from Central America.................................... 121
Surviving War in Syria 125
Wisconsin's American Indian Nations..............................156
Tehrangeles... 160
African Culture in Brazil.. 184
Fútbol—A Globalizing Force.. 191
French or English in Quebec?......................................213
Shared Sacred Sites...218
The Kurds 248
The DMZ in Korea 251
Political Control and Nunavut 268
Gerrymandering and Race... 272

Irredentism in Ukraine 279
Brexit.. 287
Women and Africa's Green Revolution 335
Coffee Production and Consumption............................. 355
Building Africa's Great Green Wall 369
Food Deserts 380
Re-Urbanizing Liverpool... 411
How Shanghai Grew 423
Informal Housing in Cape Town.................................... 438
Land-Use Change in Beijing 441
The Effects of Redlining in Cleveland 462
Milan and Urban Sustainability.....................................479
The Fourth Industrial Revolution 503
Damming the Xingu River 509
"Women-Only" Cities 531
The Development of the Grameen Bank 539
The Financial Crisis of 2007–2008 553
Reducing Waste in Fisheries.. 561

FEATURES

Examining Population Pyramids at Different Scales 83
Walls That Divide Us 131
A Portrait of Relocation Diffusion 180
Rural Survey Methods.. 313
Rural Settlement Patterns... 315
The Changing Dairying and Ranching Industries.............. 342
Precision Agriculture 373
City of the Future 416
The Shape of Cities 424
New York City's High Line 471
Designing to Scale Smart Buildings 478

INFOGRAPHICS

World System Theory... 22
Map Projection Types.. 38
A Displaced World, 2017 123
Forced Migration Due to Natural Disaster, 2017.............. 147
Patterns in Gender..165
The Indo-European Language Family............................. 204
Distribution of Language Families 207
Estimated Majority Religions, 2020 215
Cultural Iceberg 230
The Sharing of Powers 265
Citizens' Opinion of Their Government, 2018 299
Altitudinal Zonation 308
Hearths, Civilizations, and Domestication.......................324
Norfolk Four-Field System 332
Worldwide Agricultural Trade 352
World Hunger, 2015–2017 378
City of the Future 416
The Shape of Cities 424
Designing to Scale: Smart Buildings............................. 478
Industrial Revolution over Time 503

Five Economic Sectors.. 504, 570

From Raw Material to Market: The Lumber Industry 515

Where to Locate?...516, 571

Human Development Index, 2017 526

Where Your Car Is Made 575

CHARTS, GRAPHS, AND DATA SETS

Generating a GIS Map 31

Population Distribution Patterns 63

Comparing Measures of Density
(people per sq km in 2018) 68

Fertility and Mortality (2020–2025)................................ 78

Population Pyramid of Russia, 2018................................ 81

Population Pyramid of Japan, 2018................................ 81

Population Pyramid of Democratic
Republic of Congo, 2018.. 81

Population Pyramid of Germany, 2018 85

World Population Growth, 1750–2100.............................. 88

World Population Policies, 1939–2015.............................. 102

Population Pyramids, Japan, 1950 and 2019 105

Total Fertility Rate in South Korea, 1960–2017 109

Push-Pull Factors for Chinese Students Deciding
to Return to China, 1997.. 112

Top 10 Countries with the Greatest Refugee
Exodus, 2017 123

Top 10 Countries with the Most IDPs, 2017 123

Volume of U.S. Immigration by Continent
of Origin, 1820–2015 132

Swedish Immigration and Emigration Flows, 1880–2017.....134

Ireland's Net Migration, 2008–2018 139

Population Pyramid: Japan 2018 142

Population Pyramid: Niger 2018....................................142

Population Pyramid: Qatar 2018....................................142

Population Pyramid: United States 2018..........................142

Population Pyramid: India 2018 142

Personal Remittances Received, 1998–2018 146

Immigrants in the U.S. Population and Labor Force,
1980–2017 147

Global Displacement, 2007–2017 147

Life Expectancy for Women, 2017 165

Percentage of 25- to 29-Year-Olds in the U.S.
with a Bachelor's Degree or Higher, 2017 165

Placemaking.. 168

Adherents of World Religions, in Billions (2020 est.) 177

Cultural Diffusion Online..182

Types of Cultural Diffusion 183, 232, 233

Hispanic Parents in the United States Who
Speak Spanish to Their Children....................................194

Hispanic Parents in the United States Who
Encourage Their Children to Speak Spanish.....................194

Effects of Acculturation 195

Cultural Appropriation 197

Internet Use and GDP 199

Speakers of World Languages, 2019 207

World Religious Adherents (in Billions), 2020 215

Languages Spoken at Home in the United States
(Other than English), 2000, 2017 227

Languages Spoken by the Largest Numbers
of People in Real Life, 2020 231

Most Common Languages used in Websites, 2020 231

Fashion Diffusion 233

Niger-Congo Language Family 234

Denominations of Christianity 235

Federalism in the United States 265

Patriotism and Nationalism 266

Federal States vs. Unitary States 267

Gerrymandering Tactics... 270

Supranational Organizations....................................... 286

Ethnonationalism 290

Centripetal vs. Centrifugal Forces 291

Results of the United Kingdom's 2016 Referendum
on EU Membership.. 293

Projected Oil and Gas Trade Volumes Through
Two Choke Points, 2018–2040...................................... 297

State Fragility Trends... 301

Domestication of Animals... 325

Irrigation Use, 1962, 1982, 2002 337

Fertilizer Use, 1962, 1982, 2002.................................... 337

U.S. Agricultural Production, 2007 and 2017 343

The Food Supply System 344

Impact of Trade War on U.S. and Brazil Soybean Prices 346

Assumptions About the von Thünen Model 349

Leading Exporters, 2018... 352

Leading Importers, 2018... 352

World Agricultural Trade Growth, 1995–2018 352

Brazil Soybean Production and Exports.......................... 370

Empowering Women Farmers...................................... 386

Food Insecurity, 2014, 2016, 2018 389

Index of Cereal Production and Land Use, 1961–1985 393

Global Distribution of Farms Smaller Than 25 Acres 395

Global Distribution of Farms 25 Acres or More.................395

Land Use Per Ounce of Protein, by Food Type.................. 396

Global Food Waste Across the Supply Chain 397

Pressures on Biodiversity by Year 397

Population of the Largest Cities in Libya and
the United States, 2020.. 413

World City Hierarchy, 2019..421

Chicago's Railroads, 1955 429

Bike Ridership in Seattle, 2007–2018.............................. 449

Price of Downtown Apartments per Square Foot, 2018 451

Impact of Long Commutes 455

Greenbelt Towns.. 457

Largest Cities in Australia, 2020 484

Life Expectancy and Economic Growth in
the United Kingdom, 1500–2015 501

U.S. Employment by Economic Activity, 2019 505

U.S. Workforce by Gender 507

Australia's Economic Sectors, 2014–2015........................ 508

GNI per Capita in U.S. Dollars (2018) 522

Countries with Highest HDIs 526

Countries with Lowest HDIs 526

The Gender Development Index (GDI) 527

Percentage of Women in National Legislatures, 2019 529

Girls' Education Levels Around the World, 2019 536

Gender Pay Gap Comparison, 2018 537

Women in Leadership.. 538

Professional Opportunities Poll, 2019............................ 545

Complementarity: China and Kazakhstan 547

Austerity Measures 554

Outsourcing.. 556

Global Services Location Index, 2019 557

Special Economic Zones 559

United Nations Sustainable Development Goals............... 562

Multiplier Effects of New Resorts.................................. 567

Economic Sectors Algeria, 2017 570

Economic Sectors Denmark, 2017 570

Economic Sectors Haiti, 2017 570

Distribution of Commodity-Dependent and
Non–Commodity-Dependent Countries within
Each Income Group 573

Commodity-Dependent Countries 2013–2017............... 573

The Effect of Education on Birth Rates 574

NATIONAL GEOGRAPHIC CONTRIBUTORS

Enric Sala: Safeguarding Pristine Seas 4

Adjany Costa: Conserving the Delta.................................... 14

Sarah Parcak: Protecting Archaeological Sites.................... 35

Shah Selbe: Deploying Technology for
Conservation Purposes.. 47

Paul Salopek: Out of Eden, A Walk Through Time............. 60

Lillygol Sedaghat: Transforming Trash 69

Pardis Sabeti: Cracking the Genetic Code 97

Jason De León: Documenting the Stories of Migrants........119

Lynsey Addario: Documenting Journeys 126

Fred Hiebert: Discovery and Preservation 150

Sandhya Narayanan: Studying Indigenous Languages.......172

William Allard: Introducing People Across Cultures 192

Wade Davis: Preserving the Ethnosphere 217

Aziz Abu Sarah: Reconciliation Through Narrative............. 238

David Guttenfelder: Revealing Mysteries 252

Anna Antoniou: Understanding a Divided Cyprus 262

Michael Wesch: Technology's Impact on Society 282

Jerry Glover: Agriculture for a Hungry Future 304

John Stanmeyer 319

George Steinmetz: Viewing the World from Above......... 322

Tristram Stuart: Eating Ugly 347

Hindou Oumarou Ibrahim: Mapping Indigenous Climate
Knowledge 367

Jennifer Burney: Local Changes, Global Consequences.... 383

Daniel Raven-Ellison: Geography for the People 400

Michael Frachetti: Unearthing Secrets of
a Silk Road City... 406

T. H. Culhane: Empowering People with Clean Energy..... 446

Caroline Gerdes 448

Zachary Damato: A Wild Mile in the City......................... 473

Maria Silvina Fenoglio: Transforming Urban Rooftops........475

Shabana Basij-Rasikh: Educating Afghan Girls 492

Aaron Vincent Elkaim: Documenting Impacts
of the Belo Monte Dam.. 510

Amy Toensing: Widow Warriors 532

Andrés Ruzo: Sustainable Ecotourism 565

GEO-INQUIRY

Making Connections 25

The Geo-Inquiry Process 27

The Geo-Inquiry Process: Tips for Success: Ask 28

The Geo-Inquiry Process: Tips for Success: Collect............. 30

The Geo-Inquiry Process: Tips for Success: Visualize 42

The Geo-Inquiry Process: Tips for Success: Create 46

The Geo-Inquiry Process: Tips for Success: Act 46

A New Community Resource 49

Seeing Local Impacts of Population Distribution............... 85

Population in Your Community... 109

Migration in Your Community 139

Your Community's Spaces...177

Cultural Change 199

Language Diversity in Your Community 227

Local Boundaries 259

Political Boundaries Where You Live 275

Centripetal and Centrifugal Forces on a Smaller Scale...... 293

Agriculture in Your Region... 337

Reducing Food Waste 357

Food Deserts in Your Area 389

Urbanization in Your Community 429

Local Infrastructure 451

Livability in Your Community 481

Economic Structure of Your Community...........................519

Measure Development in Your Community 545

Sustainable Development in Your Community.................... 567

VIDEOS

On Human Geography by Gil Grosvenor ...... **Online Resource**

Unit 1: Site vs. Situation in New Orleans........ **Online Resource**

Unit 2: The Human Face of Migration........... **Online Resource**

Unit 3: Culture and Human Geography......... **Online Resource**

Unit 4: Maps and Boundaries...................... **Online Resource**

Unit 5: The Geography of Food Choice .... **Online Resource**

Unit 6: Reimagining Cities.......................... **Online Resource**

Unit 7: Industry and Economy .... **Online Resource**

STUDENT HANDBOOKS

Writing Handbook .... **Online Resource**

Geography Handbook .... **Online Resource**

Bering Strait

RUS.

ALASKA (U.S.)

60°N

Bering Sea

Gulf of Alaska

Aleutian Islands

Haida Gwaii (Queen Charlotte Is.)

Vancouver I.

Queen Elizabeth Islands

Ellesmere Island

Banks I.

Victoria Island

Beaufort Sea

Baffin Island

Baffin Bay

A R C T I

GREENLAND (KALAALLIT NUNAAT) (Denmark)

Jan (No

Arctic

ICELAND

Faroe Islands (Denmark)

U KIN

IRELAND

CANADA

Hudson Bay

Labrador Sea

Newfoundland

N O R T H

P A C I F I C

O C E A N

UNITED STATES

Great Lakes

30°N

Tropic of Cancer

HAWAI'I (U.S.)

MEXICO

Gulf of Mexico

Bermuda (U.K.)

N O R T H

A T L A N T I C   O C E A N

Azores (Port.) **PORTUGAL**

Madeira Islands (Port.)

Canary Islands (Sp.)

MOR

THE BAHAMAS

CUBA

DOMINICAN REPUBLIC

HAITI JAMAICA

PUERTO RICO (U.S.)

ST. KITTS AND NEVIS

DOMINICA

ST. LUCIA

BARBADOS

ST. VINCENT AND THE GRENADINES

TRINIDAD & TOBAGO

BELIZE

GUATEMALA **HONDURAS**

EL SALVADOR

NICARAGUA

COSTA RICA

PANAMA

Caribbean Sea

WESTERN SAHARA (Morocco)

CABO VERDE

MAURITANIA

SENEGAL

THE GAMBIA

GUINEA-BISSAU **GUINEA**

BU

SIERRA LEONE

LIBERIA

CÔTE D'IVOIRE (IVORY COAST)

E S

AND

VENEZUELA GUYANA

COLOMBIA

FRENCH GUIANA (France)

SURINAME

Equator

Galápagos Islands (Ecuador)

ECUADOR

K I R I B A T I

Phoenix Islands

Marquesas Islands (Fr.)

PERU

B R A Z I L

Ascension (U.K.)

St. Helena (U.K.)

SAMOA

AMERICAN SAMOA (U.S.)

Tahiti

French Polynesia (Fr.)

TONGA

Cook Islands (N.Z.)

TUAMOTU ARCHIPELAGO

LINE ISLANDS

BOLIVIA

Tropic of Capricorn

Pitcairn Islands (U.K.)

Easter Island (Chile)

PARAGUAY

S O U T

A T L A N T

O C E A

URUGUAY

Tristan da Cunha Group (U.K.)

Chatham Islands (N.Z.)

S O U T H

P A C I F I C

O C E A N

Juan Fernández Archipelago (Chile)

CHILE **ARGENTINA**

30°S

Falkland Islands (Islas Malvinas) (U.K.)

South Georgia (U.K.)

0   1,000   2,000 Miles

0   1,000   2,000 Kilometers

Scotia Sea

South Shetland Islands

South Orkney Islands

South Sandwich Islands (U.K.)

Antarctic Circle

60°S

Weddell Sea

A N T

150°W   120°W   90°W   60°W

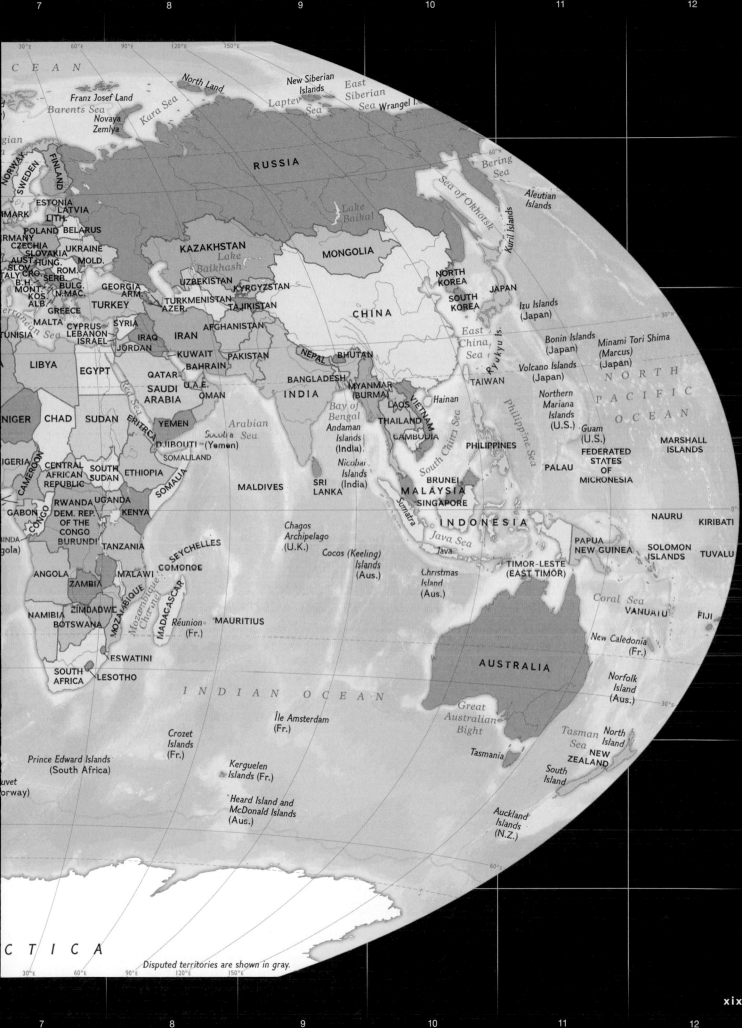

O C E A N

30°E　　60°E　　90°E　　120°E　　150°E

Franz Josef Land
Barents Sea
North Land
Kara Sea
New Siberian Islands
East Siberian Sea
Laptev Sea
Wrangel I.

Novaya Zemlya

RUSSIA

Bering Sea

Lake Baikal

Sea of Okhotsk

Aleutian Islands

NORWAY
SWEDEN
FINLAND
ESTONIA
LATVIA
LITH.
DENMARK
POLAND
BELARUS
GERMANY
CZECHIA
SLOVAKIA
UKRAINE
AUST.
HUNG.
MOLD.
SLOV.
ITALY
CRO.
SERB.
ROM.
B.H.
MONT.
BULG.
KOS.
N.MAC.
ALB.
GREECE
MALTA
TUNISIA
CYPRUS
LEBANON
ISRAEL

KAZAKHSTAN
Lake Balkhash

MONGOLIA

Kuril Islands

GEORGIA
ARM.
AZER.
TURKEY
TURKMENISTAN
UZBEKISTAN
KYRGYZSTAN
TAJIKISTAN

NORTH KOREA
SOUTH KOREA
JAPAN

SYRIA
IRAQ
JORDAN
IRAN
AFGHANISTAN

CHINA

Izu Islands (Japan)

30°N

Mediterranean Sea

LIBYA
EGYPT

KUWAIT
BAHRAIN
QATAR
U.A.E.
OMAN

SAUDI ARABIA

PAKISTAN
NEPAL
BHUTAN

BANGLADESH
MYANMAR (BURMA)

East China Sea

TAIWAN

Bonin Islands (Japan)
Minami Tori Shima (Marcus) (Japan)
Volcano Islands (Japan)

NIGER
CHAD
SUDAN
ERITREA
YEMEN

INDIA
LAOS
VIETNAM
Hainan

Ryukyu Is.

Northern Mariana Islands (U.S.)

N O R T H
P A C I F I C
O C E A N

Red Sea

Arabian Sea
Socotra (Yemen)
DJIBOUTI
SOMALILAND

Bay of Bengal
Andaman Islands (India)
THAILAND
CAMBODIA

South China Sea

PHILIPPINES

Philippine Sea

Guam (U.S.)

MARSHALL ISLANDS

NIGERIA
CAMEROON
CENTRAL AFRICAN REPUBLIC
SOUTH SUDAN
ETHIOPIA
SOMALIA

MALDIVES

Nicobar Islands (India)
SRI LANKA

FEDERATED STATES OF MICRONESIA

PALAU

GABON
CONGO
RWANDA
DEM. REP. OF THE CONGO
BURUNDI
UGANDA
KENYA

BRUNEI
MALAYSIA
SINGAPORE

CABINDA (Angola)

TANZANIA
SEYCHELLES
COMOROS

Chagos Archipelago (U.K.)

Sumatra

I N D O N E S I A
Java Sea
Java

NAURU
KIRIBATI

ANGOLA
ZAMBIA
MALAWI
MADAGASCAR

Cocos (Keeling) Islands (Aus.)

Christmas Island (Aus.)

PAPUA NEW GUINEA
SOLOMON ISLANDS
TUVALU

NAMIBIA
ZIMBABWE
BOTSWANA
MOZAMBIQUE
Mozambique Channel

Réunion (Fr.)
MAURITIUS

TIMOR-LESTE (EAST TIMOR)

Coral Sea
VANUATU
FIJI

SOUTH AFRICA
ESWATINI
LESOTHO

New Caledonia (Fr.)

AUSTRALIA

Norfolk Island (Aus.)

30°S

I N D I A N　O C E A N

Île Amsterdam (Fr.)

Great Australian Bight

Tasman Sea
North Island
NEW ZEALAND

Crozet Islands (Fr.)

Tasmania

Prince Edward Islands (South Africa)

Kerguelen Islands (Fr.)

South Island

Bouvet (Norway)

Heard Island and McDonald Islands (Aus.)

Auckland Islands (N.Z.)

60°S

A N T A R C T I C A

Disputed territories are shown in gray.

WORLD PHYSICAL

30°E   60°E   90°E   150°E

OCEAN

North *
Magnetic
Pole

Franz Josef Land

Barents Sea

Novaya
Zemlya

Kola Pen.

North Land

Kara Sea

Central
Siberian Plateau

Laptev Sea

New Siberian
Islands

East
Siberian
Sea

Wrangel I.

S   I   B   E   R   I   A

gian
a

Scandinavian
Peninsula

Baltic Sea

Northern European Plain

Ob R.

Volga R.

Ural Mountains

Western
Siberian
Plain

Yenisey R.

Lena R.

Lake
Baikal

Bering
Sea

Kamchatka
Peninsula

Sea of Okhotsk

Sakhalin

Aleutian
Islands

Kuril Islands

ALPS

be R

ca

nia

Sicily

Apennines

Black Sea

El'Brus
18,510 ft
(5,642 m)

Caspian
Depression

Caucasus
Mts.

Caspian Sea

Aral
Sea

Lake
Balkhash

Kazakh
Uplands

Altay Mts.

Tian Shan

Mongolia
Plateau

G O B I

Sea of
Japan
(East
Sea)

Yellow
Sea

Izu Islands
(Japan)

Mediterranean Sea

gar
Mts.

Suez
Canal

Euphrates R.

Zagros Mts.

Persian
Gulf

Taklimakan
Desert

Kunlun Mts.

Plateau
of Tibet

Yellow
R.

Yangtze R.

East
China
Sea

Ryukyu Is.

Bonin Islands
(Japan)

Minami Tori Shima
(Marcus)
(Japan)

Volcano Islands
(Japan)

NORTH

S A H A R A

Nile

Red Sea

ARABIAN
PENINSULA

Gulf of
Oman

Indus R.

Thar Desert

HIMALAYA

Mt. Everest
29,035 ft (8,850 m)

Xi R.

Hainan

Northern
Mariana
Islands
(U.S.)

Guam
(U.S.)

PACIFIC

OCEAN

S A H E L

Gulf of Aden

Socotra
(Yemen)

Arabian
Sea

Deccan
Plateau

Western Ghats

Bay of
Bengal

Ganges R.

Andaman Sea

Malay Pen.

South China Sea

Philippine Sea

Congo
Basin

Great Rift
Valley

Lake
Victoria

Kilimanjaro
19,340 ft (5,895 m)

Andaman
Islands
(India)

Nicobar
Islands
(India)

Sumatra

Celebes
Sea

Borneo

New
Guinea

Lake
Tanganyika

Chagos
Archipelago
(U.K.)

Cocos (Keeling)
Islands
(Aus.)

Christmas
Island
(Aus.)

Java Sea

Java

Celebes

Banda Sea

Arafura Sea

Coral Sea

Great Barrier Reef

Mauritius

Great
Sandy Desert

GREAT DIVIDING RANGE

New Caledonia
(Fr.)

KALAHARI
DESERT

Mozambique Channel

Réunion
(Fr.)

Western
Plateau

Great
Artesian
Basin

Norfolk
Island
(Aus.)

Cape of
Good Hope

I N D I A N   O C E A N

Île Amsterdam
(Fr.)

Great
Victoria Desert

Great
Australian
Bight

Mt. Kosciuszko
(2,228 m) 7,310 ft

Tasman
Sea

North
Island

30°S

C

Crozet
Islands
(Fr.)

Prince Edward Islands
(South Africa)

Kerguelen
Islands (Fr.)

Tasmania

South
Island

uvet
rway)

September extent of sea ice

Heard Island and
McDonald Islands
(Aus.)

Auckland
Islands
(N.Z.)

South Magnetic
* Pole

60°S

EEN MAUD LAND

WILKES LAND

TARCTICA

South Geomagnetic
* Pole

30°E   60°E   90°E   120°E   150°E

Elevation

feet	meters
10,000+	3,050+
5,000	1,524
2,000	610
1,000	305
500	152
0	0
Below sea level	

FOREWORD | GILBERT M. GROSVENOR

Physical geography tells you where you are. Human geography explores the interaction of humans with the world around them. It helps you envision the future and better understand the past—human geography gives humans dimension.

GILBERT M. GROSVENOR
JULY 2019

In 1979, I joined an expedition to the North Pole and jumped at the once-in-a-lifetime chance to scuba dive under massive ice blocks that thrust nearly 40 feet beneath the ocean surface. Afterward, I surveyed that harsh icescape and understood for the first time the importance of the Arctic and Antarctic as bellwethers for the future of Planet Earth. Loud cracking sounds accompanied the inevitable collisions of ice floes as nature constantly powered a million square miles of thick ice across the Arctic Ocean. I never thought of the Arctic in the same way after that.

At the time I was editor of *National Geographic* magazine and would eventually become president of the National Geographic Society, but my history with National Geographic goes back even further. My great-grandfather, inventor Alexander Graham Bell, was National Geographic's second president. He defined geography as "the world and all that's in it," and that idea has driven the organization for more than 132 years.

In fact, geography is a great tool for examining the complicated interaction between humans and the natural environment. In an era in which climate change and issues of sustainability are commanding greater attention, geography has become a more scientific, technologically oriented discipline—it gives us a good way to understand a complex, rapidly changing world.

This Human Geography course couldn't be more closely connected to National Geographic's mission to understand and preserve our world. The seven key topics that you'll study in this course have formed the backbone of the work we do in exploration, storytelling, and geography education for decades.

It's been my good fortune to work with many brilliant and dedicated women and men over the years, including marine biologists, archaeologists, mountain climbers, astronauts, photographers, and cartographers. As inspirational as their contributions to science and culture have been, I am convinced that your future contributions will rival theirs for lasting impact—you are the new Explorers. Through this Human Geography program, National Geographic hopes to be your partner in that exciting endeavor.

Those moments under the Arctic ice changed my life. You have something equally amazing in store for you, too—you have only to seek it. Start by asking those geographic questions: Where in the world? And why?

I and my colleagues at National Geographic wish you an astonishing journey.

CONTINUING NATIONAL GEOGRAPHIC'S LEGACY

Whether you're more familiar with the yellow-bordered magazine or the online interactive version, for more than a century National Geographic has told stories of intrepid explorers, ground-breaking photographers, and global geographic phenomenon.

Like the issue on migration shown here, many of those stories connect to the topics you'll study in this Human Geography course. In roles from photographer to editor-in-chief, Gil Grosvenor's vision shaped the direction of those stories.

This photo reveals two of Gil Grosvenor's passions: photography and sailing on Bras d'Or Lake in his beloved Baddeck, Cape Breton, Nova Scotia, where he grew up amidst several generations of Grosvenors.

THINKING GEOGRAPHICALLY

THE HUMAN IMPACT

Greenmarket Square in Cape Town

Humans have left an indelible imprint on every part of the globe, as evidenced here by the sprawling communities and built-up shoreline of Cape Town, South Africa. At the same time, Earth's features and processes have molded profound and enduring aspects of human societies—our cultures, economies, and politics. Human geography focuses on the interactions between humans and the physical environment.

Geographers interpret the world through a lens that allows them to make connections between local, national, regional, and global issues to better understand our human stories.

In this course, you'll use this geographic lens to investigate the movement of people, cultures, and ideas; the political organization of countries; and the development of agriculture, settlements, and linked economies. You'll build an informed global awareness and discover the factors that influence the world's livability and sustainability.

CHAPTER 1
THE POWER OF GEOGRAPHY:
GEOGRAPHIC THINKING

CHAPTER 2
GEOGRAPHIC INQUIRY: DATA, TOOLS, AND TECHNOLOGY

UNIT 1 WRITING ACROSS UNITS, REGIONS & SCALES

UNIT 1 MAPS & MODELS ARCHIVE

SAFEGUARDING PRISTINE SEAS

Biodiversity makes our life possible. The rich diversity of species on Earth helps to keep our water clean and stabilize our climate, and contributes to food security. Enric Sala, National Geographic Explorer-in-Residence and founder of the Pristine Seas project, has made it his mission to preserve the biodiversity of Earth's oceans.

LEARNING OBJECTIVE
PSO-1.B Explain how major geographic concepts illustrate spatial relationships.

A MISSION TO PROTECT A team of scientists gathered by Enric Sala left for an expedition in 2005 to the Line Islands, a cluster of coral outcrops in the Pacific Ocean roughly 1,000 miles south of Hawaii. Some of the islands are U.S. territories, while the others belong to the nation of Kiribati (kee-rih-BAHS). In this remote patch of ocean, Sala's team conducted groundbreaking research on one of the few coral reef ecosystems that remain largely untouched by human activity. These studies provided scientific support for what would become an ecological triumph.

In January 2009, President George W. Bush signed into existence the Pacific Remote Islands Marine National Monument, which placed several U.S. territories, including the American Line Islands, off limits to commercial fishing and other for-profit activities. This protected zone was expanded in 2014 by President Barack Obama to more than 745,000 square miles—covering a greater area than all U.S. National Parks on land combined. The nation of Kiribati, meanwhile, has declared a 12-mile fishing exclusion zone around its Southern Line Island, which the team and Sala explored in 2009.

In 2008, Sala founded the Pristine Seas project to expand his work in exploration and conservation. Sala's methods, models, and data are intended to establish the threshold of ecosystem health that can be used to inform conservation priorities and efforts of governments and organizations. Pristine Seas expeditions have investigated some of the most isolated places on the planet in locations ranging from the South Pacific to the high Arctic. "These remote, untouched places are the only baseline we have left for what the oceans used to be like. They are like the instruction manual for the ocean," says Sala. The Pristine Seas team includes not only researchers but also filmmakers and policy and communications specialists who support the mission to discover, inform, and advocate for changes in the ways humans interact with the oceans. To date, Pristine Seas has inspired the protection of more than 3 million square miles in 22 of the largest marine reserves on the planet.

CHALLENGES TO CONSERVATION Enric Sala admits, "It is difficult to be optimistic about the ocean in my lifetime." Indeed, while Pristine Seas has cause to celebrate notable successes in protecting a number of fragile habitats, 2.2 million square miles is a tiny fraction of the oceans' total surface area. Notwithstanding all of the zones protected by the efforts of Pristine Seas and other groups, 97 percent of Earth's oceans are still open to fishing. Much of this vast area is vulnerable to overfishing and pollution, which Sala calls "ecological sabotage."

At the same time, fishing is a means of survival for millions of people. Recognizing this fact, Sala calls for governments to better manage fisheries, improve fish farming known as aquaculture, and enforce laws against marine pollution. He argues that marine conservation actually enhances the sustainability of the fishing industry, citing the example of a fishing community in Kenya where incomes doubled because marine reserves had helped restore the health of sea life in the region's waters. "We know what works," Sala says, "we just need the political will and the vision to protect much more of our waters." ▮

GEOGRAPHIC THINKING

How might the creation of relatively small marine reserves affect natural resources and sustainability in the rest of the world's oceans?

Sala and the Pristine Seas team have completed 31 expeditions between 2009 and early 2020.

Sharks hunt off the Galapagos Islands, where Pristine Seas helped to create the Darwin and Wolf Marine Sanctuary, protecting the highest abundance of sharks known in the world.

PRISTINE SEAS EXPEDITIONS & PROTECTED AREAS

● Protected area   ● Completed expedition

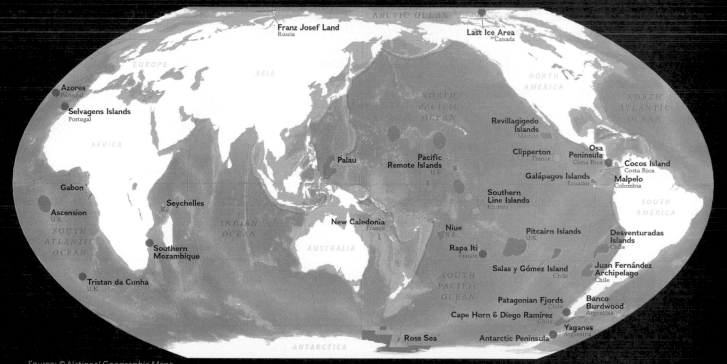

Franz Josef Land
Russia

Last Ice Area
Canada

ARCTIC OCEAN

EUROPE   ASIA   NORTH AMERICA   NORTH ATLANTIC OCEAN

Azores
Portugal

Selvagens Islands
Portugal

AFRICA

NORTH PACIFIC OCEAN

Revillagigedo Islands
Mexico

Clipperton
France

Osa Peninsula
Costa Rica

Cocos Island
Costa Rica

Palau

Pacific Remote Islands
U.S.

Galápagos Islands
Ecuador

Malpelo
Colombia

Gabon

Seychelles

Southern Line Islands
Kiribati

SOUTH AMERICA

Ascension
U.K.

INDIAN OCEAN

New Caledonia
France

Niue
N.Z.

Pitcairn Islands
U.K.

Desventuradas Islands
Chile

SOUTH ATLANTIC OCEAN

AUSTRALIA

Rapa Iti
France

SOUTH PACIFIC OCEAN

Southern Mozambique

Salas y Gómez Island
Chile

Juan Fernández Archipelago
Chile

Tristan da Cunha
U.K.

Patagonian Fjords
Chile

Banco Burdwood
Argentina

Cape Horn & Diego Ramírez
Chile

Yaganes
Argentina

ANTARCTICA

Ross Sea

Antarctic Peninsula

CHAPTER 1

THE POWER OF GEOGRAPHY: GEOGRAPHIC THINKING

CRITICAL VIEWING Rows of buildings line the Charles River in Boston, Massachusetts, a city that was founded in 1630 along the banks of the river and Boston Harbor. ▌Explain what geographers today might learn by studying the location of the city of Boston.

GEOGRAPHIC THINKING Why does geography matter?

1.1
WHAT IS HUMAN GEOGRAPHY?

CASE STUDY: New Orleans —Site vs. Situation

NATIONAL GEOGRAPHIC EXPLORER Adjany Costa

1.2
SPATIAL PATTERNS: SCALE AND REGION

CASE STUDY: India—Regional Differences in Scale

1.3
GLOBALIZATION AND SUSTAINABILITY

1.1 WHAT IS HUMAN GEOGRAPHY?

Exploring why things are located where they are can offer insights into how human activity shapes the world. Human geographers study the ways in which people use, adapt to, and change Earth, as well as how they are influenced by it. Establishing the concepts and perspectives that inform a human geographer's work will give you a context for the rest of this course.

STUDYING HUMAN GEOGRAPHY

LEARNING OBJECTIVE
PSO-1.A Define major geographic concepts that illustrate spatial relationships.

Whether you're aware of it or not, you are regularly engaged in geographic thinking. The simple act of traveling around your community requires you to know where your destination is, to plan a route, to consider distance and traffic, and to estimate how long your trip will take. When you perform these calculations, you are thinking geographically.

Geography is an integrative discipline that brings together the physical and human dimensions of the world in the study of people, places, and environments. Its subject matter is Earth's surface and the processes—continuous actions taking place over time—that shape it, as well as the relationships between people and environments, and the connections between people and places.

The discipline of geography is divided into two major areas. **Physical geography** is the study of natural processes and the distribution of features in the environment, such as landforms, plants, animals, and climate. For example, a physical geographer might focus on the movement of glaciers in different eras, or how a process like erosion changes a riverbed. **Human geography** is the study of the events and processes that have shaped how humans understand, use, and alter Earth. A human geographer studies how people organize themselves socially, politically, and economically and what impact they have on the natural environment.

Because geographers work on many of the same questions and problems as experts in other fields in the physical and social sciences, they face the challenge of differentiating geography from those fields. One distinguishing feature is geographers' focus on the relationship between humans and environments. Other disciplines tend to focus on either one or the other. Geography also recognizes the importance of where events and phenomena occur, focusing on how processes vary depending on location. For instance, a society will develop differently in a rural environment than in an urban setting. A third distinguishing feature is geographers' focus on geographic scales. You'll learn more about the importance of scale later in the chapter.

GEOGRAPHIC PERSPECTIVES

LEARNING OBJECTIVES
PSO-1.A Define major geographic concepts that illustrate spatial relationships.
PSO-1.B Explain how major geographic concepts illustrate spatial relationships.

Both branches of geography analyze complex issues and relationships from two key perspectives, or points of view. These perspectives help geographers interpret and explain spatial patterns and processes on Earth, and understand the complex relationships between nature and human societies.

The **spatial perspective** refers to where something occurs. In the same way that history is concerned with time and the chronological aspects of human life, geography is concerned with the spatial aspects—where things are located and why they are located there. When human geographers take a spatial perspective, they are studying how people live on Earth, how they organize themselves, and why the events of human societies occur where they do.

The second key perspective is the **ecological perspective**, which refers to the relationships between living things and their environments. Looking at an issue from an ecological perspective involves studying the interactive and interdependent relationships between living things, ecosystems, and human societies. This perspective helps explain human societies' dependence on diverse ecosystems for essential resources such as food and water. Taken together, these two perspectives help human geographers understand the complex relationship between humans and environments. The awareness that these and other perspectives exist is fundamental to a geographer's understanding of the world's people and places.

The essential elements of geography can be summed up neatly in the following three questions: Where? Why there? Why care? When geographers apply these questions, they are thinking geographically. Asking where something is located is the starting point for any geographic inquiry. Asking why it is located there pushes geographers to analyze the reasons behind processes and interactions. And asking why someone should care helps them establish the importance and relevance of their inquiries. Certain spatial concepts help geographers answer these questions. These concepts include location, place, space, flows, pattern, distance decay, and time-space compression.

LOCATION AND PLACE It should be no surprise by now that where things are found is an important geographic concept. **Location** is the position that a point or object occupies on Earth. Location can be expressed in absolute or relative terms. **Absolute location** is the exact location of an object. It is usually expressed in coordinates of longitude and latitude. The city of Budapest, Hungary, for instance, is located at 47.50° N, 19.04° E. With the proper means of transportation and a Global Positioning System (GPS), you could use these coordinates to get to Budapest from any other location on Earth. **Relative location** is a description of where a place is in relation to other places or features. A geographer might describe Budapest's relative location as 134 miles southeast of Vienna, Austria, or she might say that the city straddles the Danube River in the middle of the Carpathian Basin in north central Hungary.

The term **place** is related to but different from location. A place is a location on Earth that is distinguished by its physical and human characteristics. The physical characteristics of a place include its climate, landforms, soils, water sources, vegetation, and animal life; the human characteristics include its languages, religions, political systems, economic systems, population distribution, architecture, and quality of life.

When people say they feel a strong "sense of place," they are referring to the emotions attached to an area based on their personal experiences. The sense of place that people have for their hometown or certain buildings—a baseball stadium, for example—is stronger than it is for places they don't know, and it is tied to their sense of identity. Because humans create the concept of place in their encounters with the world around them, someone who grew up in Boston may strongly identify with the city or a particular neighborhood within it, just as a person who grew up in Berlin may strongly identify with that city. Their physical surroundings, the people they know, and the culture influence their perceptions. The attachment that Bostonians and Berliners form with their history, architecture, landforms, and people contribute to their identities.

Places change over time. As a society's values, knowledge, resources, and technologies evolve, the people within that society make decisions that alter the place they occupy. Cities grow, construction covers the land, wetlands are filled in, and mountains are mined for resources. Other places might shrink as people move away, and over time disappear altogether. Decisions about how to organize society and how to interact with other places cause changes as well. The relationships between places affect all involved, politically, economically, and culturally. Over a long enough period of time, empires rise and fall, climates change, and society evolves enough to change life significantly for the people who live in a place. If you've visited or seen pictures of cities that have been around for a long time, however, you've probably noticed that elements of the place's history—its original sense of place—usually remain.

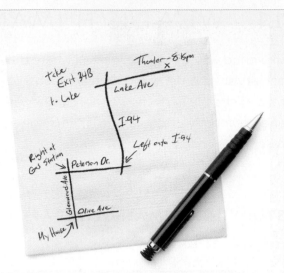

MENTAL MAPS

If you think about a place you go to regularly, you can probably imagine the route you take to get there. And you can likely draw a reasonably accurate map of your school, neighborhood, or town from memory. These internalized representations of portions of Earth's surface are called **mental maps**. Your mental map of different areas of the world depends on many factors. Your experiences, your age, where you live, and other factors contribute to the accuracy of your mental maps. For instance, what do you picture when you think of New England? How about the South, or the Pacific Northwest? Now compare your mental map to actual maps of these areas. You most likely have a clearer mental map of the area you live in than one that's far away.

Human geographers focus on two factors that influence how humans use a particular place. The first factor is **site**, which refers to a place's absolute location, as well as its physical characteristics, such as the landforms, climate, and resources. The second factor is **situation**, which refers to a place's location in relation to other places or its surrounding features. Situation describes a place's connections to other places, such as transportation routes (like roads, rail lines, and waterways), political associations, and economic and cultural ties.

When describing the site of the Spanish city of Barcelona, a geographer would say it is located on a plain with the Besós River to the north and the Llobregat River to the south. It lies between a rocky outcrop and a semicircle of mountains. It has a mild Mediterranean climate. Barcelona's situation, on the other hand, is that it is a port city on the Mediterranean Sea, which historically controlled the western portion of the sea along with Mallorca and Valencia. And because there are few navigable rivers in the region, Barcelona was well-situated as a major hub on the trade route from France to southeastern Spain.

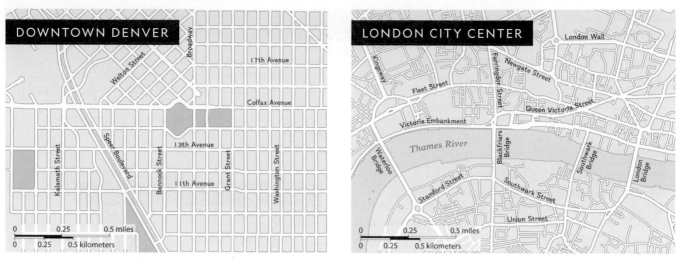

The street maps of Denver and London illustrate contrasting urban patterns—a city like London that has evolved over a long period of time looks very different from a relatively newer city like Denver. The winding roads of London bear little resemblance to Denver's angular, gridlike layout.

SPACE, PATTERN, AND FLOW As you've read, when geographers think geographically, they are considering the arrangement of things in **space**. Space in this instance refers to the area between two or more things on Earth's surface. Studying the ways in which things are **distributed**, or arranged within a given space, can help human geographers describe and analyze the organization of people, places, and environments on Earth. Density and pattern are key concepts in the examination of distribution.

Density is the number of things—people, animals, or objects—in a specific area. For example, a geographer might compare the population density of a large city to that of a rural area. Manila, the capital city of the Philippines, has over 171,000 people per square mile. A rural area like the province of Davao del Sur, on the other hand, has about 850 people per square mile. Based on this statistic, what conclusions might a geographer be able to draw about the lives of a person in Manila and a person in Davao del Sur?

Pattern—how things are arranged in a particular space—is another factor of distribution. Depending on how humans settled and developed a place, and what their needs are for it, its features might be arranged in a neat, geometric pattern, or they might be arranged in a pattern that seems more random. Studying the patterns of phenomena in space can help geographers understand different processes, such as patterns of agricultural production, urban settlement, or the distribution of fast-food restaurants in a town. In Unit 5 you'll learn about different types of rural settlement patterns and the reasons why each pattern developed. Patterns can be observed in urban areas as well. Many old cities in Europe, for example, are made up of narrow, winding roads that are inconvenient for car traffic. But Denver, Colorado, was built on a grid system, with streets that intersect at right angles, which makes the city easier to navigate. How might getting around and dealing with traffic patterns differ in London than in Denver?

Obviously, geographers are not studying a world at rest. Any given space changes over time as things move from one place to another. The study of the **flow** of people, goods, and information and the economic, social, political, and cultural effects of those movements on societies is an important aspect of human geography. You will learn about the flow of people in Chapter 5 on migration, the flow of culture in Chapter 7 on cultural change, and the flow of goods in Chapter 20 on trade.

HUMAN-ENVIRONMENT INTERACTION

LEARNING OBJECTIVE
PSO-1.B Explain how major geographic concepts illustrate spatial relationships

Regardless of where people live, they depend upon, adapt to, and modify the environment. They make decisions about how to live based on environmental features, and they make changes to the environment as a result of those decisions. Humans have always changed the landscapes they settled—using land for agriculture, tapping into natural resources, and building structures in which to live. But technologies and building techniques have given modern humans the ability to alter their environment in almost unlimited ways. Human geographers study how these changes affect both humans and the environment itself. Their views on the causes and effects of human societies' interactions with the natural environment have evolved over the years.

THEORIES OF INTERACTION In the 18th, 19th, and much of the 20th centuries, many geographers subscribed to a theory of human-environment interaction that has since been discredited, largely because some experts believe it inaccurately favors the accomplishments of certain societies over others. This theory—**environmental determinism**—argues that human behavior is largely controlled by the

A model is a representation of reality, which presents significant features or relationships in a generalized form. Models help geographers analyze spatial features, processes, and relationships. One example is the distance decay model. **Distance decay** is a key geographic principle that describes the effect of distance on interactions. The principle states that the farther away one thing is from another, the less interaction the two things will have. Cartographer and geographer Waldo Tobler's first law of geography states that while all things on Earth are related to all other things, the closer things are to one another, the more they are related. Think about an earthquake, flood, or revolution. The closer you are to any of these phenomena, the more you will be affected by it. Distance decay is connected to **friction of distance**, a concept that states that distance requires time, effort, and cost to overcome. Friction of distance applies to political, religious, and cultural movements as well, but because of modern advancements in technology and transportation, it has less impact today than in the past.

Time-space compression is a key geographic principle that is related to friction of distance. It describes the processes causing the relative distance between places to shrink. Modern transportation has greatly reduced travel times, and the internet and other forms of communication have made it easier to communicate with people anywhere on the planet and to send money around the world through online banking

transfers. Through these technologies, humans have effectively caused the distances between places to seem shorter, as they are able to cross those distances more quickly and exchange goods and information more easily. The map below illustrates time-space compression. Why might Europe and North America seem closer together to a person today than they seemed to Columbus?

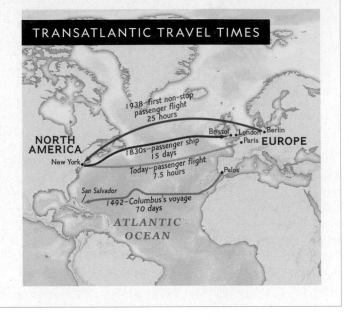

physical environment. According to the theory, a region's climate and soil fertility dictate how a society develops as it adapts to the environment. Environmental determinism has fallen out of favor, however, because it argued that the environment most suited to human development is that of western Europe and North America. This fails to take into account the fact that civilizations in other regions, such as North Africa and much of Asia, arose earlier than those in Europe and North America and were more advanced technologically and highly influential culturally for long periods of human history.

Modern geographers favor **possibilism**, a theory that argues that humans have more agency, or ability to produce a result, than environmental determinism would suggest. According to possibilism, individuals are active, not passive, agents. The environments in which they live offer individuals opportunities and challenges. Societies react to those opportunities and challenges in different ways depending on the decisions they make, their ingenuity, and the technologies available to them. The environment places some limitations on human activity, but societies have a range of options in deciding how to live within a physical environment. Think about settlements that have grown up in deserts. People divert rivers to irrigate land for agriculture and build dams and aqueducts for drinking water. They build whole cities in places that were once too barren and dry to support human life.

SUSTAINABILITY An important concept in thinking about human-environment interaction is **sustainability**, the use of Earth's land and natural resources in ways that ensure they will continue to be available in the future. Sustainable land use requires consideration of whether a particular natural resource is renewable, meaning nature produces it faster than people consume it, or nonrenewable, meaning people consume it faster than nature produces it. Solar and wind energy, for instance, are renewable resources, while coal and other fossil fuels are nonrenewable. The effects of a society's use of natural resources are important to consider as well. For example, what advice do you think a geographer concerned with sustainability might give to a government deciding what laws to pass to fight climate change?

GEOGRAPHIC THINKING

1. Explain whether the address of a restaurant is an absolute location or a relative location.

2. Describe how geographic concepts help to explain the distribution of phenomena on Earth.

3. Describe how technology "shrinks the world" using the time-space compression model.

4. Compare the theories of environmental determinism and possibilism.

CRITICAL VIEWING Lettuce and other produce grows in a garden behind center field at AT&T Park in San Francisco. Restaurants inside the ballpark use produce grown here to serve directly to baseball fans. ▮ Explain how this feature of the ballpark is an example of sustainability.

NEW ORLEANS—SITE VS. SITUATION

THE ISSUE New Orleans's proximity to resources, advantageous natural features, and transportation routes is ideal, but the land upon which it sits offers many challenges.

LEARNING OBJECTIVES

PSO-1.B Explain how major geographic concepts illustrate spatial relationships.

PSO-6.A Explain the processes that initiate and drive urbanization and suburbanization.

BY THE NUMBERS

50%
of New Orleans is at or below sea level

454,845
Population pre-Katrina

391,006
2018 population

Source: The Atlantic, United States Census Bureau

IN THE EARLY 18TH CENTURY, the French colonists who settled Louisiana needed a location for the colony's capital. They considered a variety of sites—some inland and some on the coast. After much consideration, they decided on an option that was slightly inland, on the Mississippi River. This would become the site of the city of New Orleans. Centuries later, residents of the city and the country are still grappling with the choice the original settlers made.

They knew the site wasn't ideal. Located on a sharp bend on the east bank of the Mississippi River, at the head of the delta leading to the Gulf of Mexico, and just south of Lake Pontchartrain, New Orleans floods easily and regularly and is subject to severe storms from the Gulf of Mexico. However, the city's situation was perfect. Its location at the southern end of the Mississippi meant that New Orleans would be connected to a huge area of the lands to the north. The Mississippi is the largest river system on the continent and has river links to two-thirds of the continental United States. Much of the continent's commerce traveled down the river right past the city. The city's founders decided that the advantages of the situation outweighed the disadvantages of the site. The city's situation is still valuable today—because of its location at the mouth of the Mississippi and its access to the Gulf of Mexico, New Orleans remains one of the busiest ports in the United States.

In order to deal with the site disadvantages, the city's early residents built artificial levees, or embankments, to keep the river from flooding the streets, and in the mid-1800s engineers figured out how to drain the wetlands between the river and Lake Pontchartrain, allowing the city's borders to spread out into low-lying terrain. Today roughly 50 percent of the city lies below sea level, a shallow bowl surrounded by more modern—but certainly not perfect—levees to keep the water out.

The imperfections of those levees were revealed in late August 2005, when Katrina, a destructive and deadly hurricane, slammed into New Orleans. The ten inches of rain that Katrina dumped, combined with a devastating storm surge, overwhelmed the levees that held back the waters of Lake Pontchartrain and nearby Lake Borgne. After the levees failed, water poured into the city, eventually flooding 80 percent of its land.

More than a million people evacuated the region before the storm, but tens of thousands remained because they could not or would not leave. Thousands of stranded residents took shelter at the Louisiana Superdome and the New Orleans Convention Center, but a lack of food and drinkable water and absence of sanitation created a public health emergency.

By September 6, the city had been almost completely evacuated, and fewer than 10,000 people remained. Much of the city was eventually rebuilt, and some of the displaced returned, but the population today remains lower than it was when Katrina struck. ▮

GEOGRAPHIC THINKING

Explain why New Orleans's founders decided that the advantages of the location's situation outweighed the disadvantages of its site.

Floodwaters flow over a failed levee along the Inner Harbor Navigation Canal near downtown New Orleans following Hurricane Katrina, while a trapped resident waves a white flag for help. A major flaw of New Orleans's site is found in its low-lying land along Lake Pontchartrain and the Mississippi River. Massive flooding devastated the region after Hurricane Katrina struck in 2005.

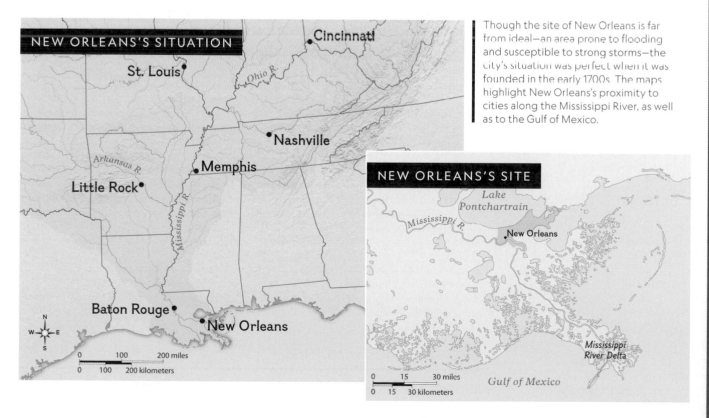

Though the site of New Orleans is far from ideal—an area prone to flooding and susceptible to strong storms—the city's situation was perfect when it was founded in the early 1700s. The maps highlight New Orleans's proximity to cities along the Mississippi River, as well as to the Gulf of Mexico.

NEW ORLEANS'S SITUATION

Cincinnati
St. Louis
Ohio R.
Nashville
Arkansas R.
Memphis
Little Rock
Mississippi R.
Baton Rouge
New Orleans

0   100   200 miles
0   100   200 kilometers

NEW ORLEANS'S SITE

Lake Pontchartrain
Mississippi R.
New Orleans
Mississippi River Delta
Gulf of Mexico

0   15   30 miles
0   15   30 kilometers

CONSERVING THE DELTA

Costa and her team are collecting scientific data that will be used to develop strategies to protect the Okavango River Basin and ensure sustainability.

LEARNING OBJECTIVE
PSO-1.B Explain how major geographic concepts illustrate spatial relationships.

As climate change worsens and world population grows, sustainability becomes an ever more important topic in human geography. It is also a major concern of biologist Adjany Costa, the assistant director for National Geographic's Okavango Wilderness Project. Costa feels that the most effective human-environment interaction is to have as little impact on the environment as possible.

The Okavango River Basin is the largest freshwater wetland in southern Africa and provides water for a million people. Its delta in northern Botswana is rich with biodiversity and is home to the world's largest remaining elephant population, plus lions, cheetahs, wild dogs, and hundreds of species of birds.

Costa is a member of a team of scientists who have embarked on a series of canoe and mountain bike expeditions into the least known, most inaccessible areas of the watershed. As Costa explains, the basin's situation—its relationship with the surrounding areas—informs her work: "It's adjacent to a protected area in Namibia and two national parks, so it would create this whole square of conservation of land and ocean that are independent of each other but can still work together in regards to conservation."

In addition to research, another major part of Costa's job is advocacy and education. She meets with community leaders to educate them about the benefits of conserving the basin. The ultimate goal of the team's work is to help establish a sustainable management plan that will protect the Okavango watershed's source rivers forever.

GEOGRAPHIC THINKING

Identify and explain the reasons why it is important to sustain the Okavango River Basin.

1.2 SPATIAL PATTERNS: SCALE AND REGION

Human geographers examine issues from different angles. They might get a broad overview of the effects of a process on a large area and then move on to study how the same process affects a small space. They group areas together into cohesive units in order to identify and organize the space they study. These tools help them to interpret Earth's complexity.

ZOOMING IN AND OUT

LEARNING OBJECTIVES

PSO-1.C Define scales of analysis used by geographers.

PSO-1.D Explain what scales of analysis reveal.

Think about an issue being covered in the news today. Is it a local, regional, national, or global issue? When answering a question like this, you are taking **scale** into account. This concept is different than scale on a map, which tells you how distance on the map compares to distance on the ground. Scale here refers to the area of the world being studied. Geographers use different scales of analysis as a framework for understanding how events and processes influence one another. For instance, a geographer might study the effects of air pollution in a city's industrial region, in the entire city, or in the country as a whole. Examining the effects of pollution at these different scales of analysis can help geographers gain a better understanding of the impacts of atmospheric processes on pollution.

The U.S. and Mississippi food insecurity maps reveal that on a national scale, about 12.5 percent of the U.S. population struggles to put food on the table. Examining the issue at a more local scale, however, it becomes clear that the problem is more serious in certain areas of the country. At the state level, Alabama, Arkansas, Louisiana, and Mississippi have food insecurity rates between 17 and 19.9 percent. Focusing on the county level reveals that in several counties in Mississippi, more than 30 percent of the population suffers from food insecurity. At an even more local level, Issaquena County in western Mississippi does not have a single grocery store, which means that many residents buy much of their food day-to-day at local convenience stores. With limited access to fresh foods,

SCALES OF ANALYSIS: FOOD INSECURITY IN THE UNITED STATES

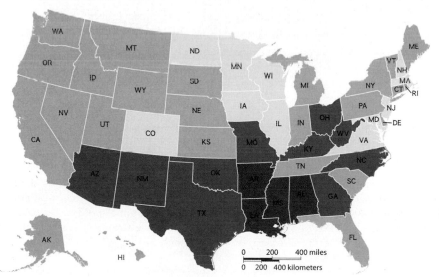

Food insecurity rates, by state
- 17–19.9%
- 14–16.9%
- 11–13.9%
- 7–10.9%

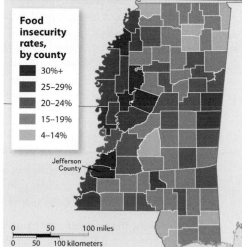

FOOD INSECURITY: MISSISSIPPI

Food insecurity rates, by county
- 30%+
- 25–29%
- 20–24%
- 15–19%
- 4–14%

READING MAPS The maps show food insecurity rates on a national scale and a local scale. The shading on the U.S. map reveals that the percentage of people who struggle with hunger is higher in certain areas of the country, such as the Southeast. Focusing on the county level in the Mississippi map reveals some of the highest rates of food insecurity in the nation. ▮ Explain what using different scales of analysis reveals about food insecurity in the United States.

some end up eating less healthy, processed convenience food rather than food with higher nutritional value. What happens at one scale affects processes at other scales, and data at different scales is necessary to fully understand issues such as food insecurity.

Observations at a local scale can also reveal details that might not be apparent at a regional scale. For instance, at the regional scale, an analysis of the population of New England reveals that 76.7 percent of the population is White, 9.6 percent is Hispanic, and 6.6 percent is African-American. Looking at the issue at a more local scale, however, reveals that Suffolk County, where Boston is located, is much more diverse, at 46.1 percent White, 19.3 percent Hispanic, and 22.5 percent African-American. In short, looking at diversity at a regional scale, New England is one of the least diverse regions in the United States. But when they look at diversity at a local scale focused on Suffolk County, geographers find a very different—and much more diverse—picture. It is important to note that scale can obscure actual spatial patterns. Suffolk may be a diverse county, but as geographers drill down even further, they find that the county-wide diversity does not apply to all Boston neighborhoods. The city is actually quite segregated. Some neighborhoods are more than 80 percent White, others are more than 80 percent African-American, and still others are more than 65 percent Hispanic.

Geographers' understanding of scale drives their research questions and data collection, and their findings then inform policy makers, hopefully to make better decisions. An issue that has a major effect on the planet, such as climate change, can be more fully understood by analyzing it at a variety of scales. For instance, scientists have determined that, globally, the planet is warming. As they drill down to a regional scale, however, the impacts differ depending on a variety of factors. Canada's Arctic region is warming at twice the global rate, potentially causing heat waves across the country and increasing risk of wildfires and drought.

In regions where climate change is occurring more slowly, its effects are more subtle. Additionally, sea level rise is not occurring uniformly across the planet. In certain regions, such as the Eastern Seaboard of the United States and in the Gulf of Mexico, sea levels have risen at higher than average rates. In other regions, like the U.S. West Coast and the oceans around Antarctica, sea levels have risen at lower than average rates. Understanding that the impacts of climate change will not be uniform helps governments prepare for problems that specifically affect their areas.

GEOGRAPHIC THINKING

1. Explain how using different scales of analysis helps geographers and other scientists understand the ways climate change is affecting the planet.

2. Describe how the analysis of the population of New England differs at a regional and local scale.

UNIFYING FEATURES

LEARNING OBJECTIVE
SPS-1.A Describe different ways that geographers define regions.

A **region** is an area of Earth's surface with certain characteristics that make it distinct from other areas. Regions are human constructs, meaning people decide how they appear. The boundaries between regions are typically not clearly defined and are often transitional, overlapping, and contested. In other words, regional boundaries can be fuzzy. For instance, the United States' Southwest is thought of as one distinct region, and El Norte (The North) in Mexico is also considered to be its own region, but because of the consistency with which the people and cultures cross the border, in some ways it is a single region. This is evident in the cities of El Paso, Texas, and Ciudad Juárez, Mexico, which share a regional economy where cultures and traditions blend and people cross the border, back and forth, on a regular basis.

Regions are a valuable tool for human geographers because they serve as an organizing technique for framing detailed knowledge of the world and for asking geographic questions. They are effective comparison tools as well. Knowing about the features of different regions is useful in discussing similarities and differences between parts of the world. Regions can be of any size, and they can act as a scale of analysis between the local, the national, and the global, helping geographers to synthesize their understanding of the world. Geographers define three types of regions based on the features that an area shares.

FORMAL REGION: THE PAMPAS

The Pampas of South America are grasslands that cover an area of 300,000 square miles. The region is defined by its moderate climate and is one of the richest grazing areas in the world.

FORMAL REGION A **formal region** is an area that has one or more shared traits. It is also referred to as a uniform region. The shared trait can be physical, such as a landform like a mountain range or a climate area like a desert. It can be cultural, such as a language or religion. Or it can be a combination of traits, defined by data such as measures of population, income, ethnicity, or precipitation. For instance, a country is a formal political region whose shared characteristics include its government, laws, services, and taxes. A smaller example of a formal political region is a state or a province within a country. The continent of Africa, with its distinct boundaries, is a formal region as well.

The Rocky Mountains make up a formal physical region in the United States, as do the Great Plains. The Pampas region of South America, shown on the "Formal Region: The Pampas" map, is defined by its moderate climate. Formal regions can also be defined by their agricultural growing season, such as temperate regions, which have long growing seasons. The corn belt, an area of the Midwest United States where corn and soybeans are the dominant crops, is a formal economic and agricultural region. The Pyrenees Mountains create a formal region along the French-Spanish border in Western Europe. People in this rugged region have developed their own culture over thousands of years.

At a more local scale, a city qualifies as a formal region as well. And within cities, shared traits can define small formal regions. The ethnic neighborhoods found in many large cities, for instance, may be considered formal regions. In the borough of Brooklyn in New York City, a large number of Hasidic Orthodox Jews live in the neighborhoods of Crown Heights, Williamsburg, and Borough Park. These neighborhoods form a region shaped by a shared religion and culture.

FUNCTIONAL REGION A **functional region** is defined as an area organized by its function around a focal point, or the center of an interest or activity. The focal point of a functional region is called a **node**. The node is the focus of the region, such as the downtown of a city. Nodes serve a particular function—often a political, social, or economic purpose—and have internal connections that tie the region together. For instance, the central business districts of some cities form the focal point for the cities' economic activity. Workers commute to this district, usually downtown, along the internal connections of roads and rail lines from other areas of the city, or from the suburbs. The central business district acts as the node for the functional region that consists of the metropolitan area.

Functional regions exist at a range of scales and can apply to a variety of geographic activities. The "Airline Flight Routes" map shows the functional region created by a major airline's flights from the Hartsfield-Jackson Atlanta International Airport to locations throughout the Americas. The airport acts as the region's node—a major hub for

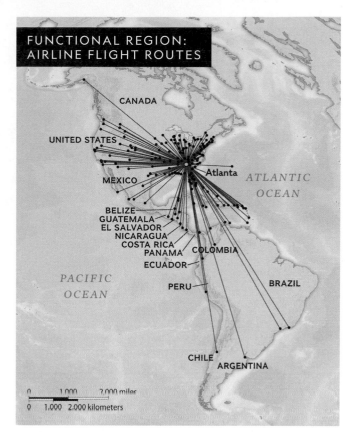

Delta Airlines flies to cities throughout the Americas from the Hartsfield-Jackson Atlanta International Airport. These cities form a functional region with the airport as the node.

The Metrorail system connects Washington, D.C., to its surrounding suburbs. L'Enfant Plaza and Metro Center serve as nodes from which six color-coded lines branch off.

PERCEPTUAL REGION: THE MIDWEST

The Midwest is a perceptual region comprising 12 states. It is defined in part by people's perceptions of the region—for example, as a largely rural area with a friendly population.

perceptions of the area—that is, their subjective understanding of the world as influenced by their culture and experience. What are the characteristics that make up the Midwest region of the United States, for example? Most people think about farms—especially corn and dairy products—and polite, down-to-earth people. The Midwest is generally not thought to be very ethnically or racially diverse, and politicians and pundits sometimes belittle it as "flyover country," meaning that it's nothing but a place you fly over to get from one coast to another. Each of these characteristics influence people's perceptions of the Midwest.

People often disagree on the boundaries of perceptual regions. Someone from the East Coast might perceive the Midwest to include Ohio, Indiana, Michigan, and parts of Pennsylvania, but people living in Minnesota, Wisconsin, or Kansas might feel strongly that they're Midwesterners. And while these regions may help to impose a personal sense of order and structure on the world, they often do so on the basis of stereotypes that may be inappropriate or incorrect. The Midwest does have large swaths of rural areas, for example, but it also contains large, diverse cities.

Outside of the United States, Eastern Europe is an example of a perceptual region. According to the United Nations, Eastern Europe consists of 23 countries including the Czech Republic, Poland, Romania, Russia, and the countries of the Balkan Peninsula. But the region exists in most people's minds based on its political, historical, and cultural characteristics. The area makes up most of what was known as the Eastern Bloc during the Cold War—the countries that were ruled by Communist governments in the years after World War II. Culturally and historically, the region was influenced by several empires. Together these characteristics define a region that exists separately in people's perceptions from Western Europe.

national and international flights. All flights from some smaller airports in the U.S. South go through Hartsfield-Jackson, making it the only connecting point for air travel between these locations.

The hub-and-spoke design of many public transportation systems form functional regions as well. The hub at the center of the system is a node, at which a great deal of economic or cultural activity occurs. From there, rail lines branch off toward the suburbs. An example is the rapid transit system of Washington, D.C., depicted in the "D.C. Metro System" map, which has six rail lines that connect the outskirts of the city to the city center.

Cities with ports, or large commercial shipping facilities, form functional regions with their surrounding areas, called hinterlands. The ports act as nodes of these regions. Goods come in on ships and are distributed to the appropriate processing plants and shipping centers in the hinterlands. At these facilities, goods are received, produced, processed, and shipped out, either through the port or into the interior of the country.

A more local example of a functional region is the service area of a pizza shop. At the node is the shop, which might limit its delivery range to a two-mile radius. The edge of the service area is the limit of the pizza shop's functional region.

PERCEPTUAL REGION A **perceptual region**,

also called a **vernacular region**, is a type of region that reflects people's feelings and attitudes about a place. A perceptual region, therefore, is defined by people's

GEOGRAPHIC THINKING

3. Quebec is a province in Canada in which 83 percent of the population speaks French as a first language. Identify Quebec's region type.

4. Compare the functional region of a pharmacy in a dense city with few drivers to the functional region of a pharmacy in a sparsely populated suburb.

5. Describe the role that cuisine, or style of food, might play in the understanding of a vernacular region.

CASE STUDY

INDIA— REGIONAL DIFFERENCES IN SCALE

THE ISSUE India has experienced impressive economic growth this century, but large portions of its population aren't experiencing a fair share of the benefits.

LEARNING OBJECTIVE
PSO-1.C Define scales of analysis used by geographers.

BY THE NUMBERS

$452.7 BILLION

GDP in 2000

2.6 TRILLION

GDP in 2017

25%

Poverty rate in rural areas

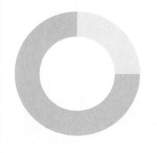

Source: World Bank

The contrast between poverty and wealth is evident in Mumbai, India, where skyscrapers rise behind an informal housing settlement on the city's outskirts.

SINCE THE TURN OF THE 21ST CENTURY, India has experienced astonishing economic growth, seeing its gross domestic product (GDP) increase from $452.7 billion in 2000 to 2.6 trillion in 2017, a 474 percent increase in the size of its economy. To put that into perspective, the U.S. economy has grown by 88 percent during the same timeframe.

However, as geographers focus on more local scales of analysis, they find that this new wealth is not distributed evenly throughout the country. Indians in some regions have become very rich, while many parts of the country remain very poor. Much of the wealth is concentrated in just a handful of states, such as Maharashtra, Kerala, and Tamil Nadu. Since economic growth began to accelerate in India 20 years ago, the wealth divide between certain regions has continued to expand.

Before the acceleration of economic growth, incomes between different states were converging. Since the acceleration, incomes have diverged, with the average person in the three richest states having three times more wealth than the average person in the three poorest states. Looking at patterns within states reveals a rural-urban divide—a large proportion of the new wealth is being generated in cities like Mumbai and Delhi. Mumbai, a port city located on the Arabian Sea in southwestern India, is considered to be the financial and commercial center of India. The country's central bank is located in Mumbai, as is a government-owned life insurance corporation, investment institutions, and the Bombay Stock Exchange. In addition to its robust service sector, the economy of Delhi, which is where the country's capital is located, has created many jobs in trade, finance, public administration, and professional services.

In the less wealthy regions of India, fewer people are living in abject poverty, but the growing wealth divide concerns geographers. Most of the country's wealth— 77 percent of the total national wealth—is held by just 10 percent of the population. Many accusations of corrupt dealings between India's politicians and the rich have been made, giving rise to anger and protests among the less wealthy. Without political reforms to fight corruption and expand social services to people who are being left behind, geographers worry the problems will continue to get worse. ∎

GEOGRAPHIC THINKING

Explain why geographers might have concerns about growing inequality in India.

CHAPTER 2

GEOGRAPHIC INQUIRY: DATA, TOOLS, AND TECHNOLOGY

CRITICAL VIEWING As part of a mapping project initiated by UNICEF, Fatima Wariou, a university student from Niamey, Niger, captures GPS coordinates in the Sahara desert. Other participants of the MAP4DEV group study the movement of the sand toward an inhabited area nearby. ▌ Explain how collecting data helps these geographers to analyze the progression of the sand.

GEOGRAPHIC THINKING What tools do geographers use to depict spatial relationships?

2.1
THINKING LIKE A GEOGRAPHER: THE GEO-INQUIRY PROCESS

2.2
GEOGRAPHIC DATA AND TOOLS

CASE STUDY: Detroit—GIS Helps Find Safer Routes

NATIONAL GEOGRAPHIC EXPLORER Sarah Parcak

2.3
UNDERSTANDING MAPS

2.4
THE POWER OF DATA

NATIONAL GEOGRAPHIC EXPLORER Shah Selbe

2.1 THINKING LIKE A GEOGRAPHER: THE GEO-INQUIRY PROCESS

Geographers use spatial analysis to explain patterns of human behavior and understand how places and societies are organized. They seek to understand where things are, why they are there, and how they develop and change over time.

THINKING LIKE A GEOGRAPHER

Geographers think spatially in terms of space, place, arrangement, and interconnections between humans and the environment. Understanding the complexities of the world, or even of a small community, involves observing the environment, aspects of culture, politics, economics, and more. Therefore, thinking like a geographer requires the integration of many topics and disciplines. Geographic thinking calls for asking questions, collecting and organizing data from a myriad of sources, making connections, and presenting data in a usable way. Only then can people make informed decisions and take appropriate action.

Using the National Geographic Geo-Inquiry Process supports geographic thinking. Tools such as maps, globes, graphs, photographs, and satellite imagery provide geographers with vast amounts of data about the world that is analyzed to understand the processes driving human geography. Following the Geo-Inquiry Process provides geographers a systematic way to examine complex issues at various scales—local, regional, or global. It also helps users make connections among various components of an issue, identify patterns, and draw conclusions to make informed predictions and decisions that can impact communities.

THE GEO-INQUIRY PROCESS

The Geo-Inquiry question is at the heart of the process. Geographers ask questions about spatial distributions, such as *Why do the majority of people migrate to urban areas?* or *Why did many settlements on rivers grow to become cities?*

Suppose local leaders have proposed building a new school in your community, but they have not determined where it should be built. To address this issue, you might first ask: *Where should the school be located?* Note that even this basic geographic question can generate multiple responses and lead to further questions depending on the purpose

---

THE GEO-INQUIRY PROCESS

The Geo-Inquiry Process is a five-step method, summarized here. As you read this chapter, you will find tips on carrying out each step.

- **ASK** In the first step of the process, you explore an issue or problem through a geographic lens that addresses the three basic questions you're already familiar with: *Where? Why there? Why care?* As you explore the problem or issue further, you reach a more complex understanding of the issue that will help narrow your focus into an overarching Geo-Inquiry question. This question will drive your project.

- **COLLECT** In the second step, you collect the data you need to answer the question. You might collect this data through interviews, fieldwork, by contacting experts or organizations, or other forms of research.

- **VISUALIZE** Once you've collected your data, you will have a large amount of information that you need to organize. Visual representation is critical. Data can be displayed in maps or through other visuals. Visuals can make complex information easier to understand and better reveal connections and patterns.

- **CREATE** In this step, you create a Geo-Inquiry story that answers your Geo-Inquiry question. This step walks people through the issue. The way you choose to create and communicate your story should be well matched to your audience.

- **ACT** This final step includes sharing your Geo-Inquiry story with decision-makers in order to inspire them to take action. Ask yourself: *What action should be taken based on the findings?*

ASK   COLLECT   VISUALIZE   CREATE   ACT

makes it easy for geographers to make connections, for instance, understanding how natural resources impact the economic activities that take place in a region.

GIS maps support geovisualization, which is the process of creating visuals for geographic analysis using maps, graphs, and multimedia. This process allows users to analyze geospatial data interactively, aiding visual thinking and providing insights into the issues geographers are studying. One common use of GIS involves comparing natural features with human activity. GIS could be used to evaluate environmental risks to a community such as flood potential or human-made risks such as industrial pollution levels. Such information can help communities plan for future sustainable development.

Geospatial technologies collect and analyze immense amounts of data—data accessible to anyone with internet access—leading to a revolution in spatial decision-making. The geospatial revolution encompasses nearly every aspect of human life, from the relatively mundane, or common, everyday activities, to the most critical of decisions. Today, in an instant, individuals and organizations can send, receive, and broadcast information about where they are, where they have been, and where they are going. Maps created out of this geospatial data have a wide variety of uses. Locally, these maps provide information on everything from recommending restaurants to finding the nearest hospital to tracking criminals. Many U.S. cities are using geospatial data to address problems with public transportation or food access in underserved communities. On an international scale, multi-layer geospatial maps can aid relief efforts after an earthquake, track global trade and shipping, document

the potential impacts of climate change, support the deployment of troops during conflict, or assist in the drawing of territorial boundaries as a part of peace-making.

GEOGRAPHIC THINKING

1. Describe the difference between quantitative and qualitative data and provide an example of each.

2. Explain what GIS is and how it is used to understand spatial patterns and relationships.

OTHER REMOTE SENSING TOOLS

LEARNING OBJECTIVES

IMP-1.B Identify different methods of geographic data collection.

IMP-1.C Explain the geographical effects of decisions made using geographical information.

A variety of geospatial technologies gather data; some do so remotely, or without making physical contact. This method of collecting data is called **remote sensing**. Most remote sensing used by geographers relies on satellites or aircraft-based sensors to collect data.

Satellites take images of sections of Earth at regular intervals to determine changes that occur on the surface. Then the remotely-sensed images are brought into GIS along with other data for comparison and analysis. Comparing satellite images can help identify phenomena such as trends in urban development or the shrinking of the polar ice caps.

Geographers use data acquired from satellite images to study environmental and developmental changes. This image of Earth at night, compiled from more than 400 satellite images, provides insights into the location of urban populations and economic development using the nighttime lights cities emit.

CASE STUDY

DETROIT— GIS HELPS FIND SAFER ROUTES

THE ISSUE Getting to and from school safely was a problem for some students in Detroit, as an economic decline contributed to abandoned houses and urban blight.

LEARNING OBJECTIVES

IMP-1.B Identify different methods of geographic data collection.

IMP-1.C Explain the geographical effects of decisions made using geographical information.

BY THE NUMBERS

672,662

population of Detroit in 2019

51,000

students enrolled in Detroit Public Schools Community District in 2019

30,000+

estimated number of abandoned houses in Detroit in 2018

Sources: World Population Review; Chalkbeat; Detroit Metro Times

At Wayne State University's Center for Urban Studies in Detroit, middle and high school students learned how to use GIS to map their neighborhoods and discover safer routes to and from school.

GEOGRAPHIC INFORMATION SYSTEMS have a wide range of real-world applications. They assist in displaying and analyzing data to make evidence-based decisions in a range of situations. In Detroit, Michigan, for example, GIS has been used to map safer school routes. Since 1999, the Detroit Public Schools Community District has used GIS to divide the district into patrol sectors and blocks. The city collects and analyzes data from each of the sectors to identify safe routes to school for students.

Nonprofit organizations and the school district also enlisted students to address urban blight, or areas in disrepair. Studies show that vacant structures are a strong predictor of assault risk. The number of vacant houses in Detroit had grown following an economic decline. One assessment put the number around 22,000, but an investigation by a Detroit newspaper suggested the number was at least 30,000. Because abandoned buildings often lack easily identifiable addresses, no one had been able to pinpoint the locations of the vacant structures. Even as the city struggled to board up or sell the vacant homes, new abandoned buildings appeared. In an innovative program called Mapping Out A Safer Community, middle and high school students used GIS software and handheld GPS to map the vacancies. The technology allowed them to identify the exact locations of abandoned buildings and vacant properties. The students then compiled their data, presented it to local government officials, and suggested areas to target for code enforcement. Using the students' information, the city boarded up abandoned buildings. The students taking action is an example of the last step in the Geo-Inquiry Process.

The student initiative was just one part of a broader data-gathering initiative, however. Members of the AmeriCorps Urban Safety Project walked the school routes and conducted surveys of parents, students, and school personnel to identify hazards. In addition to abandoned buildings, they mapped issues related to lighting, sidewalks, and dangerous intersections. This information has been used as part of a broader, federally-funded program called Safe Routes to School (SRTS) that continues to work to ensure safe travel for Michigan students to and from school. ∎

GEOGRAPHIC THINKING

Think about the mental mapping you did in Chapter 1. What would you expect to find if you followed Detroit's example in mapping routes to your school?

A forestry conservation analyst from the World Wildlife Fund (WWF) uses an unmanned drone to map an area of the Western Amazon rain forest in Brazil. Unmanned drones can be used in more locations than traditional aircraft and they provide the same data-collection capacity at a fraction of the cost. This makes them an increasingly valuable data-collection tool.

Satellites are also used for real-time decision-making. For example, satellites can track the path of a hurricane and the speed it is traveling. This data can be used to help predict where a hurricane will land. After an event, it also can be used to show the extent of damage, enabling aid to be directed appropriately. Days after Hurricane Maria devastated much of Puerto Rico in 2017, satellite images showed dramatic changes to the landscape and helped identify the hardest-hit areas.

Remote sensors mounted on aircraft or drones are another source of data. In addition to satellite images, aerial photographs were taken of the land months after Maria's damage. The photographs, along with GIS, helped the U.S. Army Corps of Engineers analyze existing and new data about the island's electrical power grid so they could make repairs and provide generators to those without power even in remote areas. Airplane-mounted sensors are also used to measure the gradual sinking of land along

the Gulf Coast to assess risk to local communities. As the technology advances and becomes less expensive, drones are making remotely-sensed data more accessible than ever. They enable scientists, including cartographers and other geographers, to take detailed measurements between features or places on Earth's surface. Drones collect data that is then brought into GIS to determine changes in land use or environmental conditions. For example, farmers can use the data to get a bird's-eye view of the condition of their crops. The use of drones to identify a cluster of diseased plants in a large field or areas in need of water helps farmers treat targeted areas of their land and save resources.

Another source of geographic data is a **global positioning system (GPS)**, an integrated network of at least 31 satellites in the U.S. system that orbit Earth and transmit location data to handheld receivers. Essentially, a GPS receiver uses the time it takes to receive a transmitted signal to measure the distance to each satellite. The receiver uses this data to pinpoint the exact location of the receiver. The accuracy of the information allows people to determine the precise distance between two points, making GPS especially useful for navigation purposes. Pilots of airplanes and ships use GPS to stay on course. Smartphones and automobiles also are equipped with GPS receivers, enabling motorists to receive instructions for the fastest or most direct route to a desired destination. GPS-based mapping systems provide users with both maps and verbal directions to follow while traveling. GPS also uses information collected from other receivers to determine the speed of travelers and where traffic is stopped. GPS is used for several geospatial applications beyond GIS.

One of the challenges that geographers face today is the enormous amount of available data. In addition to the GPS satellites that provide positioning data and satellites that collect images of Earth, there are hundreds of satellites collecting information about population, migration, soils, ocean currents, and more. Online mapping services collect and share even more data through aerial photographs and street-level cameras. The amount of real-time data, or information that is available for analysis immediately after being collected, has grown tremendously. Now internet-based supercomputer systems are being developed to help geographers manage, analyze, and share this data.

GEOGRAPHIC THINKING

3. Identify three ways geographers collect data.

4. Describe how drones have impacted the acquisition of geospatial data.

5. Explain why it is important to collect data at the appropriate scale.

6. Describe one way geographers could use GPS in their work.

LEARNING OBJECTIVES

IMP-1.B Identify different methods of geographic data collection.

IMP-1.C Explain the geographical effects of decisions made using geographic information.

NATIONAL GEOGRAPHIC EXPLORER **SARAH PARCAK**

PROTECTING ARCHAEOLOGICAL SITES

Throughout the world, expanding development and natural environmental changes can put archaeological sites at risk. Looting, the stealing of artifacts from a site, presents another challenge. The demand for ancient artifacts fuels a black market that pays looters handsomely. Archaeologist Sarah Parcak has used geospatial technologies to preserve and protect archaeological sites in Egypt.

Parcak is a professor of archaeology at the University of Alabama at Birmingham. She specializes in Egypt, which is where she had her first dig almost two decades ago. In her early work, she recognized that archaeological sites were in danger of being lost forever as a result of encroaching urban development and the rampant looting of artifacts. She posed an important geographic question: *How could her team preserve and protect these irreplaceable records of human history? This guiding question led to others. Where are Egypt's archaeological sites? What is the most efficient way to find them? Which sites are in greatest need of protection? How can we encourage people to recognize the importance of protecting these sites?*

Parcak set about gathering data to help answer these questions. She conducted extensive background research and examined satellite images showing discolored soil, changes in vegetation, or other differences in the landscape that might suggest that ancient ruins lay under the surface.

Following Egypt's political upheaval in 2011, Parcak learned from social media that people were digging illegally at various sites and stealing artifacts. Comparing satellite images of the region taken in 2010 to images taken after 2011 (such as the one above) revealed a landscape increasingly scarred by looting pits, and confirmed that the theft of artifacts was on the rise. Parcak used the satellite images and maps to show government officials where looting was taking place. The government used her data to improve its protection of the endangered sites. As a result, Parcak not only helped Egypt solve a problem that it didn't know it had, but she facilitated the preservation of ancient artifacts for future generations.

GEOGRAPHIC THINKING

Explain how geospatial technologies used for data collection have impacted geographers' work.

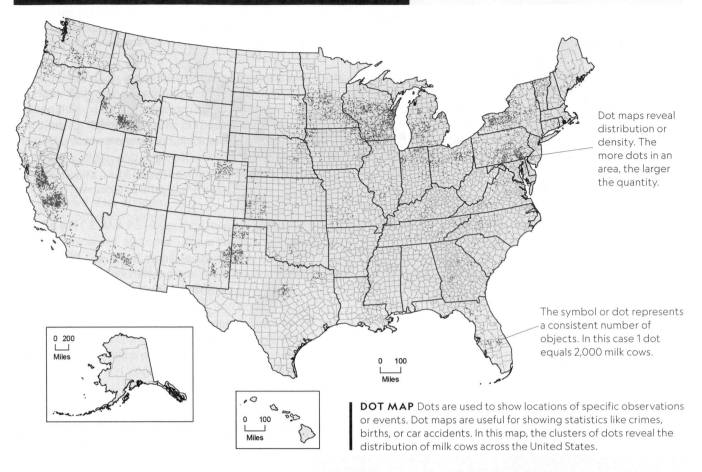

Dot maps reveal distribution or density. The more dots in an area, the larger the quantity.

The symbol or dot represents a consistent number of objects. In this case 1 dot equals 2,000 milk cows.

0 200 Miles

0 100 Miles

0 100 Miles

DOT MAP Dots are used to show locations of specific observations or events. Dot maps are useful for showing statistics like crimes, births, or car accidents. In this map, the clusters of dots reveal the distribution of milk cows across the United States.

THE GEO-INQUIRY PROCESS | TIPS FOR SUCCESS

VISUALIZE

- Begin to organize your data and consider how best to display it. Your goal is to demonstrate your understanding of the data you researched and your overall inquiry.

- Maps will probably be a key visual component of your inquiry. You can create a basemap of the area you are studying and add data layers using online mapping tools and sources.

- Consider adding images and text to your map. You can cut and paste or use online programs. Online mapping tools allow you to turn items on and off, so you can look at one type of data at a time.

- Add any first impressions you have about the area you are visualizing to your map. Attach sticky notes to printed visuals, or add markers if you are using an online mapping program.

- How you organize your data depends on the data type. Quantitative data can be organized using a spreadsheet program and then shown in graphs and charts. Add other visuals to help explain the data and further the story you're telling. Be sure that all your data is linked back to specific locations on your basemap.

- Analyze your data and notice any trends or patterns. Do the patterns relate to or answer your Geo-Inquiry question? Consider adding colors or symbols to your map to help display patterns or trends. Then analyze your map. You should be able to answer your Geo-Inquiry question at this point. If you can't, revisit your data and conduct further research.

- Finalize your map once you know it can answer your Geo-Inquiry question. Make adjustments to your maps and your other visuals so they are clear and clean. Include a title and make sure all labels are clear and relevant.

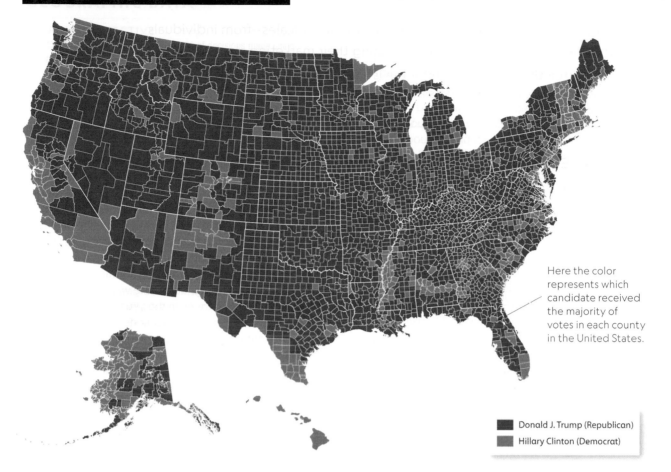

Here the color represents which candidate received the majority of votes in each county in the United States.

■ Donald J. Trump (Republican)
■ Hillary Clinton (Democrat)

CHOROPLETH MAP This thematic map uses colors or shading to represent categories of data for predetermined geographic areas such as census tracts, counties, states, provinces, or countries. Choropleth maps are useful for communicating quantitative data, such as demographics or election results.

Basemaps form the foundations of both reference and thematic maps. Many thematic maps use a basemap showing coastlines, city locations, and political boundaries. The map's theme is then layered onto this basemap. Political divisions, cities, or natural features provide reference points to help users understand the data that is presented on a thematic map, which can focus on any number of topics.

Most geographic data relates to specific points, lines, and areas. The way maps display these types of data affects analysis. Clusters are best illustrated in maps that use dots or graduated symbols, for instance. Isoline maps connect data points of equal value, like elevation, temperature, or precipitation. Choropleth maps use color or shading to display quantitative data in preset regions. Graduated symbols represent differences in size or extent of something in an area, like populations of a state or traffic volume by county. Greater numbers are represented by larger symbols.

A cartogram is a unique type of map that conveys information by making the areas on a map proportional to the variable being mapped. As one example, a cartogram might redraw the spatial features of the U.S. states according to population distribution, so that New York state or Massachusetts appears much larger than Alaska or Montana.

GEOGRAPHIC THINKING

4. Choose one of the thematic maps from this lesson. Based on specific details, describe one conclusion you can draw from the map.

5. Explain similarities and differences between dot maps and graduated symbols maps. Why might one or the other be preferable for different types of data?

THEY ARE WATCHING YOU

BY ROBERT DRAPER

The Dove satellite being held by a senior spacecraft technician at the San Francisco-based tech company Planet, is camera-equipped and able to snap two images per second. Satellites are important geographic tools that are used to investigate even small changes on Earth.

Expanding networks of satellites are providing unprecedented views of humans' influence on the land, the climate, and ourselves—documented in real time. The technology in question can monitor Earth's entire landmass every single day. It's the brainchild of a San Francisco–based company called Planet, founded by two idealistic former NASA scientists named Will Marshall and Robbie Schingler. At NASA they had been captivated by the idea of taking pictures from space, especially of Earth—and for reasons that were humanitarian rather than science-based.

They experimented by launching ordinary smartphones into orbit, confirming that a relatively inexpensive camera could function in outer space. "We thought, What could we do with those images?" Schingler said. "List the world's problems: poverty, housing, malnutrition, deforestation. All of these problems are more easily addressed if you have more up-to-date information about our planet."

A CHANGING VIEW OF EARTH In storybook fashion, Marshall and Schingler developed their first model in a garage in Silicon Valley. The idea was to design a relatively low-cost, shoe box-size satellite to minimize military-scale budgets often required for designing such technology—and then, as Marshall told me, "to launch the largest constellation of satellites in human history." By deploying many such devices, the company would be able to see daily changes on Earth's surface in totality.

In 2013, they launched their first satellites and received their first photographs, which provided a far more dynamic look at life around the world than previous global mapping imagery. "The thing that surprised us most," said Marshall, "is that almost every picture that came down showed how Earth was changing. Fields were reshaped. Rivers moved. Trees were taken down. Buildings went up. Seeing all of this completely changes our concept of the planet as being static."

WHAT SATELLITES CAN DO Today, Planet has more than 200 satellites in orbit, with about 150 so-called Doves that can image every bit of land every day when conditions are right. The company works with the Amazon Conservation Association to track deforestation in Peru. It has provided images to Amnesty International that document attacks on Rohingya villages by security forces in Myanmar. At the Middlebury Institute's Center for Nonproliferation Studies, recurring global imaging helps the think tank watch for the sudden appearance of a missile test site in Iran or North Korea.

Those are pro bono clients. Its paying customers include Orbital Insight, a Silicon Valley-based geo-spatial analytics firm that interprets data from satellite imagery. With such visuals, Orbital Insight can track the development of road or building construction in South America, the expansion of illegal palm oil plantations in Africa, and crop yields in Asia. In the company's conference room, James Crawford, the chief executive, opened his laptop and showed me aerial views of Chinese oil tanks, with their floating lids indicating they were about three-quarters full. "Hedge funds, banks, and oil companies themselves know what's in their tanks," he said with a sly grin, "but not in others', so temporal resolution [the amount of time needed to collect data] is extremely important."

Meanwhile, Planet's marketing team spends its days gazing at photographs, imagining an interested party somewhere out there who might benefit from the images. An insurance company wanting to track flood damage to homes in the Midwest. A researcher in Norway seeking evidence of glaciers eroding. But what about . . . a dictator wishing to hunt down a dissident army?

Here is where Planet's own ethical guidelines would come into play. Not only could it refuse to work with a client having malevolent motives, but it also doesn't allow customers to stake a sole proprietary claim over the images they buy. The other significant constraint is technological. Planet's surveillance of the world at a resolution of 10 feet is sufficient to discern the grainy outline of a single truck but not the contours of a human.

THE FUTURE OF PLANET On a bracing autumn evening in San Francisco, I returned to Planet to see the world through its all encompassing lens. More than a dozen clients would be there to show off how they're using satellite imagery—what it meant, in essence, to see the world as it's changing.

I zigzagged among semicircles of techies gathered raptly around monitors. Everywhere I looked, the world came into view. I saw, in the Brazilian state of Pará, the dark green stretches of the Amazon jungle flash red, prompting automatic emails to the landowners: *Warning, someone is deforesting your land!* I saw the Port of Singapore teem with shipping activity. I saw the croplands of southern Alberta, Canada, in a state of flagging health. I saw oil well pads in Siberia—17 percent more than in the previous year, a surprising sign of stepped-up production that seemed likely to prompt frantic reassessments in the world's oil and gas markets.

Planet's hosts halted the show-and-tell to say a few words. Andy Wild, the chief revenue officer, spoke of the new frontier. It was one thing to achieve, as Wild put it, "a daily cadence of the entire landmass of the Earth." Now the custodians of this technology had to "turn it into outcomes." Tom Barton, the chief operating officer, said, "I hope one year from now, we're here saying, 'We really did change the world.'"

Adapted from "They Are Watching You" by Robert Draper, *National Geographic*, February 2018

DISTANCE DECAY MODEL

A model is a represention of one aspect of reality, such as a geographic relationship, in a generalized form. It is important to examine models and compare them to real-world data to determine the degree to which they explain geographic effects in different contexts or at different scales.

The distance decay model describes a fundamental relationship in human geography: the impact of distance on interactions between locations. Specifically, the model states that the farther away two things or places are from one another, the less interaction they will have. Friction of distance—the idea that distance requires time, effort, and cost to overcome—explains some key factors that contribute to distance decay. Here, the first graph illustrates the distance decay model in its generalized form. The second graph illustrates the effects of distance decay on consumers deciding how far they will travel to shop. ▌Explain the degree to which the distance decay model explains the geographic effects of distance on individuals' shopping behavior.

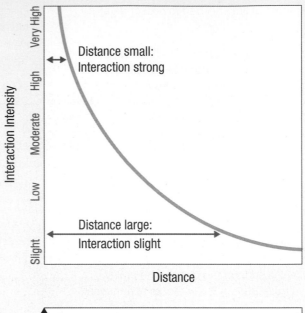

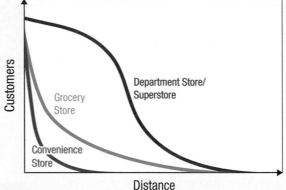

TIME-SPACE COMPRESSION

Some concepts are visually depicted in different ways. Here, time-space compression is represented by a shrinking globe, while the visual you studied in Chapter 1 highlights travel times across the Atlantic. The concept of time-space compression reflects the forces, such as improvements in transportation and communication, that can overcome the friction of distance. By compressing the amount of time it takes to travel or transmit information, these forces give the impression of lessening the space between distant locations. ▌Compare this visual with the one in Chapter 1 and identify which you think most clearly illustrates the effects of time-space compression. Explain.

ADVANCES IN TRANSPORTATION AND COMMUNICATION

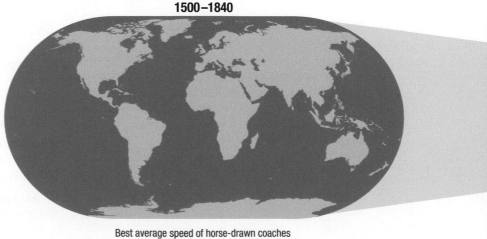

1500–1840

Best average speed of horse-drawn coaches and sailing ships was 10 mph

CHAPTER 1

WALLERSTEIN'S WORLD SYSTEM THEORY

A theory is a system of ideas that attempt to explain observed phenomena. Like models, theories explain geographic effects to varying degrees, depending on where and how they are applied.

Immanuel Wallerstein developed the world system theory to explain the global economic phenomena that he observed. Wallerstein's theory views the entire globe as a single economic system bound together through a complex network of trade and communications. It describes not only the economic ties between countries but also patterns of power across the globe.

Core countries derive the greatest benefits from the world economy and tend to dominate politically as well. Countries in the semi-periphery and periphery have less wealth and often less-stable governments, and thus find themselves in positions of lesser power. ▌ Explain the degree to which the world system theory explains the economic influence of a smaller core country such as France.

CONSUMER GOODS AND MONEY

CORE	SEMI-PERIPHERY	PERIPHERY
Economically and politically dominant on the world stage	Have core and periphery processes occurring	Often have unstable governments
Strong military and powerful allies	In the process of industrializing	Less wealth, lower levels of education than core
Highly interconnected transportation and communication networks	Often active in manufacturing and the exporting of goods	Export natural resources to core countries
Infrastructure that supports economic activity	Better transportation and communication networks than periphery	Inferior transportation and communication networks
Controls the global market	Have potential to grow into core country	Inadequate infrastructure for supporting economic activity

CHEAP LABOR AND NATURAL RESOURCES

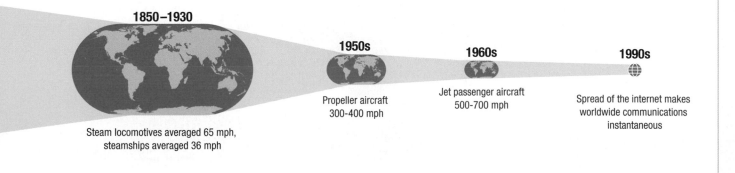

1850–1930

Steam locomotives averaged 65 mph, steamships averaged 36 mph

1950s

Propeller aircraft 300-400 mph

1960s

Jet passenger aircraft 500-700 mph

1990s

Spread of the internet makes worldwide communications instantaneous

GEOGRAPHIC SCALE

The term *scale* refers to the size of an area being studied. Examining a phenomenon at different scales reveals new perspectives that can lead to a deeper understanding. For example, geographers studying population density—the number of people relative to the amount of land—look at maps on a variety of scales.

These maps show the population densities in Asia on a national scale and the population of Pakistan on a district-wide scale. ▌Compare the maps and describe what each reveals about the population density of Pakistan. What additional information could you expect to learn from a density map of Islamabad?

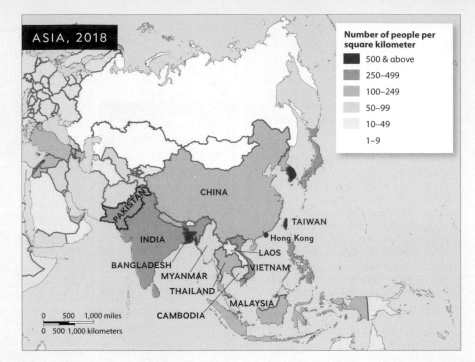

ASIA, 2018

Number of people per square kilometer

- 500 & above
- 250–499
- 100–249
- 50–99
- 10–49
- 1–9

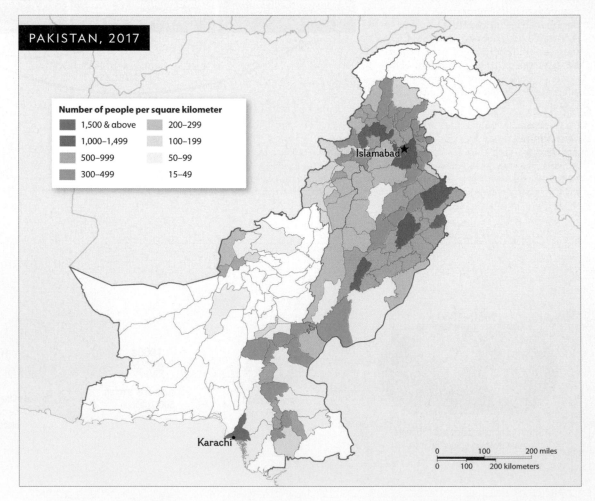

PAKISTAN, 2017

Number of people per square kilometer

- 1,500 & above
- 1,000–1,499
- 500–999
- 300–499
- 200–299
- 100–199
- 50–99
- 15–49

CHAPTER 2

SMARTPHONE MAPS

The maps many people interact with most often are found in their smartphone's GPS navigation app. One advantage of smartphone maps is their ability to display an area at a seemingly infinite variety of scales. The two smartphone maps provided show the same location at different scales. ❚ Compare the maps and describe what each scale reveals to the map user.

225 BAKER ST NW, ATLANTA, GA

CHAPTER 2

MAP PROJECTIONS

Our perceptions about countries and continents are strongly influenced by map projections. Equal-area projections accurately portray the area of a landmass, but they distort the shapes of various continents. Mercator projections preserve the continents' shapes and show accurate direction, making this projection ideal for plotting straight-line courses on navigation charts. However, the Mercator projection distorts the true area of landmasses, an effect that increases with distance from the equator. ❚ Compare the way the equal-area projection and the Mercator projection each depict the United States and Canada.

MERCATOR PROJECTION

EQUAL-AREA PROJECTION

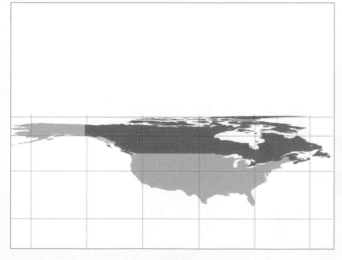

COMPARING TYPES OF MAPS

At times, it is useful to portray the same set of data on more than one type of map. Both maps show the percentage of the long-term average precipitation that has fallen over the period of one month in November. The long-term average precipitation is calculated over a 50-year base period. The dark red color indicates areas that received 50 percent or less of the long-term average precipitation. Dark green indicates areas that received 150 percent or more than the average. ▌ Compare the dot and isoline maps. Describe what each map helps viewers understand about precipitation during November 2019.

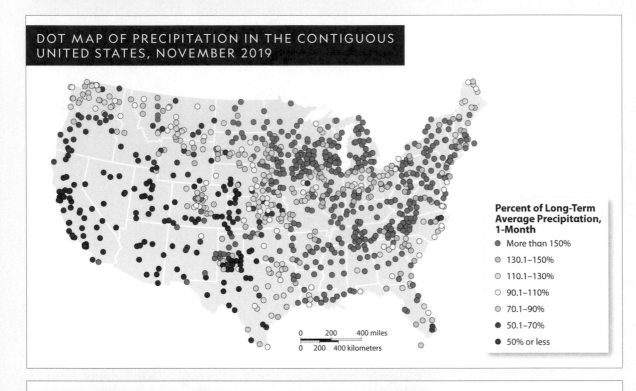

DOT MAP OF PRECIPITATION IN THE CONTIGUOUS UNITED STATES, NOVEMBER 2019

Percent of Long-Term Average Precipitation, 1-Month
- More than 150%
- 130.1–150%
- 110.1–130%
- 90.1–110%
- 70.1–90%
- 50.1–70%
- 50% or less

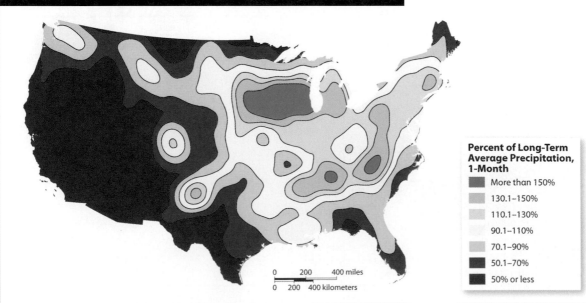

ISOLINE MAP OF PRECIPITATION IN THE CONTIGUOUS UNITED STATES, NOVEMBER 2019

Percent of Long-Term Average Precipitation, 1-Month
- More than 150%
- 130.1–150%
- 110.1–130%
- 90.1–110%
- 70.1–90%
- 50.1–70%
- 50% or less

CHAPTER 2

MAP LAYERS OF A THEMATIC MAP

AMAZON WILDFIRES IN SOUTH AMERICA, 2019

Caribbean Sea

VENEZUELA

GUYANA

SURINAME

FRENCH GUIANA (FR.)

AMAZONIA REGION

COLOMBIA

ECUADOR

A M A Z O N

Amazon

B A S I N

PERU

B R A Z I L

Brasília

BOLIVIA

PARAGUAY

Rio de Janeiro

PACIFIC OCEAN

ATLANTIC OCEAN

ARGENTINA

URUGUAY

Areas of Amazonia prone to burning each year

less   more

° **Active fire identified by satellite**

Fires shown as of August 26, 2019

300 mi
300 km

Matthew W. Chwastyk, NG Staff Sources: NASA/NOAA, VIIRS Daily Global Fire Detections; Amazonian Network of Georeferenced Socio-Environmental Information (RAISG)

This thematic map depicts where wildfires burned in the Amazon Basin in 2019. Its basemap is the shape of the South American continent. One GIS map layer shows the political borders of each country. ▌ Identify other map layers used to create this map. Explain how the map layers could be used by decision makers in South America.

POPULATION AND MIGRATION
PATTERNS AND PROCESSES

WHERE AND HOW WE LIVE

Sai Yeung Choi Street in Mongkok, Hong Kong

Issues involving world populations and their movement across the globe pop up in news sources nearly every day. Whether the concern is addressing the needs of changing populations, caring for expanding numbers of migrants, or coping with the cultural impacts of different ethnicities, languages, or religions jostling for space, it's clear to scientists across the spectrum: understanding population change and managing finite resources are foundational challenges.

The city of Shenzhen, in southeastern China, links Hong Kong to the Chinese mainland. Here, the juxtaposition of the modern city gleaming on the horizon with rice paddies in the foreground illustrates the urban expanding into the rural, and the tensions between accommodating a growing population and feeding it.

It's the human stories rising from a cultural landscape like this one that capture our imaginations—and should drive our policies.

CHAPTER 3
PATTERNS OF POPULATION

CHAPTER 4
POPULATION GROWTH AND DECLINE

CHAPTER 5
MIGRATION

UNIT 2 WRITING ACROSS UNITS, REGIONS & SCALES

UNIT 2 MAPS & MODELS ARCHIVE

OUT OF EDEN
A WALK THROUGH TIME

Geographers, historians, and archaeologists study the political, economic, and cultural effects of human migration and human interaction across the world. To tell this story of interaction and impact, National Geographic Fellow and Pulitzer-Prize winning journalist Paul Salopek is retracing the path of human migration by walking 21,000 miles over the course of several years. Salopek's online dispatches reflect what he calls the practice of "slow journalism," a reliance on forming personal bonds with people who share compelling stories with him about their everyday lives.

LEARNING OBJECTIVE
IMP-2.E Explain historical and contemporary geographic effects of migration.

TO WALK THE WORLD I am on a journey. I am in pursuit of an idea, a story, a chimera, perhaps a folly. I am chasing ghosts. Starting in humanity's birthplace in the Great Rift Valley of East Africa, I am retracing, on foot, the pathways of the ancestors who first discovered the Earth at least 60,000 years ago. This remains by far our greatest voyage. Not because it delivered us the planet. No. But because the early Homo sapiens who first roamed beyond the mother continent—these pioneer nomads numbered, in total, as few as a couple of hundred people—also bequeathed us the subtlest qualities we now associate with being fully human: complex language, abstract thinking, a compulsion to make art, a genius for technological innovation, and the continuum of today's many races.

If you ask, I will tell you that I have embarked on this project, which I'm calling the Out of Eden Walk, for many reasons: to relearn the contours of our planet at the human pace of three miles an hour. To slow down. To think. To write. To render current events as a form of pilgrimage. I hope to repair certain important connections burned through by artificial speed, by inattentiveness. I walk, as everyone does, to see what lies ahead. I walk to remember.

THE NATURAL HISTORY OF COMPASSION
The oldest hominins ever found outside of Africa were unearthed atop a rocky promontory in the Republic of Georgia, in the lush southern Caucasus. Their bones lay—gnawed on, in some cases, by giant prehistoric hyenas—beneath a medieval town. Under mossy ruins that include a church and a fortress. Under a cross. Under the sword. I think about this primordial contrast in human aspiration while walking the archaeological site.

At its most basic level, "survival of the fittest" holds that any individual whose DNA gets replicated most within a population wins the evolutionary lottery. It doesn't matter one whit how: Morality isn't biology. Indeed, selfishness is rewarded. Cheating or violence is fine. Thus, a rogue who only looks out for Number One … would, in theory, survive longest and produce the most babies. He or she would become a gold medalist in the genetic Olympics. And yet, we are not venal thugs. At least, not all the time. We grapple with our self-centered natures. Occasionally, we even lay down our lives for the weak, vulnerable, and downtrodden. For scientists this behavior is mystifying.

The most famous example is Shanidar 1, a Neanderthal man found in a cave in Iraq. His right arm was atrophied. He was partially deaf and blind. He was so crippled by arthritis and injuries, he could barely move. Still, he reached the ripe old Neanderthal age of about 40—only, it would seem, with the laborious support of other people in his clan. A useless old man was cared for.

I am walking the world. I knock on unfamiliar doors. I call out to the tents of unknown people. I slog onwards … into a vast and rumpled topography of human want and compassion. Do not be afraid. ▪

GEOGRAPHIC THINKING

Explain the historial and contemporary geographic effects of migration, as highlighted in Salopek's "slow journalism."

Top: National Geographic Fellow Paul Salopek (left) walks with his Ethiopian guide, Ahmed Elema, as they leave Herto village in the Afar region of northwestern Ethiopia. Left: The earliest clues to altruism have been found at Dmanisi, a site crowned by a medieval church and fortress. Right: A pair of Salopek's sturdy hiking boots typically last for about 1,000 miles.

CHAPTER 3

PATTERNS OF POPULATION

CRITICAL VIEWING Stone houses are built into a steep gorge in a farming village in western Iran. ▌ How might population growth or decline change this human-built landscape?

GEOGRAPHIC THINKING Where do people live, and why?

3.1
WHERE PEOPLE LIVE

NATIONAL GEOGRAPHIC
EXPLORER Lillygol Sedaghat

3.2
CONSEQUENCES OF POPULATION DISTRIBUTION

CASE STUDY: Population Distribution at the Country Scale

3.3
POPULATION COMPOSITION

3.4
MEASURING GROWTH AND DECLINE

FEATURE: Examining Population Pyramids at Different Scales

3.1 WHERE PEOPLE LIVE

People live in distinct patterns across the globe. Some of these places are densely settled, while others remain less populated. Geographers identify several physical, environmental, and human factors that help explain global population distributions. By studying these factors, geographers can make predictions about how populations will interact with Earth's different environments and change over time.

WHY STUDY POPULATION?

LEARNING OBJECTIVE
PSO-2.A Identify the factors that influence the distribution of human populations at different scales.

According to the United Nations, the global population reached 7.8 billion people in December 2019. Two-thirds of that population can be found in four regions: East Asia, South Asia, Southeast Asia, and Western Europe. During the second half of the 20th century, the world's population increased at a faster rate than ever before. And today, more people are alive than at any other time in Earth's history.

These facts compel geographers to analyze the complex reasons that populations grow and spread, and the challenges that result. They analyze where people live, differences among populations, changes within populations, and the reasons for each. **Population distribution** — where people live within a geographic area—affects the cultural, political, environmental, and economic aspects and conditions in any given area. To better understand fundamental patterns of population and the processes that affect populations, geographers study population distributions at local, regional, national, and global scales.

Global distributions of people are influenced by physical, environmental, and human factors. These factors may cause people to move to newly inhabited areas or to continue living in the same place for decades, centuries, or longer. At every scale—from local to global—there are identifiable factors that influence population distribution. These interconnected factors are liable to change, which means that populations will change with them. With a record number of people on the move, especially refugees, movement and mobility are major factors in contemporary population trends.

POPULATION DISTRIBUTION PATTERNS

Geographers analyze the patterns of population distribution to better understand the processes of population growth and movement over time. Patterns of population distribution can be described using a variety of terms, such as uniform, clustered, linear, dispersed, or random. For example, a population is said to follow a uniform pattern of distribution if it is spread out evenly over an area. Clustered populations are grouped or clumped together around a central point. A linear pattern describes a population that appears to form long and narrow lines, and a population that is spread out is **dispersed**. Random patterns describe populations that are distributed without apparent order or logic.

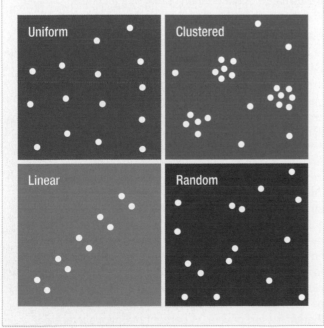

PHYSICAL AND ENVIRONMENTAL FACTORS

LEARNING OBJECTIVE
PSO-2.A Identify the factors that influence the distribution of human populations at different scales.

Humans depend on the environment for their survival, so they are more likely to settle where there are moderate climates, rich soils, and adequate water supplies. Most people tend to live in areas that are not too hot, too dry, too wet, or too cold. Coasts and waterways are often densely populated because they offer economic advantages and convenient transportation routes. Populations are most heavily concentrated at low elevations and diminish rapidly as the elevation increases.

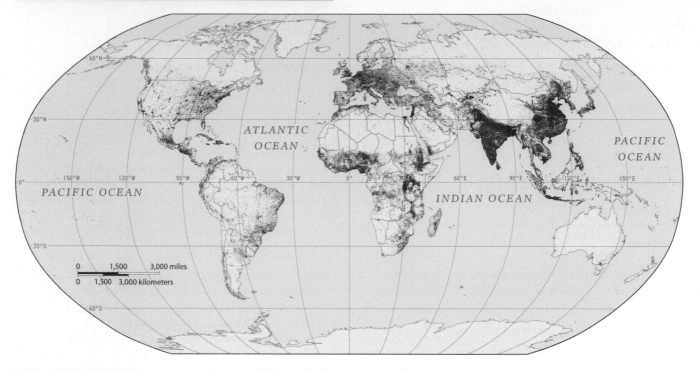

The red areas on this map represent where people live on Earth. The majority of people live in areas with low elevations, temperate climates, and accessible water.

Today, the majority of the world lives at elevations of 500 feet or less, and 80 percent of the world's population lives below elevations of 1,500 feet. Except for a few large cities such as Mexico City at 7,300 feet and Quito, Ecuador, at 9,300 feet, statistics demonstrate that most people do not live at higher elevations. It's not coincidental that the four regions—East Asia, South Asia, Southeast Asia, and Europe—where two-thirds of the world's inhabitants live occupy generally low-lying areas with fertile soil and a moderate climate.

CLIMATE **Climate** refers to the long-term patterns of weather in an area that greatly affect population distribution in direct and indirect ways. Unlike weather, which changes from day to day and even from hour to hour, climate represents the overall averages of temperature, precipitation, wind, and other atmospheric conditions year after year. The weather conditions that define a climate are normally established by averaging the weather of a specific location over decades. Climate helps shape the soil, vegetation, and agricultural opportunities of an environment.

A region's growing season, or period of the year when temperature and rainfall allow plant growth, is determined by the region's climate and is particularly important for the support of human life. Extreme climatic conditions can limit the concentration of population in an area, while areas with **temperate climates**—those with moderate temperatures and adequate precipitation amounts—are usually more densely populated.

As technology continues to develop, humans engineer new ways to live in previously uninhabitable areas. For example, rising sea levels may mobilize communities to find ways to relocate buildings to higher ground or to build seawalls. However, some places with extreme climates don't easily allow for such adjustments, like the arid Sahara in North Africa or the subarctic and polar climates in much of Canada. These areas tend to be less populated because of the extreme impact of the climate on everyday life as well as the climate's effect on the viability of agriculture.

LANDFORMS The natural features of Earth's surface, or **landforms**, also influence population distribution. People prefer lowlands due to the ease of building, planting, and transporting goods. Flat, low-lying areas like the Ganges Valley in India have deeper soil more suitable for growing crops. Habitable land has adequate water sources, relatively flat terrain, and the potential to produce food.

Areas adjacent to rivers—river valleys, deltas, and plains—typically have rich soils that agricultural communities rely on. These alluvial soils are created when the flow of rivers and streams slows, allowing particles of soil and other matter suspended in the water to settle, particularly in the lower reaches and deltas of rivers. River valleys across the world have long supported dense populations; early civilizations formed along the Nile, Tigris-Euphrates, Indus, Ganges, and Huang He rivers. Today, alluvial soil still supports agriculture as an essential, profitable sector in Egypt, despite the fact that the desert covers 95 percent of Egypt's total area.

Rocky, steep regions, such as the highlands of Tibet, are typically less populated due to the difficulty of building structures and transportation links such as roads and railways. Mountainous regions are remote and difficult to access and to live in; the air contains less oxygen than at sea level. These same areas present challenges agriculturally because higher elevations result in much colder temperatures. With every 1,000-foot rise in elevation, the average temperature drops by approximately 3° F.

WATER ACCESSIBILITY Ready access to fresh, ample water is essential for human survival and development and thus is a key factor in population distribution. People use surface water supplies like rivers, lakes, and oases and can also access underground water sources called aquifers. Today, people continue to inhabit areas with adequate water supplies. Water is needed not only for agriculture but also for industrial use, sanitation, and hygiene. Areas that are dry or that suffer from regular drought are difficult for people to inhabit; however, technology and innovation have helped some people live in drier areas.

In China, a number of physical and environmental factors, including water accessibility, influence population. Population distribution in China has remained relatively steady over time. The country has an enormous—though unevenly distributed—population. As of 2018, the country had approximately 1.4 billion people within its borders, ranking it first in the world in total population. Within China, much of the population is concentrated in the eastern half of the country along the Huang He and Yangtze river valleys.

Historically, the Yangtze River Valley has been a strong economic center because of the river and its branches, which allowed for transport and trade. Today, the valley and its waterways continue to support exceptionally high numbers of people. Major manufacturing centers are located along the Yangtze River due to the ease of transport, and this region is also important to China's agricultural production. Large numbers of people make their livings by moving goods and people along the Yangtze's many lakes, canals, and tributaries.

Many other highly populated areas in China benefit from physical factors such as the rich soil deposited from running water that makes up alluvial plains, which support intensive agriculture. This agriculturally rich economy—like the population it sustains—is rooted in the past and has carried its influence forward to the present.

HUMAN FACTORS

LEARNING OBJECTIVE
PSO-2.A Identify the factors that influence the distribution of human populations at different scales.

In addition to physical and environmental factors, changing human factors—such as economics, politics, culture, and history—influence the distribution of human populations on many scales. Geographers identify patterns that reflect how each of these factors influences population distribution.

ECONOMIC FACTORS People tend to live where they can earn a living through agriculture, natural resource extraction, manufacturing, sales, and a variety of other activities. The degree of opportunity for economic activity within an area influences population distribution. An increase in technologically advanced and global economic activities has resulted in a significant redistribution of population.

A driving force in population distribution that is often influenced by economics is **human migration**, which occurs when people make a permanent move from one place to another. Though the reasons behind migration are complex and rarely exclusive, people are often influenced to migrate for economic reasons, such as job opportunities, better working conditions, and higher pay.

One historically significant example of migration influenced by economic factors includes the movement of Europeans to North and South America, Africa, Australia, and New Zealand as part of imperialism and colonialism in the late 1800s and early 1900s. Additionally, the forced migration of millions of enslaved people to the Americas to support a developing colonial economy had far-reaching effects on population distribution as well.

The presence of natural resources in an area can also attract people to live there to extract, process, or transport the resources. Areas that provide economic opportunity may become densely populated even though the environment presents conditions that are otherwise challenging for human habitation. One example of how economic conditions prevail over environmental limitations is Norilsk, Siberia. Nearly 200,000 people in this city, which is located far north of the Arctic Circle, brave extremely harsh weather conditions every winter. Why do they live there? The region has the world's largest known deposits of nickel, an industrially important metal.

POLITICAL FACTORS People who are dissatisfied with their government or political system may voluntarily migrate to another country or region within the same country. Unstable political circumstances or war may also compel citizens to leave their home countries or regions. For example, from the 1930s to the 1950s, the Russian government forced thousands of people to move from the western regions of the country east to Siberia to develop the natural resources and economy of that region. Here, political and economic factors combined to influence population.

Similarly, in Cambodia in 1975, leaders of the Khmer Rouge forced more than 2 million residents in the capital city of Phnom Penh to migrate to the rural countryside. Under the four-year rule of the Khmer Rouge, an estimated 1.5 million to 2 million people were executed, starved, or worked to death.

Though the climate of Saudi Arabia is severe—extreme heat in summer and low rainfall—humans have found ways to make agriculture viable. Farms use center-pivot irrigation, a type of irrigation in which rotating sprinklers turn desert into farmland. Farmers must drill deep beneath the sand to unearth reserves of water used to grow vegetables, fruits, and grains to feed the population.

Governments sometimes create policy to redistribute population and encourage migration. The Brazilian government encouraged the development of central Brazil by establishing Brasilia in 1960 as the new capital city and central economic point. In the 1980s, Nigeria built its first planned city. The government chose to move its capital from coastal Lagos to inland Abuja, based on Abuja's central location within Nigeria, its accessibility, and its climate.

CULTURAL FACTORS Housing availability, safety, access to transportation, and a feeling of belonging and community are cultural factors that may serve as initial reasons to live in a certain place. Once an area is settled, it tends to stay settled and increase its population as long as the initial reasons for habitation persist.

Cultural factors that influence changes in population include religion, the roles and status of women—including the socialization of men and women within their cultural norms—and familial attitudes regarding marriage and children. For example, some societies have a strong preference for sons, which affects population composition. You will read about several of these cultural factors later in this chapter.

HISTORICAL FACTORS History, the significant events that took place in the past, is often intertwined with other physical, environmental, and human factors. The population distribution of the past can influence the population distribution of today and tomorrow. For example, humans began migrating out of Africa at least 60,000 years ago. By the end of the Pleistocene around 11,700 years ago, climate changes promoted milder conditions in more areas, resulting in major population movements and shaping the settlement patterns of humankind.

Another important migration took place between 300 and 700 C.E. during an era known as the Migration period. During this migration, people from Central Asia moved into Europe and drove groups from the region now known as Germany into what was formerly the Roman Empire. Factors such as climate change, extreme weather, economic interests, and political conflict may have influenced this migration. The population distribution that resulted from the Migration period influenced population concentrations in Europe, Northern Africa, and western Asia from that point forward.

The historical duration of settlements in a region and that region's present population concentration are often linked. Many of the densely populated areas of the world have an exceptionally long history of human habitation, while sparse populations in certain areas tend to have a less-established history of human habitation. However, the human, physical, and environmental factors that influenced population distribution in an area may change, even suddenly, which will cause a trend in population distribution to also change.

MEASURING POPULATION DENSITY

LEARNING OBJECTIVES
PSO-2.B Define methods geographers use to calculate population density.
PSO-2.C Explain the differences between and the impact of methods used to calculate population density.

By 1800, Earth's population had reached 1 billion. People concentrated in Asia, then Europe, and then Africa. Asia still has the most concentrated population today: 60 percent of the world's 7.8 billion people live in Asia. Africa is now the second most populous continent, and Europe is the third. The world's four largest population concentrations—East Asia, South Asia, Southeast Asia, and Western Europe—lie on the Eurasian landmass.

Population density, which is the number of people occupying a unit of land, is an important aspect of population. Geographers use three methods to calculate population density: arithmetic density, physiological density, and agricultural density. Each method uses a different land unit to provide key information about the pressure population exerts on the land.

ARITHMETIC DENSITY **Arithmetic density**
measures the total number of people per unit area of land. It is calculated by dividing the total population by the total land area. Though this method is used most frequently to calculate population density, arithmetic density is also called crude density because it does not account for land that is difficult to live on or uninhabitable. It is the most general of the three density measures because it provides an average density with no information about distribution patterns, such as how dispersed or clustered a population is on the land.

The island of Taiwan is a good example of how population density can vary at different scales and why geographers calculate population density in different ways. Though Taiwan has one of the highest population densities in the world, about 75 percent of its people live on just one-third of its land area. Roughly 30 percent of Taiwan's entire population lives in the greater urban area of Taipei, its largest city. The remaining two-thirds of the island is covered with high mountains, where just one-fourth of Taiwan's people live in remote rural areas and towns. To understand the interactions between Taiwan's environment and inhabitants, geographers must use several methods to measure the population density.

Particularly interesting to geographers is the direct link between population density and the available resources in an environment. This connection helps explain the degree to which interactions between people and their environment occur. In an area with a high population density, such as Taipei, the population may put great strain on the resources of the environment and its capacity to support life there.

PHYSIOLOGICAL DENSITY **Physiological density**
is the total number of people per unit of **arable land**, which is land that can be used to grow crops. Physiological density

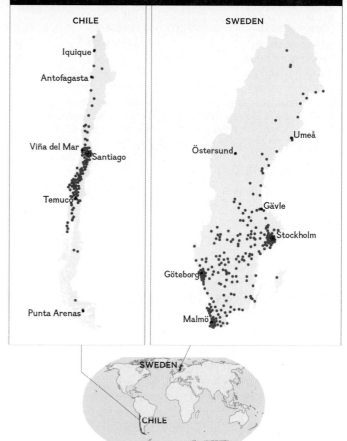

POPULATION DENSITY: CHILE AND SWEDEN

The maps show how the population is dispersed in Chile and Sweden. Both countries have low arithmetic densities, but this method provides only an average density. The maps more accurately reveal the dense settlement patterns that exist in certain areas of each country.

provides insight into whether people can sustain themselves agriculturally. The higher the physiological density, the greater the pressure on the land and its resources.

One country with greatly varying arithmetic and physiological densities is the United Arab Emirates (UAE). These densities differ due to the country's lack of arable land. The United Arab Emirates is located within an arid region, and nearly the entire country is desert. As of 2020, the total land area of the United Arab Emirates was about 32,278 square miles—but only 0.5 percent of that land was arable. The UAE's population in 2020 was about 9.7 million. Calculating the country's arithmetic density results in a measurement of only 300 people per square mile. The country's population divided by arable land area, however, measures a much higher density value—nearly 60,103 people per square mile. This example illustrates how the physiological density reveals the pressure a population exerts on the land and, for example, whether a country has to import food.

Such high population density within portions of the United Arab Emirates is a challenge. For example, 85 percent of the UAE's population lives on the west coast of the Musandam

COMPARING MEASURES OF DENSITY (people per sq km in 2018)

	Brazil	India	Japan	Kuwait	Sweden	Uganda	United States
Total Population	208,847,000	1,296,834,000	126,168,000	4,622,000	10,041,000	40,854,000	329,256,000
Arithmetic Density	64	1,022	865	672	58	439	87
Physiological Density	655	1,943	7,585	167,951	889	1,276	522
Percent Arable Land	9.7	52.6	11.5	0.4	6.5	34.4	16.6

The table compares the arithmetic density and physiological density of seven countries that span the globe. ∎ How do the two measures of density help you understand the relationship between each country's population and the environment in which the population lives?

Sources: National Geographic Atlas of the World (Eleventh Edition), World Bank

Peninsula, home to one of the region's critical commercial and financial centers. Though farming in the United Arab Emirates is extremely limited and can only be supported with irrigation, the country has been able to develop sustainability efforts within heavily crowded urban areas.

Sweden is another example of a country where the physiological density is quite different from its arithmetic density. Approximately 15 percent of Sweden's total land area lies north of the Arctic Circle and is sparsely populated. Only 6.5 percent of Sweden's land is arable, and most of the roughly 10 million people in Sweden farm and live in the southern portion of the country. In this area, the climate is milder and supports a growing season lasting about 240 days. The tundra climate of northern Sweden—located in the Arctic Circle—is a physical factor that influences population distribution in the country. Because Sweden's population distribution is far from uniform and is concentrated in the south where the climate is milder, it's important to calculate its population density in different ways to understand the interactions between its people and environment.

In both the United Arab Emirates and Sweden, physiological density provides a basic indicator of how much food-producing land is available in each country. However, neither density explains how fertile and productive the farmland really is. Central Illinois and Northern Wisconsin have similar physiological densities, but land in central Illinois is extremely fertile and productive, while farmland in Northern Wisconsin is of poorer quality. Comparing arithmetic and physiological densities helps geographers understand the capacity of the land and its resources to support the needs of the population living on it.

AGRICULTURAL DENSITY
Agricultural density measures the total number of farmers per unit of arable land. The highest agricultural densities are found in parts of Asia. Agricultural density can reveal more about a country's wealth than its population distribution. But this measurement doesn't supply data about how much technology and money can be put into cultivation. Countries with similar physiological densities but different economic conditions tend to produce vastly different amounts of food or other crops. Not all arable land is equal.

A higher agricultural density, in which there are high numbers of farmers per land unit, suggests that most of the farming taking place is providing crops and livestock for only the farmers. This practice, called **subsistence agriculture**, is common in peripheral and semi-peripheral countries where there are fewer mechanical resources available to work the land and more people are needed to care for crops and livestock. This intensive type of farming, which can include modifications such as irrigation that greatly impact the environment, requires specialized agricultural practices to get the greatest yield from small fields. It may even involve the growth and harvest of two or more crops from just one plot of land.

The different economic structures of countries may be reflected in their agricultural density measurements. A lower agricultural density, like that of the United States, is typically a result of high levels of mechanization. A country's access to technology and other resources allows for fewer people to farm extensive land areas, while still feeding many people. Though resources such as farm machinery, high-yield seeds, agricultural chemicals, and geographic information systems can be seen as beneficial in terms of yielding more crops, they can also have negative long-term effects on the environment and its ability to sustainably support populations. Subsistence agriculture and the consequences of agricultural technologies and innovations for the future are discussed in detail in Unit 5.

Agricultural density data helps geographers understand how much food is being produced. Comparing physiological density and agricultural density helps geographers analyze the overall impact on the environment and the pressures that may occur in densely populated places where settlements are encroaching on arable land. In some places, such as Rwanda where there is a large population and limited arable land, the pressures on arable land and food supplies are very high.

GEOGRAPHIC THINKING

1. Explain how physical and environmental factors influence population distribution.

2. Identify an example of how human factors influence population distribution.

3. Describe how population distribution differs from population density.

NATIONAL GEOGRAPHIC EXPLORER **LILLYGOL SEDAGHAT**

TRANSFORMING TRASH

Taiwan, a self-governing island off China's coast, was once known as "Garbage Island" but is now a world leader in recycling. Fulbright-National Geographic Storyteller Lillygol Sedaghat's work shows how Taiwan created a sustainable environment.

Sedaghat believes that everyone can learn something from Taiwan's story. Taiwan had a population of approximately 23.5 million in 2018. The terrain is largely mountainous and uninhabitable, so much of the population is concentrated along its western edge, including in Taipei City, the capital. Over the past 60 years, Taiwan transitioned from an agricultural society to an industrial one. Rapid industrialization resulted in increased consumerism and, therefore, more waste. With no formal waste management system in place until the 1980s, the fallout from trash accumulation was staggering. Yet a group of mothers pushed Taiwan to change its ways, designing an integrated waste management system that requires people in major cities today to separate their waste into burnables, recyclables, and compost so that once-used material can be recaptured and repurposed.

In fact, Taiwan is now a world leader in the circular economy (CE). Sedaghat explains the CE model as "a new theory that takes into consideration environmental, health, and social benefits with an economic model that maximizes resources throughout their life cycle." Resources are not wasted, and materials are continuously reused: the goal is zero waste. (You'll read more about sustainable development initiatives like the CE model in Unit 7.)

Sedaghat uses visual art and digital media to document recycling methods and processes used in Taiwan. Examples of her work include graphics to explain the plastics recycling process, music videos featuring sounds from Taipei City's waste management system, and blogs describing the sights and smells of Taipei's first incinerator. In May 2019, Sedaghat joined a women-led expedition team to study plastic pollution in the Ganges River as part of National Geographic's *Planet or Plastic?* initiative. The expedition is studying the amounts of and ways in which plastics enter the ocean in river systems, from the original source to the sea, through the lenses of people, land, and water. By collecting data and publishing accounts of their work, members of the expedition team are shedding light on this global crisis and identifying solutions to help tackle the issue. ∎

GEOGRAPHIC THINKING

Explain how physical and human factors may have contributed to Taiwan's waste management success.

3.2 CONSEQUENCES OF POPULATION DISTRIBUTION

Population distribution and density affect society and the environment. A population depends on, modifies, and adapts to its environment. This relationship shifts as populations grow and concentrate in some places. The impact that populations have on society and the environment may intensify to a point that is no longer sustainable.

IMPACT OF POPULATION DISTRIBUTION ON SOCIETY

LEARNING OBJECTIVE

PSO-2.D Explain how population distribution and density affect society and the environment.

The distribution and density of Earth's population reflects its landforms, soils, vegetation, climate types, available resources, and levels of economic development. People are the driving forces behind factors that impact the environment, such as pollution, resource depletion, and land degradation. Geographers want to know where people live and the consequences of population distribution—such as crowding, isolation, unequal access to services and resources, and environmental impacts—which ultimately affect the quality of human life and human society as a whole.

The more people who are born into or move to an area, the greater the need for access to adequate housing, jobs, and fresh water, and services like sanitation and health care. Providing services to clustered populations is easier than providing them to dispersed populations. The distances people are required to travel for work or social services— as well as the available modes of transportation—impact people's ability to take advantage of social services, like health care, and to support themselves.

Social services are more efficient when population distribution is clustered because the operating costs of services such as police, fire, medical, and waste collection are lower when serving a smaller, densely-populated geographic area. For example, fire response times are greater for rural areas than urban areas, due to a dispersed population as well as fewer personnel in areas where people are spread out. Populations that are dispersed throughout especially hard-to-travel terrain will likely receive fewer social services than populations dispersed on easily navigable terrain that has plenty of travel route options.

However, clustered population distributions with especially high densities necessitate greater levels of public services and resources. In areas where populations are clustered, for example, fires can pose a bigger threat to more inhabitants. This is especially true in crowded areas of decay where neglected buildings are more susceptible to catching fire. The higher the hazard level, the greater the risk, which requires more and specialized resources to mitigate.

Increases in population densities can also lead to disparities in economic growth between the areas where populations are clustered versus the areas where populations are scattered. As you have learned, these areas can be categorized as core and peripheral, and land relationships between these areas are called core-periphery relationships. There may be stark contrasts in wages, opportunities, and access to health care between the core and periphery. Unlike scattered, sparsely populated areas, evenly and densely populated areas usually have more economic development and therefore more power.

IMPACT OF POPULATION DISTRIBUTION ON THE ENVIRONMENT

LEARNING OBJECTIVE

PSO-2.D Explain how population distribution and density affect society and the environment.

As a population grows, greater pressure is placed on arable land, water, energy, and natural resources to provide an adequate supply of food. It becomes harder to maintain a balance with the environment. Greater population densities can strain resources, such as clean water, and the possibility of exhausting an environment's resources is a real concern.

The maximum population size an environment can sustain is called its **carrying capacity**. A key concept originating from biology, carrying capacity represents the threshold at which the population of a species levels off at an environmentally determined maximum because of a shortage of resources. Geographers use this term when discussing the limits that human populations face in various regions and at a range of scales. The carrying capacity of Earth, however, has yet to be determined. An area with high population density may not be considered overpopulated if the area has a high carrying capacity, which could be the result of fertile soil or modern farming methods. As a contrasting example, the huge island of Greenland has an exceptionally low carrying capacity because of its harsh, cold climate.

Greater population densities can lead to environmental degradation, which is the deterioration of the environment. When more and more humans inhabit a specific area, they may deplete and pollute the resources there. This has profound ecological consequences.

Urban areas with dense populations increasingly impact the environment through pollution and resource use. Burgeoning cities consume more resources and create pollution from additional vehicles, heating and cooling sources, and industrialization. High levels of consumption in densely populated areas also have environmental impacts through the use of large amounts of energy and the generation of excess amounts of waste. Some city officials and researchers are developing ways to use resources more efficiently and lessen the environmental impact of densely populated urban areas.

By analyzing the population density and carrying capacity of an area, geographers can better understand how a changing population interacts with its environment. Resources such as air quality, food supply, biodiversity, and safe water can be monitored to find ways to extend an environment's carrying capacity or prevent a population from exceeding the environmental limit.

GEOGRAPHIC THINKING

1. Describe how population density can negatively and positively influence society.

2. Identify which of the three methods for calculating population density would be most helpful in assessing a country's carrying capacity.

High population density and its impact on the environment is evident in the bustling, smog-filled Port of Shanghai, located on the east coast of China at the mouth of the Yangtze River. It is the world's busiest container port. In 2018, Shanghai handled 561 million tons of cargo.

POPULATION DISTRIBUTION AT THE COUNTRY SCALE

THE ISSUE Population density data can be misleading in providing an accurate description of the population distribution of an area.

LEARNING OBJECTIVE
PSO-2.D Explain how population distribution and density affect society and the environment.

BY THE NUMBERS

 **Egypt**

99,413,000
Population as of 2020

257 PEOPLE PER SQ MI
Arithmetic density

9,182 PEOPLE PER SQ MI
Physiological density

Canada
35,882,000
Population as of 2020

9 PEOPLE PER SQ MI
Arithmetic density

194 PEOPLE PER SQ MI
Physiological density

Sources: National Geographic Atlas of the World (Eleventh Edition), World Bank

WHEN COMPARING POPULATION DENSITY DATA for different geographic areas, keep in mind that arithmetic density data are most useful for small areas, such as neighborhoods. However, for larger areas, such as countries, arithmetic density data are less likely to provide meaningful measurements because they don't take into account patterns of population distribution across geographies of similar scale. Take the example of comparing the countries of Egypt and Canada.

Egypt has a low arithmetic density—only 257 people per square mile in 2020—but changing the method to calculating physiological density reveals a much higher number: 9,182 people per square mile. This value reflects the high concentration of people along the fertile Nile River Valley, which is approximately 5 percent of Egypt's land area. Almost all of the country is desert, and 95 percent of the population lives along the Nile River and its delta on Egypt's only arable land. People are further concentrated in the capital city of Cairo, which is located close to the Nile Delta. It is an expansive urban environment disproportionately larger than any other Egyptian city. By comparison, Alexandria, the second largest city in Egypt, is only 30 percent the size of Cairo. Egypt's high agricultural density, which exceeds 695 farmers per square mile, shows that Egypt requires many rural laborers to work what little arable land it has. This data also suggests that mechanical farm equipment and the type of farming practiced is less developed. Egypt's high physiological density indicates that the country is under pressure to provide people with a sufficient food supply and that importing food is a necessity.

Although Canada doesn't have people concentrated along a single river, or even in one comparatively large city, its population is concentrated along its southern border just as the Egyptian population is concentrated along the Nile River. One of the most sparsely populated countries in the world, Canada had an arithmetic density of 9 people per square mile in 2020. Much of its enormous territory is largely inhospitable and uninhabited. The arithmetic density, in this case, masks the vast, sparsely inhabited area. Canada's physiological density is 194 people per square mile, which indicates the small percentage of arable land. Ninety percent of the population lives within 100 miles of Canada's border with the United States. Environmentally, the conditions there are milder, which results in a temperate climate and longer growing seasons. The soils in these southern regions are generally fertile. People concentrated in southeastern Canada have access to the Great Lakes and the Saint Lawrence Seaway and benefit from many connections with the U.S. economy.

Both Egypt and Canada contain large, basically uninhabited areas, with most of their populations clustered in a small percentage of land area. However, sheer size also matters: Canada has nearly ten times as much land area as Egypt does, but its total population is just over one-third of Egypt's. Canada's arithmetic density is among the lowest in the world, and its physiological density is low as well—in fact, lower than Egypt's arithmetic density. These measurements show both Canada's vast size and relatively small population. Indeed, Canada is about four times as wealthy as Egypt, putting it in the global core while Egypt is in the periphery. Population density numbers tell only part of a country's story. ∎

GEOGRAPHIC THINKING

Describe how the population density maps provide a truer picture of each country's population density than arithmetic density data may provide.

Both Egypt and Canada have population densities concentrated in a small portion of each country. In Egypt, millions of people live in greater Cairo, surrounded by a desert that includes the Giza pyramids.

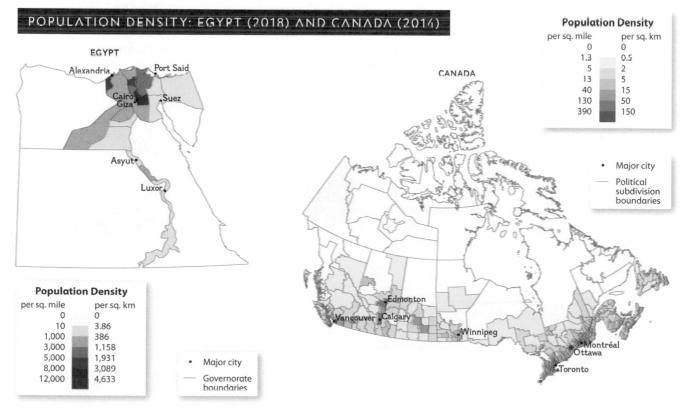

POPULATION DENSITY: EGYPT (2018) AND CANADA (2014)

EGYPT

Alexandria · Port Said · Cairo · Giza · Suez · Asyut · Luxor

CANADA

Edmonton · Vancouver · Calgary · Winnipeg · Montréal · Ottawa · Toronto

Population Density

per sq. mile	per sq. km
0	0
1.3	0.5
5	2
13	5
40	15
130	50
390	150

· Major city
— Political subdivision boundaries

Population Density

per sq. mile	per sq. km
0	0
10	3.86
1,000	386
3,000	1,158
5,000	1,931
8,000	3,089
12,000	4,633

· Major city
— Governorate boundaries

3.3 POPULATION COMPOSITION

The structure of a population is its makeup, or groups that comprise the whole, such as a population's number of men, women, and different age groups. Geographers study population structures, statistics, and trends and represent this data using diagrams, graphs, and maps. By analyzing the data, they can see a past, present, and future demographic story about a specific place. They use their analyses to evaluate similarities and differences among and within countries—and at many scales from neighborhoods to world regions—to identify cultural, political, and economic patterns across the globe.

DEPENDENCY RATIO

LEARNING OBJECTIVE

PSO-2.E Describe elements of population composition used by geographers.

The age structure of a population has significant government policy and economic implications. For example, a population with many young people needs a sufficient number of schools and eventually jobs to accommodate them. Conversely, countries with a large proportion of older people must develop retirement systems and medical facilities to serve them. Geographers analyze these and other age-related demographic studies using ratios for specific age groups. The **dependency ratio** is the number of people in a dependent age group (under age 15 or age 65 and older) divided by the number of people in the working-age group (ages 15 to 64), multiplied by 100.

Consider a population of 100 people that has 60 people in the working-age range. This population also has 30 children and 10 people age 65 or older. In this example, the dependency ratio would be 66.7. This ratio indicates that two-thirds of the population is in the working-age range. The dependency ratio is used as an indicator to measure the demand placed on the working-age population to provide for the dependent population.

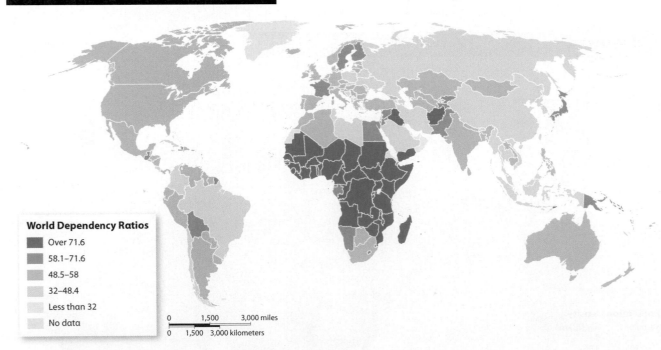

WORLD DEPENDENCY RATIOS, 2019

World Dependency Ratios
- Over 71.6
- 58.1–71.6
- 48.5–58
- 32–48.4
- Less than 32
- No data

0   1,500   3,000 miles
0   1,500   3,000 kilometers

READING MAPS This 2019 map shows each country's dependency ratio, which is the combined youth and old-age populations relative to the working-age populations. Countries with higher dependency ratios have relatively fewer people who are of working age. ▌ Which regions have the highest dependency ratios? Identify some of the economic challenges these regions might face.

Related measurements include youth dependency ratios, which compare the number of children under age 15 with the working-age population. Old-age dependency ratios are comparisons between the number of people 65 and older with those in the working-age group. However, it is important to note the assumptions when calculating dependency ratios. In reality, the workforce includes people older than 64 and younger than 15. It is also incorrect to assume that everyone ages 15 to 64 is working.

DEPENDENCY RATIOS AND ECONOMIC DEVELOPMENT The size of the dependent population relative to the size of the working-age population is a key factor influencing economic development. Dependency ratios are useful when comparing societies over time and when comparing different areas. They are also used at all levels (national, regional, local) to indicate current and future productivity at a large-scale level. Monitoring these ratios provides insight into the policies that countries may need as their population ages and changes.

The United Nations releases a dependency ratio for every country in the world. Each ratio covers a five-year period beginning in 1950. In 2015, the United States had a total dependency ratio of 51, which was the result of a youth-dependency ratio of 29 and an old-age dependency ratio of 22.1. That old-age dependency ratio was almost double the 1950 ratio of 12.6 because so many baby boomers—people born between 1946 and 1964—had reached retirement age.

The higher the dependency ratio, the more people who are not of working age, and the fewer who are in the workforce, earning income, and often paying taxes. This means that in a country with a high dependency ratio, people of working age—and the overall economy—encounter greater pressures in supporting the aging and youthful population groups. As the percentage of nonworking people rises, people who are working may face increased taxes to compensate for a larger dependent population. Ideally, an economy should have a smaller dependency ratio, with a constant flow of people entering the workforce, and a smaller number exiting the working-age population each year.

DATA BENEATH A DEPENDENCY RATIO
The global population is projected to increase to 9.7 billion by 2050, but it is also projected to stop growing and peak at 10.9 billion by 2100. In most of the world's countries, fewer babies are being born, and the number of elderly people continues to rise. In fact, the fastest-growing segment of the world population is people age 65 or older. Dependency ratios are on the rise, and countries with aging populations will continue to struggle with how to support their elderly. Although this scenario applies to most countries, others—especially countries in sub-Saharan Africa—continue to see rapid population growth, with one of the largest segments being the youngest. In this case, countries with growing younger segments could at some point have the same dependency ratio as countries with growing older segments.

Japan and Namibia are examples of countries with similar dependency ratios. In 2015, Japan's ratio was approximately 64, and Namibia's was 68. Though the difference between these ratios doesn't appear significant, the data beneath the ratios tells a different story. Japan has many elderly dependents, whereas Namibia has many youth dependents. These differences present distinct challenges. Japan's youth dependency ratio was 21.3, and its old-age dependency ratio was 42.7. Namibia's youth dependency ratio was 62.2, and its old-age dependency ratio was 5.8. This example shows that geographers must study dependency ratios in various ways and at varying scales to achieve an accurate demographic picture. Using only these numbers to compare the two countries would prevent an accurate analysis of the issues masked by the apparently similar dependency ratios.

Examining age dependency at different scales within the United States is important as well. As you have read, in 2015, the country had a total dependency ratio of 51, with an old-age dependency ratio of 22.1. Looking beyond the national rate to the dependency ratio of specific states shows patterns of age structure in certain areas. For instance, at the time of the 2010 census, Florida had an old-age dependency ratio of 28.2 with a projected old-age dependency ratio of 35.8 for 2020. Florida has the highest percentage of seniors in the United States. As a major retiree destination, this state is home to a large population who live on fixed incomes and have left their peak earning and taxpaying years behind. This age group will draw heavily upon state health care and benefits and will spend less money, which will affect the state budget and economy.

SEX RATIO

LEARNING OBJECTIVE
P30-2.C Describe elements of population composition used by geographers.

Geographers also study a population's **sex ratio** when evaluating population composition. This ratio represents the proportion of males to females in a population. In general, slightly more males than females are born. However, women tend to live five or more years longer than men do. Overall, the world has a ratio of men to women of 101:100. In Europe and North America, the ratio of men to women is 95:100. In the rest of the world, the ratio is 102:100. In peripheral countries, the number of women who die during childbirth contributes to a lower percentage of women. Societies with a high rate of emigration where men rather than women are more likely to migrate elsewhere will have more females than males. War can also create disparities because typically more men than women die in war.

Many of Asia's populations have long had a strong preference for sons. India's cultural preference for male children has led to many female children being neglected or abandoned, resulting in a high number of female deaths. This inclination can also be seen in India's sex ratio for children age 14 and younger, with 2018 estimates showing

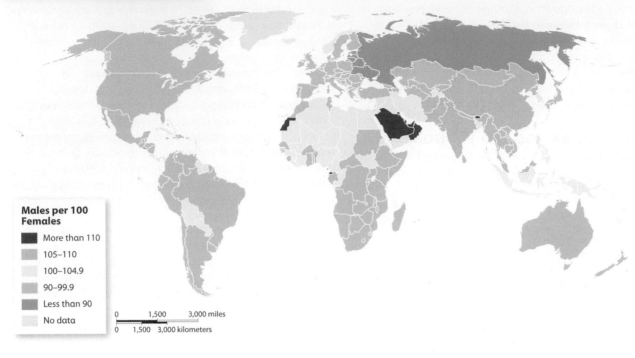

Males per 100 Females

- More than 110
- 105–110
- 100–104.9
- 90–99.9
- Less than 90
- No data

0   1,500   3,000 miles

0   1,500   3,000 kilometers

READING MAPS Some countries in Southwest Asia, such as Saudi Arabia and the United Arab Emirates, have a highly unbalanced sex ratio due to a large male migrant population. Consider Saudi Arabia, where there are 137 males for every 100 females. In 2017, only 32 percent of immigrants to Saudi Arabia were female. ▮ How might the high male population in Saudi Arabia impact the country's marriage rate, fertility rate, and the rate at which the population grows?

a ratio of 113 boys to 100 girls. In 2018, the sex ratio for the same age group in China showed an exceptionally high number of boys relative to girls: 128:100.

Many aspects of society, including political factors, have led to such an imbalance. For example, China's one-child policy that launched in 1979 and remained in effect for over 30 years has had lasting effects on the country's population structure. Under this policy, Chinese couples were allowed to have only one child, so they often sex-selected their first pregnancy. The World Health Organization defines sex-selection as "the practice of using medical techniques to choose the sex of offspring," which can include choosing specific embryos to be implanted or terminating a pregnancy after the sex of the fetus has been identified.

In some rural areas and for most ethnic minorities, couples were allowed a second pregnancy if the first child was a female. If the second (or subsequent) pregnancies were female, the result was often sex-selective abortion, infanticide, or abandonment. In many cases, male births were reported, and female births were not. Even though the one-child policy was modified in 2015 to allow for two children, its aftereffects continue to produce measurable impacts now and well into the future as China faces a rapidly aging population and shrinking workforce.

In both China and India, marriage and family determine social status and acceptance. The imbalanced sex ratio in these countries means greater competition for a bride and inevitably more single men who aren't fulfilling traditional social and economic roles. Additionally, when there is a shortage of women, the men who remain unmarried are those in the lower classes of society, who then become marginalized. In China, crime rates have exploded, with two-thirds of violent and property-related crimes in the country being committed by young unmarried men.

The sex ratio is an important social indicator as it affects marriage rates, women's labor-market participation rates, and the socialization of men and women within their cultural norms. It also impacts fertility rates, birth rates, and the natural rate at which a population grows.

GEOGRAPHIC THINKING

1. Describe the possible limitations of dependency ratios.

2. Identify three factors that may cause an imbalance in a country's sex ratio.

3. Explain why the sex ratio of a population is an important social indicator.

3.4 MEASURING GROWTH AND DECLINE

The number of births, deaths, and people moving in and out of a location all contribute to population growth and decline. But it is difficult to pinpoint and explain the reasons for these changes. By measuring specific population characteristics—including fertility and mortality—geographers can identify trends that help explain how environmental, economic, cultural, and political factors play a role in the patterns of population.

FERTILITY

LEARNING OBJECTIVE
IMP-2.A Explain factors that account for contemporary and historical trends in population growth and decline.

Demographics are data about the structures and characteristics of human populations. Though population groups can be identified and measured in different ways, geographers measure some key factors, such as fertility, to identify population trends. **Fertility**, or the ability to produce children, influences the birthrate of a population. Experts analyze the growth or decline of populations at various scales because the data impacts the natural environment and society, in the form of human health and the economy. Governments and public health officials study fertility rates to see if the population will grow, decline, or stay the same.

As world population rises, pressure increases on the agricultural and housing sectors to provide food and shelter for the added millions. Experts in public health use the data to predict and plan for health care. Fertility also affects budgets and policies surrounding education. International organizations, such as the United Nations, measure fertility to help solve international problems and make decisions about where to focus global resources.

MEASURES OF FERTILITY The **crude birth rate (CBR)** is the number of births in a given year per 1,000 people in a given population. In order to compare CBR data among countries or specific regions, a standardized measurement for CBR is used, providing the rate of births in a population of 1,000. If a country or region has a population of 1 million, and 15,000 babies were born in that

TOTAL FERTILITY RATE, 2019

Number of children born per woman

- 6 or more
- 4–5.9
- 2–3.9
- 0–1.9
- No data

0   1,500   3,000 miles

0   1,500   3,000 kilometers

READING MAPS Over the past 50 years, the global total fertility rate (TFR)—the average number of children a woman will give birth to—has been cut in half due to factors including the rising cost of raising children and increased education and employment opportunities for women. ▌ Choose a country on the map and explain how its TFR provides insight into the status of women in that country.

both genders in the United States are factors that decrease life expectancy in those countries. Climate, hygiene, crime rates, and genetics also affect life expectancy. In 2018, Japan had a life expectancy of 85.5 years, which can be attributed to accessible health care and lifestyle choices such as diet and exercise. Additionally, the Japanese government invested heavily in public health, which has resulted in a health- and hygiene-conscious culture.

In general, women live longer than men, but the average in high-income areas is six years longer, while the average in low-income areas falls to three years. Much of the difference can be attributed to the ability high-income countries have in combating diseases such as heart disease and cancer. In 2018, women in the United States had a life expectancy of 82.3 years, while men had a life expectancy of 77.8. By contrast, in some African countries, the average life expectancy for women was 64, while the average life expectancy for men was 61. The smaller gap between the genders is largely the result of AIDS and poverty, which lower the life expectancy of both groups.

In regions where the life expectancies of men and women are close, the root cause is typically a systemic issue such as poverty or inadequate medical care—or sometimes a combination of both. India had life expectancies of 67.8 for men and 70.5 for women in 2018. This small gap can largely be attributed to how gender inequality impacts the health and well-being of women. Many Indian girls and women are kept from receiving an education, are considered a drain on family finances, and are frequent victims of violent crimes.

By comparing CBRs, CDRs, and TFRs, geographers have concluded that the world has a large population of youth—the largest percentage of which is in countries in the periphery. This circumstance pressures education and health-care systems, as well as employment opportunities, within peripheral countries. People in core countries are growing older, and these populations add stresses to health care, pensions, and social protections. The worldwide population in the oldest age group, age 60 and over, is growing faster than all younger age groups. Globally, the population is aging.

Bearing in mind that scale can be an issue, geographers study fertility and mortality rates across global, national, and local scales. Regional averages can disguise significant variation among countries, and country-level measurements can mask dramatic local variations, such as urban versus rural, male versus female, and wealthy versus poor. Ethnic and cultural variations that exist within some countries, such as the vast differences among states in the United States and India, must also be considered.

The exceptionally long life expectancy in Japan can be attributed, in part, to the government's emphasis on health. For example, the town of Kamikatsu keeps the elderly population active and employed in local gardens.

VISUALIZING POPULATION COMPOSITION WITH POPULATION PYRAMIDS

LEARNING OBJECTIVES

PSO-2.E Describe elements of population composition used by geographers.

PSO-2.F Explain ways that geographers depict and analyze population

Geographers use **population pyramids** to interpret the implications of the changing structure of a population. These graphs show the age-sex distribution of a given population, which helps indicate whether the population is growing rapidly, growing slowly, or in decline. The population size of each age group affects the demand for goods and services in the region's economy. Projections and trends revealed in population pyramids inform policy makers about what goods and services are needed, such as schools, elder care, and health care, and what to plan for in the future.

Some countries have reached zero population growth or are experiencing negative growth, or decline, because of low birth rates and an old-age structure coupled with minimal net migration. Population growth rates are negative in many European countries—most notably in Russia—where the population growth rate was estimated to be -0.11 percent in 2018. Russia's trends of population growth and aging have been profoundly affected by high rates of alcoholism and suicide among its men as well as catastrophic events in the 20th century. The typical age distribution and male and female balance in the population became distorted as a result. The millions of losses incurred from World War II have caused Russia to have the lowest overall sex ratio in the world, at about 86 males per 100 females in 2018. Focusing on Russia's age-65-and-over population shows an even lower male-female ratio of 46:100.

In 1992, Russia entered a period of decline, with the number of deaths exceeding the number of births combined with the number of immigrants. In 1999, the TFR dropped below 1.2 after the economic upheaval that followed the breakup of the USSR. Drops like these will continue to impact the number of births and the rate of population growth and aging for decades to come. In turn, this downturn also affects retirement, education, and employment. Russia's low TFR of 1.6 in 2018, combined with only 17 percent of its population being below age 15, has resulted in severe labor force gaps. If the growth rate continues to decline in Russia, the population size will slowly decrease as well.

Countries with rapid population growth, such as the Democratic Republic of Congo (DRC), have a large-based and narrow-topped population pyramid, indicating a high child dependency ratio. This shape can also signify a peripheral country as it results from high birth rates that supply increasingly more people into the lowest bars, or population cohorts, of the pyramid and in turn shrink the relative number of people in the oldest stages. As the death rate declines, more people survive to reproductive ages and beyond. As these people reproduce, the pyramid base

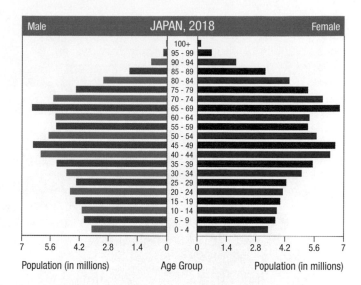

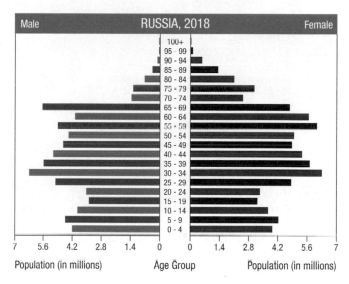

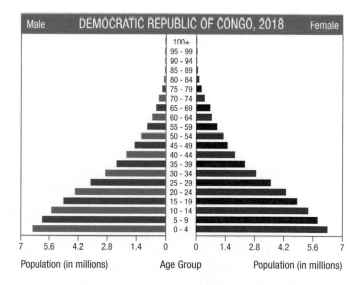

Each population pyramid reveals key factors about a country's population. For example, a pyramid such as the DRC's with a wide base tells that there are a large number of children in relation to the working-age population. ▮ What does each pyramid suggest about what the population of each country will look like in the future?

Source: CIA World Factbook

A group of young boys train at a football school in Goma in the Democratic Republic of Congo (DRC). The DRC has one of the highest child dependency rates in the world. In 2018, 41 percent of the population was under the age of 15.

widens. Peripheral and semi-peripheral countries that have experienced improvements in life expectancy but continue to have high birth rates tend to have this shape. The pattern reflects a history of rapid population growth and the potential for future rapid growth. The narrow top is the result of a smaller number of births for many years in the past (when the population was much smaller) and higher death rates at older ages.

A slowly growing population, such as the United States, has had declining fertility and mortality rates for most of the past 100 years. Because of the lower fertility rates, fewer people have entered the base of the U.S. pyramid. As life expectancy has increased, a greater percentage of the births have survived until old age. The proportion of older people in the population has been growing. This trend of the population aging was interrupted by the postwar baby boom from 1946 to 1964 when birth rates climbed again. This break in the trend can be seen in the population pyramid for the United States later in this chapter. After the baby boom factor, birth rates continued to trend downward until the late 1970s. During the 1980s, as the remaining members of the baby boom approached their childbearing years, the number of births rose again and peaked in 1990. Notice the

bulge in the 15-to-34-year-old population in the pyramid; this shows the baby boomers' children.

Despite the number of births per woman being at its lowest, the U.S. population continues to grow because of the children and grandchildren of the enormous baby boom generation. Immigration also plays a part in population growth in the United States; more people enter the country, and some of them add children to their families.

GEOGRAPHIC THINKING

1. Explain what factors may cause TFRs to be lower in core countries.

2. Describe how China's population will change in the long term, according to its 2017 TFR of 1.6.

3. Identify what technological, economic, and social factors might cause levels of mortality to change.

4. Choose a population pyramid and explain Russia's, Japan's, or Democratic Republic of Congo's current needs for goods and services and how these needs may change in the future.

EXAMINING POPULATION PYRAMIDS AT DIFFERENT SCALES

LEARNING OBJECTIVES

PSO-2.E Describe elements of population composition used by geographers.

PSO-2.F Explain ways that geographers depict and analyze population composition.

When you analyze population pyramids, you have to consider scale. The national median age in the United States in 2018 (38.2) disguised the tremendous variations that exist at state and local levels. To understand the connection between population characteristics and the demand placed on any given region, the lens through which data is examined must adjust to national, state, and local levels. For example, Virginia had a median age of 38 in 2018—close to the national median age. If geographers dig deeper into specific cities and counties, however, they uncover drastic variances and trends that differ from this average. Virginia's Lexington City and Highland County are within 80 miles of each other; yet their population compositions in 2017 were radically different.

That year, Lexington had a population of 7,113 with a median age of 21.6. It is the home of Washington and Lee University and Virginia Military Institute. Over 75 percent of students enrolled at Virginia Military Institute are male. As evidenced by the population pyramid, the city attracts high numbers of college-age men and women. Almost 20 percent of the population is 20- to 24-year-old males, and the sex ratio is 110:100. The pyramid also shows that these same college students graduate and move elsewhere rather than aging up into Lexington's population. The trend demonstrates that this cycle repeats, with more college students replacing those who left. The population percent change for Lexington is 1.09 percent growth, and a high percentage of the population, 69 percent, has never married.

By contrast, Highland County, with a population of 2,213, is one of the least-populated counties in Virginia and has a median age of 60.5. The population pyramid for Highland County shows a much larger percentage of aging population. This pyramid suggests a trend in the migration of retirees to the area. As you have read, people are less likely to live at high elevations and—at 3,000 feet—Highland County has one of the highest average elevations east of the Mississippi River. The Interstate Highway System doesn't pass through the county, and there are no colleges there. The population percent change is a 4.7 percent decline, and a high percentage of the population, 63 percent, is married. ∎

GEOGRAPHIC THINKING

Explain how the economic and health services needs of the two Virginia populations differ.

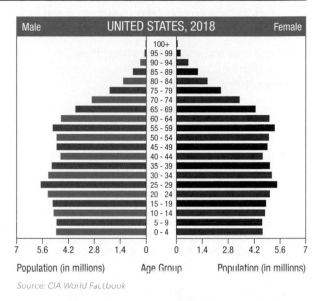
Source: CIA World Factbook

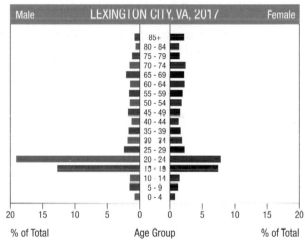
Source: U.S. Census Bureau

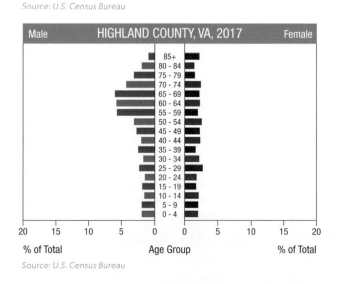
Source: U.S. Census Bureau

CHAPTER SUMMARY

Geographers study the impact that physical, environmental, and human factors have on population distribution and density to analyze population patterns.

- Physical and environmental factors that influence population distribution include climate, landforms, and water accessibility.

- Human factors that influence population distribution include economics, politics, culture, and history.

Geographers use three methods for calculating population density to uncover different information about the pressure the population exerts on the land.

- Arithmetic density is the total number of people per unit area of land.

- Physiological density is the total number of people per unit of arable land.

- Agricultural density is the total number of farmers per unit of arable land.

Geographers study the impacts of population distribution and density on society and the environment.

- Societal challenges include pressures on the government to grow the economy, provide more services, and create more jobs. Societal benefits include localized and more efficient services in densely populated areas.

- Environmental challenges include carrying capacity and the depletion of resources. Benefits include efforts to expand arable land and support ecosystems.

Geographers analyze composition data in various ways to evaluate present and future population needs.

- The dependency ratio is the number of people in a dependent age group (under age 15 or age 65 and older) divided by the number of people in the working-age group (15 to 64), multiplied by 100.

- The sex ratio represents the proportion of males to females in a population.

Geographers analyze data about fertility, mortality, and age-sex distribution to understand population trends.

- Fertility, the ability to produce children, is measured using the crude birth rate (CBR) and the total fertility rate (TFR).

- Mortality, deaths as a component of population change, is measured using the crude death rate (CDR) and the infant mortality rate (IMR).

- A population pyramid is a graph that shows the age-sex distribution of a given population to indicate whether that population is growing rapidly, growing slowly, or in decline, and to understand what this might mean for that population.

KEY TERMS AND CONCEPTS

Use complete sentences to answer the questions.

1. **APPLY CONCEPTUAL VOCABULARY** Consider the terms *distribution* and *density*. Write a standard dictionary definition of each term. Then provide a conceptual definition—an explanation of how each term is used in the context of this chapter as it relates to population.

2. Describe how physical, environmental, and human factors affect population distribution. Provide at least one example of each factor.

3. Provide an example to support the theory that past population distributions influence present and future population concentrations.

4. Explain why geographers compare physiological density and agricultural density.

5. Explain why arithmetic density is also called crude density.

6. Describe the characteristics of an area with a low agricultural density. Use a real country as an example.

7. Identify two demographic factors that geographers use to measure population groups, and define both terms.

8. Define the term *carrying capacity*. Explain its origin and how the term may relate to human populations.

9. Compare and contrast the population densities of Egypt and Canada.

10. Explain how both the crude death rate and crude birth rate can indicate population growth or decline.

11. Define *subsistence agriculture*, and explain why it is common in some countries in the periphery.

12. Identify where the highest infant mortality rates are found.

13. Explain how a region's income level affects the gap in average life expectancies between men and women.

■ INTERPRET GRAPHS

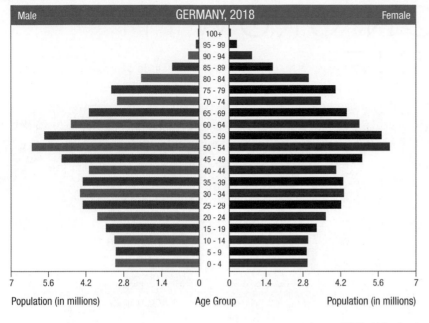

Male | GERMANY, 2018 | Female

Age groups (top to bottom): 100+, 95-99, 90-94, 85-89, 80-84, 75-79, 70-74, 65-69, 60-64, 55-59, 50-54, 45-49, 40-44, 35-39, 30-34, 25-29, 20-24, 15-19, 10-14, 5-9, 0-4

Male axis: 7 5.6 4.2 2.8 1.4 0
Female axis: 0 1.4 2.8 4.2 5.6 7

Population (in millions) | Age Group | Population (in millions)

Source: CIA World Factbook

14. **IDENTIFY DATA & INFORMATION** What type of CBR does this graph represent?

15. **PREDICT OUTCOMES** Describe Germany's dependency ratio over the next 20 years.

16. **ANALYZE VISUALS** What economic and social challenges might Germany face in 20 years?

17. **EXPLAIN PATTERNS & TRENDS** How does Germany's population continue to grow despite its death rate exceeding its birth rate?

GEO-INQUIRY | SEEING LOCAL IMPACTS OF POPULATION DISTRIBUTION

Geo-Inquiry can be used to answer questions about patterns of population where you live. Use the steps in the Geo-Inquiry process below to explore a Geo-Inquiry question at the local level.

ASK Start with an authentic, open-ended question about your community. Think about something you would like to learn more about or an issue that needs to be solved. It may be as simple as: *How does population distribution impact the environment in my community?* This is not yet a Geo-Inquiry question, because it doesn't have an action component—but it can lead to many other need-to-know questions. These will help formulate a Geo-Inquiry question such as: *How might we identify and solve the negative impact of population density on the environment in a specific location in our community?*

COLLECT Gather geographic information to answer your question. Explore local sources for statistics and data on population distributions and negative environmental issues. Look for patterns in data and create methods of data collection. Conduct interviews or surveys as needed.

VISUALIZE Analyze information you collected to identify the sources of the negative impact of population distribution on the local environment. Organize the information and create visuals such as images, videos, maps, charts, and graphs to show the relationship.

CREATE Think about the most effective way to share your Geo-Inquiry story, such as through a multimedia presentation that provides scientific data, research, and clear visuals. Keep your audience in mind, and choose elements that will inform and inspire decision-makers to take action. Decide what storytelling tool you will use and the elements you will include. Always outline or storyboard your story to ensure that your message is clear and powerful.

ACT Share your stories with decision-makers in your community. Consider how your project can help provide solutions to environmental issues within your community while taking into consideration population patterns.

ASK — COLLECT — VISUALIZE — CREATE — ACT

CHAPTER 4

POPULATION GROWTH AND DECLINE

CRITICAL VIEWING In Ankara, the capital city of Turkey, a crowd of people enjoy picnicking in a city park. Ankara is home to about 5 million people and has a high annual rate of population growth. ▌ Why might a country carefully monitor the size of its population?

GEOGRAPHIC THINKING What factors contribute to changes in population size?

4.1
WHY POPULATIONS GROW AND DECLINE

4.2
THEORIES OF POPULATION CHANGE

NATIONAL GEOGRAPHIC EXPLORER Pardis Sabeti

CASE STUDY: Zika Virus in South and North America

4.3
POPULATION POLICIES

CASE STUDY: China's Population Policies

4.4
CONSEQUENCES OF DEMOGRAPHIC CHANGE

4.1 WHY POPULATIONS GROW AND DECLINE

The trend in human population can be summarized in one word: *growth*. However, the social, economic, and geographic factors underlying this growth are nuanced and complex. Geographers analyze these factors and how they affect fertility, mortality, and migration in order to understand population changes at a range of scales, from local to global.

TRENDS IN POPULATION

LEARNING OBJECTIVE

IMP-2.A Explain factors that account for contemporary and historical trends in population growth and decline.

Earth's population has been expanding since human life began. For many thousands of years, humanity's numbers grew relatively slowly, but the rate of growth has multiplied dramatically in the past 200 years. As of 2020, the world's population numbered 7.8 billion, a nearly five-fold increase over the 1900 estimate of 1.6 billion. When plotted on a graph, the change in human population over time results in a curve that is relatively flat at the beginning and then undergoes a rapid increase in growth, producing a shape that somewhat resembles the letter J.

To analyze trends in population growth and decline, geographers look at the rate of natural increase and doubling time. The **rate of natural increase** (RNI) is the difference between the crude birth rate (CBR) and crude death rate (CDR) of a defined group of people. At the country or region scale, a high RNI can indicate rapid population growth, but because it does not take migration into account, RNI does not tell the whole story of an area's growth or decline. Considering Earth's population as a whole, however, RNI does render an accurate picture of trends. The global RNI peaked at 2.2 percent in 1963, and projections indicate that it will decline to 0.1 percent in 2100, while the actual number of humans will continue to increase. For the period of 2015 through 2020, the United Nations estimated the global RNI to be 1.1 percent.

Doubling time is the number of years in which a population growing at a certain rate will double. The formula for calculating doubling time (DT) is 70/RNI = DT. Using this formula, it is possible to calculate Ethiopia's projected doubling time in 2019 based on its RNI of 2.6 percent for that year: 70/2.6 = 26.9, or just under 27 years. The 2019 RNI for the United States was 0.3 percent, giving a doubling time of 233.3 years. Looking at doubling time can be a useful way to compare trends among countries or regions, but doubling times can change from year to year. As a country's RNI changes, its estimated population doubling time must also be recalculated.

The recent striking increase in human population growth was sparked by developments beginning in the mid-1700s.

Among the most prominent of these was the Industrial Revolution, which was launched by major technological innovations in manufacturing and profoundly affected where and how people lived and worked. The effects of the Industrial Revolution did not touch all parts of the world equally or at the same time. In general, industrialization occurred most quickly and had the greatest impact in Western Europe and North America. You will learn about the impact of the Industrial Revolution in greater detail in Chapter 18.

At the same time that manufacturing was being transformed, new understandings, practices, and technologies were increasing agricultural productivity: people could grow more food with less labor and often on less land. In addition, scientific discoveries contributed to new and better medicines, and sanitation practices began to improve. Combined with technological developments, these advances in health care helped lower rates of disease and infant mortality and improve the overall health of populations in the countries most affected by the Industrial Revolution.

As new agricultural and health-care practices spread throughout the world, they helped increase population growth in non-industrialized countries as well. The resulting strong birth rates and lower crude death rates led to a rapidly increasing worldwide RNI.

In the present day, as in the past, the world's population is not increasing at the same rate in all areas. Switching focus from the global scale to the national scale, differing population trends become apparent. Certain countries in the periphery are seeing the highest rates of natural increase. In Chapter 3, you read about the Democratic Republic of the Congo's population pyramid, which reflects its rapid population growth. In 2019, Niger, also in Africa, had the highest RNI—3.8 percent—followed by Mali (3.6 percent), Angola (3.5 percent), Uganda (3.2 percent), and the Democratic Republic of the Congo (3.2 percent). Rapid population growth can challenge a country to meet its people's needs for food, housing, medicine, schools, jobs, and other services. Experts worry that the most rapid population growth is taking place in areas that may be least equipped to support larger numbers of people.

Meanwhile, most countries in Europe have a negative RNI, meaning that the population in those places is declining or will soon begin to decline. Looking to the future, experts predict that 48 countries will show a population decline by 2050, even as Earth's overall human population continues to increase.

The changes initiated during the Industrial Revolution had a powerful and unequal effect not just on the size of the population but also on its distribution and density in different areas. As a result of the new technologies, jobs in many home-based industries, such as sewing and weaving, moved into factories, which were largely located in cities. The result was a mass migration from farms to cities, where people could find work and where population densities were higher than in rural areas. This movement contributed to **urbanization**, the growth and development of cities, and took hold more strongly in the industrialized countries that form the core. Countries in the periphery, with lower rates of industrialization, have generally remained more rural. In the present day, however, many peripheral countries are experiencing rapid urban growth as populations move from rural areas to cities.

PAST, PRESENT, AND FUTURE By the turn of the 20th century, the changes brought about by industrialization and improvements in health and sanitation had contributed to unprecedented population growth. In just 100 years, from 1900 to 2000, the world population increased from 1.6 billion to more than 6 billion. Within another two decades, that number jumped by another 1.8 billion people. Projections by the United Nations and others indicate that the world population will be nearly 10 billion by 2050.

Many researchers worry about the impact of this accelerated population growth, fearing the number of humans will exceed Earth's carrying capacity, which could bring dire consequences such as mass starvation.

Others point out that most populations cannot continue to grow rapidly and that limiting factors such as the available natural resources cause a population to level off over time. Differences in how we perceive the future depend in part on how we interpret and analyze the data. Varying scenarios can be used for forecasting population growth and total population. For example, different researchers might make different assumptions about future fertility, mortality, quality of life, and sustainability.

FACTORS THAT INFLUENCE POPULATION GROWTH AND DECLINE

LEARNING OBJECTIVES

IMP-2.A Explain factors that account for contemporary and historical trends in population growth and decline.

SPS-2.B Explain how the changing role of females has demographic consequences in different parts of the world.

Changes in population in a given place or region are driven by the balance among three factors: mortality, fertility, and migration. These are influenced by the interplay of economic, political, environmental, and cultural factors, which vary from region to region and even from place to place.

ECONOMIC FACTORS The strength of a country or region's economy can have a significant impact on both fertility and mortality. Birth rates tend to decline in times of economic hardship, particularly if people are concerned about having sufficient food and resources to support their children. Conversely, birth rates often rise during more prosperous times, when people are feeling optimistic about their future.

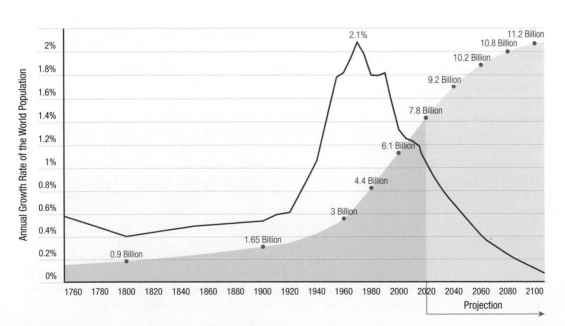

Source: OurWorldInData.org

WORLD POPULATION GROWTH, 1750–2100 This graph shows the J-shaped curve of world population growth since the beginning of the Industrial Revolution. During the millennia prior to this, population growth was relatively flat. The data projected out to 2100 predicts that the global population will reach 11.2 billion, even as the population growth rate falls to 0.1 percent

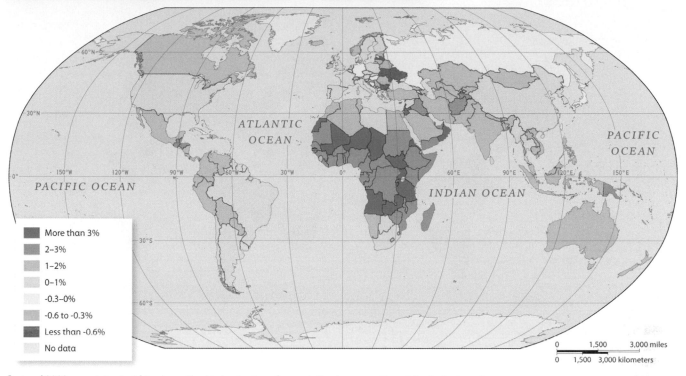

Legend:
- More than 3%
- 2–3%
- 1–2%
- 0–1%
- -0.3–0%
- -0.6 to -0.3%
- Less than -0.6%
- No data

0   1,500   3,000 miles
0   1,500   3,000 kilometers

As of 2020, countries in Africa have the highest rates of population increase. Countries in Eastern Europe are seeing the greatest rates of population decrease.

Access to health care, a key factor in fertility and mortality, can also be largely dependent on the economy. In general, wealthier countries can provide better access to health care, advanced medical treatments, good nutrition, and clean water, all of which can help prevent or cure disease and lower the crude death rate. Good-quality pre- and post-natal health care and nutrition may also make it easier for women to carry their babies to term and lower a country's infant mortality rate.

Types of economic activity also influence families' decisions about childbearing, and thus fertility rates. Families tend to be larger in agriculturally-based economies, where children are considered essential for labor. In industrial and post-industrial economies, on the other hand, children may be viewed as an economic burden, leading to a lower crude birth rate.

POLITICAL FACTORS War, peace, and government policy play an important role in population trends. At different times, governments in different parts of the world have adopted measures attempting to control the rate of population growth in their countries. Some governments, concerned about population growth, aim to dissuade families from having too many children by offering incentives or disincentives—measures intended to discourage a certain behavior. China went a step further with its policy permitting only one child per couple. China's total fertility rate, birth rate, and rate of natural increase all dropped during the years the law was in force.

On the other hand, countries with declining populations may enact policies that encourage people to have children. Singapore, for instance, offers tax breaks and extended maternity leave. South Korea, Sweden, France, and Iran have also passed policies that favor families with children. You will read more about China's and Singapore's policies on fertility later in this chapter.

War contributes to population decline in ways both obvious and more subtle. In addition to a higher mortality rate as the result of combat-related deaths and inevitable civilian casualties, war often results in food shortages or mass migration away from the conflict. At the end of 2018, for example, 5.7 million people had fled Syria's civil war to become registered refugees in neighboring countries. War also may influence the birth rate, as soldiers on the front lines are separated from their spouses or partners. Additionally, just as people tend to have fewer children in times of economic hardship, they also hesitate to start families in times of conflict. A war can have a long-term impact on the demographics of a country or region by reducing the number of people of childbearing age. For example, France experienced a drastic reduction in the number of births immediately following World War I, a conflict that killed more than a million French soldiers.

In contrast, the onset of peace after a long war or political strife may cause a spike in population. For instance, many countries, including the United States, experienced an increase in the birth rate during the two decades following World War II—a period known as the Baby Boom.

POPULATION GROWTH AND DECLINE **89**

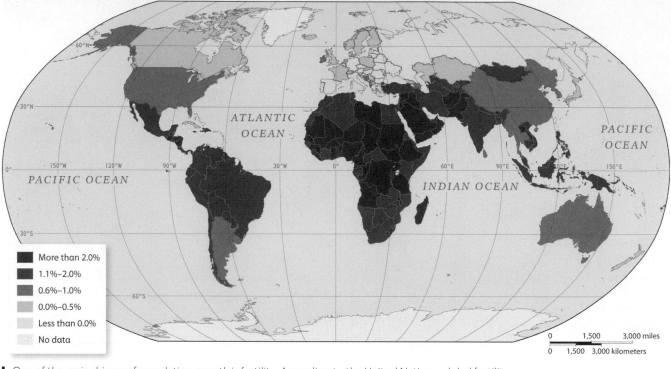

■	More than 2.0%
■	1.1%–2.0%
■	0.6%–1.0%
■	0.0%–0.5%
■	Less than 0.0%
■	No data

One of the main drivers of population growth is fertility. According to the United Nations, global fertility is now 2.5 children per woman, but the rate varies considerably across the world. Singapore, a country in Southeast Asia not visible on this small-scale map, has the lowest total fertility rate (TFR), with just 0.82 children per woman. Eight countries—all in Africa—have TFRs of more than 5.5 children per woman.

ENVIRONMENTAL FACTORS Natural disasters are just one environmental factor that can radically affect a region's population. Examples of such events abound: between 1 million and 4 million people lost their lives in floods in China in 1931; in 2004, an earthquake in the Indian Ocean caused a tsunami that killed almost 228,000 people; and a 2010 earthquake in Haiti resulted in 316,000 deaths.

Famine and the spread of deadly disease can have a similar impact. For instance, the world's population experienced a radical dip in the 1300s as the result of the bubonic plague, which swept through much of Europe and Asia. According to some estimates, perhaps 60 percent of Europe's population was wiped out.

Famine is often caused by drought, a natural disaster, or by political factors such as war. It may affect a population not only through deaths by starvation but also by lowering fertility rates due to poor maternal health. In China, a famine that began in 1876 killed upwards of 9 million people. Since the year 2000, famines in Sudan, Uganda, Somalia, and the Democratic Republic of the Congo have cost more than 3 million lives.

Environmental factors also affect population distribution within regions and worldwide by encouraging migration. During the Great Famine of 1845–1849, for example, around 1 million people in Ireland died when a crop disease destroyed potato harvests, and nearly 2 million Irish people emigrated to the United States and other countries.

CULTURAL FACTORS Cultural expectations play an important role in fertility rates. In societies where women tend to marry at a relatively young age and large families are the norm, the birthrate can be expected to be higher. In Afghanistan, where girls often marry before they turn 18, the crude birth rate in 2018 was 37.5. (A CBR of greater than 30 is considered high.) Religion also has historically played an important role in a family's decisions to have children. Some conservative Islamic and Christian leaders, for example, have explicitly taught against using various forms of contraception.

Family planning—availability and access to contraceptive options—also has an impact on birth rates. Societies that discourage the use of contraception, often due to religious beliefs, tend to have higher birth rates than those that do not. As many people worldwide are becoming more secular (that is, not following a religion), they are often ignoring religious rules about birth control. Catholic teaching still forbids contraception, for example, but birth rates in many traditionally Catholic countries such as Ireland remain low.

Another factor that may influence population growth is education, particularly as it relates to medicine, prenatal care, health care, and nutrition. More information results in fewer infant deaths (a lower IMR), a lower CDR, and greater life expectancy. While these factors might tend to increase population, this effect may be balanced by better education about contraception, which may result in a lower TFR.

This female construction worker in China gives orders during work on the Three Gorges Dam, the world's largest hydroelectric dam, which was completed in 2006. Countering worldwide trends, the percentage of Chinese women working outside the home has been steadily declining in recent years, from 73 percent in 1990 to 61 percent in 2019.

THE CHANGING ROLE OF FEMALES Changing social, economic, and political roles for women have influenced patterns of fertility. In many core countries, women in previous generations tended to stay home and raise children upon marriage. Today in those countries, women are more likely to remain in the workplace full-time as they balance parenting and household responsibilities. Professional women are postponing having children until after they have established their careers, thus reducing their childbearing years. In addition, some women may choose not to have a family at all—or to have fewer children— because they don't want to take time out of the workforce. Combined with the availability of effective birth control options, the improved status and decision-making power of women contributes to a lower birth rate.

In many cultures, however, strict gender division remains the norm. In patriarchal societies, male babies are still preferred over female babies, girls receive less education, and women have few rights. According to UNESCO (United Nations Educational, Scientific and Cultural Organization), fewer than 40 percent of countries provide girls and boys with equal access to education. Studies indicate that women who receive more schooling have a lower TFR, at least in part because they tend to marry later.

In many countries, too, women are discouraged from working outside the home, and cultural expectations call for them to care for elderly members of the family, as well as their own husbands and children. Evidence suggests that the chronic stress associated with caring for elderly parents contributes to poor health outcomes for caregivers.

According to some recent evidence, increases in political power for women may also affect mortality. One study conducted in 2019 examined countries that in the 1990s had established gender quotas for their legislatures. In other words, each country's legislative body was required to have a certain minimum number of women. Researchers found that these countries had experienced an estimated 9 to 12 percent decrease in maternal mortality rates. Other studies have found that greater political power for women—as demonstrated by voting rights and the number of women serving in the legislature—correlates with a lower infant mortality rate.

GEOGRAPHIC THINKING

1. Identify which factors affected population growth beginning in the mid-1700s, and explain which factors had the greatest influence.

2. Explain whether population projections are more likely to be accurate over the short term or the long term.

3. Compare cultural perceptions of the role of women in different parts of the world; explain how they affect a country's RNI.

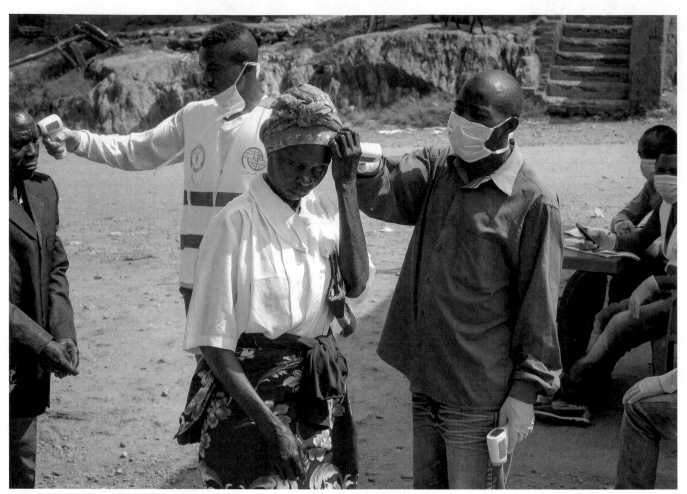

CRITICAL VIEWING In 2019, an outbreak of the Ebola virus had killed thousands of people in the Democratic Republic of the Congo. People crossing the border into Uganda had their temperatures taken as a way of checking for symptoms of the highly contagious disease. ▌ What are some of the challenges of preventing the spread of communicable diseases like Ebola?

In addition, a highly mobile population and global economy increase the risk of deadly communicable diseases spreading rapidly. The 2010s, for example, witnessed the outbreak of Ebola, a deadly virus that was first identified in 1976 in tropical Africa. The first incidence occurred in March 2014 in a rural region of southeastern Guinea, but the disease soon spread to other parts of that country, as well as to neighboring Liberia and Sierra Leone. Ebola is very contagious through direct contact with an infected person or animal, so it has the capacity to spread quickly. Many people contracted Ebola by caring for an infected relative at home or preparing a body for burial according to tradition. At the same time, medical services in the affected countries were not sufficiently staffed or prepared for such an emergency.

By the time the outbreak was declared over in June 2016, there were 28,610 reported cases of Ebola, causing 11,308 deaths. In 2018, a new Ebola outbreak was declared in the Democratic Republic of the Congo, and by late 2019 more than 2,000 people had died of the disease.

Many are concerned about the possibility of viruses or antibiotic-resistant strains of bacterial diseases spreading

on a more global scale, traveling across oceans with infected airline passengers. While it has a lower death rate than Ebola, the COVID-19 virus illustrates this concern. First appearing in the city of Wuhan, China, in December 2019, COVID-19 was found in locations in Asia, Europe, and North America within months. By the beginning of March 2020, the disease was believed to have infected 89,000 people worldwide and caused 3,000 deaths.

GEOGRAPHIC THINKING

1. Explain how Malthus's theory was affected by the time and place in which he lived.

2. Explain the degree to which the Demographic Transition Model effectively explains population changes.

3. Describe limitations of the Epidemiological Transition Model.

4. Explain how the present-day Ebola outbreaks fit into Stage 5 of the Epidemiological Transition Model.

CRACKING THE GENETIC CODE

When she's not making music with her indie rock band Thousand Days, Pardis Sabeti is a genetic researcher and professor at Harvard University.

LEARNING OBJECTIVE
IMP-2.A Explain factors that account for contemporary and historical trends in population growth and decline..

In her groundbreaking research on the evolution of disease, Pardis Sabeti wields the power of math in a quest to protect the human population.

"Humans and virulent microbes are both governed by genetic codes that allow them to evolve over time," Sabeti explains. "There's also a constant evolutionary arms race going on between the two. Humans develop genetic resistance to particular diseases, while microbes develop resistance to antibiotics and our immune defenses. Unlocking the genetic codes of humans and pathogens can help us understand how to intervene." Work like Sabeti's may someday help prevent communicable diseases from making the comeback predicted in Stage 5 of the Epidemiological Transition Model.

To this end, Sabeti developed methods for computers to analyze the DNA of groups of people in search of clues to disease resistance. Specifically, she is looking for genetic mutations that have become very common very quickly in certain populations. These mutations can help researchers identify genes associated with the ability to resist diseases such as malaria.

One of Sabeti's genome scans found evidence for a recent genetic adaptation that may be linked to resistance to the Lassa virus, an extremely dangerous pathogen. Sabeti has worked in Nigeria over the decade since, identifying individuals who have been exposed to the virus but have suffered few effects, and analyzing their genomes to uncover the parts associated with this resistance. This decade-long project is not only exploring how certain people develop resistance, but also helping develop improved diagnostics to quickly test for Lassa exposure and identify which strains of the virus are the most infectious. Armed with mathematics and tools for genetic analysis, Pardis Sabeti aims to develop comprehensive approaches to treating and preventing outbreaks not just of Lassa but of many deadly infectious diseases. ▌

GEOGRAPHIC THINKING

Explain how Pardis Sabeti is using quantitative data to have an impact on mortality.

ZIKA VIRUS IN SOUTH AND NORTH AMERICA

THE ISSUE In 2015, hundreds of thousands of cases of Zika virus infection were reported in Brazil. The virus spread to other parts of the Americas and the Caribbean.

LEARNING OBJECTIVE
IMP-2.B Explain theories of population growth and decline.

BY THE NUMBERS

707,133

Zika virus cases reported in the Americas between May 2015 and December 2016

60

countries worldwide reporting cases of Zika virus in 2015–2016

2

U.S. states reporting cases of Zika in 2016: Florida and Texas

Source: Center for Disease Control

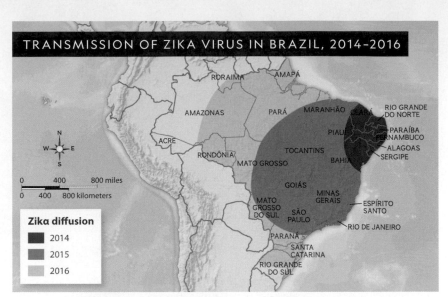

The Zika virus rapidly spread through Brazil in the years 2014–2016. A 2019 study by the journal *Nature Microbiology* predicted that in future years, warming global temperatures caused by climate change will foster conditions favorable to the mosquitoes that spread Zika and other diseases.

ONE UNPREDICTABLE FACTOR that influences population size is the spread of disease. Scary new viruses sometimes seem to emerge abruptly, and too often they re-emerge after being inactive for years or decades. One such virus is Zika, which was first discovered in 1947 in monkeys in Uganda. Five years later, the first human diagnoses of the Zika virus were made in Uganda and Tanzania. In May 2015, the virus made front-page news due to a major outbreak in Brazil, on the other side of the Atlantic Ocean. By November of that year, the Brazilian government had declared a national public health emergency, and by November 2016, more than 200,000 cases of Zika infection had been reported there. The virus soon spread to other parts of North, Central, and South America and the Caribbean.

Researchers point to several factors that contributed to the rapid spread of the disease. The Zika virus is carried by the *Aedes aegypti* mosquito, a species that lives in tropical and subtropical regions. These mosquitoes reproduce in puddles and other standing water, and crowded living conditions in warm climates provide excellent breeding grounds. Although mosquitoes are the most common means of transmission, the virus can also be diffused through sexual activity. In addition, scientists say that the population of the Americas was susceptible to the disease because unlike Africans, who had built up resistance to Zika, they had no previous exposure to the virus. Symptoms of Zika are often mild, so infected people may unknowingly spread the disease locally or travel to a new place after contracting it.

One of the reasons the Zika virus is so frightening is that it affects the brain development of a fetus and can cause microcephaly—a smaller than normal head size—and other malformations. Thus, Zika is especially damaging when a pregnant woman is infected. To address the crisis, governments engaged in public education campaigns and took measures to eradicate the *Aedes aegypti* mosquitoes. In the United States, the Centers for Disease Control and Prevention cautioned pregnant women to avoid traveling to areas where Zika had been detected. ∎

GEOGRAPHIC THINKING

Explain whether the spread of the Zika virus challenges aspects of the Epidemiological Transition Model.

4.3 POPULATION POLICIES

Governments occasionally try to influence population trends through policy, in some cases trying to spur population growth and in other cases trying to limit it. Their goal is to avoid out-of-control increases in numbers that could stress resources, while at the same time maintaining a vigorous workforce and strong economy.

TYPES OF POPULATION POLICIES

LEARNING OBJECTIVE

SPS-2.A Explain the intent and effects of various population and immigration policies on population size and composition.

Government policies enacted to influence the natural rate of increase fall into two categories. Those designed to curb population growth by discouraging citizens from having children are known as **antinatalist**, and they are usually a reaction to concerns about population growth exceeding resources. The goal of these policies is to reduce the risk of potential famine or disease due to overuse of natural resources and to ensure that there are sufficient schools, jobs, and services to support the future population.

In contrast, **pronatalist** policies encourage births and aim to accelerate population growth. Governments enact pronatalist policies for a variety of reasons, including to address concerns about an aging population. Low birth rates and fertility rates in some countries give rise to concerns about the size of the workforce and its ability to meet future economic needs as older workers retire. Some experts also argue that stronger birth rates promote a stronger economy, or that having a family promotes personal well-being.

CRITICAL VIEWING Countries monitor their population trends by looking principally at two areas: birth rate and flow of immigration. In 1979, China began a program to control its birth rate by enacting an antinatalist one-child-only policy. Billboards like these depicted happy one-child families. ▌ How might this billboard have affected Chinese citizens' feelings about the country's One-Child Policy?

CHINA'S POPULATION POLICIES

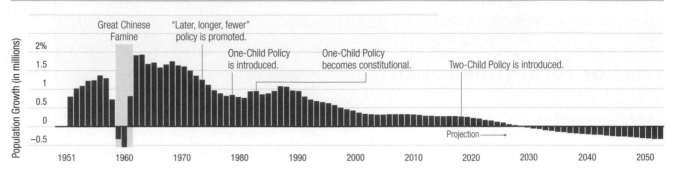

ANNUAL POPULATION GROWTH OF CHINA China's One-Child Policy resulted in a drop in the country's fertility rate. By the early 2010s, with projections anticipating an alarming decline in population, the government ended the policy.

Source: U.S. Census International Data Base

THE ISSUE China issued its One-Child Policy to avoid problems with population growth. Now it is experiencing unforeseen impacts of the measure's success.

LEARNING OBJECTIVE
SPS-2.A Explain the intent and effects of various population and immigration policies on population size and composition.

BY THE NUMBERS

970 MILLION
China's population in 1979

1.4 BILLION
China's population in 2017

2.8
China's fertility rate in 1979

1.7
China's fertility rate in 2019

Sources: Center for Disease Control; World Data Atlas

IN 1979, concerned that the country's resources would be unable to support its growing population and that earlier measures to limit population growth had not shown sufficient results, the communist government of China enacted its One-Child Policy. Any couple who had a second child would be required to pay a fine that only the very rich could afford. In addition, families with more than one child were ineligible for government assistance. The only exemptions given were to members of some ethnic minorities or in cases where the firstborn child had a disability. The government also offered incentives to families who limited themselves to one child, including better employment opportunities and higher wages.

Even before enacting an official policy, China had worked to decrease its population by encouraging people to marry later and have smaller families. As a result, the fertility rate had fallen from a high of 6.1 children per woman in 1968 to 2.8 in 1979. By the 2010s, China's fertility rate was holding steady at about 1.6 children per woman. The poicy is estimated to have prevented up to 400 million births.

China's One-Child Policy had unintended consequences, however. The elderly population grew more than anticipated because improvements in medicine and health care increased life expectancy. Eventually, government leaders began to worry that there were too few workers to support the aging population. In addition, the cultural preference for boys led to a gender imbalance. Infant girls were sometimes abandoned or given up for international adoption. Instances of abortions of female fetuses and female infanticide were also reported.

In 2015, China abandoned the policy and replaced it with one that allows any couple to have two children. Some experts believe this change will not affect the population growth rate any time soon, for several reasons. Many Chinese women are past their childbearing age. Many men are having trouble finding wives because of the gender imbalance. Young couples often live in cities, where the high cost of living may deter them from having children. And couples are getting married later in life, a cultural change the government itself had encouraged. Immigration—often involuntary—may come to play a role in China's future population. In recent years, news organizations have reported that some criminal groups have begun luring or kidnapping women in neighboring countries for forced marriages or childbearing. China will be coping with the impacts of its One-Child policy for decades to come. ∎

GEOGRAPHIC THINKING

Identify the ways in which China's One-Child Policy was both successful and unsuccessful.

In the east African country of Tanzania, family planning information is distributed by community-based organizations as well as by mass media campaigns funded by the United States Agency for International Development (USAID). In 2018, Tanzanian president John Magufuli ordered USAID to stop running commercials, citing concerns about a shrinking labor force.

RESULTS AND CONSEQUENCES

LEARNING OBJECTIVE

SPS 2.A Explain the intent and effects of various population and immigration policies on population size and composition.

Both pronatalist and antinatalist policies have had mixed success. Results generally depend on how well the population accepts the fundamental principles proposed by its government. If citizens agree that it is to their advantage to have more or fewer children, they will more likely comply with government policies. It is impossible to force people to have more children; pronatalist policies generally are fueled by a sense of ethnic or national pride and tend to succeed where there is a strong sense of nationalism or anti-immigrant sentiment. Pronatalist policies may include financial support, such as free daycare, to make it less expensive to have and raise children. Antinatalist policies, on the other hand, generally include elements such as contraception education and family planning support, as well as financial incentives. A few countries have attempted to control the population through forced sterilization, but these policies tend to have little impact on the total population growth.

India's government was among the first to control its citizens' fertility in an effort to curb population growth.

In the 1970s, India enacted aggressive mandatory sterilization campaigns, mostly targeting men. In many cases, men were sterilized without their consent; in others, the men consented in exchange for land or for not being cited for riding a train without a ticket. In 1976 alone, the Indian government sterilized 6.2 million men. In more recent years, India has focused its sterilization efforts on women, generally targeting very poor areas, where the payment for sterilization may amount to more than two weeks' wages. India's government insists that its sterilization programs are voluntary and claims they are essential to limit population growth in the country, which is projected to become the most populous one on Earth by 2030. India has also implemented media campaigns to promote contraception and family planning, as well as financial aid for people seeking birth control from health care centers.

Nigeria initiated its antinatalist policy in 1998 with the goal of reducing the total fertility rate from more than 6 to 4 births per woman. The government sought to encourage contraception and worked with international donors to increase family planning education and the availability of contraceptives. The policy encountered opposition from Nigeria's Catholic and Muslim communities, which both frown on birth control. Twenty years later, the country's fertility rate is still nearly 5 children per woman—one of the highest in the world.

CRITICAL VIEWING Vans in Idumota Market in Lagos, Nigeria, pick up workers returning home from work. Some worry that Lagos will be unable to meet the needs of its growing population.
▮ What challenges resulting from Nigeria's growing population do you see in the photo?

Nigeria's crude death rate. Predictions that rapid growth would contribute to economic decline have not borne out; in fact, Nigeria's GDP grew at 7 percent per year from 2000 to 2014, though it has slowed since then. Nevertheless, some researchers say its population is one of Nigeria's greatest resources. At the same time, many middle-class and wealthier Nigerians with highly skilled jobs are moving to Europe, the United States, and Canada, a trend that causes some concern for the future of Nigeria's economy.

CONSEQUENCES OF AN AGING POPULATION

LEARNING OBJECTIVE
SPS-2.C Explain the causes and consequences of an aging population.

In Chapter 3, you read about the dependency ratio, which is the number of people in a dependent age group (under age 15 or older than 64) divided by the number of people between the ages of 15 and 64. In many countries,

particularly core countries, the dependency ratio is increasing due to the number of elderly people. Countries with aging populations generally have lower TFRs, often below 2.1 children per woman. When represented by a population pyramid, the higher tiers are larger than the bottom ones.

In 2018, 9 percent of the world's population was 65 or older, and projections suggest that this number will increase to 16 percent by 2050. Aging populations are not equally spread across the world, however. In 2018, 13 countries had populations in which 20 percent or more of the population was over 65. Some projections suggest that 82 countries will have a similar top-heavy population pyramid by 2050.

The average global life expectancy of roughly 72 years for those born in 2019 represents a significant rise over the life expectancy of 66.5 years for those born in 2000. In some regions of the world, life expectancy has risen even more significantly. This change, coupled with decreased fertility rates, is the main reason for the aging population in many countries.

In general, people are living longer because they have better access to medical care, especially in core countries. A better understanding about healthy lifestyle habits also contributes to longer lifespans. Improved detection and treatment of infectious and degenerative diseases in countries at all levels of development is another factor in the overall life expectancy rise. As you have seen, many of these changes are captured in the Epidemiological Transition Model.

Although living longer is a positive development, it is not without challenges. "An aging society is literally and figuratively a 'dying society,'" cautions Mark Bockenhauer, a professor of geography and a former Geographer-in-Residence at the National Geographic Society. "Without young people coming into the society, and their energy, work, and new ideas, the future cannot be bright."

Like any other change in population size or structure, an aging population has both short- and long-term effects on the economy, culture, and politics of a city, country, or region. Societies cannot avoid an aging population; they must adapt by confronting the challenges and taking advantage of the benefits this demographic change can bring about.

SOCIAL EFFECTS A graying population can challenge traditional family dynamics. In many cultures, for example, multigenerational families have long been the norm. It is expected in some societies for the bride to move in with her husband's family, allowing the couple to care for his parents as they age. In recent decades, however, fewer newlyweds are opting for this living arrangement. Social changes like this one, coupled with demographic change, mean that fewer young people are available to care for aging parents at home. In response, some countries have begun building living facilities for the elderly, changing the social fabric of the culture.

India provides an example of this phenonenon. Traditionally structured Hindu families in India live in multigenerational households incorporating grandparents, aunts and uncles, and cousins. Brides move in with their husband's family, and elderly parents are cared for in the home. Recently, however, increasing numbers of young people have been moving away from their homes to seek better-paying jobs, and women are entering the workplace in greater numbers. These factors, as well as changes in cultural attitudes, have led many younger Indians to form nuclear households—that is, homes consisting solely of parents and their children. Some social commentators in India have criticized this trend and the resulting increase in elderly people moving into senior living facilities.

At the same time, the social benefits of a larger elderly population cannot be overlooked. Retired grandparents may be available to care for grandchildren, enabling both parents to return to work without the added cost of daycare. When parents are unable to raise their children, often it is the grandparents who step in. Elderly people also play a key role in maintaining social networks that bind families and groups together and, through their engagement in community life, can help change negative societal attitudes toward aging.

ECONOMIC EFFECTS Perhaps the largest economic challenge of an aging population comes from the fact that retirees pay less in income taxes, which in most countries is a major revenue source for the government. In many countries, including the United States, Germany, and Italy, record numbers of people are supported by government-sponsored retirement programs such as the United States'

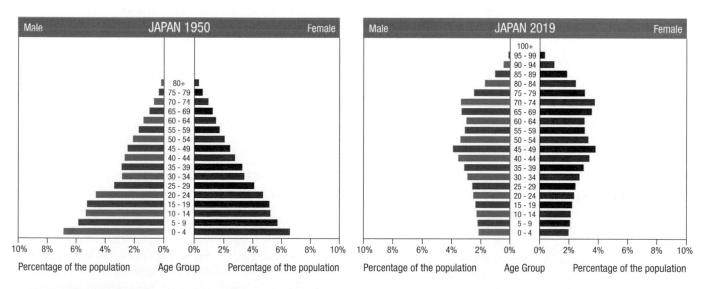

POPULATION PYRAMIDS, JAPAN, 1950 AND 2019 It is projected that by the year 2060, 40 percent of Japan's population will be over the age of 65. Japan is feeling the impact of its rising elderly population in every area of modern life, from a reduced workforce in dire need of new workers to supermarkets needing more parking spaces near entrances to accommodate less mobile older customers.

More than 25
15–25
10–14.9
5–9.9
Less than 5
No data

0   1,500   3,000 miles
0   1,500   3,000 kilometers

READING MAPS The elderly dependency ratio is the number of people age 65 or older relative to the working-age population.

Social Security system. On average, retirees are living longer, adding to the costs of these programs, which are largely financed by taxes paid by younger people who are still in the workforce. As the cost of public retirement programs rises, taxes may also go up, or benefits for the retirees may be reduced.

People also rely on their private savings to maintain their lifestyles in retirement. Living 20 or 30 years beyond retirement is no longer unusual, and some retirees run out of their personal savings long before the end of their lives. In response, research suggests that in many countries people are postponing retirement and working longer. In some cases, retirees may return to work if their savings cannot support their retirement.

Health care is the other most notable cost associated with an aging population. Because people live longer, they often are ill or unable to fully care for themselves for a longer period of time. Statistics suggest that the cost of long-term care in the United States may double over the next 20 years.

The financial consequences of health care can span generations. When an aging parent requires round-the-clock care for a serious physical or mental condition, an adult child may have to choose a less demanding job or leave the workforce altogether in order to care for that parent. In some places, the increased need for medical specialists who care for the elderly has outstripped supply. Countries and communities may need to reconsider how services are provided. Sweden, for instance, has implemented an approach whereby mobile teams provide flexible home care for elderly residents.

These challenges can be partially offset by several economic benefits of an aging population. Older adults spend money on food, clothing, housing, and entertainment just as younger adults do, and they may stimulate growth in many economic sectors. For instance, seniors use services such as specialized health care and in-home caregivers. In recent decades, the number of geriatric phyisical therapists, or physical therapists who specialize in working with elderly patients, has grown considerably. One estimate placed the value of the elder care industry in the United States at $400 billion in 2018. Retirees also contribute countless hours in volunteer work, which may reduce the government's burden. In addition, the elderly are less likely to commit crimes and do not attend public school, both of which represent major expenditures for local governments in many countries around the world.

POLITICAL EFFECTS An aging population may also shape the political landscape of a country or region. Changes in the voting demographic may influence who is elected and what policies are enacted. In some countries, elderly citizens have a strong voice in politics. In the United States, for example, the percentage of people aged 65 and older who vote in elections is consistently greater than that of any other age group. Some research has indicated that older voters see pensions and health care as their top priorities, with education and environmental concerns farther down the list. Yet older populations are diverse in

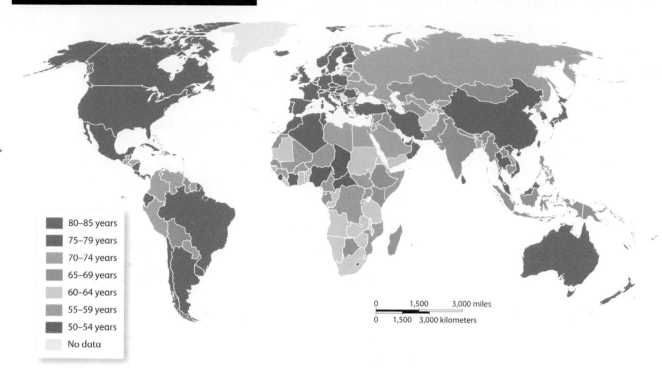

80–85 years
75–79 years
70–74 years
65–69 years
60–64 years
55–59 years
50–54 years
No data

0   1,500   3,000 miles
0   1,500   3,000 kilometers

READING MAPS The elderly dependency ratio in the "Elderly Dependency Ratio, 2018" map can be compared with the life expectancy numbers in this map to better understand age-related demographics. For example, Nigeria has an elderly dependency ratio of 5–9.9 and an average life expectancy of 50–54 years. It makes sense that these numbers correspond because a low life expectancy would leave fewer elderly people in the population in relation to number of people aged 15 to 64. ▮ Compare the statistics for one or two other countries on this map and the "Elderly Dependency Ratio, 2018" map and explain how they might be related.

their opinions. Researchers also concluded that as younger generations become seniors themselves, they will likely carry their own varying priorities into the voting booths.

Political effects of an aging population are often intertwined with economic effects. In the United States, Social Security is a regular topic of debate among citizens and lawmakers, as the Baby Boom generation leaves the workforce to enter retirement, adding to strains on the Social Security system. How to fund and maintain public retirement programs poses difficult policy questions for lawmakers worldwide. Germany and the United Kingdom have dealt with this problem by allowing larger numbers of immigrants of working age into the country to expand the workforce and relieve some of the tax burden.

Some countries, too, are attempting to control costs by raising the retirement age. The United Kingdom and the United States have both increased the age at which retirees can claim full benefits and plan to phase in more changes in the future. In some countries in the European Union, including Finland, Denmark, Greece, and Italy, the retirement age is being linked to life expectancy. Policy decisions relating to public retirement plans have economic impacts for both older and younger generations.

Immigration, mentioned previously as a way of adapting to the economic challenges of a shifting dependency ratio, also has a political dimension. Governments set immigration policies in response to a variety of economic and social pressures. In Germany, as in other European countries, increased immigration has been unpopular among many citizens, contributing to divisions within the society. In other places, immigrants are welcome solutions to the problem of providing quality services to a growing population. You will explore the social, political, and economic dimensions of immigration in Chapter 5.

GEOGRAPHIC THINKING

1. Identify the stages in the Demographic Transition Model where you expect to find countries with a high elderly dependency ratio. Explain what the DTM helps you understand about these countries.

2. Compare the positive and negative economic effects of an aging population.

3. Explain how changes in a country's working-age population can affect the country both economically and culturally.

■ CHAPTER SUMMARY

The three main factors that cause changes in population size and structure are fertility, mortality, and migration. These factors are influenced by economic, political, environmental, and cultural factors.

- A wide range of changes that occurred during the Industrial Revolution caused the global population to start growing exponentially.

- The changing role of women is impacting the fertility rate in many places.

- An increase in life expectancy is contributing to population growth and influencing the composition of the population in many countries.

- Geographers use the rate of natural increase (RNI) and doubling time to explain changes in population size. The RNI is the difference between the crude birth rate and the crude death rate. Doubling time is calculated by using the formula 70/RNI to obtain the number of years a population will take to double in size.

Several models and theories have been developed to help explain and forecast changes in population.

- Malthus's theory suggests that population growth will outpace food production.

- The Demographic Transition Model (DTM) portrays five stages of population development and is based on trends related to birth rates and death rates.

- The Epidemiological Transition Model (ETM) seeks to explain trends in population by examining the principal causes of death at different stages.

Countries adopt policies to address needs related to the size of their population.

- Antinatalist policies are designed to address future problems due to overpopulation by discouraging people from having large families.

- Pronatalist policies are designed to address problems associated with a declining population by encouraging people to have children.

- Governments also use immigration policies to address population issues.

Although the population is growing rapidly in some countries (especially in Africa), other countries (especially in Europe) are experiencing declining population rates.

An increasing number of countries have aging populations, which lead to a higher dependency ratio.

- Social effects of an aging population include challenges to traditional family structures.

- Political and economic effects include changes to policies relating to public retirement funds.

■ KEY TERMS AND CONCEPTS

Use complete sentences to answer the questions.

1. **APPLY CONCEPTUAL VOCABULARY** Consider the term *urbanization*. Write a standard dictionary definition of the term. Then provide a conceptual definition—an explanation of how the term is used in the context of the chapter.

2. What challenges might a country like Japan face in bringing up its rate of natural increase?

3. How does the environment affect the growth and distribution of population?

4. What is the significance to geographers and demographers of a population that follows the shape of the letter J when plotted on a graph?

5. Compare and contrast the Demographic Transition Model and the Epidemiological Transition Model.

6. What factors could cause a population's doubling time to increase or decrease?

7. What present-day trends might reinforce Malthus's concern about overpopulation?

8. Define and give examples of antinatalist policies.

9. Define and give examples of pronatalist policies.

10. What changes might a neo-Malthusian thinker project for a country with an aging population and an immigration policy such as Germany's?

11. Very few countries are thought to be in Stage 5 of the Demographic Transition Model at present. Do you think many more countries will experience Stage 5? Why or why not? What would be the consequences?

12. What evidence is there that antinatalist or pronatalist policies can be difficult to reverse? Why do you think this is the case?

13. What does a country's elderly dependency ratio help explain about its politics, economy, and culture?

■ INTERPRET GRAPHS

Study the graph and then answer the following questions.

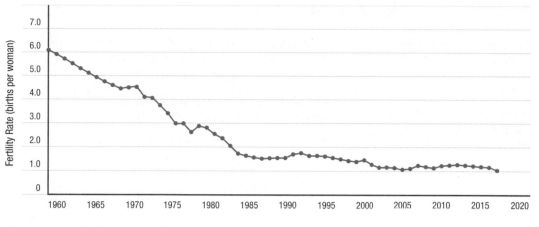

■ TOTAL FERTILITY RATE IN SOUTH KOREA, 1960–2017

Source: The World Bank

14. **ANALYZE DATA & INFORMATION** Based on the graph, is South Korea experiencing positive or negative population growth? Explain.

15. **ASK QUESTIONS** What other information would you need to determine Korea's overall population growth rate (or decline)?

16. **PREDICT OUTCOMES** What types of challenges might South Korea anticipate based on the population trends shown in the chart?

17. **ANALYZE DATA** Do you think South Korea's natalist policies have changed between 1960 and today? Why or why not?

GEO-INQUIRY | POPULATION IN YOUR COMMUNITY

Consider how you can use the Geo-Inquiry Process to explore how population grows or declines in your community. Use the steps below to explore changes in the size and structure of your city, town, or county.

ASK Start with an authentic, open question about your community. It may be as simple as: *How can local government better prepare for changes in population size?* Use the Geo-Inquiry Process to expand this question and ask other need-to-know questions to help formulate an answer and possible proposal for action. For example: *Which areas of the community are experiencing the greatest growth or decline? What groups within the community have the fastest rate of change? What impact will population growth or decline have on services?*

COLLECT Decide how to gather geographic information to answer your question. Explore local sources of information, such as Census Bureau records on your community's past and current population, county records on development or land use, or graphics created by the local government planning board showing how the community has changed or is expected to change.

VISUALIZE Analyze the information you collected to draw conclusions. Use maps, charts, or graphs to help you understand both the data and the patterns it contains. Consider which visuals would help others understand the population changes in the community.

CREATE Focus on how to tell a Geo-Inquiry story that will answer the Geo-Inquiry question and convince others of any proposal you have created. You may choose to create a storyboard outline of the highlights that are most important to share and add details that support your proposal. Consider how you can use images, videos, and visual aids to illustrate your findings.

ACT Share your story with other stakeholders in the community. Decision makers will be interested in learning about your findings and how your investigation can support better plans for the community's future.

ASK   COLLECT   VISUALIZE   CREATE   ACT

CHAPTER 5
MIGRATION

CRITICAL VIEWING Rohingya refugees carry their belongings through a rice paddy in Bangladesh after fleeing from Myanmar. ▌What cultural and economic effects might this migration have on Bangladesh?

GEOGRAPHIC THINKING How does migration shape our world?

5.1
WHY DO PEOPLE MIGRATE?

5.2
TYPES OF MIGRATION

NATIONAL GEOGRAPHIC EXPLORER Jason De León

CASE STUDY: Migration from Central America

5.3
REFUGEES AND INTERNALLY DISPLACED PERSONS

CASE STUDY: Surviving War in Syria

NATIONAL GEOGRAPHIC PHOTOGRAPHER Lynsey Addario

5.4
MIGRATION AND POLICY

FEATURE: Walls That Divide Us

5.5
EFFECTS OF MIGRATION

5.1 WHY DO PEOPLE MIGRATE?

When people migrate, they take with them their customs, values, and beliefs—in short, their culture—creating a link between their origin and destination. Geographers study these links to better understand how migration affects populations and, in turn, changes the world culturally, politically, and economically.

WHAT IS MIGRATION?

LEARNING OBJECTIVE
IMP-2.C Explain how different causal factors encourage migration.

Humans have been on the move for two million years. Explorers have journeyed across oceans in search of resources, and armies have crossed continents to establish empires. Human mobility has transformed the planet through the spread of cultures and ideas. **Mobility** includes all types of movement from one location to another, whether temporary or permanent or over short or long distances. Temporary, repetitive movements that recur on a regular basis are called **circulation**. This might involve short distances, like walking a few blocks or riding the bus a few miles to school each day, or it might mean long-distance movement like the seasonal routines of farm workers or retirees traveling thousands of miles. The permanent movement of people from one place to another is called **human migration**.

Human movement affects the population of both the place of origin and the destination. **Emigration** is movement away from a location, and **immigration** is movement to a location. The difference between the number of emigrants and immigrants in a location such as a city or a country is the **net migration**. If more people emigrate from Japan than immigrate to Japan, the entire population decreases, creating a negative net migration. If fewer people emigrate from France than immigrate to France, the population rises and the net migration is positive.

Long-distance migrations can be dangerous, time consuming, and physically or mentally demanding. People—young, old, weak, strong, entire families—die trying to migrate. So why do people do it? Geographer Ernst Ravenstein studied the movements of migrants in England during the 19th century and proposed several principles or "laws" that describe trends in migration. Through his observations, Ravenstein concluded that economic conditions push and pull people in predictable directions. He also noticed that population size and distance affect migration.

Ravenstein's thinking laid the groundwork for the **gravity model**, which geographers derived from Newton's law of universal gravitation in order to predict the interaction between two or more places. (A diagram of the gravity model appears in the Maps and Models Archive at the end of this unit.) When used to describe migration patterns, the model suggests that as the population of a city increases, migration to the city increases, and as the distance to a city grows, migration to that city decreases. While economic circumstances play a major role in migratory decisions, environmental and political conditions, as well as demographic and cultural factors, also drive migration.

GEOGRAPHIC THINKING

1. Compare human migration and circulation.

2. Describe factors that might encourage young adults to migrate more often than families.

MODEL: RAVENSTEIN'S LAWS OF MIGRATION

Ravenstein first published his laws of migration in a British journal in 1885.

1. Migration is typically over a short distance.

2. Migration occurs in steps, like from a rural area to a nearby city, and then perhaps on to a larger city.

3. Long-distance migrants often move to places of economic opportunity (urban areas).

4. Every migration generates a movement in the opposite direction, or a counter flow (not necessarily of the same number of migrants).

5. People in rural areas migrate more than people in cities.

6. Males migrate over longer distances than females.

7. Most migrants are young adult males.

8. Cities grow more by migration than by natural increase.

9. Migration increases with economic development.

10. Migration is mostly due to economic factors.

CRITICAL VIEWING Freshwater flooding caused by Hurricane Florence, which struck the Carolinas in September 2018, left many homes in Lumberton, North Carolina, completely uninhabitable. Adverse physical conditions such as flooding can push people from impacted regions. ❚ What other factors related to Florence might influence a Lumberton resident's decision to rebuild or relocate?

ENVIRONMENTAL CONDITIONS A variety of environmental factors can also influence migration decisions, pushing or pulling people to relocate. A desirable climate or landscape can pull migrants to certain regions. Adverse physical conditions, including intense heat, drought, or substantial flooding, can push people from affected regions. Hurricane Katrina, the storm that battered the Gulf Coast of the United States in 2005, displaced hundreds of thousands of people and flooded much of the city of New Orleans. One year after the storm, almost 50 percent of residents had returned as the city continued to rebuild. But some residents with fewer ties to the city, including renters and people with no family members in Louisiana, simply relocated. For others, the damage to their homes was too extensive and costly to return and rebuild.

Scientific evidence indicates that climate change contributes to crop failure and water scarcity, intensifies storms, and causes sea levels to rise, displacing people from their homes around the world. Scientists predict at least 50 million people will be displaced from their communities by 2050 because of problems related to climate change, and the figure likely will be higher. Some people will adapt to the new environmental conditions by voluntarily leaving home. Others will be forced to become migrants as more areas, especially island, coastal, or desert communities, become uninhabitable.

GEOGRAPHIC THINKING

3. Describe the types of factors that influence people's decision to migrate.

4. Explain how people's perceptions affect migration.

5. Explain why different communities have different push and pull factors.

5.2 TYPES OF MIGRATION

Think about why someone might decide to leave the place he or she calls home, and all that is involved in making such a move. How strong do the push and pull factors have to be to cause that person to endure the hardships of migration?

VOLUNTARY MIGRATION

LEARNING OBJECTIVES
IMP-2.C Explain how different causal factors encourage migration.
IMP-2.D Describe types of forced and voluntary migration.

Geographers distinguish between two types of migration: **voluntary migration**, in which people make the choice to move to a new place, and **forced migration**, in which people are compelled to move by economic, political, environmental, or cultural factors. In many cases throughout history, people have been enslaved through violent action by others and forced to move. But other instances blur the line between voluntary and forced migration.

People voluntarily migrate for many reasons. As you have read, push factors such as joblessness or drought might cause them to leave their current home; pull factors like economic opportunity or a mild climate might draw them to a new home. Whatever reasons migrants have for moving, these factors must outweigh the inconvenience of having to travel with everything they own or to leave possessions behind, as well as the uncertainty of what life will be like in the new location.

Crossing an international border brings an additional set of challenges. It often requires immigrants to travel long distances under difficult conditions, to seek permission to enter the destination country, and once they've arrived, to attempt to adapt to the culture—the language, customs, and indeed, every aspect of life in a new country. The United States hosts the largest number of immigrants (50 million in 2017), followed by countries such as Germany and Russia. The countries losing the most emigrants are India, Mexico, Russia, China, Bangladesh, Syria, Pakistan, and Ukraine. The single largest flow of immigrants from one country to another is from Mexico to the United States.

While about half of all foreign-born residents in the United States come from Latin America (primarily from Mexico, Central America, and the Caribbean), the fastest-growing group of immigrants comes from Asia. Between 2010 and 2017, Asians comprised 41 percent of all U.S. immigrants. China and India contribute the largest proportion of Asian immigrants, with many settling in New York City. On the other side of the the country, the city of Los Angeles is home to large groups of Filipino, Vietnamese, and Korean immigrants. Sizeable Asian-American communities have sprung up in the South as well, in Atlanta, Georgia; Raleigh,

North Carolina; and Austin, Texas. More and more, these new Asian residents are highly educated. Between 2000 and 2009, 30 percent of Asians arriving in the United States had a college degree. From 2010 to 2017, that number rose to 45 percent.

Overall, the tendency is for people to emigrate from countries of the periphery and semi-periphery and immigrate to countries with stronger economies. As of 2017, about 3.5 percent of the world's population—or 258 million people—were living outside the country in which they were born. The median age of international immigrants in 2017 was 39.2, and 48.4 percent of immigrants were women.

In **transnational migration**, immigrants to a new country retain strong cultural, emotional, and financial ties to their country of origin and may regularly return for visits. In a sense, transnational migrants live in two cultures—and two countries—at once. Often, they send money to help support their families back home. They also use technologies such as social media to keep in close touch with the families and friends they left behind. Today there are three major flows of transnational migration in the world: from Latin America to North America, from Southwest Asia to Europe, and from Asia to North America.

Despite the large number of immigrants living around the world, it is more common for people to move from place to place within a particular country. Movement within a country's borders is called **internal migration**. Recall Ravenstein's laws, which state that most migration occurs over short distances. Moving a short distance is significantly easier than moving a long distance, both physically and psychologically. This is because of the **friction of distance**, a concept that states that the longer a journey is, the more time, effort, and cost it will involve. Consider the similarities and differences among cities around the world. How do towns and cities that are close together tend to be similar? How do towns and cities in different countries, regions, or hemispheres tend to differ? (See Unit 6 on cities and urban land use.) Factors such as language, customs, and climate can present difficult hurdles for international migrants. When moving from place to place within a country as internal migrants, however, they may face smaller changes—people likely speak the same language and may have similar social and cultural traditions.

Internal voluntary migrations often happen in waves or patterns. For instance, in the years following World

time but later decide to stay permanently. In fact, today, between 2.5 and 4 million people of Turkish descent live in Germany, making up the country's largest immigrant group. With globalization and improved transportation, however, **circular migration**—when migrant workers move back and forth between their country of origin and the destination country where they work temporary jobs—is becoming more common. The money workers earn in the destination countries may have greater purchasing power in their home countries, where prices are lower.

MODEL: DISTANCE DECAY

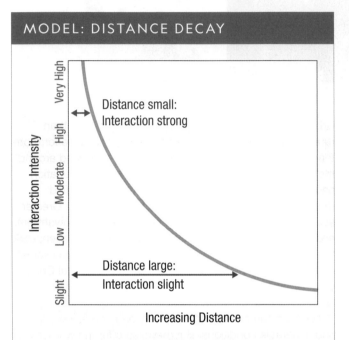

The farther away an object is, the harder it is to see clearly. This statement also applies to an important geographic concept and model called **distance decay**. The term is used to describe how distance affects interactions between locations. For example, people know more about their own town or a nearby city than they do about a city in another country. And the farther away a place is, the less people tend to know about it. Distance decay can affect where migrants decide to move. But today the effects of distance decay are lessened as technology connects us in new ways and puts knowledge about distant locations at the fingertips of anyone with an internet connection. ▌ How do you think the construction of new roads or railways and improvements in communication technology, affect distance decay?

FORCED MIGRATION

LEARNING OBJECTIVE
IMP-2.D Describe types of forced and voluntary migration.

For many, the concept of home brings to mind feelings of comfort, safety, and identity. People grow attached to the places they live, and it would take quite a lot of persuasion to convince them to move. But not everyone who leaves their home does so by choice.

As you have read, forced migration occurs when people are compelled to leave their homes by extreme push factors. People might be forced to move because of conflict, political upheaval, or natural disaster. They might be fleeing from persecution due to their ethnicity, religion, or social or political beliefs. They might be escaping the violence of war. **Refugees**, for instance, are people who are forced to leave their country for fear of persecution or death. Because of the danger they face at home, refugees may be granted special status when they attempt to enter a new country. They have the right to request **asylum**, or the right to protection, in the new country. Migrants who do not meet the definition of refugee established by the United Nations High Commissioner for Refugees (UNHCR) are not eligible for asylum and must find another avenue to enter a foreign country. **Internally displaced persons** are people who have been forced to flee their homes but remain within their country's borders. Internally displaced persons include those running from conflict and those evacuating their homes because of a natural disaster such as flooding, an earthquake, or a hurricane.

In 2018, 2.3 million people around the world were driven from their homes, according to the UN. This brought the total number of forcibly displaced people in the world to 70.8 million. Of those, about 41 million were internally displaced persons. More than 25 million were refugees who had fled to escape conflict or persecution in places such as the Democratic Republic of the Congo, South Sudan, and Myanmar. And 3.5 million were asylum seekers waiting to learn if they would be granted refugee status.

For people forced from their homes, migration can be significantly more difficult than when the move is voluntary. Especially if they are fleeing from violence, people often do not have time to plan properly. They might have to leave with only the possessions they can carry, with no idea where their journey will take them. For many, like the millions of refugees who have fled from the civil war in Syria since 2011, the journey itself is fraught with danger, and they often end up living in harsh locations such as refugee camps for months or years.

Many Rohingya people, members of an ethnic minority in Myanmar, have experienced forced migration. The Rohingya are Muslims in a majority Buddhist country, and they have faced persecution for years. Their citizenship was denied by a law passed in 1982, leaving them "stateless" and subjecting them to extreme difficulties with employment, heath care, and more. In August 2017, Myanmar's military carried out widespread attacks on the Rohingya, burning villages and torturing and killing many individuals. Since then, hundreds of thousands of Rohingya have fled Myanmar for Bangladesh, making a dangerous journey through jungles and over mountains, or risking a harrowing sea voyage across the Bay of Bengal. Most of those who have reached Bangladesh are women and children. Forty percent are under the age of 12. The UNHCR documented this humanitarian crisis, finding that 723,000 Rohingya had

DOCUMENTING THE STORIES OF MIGRANTS

De León collaborated with artist Amanda Krugliak on an exhibit called State of Exception/Estado de excepción, which includes a wall of discarded backpacks left by Mexican migrants in the Sonoran Desert.

LEARNING OBJECTIVE
IMP-2.C Explain how different causal factors encourage migration.

People view undocumented migration into the United States from many perspectives, often focusing on immigrants' effects on the politics, culture, and economy of the United States. Jason De León may be the first to study migration patterns from an unusual perspective—that of an archaeologist.

A spiky cactus bristles in the scorching Sonoran Desert sun. Caught on its thorns—a baby's diaper. Miles away, a tattered backpack contains one roll of toilet paper, a love letter, and a prayer card. Beside it, a tiny child's shoe. Until Jason De León, a National Geographic Explorer and the founder of the Undocumented Migration Project, arrived on the scene, such items were considered garbage or never discovered at all.

As an archaeologist, De León applies scientific techniques to gain a deeper understanding of the migrants' experiences, paying particular attention to vulnerable groups such as women, children, and LGBTQIA+ individuals. De León studies artifacts he finds in the desert's harsh landscape, left behind by migrants from Mexico, Central America, and places farther south. In addition to collecting the objects they leave behind, he conducts interviews to help reveal the meaning of the items. De León explains, "We use archaeological surveys, linguistics, forensics, and ethnography to document how people prepare to cross the border, who profits from helping them, how they deal with physical and emotional trauma during their journey, and what happens to those who don't make it."

His goal is to learn more about the societal impact of immigration on those affected, including migrants, law enforcement officers, smugglers, and everyday citizens. "It's an emotional subject, but my focus is science first," says De León.

GEOGRAPHIC THINKING

Describe how the migration data De León collects might help him identify patterns and trends among vulnerable groups of migrants.

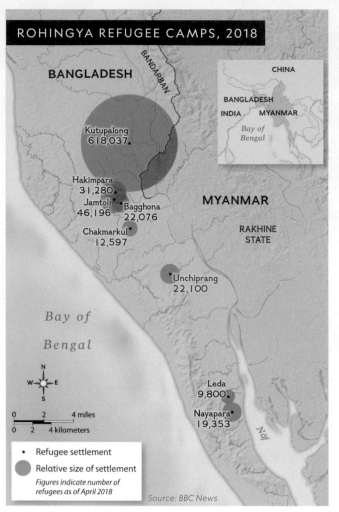

ROHINGYA REFUGEE CAMPS, 2018

BANGLADESH

BANDARBAN

Kutupalong
618,037.

Hakimpara
31,280.

Jamtoli
46,196

Bagghona
22,076

Chakmarkul
12,597

MYANMAR

RAKHINE
STATE

Unchiprang
22,100

Bay of

Bengal

Leda
9,800.

Nayapara
19,353

Naf

CHINA

BANGLADESH

INDIA   MYANMAR

Bay of
Bengal

N
W   E
S

0   2   4 miles

0   2   4 kilometers

• Refugee settlement

● Relative size of settlement

*Figures indicate number of
refugees as of April 2018*

Source: BBC News

Kutupalong is the largest refugee settlement in the world,
housing more than 600,000 Rohingya refugees in an area
covering just 5 square miles.

fled their homes by August 2018, with most sheltered in a
single, enormous refugee camp in Bangladesh. Their future
is, like that of most refugees, uncertain.

The largest forced migration in history was the transatlantic
slave trade. From the 16th to the 19th centuries, between 10
and 12 million men, women, and children were transported
from Africa to the Americas. They were captured by their
enemies or by European or African slave traders and forced
onto crowded ships bound for North, Central, and South
America and the Caribbean. Many died on the horrific
voyage across the Atlantic, and those who survived were
sold into lives of hard labor, often on sugar, tobacco, and
cotton plantations. The slave trade had a devastating
effect in Africa as well. People lived in fear of capture, and
depopulation, especially of working-age adults, gutted
families and societies.

Slavery was outlawed in the United States more than
150 years ago, but a form of the institution still exists in the
world today. **Human trafficking** is defined by the United
Nations as "the recruitment, transportation, harboring,
or receipt of persons by improper means (such as force,

abduction, fraud, or coercion)." Victims are often illegally
sold into forced labor, domestic servitude, and sexual
exploitation. Human trafficking is a form of modern-day
slavery, and according to the U.S. Department of Homeland
Security, millions of people are trafficked around the world
each year, including within the United States.

Traffickers prey on vulnerable people, such as homeless
and runaway youths, poor immigrants, and people who
have suffered physical and psychological trauma. They often
smuggle their captives across international borders because
victims find it more difficult to seek help in a foreign country.
Nearly every country in the world is affected by human
trafficking, either as a country of origin, a country of transit,
or a destination country for victims.

Consequently, human trafficking frequently goes unreported
and is considered a "hidden crime." Despite its invisibility, it
is both a grave violation of human rights and a major issue—
experts estimate the crime brings its perpetrators billions of
dollars each year. It is the second most profitable form of
international crime, after drug trafficking.

THE GRAY AREA   Despite the terms' clear definitions,
it can at times be difficult to distinguish between voluntary
and forced migration. Consider the example of the Irish who
immigrated to the United States in the 1800s. The emigrants
who left Ireland during the Potato Famine of 1845–1849
were forced out by starvation, but the wave of Irish migration
had actually begun earlier, in the 1820s. The country was
under colonial rule by the British, and until 1829, Irish
Catholics were prohibited from owning land, carrying
weapons, and voting. In addition, the Industrial Revolution
that swept England beginning in the mid-1700s left Ireland
behind. The smaller country's agricultural economy and real
estate values suffered, leaving the Irish even poorer.

For many, the conditions had become too difficult, and
Irish citizens boarded ships bound for cities in Great Britain
such as Liverpool and Glasgow, or they made the long
sea journey to the United States to make a new life for
themselves in cities such as New York and Boston. But
many others remained behind in Ireland under the same
conditions. The question for geographers, then, is this:
when that wave of Irish immigrants boarded those ships,
could their experience be described as voluntary or forced
migration? Over the centuries and across the globe, myriad
migrants have made their way—and continue to advance—
in this "gray area."

GEOGRAPHIC THINKING

1. Explain how a region's climate, economy, politics, and
culture might affect migration to and from the area.

2. Explain the degree to which friction of distance might
explain the decisions of Irish people considering chain
migration in the late 1800s.

CASE STUDY

MIGRATION FROM CENTRAL AMERICA

THE ISSUE After the U.S. Refugee Act became law in 1980, Central American immigrants, fleeing instability and violence in their countries of origin, have sought asylum in the United States.

LEARNING OBJECTIVE
IMP-2.D Describe types of forced and voluntary migration.

BY THE NUMBERS

350,000

Central American immigrants living in the United States in 1980

3.4 MILLION

Central American immigrants living in the United States in 2015

42%

of people apprehended at the U.S. southern border in 2016 came from the Northern Triangle

Source: The Brookings Institution

A mother and two young daughters, part of a caravan of thousands traveling from Central America to the United States in 2018, flee tear gas fired by U.S. Border Patrol agents over the security fencing that separates the United States from Mexico.

BEGINNING IN THE 1980s, the number of immigrants arriving in the United States from Central America rose dramatically. The reasons for this increase are numerous, including unstable political conditions and a lack of jobs, as well as high homicide rates and widespread gang violence in their home countries.

In 1980, immigrants had a new reason to consider coming to the United States. Congress passed the Refugee Act, which raised the ceiling for refugees allowed into the United States each year from 17,400 to 50,000. The act also affected who would be considered a refugee. Previously, the United States had granted refugee status only to those fleeing from a communist regime. The new law followed UN protocols, defining a refugee as anyone with a "well-founded fear of persecution on account of race, religion, nationality, membership in a particular social group, or political opinion."

Today, many of those seeking asylum in the United States come from El Salvador, Guatemala, and Honduras—the "Northern Triangle" of Central America. These countries, according to the aid organization Doctors Without Borders, are experiencing "unprecedented levels of violence outside of war zones." They have some of the highest homicide rates in the world, and kidnapping, extortion, and corruption are common. Sexual violence and violence against women are also widespread. Fear of these crimes has driven many from their homes, including families and unaccompanied children. Between 1980 and 2015, the number of Central American immigrants living in the United States rose by nearly a factor of ten, from 350,000 to 3.4 million.

In recent years, however, the United States decided that the difficult circumstances in the Northern Triangle do not rise to the level of persecution. In an effort to stem the flow of immigrants from this region, the U.S. government tightened restrictions on would-be immigrants. Many who arrive in the United States seeking asylum are deported back to their home countries. The irony is that the majority of the crime in these countries is committed by drug cartels and gangs, which are driven by demand for illegal drugs in the United States—and much of the violence is committed using weapons manufactured in the United States. ▌

GEOGRAPHIC THINKING

Explain whether the migration patterns of people coming from Central American countries to the United States are examples of forced or voluntary migration.

5.3 REFUGEES AND INTERNALLY DISPLACED PERSONS

Conflict and instability have driven millions from their homes, creating a widespread crisis that is one of the most challenging issues in the world today. For governments, it is a political and administrative issue. For the people forced to flee, it can be a matter of life or death.

CHALLENGING OBSTACLES

LEARNING OBJECTIVE
IMP-2.D Describe types of forced and voluntary migration.

As you have read, migrants who seek asylum in another country are known as refugees and those who remain within their home country's borders are known as internally displaced persons (IDPs). In either case, they are likely fleeing into unfamiliar territory by any means available. They must rely on the help of others and may be forced to pay to be smuggled to safety or over borders. They must also navigate the natural obstacles of unknown topography and weather conditions. International border restrictions cause many refugees to take dangerous alternate routes. If crossing a border illegally, refugees live in fear of being apprehended by authorities. Getting caught could mean being separated from family members or being deported back to the homeland they are trying to escape.

OBTAINING REFUGEE STATUS Today, refugees can seek asylum in any of the 145 countries that have ratified the 1951 Refugee Convention. The document was created by the United Nations to address the many people displaced by World War II. Originally, the UN defined refugees as people who leave their home countries out of fear of persecution. In 1967, it expanded its definition to include people escaping any conflict or disaster, such as the famine in Ethiopia in 1984–1985 that forced hundreds of thousands to leave the country rather than face starvation.

Official refugee status must be granted by the country providing asylum or by an international agency. Obtaining refugee status can be a long and difficult process. This is especially true when applicants have little documentation to prove their situation complies with the official definition of a refugee. Factors such as illiteracy, severe trauma, and memory loss can make it difficult for refugees to tell a convincing story. Once an asylum seeker is approved for refugee status, the host country is expected to provide civil rights, the right to work, and access to social services.

The United Nations High Commissioner for Refugees (UNHCR), established in 1950, continues to be an international resource for refugees and for countries offering asylum. Organizations such as the UNHCR work to help displaced people find safety, health care, and shelter, and apply for refugee status. In recent years, the number of refugees has reached record highs, and fewer refugees have been able to return to their home country—or **repatriate**—due to ongoing conflicts. Consequently, organizations have needed to plan and construct more long-term camps where refugees can find support for the needed adaptations to a new location—and new hope for the future.

TOP REFUGEE COUNTRIES OF ORIGIN A large portion of the refugees in the world come from just a few different countries. In 2017 for instance, more than a fifth of the world's 25.4 million refugees were Palestinians, and two-thirds of the remainder were from Syria, Afghanistan, South Sudan, Myanmar, or Somalia.

These countries and their people have been ravaged by war, violence, and persecution. In South Sudan, for instance, a civil war that began in 2013 has embroiled most of the country in conflict and violence. As the war has reached the fertile land in the south, farmers have not been able to produce as much food, bringing famine and food insecurity to much of the country. By 2018 these issues had forced more than 4 million people from their homes, or 1 out of every 3 South Sudanese citizens. More than 1.7 million of them remain within South Sudan's borders; over 2.4 million have managed to escape to neighboring countries.

THE HIDDEN CRISIS OF IDPS News stories about boats full of refugees making dangerous sea crossings or caravans traveling long distances on foot draw attention to the plight of refugees. But the struggles of internally displaced persons do not always receive as much coverage. Stories of IDPs are often subsumed by the narrative of the larger conflict taking place in their country. Therefore, despite the fact that there are significantly more IDPs than refugees in the world—about 15 million more in 2018—the refugee crisis is more well-known and better understood.

IDPs remain within their country's borders for a number of reasons. Some choose to stay close to the homes they were forced to leave, hoping the factors that pushed them out will improve. Others don't have the money or the physical means to make a long journey. Still others might be trapped

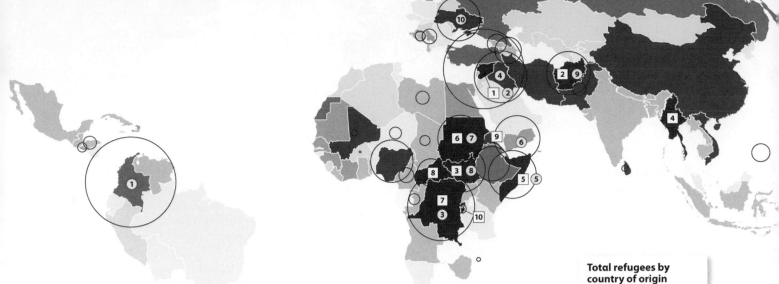

Total refugees by country of origin

- More than 1,000,000
- 500,001–1,000,000
- 100,001–500,000
- 50,001–100,000
- 20,001–50,000
- 5,001–20,000
- 2,001–5,000
- 501–2,000
- 0–500

IDPs by country

- 2,000,000–7,700,000
- 1,000,000
- 100,000

A DISPLACED WORLD, 2017

How many people were displaced in 2017, and where were they from? Darker shaded countries produced the most refugees. (The top ten countries of origin are numbered with white boxes.) Blue circles appear above countries with IDPs. (The top ten countries with the most IDPs are numbered in blue below.)

TOP 10 COUNTRIES WITH THE GREATEST REFUGEE EXODUS, 2017

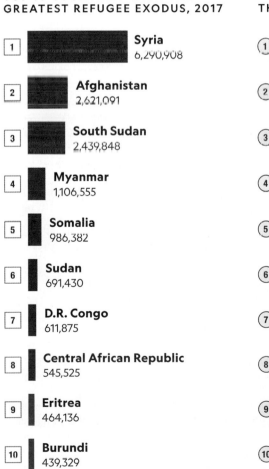

#	Country	Number
1	Syria	6,290,908
2	Afghanistan	2,621,091
3	South Sudan	2,439,848
4	Myanmar	1,106,555
5	Somalia	986,382
6	Sudan	691,430
7	D.R. Congo	611,875
8	Central African Republic	545,525
9	Eritrea	464,136
10	Burundi	439,329

TOP 10 COUNTRIES WITH THE MOST IDPs, 2017

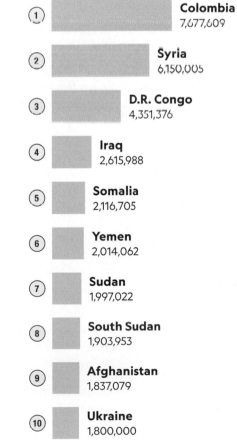

#	Country	Number
1	Colombia	7,677,609
2	Syria	6,150,005
3	D.R. Congo	4,351,376
4	Iraq	2,615,988
5	Somalia	2,116,705
6	Yemen	2,014,062
7	Sudan	1,997,022
8	South Sudan	1,903,953
9	Afghanistan	1,837,079
10	Ukraine	1,800,000

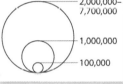

40 MILLION
internally displaced people (IDPs) worldwide

25.4 MILLION
refugees worldwide

3.1 MILLION
asylum seekers of which **173,800** were solitary or unattended children

Sources: United Nations High Commissioner for Refugees (UNHCR), Internal Displacement Monitoring Centre (IDMC); data from 2017

in the area by the violence or conflict they're attempting to flee in the first place.

While refugees rely on the protection of a foreign government for their safety, IDPs remain under the laws—and therefore the protection—of their own government. Sometimes, however, the government is involved in the conflict the IDPs are attempting to flee and is unable or unwilling to provide protection. In addition, armed conflict or an unfriendly government often make it difficult for aid organizations to reach IDPs. All of this makes IDPs a particularly vulnerable group.

CLIMATE'S ROLE Changes in environmental conditions—floods, drought, volcanic eruptions—have always spurred migrations. But as climate change intensifies these effects, a new category of migrant has emerged: climate refugees. Scientists predict that in the coming years, many people living in coastal areas will be forced to move due to rising sea levels. Increasing temperatures are already diminishing agricultural production in some areas, while rising sea levels are taking some farmland out of production.

While climate refugees haven't been given an official definition yet, their numbers are on the rise—since 2008, severe weather has driven an average of 22.5 million people from their homes each year. Though the term "climate refugee" seems to imply international movement, more than half of the people fleeing natural disasters each year become internally displaced persons.

Climate change creates new patterns of displacement. For example, Bangladesh's southern coast was a traditional source of agriculture and trade for tens of thousands of years. Within the last decade, however, unpredictable flooding and severe erosion have caused people to flee the area. Most have wound up in the urban slums of Dhaka, one of the world's fastest-growing cities. Bangladesh's southeast coast is also where 1 million Rohingya refugees live in settlements, shown on the "Rohingya Refugee Camps, 2018" map earlier in this chapter, following Myanmar's acts of genocide. Deforestation and other environmental impacts caused by the presence of so many refugees have compounded the effects of erosion and other natural disasters in the area.

GEOGRAPHIC THINKING

1. Compare an internally displaced person and a refugee.

2. Identify three reasons—one political, one social, and one environmental—why refugees flee their homeland.

3. Describe the predicted impacts of climate change on migration patterns.

CRITICAL VIEWING Food is distributed to young victims of Hurricane Maria in Puerto Rico, where 86,000 residents were displaced by the storm in 2017. Economic and infrastructure problems on the island worsened exponentially after Maria hit, and in 2018, 123,000 more people left Puerto Rico than moved there. ▮ How can a storm's short- and long-term impacts on an area affect patterns of migration?

CASE STUDY

SURVIVING WAR IN SYRIA

THE ISSUE The civil war that broke out in Syria in 2011 has led to a humanitarian crisis, with nearly 13 million Syrians forced to flee their homes.

LEARNING OBJECTIVE
IMP-2.D Describe types of forced and voluntary migration.

BY THE NUMBERS

6.6 MILLION
Syrians internally displaced as of 2018

5.6 MILLION
Syrians registered as refugees as of 2018

10%
of Syrian refugees live in refugee camps in Southwest Asia

80%
of Syrian refugees live in urban areas in Southwest Asia

Sources: Pew Research Center; UNHCR

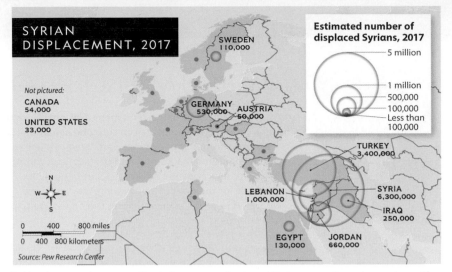

SYRIAN DISPLACEMENT, 2017

Not pictured:
CANADA 54,000
UNITED STATES 33,000

SWEDEN 110,000

GERMANY 530,000 AUSTRIA 50,000

Estimated number of displaced Syrians, 2017
5 million
1 million
500,000
100,000
Less than 100,000

TURKEY 3,400,000

LEBANON 1,000,000   SYRIA 6,300,000   IRAQ 250,000

EGYPT 130,000   JORDAN 660,000

N W E S

0   400   800 miles
0   400 800 kilometers

Source: Pew Research Center

Numbers on the map estimate how many displaced Syrians were in each country, with the majority remaining in Syria as IDPs. Notice that most Syrian refugees stayed in neighboring countries, while a smaller fraction migrated to other regions.

IN 2011, peaceful protest marches in Syria rapidly turned into a full-scale civil war. The marches were part of a wave of demonstrations, known as the Arab Spring, that occurred in Southwest Asia and North Africa beginning in 2010. Some earlier pro-democracy demonstrations, such as those in Tunisia, Egypt, and Libya, had been successful in overthrowing governments believed to be oppressive. Syrian pro-democracy activists were hopeful that peaceful protests calling for the resignation of President Bashar al-Assad would also succeed. By March 2011, demonstrations had spread throughout Syria. However, government troops responded by imprisoning, killing, and torturing demonstrators, including children.

What started as a demonstration by civilians quickly escalated into a complex war among religious groups within Syria. The violence against demonstrators spurred rebel groups to engage in combat with government troops, leaving civilians caught in the crossfire. Since 2011, the war has increased in complexity as more rebel factions formed and governments outside of Syria, such as Turkey, Russia, and the United States, backed different participants. Syrian neighborhoods became battlefields where families lived in fear of bombs, gunfire, imprisonment, and chemical weapons. It is estimated that the war has left more than 500,000 dead or missing.

By 2018, about 12 million Syrian civilians had been forced from their homes. More than 6 million were internally displaced. Of these, about 3 million fled to remote, besieged areas within the country. Most internally displaced Syrians live on the edge, struggling to find safe, affordable, healthy places to live. In 2019, U.S. president Donald Trump withdrew the majority of American troops from Syria, and the Turkish army advanced into the country. The Turkish government claimed it would establish a "safe zone" in Syria for the refugees Turkey had accepted during the war, but the invasion in reality unleashed another wave of displacements.

Since the uprising began, more than 5.6 million Syrians have fled the country and are registered as refugees. The majority of Syrian refugees went to urban areas in the region, including cities in Turkey, Jordan, Lebanon, Iraq, and Egypt. Just 10 percent settled in refugee camps in neighboring countries. About 1 million Syrian refugees fled to Europe. After obtaining asylum, refugees struggled for social acceptance and economic opportunities in their new country of residence. ∎

GEOGRAPHIC THINKING

Explain the degree to which distance decay and the gravity model apply to the pattern of Syrian displacement shown in the map.

DOCUMENTING JOURNEYS

Addario has traveled to countries across the world to document refugees crossing borders throughout the ongoing refugee crisis.

LEARNING OBJECTIVE
IMP-2.E Explain historical and contemporary geographic effects of migration.

After studying international relations, National Geographic photographer Lynsey Addario had a thought: photojournalism could be a marriage between international relations and art, telling stories with pictures. Fast-forward a few years, and Addario is one of National Geographic's most accomplished conflict photographers. Refugees and the contemporary effects of migration are a primary focus of her work. "My philosophy has always been that I'm there for the people I'm covering," says Addario. "I'm just a messenger documenting whatever is going on and bringing their message to people in power who may be able to do something about it."

Addario's journalism uncovers how location affects human experiences. In addition to documenting forced migration and refugees, Addario exposes life and conflict in Afghanistan since the fall of the Taliban, stark reality in sub-Saharan Africa, and the often hidden experiences of women in Southwest Asia (also referred to as the Middle East). Yet even after winning numerous prestigious awards—including a Pulitzer Prize—Addario confesses she still panics before a new assignment, concerned that her photographs won't capture the story. Even so, Addario believes she understands how to photograph people better than she did when she started. For one thing, she's learned how important it is to form a deep connection with people before she turns her lens toward them. ▮

CRITICAL VIEWING In the village of Selea, in the West Darfur region of Sudan, women await food and other aid being distributed by international humanitarian organizations in 2008. Civil war in the region resulted in a massive refugee crisis, with millions displaced from their homes and forced to migrate within Sudan or seek refugee status outside the country. ▮ What does the photo suggest about the reasons people migrate?

CRITICAL VIEWING Top: Thousands of ethnic Kurds from Syria cross the border between northern Syria and Iraqi Kurdistan in 2013, hoping to find better economic opportunity—and safety—within the Kurdish region of Iraq. Bottom: After a night sea voyage from Tripoli to Sicily, a raft filled with 109 African migrants is rescued in 2014. What do these photos convey about the challenges of migration?

5.4 MIGRATION AND POLICY

Since governments were first formed and national borders established, the movement of people has been affected by the border rules—or policies—of governments. Geographers analyze historical migrations to understand the effects migration patterns and policies have had on migrants and the places to which they move.

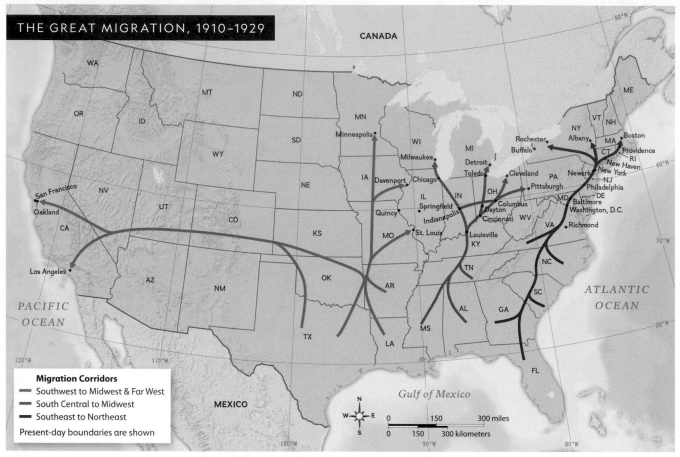

THE GREAT MIGRATION, 1910–1929

Migration Corridors
— Southwest to Midwest & Far West
— South Central to Midwest
— Southeast to Northeast
Present-day boundaries are shown

READING MAPS The map highlights the migration corridors that were established in the contiguous United States during the first part of the Great Migration. ▌ What social and economic impacts might these patterns of internal migration have had on the North, the South, and the West?

HISTORICAL U.S. MIGRATIONS

LEARNING OBJECTIVES
IMP-2.C Explain how different causal factors encourage migration.
IMP-2.D Describe types of forced and voluntary migration.

U.S. policy and government action have influenced a number of important migrations in American history. One of the earliest and most infamous examples of this influence was the Trail of Tears, the forced internal migration of approximately 100,000 Cherokee, Creek, Chickasaw, Choctaw, and Seminole people from their land in the southeastern United States. The five tribes' lands, which were already attractive to European-American settlers, became even more desirable to the United States when gold was discovered there. The takeover was finalized with the passing of the Indian Removal Act of 1830, which authorized the U.S. Army to force the tribes to move to one shared territory in Oklahoma.

Numerous voluntary migrations have also taken place throughout U.S history. In fact, internal migrations happen more frequently than international migrations, due to the friction of distance. The following historical examples illustrate voluntary internal migrations, some occurring after an international migration to the United States. They highlight both **interregional migration**—or movement from one region of the country to another—and **intraregional migration**, or movement within one region of the country. In each example, consider how U.S. policy played a role, what unintended effects may have resulted, and whether the goal behind the policy was achieved.

THE GREAT MIGRATION The Great Migration was a voluntary internal migration that occurred during the 20th century in the United States. Between 1916 and 1970, more than 6 million African Americans moved from the South to industrialized cities in the Northeast, Midwest, and West. The Great Migration altered the demographic makeup of the country. When it began, 90 percent of African Americans lived in the South. By the 1970s, 47 percent of African Americans lived in the North, Midwest, and West.

Strong push factors propelled African Americans to leave the South. Racial discrimination and violence were rampant, and segregation laws known as Jim Crow laws severely restricted African-American livelihood. Moreover, a pest called the boll weevil wreaked havoc on cotton crops. Employed as sharecroppers or tenant farmers, most African Americans were ruined financially when a cotton crop failed. The main pull factor was economic opportunity, in the form of factory and mill jobs. Work opportunities opened up when the United States entered World War I and millions of men enlisted. Furthermore, U.S. immigration policy of the 1920s set **quotas**—or limits on the number of immigrants allowed into the country each year. This slowed the flow of Europeans into northern cities, leaving many jobs open in urban factories.

News of economic opportunities from growing African-American communities in cities like Chicago, Detroit, and Baltimore spread among families and friends in southern communities. This caused migration waves to flow steadily from the South. Chain migration played a role in the Great Migration as **kinship links**—or networks of relatives and friends—led migrants to follow the same paths and settle in the same places as those who migrated before them. The move was an expensive struggle. Migrants often made the journey in stages, stopping to work in places on the way before continuing on. For many, this step migration to the final destination consisted of numerous stops and took years. For example, a sharecropping family from rural Alabama might have stopped in Nashville, Louisville, and Indianapolis on their years-long migration to Detroit. In each of these cities an intervening opportunity, in the form of a job or affordable place to live, would have held them for months or years. Intervening obstacles, such as a lack of funds or a sick family member, might also have paused the migrants' progress. Or the family might have stayed in one of those cities permanently without ever reaching their intended destination of Detroit.

SOMALI MIGRATION Internal migrations still happen today in the United States. One contemporary example involves a refugee group from Somalia in East Africa. Somali refugees have been resettling in the United States since 1990. U.S. resettlement locations for this group are spread throughout the country in large cities such as Minneapolis, Houston, Atlanta, Boston, and San Diego. After making their international migration as refugees to U.S. resettlement locations, many make an internal secondary migration to other U.S. towns or

American Jacob Lawrence painted Panel 28 of his 1941 series, *The Migration of the Negro*. The 60-painting collection honors southern African Americans, including his parents, who moved to cities in the North and West during the Great Migration.

Jacob Lawrence, "Panel 28, "from "The Migration Series", credit: © 2017 The Jacob and Gwendolyn Knight Lawrence Foundation, Seattle / Artists Rights Society (ARS), New York

cities where large Somali communities have emerged. This secondary migration has caused growing Somali communities to form in Minneapolis, Minnesota; Columbus, Ohio; and Lewiston, Maine.

As Somali communities in the United States continue to grow, chain migration plays a stronger role. The increase in Somalis living in a given location causes more kinship links to form. Growing networks of Somali relatives and friends attract even more Somalis to the community. One such example of this can be seen in Minneapolis, which has the largest Somali community in North America. Not far from this urban center, a Somali community in the small city of St. Cloud, Minnesota, has grown. Some Somali refugees resettled directly in St. Cloud. Others migrated internally from within the United States, attracted to the small-town life and manufacturing jobs available there. Internal migration has trickled even farther as a few Somalis moved from St. Cloud to tiny, nearby agricultural towns such as Cold Spring, Minnesota.

HMONG MIGRATION Another example of internal migration as a secondary migration occurred after Hmong refugees from Laos began moving to the United States in 1975. The Hmong had fought alongside U.S. soldiers in Laos during the Vietnam conflict. When the conflict ended, the new Laos government threatened to capture and kill Hmong soldiers and families who had sided with the United States. For the two decades that followed, more than 200,000 Hmong fled Laos to neighboring Thailand, where some spent up to ten years in refugee camps awaiting resettlement. Most moved to the United States, with fewer moving to France, Canada, and Australia. Hmong refugees were widely dispersed in the United States. Many made internal secondary migrations to more populated Hmong communities in California, Minnesota, and Wisconsin. Leading factors that drove the Hmong resettlement pattern were kinship links and economic opportunity or sponsorship.

Numerous Southeast Asians, including Vietnamese and ethnic Chinese peoples, fled when the Vietnam conflict ended in 1975. As they sought asylum in the United States, it became apparent, given the circumstances, that American policy was too restrictive in its admission of refugees. The U.S. government quickly enacted the 1975 Indochina Migration and Refugee Assistance Act, which allowed 300,000 refugees from Southeast Asia into the country.

WHAT DRIVES POLICY?

LEARNING OBJECTIVE
IMP-2.E Explain historical and contemporary geographic effects of migration.

Governments use immigration policy to achieve several purposes. The main goal behind the creation of most immigration policy is to meet labor market needs. A secondary aim is to maintain current levels of immigration. Policies are also commonly structured to attract skilled workers, promote the well-being of immigrants and their integration into society, and address illegal immigration. Illegal immigration, in particular, has become an exceedingly complex issue to tackle. Related challenges such as age and gender discrimination, exploitation, and abuse of immigrants are difficult problems to uncover and address effectively.

Government policies intended to limit immigration have sometimes focused on the number of immigrants from a certain country or region. These limits may have as much to do with xenophobia—or fear and hatred of foreigners—as they do with the good of the country. In contrast, loosening quotas on immigrants from specific countries increases population diversity in the host country.

Contemporary and historical examples of factors that have driven government immigration policy include gender or age, asylum regulations, and other immigration-related legislation. By examining factors such as these, geographers can better identify how government immigration policies can foster positive patterns, limit negative patterns, and achieve a balance that works in conjunction with other existing policies.

RISKS FOR FEMALE IMMIGRANTS Gender and age play a role in the types of opportunities and risks that immigrants face. For instance, female immigrants face different opportunities and risks than their male counterparts. This is true even though the numbers of female and male immigrants are about equal. In 2017, nearly 50 percent of all international immigrants were female. That year, female immigrants outnumbered male immigrants in Europe, North America, Oceania, and Latin America and the Caribbean.

If women are moving from a region with restrictive laws or traditions, their new home might offer more access to education, jobs, and status. These opportunities can increase as they further their education and grow more accustomed to their new culture. But in general, female immigrants are more vulnerable than males to violence, human trafficking, and sexual discrimination. Understanding the positives and negatives of female migration helps organizations like the United Nations Entity for Gender Equality and the Empowerment of Women push the international community to develop policies that reflect the needs of female immigrants.

ASYLUM IN THE EUROPEAN UNION The European Union's early-21st century refugee crisis was exacerbated by a policy requiring asylum seekers to remain in the first EU country entered and to apply for asylum there. Immigrants who traveled on to other EU countries risked being deported back to the first EU country they entered. The policy posed a great strain on border countries along the Mediterranean—such as Greece, Italy, Spain, and Malta—which experienced a mass influx of illegal entries by boat, most noticeably from 2014 to 2017.

During the overflow, asylum seekers broke past the entry-point countries' borders and headed for Germany, Sweden, and other EU countries with more robust economies. These countries temporarily ignored the regulation to address the refugee crisis, accepting many asylum applications.

U.S. RESTRICTIONS The Chinese Exclusion Act was the first U.S. policy to broadly restrict immigration. Passed in 1882, it was meant to suspend Chinese immigration for a period of 10 years. However, its ongoing renewal by Congress kept the suspension constant for more than 60 years. By 1924, the act was expanded to include nearly all Asian groups. This greatly reduced the number of immigrants from an entire continent for decades. The act was finally repealed in 1943, but quotas enacted in the 1920s continued to severely limit the number of Asian, Arab, and African immigrants allowed into the United States. Not until the passage of the 1965 Immigration and Nationality Act was a more inclusive policy instituted.

This aerial view of the U.S.-Mexico border highlights the division between the residential area (right) stretching to the border fence in Tijuana, Mexico, and the open landscape outside San Diego, California. Parts of these homes and structures are slated for demolition as the border fence is replaced with a larger barrier.

WALLS THAT DIVIDE US

LEARNING OBJECTIVE

IMP 2.E Explain historical and contemporary geographic effects of migration.

The recent unprecedented rise in the number of refugees and immigrants has prompted some world leaders to construct walls and fences along sections of their countries' borders. When the Berlin Wall was torn down in 1989, 15 other border walls still stood in various parts of the world. By 2018, more than 70 walls had been completed or were under construction. Most of the walls are in Europe, a continent that in the second half of the 20th century had seen a strong movement toward open borders, particularly within the member countries of the European Union. That movement encountered some resistance in the beginning of the 21st century and was cited as one of the reasons Great Britain left the European Union in 2020.

Though countries insist that border walls increase security and reduce illegal immigration, barriers are also about politics and can signal a nation's attitude regarding outsiders. For example, a 400-mile wall along the West Bank in Southwest Asia dividing Israelis from Palestinians reduces Palestine's territory and restricts Palestinians' movements. The wall is a constant reminder of Israel's occupation of the region and can provoke anger, resentment, and violence against the Israelis. A more secure wall built by Spain in Morocco in 2005 has significantly reduced the number of people entering Spain from the north coast of Africa illegally. But the wall hasn't stopped immigration completely. Imigrants find new, often riskier, routes around the barrier or enter Spain from neighboring countries. Many immigrants now enter European countries by way of a dangerous journey across the Mediterranean Sea.

Throughout history, walls and fences have separated populations literally and figuratively, intensifying the divisions between people. Americans are greatly divided over the building of a wall spanning the 2,000-mile border with Mexico—an idea introduced by U.S. President Trump's administration to keep undocumented immigrants out of the United States. A Pew Research Center survey in 2018 revealed that younger generations were less likely to favor a wall, while non-Hispanic Whites were more than twice as likely to favor it as African Americans or Hispanics. Some people question whether a wall to stop illegal immigration is even feasible or necessary, or if it will instead put refugees escaping violence in greater danger. ▐

GEOGRAPHIC THINKING

Identify the consequences that a border wall along the entire 2,000-mile U.S.–Mexico border could have on the United States and on Mexico.

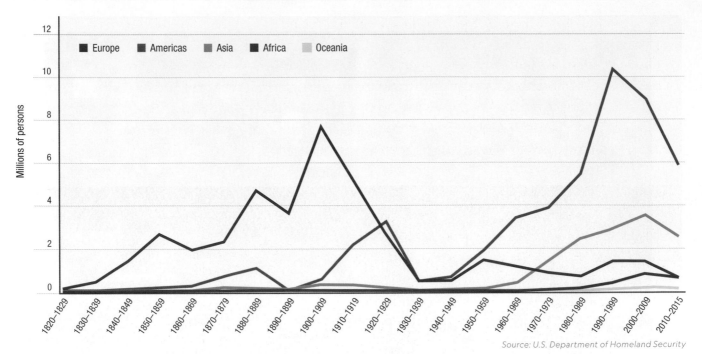

VOLUME OF U.S. IMMIGRATION BY CONTINENT OF ORIGIN, 1820-2015
Spikes and dips in the immigrant populations coincide with the changes that took place to U.S. quota laws and immigration policies over time. Notice that the last time span shows data for just five years, whereas the other time spans represent data for ten years.

Source: U.S. Department of Homeland Security

In the aftermath of the 9/11 terrorist attacks on the United States, the U.S. government developed stricter border protection and immigration requirements. Tougher border patrols and immigration laws in the United States pushed immigrants crossing the U.S.–Mexico border, many of whom fled violence in Central America, to fall victim to smugglers and human traffickers. Afraid to seek help from U.S. authorities for fear of deportation, victims endured situations of forced labor or prostitution. In addition, certain U.S. visa programs have been criticized for not protecting against exploitation and abuse. Each year, more than 1 million temporary foreign workers—or guest workers—are employed in the United States. Once in the United States, temporary workers' visas almost always link them to a single employer, with no option to seek another employer if the immigrant is mistreated.

More recently, U.S. immigration policies have stirred debate about tougher restrictions that may infringe on the human rights of immigrants. For example, a 2017 policy meant to keep terrorists out of the country restricted entrance of foreign nationals from seven Muslim-majority countries and was criticized as being a "Muslim ban." Also, legislation known as Deferred Action for Childhood Arrivals (DACA) that protected immigrants who had entered the United States illegally as children was revoked in 2017. With its repeal, the program stopped accepting applications for work visas and for protection against deportation. Those who remained in the United States under DACA were expected to lose legal status within the next few years. Equally controversial in 2018, a "zero-tolerance" immigration policy in the United States led to children being separated from their parents

and held in shelters scattered across the country. The policy required that adults illegally crossing the U.S.–Mexico border be criminally prosecuted. Because it is illegal to send children to jail with their parents, families who were caught crossing the border were split up, with parents being sent to one facility and children to another.

Restrictive immigration policies affect migration patterns. In addition to the immediate effects of deporting immigrants or turning them away at borders, policies like these can impact international migration flows. People who are planning to leave their home country but are not welcome in the country of their choice because of restrictive policies might decide to settle somewhere else, or not to move at all.

GEOGRAPHIC THINKING

1. Explain how migration policy created to meet labor market needs reflects Ravenstein's laws.

2. Identify what factors may cause a country to create a stricter immigration policy. Give examples.

3. Explain the degree to which changes in immigration policy affected the number of Asian immigrants entering the United States over time. Use the graph above to explain your answer.

4. Compare how step migration and chain migration play a role in the resettlement of refugees.

5.5 EFFECTS OF MIGRATION

Migration changes both the places of origin and, of course, the destinations. And migration affects more than just those who migrate—it impacts the family, friends, and the rest of the communities on either side of the journey. When enough people move to or from a particular place, those impacts stretch beyond the individual to influence that place economically, culturally, and even politically.

Somali Muslims pray together during an evening soccer tournament at Hamline University in St. Paul, Minnesota. Cities such as Minneapolis and St. Cloud have become destinations for Eastern African immigrants. Some Somalis came to Minnesota as refugees and were settled by nonprofits and religious groups. Others moved to the state to be part of these large Somali communities.

ECONOMIC CONSEQUENCES

LEARNING OBJECTIVE
IMP-2.E Explain historical and contemporary geographic effects of migration.

While a move drastically changes the life of an individual, a single migrant moving from one place to another has little effect on either location. But migration pathways and chain migration can push the number of migrants high enough for impacts to be felt in both the sending and receiving communities. Geographers examine these effects in terms of the economic costs and benefits that migrants have on their destinations and their places of origin.

DESTINATION COUNTRIES Recall that the overall trend in international migration is from less economically developed countries to more economically developed countries. One benefit to core countries receiving immigrants is that immigrants become a source of labor. They are often more willing than native-born citizens to accept less desirable, lower-paying work, such as agricultural, construction, and service sector jobs. This is true of immigrants in general, but especially true of those living in a country illegally. In addition, immigrants who are educated or skilled are often willing to work for less pay than their native-born counterparts. And qualified immigrants can reduce the **skills gap**—a shortage of people trained

The vibrant colors of Cuban culture are on full display in Miami's Little Havana. 8th Street—or *Calle Ocho* as it's known—is the neighborhood's main thoroughfare, lined with murals celebrating the country's rich culture and history, restaurants serving Cuban cuisine, and many shops, galleries, and museums. In Maximo Gomez Park, better known as Domino Park, locals and tourists alike come to witness the older generation of Cuban immigrants engage in an intense game of dominoes.

change too much. They feel their country's traditions are endangered by the introduction of new customs. These attitudes can lead to prejudice against immigrants. Some countries have implemented policies to protect their culture from change. In the Netherlands, for instance, immigrants must take classes in Dutch culture to become citizens. The topic of immigration can also lead to strain within the receiving society as pro- and anti-immigration groups engage in public demonstrations, sometimes even becoming violent. In recent years, demonstrators on both sides of the issue have clashed in North America and Europe.

Because of the challenges involved in migrating to a foreign country, immigrants tend to cluster together, creating segregated neighborhoods like Little Havana or Chinatown. While these neighborhoods help immigrants retain their traditions and customs, they can also prevent them from fully acclimating to their new country. Conversely, many immigrants, as well as children of immigrants born in the receiving country, tend to lose some of their cultural identity as they adjust to the way of life in their new home.

COUNTRIES OF ORIGIN

Immigration's social benefits for the source country are connected to the economic benefits. Remittances can improve the quality of life of families in the source country, which can in turn help support the economy. In Jalpan de Serra, a city in Querétaro, Mexico, people flock from surrounding towns and villages to collect remittances sent from family members living in the United States. A worker in Mexico averages about $55 per week, which is less than an immigrant working construction or harvesting fruit in the United States can make in a single day. The extra money sent home as remittances pays for nicer clothes, better food, appliances, and other necessities and small luxuries for the immigrant's family in Mexico. Legal and illegal immigrants send about $28 billion in remittances home to Mexico each year.

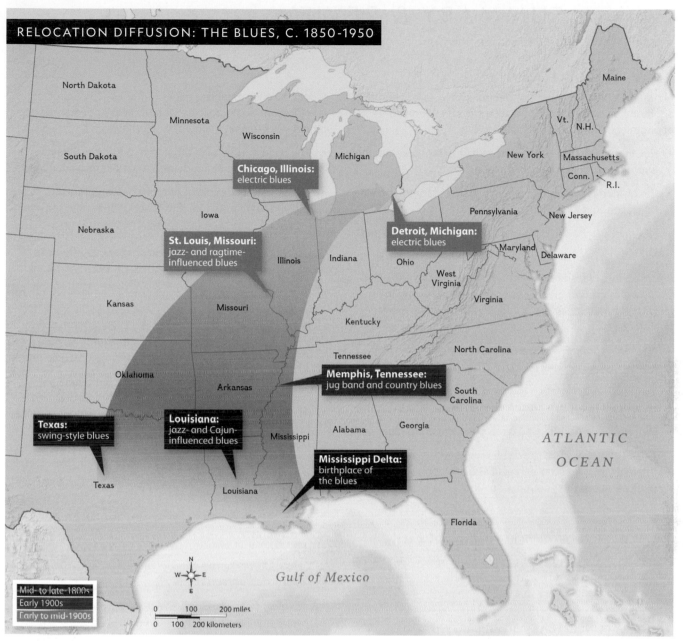

RELOCATION DIFFUSION: THE BLUES, C. 1850-1950

Chicago, Illinois: electric blues

St. Louis, Missouri: jazz- and ragtime-influenced blues

Detroit, Michigan: electric blues

Memphis, Tennessee: jug band and country blues

Texas: swing-style blues

Louisiana: jazz- and Cajun-influenced blues

Mississippi Delta: birthplace of the blues

Mid- to late-1800s
Early 1900s
Early to mid-1900s

ATLANTIC OCEAN

Gulf of Mexico

READING MAPS The music known as the blues originated on slave plantations in the Mississippi Delta and spread north and west as African Americans migrated during the Great Migration. As it spread, each region left its mark, combining the blues with jazz, gospel, country, and ragtime music. ▌ What cultural effects might this example of relocation diffusion have on the Midwestern United States?

On the other hand, migration can have a disrupting effect on the social structure of a place of origin. For example, the rural villages surrounding Jalpan de Serra have lost many young men to migration. It's difficult to make a living on the area's small, overworked farms, so young men are drawn to the promise of higher wages in the United States. Older mothers often don't see their sons and daughters who emigrate for years, and young women who stay in their hometowns have trouble finding life partners with whom to start a family. Life in these rural villages has been completely altered. The effect on the dependency ratio is the opposite of the change immigrants bring to destination countries—in many of these villages, it is mostly older people and young children who remain.

GEOGRAPHIC THINKING

1. Explain how remittances act as both a benefit and a cost to countries of origin and destination.

2. Compare the positive and negative economic effects of migration for countries of origin and destination.

3. Describe how the ethnic diversity resulting from migration benefits the destination country.

4. Explain how Ravenstein's laws are represented by the large-scale immigration of Cubans to Miami.

SUMMARY & REVIEW

■ CHAPTER SUMMARY

Migration is the movement of people from one location to another. It is influenced by the interplay of environmental, economic, cultural, and political factors.

- Pull factors encourage migration to a place; push factors encourage migration from a place.

- Emigration is migration from a location; immigration is migration to a location.

- Net migration is the difference between emigration and immigration.

Geographers classify different types of migration. In voluntary migration, people choose to migrate, and in forced migration, they are compelled to move by extreme push factors.

- Internal migration—movement within a country's borders—can be interregional or intraregional.

- Transnational migration involves individuals who have emigrated but retain close ties to their country of origin.

- Refugees are people who have been forced to migrate to another country.

- Internally displaced persons (IDPs) are people forced to migrate within their country.

Most countries establish migration policy to control immigration. Some policies work to help immigrants while others work to limit the number of immigrants.

- The main purposes of most immigration policies are to meet labor market needs and maintain migration levels.

- Quotas set limits on the number of immigrants allowed to migrate to a particular country and may set preferences for who is allowed into the country.

Geographers study the economic and social effects of migration on the countries of both destination and origin.

- In destination countries, immigrants can fill labor needs and reduce the skills gap, as well as add diversity and cultural variety. Costs include a reduced number of jobs available for native-born citizens and possible discomfort with cultural changes brought by immigrants.

- In countries of origin, the gap left by emigrants can reduce unemployment and strain on resources, and remittances sent home by immigrants can help support the economy. Costs include brain drain—the loss of trained workers—and disruption of the social structure.

■ KEY TERMS AND CONCEPTS

Use complete sentences to answer the questions.

1. **APPLY CONCEPTUAL VOCABULARY** Consider the terms *mobility* and *refugee*. Write a standard dictionary definition of each term. Then provide a conceptual definition—an explanation of how each term is used in the context of this chapter.

2. How are the terms *kinship links* and *chain migration* related?

3. Define the term *net migration* using the concepts *emigration* and *immigration*.

4. Describe how push factors and pull factors affect a person's decision to migrate. List examples of both push factors and pull factors.

5. Give examples of a demographic pull factor and a demographic push factor.

6. Compare the terms *voluntary migration* and *forced migration*. Cite examples of each.

7. How are the terms *internal migration* and *internally displaced person* related?

8. Explain how a refugee is different from a guest worker. Give an example of each.

9. Provide an example of an intervening obstacle. Then, provide an example of an intervening opportunity.

10. Explain how the terms *asylum* and *transnational migration* are related.

11. Define the term *brain drain* using the concept *skills gap*.

12. Explain the relationship between the terms *distance decay* and *friction of distance*.

13. Explain the degree to which the gravity model could impact relocation diffusion.

14. Define the term *quota* in relation to migration policy. Cite an example of when, how, and why a quota was used in the world.

15. Describe how the terms *remittance* and *guest worker* are related.

■ INTERPRET GRAPHS

Study the graph and then answer the following questions.

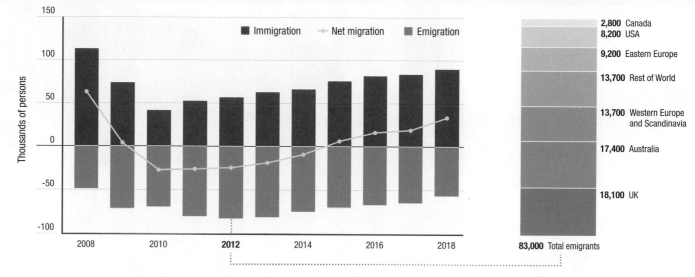

■ IRELAND'S NET MIGRATION, 2008–2018

Source: Irish Central Statistics Office, Population and Migration Estimates

16. IDENTIFY DATA & INFORMATION In what year was emigration highest in Ireland? In what year was immigration highest?

17. ANALYZE VISUALS How did the rise in both immigration and emigration affect Ireland's net migration in the year 2011?

18. DESCRIBE SPATIAL RELATIONSHIPS Describe Ireland's pattern of migration between the years 2008 and 2018.

19. APPLY MODELS & THEORIES How does the number and location of emigrants from Ireland in the year 2012 support the gravity model of migration?

GEO-INQUIRY | MIGRATION IN YOUR COMMUNITY

Consider how you can use Geo-Inquiry to answer questions about migration where you live. Use the steps in the Geo-Inquiry Process to create an actionable answer to your Geo-Inquiry question.

ASK Start with an authentic supporting question about your neighborhood. It may be as simple as: *How can we make our school or community more welcoming for newcomers?* Use the Geo-Inquiry Process to expand this question. Additional need-to-know questions might include: *What are the current trends in immigration to our community? How does local migration impact our community?*

COLLECT Decide how you could gather geographic information to answer your first question. Explore local sources for data on immigrants in your community.

VISUALIZE Analyze the information you collected on immigration to your community to draw conclusions. Organize the information and use it to create a map that can be made accessible to others.

CREATE Focus on ways to tell a Geo-Inquiry story, such as persuasive writing and providing data and other information, keeping your audience in mind. Create a list of the elements that you will use to tell your Geo-Inquiry story, such as specific images, videos, compelling storylines, and clear charts and graphs. Outline or storyboard your story, and then tie all of your elements together using a storytelling tool.

ACT Share your stories with others in your community. Consider how your project can improve the situation of immigrants in your community or school.

ASK   COLLECT   VISUALIZE   CREATE   ACT

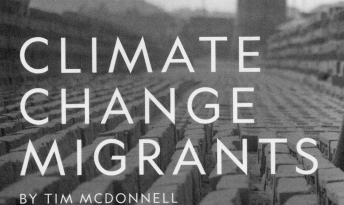

CLIMATE CHANGE MIGRANTS

BY TIM MCDONNELL

A teenage boy works at a brick field in Bhola, Bangladesh. Brick fields in urban areas are a common destination for coastal climate migrants, especially young men.

Golam Mostafa Sarder starts every day before dawn, rising from a thin reed mat in the shed that he shares with 15 roommates. Each has just enough space to lie flat. Outside the shed's open doorway, in the outskirts of Dhaka, the sprawling megacity capital of Bangladesh, is the brick factory where Golam and his neighbors work for 15 hours a day, seven days a week, at least six months a year. His home in Gabura, a remote village on the country's southwestern coast, is more than a day's journey from the city by bus, rickshaw, and ferry.

Golam's job is to push wheelbarrows of mud down the production line. Waist-high rows of drying bricks spiral off from a towering kiln that belches smoke over an area the size of a city block. Golam has never heard of global warming. But he says he knows one thing for sure: "If the river didn't take our land, I wouldn't need to be here."

CLIMATE-DRIVEN DISPLACEMENT
Fifty-five million people in Bangladesh live along the southern coast, a lush honeycomb of island villages, farms, and fish ponds linked by protective embankments. During the rainy season more than one-fifth of the country can be flooded at once. Climate change is disrupting traditional rain patterns—droughts in some areas, unexpected deluges in others—and boosting silt-heavy runoff from glaciers in the Himalaya Mountains, leading to an increase in flooding and riverbank erosion. Meanwhile, sea-level rise is pushing saltwater into coastal agricultural areas and promising to permanently submerge large swaths.

Over the last decade, nearly 700,000 Bangladeshis were displaced on average each year by natural disasters. As people flee coastal areas, most are arriving in urban slums, or informal housing, particularly in Dhaka, one of the world's fastest-growing megacities. The city is perceived as the country's bastion of economic opportunity, but it is also fraught with extreme poverty, public health hazards, human trafficking, and its own vulnerability to floods.

A CITY ALTERED BY CLIMATE CHANGE
For climate migrants who arrive in Dhaka, life is seldom easy. Men and boys work in brick factories, drive rickshaws, and build skyscrapers. Women and girls clean houses, stitch Western fashions, and raise families—often fending off sexual violence at multiple steps along the way. Education is a luxury; rent is preposterous. As a result, 40 percent of the city's residents live in slums, hundreds of which are spread across the city. According to the International Organization for Migration, up to 70 percent of the slums' residents moved there due to environmental challenges.

Slums emerge unplanned and unsanctioned in the backyards of glassy skyscrapers, straddling railroad tracks, on stilts above water-logged floodplains, on the fringes of construction sites. Single beds are frequently shared by five or more family members. Sewage runs freely. Structure fires spread easily. Most electricity, when it's working at all, is tapped illegally from the grid. Insect infestations are inescapable. Skin and gastrointestinal diseases transmitted by dirty water are routine, and the infant mortality rate is twice that of rural areas. Rent money flows into a real estate black market controlled by corrupt local officials and businessmen.

"It's very hard to get a living here," says Sahela Begum, who moved to Dhaka with her four young daughters after losing her home along the Padma River. "But my life is my childrens' life. If I can make a good future for them, that's the best thing I can hope for."

CITIES FOR CLIMATE MIGRANTS
When Bangladesh gained independence in 1971, the population was 91 percent rural. Today, nearly one-third of the population lives in cities. Throughout that process of growth, "low-income people were totally left out of the development framework of the city," says A.Q.M. Mahbub, an urban studies researcher at the University of Dhaka. Affordable housing and public transit connecting the city center to suburbs were never priorities.

Local officials tend to view slum dwellers as illegal squatters, rather than residents with a right to basic services, preferring to leave slum residents reliant on aid from local and international non-governmental organizations. "If we invest money directly in slum areas, or give them an electricity supply, they will start to think, 'O.K., we have these facilities, so we have the ownership of this land,'" says a senior official at a government agency that manages the city's infrastructure. "Once we give them improved services, they become permanent."

Many of the country's leading public policy experts think that attitude—that climate migrants are a regrettable burden—is short-sighted. Mongla, a port town on the country's south-central coast, is one of several emerging "secondary cities," models of climate-savvy urban planning where investments in sea walls and other adaptive infrastructure are being paired with blue-collar job opportunities, as well as affordable housing, schools, and hospitals.

In the last five years, Mongla's population has jumped nearly 60 percent to 110,000, and the price of land has skyrocketed. The town's positive reputation is spreading. "Because of salinity and flooding, there's not much opportunity in my village. But here, I can make good money," says Mohammed Kabir Hossain, who drives a rickshaw. He came to Mongla a few years ago. "A lot of people are coming here from across southern Bangladesh, especially those who are unwilling to go to Dhaka." ▮

Adapted from "Climate Change Creates a New Migration Crisis for Bangladesh" by Tim McDonnell, nationalgeographic.com, January 2019

WRITE ACROSS UNITS

Unit 2 explored factors that influence changes in population and how population changes and migration profoundly affect a country's development. This article reveals how one factor, climate change, is affecting Bangladesh, not only altering the lives of those experiencing a natural disaster, but also those who take in climate migrants. Use information from the article and this unit to write a response to the following questions.

LOOKING BACK

1. What geographic questions does the article pose about the situation in Bangladesh? UNIT 1

2. What economic impact can climate change migrants have on their destinations? UNIT 2

LOOKING FORWARD

3. What aspects of Bangladesh's culture are depicted in the article? Explain how one human-environment interaction mentioned in the article is affecting the cultural landscape. UNIT 3

4. How do political attitudes affect treatment of Bangladesh's climate migrants? UNIT 4

5. What effects is climate change having on the agricultural areas of Bangladesh, and how might those effects be felt by the entire population of the country? UNIT 5

6. Describe how climate migration is putting pressure on Dhaka's urban infrastructure. UNIT 6

7. What can you infer about Bangladesh's level of development from the article? UNIT 7

WRITE ACROSS REGIONS & SCALES

Research a community in a region outside of South Asia that has been directly affected by climate change or by the arrival of climate migrants. Write an essay comparing this community with either Dhaka or Mongla in Bangladesh. Drawing on evidence from this unit and the article, address the following topic:

Describe how a community can prepare for changes in population due to climate change. What might the ideal city for climate migrants look like?

THINK ABOUT

- the factors that city officials must take into account as the population increases or decreases

- the similarities and differences in how each community handles the direct and indirect effects of climate and population change

CHAPTER 3

POPULATION PYRAMIDS

A population pyramid illustrates the age and gender characteristics of a country's population and may provide insights about economic development and social circumstances, such as gender equality, ethnic tensions, or health conditions. The population is distributed along the horizontal axis. The male and female populations are represented as horizontal bars along the vertical axis according to age. The shape of the population pyramid may evolve based on fertility, mortality, and international migration trends. A country with a wide pyramid base likely has high fertility rates. A country with a narrow base likely has low fertility rates. ▮ Compare the population pyramids shown here. Explain what they might indicate about the birth and death rates, or about migration trends in each country.

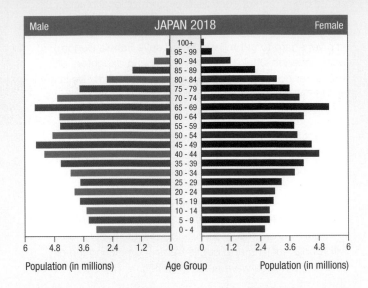

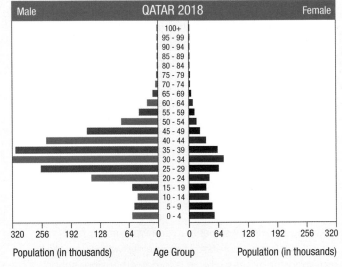

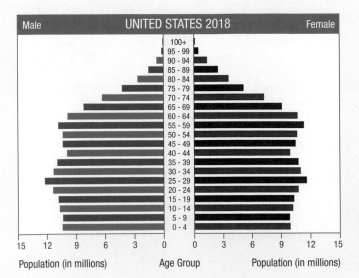

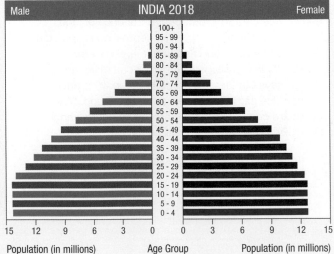

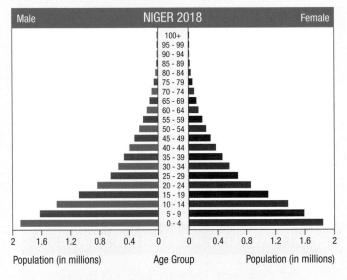

Source: The World Factbook

CHAPTER 4

DEMOGRAPHIC TRANSITION MODEL

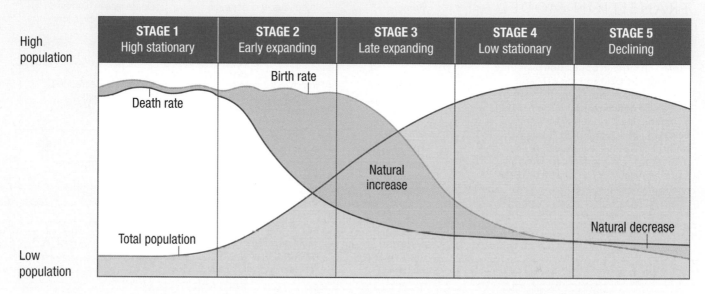

High population

| STAGE 1 High stationary | STAGE 2 Early expanding | STAGE 3 Late expanding | STAGE 4 Low stationary | STAGE 5 Declining |

Death rate

Birth rate

Natural increase

Total population

Natural decrease

Low population

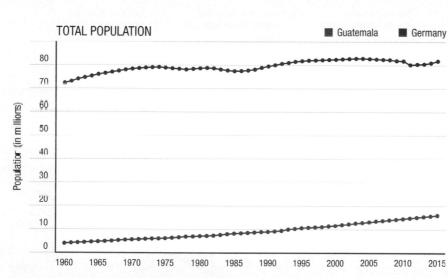

TOTAL POPULATION

■ Guatemala ■ Germany

Population (in millions)

80
70
60
50
40
30
20
10
0

1960 1965 1970 1975 1980 1985 1990 1995 2000 2005 2010 2015

The demographic transition model (DTM) is a useful tool for analyzing a country's population and development. The model illustrates the interaction between a country's birth rate, death rate, and population. Historically, countries move through the stages of the demographic transition model as they develop. ▮ Based on the total population and birth and death rates provided, identify the stages for Germany and Guatemala. Explain your answer.

BIRTH RATE, CRUDE (per 1,000 people)

Population (in millions)

50
45
40
35
30
25
20
15
10
5

1960 1965 1970 1975 1980 1985 1990 1995 2000 2005 2010 2015

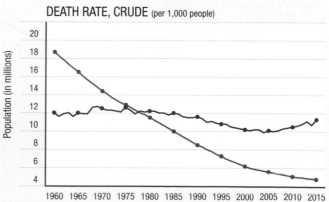

DEATH RATE, CRUDE (per 1,000 people)

Population (in millions)

20
18
16
14
12
10
8
6
4

1960 1965 1970 1975 1980 1985 1990 1995 2000 2005 2010 2015

CHAPTER 4

EPIDEMIOLOGICAL TRANSITION MODEL

The epidemiological transition model (ETM) depicts patterns of diseases and causes of death and uses them to explain changes in population over time. Although the DTM and the ETM are often compared, the stages in the two models do not correspond. The ETM is an independent model for explaining how populations grow and, perhaps, eventually decline. ▮ Research online to find the life expectancy for Australia. Identify the country's stage in the ETM and explain your answer.

STAGES	DESCRIPTION	EFFECTS
1. Famine	Infectious and parasitic diseases mostly cause human death; animal attacks also cause deaths	Death rate is high and life expectancy is low
2. Pandemic Disease	Improved sanitation, nutrition, and medicine lower spread of infection	Death rate decreases and life expectancy increases
3. Degenerative and Human Created Diseases	Fewer deaths from infectious disease and increase in diseases related to aging (heart attack/cancer)	Death rate is low and life expectancy increases
4. Delayed Degenerative Diseases	Medical advances reduce or delay incidences of diseases related to aging	Life expectancy is at its highest
5. Reemergence of Infectious Disease	Infectious and parasitic diseases become resistant to antibiotics and increase	Life expectancy decreases

CHAPTER 4

MALTHUS'S THEORY OF POPULATION GROWTH

In 1798 Thomas Malthus argued that population grew exponentially while food production grew arithmetically. He predicted that population growth would surpass food production, leading to a hunger crisis. While agricultural advancements and globalization have caused food production and distribution to grow faster than Malthus predicted, neo-Malthusians have broadened the model, arguing that pressure on resources from overpopulation leads to dire consequences such as famine and war. ▮ Explain how a neo-Malthusian might apply Malthus's theory to climate change.

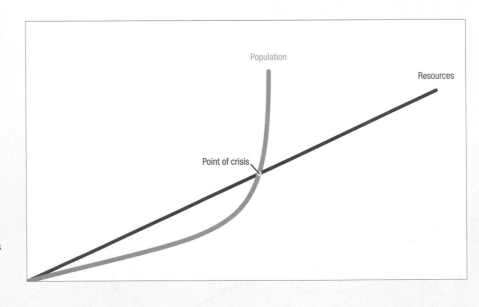

CHAPTER 4

MAPPING NONCOMMUNICABLE DISEASES

The United States is considered to be in Stage 4 of the ETM. In this stage, noncommunicable diseases (NCDs), including heart disease, cancer, and diabetes, are the dominant cause of death. The number of people and communities affected by these diseases is growing due to insufficient physical activity, unhealthy diet, and the harmful use of tobacco and alcohol among other factors. ▮ Explain how the information in the map below can be useful for reducing NCD death rates in the United States.

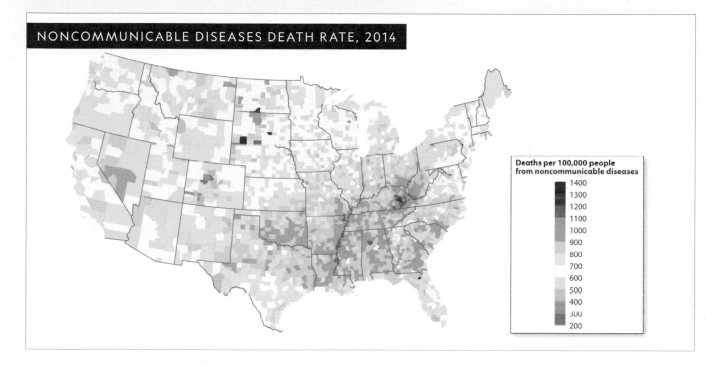

NONCOMMUNICABLE DISEASES DEATH RATE, 2014

Deaths per 100,000 people from noncommunicable diseases

1400
1300
1200
1100
1000
900
800
700
600
500
400
300
200

CHAPTER 5

RAVENSTEIN'S LAWS OF MIGRATION

Ravenstein's laws were developed by geographer Ernst Ravenstein in 1885 to describe trends in migration. Ravenstein concluded that factors such as economic conditions, population size, and distance affect whether people migrate and where they move to. While Ravenstein's laws are still relevant today, some are more relevant than others. For instance, Ravenstein stated that most migrants are young adult males. In 2017, however, 48.4 percent of migrants were women, nearly equaling male migrants. ▮ Explain whether Ravenstein's laws apply equally to voluntary and forced migration.

1. Migration is typically over a short distance.

2. Migration occurs in steps, like from a rural area to a nearby city, and then perhaps on to a larger city.

3. Long-distance migrants often move to places of economic opportunity (urban areas).

4. Every migration generates a movement in the opposite direction, or counter flow (not necessarily of the same number of migrants).

5. People in rural areas migrate more than people in cities.

6. Males migrate over longer distances than females.

7. Most migrants are young adult males.

8. Cities grow more by migration than by natural increase.

9. Migration increases with economic development.

10. Migration is mostly due to economic factors.

CHAPTER 5

GRAVITY MODEL

The gravity model predicts the amount of spatial interaction, such as migration, tourism, or trade, that will occur between two or more places. According to the model, the level of interaction between two cities depends on the size of the cities' population and the distance between them. The larger the population, the more interaction a city will receive. And the shorter the distance between two cities, the more they will interact with each other. ▮ Describe the gravity model using Delhi, Kolkata, and Rajkot as examples.

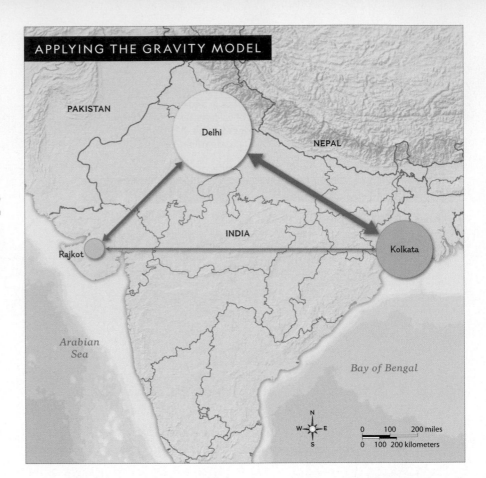

CHAPTER 5

REMITTANCES

Remittances are the money earned by emigrants abroad and sent back to their home countries, usually to family members. This money plays an important role in the economies of many countries. In some countries, such as those shown in the graph, remittances represent a significant percentage of the gross domestic product (GDP), which is the total value of all goods and services produced by a country in a year. ▮ Explain how the importance of remittances to the economies of the countries shown in the graph has changed since 1998.

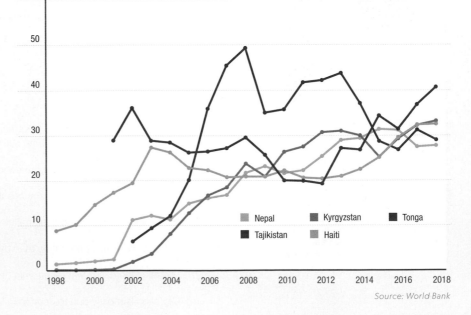

PERSONAL REMITTANCES RECEIVED, 1998–2018 (% OF GDP)

Nepal · Kyrgyzstan · Tonga · Tajikistan · Haiti

Source: World Bank

CHAPTER 5

MIGRATION DATA

Displaying geographic data in a graph or chart allows you to quickly compare two or more statistics or visualize how trends have developed over time. Study the following infographics and use the questions below to help you analyze the migration data. ▌ Explain what this graph tells you about immigrants in the U.S. labor force.

IMMIGRANTS IN THE U.S. POPULATION AND LABOR FORCE, 1980-2017

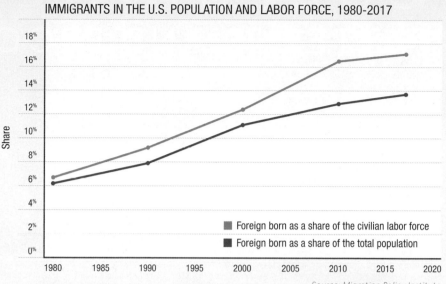

■ Foreign born as a share of the civilian labor force
■ Foreign born as a share of the total population

Source: Migration Policy Institute

GLOBAL DISPLACEMENT, 2007–2017

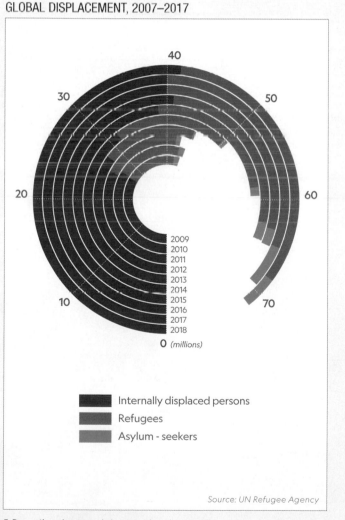

2009
2010
2011
2012
2013
2014
2015
2016
2017
2018
0 *(millions)*

■ Internally displaced persons
■ Refugees
■ Asylum - seekers

Source: UN Refugee Agency

▌ Describe the trend depicted in the graph.

FORCED MIGRATION DUE TO NATURAL DISASTER, 2017

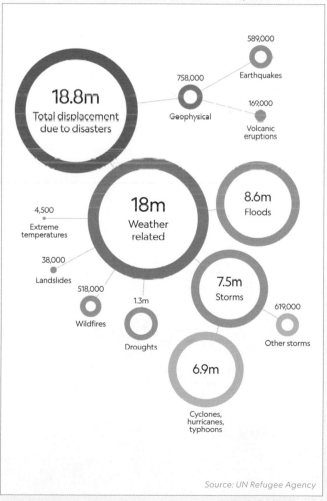

18.8m
Total displacement due to disasters

758,000
Geophysical

589,000
Earthquakes

169,000
Volcanic eruptions

4,500
Extreme temperatures

18m
Weather related

8.6m
Floods

38,000
Landslides

518,000
Wildfires

1.3m
Droughts

7.5m
Storms

619,000
Other storms

6.9m
Cyclones, hurricanes, typhoons

Source: UN Refugee Agency

▌ Describe in a sentence or two the role that weather plays in forced migration.

CULTURAL
PATTERNS AND PROCESSES

WHO WE ARE

Village church in Machuca, Chile

Culture is a mix of tangible objects and intangible concepts—embodied in buildings, books, and paintings as well as in languages, religious ideals, and attitudes toward women. Human cultures are intimately tied to the places where they arise and where they spread.

People from diverse perspectives not only endow existing landscapes with lasting meanings but also create new landscapes that reflect their cultural visions. In Bolivia, participants in La Paz's Fiesta del Gran Poder, or the Festival of the Great Power (shown here), blend indigenous Aymaran dress and folklore with Catholic themes as they celebrate their belief in Jesus Christ.

Over time, cultures transform, as do the places they help mold. Rarely have cultural landscapes evolved as swiftly as they do today, with globalizing forces such as communication and transportation technology driving the pace.

CHAPTER 6
CONCEPTS OF CULTURE

CHAPTER 7
CULTURAL CHANGE

CHAPTER 8
SPATIAL PATTERNS OF LANGUAGE
AND RELIGION

UNIT 3 WRITING ACROSS UNITS,
REGIONS & SCALES

UNIT 3 MAPS & MODELS ARCHIVE

DISCOVERY AND PRESERVATION

As a field archaeologist, National Geographic Archaeologist-in-Residence Fred Hiebert travels the world to unearth remains of ancient civilizations. As a museum curator, he looks for innovative ways to educate present-day audiences about these cultures. And as an advocate for preservation, he strives to make sure that irreplaceable artifacts will be available for future generations.

LEARNING OBJECTIVE
PSO-3.A Define the characteristics, attitudes, and traits that influence geographers when they study culture.

ANCIENT GEOGRAPHY Fred Hiebert is always conscious of the ways geography influenced the location and cultural practices of ancient civilizations. He defines geography as the ability to identify regions and put them in context in terms of conflict, history, and culture. He's applied that understanding to archaeological digs in locations such as Peru, the Black Sea, Afghanistan, and Jerusalem.

In 2014, Hiebert curated a landmark exhibition called *Peruvian Gold: Ancient Treasures Unearthed* at the National Geographic Museum in Washington, D.C. Hiebert linked Peru's geography to its archaeological richness and cultural diversity. He explains, "What makes Peru one of the great centers of civilization is its geography," describing the country's high mountains, valleys, and coastal deserts. Hiebert believes curating and displaying Peru's intriguing artifacts helps people connect the present with the distant past—which enriches the lives of all who come to see them.

Hiebert also curated *The Greeks: Agamemnon to Alexander*, an international 2016 exhibition that explored 5,000 years of ancient Greece through more than 500 artifacts from 22 Greek museums. Greece's geographic diversity includes a mountainous mainland and thousands of islands dotting the Aegean, Adriatic, and Ionian seas. "Greece's challenging geography is also one of its greatest assets," Hiebert says. "The ancient Greeks adapted to living on islands, coastline, rugged terrain, and hard-to-farm land, which helped them establish a unique identity."

PAST AND PRESENT "Culture—the past, the remains of our history—is nonrenewable," Hiebert told an audience at National Geographic headquarters in Washington, D.C. He was talking about the urgent need to protect archaeological sites from looters who remove artifacts and sell them to collectors. These thefts rob archaeologists of the chance to study such objects in their proper context and deprive the general public of the chance to learn from and enjoy them.

Hiebert also pointed out that archaeological treasures are sometimes at risk of deliberate destruction. Demolishing cultural pieces violates international conventions of war. Some conflicts seek to negate cultures and demoralize populations. He highlighted a 2001 incident in which the ruling Taliban party in Afghanistan dynamited a pair of monumental statues of Buddha dating to about 500 C.E. Taliban members also smashed artifacts in Afghanistan's National Museum. Fortunately, the museum's curators had the foresight to remove and hide many of its most valuable artifacts years before the Taliban's rampage. Hiebert was instrumental in rediscovering these objects. In 2004, he curated National Geographic's exhibition *Afghanistan: Hidden Treasures from the National Museum*. Clearly, preserving artifacts from disappearance or destruction serves the needs of archaeologists in search of knowledge.

Museum exhibitions are not Hiebert's only method for sharing connections with antiquity. National Geographic reaches nearly 400 million individuals through print, video, and digital media. Hiebert uses all these 21st-century modes of communication to make the ancient world come alive for people who may never step inside a museum. His curation of *The Greeks* exhibition led to National Geographic's involvement in the 2016 restoration of the Edicule—believed by the faithful to be the tomb of Christ—in the Church of the Holy Sepulchre in Jerusalem as well as the 2017 "Tomb of Christ" 3-D exhibition in the National Geographic Museum. ▮

GEOGRAPHIC THINKING

Explain how Fred Hiebert's definition of geography influences his perceptions of ancient cultures, and describe what his work might convey to others.

Top: Fred Hiebert's role as an archaeologist leads him to more than "lost" artifacts—he can also search for lost people. In 2019, Hiebert and anthropologist Jaime Bach inspected a site on Nikumororo Island, Kiribati, to look for evidence of Amelia Earhart's 1937 plane crash. Bottom left: The drinking vessel made by the Recuay culture in Peru around 300 c.e. whistled when liquid was poured from it. Bottom right: The original Mask of Agamemnon, named for the mythical Greek king, dates to the 16th century b.c.e.

CONCEPTS OF CULTURE

CRITICAL VIEWING In 2016, the Standing Rock Sioux Tribe protested the construction of the Dakota Access Pipeline on the grounds that this oil pipeline would disturb their reservation in North Dakota. ▌ For what reasons might a cultural group like the Standing Rock Sioux Tribe want to protect their territory?

GEOGRAPHIC THINKING How do location and resources influence cultural practices?

6.1
**AN INTRODUCTION
TO CULTURE**

CASE STUDY: Wisconsin's
American Indian Nations

6.2
**CULTURAL
LANDSCAPES**

CASE STUDY: Tehrangeles

6.3
**IDENTITY
AND SPACE**

6.4
**CULTURAL
PATTERNS**

NATIONAL GEOGRAPHIC
EXPLORER Sandhya Narayanan

6.1 AN INTRODUCTION TO CULTURE

Evidence of people's culture, or way of life, can be found in the places where people live. Cultural geography is the study of the ways humans organize space and the varying characteristics and patterns of the places people create.

CULTURE

LEARNING OBJECTIVE

PSO-3.A Define the characteristics, attitudes, and traits that influence geographers when they study culture.

As the heartbeat of human geography, **culture** refers to the beliefs, values, practices, behaviors, and technologies shared by a society and passed down from generation to generation. Some elements of culture, such as clothing, literature, food, and music, are relatively easy to identify and experience. Other cultural attributes, however, are not as easily observed. For example, a group's festivals or holidays might be obvious, but their attitudes and values may not be so visible.

To illustrate the many types of cultural attributes, geographers often use the metaphor of a "cultural iceberg." The exposed tip of the iceberg represents everything fairly easy to observe about culture, such as language, the arts, land-use patterns, and personal behavior. The larger, submerged part of the iceberg represents the subconscious values and thought patterns in culture that are generally unseen, such as a group's beliefs, values, and rules. This invisible part of a culture strongly influences the visible part.

At the tip of the cultural iceberg are material objects shared by a group, such as food and clothing, as well as language and other shared cultural practices, which include activities that most group members do. Each attribute is considered to be a **cultural trait**. Cultural traits can vary widely across regions and even within societies. For example, a cultural trait many Muslim women follow is wearing a hijab in public, so their hair and ears are completely covered by a scarf outside of the home. However, not every Muslim woman wears a hijab. Hijabs are common for religious, cultural, and social reasons. In other places and among other groups, Muslim women will wear no head covering at all. Another cultural trait is how people greet one another. A handshake may be acceptable in one group but not in another.

Cultural traits can be artifacts, sociofacts, or mentifacts. **Artifacts** are the visible objects and technologies that a culture creates, such as houses and buildings, clothing, tools, toys, and land-use practices. Artifacts change readily. Some objects are basic necessities (buildings), while others can be used as part of a culture's religious or societal expression (clothing) or for recreation (toys). **Sociofacts** are structures and organizations that influence social behavior, such as families, governments, educational systems, and religious organizations. Slower to change than artifacts, sociofacts define the way people act around others and establish rules that govern behavior. **Mentifacts**—the central, enduring elements of a culture that reflect its shared ideas, values, knowledge, and beliefs—are the slowest to change. Examples include religious beliefs and language, which you will read about later in this chapter.

A *quinceañera* is a traditional celebration in Latino communities around the world during which a 15-year-old girl is said to move from girlhood to womanhood. Here, a young woman named Lacey celebrates her 15th birthday in Culiacán, Mexico. A girl's *quinceañera* dress can be considered an artifact.

CULTURAL DYNAMICS

LEARNING OBJECTIVE
PSO-3.A Define the characteristics, attitudes, and traits that influence geographers when they study culture.

Culture is socially constructed, which means it's created jointly by people rather than by individuals. Culture is also naturally dynamic: it's subject to change, and it transforms in response to countless environmental, human, and technological forces. The speed at which a culture transforms and the aspect of a culture that changes varies from society to society.

For example, the role of women in U.S. culture changed rapidly in the 1960s. A growing population and booming job market enticed women to pursue paying careers. They moved beyond the established social expectation for them to remain at home, working as unpaid housewives. As these societal values changed, education and job opportunities for women expanded. From 1964 to 1974, the number of women working outside the home grew by 43 percent. Simultaneously, the women's rights movement helped women take more prominent roles in the workplace and in society. Women's labor participation rate grew steadily until its plateau in the early 2000s, at which point it was projected to remain above 55 percent through 2020. (You will learn about labor-market participation in Chapter 19.) Again, cultural expectations changed, which permanently altered the U.S. workforce.

Sociofacts, such as the role of women in society, play out in regions all over the world. In Kenya, the *sepaade* tradition—which was developed during the mid-19th century—required that some women could not marry until all their brothers had married. Many women didn't marry until they were beyond child-bearing age. By 1998, a variety of social, technological, and environmental factors had altered how Kenyans regarded this custom. A cultural value shifted, and as a result, the tradition ended.

WHEN CULTURES MIX Cultural change can occur when groups from one culture move to a new place that is home to a different culture. People may retain some or much of their original culture while taking on traits of the new-to-them culture. Over time, immigrants may lose some of their original cultural traits, and the cultural traits they maintain can eventually differ from those of their home countries.

One example can be seen in the way Spanish is spoken throughout the United States. Many people who originally immigrated to the United States from Spanish-speaking countries continue to speak Spanish at home. However, while children born to these families in the United States often learn Spanish, they learn it as a heritage language, a minority language learned primarily at home in informal settings. A heritage language differs from the Spanish spoken in their family's country of origin and serves as an illustration of how a cultural trait—language—can become different as two cultures come together.

CULTURAL NORMS AND DIFFERENCES As you have read, the effects of distance decay have been reduced through innovations in transportation and communication. Regardless of geographic location, people now can connect with other people and communities easily via the internet, social media, and smartphones. Also, global travel is easier than ever. The increased use of these technological advances has led to rapid, far-reaching cultural changes. Trends in music, dance, fashion, and food now bounce around the world in a matter of seconds. These examples of **popular culture**—defined as the widespread behaviors, beliefs, and practices of ordinary people in society at a

Buddhist monks at Fuguo Monastery in Yunnan Province, China, playing basketball—a sport more typical to the United States—is an example of cultural mixing.

Free
Partly free
Not free
Not assessed

0   1,500   3,000 miles
0   1,500   3,000 kilometers

READING MAPS An analysis of internet freedom conducted during 2017 and 2018 showed that government censorship and surveillance of the internet varied widely around the world. For example, China's Cyber Security Law makes it illegal to transmit banned content. ▌ How does this map support the claim that U.S. popular culture influences the world?

given point in time—tend to change quickly. And with increased communication and transportation technology, the rate of change continues to accelerate. Even television has drastically expanded cultural reach across the world. For example, slang from U.S. movies and TV shows often weaves its way into the cultures of other countries thanks to the power of global broadcasting.

In contrast to popular culture, **traditional culture** is comprised of long-established behaviors, beliefs, and practices passed down from generation to generation, such as languages, food, ceremonies, and customs. **Cultural norms**, or the shared standards and patterns that guide the behavior of a group of people, play an important role in upholding traditions and keep traditional culture from changing. In some countries, cultural norms may even be tightly governed. Some societies requiring strong conformity may limit people's exposure to popular culture by forbidding them from accessing the internet and social media. Societies with more relaxed cultural norms are more likely to embrace the influences of popular culture.

People around the world have a wide range of attitudes toward cultural differences. One such attitude is **ethnocentrism**, the tendency of ethnic groups to evaluate other groups according to preconceived ideas originating from their own culture. Ethnocentrism exists in varying degrees. More profound ethnocentrism may

include the belief that one's own cultural group is superior, which may result in overt or clear discrimination against other groups.

In contrast, the attitude known as **cultural relativism** is the evaluation of a culture solely by its unique standards. This approach requires putting aside one's own cultural criteria to understand the context behind the cultural practices of another culture. Critics of cultural relativism challenge the belief that it is appropriate to accept extreme cultural practices, such as violations of human rights, as long as the cultural context behind such practices is understood. Such detractors suggest that cultural relativism allows societies to transcend the limits of what is morally acceptable, justifying extreme cultural practices through cultural context.

GEOGRAPHIC THINKING

1. Define *artifacts*, *sociofacts*, and *mentifacts* and compare the differences among them.

2. Identify and describe an example of a cultural trait from your own culture that has changed over time.

3. Explain how cultural relativism might impede attempts to have international agreements on practices such as genocide or child labor.

WISCONSIN'S AMERICAN INDIAN NATIONS

THE ISSUE The state of Wisconsin officially recognizes the cultural significance of the Wisconsin American Indian Nations, which has affected the state's own cultural values and practices.

LEARNING OBJECTIVES

PSO-3.C Explain how landscape features and land and resource use reflect cultural beliefs and identities.

PSO-3.D Explain patterns and landscapes of language, religion, ethnicity, and gender.

BY THE NUMBERS

50,094

American Indians and Alaska Natives in Wisconsin (2017 estimate)

11

federally recognized tribes in Wisconsin as of 2019

12

states observe Indigenous Peoples' Day as of 2019; Washington, D.C., also commemorates this holiday

Sources: 2013–2017 American Community Survey; Wisconsin Tribal Judges Association; Smithsonian magazine, October 2019

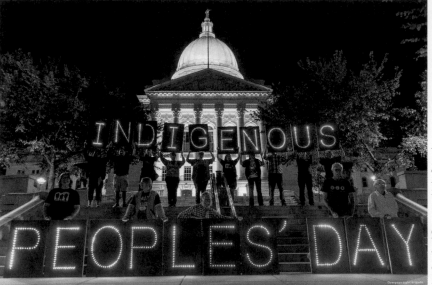

Joe Brusky / Overpass Light Brigade

In 2019, Wisconsinites celebrated an executive order designating the second Monday in October as Indigenous Peoples' Day instead of Columbus Day. While the latter remains a federal holiday, states and localities can choose not to observe it. Indigenous Peoples' Day recognizes and honors the contributions of American Indian nations.

IN AN EFFORT TO COMBAT MISUNDERSTANDINGS and misinformation about American Indians, the state of Wisconsin and its tribal leaders passed Wisconsin Act 31 in 1989. (Other indigenous peoples may refer to themselves as Native Americans, Alaska Natives, First Nations, First Peoples, or by their tribal or cultural names.) The statute was developed to ensure that Wisconsin's students had access to accurate information about the history, culture, and tribal sovereignty of the state's federally recognized American Indian nations and tribal communities. Required instruction under Wisconsin Act 31 includes educational programs that teach about terminology, value systems, and connecting cultures from the past to the present. The purpose of the act is to bridge cultural gaps and develop unity through mutual respect and understanding.

Higher educational institutions within Wisconsin have also taken steps to honor American Indian heritage by using language that promotes unity and understanding among different communities within their respective regions. St. Norbert College in De Pere, Wisconsin, adopted a land acknowledgment statement in 2018 that reads, in part, "In the spirit of the Norbertine value of *stabilitas loci*, a deep commitment to the local community, we acknowledge this land as the ancestral home of the Menominee nation, which holds historical, cultural, and sacred significance to the community." This declaration serves as a first step in acknowledging both the historical and ongoing contributions of American Indians, and similar statements are being implemented by colleges and universities globally.

To further honor Wisconsin's American Indian history, Governor Tony Evers signed an executive order in 2019 to declare the state's first Indigenous Peoples' Day. (Columbus Day remains a federal holiday.) By renaming and repurposing Columbus Day, Wisconsin and several other states—and a large number of U.S. cities as well—use Indigenous Peoples' Day to transform a traditional celebration of colonialism, honor the historical and contemporary cultures of indigenous people, oppose current injustices against them, and recognize that original inhabitants of the Americas have shaped regional culture. ▮

GEOGRAPHIC THINKING

Explain why the passing of Wisconsin Act 31 is culturally significant.

6.2 CULTURAL LANDSCAPES

Every place and region has its own distinct, definable characteristics. These characteristics assemble to form the cultural landscape of a place or region. Made up of natural and cultural features, each cultural landscape is unique.

The terraced rice paddies in Shiroyone Senmaida, Japan, have been registered by the United Nations as Globally Important Agricultural Heritage Systems (GIAHS). The 20,000 solar-powered LED lights provide them with a modern look that attracts visitors and highlights the paddies' cultural importance.

DEFINING CULTURAL LANDSCAPES

LEARNING OBJECTIVES

PSO-3.B Describe the characteristics of cultural landscapes.

PSO-3.C Explain how landscape features and land and resource use reflect cultural beliefs and identities.

PSO-3.D Explain patterns and landscapes of language, religion, ethnicity, and gender.

A natural landscape that has been modified by humans, reflecting their cultural beliefs and values, is a **cultural landscape**. It is the human imprint on the landscape, and it offers clues about cultural practices and priorities, both past and present. Geographers study cultural landscapes to answer questions such as these: What does the landscape communicate about the culture of the people who shaped it? How did they adapt the natural environment to fit their cultural practices and societal needs? And in terms of **identity**—how humans make sense of themselves and how they wish to be viewed by others—how do cultural landscapes influence and reflect a group's identity, and vice versa?

Every landscape is a cultural landscape, and each one has been shaped by a unique series of human activities over time. Humans have interacted with Earth's natural landscapes and resources for hundreds of thousands of years, creating varied cultural landscapes to meet their needs and express their values and beliefs.

Material expressions of culture found in cultural landscapes are evidence of how people live to meet their needs and aspirations. For example, geographers have examined the cultural landscape of the Shiroyone Senmaida rice paddies in Japan, shown in the photograph. Shiroyone is part of an agricultural tradition that has been in place for more than 1,300 years. The terraces built there support the local industry of rice production and create a habitat for local wildlife. The population that gathered—and continues to gather—in this region has shaped a unique cultural landscape, defined by agricultural practices. The terraced rice paddies are visible manifestations of a coherent, organized culture that can maintain them.

Early-20th-century geographer Carl Sauer saw cultures and societies as both developing out of and being affected by landscape. He famously stated, "The cultural landscape is fashioned from a natural landscape by a culture group. Culture is the agent, the natural area is the medium, and the cultural landscape is the result." He perceived the human impact on landscapes to be a reflection of culture and asserted that geographers could only understand a culture by first learning to read its landscape. One example can be seen in the U.S.–Mexico borderlands, which share the same physical environment of mountains, deserts, and grasslands but have different cultural landscapes as a result of the differences between Mexican and U.S. cultures. Visually apparent differences are readily seen when comparing the land use, agricultural practices, and architecture that exist on each side of the border.

Sauer also suggested that people need to understand the past to understand the present. He believed that cultural landscapes offered clues about the cultural practices and activities of a region's past inhabitants. Geographers call this **sequent occupance**—the notion that successive societies leave behind their cultural imprint, a collection of evidence about human character and experiences within a geographic region, which shapes the cultural landscape.

Consider New Orleans, Louisiana, as an example of sequent occupance. Its landscape reflects numerous cultures that have shaped the city over time. As each group sequentially occupied this space, its members instilled some of their values, economic practices, languages, and customs into the landscape. American Indians initially inhabited the region in which present-day New Orleans exists. After European colonization of the Americas, it was a French city and then a Spanish city before becoming part of the United States due to the land deal known as the Louisiana Purchase. African-American culture had a tremendous influence on New Orleans and the city's cultural landscape. Enslaved Africans and African Americans made New Orleans's Congo Square (now Louis Armstrong Park) their own. It is not coincidental that this location in the historically African-American Tremè neighborhood is the birthplace of jazz, a uniquely American art form created by African Americans.

EXAMPLES OF CULTURAL LANDSCAPES

LEARNING OBJECTIVES

PSO-3.B Describe the characteristics of cultural landscapes.

PSO-3.C Explain how landscape features and land and resource use reflect cultural beliefs and identities.

PSO-3.D Explain patterns and landscapes of language, religion, ethnicity, and gender.

Landscapes you encounter every day as you walk or drive through your community, as ordinary as they may seem, are still unique cultural landscapes. Geographers analyze such landscapes to understand the cultures of the people who create them. Cultural landscapes can undergo both slow and rapid changes over time. These changes are accelerated by human factors and processes—such as technology, industrialization, urbanization, globalization, and sustainability initiatives—all of which are influenced by culture. By studying examples of different cultural landscapes, including neighborhoods, building styles, and land-use patterns, geographers can better understand the relationship between culture and landscape.

ETHNIC NEIGHBORHOODS **Ethnicity** is the state of belonging to a group of people who share common cultural characteristics. Large cities typically contain minority clusters, who may, if their numbers and duration of residence allow, form **ethnic neighborhoods**—cultural landscapes within communities of people outside of their areas of origin. Chinatown in Vancouver, British Columbia, is an example of how the history, tradition, and social practices of an ethnic group can transform a landscape into one that is responsive to a community's needs. But why do ethnic neighborhoods form? Processes of exclusion, segregation, and discrimination certainly cause minority groups to band together to maintain their identity. The advantages of uniting in a certain area can help a cultural group set themselves apart to practice their customs in their own neighborhood schools, places of worship, stores, and businesses. Attitudes that exist within the surrounding communities may draw visitors and businesses into an ethnic neighborhood, or they may promote discrimination against the ethnic neighborhood's residents and businesses.

The Goutte d'Or neighborhood of northern Paris, also known as "Little Africa," is another example of an ethnic neighborhood. The city of Paris appeals to emigrants from French-speaking African countries such as Mali and Senegal for an obvious reason: the common language. For decades, African immigrants have settled in Goutte d'Or, and consequently, the cultural imprint of West Africa is present everywhere there—from the foods served in restaurants to the rich fabrics sold at the local open-air market. Additionally, the exceptional textile-making skills of African immigrants have propelled this Parisian neighborhood into one of France's creative hubs.

TRADITIONAL ARCHITECTURE **Traditional architecture**—established building styles of different cultures, religions, and places—was originally influenced by the environment and is based on localized needs and construction materials. It tends to reflect local traditions, and usually evolves over time to reflect the environmental, cultural, and historical context in which it exists.

In the 1500s in what is now the U.S. Southwest, Spanish colonizers found mud homes built by the Pueblo people. The Spaniards later combined the Spanish-Moorish adobe building technique with the traditional, regional style of the original American dwellings. (The Spanish word *adobe* is derived from the Arabic term *al-tob*, which means "mud-brick," and can describe either the material or the method

of construction.) The original materials of wood, stone, and puddled adobe—sun-dried mud—were readily available resources that kept homes cool during the day and warm at night. The construction materials have been adapted over time and, with added modern energy conveniences, this style of home remains prevalent in states such as Arizona and New Mexico, where adobe continues to provide an energy-efficient material in hot, dry climates. Traditional architecture often reflects a historical association, continuity, and ties with the origins of a culture or place.

The round, movable homes—called gers—of Mongolian nomads reflect a nomadic lifestyle, dependency on traditional herding practices, and interactions with nature. As of 2017, approximately 1 million nomads lived on the vast, open plains of Mongolia. They principally herd sheep and goats, but many nomads also have cows, horses,

dogs, camels, and yaks. In addition to milk and meat, these animals provide wool for the felt sidings that keep the gers warm and dry. Nomadic Mongolians set up their mobile dwellings between summer pastures and winter feeding lands where they can shelter from the powerful, icy winds. This confluence between humans and their environment illustrates how established practices and natural elements are woven together into a cultural landscape.

POSTMODERN ARCHITECTURE Postmodern architecture emerged in the 1960s as a reaction to "modern" designs, which emphasized form, structure, and materials. Some people thought modern architecture could solve urban social problems. During the 1950s and 1960s, many urban renewal projects destroyed historic buildings— and even entire neighborhoods—in cities large and small.

TEHRANGELES

THE ISSUE The concentration of Iranians living in the Los Angeles community known as Tehrangeles forms a cultural landscape that preserves some of their native language and traditions.

LEARNING OBJECTIVES

PSO-3.B Describe the characteristics of cultural landscapes.

PSO-3.D Explain patterns and landscapes of language, religion, ethnicity, and gender.

A U.S. flag flies near a Persian restaurant in Tehrangeles, an Iranian neighborhood in Los Angeles that makes up a unique cultural landscape. The name *Tehrangeles* is a blend of two place names: Tehran (the capital of Iran) and Los Angeles.

BY THE NUMBERS

40%+

of all people of Iranian ancestry in the United States live in California (2019 article)

220+

languages spoken in Los Angeles (2017 estimate)

87,000

people of Iranian descent live in Los Angeles (2019 article)

Sources: Los Angeles Times, LA Tourism & Convention Board, U.S. Census Bureau

LOS ANGELES IS A LARGE, DIVERSE CITY filled with ethnic communities such as Chinatown, Koreatown, and Little Armenia. On the city's west side lives a concentration of Iranians who form a neighborhood known as Tehrangeles. Tehrangeles started as a small community of immigrant students and entrepreneurs in the 1960s and has evolved into the largest community of Iranians outside of Iran. The main driver of the community's growth was the 1979 Iranian Revolution, when the last shah of Iran was overthrown and the government was transformed into an Islamic republic. Many Iranians fled the oppressive new regime, and thousands of them settled in Los Angeles. In the years that followed, chain migration drew more Iranians to the community to be with their families, and the Iran-Iraq war of 1988 pushed others to leave their native country.

Los Angeles is an appealing destination because many immigrants find that it reminds them of Iran: the mountainous landscape, the climate, and even the car culture. The community has offered a safe haven for Iranians during times of conflict between Iran and the United States, such as the hostage crisis of 1979, which exposed sharp feelings and subsequent actions of prejudice against Iranians. The Iranians who helped establish Tehrangeles are now in their 70s and 80s and are bonded to the community by their role in its history as well as their contributions to cultural preservation. Members of the younger generation inherit Iranian traditions from their elders and embrace their American identity at the same time.

What distinguishes this prosperous neighborhood of middle-class homes from any other in Los Angeles? Its Iranian character might not be readily apparent when traveling through Tehrangeles, but it's there; for example, children learn to play traditional Iranian instruments, and rug shops sell exquisite Persian rugs. Traditional Iranian restaurants exist near those that offer Iranian fast food such as "Persian pizza," which is made with Persian ingredients and spices. Iran's primary language, Farsi, is spoken throughout the community and appears on the signs of many shops and restaurants. Some businesses display only Farsi names, while others have signs in both English and Farsi. Similarly, some businesses fly only the Iranian flag while others display both U.S. and Iranian flags. In addition, Tehrangeles is a media hub, broadcasting several Farsi language television stations and a Farsi radio station. ∎

GEOGRAPHIC THINKING

Describe how Tehrangeles illustrates the connections among language, ethnicity, and geography.

Postmodernism was, as historian Mary McLeod wrote, "a desire to make architecture a vehicle of cultural expression."

In contrast to the restrictions of modernism, postmodern architecture values diversity in design, and public spaces that can be enjoyed by anyone are integral. Urban skylines can reflect a city's robust economy. In recent decades, Dubai has become a global center for commerce. Highly visible from great distances, its skyscrapers—including Burj Khalifa, one of the of tallest structures in the world—represent both rising power and economic strength. As part of the cultural landscape, skylines make the most effective use of space in a crowded city and reflect the local culture's admiration of the values of ambition and success.

LANDSCAPES OF RELIGION AND LANGUAGE

LEARNING OBJECTIVES

PSO-3.C Explain how landscape features and land and resource use reflect cultural beliefs and identities.

PSO-3.D Explain patterns and landscapes of language, religion, ethnicity, and gender.

From the markets of Goutte d'Or to the restaurants of Tehrangeles, each diverse cultural landscape you have read about contains evidence of how it has been constructed to reflect the cultures of its inhabitants. These cultural practices might be seen in the land-use patterns, the types of housing, the transportation systems, or other cultural landscape features. Two of the most deeply influential aspects of culture—religion and language—leave distinct and identifiable imprints on almost any cultural landscape.

RELIGION Religion is a system of spiritual beliefs that helps form cultural perceptions, attitudes, beliefs, and values—the motives behind observable cultural behaviors and practices. Although these deep cultural foundations may be less visible, religion significantly impacts cultural landscapes. As a mentifact, religion is the slowest type of cultural trait to change, and because it is central to the shared beliefs and ideas of a group, it is reflected in the sociofacts and artifacts of that group's culture.

While immigrants and their descendants often adopt the language and other cultural traits of their new country, they typically continue to uphold the religious beliefs and practices of their home country or region. A person's religion reflects his or her core beliefs, which contributes to his or her cultural values and identity. And there is a strong connection between religion and ethnicity—so strong that the effects of both are evident in an ethnic group's lifestyle and value system. In fact, some major world religions are so closely connected to the cultural identities of certain countries that it is difficult to think of the country without thinking of the religion, too. Buddhism, for example, is closely linked with the cultural identity of Thailand, and Hinduism is a prominent part of India's cultural identity.

Each religion has a different spatial organization. The practices of the religion influence where the culture worships, which then affects the design and architecture of its places of worship. Members of some religions assemble for congregational worship or community assembly in churches, mosques, and synagogues. Others worship or observe religious practices individually in smaller pagodas, temples, or shrines.

The Kaaba, a square stone building in the center of the Great Mosque in Mecca, Hejaz, Saudi Arabia, is considered to be the most sacred Islamic shrine. Wherever they are in the world—even on airplanes—Muslims make sure to face the Kaaba during their five daily prayers. They also bury their dead facing Mecca. Adult Muslims are expected to make a **pilgrimage** to Mecca called the hajj at least once during their lifetime to walk around the Kaaba. A pilgrimage is a journey to a holy place for spiritual reasons. In contrast, Hinduism's temples are meant to house shrines devoted to certain gods, rather than provide places for congregational worship. Individual Hindus practice private worship, alone or with family members, performing rituals that include making offerings and repeating mantras—sounds or words—three times a day.

LANGUAGE Language is the carrier of human thoughts and cultural identities. As you might expect, each distinct system of communication has a significant imprint on the cultural landscapes people inhabit, linking language to sequent occupance. Nearly all languages have a literary tradition, or some form of written communication. Visible language is a clue to the identities of the people who live in that area, and it threads its way into daily life within a cultural landscape through place names and street names—and even public murals. These uses of language often reflect the linguistic heritage of a particular geographic location.

Place names, or **toponyms**, help define what is unique about a place, such as its geographic features or history. Coconut Creek, Florida, for example, was named for the large number of coconut trees planted by developers before the area became a city. Big Bend National Park in Texas was established in 1944 alongside a large, natural curve of the Río Grande. A toponym such as Battle Creek, Michigan, provides insight into a city's history, while a French street called Avenue Charles de Gaulle pays homage to a famous individual.

GEOGRAPHIC THINKING

1. Describe the characteristics of a cultural landscape.

2. Describe evidence that might help you identify the languages used in ethnic neighborhoods.

3. Explain the degree to which architecture can reflect cultural beliefs and identity.

With improvements in transportation and crowd control and rising global wealth, more than 2 million Muslims make the hajj—or pilgrimage to Mecca—every year. As a result, the government of Saudi Arabia has expanded its facilities in Mecca to handle the large number of pilgrims.

6.3 IDENTITY AND SPACE

A single space in a cultural landscape—a person's workspace, for example—will likely reflect some part of that individual's identity. A person's age, ethnicity, and gender can often be "read" in that space. Geographers apply this same principle to help understand the ways that identities of groups are reflected in the cultural landscape.

SHAPING SPACE THROUGH IDENTITY

LEARNING OBJECTIVE
PSO-3.C Explain how landscape features and land and resource use reflect cultural beliefs and identities.

So who are you, anyway? You read that identity is how humans make sense of themselves and how they wish to be viewed by others. Culture, ethnicity, and gender are major factors that establish a person's identity. And identity affects how people occupy space in society and shape the landscape. People's cultural beliefs and identities influence how they use the land they occupy and its resources.

The artifacts found in a person's workspace or home can tell you quite a bit about that person's life. Things like photographs, books, artwork, and technology can reveal what a person values and what that person finds less important. On a broader scale, neighborhoods reflect the cultural attitudes of their residents. For instance, the churches, restaurants, and shops of an ethnic neighborhood show how cultural attitudes and practices affect the way space is used. Ethnic neighborhoods are examples of concentrated populations of an ethnic group that retain elements of the culture of origin while functioning within the new culture. In fact, however, all neighborhoods are landscapes that reflect a unique set of beliefs and attitudes.

LANDSCAPE FEATURES AND IDENTITY Homes within neighborhoods may display features that reflect the residents' cultural beliefs or identity. People use landscapes to communicate their religious beliefs. For example, regardless of where they are located geographically, it is not unusual for people who practice Catholicism to have a statue of the Virgin Mary or a cross on a wall inside their home as a symbol or reminder of their faith. A Buddhist may build a garden that reflects the Buddhist principles of peace, serenity, goodness, and respect for all living things. A statue of Buddha in that garden would face the home, a position that Buddhists believe results in abundance.

Czech communities in the United States have created cultural landscapes that reflect both their religion and ethnicity. Religious monuments are significant components of the Czech Republic's architectural heritage and identity, and Czech immigrants brought the tradition of erecting them along roads when they immigrated to Wisconsin in the mid-1800s. These stone or metal shrines were three to four feet high and were typically inscribed with a scripture verse in Czech and topped with a crucifix. Similarly, Czech immigrants and their descendants have left their mark on the landscape in Fayette County, Texas, where they hold traditional Czech festivals, operate bakeries specializing in Czech pastries, and have built the famous "Painted Churches of Texas"—churches that are unassuming from the outside but painted in vivid colors on the inside.

In the western United States, residents sometimes mark treeless hills and slopes with one or more gigantic capital letters to signify the names of towns or schools. Often, these mountain monograms or cultural signatures are constructed using whitewashed rocks, and they represent an invented regional tradition by which residents demonstrate their community or school pride. This practice of imprinting the landscape remains concentrated in the West and has become a means of regional identification over the past hundred years.

LAND AND RESOURCE USE Amish immigrants first arrived in eastern Pennsylvania in the 18th century, and a large Amish settlement still thrives there today. Sizable Amish agricultural communities can also be found in Ohio, Indiana, and Missouri. The landscapes inhabited by these communities are distinct—large plots of farmland whose characteristics reflect the Amish identity. People who subscribe to the Old Order Amish refuse modern conveniences like cars, trucks, modern farming equipment, and even electricity, instead using horses and plows and gas- or battery-operated lights. They view their farming practices as coinciding with their values of discipline and hard work. Members of the community help each other farm, and Amish "barn-raisings" are an integral cultural tradition. Amish women are renowned for their baked goods that provide a source of income and are often made using milk, eggs, and produce from their own farms. Simple living, community cooperation, and acting as stewards of the land are values that the Amish identify with and are reflected in how they farm the land and use its resources.

The Inupiat people offer another example of the ways in which a culture's identity is connected to its use of land and resources. The Inupiat live on the North Slope, an Arctic coastal plain north of the Brooks Mountain Range in northeastern Alaska. The area stretches over 89,000 square miles from the Brooks Range to the coastline of the Arctic

In the Indian city of Delhi, women-only train cars have been introduced to the city's metro system in an attempt to provide safer spaces for Indian women. Public awareness of sexual harassment and sexual violence against women in India has risen sharply since the 2010s.

Ocean. They hunt marine and land mammals, fish, and migratory birds to feed their population—which totals fewer than 10,000 people in eight small communities—and sustain their economic livelihoods and cultural lifestyles. Hunting also serves as a vehicle to pass on tribal knowledge. The most culturally significant resource harvested on the North Slope is the bowhead whale, which the Inupiat have hunted for a thousand years. At an early age, children are taught about subsistence whaling as a culturally acceptable practice (as opposed to commercial whaling) and play a part in the harvest to ensure survival of this central part of the Inupiat culture. Subsistence whaling is also culturally important because sharing resources is a valued tradition for the North Slope people.

WOMEN AND GENDERED SPACES

LEARNING OBJECTIVE
PSO-3.C Explain how landscape features and land and resource use reflect cultural beliefs and identities.

When a society has strict roles for men and women, certain spaces may be designed and deliberately incorporated into the landscape to accommodate gender roles. These spaces, called **gendered spaces**, can exist in homes, workplaces, and public areas. Depending on the cultural and societal factors that establish them, gendered spaces can be supportive, positive places or restrictive places.

Throughout history and across the world, gendered spaces have been more restrictive for women than for men. Traditional gender roles often keep women from playing a part in certain aspects of society and push them to fulfill cultural expectations that can be limiting.

In the rural areas of some countries, gender differences tied to laws or cultural beliefs about land ownership influence how men and women use land. For example, in Kenya, it's much more likely that a man will own land because women in this country don't have equal property rights, and property rights normally pass from father to son. In fact, since 2013, less than 2 percent of title deeds issued in Kenya have been granted to women. However, according to the World Bank, more than three-quarters of the farms in Kenya are run by women. They do much of the country's agricultural work while the men own and control the vast majority of the farmland.

For both men and women, some spaces are perceived to be inclusive while others are perceived to be exclusive. Urban planners all over the world recognize that women experience city life differently than men. In the United States, 10 million of the 18 million women who own homes live alone, and demand has increased for housing that provides increased safety and affordability and requires little maintenance. In general, women place more value on safety than men do, preferring urban spaces with well-lit parks and parking areas. Some urban places have

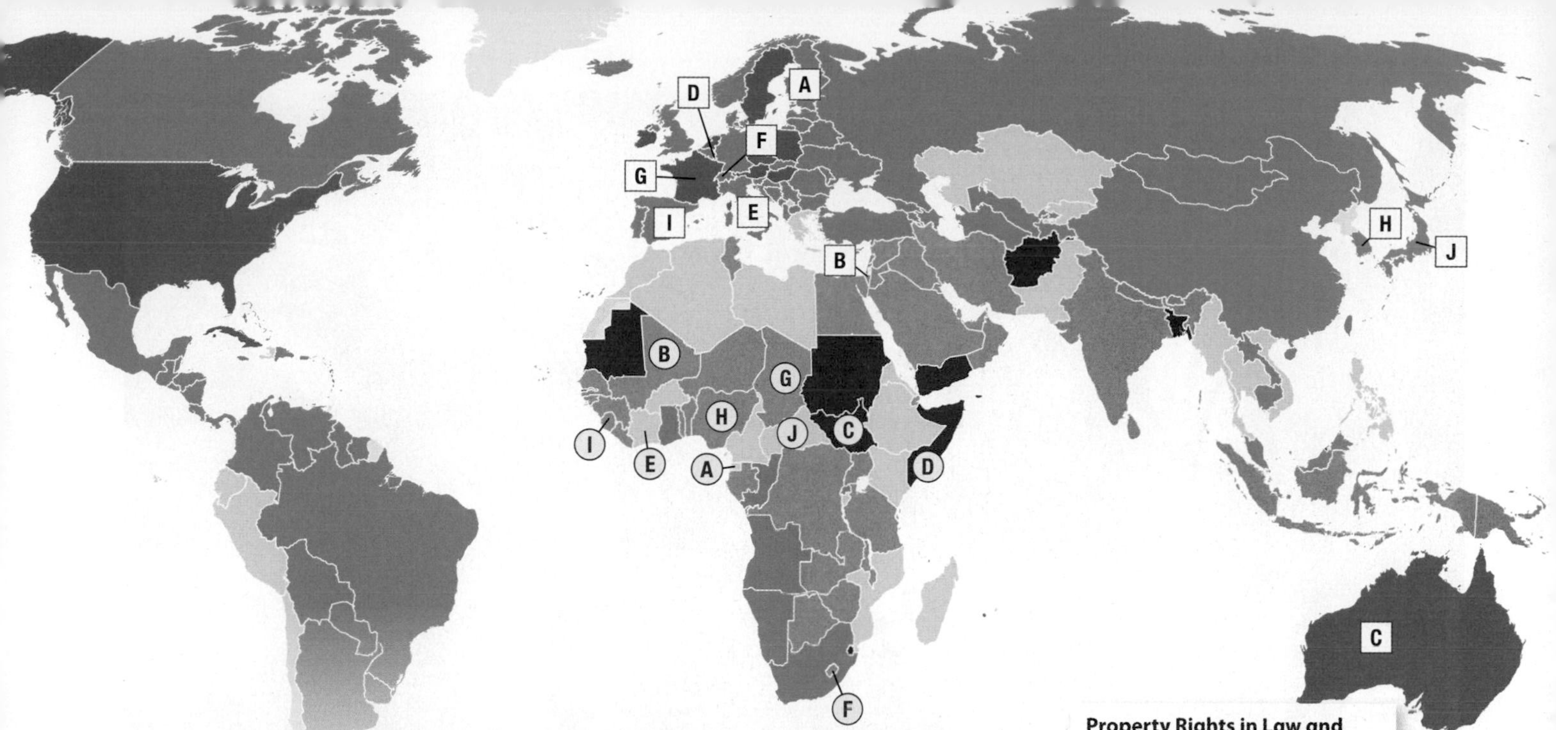

PATTERNS IN GENDER

The right to an education and the right to own property have been critical areas of progress for women throughout human history. In the United States, a country in which women have more rights than in many other places around the world, more women than men have college degrees. But millions of women worldwide—in as many as half of all countries—still face discrimination in property rights: some discrimination enshrined in law, some in practice, and some in both. ▮ Use the map and the life expectancy data to identify patterns between the highest and the lowest average life expectancies for women and their property rights.

Property Rights in Law and Practice for Women, 2017

- Almost no discrimination in law and practice
- Almost no discrimination in law; some discrimination in practice
- Moderate discrimination in law and practice
- Moderate discrimination in law; more discrimination in practice
- Significant discrimination in law and practice
- No data

LIFE EXPECTANCY FOR WOMEN, 2017

	A	B	C	D	E	F	G	H	I	J
	84.4	84.6	84.7	85.4	85.6	85.6	85.7	85.7	86.3	87.3
	Finland	Israel	Australia	Luxembourg	Italy	Switzerland	France	South Korea	Spain	Japan

COUNTRIES WITH THE HIGHEST AVERAGE LIFE EXPECTANCY FOR WOMEN

74.7 Global Average

COUNTRIES WITH THE LOWEST AVERAGE LIFE EXPECTANCY FOR WOMEN

Eq. Guinea	Mali	South Sudan	Somalia	Côte d'Ivoire	Lesotho	Chad	Nigeria	Sierra Leone	CAR*
59.3	59.2	58.9	58.4	58.3	56.2	55.1	54.8	54.7	54.4
A	B	C	D	E	F	G	H	I	J

*Central African Republic

PERCENTAGE OF 25- TO 29-YEAR-OLDS IN THE U.S. WITH A BACHELOR'S DEGREE OR HIGHER, 2017

Women ● Men ●

American Indian/ Alaska Native	Hispanic	Black	White	Asian/ Pacific Islander
19% / 8%	22% / 15%	24% / 22%	47% / 38%	64% / 58%

Sources: The Women's Atlas, World Bank, National Center for Educational Statistics

In Judaism, a bar mitzvah celebration takes place on a boy's 13th birthday, which marks the day when a boy becomes accountable for his own actions and sins. The corresponding ritual for girls is called a bat mitzvah, and takes place when a girl is 12 or 13.

responded to that preference by introducing spaces where men are not allowed. In Mexico City, for instance, the public transportation system includes bright pink buses that are available to women and children only.

Gendered spaces can offer women more than just physical safety; they can be places where women feel emotionally safe as well. In some regions of India, for example, women are discouraged by the culture from openly sharing their viewpoints in the company of men. To address this issue, the Zenana Bagh, or "women's park," was created in Delhi as a safe place for Indian women to gather for prayer and to openly discuss religious, environmental, and political issues.

Until recently, restaurants in Saudi Arabia were required to have separate entrances for men and women, and screens were set up to divide men-only areas from areas where families and tables with only women could eat. In December 2019, however, these restrictions were eased by the government and restaurants were no longer required to segregate by gender.

What happens when societal conventions related to gendered spaces are broken? During a political revolution in Egypt in 2011, women joined demonstrators in Tahrir Square, a public space they had once been prohibited from entering. Many of these women were threatened and physically attacked while demonstrating. In Egyptian culture, men and women are often expected to follow strict gender roles, with a woman's role mostly limited to serving men in domestic capacities within a household. The events of Tahrir Square demonstrate how men can carry over dominant behaviors from the domestic sphere into the public sphere.

Geographers can use spatial analysis and maps to identify and highlight gendered spaces. Mapping gendered spaces can reveal patterns that might otherwise be overlooked. Geographers can also help identify where gendered spaces are compartmentalized in society and determine the accessibility of resources. For example, they could use gender-based mapping to analyze land ownership in Africa. This type of mapping can be used to show the ways in which women are discriminated against.

LGBTQIA+ SPACES

LEARNING OBJECTIVE
PSO-3.C Explain how landscape features and land and resource use reflect cultural beliefs and identities.

According to the Human Rights Campaign, **gender identity** is "one's innermost concept of self as male, female, a blend of both or neither—how individuals perceive themselves and what they call themselves. One's gender identity can be the same or different from their sex assigned at birth." Many factors contribute to a person's gender identity, and can include a culture's mentifacts. The gender with which a person identifies may also differ from the gender perceived by society, and this can profoundly affect how certain individuals participate in society and shape the landscape.

The LGBTQIA+ community is an inclusive group of people whose gender identity, sexuality, or both do not fall within "traditional" cultural norms. This community generally celebrates diversity, pride, and individuality, and provides a place for members to feel safe and accepted. Over the

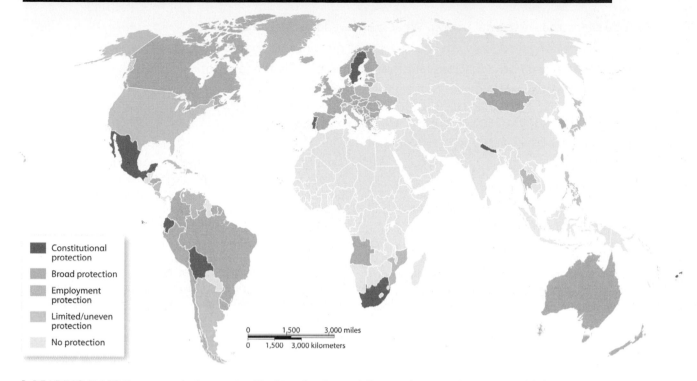

Constitutional protection

Broad protection

Employment protection

Limited/uneven protection

No protection

0   1,500   3,000 miles
0   1,500   3,000 kilometers

READING MAPS Every year, the International Lesbian, Gay, Bisexual, Trans and Intersex Association publishes a report on sexual orientation laws across the world. As of 2019, consensual same-sex acts between adults are punishable by death in 11 countries. ▌What conclusions can you draw about regions that discriminate against sexual orientation?

years, the LGBTQIA+ acronym has evolved to be more inclusive, but its most recent form stands for lesbian, gay, bisexual, transgender, queer or questioning, intersexual, and allied or asexual. The plus sign at the end represents anyone not included in the abbreviation whose gender identity differs from traditional expectations.

SAFE SPACES AND NEIGHBORHOODS

Social media, school-based groups, sports leagues, and performance groups have created **safe spaces**, or spaces of acceptance for people such as members of the LGBTQIA+ community who are sometimes marginalized by society. Safe spaces exist within larger, more traditional landscapes where LGBTQIA+ people can share interests and experiences with others who identify with the community. Community centers throughout the world, such as The Center in New York City, offer advocacy, health and wellness support, and access to cultural events.

A number of urban neighborhoods, such as Midtown in Atlanta and Schöneberg in Berlin, have become cultural landscapes with many safe spaces for LGBTQIA+ people. Such communities formed years ago when gays and lesbians moved into and renovated urban neighborhoods to form places free of discrimination. However, areas such as Boystown in Chicago and Shoreditch in the East End of London are now attracting residents from outside the LGBTQIA+ community. **Gentrification**, or the renovations and improvements conforming to middle-class preferences,

has driven up the demand for housing and the cost of living in these neighborhoods, making it difficult for less affluent, more vulnerable LGBTQIA+ populations to live there. Some LGBTQIA+ businesses have also been forced out of their neighborhoods, changing the cultural landscape.

The term **third place**, coined in the late 1980s, refers to a communal space such as a coffee shop, fitness center, or bookstore that is separate from home (first place) or work (second place). In all communities, having a physical third place is important; individuals need social spaces where they can develop a sense of self, let their guard down, and form relationships with others. The need for accessible, safe, and welcoming third spaces is especially important for groups such as members of the LGBTQIA+ community, who feel marginalized by mainstream society.

By 2019, more than 20 U.S. states and the District of Columbia had adopted legislation to prevent the bullying of LGBTQIA+ students in Grades K–12. Various organizations help schools create safe environments by offering educator guides and "safe space kits" to help teachers and students.

GEOGRAPHIC THINKING

1. Describe an example of a gendered space for women.

2. Explain how educational institutions might further develop or create safe spaces for LGBTQIA+ students.

6.4 CULTURAL PATTERNS

Think about a place that is special to you. What makes it so remarkable? Good memories of a place can affect how you interpret that geographic space. All humans associate feelings with locations, and geographers study these emotions because they help explain patterns found in cultural landscapes.

SENSE OF PLACE

LEARNING OBJECTIVE
PSO-3.D Explain patterns and landscapes of language, religion, ethnicity, and gender.

Geographers claim that when people develop a **sense of place**, they fill a geographic location with meaning by connecting memories and feelings to it. As memories and stories of a place accumulate, transform, and even fade over time, an individual's sense of place will continue to adjust, which impacts that person's understanding of that place. Hearing new stories about your childhood home may add new dimensions to your sense of place for that home. Even fictional stories associated with a location can contribute to a sense of place. A classic example would be a movie that shows King Kong climbing the Empire State Building and having that event shape your sense of place about the famed New York City skyscraper.

Placemaking is a community-driven process in which people collaborate to create a place where they can live, work, play, and learn. Placemaking facilitates creative patterns of use of a landscape, and in turn the landscape reflects the culture, feelings, experiences, and perceptions of the people who use the place. Placemaking is a dynamic process that adapts to the needs of the physical, cultural, and social identities that participate in defining and using a specific place.

People's sense of place shapes their identities, which can manifest itself in a range of scales. Residents of South Boston also identify as New Englanders, just as residents of Colorado identify themselves as Westerners. Examples of the perceptual or vernacular regions (defined by a person's perception and sense of place) in the United States are the West, the Midwest, the East Coast, and the South. Each perceptual region has distinct environmental, cultural, and economic features that cause people to perceive it as unique from the others. The West, for example, is commonly viewed as a place of adventure and opportunity where the outdoors represents a way of life, whereas the East Coast is known for its large cities, industry, and diversity.

PLACEMAKING The Project for Public Spaces (PPS) is an organization that helps people build public spaces that support local communities. This PPS infographic is a tool designed to help communities evaluate public places. The inner circle shows a place's most important qualities, the middle circle describes intangible attributes, and the outer circle shows measurable data. ▌ With a partner, use the intangible attributes in the middle circle to evaluate your school in each of the four qualities shown in the center circle. Then use the outer circle to identify one piece of data you would like to measure as part of your evaluation.

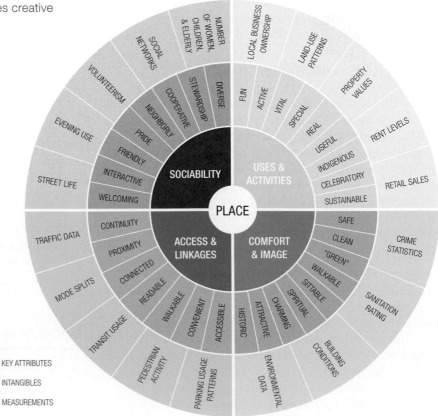

KEY ATTRIBUTES

INTANGIBLES

MEASUREMENTS

The Valley of the Gods is an area within the Bears Ears National Monument in Utah. Its topography provides a classic example of the landscape of the American West.

LANGUAGE, RELIGION, AND ETHNICITY

LEARNING OBJECTIVE

PSO-3.D Explain patterns and landscapes of language, religion, ethnicity, and gender.

You already know the importance of language, religion, and ethnicity to culture and the cultural landscape. So it should come as no surprise that these factors contribute to a person's sense of place. The distribution of cultural traits creates unique landscapes with which people identify. Language, religion, and ethnicity all work together to form regions. For instance, the Southwestern United States is shaped by the Spanish language, Catholicism, and Hispanic migration. Geographers identify the patterns and landscapes that exist for individual languages, religions, and ethnicities by examining various regions.

LINGUISTIC PATTERNS Languages and words play a crucial role in the establishment of landscape. The speech patterns of members in a group within a geographical area distinguish these people from other groups and also shape their sense of place. Within a single language there may be wide variations in grammar, vocabulary, and the pronunciation of words. These variations are often regional and provide clues to migration and settlement patterns and the historical development of each region.

Early settlers to the United States established themselves in different areas along the East Coast. Eventually, settlers moved, and more migrants came to America contributing to the growth of American **dialects**. A dialect is a variation of a standard language specific to a general area. It is distinguished by differences in pronunciation, degree of rapidity in speech, word choice, and spelling. As groups settled in different regions, their unique ways of speaking contributed to the cultural landscape and became part of the regional identity. Vocabulary is one way groups distinguish themselves. The use of the second person plural varies among people living in the South, the Midwest, New England, and other U.S. regions: *you, y'all, you guys, youse guys,* or *you'uns*.

In addition to geographic location, social factors such as class, race, or ethnicity can also impact language patterns. In New England, for example, a distinction is sometimes made between people in the upper and working classes based on dialect. The so-called Boston Brahmin dialect is historically associated with people who shaped the New England cultural landscape, including the descendants of the American founders and the powerful and wealthy. In contrast, the traditional Boston accent, with its "lost *r*'s" ("pahk the cah" instead of "park the car") and other unique grammatical constructs, is traditionally linked to the working class. Another example of societal factors influencing language patterns is African-American English (AAE), a distinct dialect that developed because many African Americans were socially isolated, even after emancipation.

The southern United States uses a regional variety of English that distinctly sets it apart from other regions. The dialects and accents of the South have become part of the region's identity. Despite stereotypes, there are linguistic variances in Southern American English (SAE), some of which can be attributed to geographical location and many of which are determined by whether a person lives in a city or a rural area, as well as that individual's family history. For example, a person from Georgia has a different southern accent than a person from Texas. SAE garners a great deal of attention because it is so widely recognized. While some southerners may work to modify their accents, most maintain them as part of their cultural identity. Regional dialects aside, the United States acknowledges the existence and use of Standard English (SE) as an idealized norm, but to what degree SE is used or adopted depends largely on location.

Certain places in the world have more involved language structures in which language use, identity construction, and place formation are intertwined. Complex regional patterns such as these can be found in Hualien County, Taiwan, an agricultural township that spans the island's Coastal Mountain Range and the East Rift Valley. Rich in indigenous diversity, this region is packed with various ethnic groups, including Taroko, Amis, and Han.

The Hualien County government reports that there are at least nine languages spoken in the region. In Hualien, different ethnic groups name places based on how each group views and uses the surrounding landscape as well as the group's historical legacy. Mandarin Chinese is the most common language, but different ethnic groups will switch from Mandarin to an indigenous language when referring to place names. Groups do this because places have different cultural meanings to different groups and switching languages emphasizes the identity of the speaker. In this example, indigenous place-naming coincides with indigenous knowledge and experience, much of which centers around a relationship with a certain place.

The Basque are an ethnic group with a population of approximately 1 million people who live in the western Pyrenees and along the Bay of Biscay in Spain and France in an area comprising about 3,900 square miles. The Basque language (also called Euskara) is spoken by the Basque people and is a unique contributor to placemaking and the Basque landscape. This language has eight different dialects and no common link to modern languages. The rugged Pyrenees have long provided a natural fortress of safety and seclusion for the Basque homeland. This isolated existence helped preserve the language in the face of heavy language competition. As one of the oldest living languages, the Basque language has become symbolic of the Basque people's cultural identity as they are one of the oldest ethnic groups in Europe. In an effort to help protect this language, knowing how to speak and write it is a requirement to work for the Spanish Basque government, and the language is being taught in some schools across the region today.

RELIGIOUS PATTERNS Religions tend to organize space in distinctive ways, based on how the religion is organized, its beliefs, and how it is practiced. These three factors also impact the distribution of **adherents**, or the people who are loyal to a belief, religion, or organization. Some religions appeal to a wide variety of people across the globe, no matter their race, ethnicity, or class, and other religions appeal to a specific ethnic group living in particular regions of the world.

Religions are often organized into smaller groups including branches, denominations, and sects. A branch is a large fundamental division within a religion. Protestant, Catholic, and Eastern Orthodox are the major branches of Christianity. Sunni and Shiite are two branches of Islam. A branch is sometimes divided into **denominations**, which are separate organizations that unite a number of local congregations. Lutheran, Methodist, and Baptist are a few denominations of the Protestant branch. A **sect** is a relatively small group that has separated from an established denomination.

Sometimes the terms *branch*, *denomination*, or *sect* are used interchangeably, but it is important to understand that geographers use these terms to define these types of organizations to study all religions' influence on the landscape. It is also relevant to note that religions transition between these types of organizations—for instance, from sect to major religious branch—as their popularity or acceptance grows or diminishes.

In the United States, the distribution of adherents of various religions and denominations follows a regional pattern, which is also related to ethnicity. According to the Public Religion Research Institute (PRRI), a U.S. nonprofit organization, the number of White evangelical Protestants is twice as large in the South (22 percent) and Midwest (20 percent) as it is in the Northeast (8 percent). White evangelical Protestants account for 12 percent of residents in the West. In contrast, Catholics represent a much larger share of the northeastern region: 29 percent of residents of the Northeast identify as Catholic, compared to 21 percent of Westerners, 19 percent of Midwesterners, and 17 percent of Southerners. In Chapter 8, you will learn in detail about the regional distribution of adherents in the United States.

Places of worship are closely related to how a religion is practiced, and they also represent a physical connection between religion and the cultural landscape. Places of worship, including churches, synagogues, temples, and other sacred places, are sites where worshipers sometimes

CRITICAL VIEWING The location of the Basque homeland in a remote and mountainous area of Spain has insulated its language from external influences. As a result, certain dialects of the Basque language have remained largely unchanged since the Roman era in the second century B.C.E. ∎ Explain how the Basque language contributes to a sense of place.

STUDYING INDIGENOUS LANGUAGES

Sandhya Narayanan studies indigenous multilingualism and the factors affecting how these languages are spoken by younger generations in the Puno region of Peru. The local community gathers at the foot of Allin Qhapaq annually to make offerings and watch performances of traditional dances and songs.

LEARNING OBJECTIVE
PSO-3.D Explain patterns and landscapes of language, religion, ethnicity, and gender.

Growing up in a multilingual home in multilingual communities led Sandhya Narayanan to research indigenous languages, focusing on how multilingualism affects a culture and the future of language.

The high-altitude plain in the Andes Mountains in South America has been home to speakers of Quechua, Aymara, and other indigenous languages for centuries. Spanish is also a vital part of the linguistic mix in this region. The Puno region of Peru, on the border of the Quechua and Aymara regions, is the perfect place to study the interactions among cultural landscapes. The Puno region drew linguistic anthropologist and National Geographic Explorer Sandhya Narayanan to its local marketplaces. There, women have traditionally sold produce and craft goods to consumers from the area's diverse linguistic communities, making it a living laboratory for the study of the historical effects of multiple languages on the region.

Through fieldwork that includes interviews, recordings, observations, and conversations with local consultants, Naranayan has noted a generation gap, as members of the younger generation tend to employ Spanish exclusively to communicate. Interestingly, this is not youthful rebellion against the traditional languages but a practice created by parents who discourage learning indigenous languages. Naranayan says, "There's an idea that children won't advance if they don't speak Spanish, and that speaking an indigenous language jeopardizes their ability to learn Spanish." Members of that younger generation see this practice as a loss that disconnects them from their traditional culture and heritage.

Are these language dynamics at play in other multilingual areas? Narayanan may explore this question in future research, as she intends to do similar fieldwork in India.

GEOGRAPHIC THINKING

Compare how and why different generations in the Puno region of Peru may have differing senses of place.

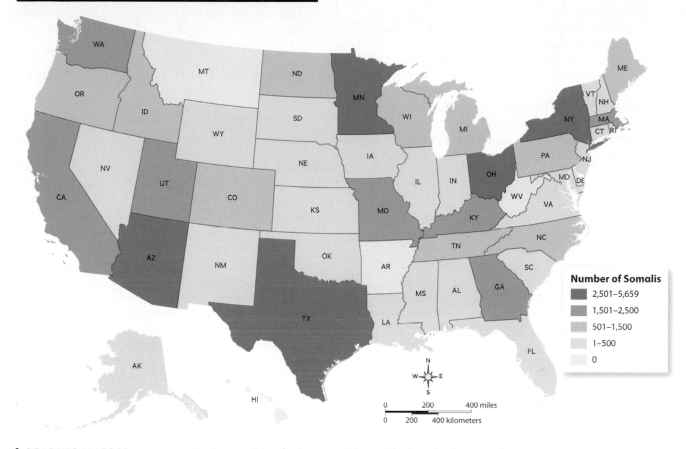

SOMALI REFUGEE ARRIVALS, 2010–2016

Number of Somalis
- 2,501–5,659
- 1,501–2,500
- 501–1,500
- 1–500
- 0

READING MAPS Minnesota remains the top state of primary resettlement for Somali refugees, with almost 12 percent of total Somali refugees settling there. New York State is second with 8 percent.
▌ How might this map be used to attract more Somalis to the United States?

gather or have spiritual significance or power. Mosques are community spaces where Muslim worshipers assemble for prayer or to celebrate holy festivals. Each mosque has a minaret, or tower, where a man summons people to worship. In contrast, pagodas in China and Japan are designed to hold relics of the Buddhist religion, not as sites of community worship. Pagodas are tall, ornate structures with balconies and slanting roofs.

Patterns related to the selection of sacred places contribute to a regional cultural landscape and can be expressed through interactions with the natural environment, human-made features or design, and even through culture and lifestyle. For example, some religions choose sacred sites based on places that were significant in the lives of various religious founders or leaders. Lumbini, Nepal, where Buddha was born; Bodh Gaya, India, where he received enlightenment; and Sarnath, where he first preached, are all considered sacred sites and are heavily visited by Buddhist pilgrims from around the world. The Maya Devi Temple in Lumbini is considered Buddha's birthplace, and in 2019, the surrounding site was being developed as a pilgrimage center. Sacred Buddhist spaces, including pagodas and stone stupas (dome-shaped Buddhist shrines), and

Buddhist texts written in Pali and Sanskrit languages and other ancient languages of India contribute to a sense of identity and form the regions where Buddhism is prevalent in East and Southeast Asia. Ethnicity is another factor that helps define a region.

ETHNIC PATTERNS Patterns of ethnicity are deeply linked to religion and language. The Somali in Minnesota exemplify how ethnicity, religion, and language contribute to a sense of place within a specific region. As you read in Chapter 5, the largest community of Somalis in North America lives in Minneapolis, where Somalis continue to shape the cultural landscape both in their ethnic neighborhoods and throughout the state. In 2017, Somalis represented the second-largest group of foreign-born Minnesotans, with a population of 27,373. The Cedar-Riverside neighborhood of Minneapolis, which houses the largest concentration of Somalis in the city, is also home to Dar Al-Hijrah, the oldest mosque in Minnesota. The mosque has become part of the cultural landscape, signifying an important component of Somali identity and providing a space for religious worship, an Islamic school, and community gatherings. More than 30 mosques now exist in the metropolitan area of Minneapolis and St. Paul.

Overcoming the language barrier has been challenging for Somalis. Many of them arrived in Minnesota proficient in multiple languages, like Somali and Arabic, but gaining English proficiency made their transitions difficult. Somali families have started charter schools to support Somali language preservation and make it easier for students to adhere to religious practices. Demographics reveal that half of the Somali population in Minnesota is aged 22 years or younger. As this young population ages, its economic and cultural influence in the state will likely continue to grow. The first Somali American (and first of two Muslim women) secured a seat in Congress in 2018, and immigrant entrepreneurs, in general, currently contribute $489 million annually to Minnesota's economy.

Regionally, why Minnesota instead of other states? Though Minnesota may not seem like an obvious destination for Somali immigrants, highly active volunteer agencies there have contracted with the U.S. State Department to help refugees learn English, find housing, access health care, and start a new life in the United States. For similar reasons, Minnesota is a population center for Hmong refugees. When ethnic groups find that public and private institutions are welcoming and supportive, the news spreads back to the home country or region and influences where second waves of relatives and friends choose to settle.

Historically, three major ethnic groups formed clusters in particular regions in the United States: Hispanics in the Southwest, African Americans in the Southeast, and Asian Americans in the West. Over time, these patterns have changed through migration and new immigrant flows. The U.S. population overall has been moving southward and westward in recent decades. However, certain ethnic patterns in the United States have prevailed and continue to enhance the placemaking of the region. For example, the main urban ethnic neighborhoods established in U.S. cities during the 19th century were home to the Catholic Irish, Italians, Polish, and East European Jews. In Chicago specifically, patterns of Irish, Italian, and Polish neighborhoods have changed over a period of almost 60 years. African-American and Hispanic immigration to these neighborhoods has changed the landscape. Today, all of these groups have a strong presence in the form of churches, restaurants, stores, and art exhibits—many of which reflect their native languages and all of which contribute to a sense of place within a culturally diverse city.

Africa is made up of more countries than any other continent, and its cultural landscape is a collection of hundreds of ethnic groups. Some groups formed before the precolonial period, and others emerged because European colonial governments categorized groups by differences that often held little meaning to the people themselves. Colonialism forced Africa into a period of intense environmental, political, social, and religious change as European powers created new political realms and divided existing ones. Established cultural groups that had long been in existence became split, and other groups—different

from one another—were forced to live together. The cultural tensions created by this politically motivated restructuring created deep strains and tumultuous conflict that still exists today and has become part of the global cultural landscape.

PATTERNS OF UNITY AND DIVISION

LEARNING OBJECTIVE
PSO-3.D Explain patterns and landscapes of language, religion, ethnicity, and gender.

A force that unites a group of people is called a **centripetal force**. Cultural traits act as centripetal forces when they create solidarity among a group of people and provide stability. A common language or a popular national sport can unite citizens. Conversely, a force that divides groups of people is called a **centrifugal force**. Cultural traits that sow division between the people of a country or region—sometimes leading to violence, civil unrest, or war—act as centrifugal forces. A state with two or more ethnic groups aiming for their own political status and wishing to separate and form their own country can be a dominant centrifugal force. The former Soviet Union, which broke up into 15 independent countries, is an example of a multinational state that experienced the effects of centrifugal forces. Centripetal and centrifugal forces and how they affect patterns of political geography will be covered in Chapter 11. Here, you'll focus on how these forces relate to culture.

CENTRIPETAL FORCES Shared religion, language, or ethnicity can create a shared sense of identity—which can act as a centripetal force. Even very diverse cultures may have centripetal forces that help hold them together. A dominant religion, such as Roman Catholicism in Mexico or Brazil, can be an extremely strong centripetal force. Similarly, a shared language helps unify people by facilitating communication. As a flood of immigrants came to the United States in the 19th century, many learned English, which helped unify these people from diverse cultures. A shared ethnicity can be a strong centripetal force as well. Although China has 55 ethnic minorities, more than 91 percent of the country's population is Han Chinese. This shared ethnicity serves as a unifying force.

CENTRIFUGAL FORCES Religion, language, and ethnicity—which were just identified as centripetal forces—can also act as centrifugal forces under different circumstances. For example, the official "language of the Union" of India is Hindi. Hindi and English are both used in parliament, and India's constitution includes 22 official regional languages as well. Because language is so critical to communication, having several languages within a country can be a dividing force. Ethnicities are often extremely divisive as well. Conflict between ethnicities in many parts of the world has escalated to genocide or ethnic cleansing.

RELIGIOUS AFFILIATION IN NORTHERN IRELAND, 2011

Derry

NORTHERN IRELAND

Omagh

Belfast

Lisburn

Newry

IRELAND

Areas where Protestants dominate
Areas where Catholics dominate

READING MAPS A research project mapped where Protestants and Catholics resided in Northern Ireland in 2011. ▮ Explain how the map supports the idea that religion has been a centrifugal force in Northern Ireland.

For example, the country of Azerbaijan in western Asia has seen ongoing disputes between ethnic Azerbaijanis and Armenians. Disagreements over territorial issues, specifically the Nagorno-Karabakh region along the border between Armenia and Azerbaijan, have fueled the continuing clashes since the late 1980s, resulting in bloodshed and political and ethnic tension. The Nagorno-Karabakh region was established within Azerbaijan's borders by the Soviet government in the 1920s. Approximately 95 percent of the population living within this region is Armenian. When the Soviet Union collapsed, the region declared independence, and the Armenians and Azerbaijanis have been fighting for control ever since.

Religion has been a centrifugal force in Northern Ireland for many decades, as Catholics and Protestants have fought for control. Much of the conflict has been grounded in politics and cultural identity. Protestants, who have largely identified as British because of their British ancestors, have desired to remain part of the United Kingdom, while the majority of Catholics, who have seen themselves as Irish, has wanted a united Ireland free from British rule.

In the last few decades, violence between the two groups has ceased thanks to an agreement between the British and Irish governments, and most of the political parties

in Northern Ireland, about how Northern Ireland should be governed. An end to clashes isn't the only newer development. A significant demographic shift—a rapid increase of the Catholic minority—has occurred within the country. Geographers cataloged the impact of these changes by using census data to map areas where Protestants and Catholics live. The data reveals the deep divisions that remain in the country. Most Catholic and Protestant children are taught in separate schools, and their families live in segregated neighborhoods. Rivers and other natural features often serve as borders between Catholic and Protestant areas, but there are also human-made borders called peace walls.

GEOGRAPHIC THINKING

1. Explain the linguistic patterns of the United States.

2. Explain how placemaking impacted the Somalis in Minnesota and shaped the cultural landscape.

3. Describe an example of how language, religion, or ethnicity work together to form regions.

4. Compare how one factor can be both a centripetal force and a centrifugal force.

SUMMARY & REVIEW

■ CHAPTER SUMMARY

Culture is the beliefs, values, practices, behaviors, and technologies shared by a society. Elements of a shared cultural practice, or cultural trait, fall into three categories.

- Artifacts are the visible objects and technologies a culture creates.

- Sociofacts are the structures and organizations that influence social behaviors.

- Mentifacts are the central, enduring elements of a culture that reflect its shared ideas, values, knowledge, and beliefs.

Different cultural aspects change and spread at different rates, depending on the degrees of technology and cultural attitudes involved.

- Popular culture reflects widespread behaviors, beliefs, and practices of a society at a given point in time.

- Traditional culture reflects long-established, shared experiences that are passed from generation to generation. There are two prominent cultural attitudes.

  - Ethnocentrism is the tendency of ethnic groups to evaluate other groups according to preconceived ideas originating from their own culture.

  - Cultural relativism is the evaluation of a culture by its own standards.

A cultural landscape is a natural landscape modified by humans, reflecting their cultural beliefs and values.

- Sequent occupance is the notion that successive societies leave behind a collection of evidence about human character and experiences within a geographic region, which shapes the cultural landscape.

- Large cities typically contain many ethnic neighborhoods, which are cultural landscapes within communities of people outside of their areas of origin.

- Traditional architecture and postmodern architecture are two building styles that reflect different cultures, religions, and places in cultural landscapes.

- Religion, a system of spiritual beliefs, greatly impacts cultural landscapes because it drives much of what is hidden beneath the observable surface of culture.

- Language, the carrier of human thoughts and cultural identities, is a distinct system of communication and usually has a literary tradition, or some written form.

Identity is how humans make sense of themselves and how they wish to be viewed by others. Landscape features, land and resource use, and attitudes toward gender shape the use of space in a cultural landscape.

The subjective feelings people associate with a geographic location are known as sense of place. Placemaking is how people collaborate to create a place where they can live, work, play, and learn. Patterns of language, religion, ethnicity, unity, division, centripetal forces, and centrifugal forces contribute to a sense of place, enhance placemaking, and shape the global cultural landscape.

■ KEY TERMS AND CONCEPTS

Use complete sentences to answer the questions.

1. **APPLY CONCEPTUAL VOCABULARY** Consider the terms *centripetal force* and *centrifugal force*. Write a standard dictionary definition for each term. Then provide conceptual definitions—an explanation of how each term is used in the context of this chapter.

2. Explain why geographers often use the metaphor of an iceberg to illustrate the concept of *culture*.

3. Provide examples of how artifacts, sociofacts, and mentifacts can be both similar and different around the world.

4. Explain why some places have stricter cultural norms than other places.

5. Explain the correlation of ethnocentrism with the Wisconsin American Indian Nations Case Study.

6. Define the term *sequent occupance* and provide an example of it.

7. Describe the characteristics of an ethnic neighborhood using an example.

8. Explain why places of worship are often featured prominently in cultural landscapes. Provide an example.

9. How can a person's identity shape a place? Give two examples in your response.

10. Explain the origin of the term *gendered space* and tell how cities are creating safer gendered spaces today.

11. Compare the building styles of traditional architecture and postmodern architecture and how they shape cultural landscapes.

■ INTERPRET GRAPHS

Study the graph and then answer the following questions.

❙ ADHERENTS OF WORLD RELIGIONS, IN BILLIONS (2020 EST.)

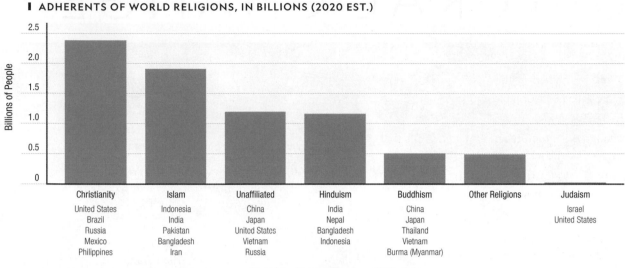

Source: The Pew-Templeton Global Religious Futures Project

12. **IDENTIFY DATA & INFORMATION** What information about religion does the bar graph show?

13. **DESCRIBE SPATIAL PATTERNS** What is spatially significant about the countries with the most adherents?

14. **ANALYZE VISUALS** What generalizations can you make about Hinduism based on the bar graph?

15. **MAKE INFERENCES** What conclusions can you draw about the influence of Christianity on the global cultural landscape?

GEO INQUIRY | YOUR COMMUNITY'S SPACES

Consider how you can use Geo-Inquiry to answer questions about concepts of culture and their impact on your community. Use the steps in the Geo-Inquiry Process below to discover patterns of safe spaces and third places on a local level.

ASK Start with an open-ended Geo-Inquiry question. It may be as simple as: *How might we better communicate safe spaces for LGBTQIA+ members in our community?* Use the Geo-Inquiry Process to expand this question and ask related questions: *What safe spaces or third places exist, if any? Is there a need for more safe spaces or third places in my school or community? Are any groups unintentionally excluded from these spaces?*

COLLECT Describe how you could gather geographic information to answer your questions. Create a map of your community's safe spaces or third places. Interview people who occupy these spaces to find out how they learned about them, how they feel about them, and if there is a need for more spaces. Document your findings.

VISUALIZE Analyze the information you collected. Use the data to identify patterns, find gaps, draw conclusions, and identify needed actions. Organize the information and think about how you can best present it in a format, such as a chart or map, to share with others. Create drafts to help you plan and revise for clarity.

CREATE Create a list of the elements that you will use to tell your Geo-Inquiry story, such as specific images, videos, compelling storylines, and clear charts and graphs. Outline or storyboard your story, then tie all your elements together using a storytelling tool. Focus on ways to tell a Geo-Inquiry story, such as a multimedia presentation that provides data, research, and visuals in a manner that moves the audience to action.

ACT Identify the audience who would benefit most or decisions makers who can implement your proposed action. Consider how you can use social media to expand your project's reach and help implement your proposal.

ASK   COLLECT   VISUALIZE   CREATE   ACT

CHAPTER 7

CULTURAL CHANGE

CRITICAL VIEWING A woman sells goods at the Siti Khadijah market in Malaysia. ▮ How might a region's cuisine reveal details about its culture?

GEOGRAPHIC THINKING What are the causes and consequences of cultural change?

7.1
CULTURAL
DIFFUSION

FEATURE: A Portrait of
Relocation Diffusion

CASE STUDY: African Culture
in Brazil

7.2
PROCESSES OF
CULTURAL CHANGE

CASE STUDY: Fútbol—
A Globalizing Force

NATIONAL GEOGRAPHIC
PHOTOGRAPHER William Allard

7.3
CONSEQUENCES OF
CULTURAL CHANGE

7.1 CULTURAL DIFFUSION

Cultures are not set in stone. Cultural ideas, practices, and innovations change or disappear over time. Cultural change results from both internal pressures within a group of people and through external contact with others. By studying the processes that cause cultural change, geographers can gain a better understanding of culture and its impact on human societies.

RELOCATION DIFFUSION

LEARNING OBJECTIVE
IMP-3.A Define the types of diffusion.

The process by which a cultural trait spreads from one place to another over time is called **diffusion** . A trait often originates in a **cultural hearth** and initially diffuses, or spreads, from there. As you've read, flow is an important concept in human geography. And just as geographers study the flow of humans in migration, they also study how cultural ideas, innovations, and trends flow in spatial patterns. Historically, diffusion occurred through imperialism and colonialism, which drove exploration, military conquest, missionary work, trade, and migration. Today, diffusion continues through some of the same historical ways, but it also occurs through mass media and the internet. Diffusion has introduced customs, traditions, language, technology, means of communication, consumer products, and other aspects of culture to people across the planet. There are two broad categories of diffusion: relocation diffusion and expansion diffusion.

Relocation diffusion, as you read in Chapter 5, is the spread of cultural traits or ideas through the movement, or relocation, of people—either individuals or groups. Throughout history, people migrating to new places have brought artifacts and mentifacts of their culture with them. Religions, for instance, often spread through relocation diffusion as people bring their deeply held beliefs with them and continue to practice the rites and rituals of their faith in their new homes.

Beginning in the late 15th century, as Europeans moved to the Americas, they brought aspects of their culture with them. The languages spoken by most people in North and South America today—Spanish, English, Portuguese, and French—are the result first of relocation diffusion, then expansion diffusion. Europeans also brought Christianity and Judaism, changing the religious beliefs and practices of many with whom they came into contact, often through force and conquest.

Relocation diffusion is also illustrated in the example of the African diaspora, the spread of people of African descent from their ancestral continent to other parts of the world as a result of forced migration. The huge number of people—10 to 12 million—taken from their homes in Africa during the transatlantic slave trade inevitably left its mark on the cultures of the Americas. The men, women, and children brought over on the slave ships carried their cultures with them, and despite the brutal conditions under which they lived, many of their cultural traits and practices survived. They made instruments for playing traditional African music, which is community-based, with everyone participating by playing, singing, or dancing to the rhythmic beats. Aspects of African agricultural practices spread to the Americas through farming techniques, food preparation methods, and specific ingredients. Enslaved Africans popularized new foods such as okra, melons, and bananas and contributed new techniques for farming rice. They made clay pottery, baskets, and clothing with African designs. Over time, some of these cultural traits were adopted by the greater population. Traditional African music influenced the blues and jazz, which went on to influence rock music. The farming techniques the Africans brought with them greatly improved rice production in the South.

Another migration—this one occurring in the aftermath of American slavery—provides an example of relocation diffusion on a regional scale, within a country. As you know, the Great Migration was the internal migration of millions of African Americans from the rural South due to the push factors of racial discrimination, segregation laws, and widespread financial difficulties. Large numbers of African Americans moved to industrialized cities in the Northeast, Midwest, and West between 1916 and 1970. The culture they brought with them—the literature, music, theater, and visual art they created—spread to these new regions as people living in these places adopted some of the cultural traits introduced to them by the migrants.

Relocation diffusion can occur at an even smaller scale as well. When a CEO leaves one company and goes to work for another company, for instance, he or she will often take ideas, tools, or systems that made the original company successful and bring them to the new company. In fact, observers of the business world describe the aspects of a company that affect employees' daily work environment as a "company culture." A positive culture can lead to a more successful company than a negative culture, and a new CEO might be hired specifically to make positive changes to the company culture. These changes occur through a combination of relocation and expansion diffusion.

CRITICAL VIEWING Left: Paintings of Charlie Lewis (top) and Ossa Keeby, two of the former slaves who helped found Africatown. Right: Lewis's great-great-granddaughter Lorna Gail Woods (top) and Keeby's descendant Karliss Hinton. ▌Explain the role that relocation diffusion played in the lives of the Africatown residents pictured in the paintings and photos.

A PORTRAIT OF RELOCATION DIFFUSION

The effects of relocation diffusion as a result of the African diaspora can be seen today in Africatown, Alabama. The town was founded by former slaves who had been brought to the United States on the *Clotilda*—the last known slave ship to arrive in the country. The *Clotilda* landed illegally near Mobile, Alabama in 1860, 52 years after the import of slaves had been outlawed. Transported across the Atlantic Ocean in a clear example of forced migration, the enslaved Africans on the ship formed tight bonds with one another.

After slavery was abolished in 1865, the former slaves worked and saved and pooled their money together to buy land to establish their own community. The inhabitants planted gardens and fruit trees, built a church that faced east toward Africa, and passed their cultural traditions down to their children and their children's children. Africatown is still inhabited by the descendants of these former slaves today, and the sunken remains of the *Clotilda*, which evaded researchers for decades, were discovered in 2019 along the Mobile River.

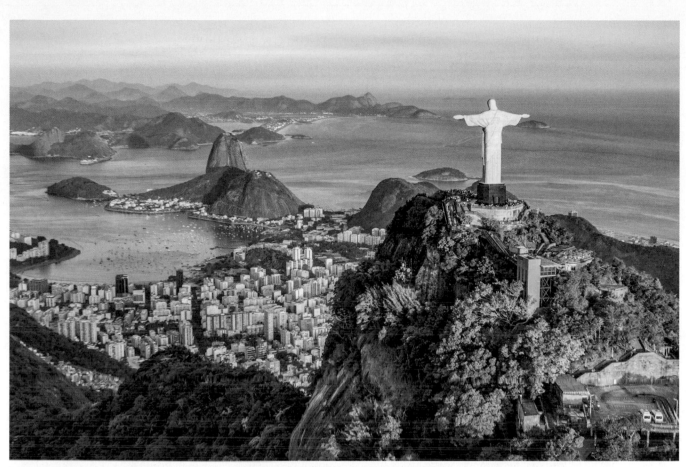

The Christ the Redeemer statue in Rio de Janeiro signifies the relocation diffusion that took place when Portuguese colonists brought their language and religion with them to Brazil in the 1500s. Today, Brazil has the largest Roman Catholic population in the world, with an estimated 126 million Catholic Brazilians.

EXPANSION DIFFUSION

LEARNING OBJECTIVE

IMP-3.A Define the types of diffusion.

Expansion diffusion occurs when an aspect of culture spreads outward from where it originated. As it spreads, the trait also remains in its place of origin—that is, it expands outward from its hearth. The main difference between relocation diffusion and expansion diffusion is that with expansion diffusion, cultural traits move even though the people who are a part of that culture do not relocate. There are three types of expansion diffusion: contagious diffusion, hierarchical diffusion, and stimulus diffusion. The three types differ in the spatial patterns by which an idea or trait spreads and in the mechanisms that trigger the flow.

CONTAGIOUS DIFFUSION **Contagious diffusion** occurs when an idea or cultural trait spreads adjacently, or to people or places that are next to or adjoining one another. Contagious diffusion occurs among people of all social classes and levels of power. An outbreak of a disease, when it spreads through direct person-to-person contact and expands outward to people living nearby, is an example of contagious diffusion. A less destructive example is when a new slang word spreads through a school as more and more students hear their friends and acquaintances say it and begin using it themselves.

Originally, contagious diffusion referred only to the spread of a trait outward from person to person through direct contact. However, technology has changed the ways in which people connect with one another. The internet or social media can cause a song, fad, or idea to spread independent of proximity to its point of origin. The contact between people online is virtual, but a meme can be created by anyone who has access to the internet and spread to everyone that person has contact with online. They, in turn, can spread it to all of their contacts, and on and on.

Because traits that spread through contagious diffusion are available to people without regard to social status, wealth, or power, they can spread quickly and widely. Contagious diffusion is sometimes compared to a wave spreading through a population.

HIERARCHICAL DIFFUSION A hierarchy is a system through which people or groups are ranked one above the other according to their size or status. **Hierarchical diffusion** is the spread of an idea or trait from a person or place of power or authority to other people or places. A cultural trait that becomes popular in a large urban center will spread down the urban hierarchy to mid-sized cities and then on to small cities, towns, and villages. Traits can diffuse hierarchically through people as well. A new fashion trend, for instance, might start when a popular celebrity or public figure introduces a clothing style, hairstyle, or other fad, prompting others to adopt it. Such trends are often then reinterpreted and recreated to be sold more affordably in department stores to the general public.

Professional innovations can spread hierarchically as well. A farmer might adopt a new planting or plowing method that is more effective but can only be adopted by neighboring farms that can afford the new equipment. The innovation then spreads across the region among wealthier farmers. If it becomes popular enough that the equipment becomes cheaper, it could then diffuse to smaller farms.

Hierarchical diffusion can also occur from the bottom of the hierarchy to the top. This is sometimes referred to as reverse hierarchy. Blue jeans, for example, were initially designed for miners during the 1849 California Gold Rush. Soon, cowboys and other laborers were wearing jeans because they could stand up to hard work. The durable garment became a symbol of the American West and the working class, and as such it traveled up the hierarchy to be embraced in the 1950s by actors like Marlon Brando and James Dean. From there, blue jeans traveled back down the hierarchy, becoming popular with teens and college students, and eventually becoming a staple of the American middle-class wardrobe. Today, blue jeans are worn by people around the world. Original blue jeans are still appreciated for their rugged wear, but designer brands have also adopted this aspect of the culture.

STIMULUS DIFFUSION The third type of expansion diffusion— **stimulus diffusion** —occurs when the fundamental idea behind a cultural trait stimulates a new innovation. In stimulus diffusion, the trait itself does not spread, but it triggers an idea that leads to a new cultural trait. In the early 19th century, blacksmith John Deere found that wood and cast-iron plows, common in the eastern United States at that time, didn't work well in the heavier soils of the Illinois prairies. By 1838, in an example of stimulus diffusion and experimentation, he successfully modified the older design into a steel-bladed plow that did the trick—and made his name synonymous with American agriculture. More recently, in 2014 Elon Musk, the CEO of Tesla, a company that makes electric cars, announced that anyone could freely use the company's patents to advance electric car technology. Musk made the decision in hopes

CULTURAL DIFFUSION ONLINE

How does culture diffuse online? Is the spread of an idea over the internet an example of contagious or hierarchical diffusion? The answer is: it depends.

On one level, all online activity is hierarchical, because not everyone has access to the internet, or speaks the language in which a meme or trend is shared. Those who do have an internet connection, however, can access a seemingly infinite amount of information, so the internet is often thought of as a place where everyone is equal. When an idea, trend, or meme is passed between contacts online without regard to status or wealth, it is an example of contagious diffusion. Indeed, the phrase "going viral" refers to an idea spreading over the internet through virtual contact in the same way that a contagious disease spreads through physical contact.

Even online, however, hierarchies exist. A popular social media star has much more influence than the average user. A fashion trend posted to an account with millions of followers can spread around the world quickly, and the opinions of popular influencers might be accepted more readily than opinions shared by acquaintances on social media. This type of expansion—the spread of an idea through an influencer—is an example of hierarchical diffusion.

that his technology will trigger others to come up with innovations to make electric cars better and more popular, fighting climate change as a result.

A MIX OF DIFFUSION TYPES It is useful to learn about the different types of diffusion individually, but in the real world, culture usually spreads through a combination of diffusion types. A cultural trend might start out diffusing hierarchically and then continue to spread through contagious diffusion. For instance, when the major networks first started broadcasting regular television programming in 1947, fewer than two percent of households owned a TV set. It was an expensive luxury that spread through hierarchical diffusion, beginning with large cities and eventually spreading to smaller and smaller cities and towns. When a television station began broadcasting in a town, people would gather to watch in the homes of those who had TVs or in public places like bars. As the medium became more popular and TVs became more affordable, television spread through contagious diffusion, from household to household. By 1956, 70 percent of American households had a TV.

GEOGRAPHIC THINKING

1. Explain how relocation diffusion through forced migration might differ from relocation diffusion through voluntary migration.

2. Introduced by Italian immigrants, pizza spread from Italian neighborhoods of New York City outward to every corner of America. Explain how this spread represents both relocation and expansion diffusion.

3. Compare the three types of expansion diffusion and explain how each is affected by wealth and power.

RELOCATION DIFFUSION

Cultural traits spread through the movement of individuals or groups.

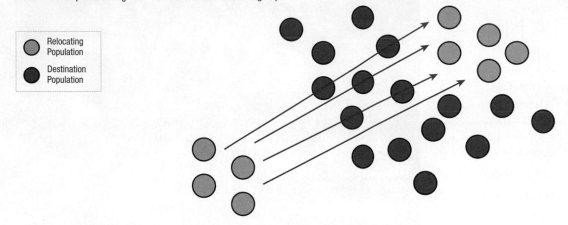

Legend:
- Relocating Population
- Destination Population

EXPANSION DIFFUSION

Cultural traits spread independently of the movement of people.

1. CONTAGIOUS DIFFUSION

Traits spread from person-to-person contact regardless of social class or level of power.

2. HIERARCHICAL DIFFUSION

Traits jump from powerful places or people to other powerful places or people, then spread down the hierarchy (or up from the bottom of a hierarchy to the top).

Legend:
- Hearth
- Early Diffusion
- Later Diffusion
- Non-powerful Place or Person
- Powerful Place or Person

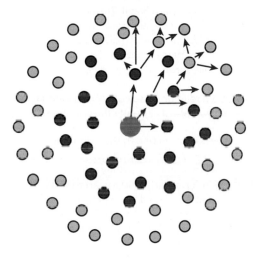
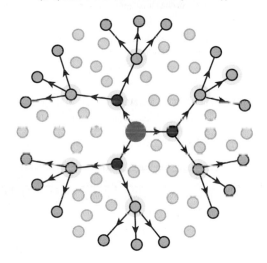

3. STIMULUS DIFFUSION

Traits spread to another culture or region but are modified to adapt to the new culture.

Legend:
- Original Trait
- Early Adaptations
- Later Adaptations

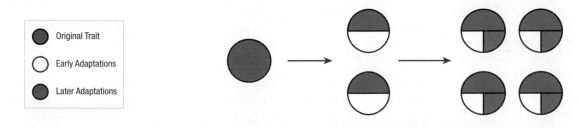

TYPES OF CULTURAL DIFFUSION Cultural traits and ideas can spread across space and time in different ways. In general, culture originates from a cultural hearth, such as an urban area, and spreads to smaller cities and towns. ❚ Explain which type of cultural diffusion results in the greatest change to a cultural idea or trait, and why.

AFRICAN CULTURE IN BRAZIL

THE ISSUE Descendants of the West Africans brought to Brazil as enslaved labor from the 16th–19th centuries have left an indelible mark on the country's vibrant culture, including its Carnival celebrations.

LEARNING OBJECTIVES

IMP-3.A Define the types of diffusion.

SPS-3.A Explain how historical processes impact current cultural patterns.

BY THE NUMBERS

1888

the year Brazil became the last western country to ban slavery

37%

of all Africans enslaved during the transatlantic slave trade were in Brazil

MORE THAN 50%

of Brazilians identify as having African heritage

Source: World Population Review

An African drumming band performs during Carnival in Pelourinho, the historical center of Salvador, Brazil. West African culture remains a dynamic part of Carnival celebrations in the city, as well as in everyday life in Brazil.

THE CITY OF SALVADOR knows how to throw a party. It's the capital of Bahia, a state in northeastern Brazil. The city has about three million residents, but each year over a million more are drawn to its Carnival festival, which goes on for the six days leading up to the Christian observance of Lent. The celebrations include parades, shows, street parties, and the pounding beat of drumming bands that can be heard for miles around. Brazil's diverse culture is on full display during the festivities, and while its history as a Portuguese colony is reflected in the country's language and main religion, many other cultural traits have roots that trace back to West Africa—an example of cultural diffusion through forced migration.

Portuguese settlers in Brazil began the brutal process of importing West Africans as enslaved labor in the 16th century and continued the practice for approximately 300 years. In that time, four million Africans were stolen from their homes, chained and brought to Brazil in slave ships, and forced to work on sugar plantations and in the mining industry. Brazil enslaved more people than any other country—37 percent of all Africans enslaved in that time period—and did not abolish slavery until 1888, the last western country to do so. Today more than half of Brazilians identify themselves as having African heritage.

This heritage is evident in the country's culture, for even when migration is forced and people leave their homes with none of their belongings, they carry their culture in their hearts and minds. And when they arrive at their destination, they continue, as they are able, to play the music, make the food, recreate the fashion, and tell the stories of their homeland. The cultural ideas and traits they bring with them change as they interact with the people in the destination country, combining into a new form of cultural expression with roots in the old. Samba, an African-influenced style of music and dance that is one of the defining features of Carnival, developed in the country's predominantly Black neighborhoods. Candomblé, a religion that mixes Christian and African rituals and traditions, originated in Bahia and today has about two million followers in South America. The elaborate costumes and decorations of Carnival, with their vibrant colors, are influenced by West African cultures as well. ∎

GEOGRAPHIC THINKING

Explain how aspects of Salvador's Carnival celebration are an example of cultural diffusion through forced migration.

7.2 PROCESSES OF CULTURAL CHANGE

Cultural patterns are shaped by processes occurring at global, regional, and local scales. Historically, cultures came into contact with—and altered—one another through colonialism, imperialism, and trade. While these processes are still at work, other processes, such as urbanization and globalization, are currently causing changes to cultural ideas and practices through the media, technology, politics, economics, and social interaction.

HISTORICAL CAUSES OF DIFFUSION

LEARNING OBJECTIVE
SPS-3.A Explain how historical processes impact current cultural patterns.

The cultural patterns seen in the world today have their roots in the past. Countries with strong military and economic power have always imposed elements of their cultures on countries with less power. Trade between different cultures has also facilitated the spread of ideas. Migrations of all kinds have impacted cultures worldwide. The effects of these interactions are observable in cultures around the world.

COLONIALISM AND IMPERIALISM Many countries have sought to gain power, wealth, or other advantages through policies of colonialism and imperialism. As you know, colonialism is when a powerful country establishes settlements in a less powerful country for economic or political gain. Imperialism is a related concept, occurring when a country enacts policies to extend its influence over other countries through diplomacy or force. These two processes have had a strong influence on cultural patterns in the world. The dominance of European countries on the world stage in the 17th, 18th, and 19th centuries, and those countries' policies of colonization and imperialism, reshaped the world map and spread European culture in ways that still resonate today.

For instance, in the 17th century the Netherlands established a colony on the southern tip of Africa as a supply port for Dutch East India Company ships trading with Asia. Settlers moved there to farm the land in order to provide food for the Dutch ships. Because there were no sources of local labor, they brought slaves with them. The Dutch introduced cruel policies against the enslaved and native peoples, as well as new land ownership laws and farming techniques that were advantageous to Dutch settlers. Over the next several decades, Dutch influence spread, giving rise to a new language, Afrikaans, which integrates the languages of the native groups of southern Africa into the Dutch language. The culture of the area was forever changed. Descendants of these original Dutch colonists (along with some of German and French Huguenot descent) established apartheid in South Africa in 1948, a racist policy of segregation that wasn't repealed until 1994.

In the 19th century, European countries increased their imperialist activity, racing to establish colonies across Africa that would give them access to the raw materials found there as well as control over shipping routes and ports. At a conference in Berlin in 1884, the European empires met, with no African members present, and split up Africa to avoid fighting for control. The European countries drew borders through African territories and then took control of the areas within those boundaries, changing the cultures of people throughout Africa. The effect on culture is particularly evident in the languages of varied African countries.

The cultural impact of European imperialism can be seen in Asia as well. The British East India Company, for instance, had taken control of parts of India in the 1700s and ruled most of India by the 1820s. The British government took control of India in 1858 and held power there until it granted the territory independence in 1947, dividing the land into separate countries that are today India, Pakistan, and Bangladesh. The effects of British rule on India's culture are evident in many ways, such as the language (125 million Indians speak English), religion (Christianity is the third most popular religion), and recreation (cricket, soccer, and field hockey, all introduced by the British, are extremely popular).

MILITARY CONQUEST Some of the most significant cultural changes have occurred when powerful military leaders took over new lands. Military conquest can cause cultural change to take place more rapidly than through processes like trade or migration, because the conquerors impose their way of life on the conquered people. In the 300s B.C.E., Alexander the Great spread Greek culture throughout his empire, which at its height extended from Macedonia and Greece into Egypt and northern India. He established cities in the conquered lands, including Alexandria, Egypt, which became a cosmopolitan center of learning. He also encouraged the men of his army to marry the local women. Greek culture became entwined with those local cultures, bringing about changes so significant that historians have a name for it: the Hellenistic Age.

Hundreds of years later, the Spaniards conquered the Aztecs of Mexico and the Inca of Peru. Spanish conquistadors, or conquerors, had many goals, including the discovery of fabled riches, but their main stated goal

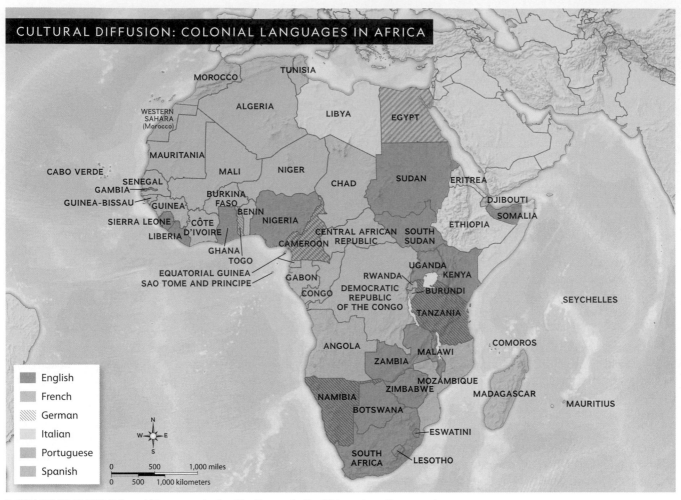

CULTURAL DIFFUSION: COLONIAL LANGUAGES IN AFRICA

Legend:
- English
- French
- German
- Italian
- Portuguese
- Spanish

READING MAPS When Africa was colonized by Europe in the 19th century, European languages became the official language in those African colonies. Today, most Africans speak both colonial languages and indigenous African languages, or a combination of the two. ▌ Explain how the map illustrates cultural diffusion and its impact on Africa during European colonization.

was to spread Christianity. They also spread other aspects of their culture. Today, Spanish is the main language of most of Central and South America, and Catholicism is the most practiced religion.

As global forces—such as the Spanish conquest of much of Central and South America—come to bear on a society, interactions between different cultures can lead to new forms of cultural expression. In this case, Spanish became the region's **lingua franca**, or common language used among speakers of different languages, as the conquered peoples adopted the language of the conqueror. A lingua franca might also develop through more peaceful means, however. Through trade, speakers of different languages might develop a simplified combination of two languages or a third language altogether. And while a lingua franca might become the official language of a country, as Spanish has in many South American countries, many people still speak their indigenous languages as well. Today, English is a lingua franca around the world. The historical expansion of the British Empire, and later the United States' dominance on the world stage, has made English the dominant language in business, political, and cultural transactions

around the globe. It is also the predominant language of the internet, and throughout the world, all airline pilots must communicate in English with air traffic controllers.

Sometimes, rather than leading to the adoption of a common cultural trait, interactions between cultures can result in two or more cultural elements blending together. This process is called **creolization**. It occurs when people incorporate particular elements from an incoming culture and endow them with new meanings. A creole language, for instance, results from the blending of two or more languages that may not include the features of either original language. Haitian Creole is the blend of French and several African languages. (You'll learn more about the spread of language and religion in Chapter 8.)

TRADE Trade brings people together. They interact in order to buy and sell goods, and as you've seen, interaction between people from different places leads to an exchange of ideas, values, technologies, and practices. Geographers examine trade patterns from the past to determine how historical processes impact current cultural patterns.

The Silk Road, an ancient network of trade routes that stretched from East Asia to the Mediterranean, brought about an unprecedented exchange of ideas that transformed cultures from China to Europe in ways that can still be observed today. For instance, along with luxury items such as Chinese silk, Roman glass, and Arabian spices, Buddhism also spread via the Silk Road. The process of religious diffusion was facilitated by the towns that sprang up along the Silk Road, as Buddhist temples were built to attract Buddhist merchants. And as Buddhism spread westward along these trade routes, Christianity spread eastward along the Silk Road through Asia to China.

Silk Road traders from many cultures along the way also helped spread new ideas related to medicine, mathematics, astronomy, and technology. Paper-making methods and printing technology spread from Asia to Europe and gave rise to Gutenberg's printing press, leading to the spread of knowledge and religion. New ship designs and tools such as the astrolabe enabled traders and explorers to travel farther. Seeking new trade routes, European explorers happened upon the Americas, lands previously unknown to them. As European countries scrambled for control of these lands, trade between Europe and the Americas continued to transform cultures on both sides of the Atlantic Ocean.

Today, trade and culture sometimes go hand in hand. For instance, American entertainment, such as movies, television, and music, is popular around the world. And while people in other countries enjoy the boost to the economy that trade with the entertainment industry brings, they sometimes resent the effect the media has on their culture. In order to stop their culture from becoming too Americanized, many countries take measures to ensure that there is room in the marketplace for their own entertainment. Some restrict the number of American films that can be exhibited each year. Others use government funds to subsidize their own film and music industries.

MIGRATION As discussed, migration has helped to shape the patterns and practices of culture through the spread of ideas and cultural traits between countries and regions. Global patterns of language developed in large part because of migration.

The Romance languages, which include French, Italian, Spanish, Portuguese, and Romanian, evolved from Latin, which spread across much of Europe with the expansion of the Roman Empire. As Europeans settled in the Americas, Africa, and Asia, the Romance languages spread throughout the world. Today more than 900 million people speak a Romance language as their first language.

Like other aspects of culture, language is constantly changing. People who migrate to new areas introduce words for unfamiliar things they see or experience. And as they come into contact with people who speak different languages, words or phrases from the foreign language may be folded into the dominant language. The result is that people in different places may speak different dialects of the same language. Isolation can also influence vocabulary and

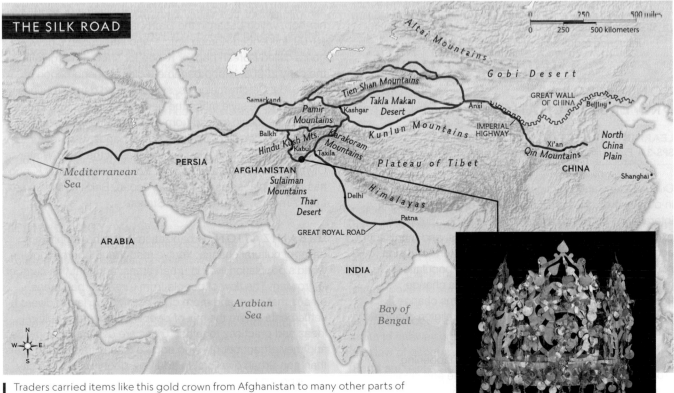

THE SILK ROAD

Traders carried items like this gold crown from Afghanistan to many other parts of the world along the Silk Road. This trade network facilitated not only the spread of goods from places like Southwest Asia, but also the culture of those regions.

Tobler's law is related to the distance decay model, which suggests that the farther people are from the hearth of an idea or cultural trait, the less likely they are to be affected by it. The model also suggests that as an idea or trait travels, the friction of distance takes effect and the idea "decays," or changes. As a cultural trait makes its way from location to location, the people who adopt it might alter it—intentionally or unintentionally. The trait might even die out and disappear altogether. Distance decay explains why people in different parts of the world who speak the same language speak with different accents or why people have different rites and rituals for the same religion. It also explains why people in one region might have a practice or tradition that seems very foreign to those in another part of the world. Arranged marriages, for example, are part of the tradition of many people in South Asia but are highly unusual in the United States today.

Because of time-space compression, distance decay no longer has the same impact on cultural interaction that it once did. Cultural convergence, therefore, occurs much faster today than in the past. Remember that time-space compression describes the shrinking of the world due to improvements in communication and transportation technologies. It shows how technology has overcome the friction of distance by shortening the time it takes to travel or communicate between two places, making places seem closer together. With each progression in technology, ideas flow faster, and people and goods move more quickly. Their values, ideologies, behaviors, arts, and customs begin to reflect these interactions, driving cultural convergence. As globalization, communication, and transportation technologies make interactions easier and more frequent, cultures often share traits and mimic one another.

Cultural convergence can be observed in the ways in which aspects of Hispanic culture have spread to the United States. Quinceañeras, which you read about in Chapter 6, are popular among Hispanics living in the United States. During the Christmas season, the soft glow of luminarias—traditional Mexican lanterns—illuminate pathways, squares, and churches in many places in the Southwest. And Tex-Mex food, which evolved along the border of the United States and Mexico, is an Americanized version of Mexican cuisine, adapting spicy Spanish, Mexican, and Native American flavors.

CULTURAL DIVERGENCE

LEARNING OBJECTIVE
SPS-3.A Explain how historical processes impact current cultural patterns.

Just as increased interaction can cause cultures to become more similar, conflicting beliefs or other barriers can cause two cultures to become less similar. This process is called **cultural divergence**. Divergence can happen when a person or group moves away from their core culture and is exposed to new cultural traits.

Contemporary drivers of change, most notably communication technologies, can cause cultural divergence. Access to technology may vary considerably from one culture to another. As technology speeds up cultural change, the divide will grow between people who have smartphones, the internet, and other technologies and those who lack these technologies. In addition, different cultures may view new technologies differently. Some cultures may reject new technologies, contributing to cultural divergence. The Amish people, a traditional Christian group in North America, do not use many conveniences of modern technology, such as cars, telephones, and even electricity, because they believe these technologies have a negative effect on community and family life.

Divergence can also happen due to physical barriers, such as mountains or rivers, which might separate groups of people living in different parts of a cultural region. As time passes, geographers observe that each group may develop different cultural traits. For example, the indigenous peoples of the islands of Polynesia are separated by the Pacific Ocean and by the politics of the countries that control particular islands or groups of islands. The culture of Polynesians in New Zealand differs greatly from that of Polynesians living in Hawaii or Samoa. The cultures of the different islands evolved differently in response to their particular physical geographies and natural resources, as well as colonizing forces, particularly Britain's annexation of New Zealand in 1840.

BARRIERS TO DIFFUSION Besides physical barriers like mountains, rivers, oceans, deserts, swamps, and rain forests, cultural and political barriers can slow or stop the spread of culture as well. Cultural barriers include taboos or bans on certain practices. In the Hindu religion, cows are sacred, so it is a taboo to eat beef. McDonalds found a way around this barrier in India by developing a special menu with vegetarian items. Muslims are banned from drinking alcohol. Language can act as a cultural barrier to diffusion as well. People cannot adopt a cultural idea or trait if they don't understand the language in which it is communicated.

Political barriers include policies and borders. For instance, a country that allows free expression and does not place limits on communication technologies like the internet will be much more open to the diffusion of new cultural traits than a country that places restrictions on speech and technology.

GEOGRAPHIC THINKING

3. Explain how communication and transportation technology have affected the distance decay model.

4. Describe how religion can be a strong force of cultural divergence.

CASE STUDY

FÚTBOL—A GLOBALIZING FORCE

THE ISSUE The popularity of soccer transcends geopolitical boundaries.

LEARNING OBJECTIVE
SPS-3.A Explain how historical processes impact current cultural patterns.

Megan Rapinoe (far right) helped lead the United States to victory in the 2019 FIFA Women's World Cup in Lyon, France—a match watched by viewers around the world.

BY THE NUMBERS

3.5 BILLION

people watched the 2018 Men's World Cup

22%

more U.S. viewers watched the 2019 Women's Final than watched the 2018 Men's Final

4%

of the world's population actively play soccer

211

member countries belong to FIFA

Source: FIFA

SOCCER ... FOOTBALL ... FÚTBOL ... It's called different things in different parts of the world, but this sport is loved around the globe. According to FIFA, soccer's official governing body, over 265 million people play the sport. Recent surveys show that more than four in ten people consider themselves fans, making soccer the world's most popular sport. In some countries, more than 75 percent of survey respondents say they follow soccer.

International rules for soccer were officially set in 1863, but soccer was already being played in countries across the globe. It spread from its hearth in England through trade and colonialism. By the time the colonial era ended, the sport had become an integral part of the culture in many of England's former colonies. One of the reasons for soccer's popularity is that it can be adapted to local circumstances. In many peripheral countries, children make balls out of whatever materials are available and play on abandoned fields or lots. The game can be learned and played for free, and yet the pros play in stadiums that hold as many as 100,000 fans. In 2019, the three highest paid athletes in the world were soccer players.

FIFA has 211 member countries, each of which has leagues at all levels. The result is a common culture grounded in the sport. Refugees who move from one part of the world to another take comfort in soccer as a common bond. Elite players might migrate to play in a league a country—or even a continent—away. Many professional teams have fans who live halfway around the world.

Every four years, players from around the world join national teams to participate in the World Cup. The Men's World Cup has been held since 1930, and the Women's World Cup since 1991. Countries compete to host the tournaments, which are attended by hundreds of thousands of fans and watched by millions. Worldwide, more than 3.5 billion people watched at least some part of the 2018 Men's World Cup, with 1 billion tuning in for the final match between France and Croatia. The 2019 Women's World Cup Final had 22 percent more U.S. viewers than the men's final, with 14.3 million U.S. viewers watching the United States defeat the Netherlands. Soccer, football, or fútbol—whichever name you prefer—is a globalizing force that has created a common culture that crosses boundaries. ∎

GEOGRAPHIC THINKING

Identify a question that you might pose to determine whether the popularity of soccer will continue to grow.

William Allard's photos put people front and center, allowing viewers to make their own connections across cultures.

LEARNING OBJECTIVE

SPS-3.A Explain how historical processes impact current cultural patterns.

INTRODUCING PEOPLE ACROSS CULTURES

For more than 50 years as a National Geographic photographer, William Allard has been known for his vivid, memorable portrayals of people in their daily lives. "I really believe if you can make that picture well enough, you can introduce someone who might be a continent removed, a language removed—somehow that viewer can get the feeling that they know something about the person in the picture," he says.

On assignment in 1969 to photograph Surprise Creek, a Hutterite community in central Montana, Allard connected deeply with the families he met. The Hutterite religious group arose from the same movement as the Amish, and like the Amish they live apart from mainstream U.S. culture. The first Hutterites arrived in North America in the 1870s, and today hundreds of Hutterite communities, called colonies, dot the northwestern United States and southwestern Canada. Hutterites are guided by a strong, Bible-based faith and adhere to traditional ways of dress and behavior, including firmly defined roles for men and women. At the same time, they do not avoid technology to the same extent as the Amish. They use the latest in agricultural machinery on their farms, have televisions in some colonies' common areas, and some colony members even maintain a website about Hutterite life.

In 2005, Allard photographed and wrote another article about the Hutterites of Surprise Creek. It was a personal essay about his friendship with colony members, and it recounted the heartfelt support they offered when Allard learned his son had died after a battle with cancer. Sharing his own emotions in words and pictures, Allard once again introduced viewers to the people of a unique American culture.

CRITICAL VIEWING According to Allard, Hutterite children are great at entertaining themselves, despite the fact that TVs and computers aren't allowed in homes. ▮ Explain the degree to which the Hutterite community represents an example of cultural divergence.

CRITICAL VIEWING Top: No matter the activity, Hutterite girls wear traditional dresses or skirts and head scarves. Bottom: Guests blow bubbles at a Hutterite wedding reception. Weddings are celebrated with a shivaree—a big, joyous meal with singing. Explain how these photographs illustrate the cultural processes at work in the Hutterite community.

7.3 CONSEQUENCES OF CULTURAL CHANGE

By now you should understand how colonialism, imperialism, globalization, and urbanization have impacted—and continue to impact—cultural patterns. Geographers also identify ways in which cultural diffusion affects societies as people and groups adopt or reject the cultural artifacts, sociofacts, and mentifacts they come into contact with.

ACCULTURATION

LEARNING OBJECTIVE
SPS-3.B Explain how the processes of diffusion result in changes to the cultural landscape.

When cultures come together, either through migration or some form of expansion diffusion, one effect is **acculturation**, where people within one culture adopt some of the traits of another while still retaining their own distinct culture. It often occurs as the result of prolonged contact between two or more cultures and can happen at a group or individual level.

Acculturation can occur with almost any cultural trait. It is often discussed in terms of a minority culture that adopts elements of a majority culture. Immigrants to a new country, for instance, go through a process of adapting to their new cultural context—they often learn the language, wear the fashions, and follow some of the customs of their adopted

country. In the process of taking on these new traits, some aspects of the original culture can be lost over time. As the graphs illustrate, 97 percent of Hispanic immigrants speak Spanish to their children at home, while 71 percent of second-generation Hispanic immigrants share their native language with their children. The number falls to less than half for third-generation immigrants and beyond.

Fashion offers a clear example of acculturation. Muslim women who immigrate to a Western country from a Muslim-majority country might adopt aspects of their new culture by wearing many of the popular fashion trends of their adopted country but still retain their own culture by continuing to wear the traditional hijab.

Destination countries experience acculturation as well. Currywurst, a popular food sold by street vendors in Berlin, Germany, combines a traditional German sausage with curry powder—a spice from India—and ketchup, which originated in the United States.

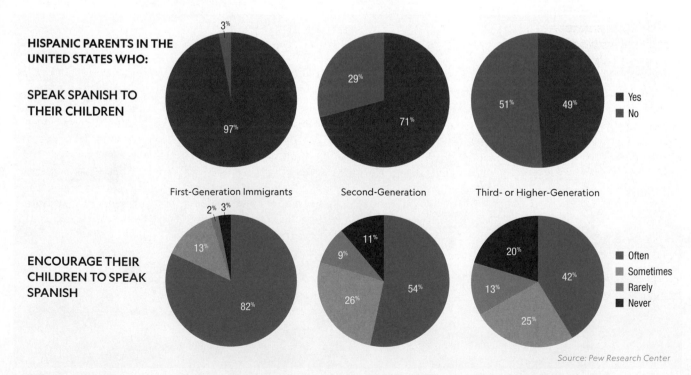

Source: Pew Research Center

CRITICAL VIEWING Acculturation has caused the number of Spanish-speaking Hispanics in the United States to decline. Notice that the graphs show declining numbers of both Hispanic parents who speak Spanish to their children (top) and Hispanic parents who encourage their children to speak Spanish (bottom). ▮ Describe how the two sets of graphs relate to each other, and explain the overall trends depicted in the graphs.

Effects of Acculturation

Integration	**Assimilation**	
Follows practices of both culture of origin and host culture	Follows practices of host culture; rejects practices of culture of origin	**Does the individual adopt the traits of his or her new culture?**
Low stress predicted	Moderate stress predicted	
Separation/Segregation	**Marginalization**	
Follows practices of culture of origin; rejects practices of host culture	Rejects practices of both culture of origin and host culture	
Moderate stress predicted	High stress predicted	

Yes ←——————————→ No

Does the individual maintain his or her cultural heritage?

The table shows the results of cultural psychologist John W. Berry's research on acculturation.

Geographers studying acculturation point out the complicated nature of the process. Factors such as age, personality, upbringing, education, and many others determine how comprehensively immigrants incorporate a new culture into their life. Some immigrants adopt the receiving culture wholeheartedly and drop as much of their heritage culture as possible, while others go in the opposite direction, holding onto as much of the culture they grew up with as possible. Some adopt elements of the new and retain elements of the old, and some marginalized immigrants reject both the receiving and heritage cultures. Cultural psychologist John W. Berry studied the ways in which individuals choose to acculturate and the effects of these choices. Berry found that no matter how people attempt to handle the collision of two or more cultures in their lives, they will experience some stress. Those who integrated elements of both their original and adopted cultures into their lives experienced the least amount of stress, and those who rejected both cultures experienced the most. People who accepted the adopted culture and rejected their original culture, and people who retained their original culture and rejected the new culture, both experienced moderate amounts of stress.

ASSIMILATION

LEARNING OBJECTIVE
SPS-3.B Explain how the processes of diffusion result in changes to the cultural landscape.

Assimilation is a category of acculturation in which the interaction of two cultures results in one culture adopting almost all of the customs, traditions, language, and other cultural traits of the other. An individual or group that has fully assimilated into a culture will be indistinguishable socially and culturally from others in the culture. It is the most comprehensive form of acculturation, and it might happen voluntarily or be forced upon a group by a dominant culture. But since it involves replacing deeply held beliefs and cultural practices, complete assimilation is rare.

In Chapter 6, you read about the U.S. government removing American Indian children from their families and forcing them to attend boarding schools where they had to speak English and take on English names. This is a very clear case of forced assimilation. Sometimes, however, the line between forced and encouraged assimilation can be blurry. To encourage immigrants to assimilate, Germany requires them to pass an oral and written language test for permanent residency and citizenship.

Voluntary assimilation can occur when it is advantageous for an immigrant group to fit in with its adopted culture. When Europeans immigrated to the United States in the 1800s, they often faced prejudice from anti-immigrant groups. By assimilating into the culture, they were more likely to find employment and avoid persecution.

The downside of assimilation is the loss of cultural identity—the traditions, languages, holidays, and practices that make a culture unique. Historically, there are many examples in which colonial forces and imperialism have minimized or banned cultural traditions. Whole languages have faded out completely as people from colonized groups have been forced to learn the colonizer's language. But assimilation can happen in a less extreme manner as well. Traditions might be lost as generations die off and children of immigrants naturally absorb the practices of the adopted culture.

SYNCRETISM

LEARNING OBJECTIVE
SPS-3.B Explain how the process of diffusion results in changes to the cultural landscape.

Sometimes traits from two or more cultures blend together to form a new custom, idea, value, or practice. This process of innovation combining different cultural features into something new is called **syncretism**. Cultural syncretism is an effect of diffusion that can occur through circumstances such as immigration, military conquest, marriages between groups, and others. The result is a combination of two cultures to create new ideas, values, or practices.

Religious syncretism is common around the world. Indeed, as many religions found a foothold in new areas, they incorporated traditional customs into their rites, rituals, and beliefs. Santería, for instance, is a religion that developed in Cuba as a syncretic hybrid of a traditional African religion and Roman Catholicism. Ethnic Yorubans of West Africa who were enslaved and transported to Cuba brought with them a religion in which practitioners worship deities called *orishas*, who are thought to be messengers between humans and the divine. The religion was influenced by Roman Catholicism, which was already present in Cuba, and developed into Santería, which blends the *orishas* with Roman Catholic saints. Since its development in Cuba, the syncretic religion has spread through relocation and expansion diffusion to groups of people in Latin America and the United States.

Cultural syncretism is often evident in celebrations. Halloween, for instance, has its roots in both Christian and pagan practices. In Mexico, the Day of the Dead is celebrated from October 31 to November 2 to coincide with two Catholic feast days, but the festival's origins are rooted in traditional celebrations of indigenous peoples.

Syncretism occurs in music as well, as new musical styles often combine the musical traditions of several different cultures. Bluegrass music, which was developed in the Appalachian region of the United States, fuses Irish and Scottish musical traditions with African-American influences. As the popularity of bluegrass spread across the United States and to other parts of the world, younger bluegrass musicians incorporated influences from rock music.

MULTICULTURALISM

LEARNING OBJECTIVE
SPS-3.B Explain how the processes of diffusion result in changes to the cultural landscape.

Sometimes diverse cultures coexist within a shared space. People in these spaces do not belong solely to one culture or another. They may share some cultural features with others around them while retaining some of their original cultural traits. This **multiculturalism** often occurs in large cities, where people from many different cultures live in close proximity. The United States is a classic example of a multicultural country. Although Americans share a dominant culture based on democratic ideals, there are many different ethnicities that retain aspects of their own cultures, as evident in the varied cuisines, religions, arts, and languages found within the country.

Multiculturalism can create an atmosphere of acceptance and lead to a rich, vibrant blend of cultural traits. In Canada, for instance, multiculturalism is an official policy. In 1971, the government adopted the stance that multiculturalism was a fundamental right of all citizens, and that by keeping their cultural identities and taking pride in their ancestry, all Canadians would become more open and accepting of diverse cultures. This climate of tolerance has contributed to an influx of skilled workers and foreign investment that has bolstered Canada's economy. In addition, the marriage rate between native-born Canadians and immigrants has risen and immigrants report approximately the same level of satisfaction with their lives in Canada as native-born citizens.

The coexistence of cultures is not always easy. Sometimes people can feel caught between two cultures. These difficulties are typical of cultural changes caused by diffusion, and their severity depends on a range of factors, such as the degree of cultural difference. In Australia, a recent study of immigrant families from Africa, Burma, Nepal, India, Afghanistan, Bangladesh, and Iraq found that many immigrants struggled as they attempted to balance the need to acculturate with the desire to retain their culture. In particular, researchers noted challenges that relate to the clash between Western ideals and the traditional values of the countries of origin.

Young women celebrate *Día de los Muertos*, or Day of the Dead, by dressing up and painting their faces. Throughout Mexico, and in U.S. locations where people of Hispanic descent live, people honor family members who have passed away by singing, dancing, and holding parades and parties during this holiday.

In London, Ontario, people from diverse cultures take part in a Canadian citizenship ceremony to celebrate Canada Day. Multiculturalism is an accepted and celebrated part of life in Canada.

CULTURAL APPROPRIATION

Cultural appropriation is the act of adopting elements of another culture. It is usually used to describe the adoption by a dominant culture of one or more elements of a minority culture. The term was coined in the 1960s to critique the effects of colonialism, and it is used today to describe any intentional adoption of cultural traits of another culture. The term is most often used to describe instances when such adoption is inappropriate or out of context.

Cultural appropriation is controversial. Some people complain that it is disrespectful to adopt cultural traits that have meaning to a group of people without fully understanding or embracing the meaning behind these traits. In some cases, participating in a custom, tradition, or celebration has sparked cultural debate, as has wearing the clothing or hairstyles of another culture. The cultural appropriation controversy often gets attention at Halloween, as people's choice of costumes may reinforce racial, ethnic, or cultural stereotypes.

Not everyone agrees that cultural appropriation should be avoided, however. Some people claim that concerns about cultural appropriation demonstrate an oversensitivity. Others argue that the appropriation of cultural traits is a natural aspect of positive change, as cultures "try on" the traits of others.

The cultures of Africa and Asia are **collectivist cultures**, where people are expected to conform to collective responsibility within the family and to be obedient to and respectful of elder family members. These expectations are at odds with the spirit of individualism and independence of the culture of Australia. The disparity between these sets of values can make it difficult for young people to assimilate into the new culture and can lead to conflict at home. The fact that these issues are less obvious than other challenges of acculturation, such as learning a new language, means that they can be even more difficult to overcome.

GEOGRAPHIC THINKING

1. Compare acculturation and assimilation.

2. Identify and describe the advantages and disadvantages of multiculturalism. Do the benefits outweigh the downsides? Explain.

3. Explain whether Australia's problems with multiculturalism would be solved by adding a government policy of acceptance and tolerance like Canada's. Why or why not?

4. Explain how cultural appropriation is different from acculturation.

CHAPTER 8
SPATIAL PATTERNS OF LANGUAGE AND RELIGION

CRITICAL VIEWING In 2016, the Tunisian-French artist known as eL Seed painted a mural across a group of 50 buildings in one of the poorest neighborhoods in Cairo, Egypt. The mural is Arabic calligraphy and it quotes a Coptic Christian bishop: "If one wants to see the light of the sun, he must first wipe his eyes." ▮ In what ways do both language and religion play a role in the mural?

GEOGRAPHIC THINKING How do language and religion affect each other's spread?

8.1
PATTERNS OF LANGUAGE

8.2
THE DIFFUSION OF LANGUAGE

CASE STUDY: French or English in Quebec?

8.3
PATTERNS OF RELIGION

NATIONAL GEOGRAPHIC EXPLORER Wade Davis

CASE STUDY: Shared Sacred Sites

8.4
UNIVERSALIZING AND ETHNIC RELIGIONS

8.1 PATTERNS OF LANGUAGE

More than 7,000 distinct languages are spoken in the world today. Geographers group these languages according to various factors, including their shared origins and how they have evolved. Comparing languages and studying their history is a window into the interactions of people over space and time.

LANGUAGE AND CULTURE

LEARNING OBJECTIVE
PSO-3.D Explain patterns and landscapes of language, religion, ethnicity, and gender.

Language is an important vehicle by which culture is transmitted and preserved. Through language, whether oral or written, a culture's values, beliefs, traditions, and norms are shared and passed down. Language can identify and differentiate a culture, unifying the people who speak a common tongue and separating them from those who speak other languages. For example, the hundreds of millions of people in the world who speak Arabic share a common bond, whether they come from Saudi Arabia, Nigeria, the United States, or New Zealand. The differences among languages reflect the differences among cultures, and language is sometimes used to highlight those differences. In 2019, Ukraine's parliament enacted a law making Ukrainian the official state language. The law called for any print media published in Russian (but not English) to also be published in an equal number of copies in Ukrainian. The law was aimed at diminishing the use of Russian and weakening the spread of Russian media in Ukraine, while strengthening the Ukrainian culture by protecting the use of its language.

Language and culture both reflect and shape our ways of life. The Kuuk Thaayorre, an Aboriginal people living in northern Australia, use their words for north, south, east, and west to describe the location of people and objects. They do not have words such as *left*, *right*, *in front*, or *behind*. While an English speaker might refer to his or her left hand, a Kuuk Thaayorre individual refers to the north, south, east, or west hand—depending on the direction he or she faces. These two approaches of spatial thinking are affected by both cultural differences and the language English speakers and the Kuuk Thaayorre have available to them.

As the needs of a culture change, so does its language. Throughout history, people have created and borrowed words to describe new experiences and encounters that are made possible through migration, trade opportunities, and technological advances. For example, the term *text* has evolved to refer to the way people share messages by cell phone. As people migrate, their native languages intermingle, and new languages evolve. Occasionally, the language brought by migrants to a different region even replaces the original language of that region entirely.

Linguists and geographers study the methods and sequences of the diffusion of different languages, looking for connections between languages that will help describe human movement and development. Mapping the locations of where different languages are spoken is an important step in seeking connections among them. A system for comparing and categorizing languages aids this process.

CATEGORIZING LANGUAGES

LEARNING OBJECTIVE
IMP-3.B Explain what factors lead to the diffusion of universalizing and ethnic religions.

While languages like Spanish and Portuguese are distinct, speakers of these two languages can usually understand each other because the languages are closely related. Linguists use the similarities and differences among languages to organize them into categories with increasing degrees of differentiation from a common language. From closest to the common language to farthest from the common language, the levels of organization are (in order): families, branches, groups, and dialects.

LANGUAGE FAMILIES A **language family** is the largest grouping of related languages and includes those languages that share a common ancestral language from a particular hearth or origin. Ancestral languages are not extant, meaning they are not being actively used anymore. In fact, they are not even identifiable from written records because they developed in ancient times before any culture developed a writing system. Therefore, linguists infer the existence of these ancient languages based on similarities in grammar and root words in existing languages, rather than based on clear written evidence. The first language family to be proposed was Indo-European—a diverse language family that includes most of the languages of Europe and many languages of South and Southwest Asia, ranging from Hindi to German, for example. Indo-European was described by a British scholar in the 1780s based on similarities he found between Greek, Latin, and Sanskrit, an ancient language of South Asia.

Ethnologue—a respected organization that catalogs languages—has identified 142 language families. Six of those are major language families, and together they account for 63 percent of all living languages and 85 percent of the world's population. Nearly 6 billion people speak a language that is included in the six major language families. Indo-European languages, with more than 3.2 billion speakers, make up the largest language family with the widest distribution. This family includes speakers in North America, South America, Europe, and South Asia, followed by the nearly 1.4 billion speakers of Sino-Tibetan languages in East and Southeast Asia.

Some languages are not assigned a language family. An isolated language, or **isolate**, has no known historic or linguistic relationship with any other known language. Isolates may occur because related languages have gone extinct. Basque—the native language of about 1 million people living in the Basque region of northeastern Spain and southwestern France—is one such example. Huave, an American Indian language of the Oaxaca state in Mexico, is another. The rugged mountainous terrain of each of these regions has helped to isolate each community and preserve its languages.

LANGUAGE BRANCHES The next level in the language hierarchy is the **language branch**. This collection of languages within a family share a common origin and were separated from other branches in the same family thousands of years ago. Languages among various branches may show some similarities in grammatical structure, but are so distinct that speakers of languages from two branches cannot understand each other. For example, in the Indo-European family, the Romance branch—which derives from Latin and includes French, Italian, Spanish, and Portuguese—is very different from the Germanic branch, which includes German, English, Dutch, and the Scandinavian languages. Both of those branches differ significantly from the Slavic branch, which includes Russian, Polish, Czech, and Bulgarian. All three of these branches have a distinct geographic distribution, with the Germanic languages found mainly in northern Europe, the Romance languages largely in southern Europe, and the Slavic languages mostly in eastern Europe.

Language is closely tied to culture, as evidenced by this signboard of ads for retail stores written in Hangul, the language of South Korea. The name of one American business, Baskin-Robbins, appears in English.

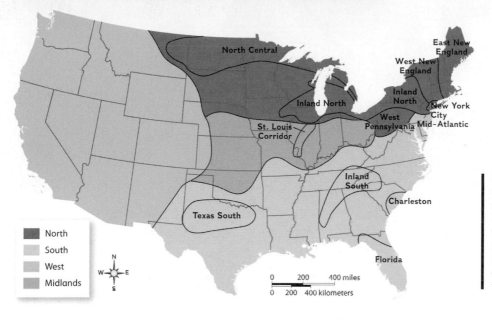

North Central
East New England
West New England
Inland North
New York City
Inland North
West Pennsylvania
Mid-Atlantic
St. Louis Corridor
Inland South
Charleston
Texas South
Florida

North
South
West
Midlands

N
W   E
S

0   200   400 miles
0   200   400 kilometers

READING MAPS The contiguous United States has four main dialect regions: North, South, West, and Midlands. Subdialect regions are areas within a larger dialect region that share certain dialect characteristics. ▮ Describe two patterns of language development that you can infer from the map.

LANGUAGE GROUPS **Language groups** are languages within a branch that share a common ancestor in the relatively recent past and have vocabularies with a high degree of overlap. Speakers of different languages within a language group will recognize many similar words in each other's languages. Using the example of Spanish and Portuguese again, speakers of these two languages typically can understand each other because Spanish and Portuguese belong to the same language group within the Romance language branch.

DIALECTS Language branches and groups are divided further into individual languages and dialects. A dialect is a variation of a standard language distinguished by differences in pronunciation, degree of rapidity in speech, word choice, and spelling. Speakers of the same language sometimes talk with a unique dialect. Various Spanish dialects are spoken throughout regions of Spain and in Latin American countries. So a native resident of Spain will understand a native resident of Mexico but may use distinct pronunciation for some of the same words. For example, the Spanish word *guagua* refers either to a baby or a bus depending on the speaker's dialect. Similar variations in words and meanings exist in all countries and across all languages.

English has numerous dialects, a result of the large number of primarily English-speaking countries distributed around the world, including Australia, the United States, those in the Caribbean, and, of course, those in the United Kingdom. Both migration and isolation play a role in diversifying the English dialect spoken in each of these countries and within regions in the countries.

The migration of colonists from Europe to North America during the 17th century contributed to the American English dialects. The drawl, or long, drawn-out vowels, characteristic of the southern dialect reflects the speech of southern England, source of the first southern settlers. African Americans formed their own dialect by mixing English and their native West African languages. Other groups who came to the English colonies, like the Scots-Irish settlers of Appalachia or Germans who settled in Pennsylvania, contributed to the development of regional dialects as well.

As people moved west, the dialects that had developed in the original colonies blended to create a less distinct western accent. Immigrants of the 19th and 20th centuries, including the Irish, Scandinavians, Italians, and Eastern European Jews, influenced the dialects that developed both along the Atlantic coast and inland. Expansion north from Mexico into areas from Texas to California that had originally been settled by Spanish speakers influenced the dialects of the Southwest. The separation of English speakers across oceans works to preserve the differences in the English language, but that may be short-lived. Communication technologies and social media continue to transform the English language by allowing constant interaction among people who speak a multitude of different languages.

GEOGRAPHIC THINKING

1. Describe how and why language differentiates one culture from another.

2. Explain why languages change as cultures change. Give two examples as part of your answer.

3. Explain how the categorization of languages provides insights into human history.

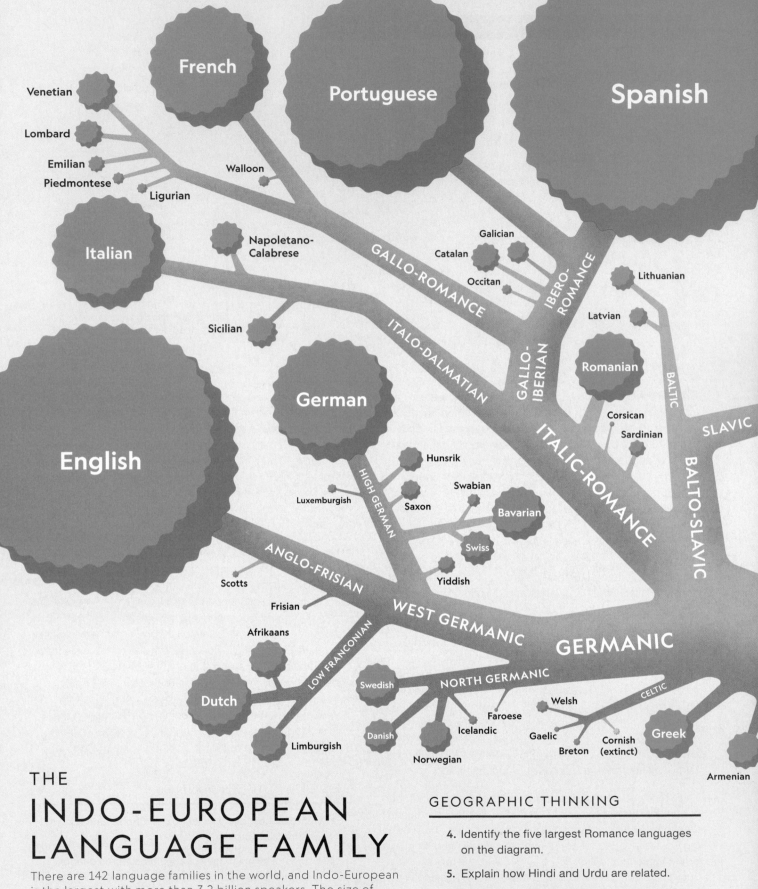

THE
INDO-EUROPEAN
LANGUAGE FAMILY

There are 142 language families in the world, and Indo-European is the largest with more than 3.2 billion speakers. The size of the leaves on the diagram approximates how many people speak that language and not every Indo-European language is represented.

GEOGRAPHIC THINKING

4. Identify the five largest Romance languages on the diagram.

5. Explain how Hindi and Urdu are related.

6. Explain how the diagram illustrates the increasing differentiation of languages as one moves from ancestral languages to dialects.

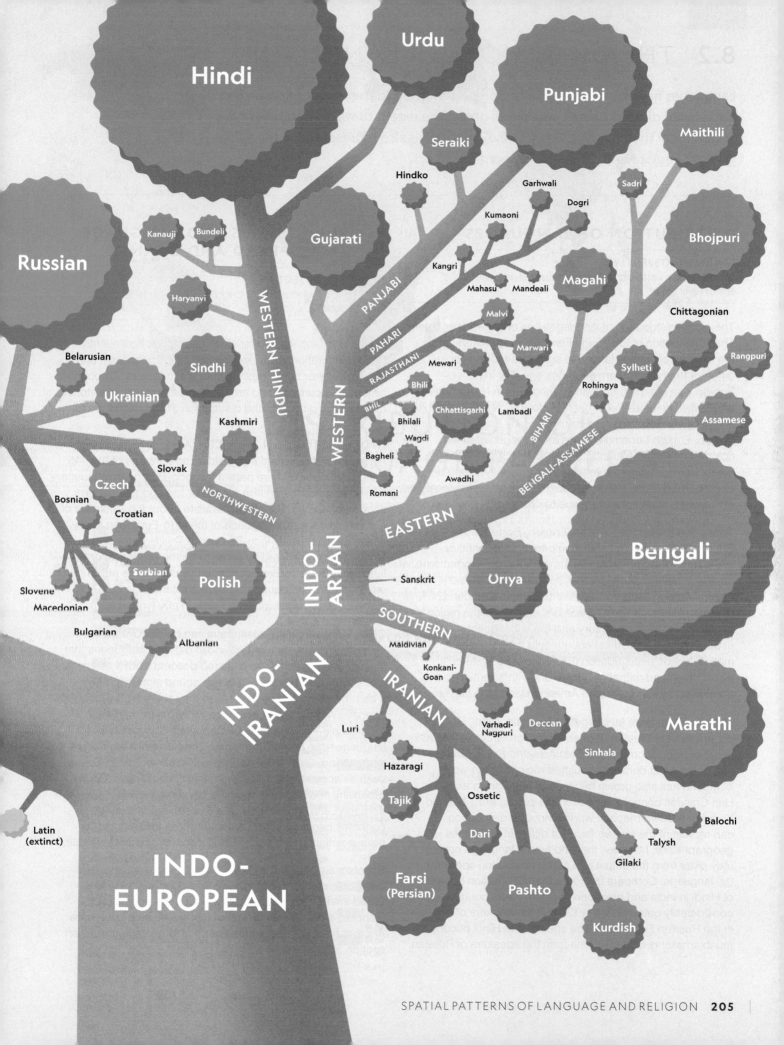

Hindi

Urdu

Punjabi

Seraiki

Maithili

Hindko

Garhwali

Sadri

Bhojpuri

Russian

Kanauji

Bundeli

Gujarati

Dogri

Kumaoni

WESTERN HINDU

PANJABI

Magahi

Haryanvi

Kangri

PAHARI

Mahasu

Mandeali

Chittagonian

Belarusian

Sindhi

RAJASTHANI

Malvi

Sylheti

Rangpuri

Ukrainian

Kashmiri

BHIL

Mewari

Marwari

Rohingya

WESTERN

Bhili

Assamese

Slovak

NORTHWESTERN

Bhilali

Chhattisgarhi

Lambadi

BIHARI

Czech

Bagheli

Wagdi

Bosnian

Croatian

Romani

Awadhi

BENGALI-ASSAMESE

EASTERN

Bengali

Slovene

Serbian

Polish

INDO-
ARYAN

Sanskrit

Oriya

Macedonian

Bulgarian

Albanian

SOUTHERN

Maldivian

Marathi

INDO-
IRANIAN

Konkani-
Goan

IRANIAN

Varhadi-
Nagpuri

Deccan

Luri

Sinhala

Hazaragi

Tajik

Ossetic

Balochi

Latin
(extinct)

Dari

Talysh

Gilaki

INDO-
EUROPEAN

Farsi
(Persian)

Pashto

Kurdish

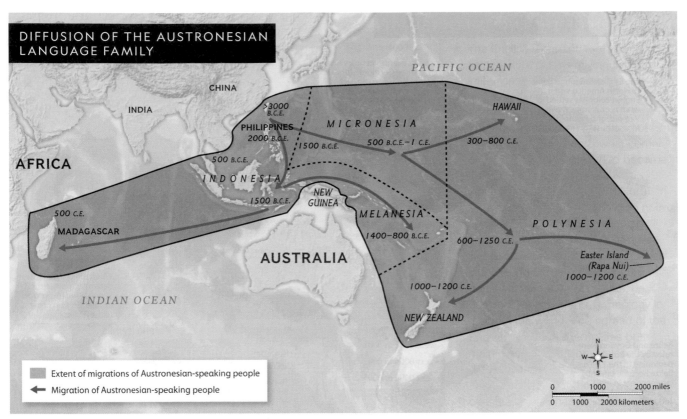

DIFFUSION OF THE AUSTRONESIAN LANGUAGE FAMILY

READING MAPS The Austronesian language family has spread among many islands of different regions. ❚ How does the map support the idea that geographic proximity facilitates the diffusion of language? In what way does the Austronesian language family example also offer a counterargument?

Ocean and colonizing Madagascar in the first century C.E. Africans didn't sail to Madagascar until centuries later. The Austronesian languages had been firmly established on the island by the time Africans arrived, and that language family still prevails in Madagascar today.

IMPACTS OF LANGUAGE DIFFUSION

LEARNING OBJECTIVE
IMP-3.B Explain what factors lead to the diffusion of universalizing and ethnic religions.

The spread of language impacts cultures in different ways. Earlier in this unit, you read about the interaction of cultures and cultural convergence or divergence, which causes the cultures to become more similar or dissimilar. One culture either adopts another's language, the languages blend to form a new language, or the languages become isolated from each other and are preserved.

Sometimes, as a result of diffusion, cultures borrow from another language. Such words as *kindergarten*, *coffee*, and *karate* are now common English words that originated in the German, Turkish, and Japanese languages, respectively. Today, the existence of the internet, plus widespread access to movies in English and to American and British TV shows, affects worldwide language use, causing language and thus cultural convergence through these lines of communication.

Convergence is evident in the development of blended languages like "Spanglish," a form of expression spoken by some Hispanics living in the United States that combines English and Spanish grammar and vocabulary. For example, one might ask *"Are you ready?"* in English, or *¿Estás listo?"* in Spanish. The Spanglish version of this question is a combination of both languages: *"¿Estás ready?"* Sometimes English words are transformed into Spanglish, taking on spelling, construction, or pronunciation from Spanish. The English verb "to click," as in clicking on a website, would become in Spanglish, *"clickear."* The *-ear* at the end of the word is a common verb ending in Spanish. Many Spanglish words come from business or technology, reflecting the dominance of English in these fields.

Language divergence is also a result of the formation of group boundaries, or barriers that separate people into groups. Causes for these boundaries include topography and cultural distinctions. Both are at play in the world's most linguistically diverse country, Papua New Guinea, which is less than one-twentieth the size of the United States, with more than 800 languages. The mountainous terrain and proliferation of islands result in populations occupying small, isolated pockets of land and promote the development of distinct languages. Strong in-group identification leads these populations to protect their linguistic autonomy and reject the language of other communities when there is contact.

Another example includes the people of North and South Korea, who come from the same ethnic group and both speak Korean, but have been separated politically since 1945. During this relatively short period of isolation, significant language differences have developed between the two countries. Since South Korea is open to trade and political contact, many foreign words have been incorporated into South Korea's version of the Korean language. The communist government in North Korea has resisted the introduction of foreign interactions—and consequently, foreign words. Those that did enter the language were often Russian, reflecting the influence of the long-time North Korean political ally. The Korean word for *friend*, *tongmu*, was once used widely across the Korean peninsula. However, when the North Koreans began using *tongmu* to mean "a fellow socialist citizen" just like the Russian word *comrade*, the South Koreans stopped using the word *tongmu*, replacing it with the word *chingu*.

The people of some countries or cultures have assembled formal bodies and written decrees aimed at preserving their language in the face of language diffusion. The Arab Academy of Damascus, founded in 1919, has the goal of setting standards for the Arabic language, creating Arabic equivalents for scientific terms and promoting the growth of Arabic content on the internet. The French—who established their language academy in 1635—resist the promotion of English and even had a law banning its use exclusively to teach university classes. In Israel, Hebrew was established as the official language when the state formed in 1948 to differentiate from other languages spoken in the region.

THE INFLUENCE OF POWER You have read that power, whether economic, political, or military, impacts cultural change. Power influences which languages become dominant and subordinate. Dominant languages tend to be distributed widely or spoken by a large number of people, and subordinate languages are in danger of disappearing.

Linguists disagree over whether the subordinate or dominant group, or a combination of the two, is the primary force behind the development of creole languages. Recall that a creole language is a blended language that arises to facilitate communication among the dominant and subordinate groups with diverse languages in a colonial system. Some scholars believe population size and duration of interaction between the cultures influence how languages develop. In the case of Haitian Creole, which has a strong African influence, Africans outnumbered the French colonists in Haiti, and the French controlled the island for less than 200 years. Over time, the influence one language has over the other lessens, and creole languages develop their own vocabularies and more complex grammar.

While commerce and trade often necessitate the development of a lingua franca, a common language between speakers of different languages also develops for diplomacy. A lingua franca can help governments and organizations build international relationships. Speakers of

local languages sometimes adopt the imperial language, either through contact with native speakers of that language, or due to the prestige the language carries. Arabic became a lingua franca as the Islamic Empire spread throughout Southwest Asia and North Africa, not only to facilitate commerce and diplomacy, but as part of the diffusion of the Islamic religion.

Today, English is the dominant language used in the fields of science, technology, and diplomacy. The economic power of the United States influences the use of English in global commerce as well. English is also the lingua franca of numerous university programs around the world. Non-native English speakers learn English to increase their career opportunities and improve their ability to attend an international university.

Power also influences toponyms, or place names. As regimes change throughout the world, leaders sometimes change the names of the cities or streets under their control. The Russian city of St. Petersburg was founded in the 18th century by Czar Peter the Great. After the Russian Revolution, which put communists in control of

The city of St. Petersburg is an example of how changes in political power impact toponyms. The name of the city changed each time power in the region shifted, either to pay homage to a leader or to restore a name some believe is more appropriate.

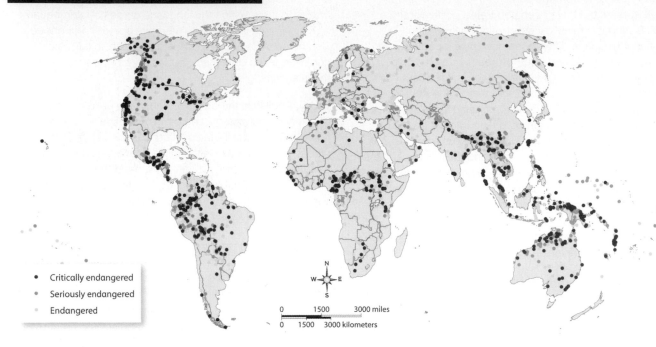

Critically endangered

Seriously endangered

Endangered

READING MAPS A group of geographers, linguists, academics, and other experts have joined together to form the Endangered Languages Project, which tracks languages in danger of disappearing and encourages the sharing of information on how to preserve them. This map from the Endangered Languages Project identifies three categories of endangered languages. ▌ What do you notice about the pattern of languages that are under threat across the world?

what became the Soviet Union in 1918, the city's name was changed to Petrograd—a Russian form of the name. That name remained until the death of the communist leader Vladimir Lenin, when the city was renamed as Leningrad. When the Soviet Union collapsed in 1991, the city was once again named St. Petersburg.

Many cities in India have had several names over the centuries, each name revealing something about the culture of the people who chose that name. In 2018, the government of the state of Uttar Pradesh changed the 500-year-old name of the city Allahabad, which means "place where Allah lives," back to its original name of Prayagraj, which means "place of sacrifice." These toponym changes reflect the religious beliefs of those controlling the city; the Muslim emperor Akbar gave the city its Muslim name in 1580, and Hindu political leaders made the change in 2018.

ENDANGERED LANGUAGES Language diffusion sometimes results in endangered languages—the languages of small groups of people, often of indigenous cultures, that become in danger of disappearing due to declining populations and cultural pressures. Experts identify language hotspots that have a high degree of linguistic diversity—determined by the number of language families present in an area—and several levels of endangerment, based on the number and age of native speakers. Some languages succumb to these pressures. According to

UNESCO, about 230 languages became extinct from 1950 to 2010, and a language dies every two weeks.

Social scientists, linguists, and native speakers are making efforts to preserve endangered languages, and some with considerable success. In 1983, only about 50 children spoke Hawaiian. An effort to teach the language in the state's schools has made it far more widespread. In Wales, part of the United Kingdom, champions of the Welsh language won the establishment of a Welsh-only public television channel that televises Welsh language programming. In Japan, members of the Ainu are taking steps to preserve their language, which dates from Neolithic times. They include free Ainu courses at various sites on the island of Hokkaido; publication of books and stories from the Ainu oral tradition in both Ainu and Japanese; and creation of an Ainu radio station. Groups like the Endangered Language Fund, Cultural Survival, and UNESCO's Languages in Danger program seek support to preserve endangered languages.

GEOGRAPHIC THINKING

1. Identify an example of hierarchical diffusion affecting language.

2. Describe how the diffusion of language creates unity.

3. Explain how changes in regime affect toponyms.

CASE STUDY

FRENCH OR ENGLISH IN QUEBEC?

THE ISSUE The French-speaking majority in the Canadian province of Quebec wants to preserve French language and culture in the predominantly English-speaking country.

LEARNING OBJECTIVE
SPS-3.A Explain how historical processes impact current cultural patterns.

BY THE NUMBERS

7.9 MILLION
French speakers in Canada

6.9 MILLION
French speakers in Quebec

26.2 MILLION
English speakers in Canada

1.1 MILLION
English speakers in Quebec

6.9 MILLION
bilingual speakers in Canada

3.6 MILLION
bilingual speakers in Quebec

Source: Statistics Canada

In 2013, protesters demonstrated against language Bill 14 in Montreal. The bill would have strengthened the use of French in Quebec's small businesses and schools. Opposers of the bill, however, favored greater bilingualism in the province.

CANADA IS A BILINGUAL COUNTRY with two official languages: French and English. In the past, cultural and political conflict between French Canadians and English Canadians has led Quebec's majority French-speaking citizens to call for the separation of the province from the rest of Canada. Quebec is the second largest province in the country. A large portion of francophones (people who speak French) in Quebec believe the Canadian government will never respect the French language and culture that is so prominent there.

Tensions reached a peak in 1995 when the provincial Partí Québécois government proposed a referendum to give Quebec greater sovereignty but still remain in Canada. The measure was defeated by a mere 55,000 votes.

In 2013, the Partí Québécois introduced Bill 14 into legislation. The bill proposed amendments to Quebec's French language charter, which already ensures the only official language of Quebec is French. Amendments included governmental power to revoke a city's bilingual status if the anglophone population (people who speak English) dropped below 50 percent, and businesses with more than 25 employees were to make French their everyday work language. The bill died, and the current government party, the Coalition Avenir Québec, has not raised the issue, instead prioritizing tax cuts and immigration issues as part of their agenda.

Still unsettled is the tension over French dominance and bilingualism. Quebec has grown more multicultural, particularly in and around Montreal, which holds two-fifths of Quebec's population. As more French speakers moved from the city to its suburbs, the provincial government passed a law unifying the city and its suburbs into one municipal unit to maintain Montreal as a French-speaking city.

English speakers chafed at this new law, irritated that the government went to such lengths to diminish bilingualism. The law also shows that efforts to negotiate language and cultural differences remain a struggle. ▌

GEOGRAPHIC THINKING

Explain how immigration might affect the goals of Quebec's French-speaking citizens.

8.3 PATTERNS OF RELIGION

Interaction among people over the centuries has contributed to the creation, evolution, or splintering of thousands of religions that attract different groups of people. The distribution of religions today varies, based on their different hearths, teachings, values, and patterns of diffusion.

RELIGION AND CULTURE

LEARNING OBJECTIVE
PSO-3.D Explain patterns and landscapes of language, religion, ethnicity, and gender.

Religions deeply impact individuals and cultures. They shape cultural beliefs and traditions and serve as a reflection of how people think about the world. As an integral part of culture, religious beliefs can cause political divisions within a country and can impact the environment. According to the Dalai Lama, a Buddhist leader, the Buddhist view is that humans have a responsibility to protect nature. Some Christians hold the view that God gave humans authority over all creation, to use it as they wish. Others argue that humans have a moral responsibility to exercise stewardship over the entire natural world, which echoes Buddhist values.

The beliefs and traditions shaped by different faiths have played an important role throughout the history of the world because religions are so closely tied to identity and ethnicity. This has impacted how religions have spread and where certain religions are practiced today.

PATTERNS OF DISTRIBUTION

LEARNING OBJECTIVE
IMP-3.B Explain what factors lead to the diffusion of universalizing and ethnic religions.

To understand the geographic distribution of religions worldwide, geographers consider the places of origin, extent and methods of diffusion, and contemporary cultural processes of different religions. Some religious groups are concentrated within a region, while others are dispersed with a presence on several continents. Practices and belief systems attract different people and impact a religion's distribution. Historically, for example, many Hindus perceived to be of a lower caste were attracted to Islam because its teachings value all humans equally. Some Europeans became Protestants because of disagreements with Catholic principles and to break from oppression.

Like the previous world languages map, the "Estimated Majority Religions" map is a snapshot in time, documenting current patterns of distribution—not those of earlier centuries. Christianity is the dominant religion in most

Voodoo is an ancient religion with roots in the West African nation of Benin, which officially acknowledged it as a religion in 1989. It is practiced by about 60 million people worldwide. Practitioners of Voodoo gather in Ouidah, Benin for an annual religious festival, which includes elaborate ceremonial costumes.

of Europe, the Americas, central and southern Africa, as well as in Australia and New Zealand. With origins in Southwest Asia, the spread of Christianity has occurred as a result of relocation diffusion (migration) and expansion diffusion (conquest and missionary work). Islam, which also originated in Southwest Asia, is the main religion in Central Asia, Indonesia, Southwest Asia, and North Africa, as well as portions of southeastern Europe and India. Trade, conquest, missionaries, and leaders adopting Islam as the religion of their people contributed to its current distribution. Hinduism is distributed near its hearth in Asia and hasn't spread far beyond the borders of India. While Buddhism has spread across countries, fewer adherents remain in and around its hearth of India, now dominated by Hinduism. Folk religions are strong in many areas of rural Africa and the interior Amazon Basin and northern North America, locations with large indigenous populations. Though they display significant differences, these traditional religions are sometimes grouped under the name *animism*, which denotes a belief that humans share the world with numerous spirits whose actions can help or hurt humans.

The global scale of the "Estimated Majority Religions" map makes interpreting the locations of where different religions are practiced a bit misleading. The map displays the religion that is most widely practiced in a country or

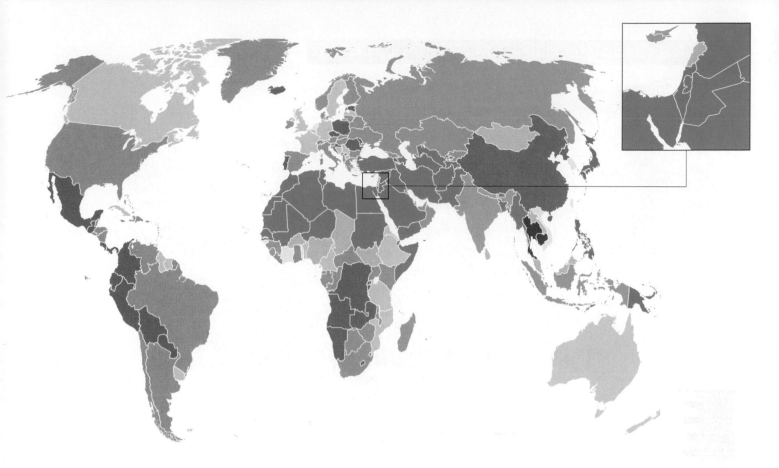

ESTIMATED MAJORITY RELIGIONS, 2020

The coloring of each country corresponds to its majority religion, and the darker the shade, the greater the prevalence of that religion. No folk religion is the majority in any country. Guinea Bissau, Ivory Coast, Nigeria, Singapore, South Korea, Taiwan, Togo, Vietnam, and Macau (autonomous region) have no clear majority religion. ▌ Explain how the map and chart work together to provide a deeper understanding of the distribution of religion in the world.

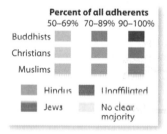

Percent of all adherents
50–69% 70–89% 90–100%

Buddhists
Christians
Muslims

Hindus   Unaffiliated
Jews   No clear
                majority

WORLD RELIGIOUS ADHERENTS (IN BILLIONS), 2020

Christians
2.383B

Muslims
1.907B

Unaffiliated
1.194B

Hindus
1.161B

Buddhists
0.507B

Folk Religion
0.430B

Other Religions
0.061 B

Jews
0.015B

🧍 = 25 million adherents

Source: Pew Research Center

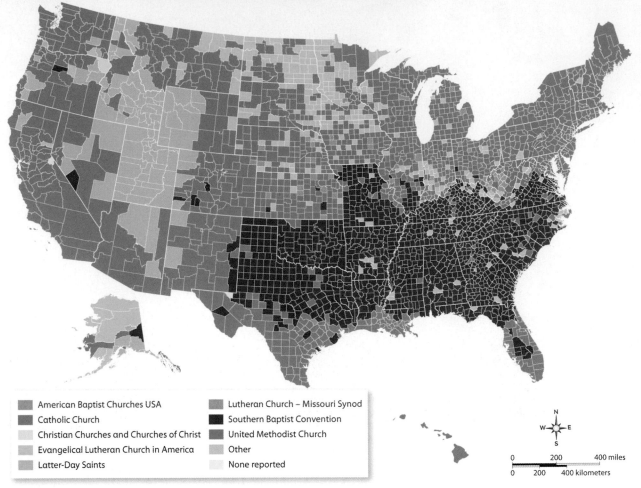

American Baptist Churches USA
Catholic Church
Christian Churches and Churches of Christ
Evangelical Lutheran Church in America
Latter-Day Saints
Lutheran Church – Missouri Synod
Southern Baptist Convention
United Methodist Church
Other
None reported

N · W · E · S

0   200   400 miles
0   200   400 kilometers

READING MAPS Every ten years, a study is conducted of religious adherents in the United States. You might notice that some major religions, such as Judaism, aren't on the map. Judaism has many adherents in large metropolitan areas such as Los Angeles and New York City, but it is not the majority religion in any U.S. county. ▌ Does the map support the idea that historical settlement patterns and religious patterns are aligned in this country? Explain your thinking.

region, not accounting for the relative mix of faiths in a given area. For example, the prevalence of Islam found in North Africa decreases when moving south. But it is unclear if the remaining population in the Muslim-majority areas is Christian, follows traditional religions, or practices some other faith. Additionally, some individuals embrace more than one belief system. Recall that some Roman Catholics in Latin America and the United States practice rituals that belong to traditional African-based beliefs called Santería. In some countries, including China, the largest number of people are not affiliated with any religion.

REGIONAL PATTERNS Patterns revealing greater religious differentiation are evident with different scale maps. Consider the "Majority Religious Adherents by U.S. County" map, depicting Roman Catholicism as the chief religion across much of the country, though Southern Baptists dominate the South. Historical settlement patterns help explain present-day locations of religious groups. For example, in the 1850s, many Germans and Scandinavians

who identified as Lutheran settled in Pennsylvania and eastern Ohio and moved throughout the upper Midwest attracted by employment opportunities. Their settlement is still reflected in the distribution of Lutheranism today. The Church of Jesus Christ of Latter-day Saints, or the Mormon Church, which originated in New York State, dominates in Utah and is significantly represented throughout the West. Early followers of the faith were not welcome in certain established parts of the United States, so they migrated west to largely unsettled territories where they could practice their religion freely. Mormons have remained in this area for more than 150 years.

GEOGRAPHIC THINKING

1. Compare the spatial distribution of Christianity, Islam, and Buddhism.

2. Identify where Christianity, Islam, and Hinduism originated.

NATIONAL GEOGRAPHIC EXPLORER **WADE DAVIS**

PRESERVING THE ETHNOSPHERE

Wade Davis, National Geographic Explorer-in-Residence, has lived with indigenous peoples throughout the world. He took the above photo of the Great Mosque of Djenne in Mali while following Arab merchants who sell local salt.

LEARNING OBJECTIVE

PSO-3.D Explain patterns and landscapes of language, religion, ethnicity, and gender.

Wade Davis immerses himself in different cultural landscapes all over the world, always with the goal to learn from indigenous peoples what it means to be human.

When Davis travels, he visits sacred sites and participates in—or simply contemplates—cultural rituals and ceremonies. Each culture, he says, demonstrates "that there are other ways of being, other ways of thinking, other ways of orienting yourself in the world," which has allowed people to successfully live in the harshest locales, including deserts and the Arctic, for centuries. Davis is dedicated to learning as much as possible about the collective thoughts, ideals, myths, intuitions, and inspirations originating from the imagination of the people of every culture, the sum of which he calls the ethnosphere.

Central to his efforts to understand a culture is the need to comprehend peoples' religious beliefs, which impacts the diffusion and distribution of a religion. While religious practices vary across locations because of the resources available to the people, Davis believes that religion exists to help all people find order in their universe. The search for order is manifested in myriad ways. As he was told during his study of Voodoo in Haiti, "You white people go to church to speak about God. We dance in the temples and become God."

Davis calls the ethnosphere "humanity's great legacy," and he notes that losing any of the diverse languages, traditions, and sacred spaces around the world diminishes the ethnosphere. At risk is losing the vast archive of knowledge and expertise of elders, healers, and others. Davis tells their stories of the natural and spiritual world in an attempt to document and preserve the catalog of human knowledge that will help us adapt to the common problems we all face, no matter our culture or where we live. ▮

GEOGRAPHIC THINKING

Explain how learning about peoples' religious beliefs helps to define what it means to be human.

SHARED SACRED SITES

THE ISSUE Disputed land in India sacred to Hindus and Muslims has caused tensions between both religious groups for decades.

LEARNING OBJECTIVE
SPS-3.A Explain how historical processes impact current cultural patterns.

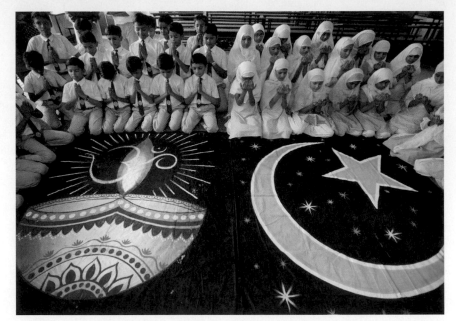

India is home not only to 94 percent of the world's Hindus, but also to the second-largest Muslim population living in a single country (after Indonesia). These Hindu and Muslim children are praying for peace at their school in the city of Ahmedabad.

BY THE NUMBERS

199.8 MILLION

people living in
Uttar Pradesh (2011)

79.7%
Hindu

19.3% ☪
Muslim

1%
Other

Source: World Population Review, Census Organization of India

THE BIRTH AND SPREAD OF RELIGIONS spanning centuries has resulted in examples where one geographic location is significant to more than one faith. Angkor Wat, located in Cambodia, was first a Hindu temple and later turned into a Buddhist temple. Jerusalem's Old City remains a sacred place to three major religions—Judaism, Christianity, and Islam. Hindus and Muslims both consider a three-acre plot of land in Ayodhya, a city in the state of Uttar Pradesh, in India, sacred to both of their religions.

Hindus believe the site was the birthplace of their revered god Rama and that a Hindu temple was once located there. Some believe the temple was demolished by the Mughal empire, a Muslim empire that ruled northern India from the early 16th century to the mid-18th century, to build an Islamic mosque called Babri Masjid. The mosque stood on the disputed site until 1992 when Hindu extremists destroyed it, sparking nationwide riots.

Ownership of the land was debated in Indian courts for decades. A group that oversees Sunni Islamic properties argued that there is no proof of the Hindu temple ever existing. Hindus presented the courts with ancient texts that purportedly describe Ayodhya as a holy Hindu city. Finally, in 2019, the Supreme Court of India unanimously ruled in favor of the Hindus, giving them permission to construct a temple at the site. The court also ruled that Muslims will be given land to build a mosque at a prominent alternative site in Ayodhya.

India's Muslims are divided about the ruling. Some would like to contest the decision, viewing it as a statement about Muslims' place in India as second-class citizens. They also fear that the decision would embolden Hindu extremists to target the new mosque in the future. Others are accepting of the fact that five acres will be provided to build a new mosque in another location. They believe accepting the decision is the first step toward easing tensions between Hindus and Muslims regarding the dispute. The prime minister of India, Narendra Modi, praised the court's decision but called for unity among both groups. ▌

GEOGRAPHIC THINKING

Describe how historical events have impacted the interactions between some Hindus and Muslims in Uttar Pradesh.

8.4 UNIVERSALIZING AND ETHNIC RELIGIONS

Geographers rely on their own knowledge of history and the scholarship of historians when they examine how religion affects patterns of culture. An in-depth account of religious history is beyond the scope of this course, but knowing a few key milestones for each of the major world religions will help you put events and concepts in context.

UNIVERSALIZING RELIGIONS

LEARNING OBJECTIVE
IMP-3.B Explain what factors lead to the diffusion of universalizing and ethnic religions.

Universalizing religions attempt to appeal to a wide variety of people and are open to membership by all, regardless of a person's location, language, or ethnicity. Examples of universalizing religions are Christianity, Islam, and Buddhism, as well as faiths with fewer adherents including Sikhism, Baha'i, and the Church of Jesus Christ of Latter-day Saints.

By nature, universalizing religions are open to diffusion, and two in particular—Christianity and Islam—have become the largest world religions today. At different periods in history, different processes of diffusion have spread religions. Often more than one type of diffusion is reflected as different elements of human interaction occur in different places. Universalizing religions have commonly spread through relocation and expansion.

CHRISTIANITY Started in what is now the West Bank and Israel around the beginning of the common era, **Christianity** has spread to all continents. The religion is based on the teachings of Jesus, a man believed by the faithful to be God's son. Jesus taught his followers that they should love and care for their fellow humans.

The Christian religion spread around the world through relocation and expansion diffusion as a small group of followers called disciples carried the Christian message throughout the Roman Empire and Mediterranean region. In the 300s, the emperor Theodosius declared Christianity the official religion of the Roman Empire, an example of hierarchical diffusion.

For the next 1,000 years, Christian missionaries traveled to promote the religion in new regions, spreading Christianity from Rome throughout Europe. Church officials made their faith more welcoming by absorbing some of the beliefs and practices of local groups. These actions are an example of the acculturation discussed in Chapter 7. For example, pagan Europeans converted readily when Christianity adapted and included their beliefs and practices, such as the Celtic holiday Samhain. By the 10th century, Christianity had spread throughout most of Europe as far east as Russia, though some areas—such as Sweden in the

12th century—did not become Christian until later. Some Europeans were forced to adhere when their monarchs coverted to Christianity, which occured in Lithuania. Throughout the Crusades (1096-1204), Christians in Europe fought non-Christians, including Muslims, to conquer Palestine and retake Spain. During the wars, the rulers of Spain used a powerful court called the Spanish Inquisition to punish non-Christians who would not convert or who secretly practiced their former religion. Christianity became strong in northern Africa from Roman times and in Ethiopia from the 4th century when, through hierarchical diffusion, the king converted and adopted it as the state religion, also forcing the people to adhere.

In the 11th century, differences over the organization and doctrine (or teachings) within the church led to a split that resulted in the divergence of religious groups and the formation of two distinct Christian branches called Roman Catholicism and the Eastern Orthodox tradition.

The Roman Catholic Church grew in wealth and power, raising concerns of corruption and causing the Catholic Church to fracture, spurring a third Christian branch called Protestantism. European geopolitics affected the Protestant branch, and the development of denominations, or separate church organizations, was shaped not only by differences in doctrine and ritual but also nationalism, or a strong sense of national identity. A recent estimate placed the total number of Christian denominations at more than 30,000. Independent nation-based organizations such as the Greek Orthodox Church, the Bulgarian Orthodox Church, and the Russian Orthodox Church are all examples of denominations of the Eastern Orthodox branch of Christianity.

The next significant period of Christian diffusion began in the 15th century and brought Christianity to areas beyond Europe through imperialism and colonialism. Emigrants left Europe to settle in new colonies in the Americas, and later in Australia, New Zealand, and southern Africa. In addition to relocation, Christianity continued to spread through expansion diffusion. Power dynamics and persuasion by missionaries led to the conversion of many Native Americans and enslaved Africans to Christianity while incorporating their previous spiritual beliefs. Missionaries also brought Christianity to Asia, and it took strong hold in the Philippines in the 16th century. Christianity gained less of a stronghold in places like China and Japan during this age of European expansion. Rulers and their advisors worried that the spread

CHAPTER 8

NIGER-CONGO LANGUAGE FAMILY

The majority of people in Africa—around 85 percent—speak a language in the Niger-Congo family. It is estimated that around 1,400 Niger-Congo languages exist, but most of them can be classified into distinct language groups. The nine major Niger-Congo language branches are shown in green ovals in the diagram. (Linguists do not agree on the exact classification of Dogon, hence the dotted line.) ▌ Identify the types of information in this diagram that would be unavailable on a map of languages spoken in Africa today. Describe how linguists may have reached their conclusions about how the languages are related.

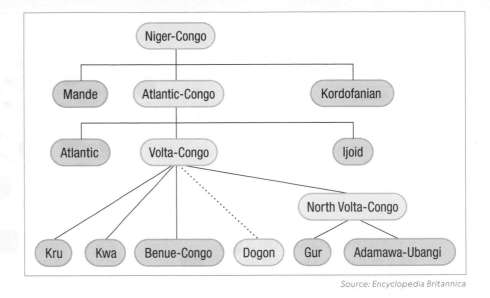

Source: Encyclopedia Britannica

CHAPTER 8

RELIGIOUS INFLUENCE

The "Estimated Majority Religions, 2020" map in Chapter 8 shows the majority religion in each country but does not include data about the number of people who practice that religion. This map shows the percentage of people in each country who replied "very important" in a survey about the importance of religion in respondents' lives. ▌ Compare the two maps, and explain how data from both of them can help researchers consider the extent to which religion influences culture.

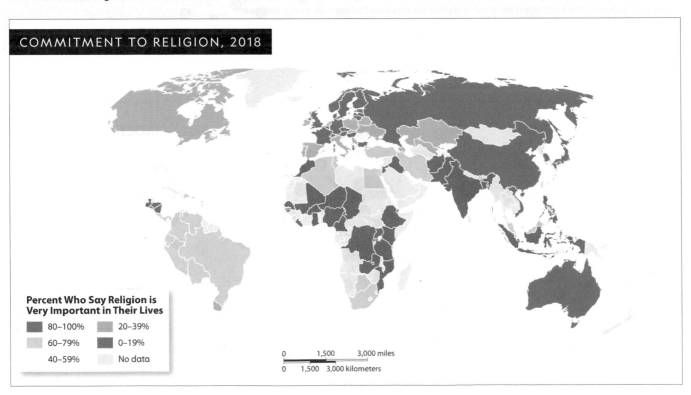

COMMITMENT TO RELIGION, 2018

Percent Who Say Religion is Very Important in Their Lives

- 80–100%
- 60–79%
- 40–59%
- 20–39%
- 0–19%
- No data

0   1,500   3,000 miles
0   1,500   3,000 kilometers

CHAPTER 8

DENOMINATIONS OF CHRISTIANITY

Christianity is a widespread religion with numerous denominations, or separate church organizations that unite a number of local congregations. This diagram traces the principal organizations in the development of Christianity, although many additional denominations exist. ▮ Identify the two church organizations that have the highest number of connected denominations. Then explain how diffusion may have led to the creation of Christianity's multiple denominations.

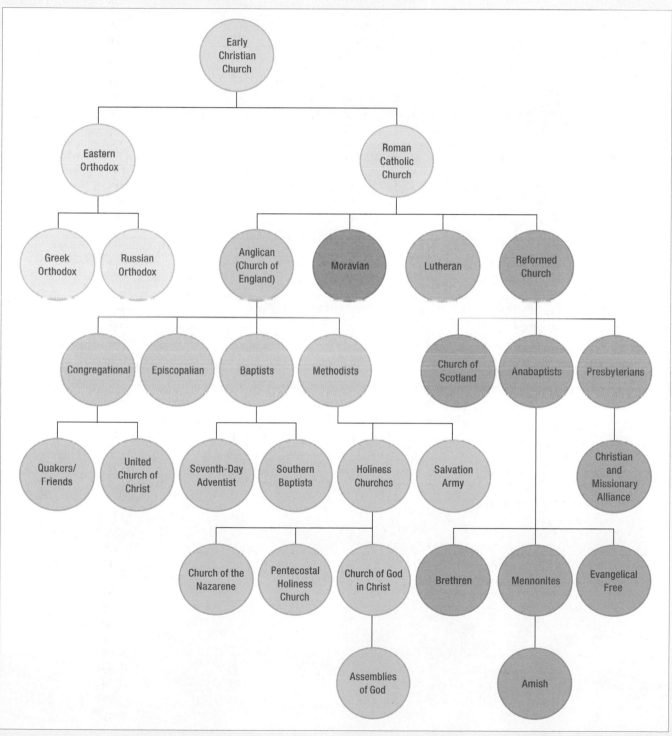

Source: *Thinking Through Christianity*

POLITICAL
PATTERNS AND PROCESSES

DIVIDING LINES

Imjingak Park, South Korea

What could be simpler or more definitive than boundary lines on a map? In fact, the reality represented by those lines is complex and almost never clear cut. International borders are a reflection of political power, and they result from an interplay of cultural, historical, economic, and other forces.

Some borders, like the 2.5-mile wide strip of land that separates North Korea from South Korea, act as buffer zones between hostile countries. This border is known as the Demilitarized Zone (shown here) and it's one of the most heavily guarded and fortified places on Earth. Still, tourists—like these visitors from South Korea—are often drawn to borders, the symbolic and literal dividing lines between peoples and cultures.

For geographers, borders on a map are just the starting point for understanding the many ways that groups define themselves and each other and lay claim to their spaces on the globe.

CHAPTER 9
THE CONTEMPORARY POLITICAL MAP

CHAPTER 10
SPATIAL PATTERNS OF POLITICAL POWER

CHAPTER 11
POLITICAL CHALLENGES AND CHANGES

UNIT 4 WRITING ACROSS UNITS,
REGIONS & SCALES

UNIT 4 MAPS & MODELS ARCHIVE

RECONCILIATION
THROUGH NARRATIVE

National Geographic Explorer Aziz Abu Sarah calls the strife in Israel "one of the oldest, most complicated conflicts in the world." Both Jews and Palestinians, most of whom are Arab Muslims, claim centuries-old cultural, religious, and national ties to the land. Since the formation of the modern-day state of Israel, the country's government and its Palestinian residents have been grappling over territory and other rights using words, slingshots, tear gas, bullets, and even rockets.

LEARNING OBJECTIVE
PSO-4.C Describe the concepts of political power and territoriality as used by geographers.

GROWING UP PALESTINIAN When Abu Sarah was a young boy attending a Palestinian elementary school near Jerusalem, conflict was an everyday fact of life. His mother made certain he had an onion with him every day when he went to school, because an onion's fumes were thought to counteract the effects of teargas, which Israeli soldiers sometimes use when clashes with Palestinian protesters become violent. Later, Abu Sarah became a dedicated participant in the fight against the Israeli government, motivated by an urge toward revenge for the death of his older brother, who perished after spending a year in an Israeli prison. As a teenager, Abu Sarah wrote prolific articles for anti-Israeli publications and took part in violent confrontations, throwing stones at Israeli soldiers.

When Abu Sarah was 18, he decided to learn Hebrew, because it is difficult to work and live in Jerusalem without knowing the language. He found himself the only Palestinian in a classroom full of Jews from other countries who had recently immigrated to Israel. Bonding with his classmates over relatively frivolous connections such as a shared love of country music—which Abu Sarah claims is practically unheard of among his fellow Palestinians—led to deeper conversations about personal experiences and values. These exchanges humanized Israeli Jews in Abu Sarah's eyes. "I knew after that class where the problem is," he says. "When you don't know somebody, you're going to hate them, and you're going to fantasize about their horns and tails. … You start thinking they're less of a human than you."

CHANGING NARRATIVES When describing his work as a peace activist and cultural educator, Abu Sarah often uses the words "narrative" and "reconciliation." He seeks out ways to foster meaningful, in-person encounters between Israelis, Palestinians, and others involved in the conflict, because sharing personal narratives helps individuals find commonalities and perceive one another as fully human. By building empathy, Abu Sarah hopes to foster a spirit not only of tolerance but of reconciliation— a true coming together.

To this end, Abu Sarah speaks frequently to groups in churches, synagogues, and mosques, as well as working to share his message across all media. In a series of videos for National Geographic, he stood on both sides of skirmishes between Israeli soldiers and Palestinian protesters to gather their stories firsthand. Abu Sarah has also taken on the role of social entrepreneur, or one who founds a business that aims to solve a social problem. His company organizes tours of Israel and the Palestinian territories narrated by diverse guides who share multiple points of view—Palestinian and Israeli; Jewish, Muslim, and Christian. While Abu Sarah is optimistic about the power of narrative and personal connections, he knows the wall of ignorance separating Jews and Palestinians is an imposing barrier. "What needs to be done is put cracks in that wall," he says. "One of my colleagues says what we [as peace activists] do is bang our heads against that wall until we break it down." ▮

GEOGRAPHIC THINKING

Describe how people's narratives can affect the expression of territoriality in their communities.

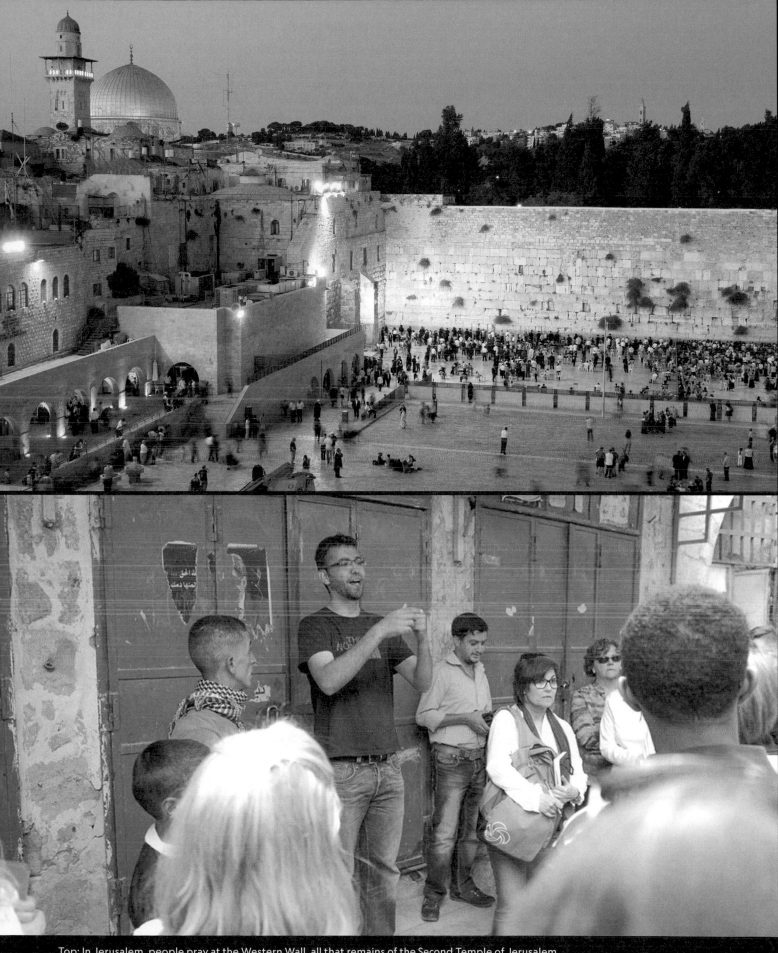

Top: In Jerusalem, people pray at the Western Wall, all that remains of the Second Temple of Jerusalem, an ancient Jewish holy site. The gold dome in the background is the Dome of the Rock, an Islamic shrine built on a site that is sacred to Muslims, Jews, and Christians. Bottom: Aziz Abu Sarah leads a tour group.

CHAPTER 9

THE CONTEMPORARY POLITICAL MAP

CRITICAL VIEWING A military parade through the Arc de Triomphe is part of the Bastille Day celebrations in Paris, France, on July 14, 2019. Demonstrations of national pride such as this one help define and unite nations. What might this celebration suggest about the political situation in France?

GEOGRAPHIC THINKING How do maps reflect political borders around the world?

9.1
THE COMPLEX WORLD POLITICAL MAP

9.2
POLITICAL POWER AND GEOGRAPHY

9.3
POLITICAL PROCESSES OVER TIME

CASE STUDY: The Kurds

9.4
THE NATURE AND FUNCTION OF BOUNDARIES

CASE STUDY: The DMZ in Korea

NATIONAL GEOGRAPHIC PHOTOGRAPHER David Guttenfelder

9.1 THE COMPLEX WORLD POLITICAL MAP

Take a close look at a political map of the world. Notice how lines—straight and crooked, solid and dashed—divide the land into countries. Who created these spaces and gave them their particular boundaries? On a world political map, geographers see the impact of people's need to control territory and exert power.

ORGANIZING SPACE

LEARNING OBJECTIVES

PSO-4.A For world political maps: a. Define the different types of political entities. b. Identify a contemporary example of political entities.

PSO-4.B Explain the processes that have shaped contemporary political geography.

When studying a map or globe, human geographers are interested in understanding how and why countries and regions of the world came to be organized politically. As you have learned, the world political map has changed enormously since the first civilizations began to mark their territory and establish governments. Early civilizations had vague, loosely defined boundaries. Over the centuries, however, as groups established themselves and claimed land through means both peaceful and not, these lines—the borders between groups—often became more clearly defined. **Political geography** is the study of the ways in which the world is organized as a reflection of the power that different groups hold over territory.

Although we tend to view maps as representations of settled facts, political maps can express particular interpretations of the world. For example, the government of China does not recognize the island of Taiwan, off China's east coast,

as a separate country. The United States, however, does consider Taiwan to be independent. So a map of China approved by the Chinese government looks different from one published by a mapmaker in the United States. Travelers might experience the same phenomenon when using online map applications in different countries. If a boundary dispute exists, the border could appear in a different place depending on which country a person is standing in when accessing a smartphone map.

STATES States are created by humans as a way to organize and manage themselves. A **state** is a politically organized independent territory with a government, defined borders, and a permanent population—in short, a country. State governments have power over a population that works together to contribute to an economy and is connected by transportation and communication systems. A state has **sovereignty**, which is the right of a government to control and defend its territory and determine what happens within its borders. If a state is not recognized as an independent country by other states, it is not considered sovereign. The use of the term *state* can occasionally be confusing for students in the United States. An independent state such as Sweden is not the same as a U.S. state such as Nebraska.

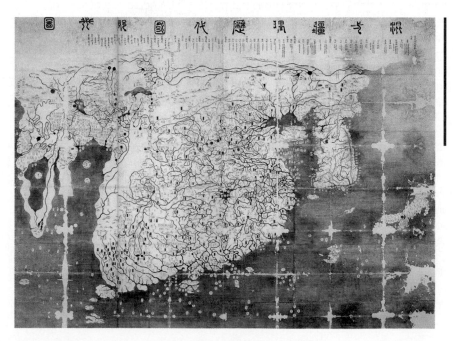

This map of the Eastern Hemisphere, known as the Kangnido Map, was created by a Korean geographer in the 15th century. The mapmaker's inaccurate size of Korea (the peninsula to the right of the large landmass) in relation to the rest of Asia is an example of how maps can express skewed interpretations of the world. The Kangnido Map also shows Africa (far left) to be much smaller than its actual size and a barely visible Europe.

Countries that recognize
Palestine as a state

Palestinian territories

0   1500   3000 miles
0   1500   3000 kilometers

READING MAPS Since the 20th century, the Palestine region (see inset) has been a source of persistent conflict as Jewish Israelis and Arab Palestinians fight for control of territory. In 2019, 137 members of the United Nations recognized Palestine as a state, while 56 did not. ▌ Why do you think a larger number of UN member countries recognize Palestine as an independent state?

The world is organized into a number of diverse sovereign states. Some, like China and Canada, cover vast territories, while others, such as Belize and Togo, are very small in size. The number of independent states around the globe often changes in response to pressures from political circumstances. In 1991, when the Soviet Union dissolved, 15 republics that had been part of that massive state, including Estonia, seceded and declared their independence. Following Estonia's declaration, other countries recognized it as a sovereign state. Among its first steps, the new Estonian government reestablished its military and its currency, the kroon, which immediately became a symbol of the country's independence. Other former Soviet republics, including Ukraine and Belarus, also took steps to establish their sovereignty and were recognized by the international community.

There is no general agreement on the number of independent states around the globe. The United Nations recognizes 195 countries, but not every member state of the UN agrees on which countries are independent and which are not. For example, the UN as an organization recognizes Palestine as an independent state, but 56 of its member countries do not. On the other hand, Kosovo, which had been part of Serbia but declared its independence in 2008, is not recognized as an independent state by the United Nations. However, 111 UN members do consider Kosovo to be sovereign.

NATIONS States should not be confused with **nations**. Whereas states are political entities, nations are cultural entities, meaning that they are made up of individuals who have forged a common identity through a shared language, religion, ethnicity, or heritage—often all four of these. Some define a nation as including a "reasonably large population," while others argue that the size of the population does not matter. The people of a nation share a common vision of the future, which produces an undeniable feeling of togetherness.

Several examples of nations exist within the United States. Native Hawaiians, for example, are descendents of Polynesian people who landed on the Hawaiian islands more than a thousand years ago and are united by their common history, culture, and language. In the western United States, the Navajo people are also a nation bound by tradition, history, and a common language. In fact, the U.S. government recognizes 573 native, or tribal, nations living on United States territory.

NATION-STATES In a **nation-state**, the territory occupied by a group who view themselves as a nation is the same as the politically recognized boundaries of the state they call their own. The concept of a nation-state is an ideal; no existing country can be described as a pure nation-state, because all are home to at least small ethnic or cultural minorities who might consider themselves as a nation within their country. Still, some countries come closer than others to the definition of a nation-state. Estonia, following its independence from the Soviet Union, is often viewed as a nation-state because most of its people share a common identity in terms of ethnicity and language. In Asia, Japan is commonly used as an example of a nation-state because nearly all its people share a common culture. Examples of other countries often identified as nation-states include Iceland, Iran, Albania, Croatia, Poland, and France. However, some critics challenge this categorization. France, for example, is home to diverse minority ethnic communities originating from North Africa, sub-Saharan Africa, and Southeast Asia. A 2017 study found that around 5 percent of the French population was non-white and non-European.

The concept of the nation-state first emerged in Europe, which until the 20th century was ruled by a small group of monarchs. A map of Europe from the early 19th century looks similar to a modern map in some places, but very different in others. France mostly looks as it does today, but the territories to the east of France do not.

Toward the end of the 19th century, however, the idea of drawing state borders to match national identities was taking hold, and when the victorious Allied leaders met in 1918 after the end of World War I to redraw national boundaries in Europe, they had this ideal in mind. Poland, for example, which had been divided among Russia, Germany, and Austria-Hungary, was reunited. The rest of Europe, too, was largely composed of countries intended to be nation-states. But even today, some European countries lack the unity that defines most of the continent's nation-states. In Spain, both the Basque people and the Catalans, ethnic groups living in parts of northern Spain, have strong national identities, and each group has agitated for independence from Spanish rule.

MULTISTATE NATIONS AND MULTINATIONAL STATES A **multistate nation**

consists of people who share a cultural or ethnic background but live in more than one country. Ethnic Russians are considered to be a multistate nation, because sizeable numbers of them live outside of Russia. They form substantial minorities in several countries that once belonged to the Soviet Union. Some consider the two

Koreas as one nation but two states, while others disagree with this view.

Multistate nations can pose challenges to political borders because people may feel a stronger affinity for a neighboring state that is home to others in their ethnic group than to their own state. Surveys of ethnic Russians living in Estonia, Latvia, and Ukraine, for example, show strong pro-Russia attitudes. Sometimes this situation leads governments to establish a policy of **irredentism**, attempting to acquire territories in neighboring states inhabited by people of the same nation. Russia was accused of irredentism when it attempted to annex territory in Ukraine that has a significant Russian population. You will learn more about irredentism and the case of Ukraine in Chapter 11.

A country with various ethnicities and cultures living inside its borders is a **multinational state**. Multinational states

READING MAPS State boundaries in Europe today primarily reflect the ideal of nation-states. Prior to World War I, however, this was not always the case. ❚ Identify the boundary changes that have taken place in Germany between 1914 and today. How do these changes reflect the trend of drawing state borders to match national identities?

sometimes struggle to create a sense of unity among different peoples. Iraq, for example, has long suffered from internal conflict because of a lack of shared identity among its Sunni, Shia, and Kurdish populations. Sometimes multinational states split up because the differences are unbridgeable, like Yugoslavia after the breakup of the Soviet Union. Other times, multinational states are able to forge a national identity despite the presence of many different ethnicities, cultures, and religions. Although culture and ethnicity have sometimes been a source of conflict, the United States has been broadly successful in integrating and assimilating different groups after they immigrate. In reality, because of global migration and the diverse nature of boundaries, most countries today are multinational states.

AUTONOMOUS AND SEMIAUTONOMOUS REGIONS Some countries contain regions that are either **autonomous** or **semiautonomous**, meaning they are given some authority to govern their own territories independently from the national government. In China, the territory of Hong Kong has been autonomous, using a system of government and currency that differs from the ones used throughout the rest of the country. In the United States, American Indian reservations are semiautonomous places with the authority to operate under certain different laws. This is the reason gambling casinos are permitted on Indian reservations even when they are not legal in the states where the reservations are located. Despite their semiautonomy, the view of the U.S. government is that

Native American nations are not sovereign, because their power is limited. Some tribal nations disagree with this interpretation, and the nature of tribal sovereignty in the United States is a topic of serious ongoing debate.

STATELESS NATIONS The term **stateless nation** describes a people united by culture, language, history, and tradition but not possessing a state. Tribal nations in the United States are stateless nations. Similarly, the Basque people in Spain have a unique culture and language, but despite the formation of secessionist organizations in the past, they do not have a separate, independent state. The Palestinians are considered a stateless nation because much of the world does not recognize Palestine as an independent state. Before Israel was established in 1948, the Jewish people were considered to be a stateless nation.

GEOGRAPHIC THINKING

1. Identify how maps can be a tool used to express power.

2. Explain why Kosovo seeks recognition as a sovereign state by the United Nations as a whole.

3. Explain your argument to answer the following question: Is the United States a nation-state?

9.2 POLITICAL POWER AND GEOGRAPHY

Territory is a powerful word describing a concept that's meaningful on many scales. At the individual level, your family might view your home as personal territory, protected by a fence around the yard or apartment doors that lock against intruders. States, too, place tremendous value on claiming, controlling, and defending the land that they consider their territory.

ISSUES OF SPACE AND POWER

LEARNING OBJECTIVE
PSO-4.C Describe the concepts of political power and territoriality as used by geographers.

Looking beyond your personal space, you can quickly perceive the countless ways different groups or entities claim their territories. For example, schools typically have home courts or fields, mascots, logos, and slogans that

give them a unique identity. Communities of all sizes also define themselves using markers such as signs, slogans, and sometimes nicknames like "The Big Apple" or "City of Brotherly Love." In many cities and towns, gated communities are neighborhoods surrounded by literal fences to ensure that only residents or people invited by residents can enter. At the national scale, countries control their land by forming borders, and they establish a national identity in a variety of ways, including through their names, flags, anthems, and citizenship requirements.

Along some parts of its border with Mexico, the United Sates has erected a fence to outline its territory. A photograph of the eyes of a young undocumented immigrant, known as a "Dreamer," spreads across this fence in Tecate, Mexico. The border has been the site of tension between immigrants and border patrol agents, but the artwork is meant to be used as a giant shared picnic table among residents on both sides of the wall.

These are all examples of **territoriality**, a concept that has multiple dimensions. Geographer Robert Sack defines territoriality as the "attempt by an individual or group to affect, influence, or control people, phenomena, and relationships by delimiting and asserting control over a geographic area." It is also an expression of a group's historic and personal links to a place—the connection of people, their culture, and their economic systems to the land. According to Sack, territoriality is the basis for the power that people try to exert and the political spaces they create. Governments form around these spaces, build political power, and establish sovereignty, which allows them to control their territory and protect it from outside interference. Sovereign countries, under international law, are permitted to defend their borders militarily and establish the laws that govern the people who live there.

CONTROLLING PEOPLE, LAND, AND RESOURCES

LEARNING OBJECTIVE

PSO-4.C Describe the concepts of political power and territoriality as used by geographers.

To assert and maintain political power, states impose control over the people, land, and resources in their territories. At times, states also attempt to control resources outside of their territories using tools of trade, diplomacy, or war.

NEOCOLONIALISM As you have learned, European countries began to establish colonies throughout the world starting in the 16th century, gaining control over lands in Africa, Asia, the Americas, and elsewhere. The term **colonialism** describes this practice of claiming and dominating overseas territories.

Although most former colonies have declared independence and claimed their sovereignty, **neocolonialism** endures in the use of economic, political, cultural, or other pressures to control or influence other countries, especially former dependencies. Neocolonialism is seen in many former African colonies that are free states but have economies that rely on outside investment and are therefore vulnerable to excess influence by outside powers. To cite one example, Kenya, in eastern Africa, needed to replace aging railroad infrastructure to transport cargo across the country. In 2014, the Kenyan government agreed to pay a company owned by the Chinese government to build a railroad line from Nairobi, the capital, to the city of Mombasa. The cost of the project was $3.8 billion, an amount that critics say will place Kenya in debt to China for many years. It also leaves China in control of decisions about when and how to build the railroad, which has not yet been completed.

CHOKE POINTS A **choke point** is a narrow, strategic passageway to another place through which it is difficult to pass. Because they are limited in size and because there is a great deal of competition for their use, choke points can be sources of power, influence, and wealth for the countries that control them. Waterway choke points can be straits, canals, or other restricted passages.

Choke points have historically played a significant role in military campaigns, as large armies or navies have difficulty moving through narrow passages. A classic example of a land-based choke point is Thermopylae, a mountain pass in Greece where a Greek force estimated at 7,000 men was able to hold off an invading Persian army of between 70,000 and 300,000 soldiers for three days in 480 B.C.E.

Today, waterway choke points command the most attention and are a cause for international concern because high volumes of crucial commodities, such as oil and food, pass through them. The Strait of Malacca—between Malaysia, Indonesia, and Singapore—is a choke point for all goods shipped by sea between Europe, Africa, Southwest Asia, and South Asia to East Asia. In 2017, more than one-quarter

CASE STUDY

THE KURDS

THE ISSUE Even though the Kurdish people have a long history as a distinct ethnic group and view themselves as a nation, they do not have their own state, despite years of trying.

LEARNING OBJECTIVE

PSO-4.B Explain the processes that have shaped contemporary political geography.

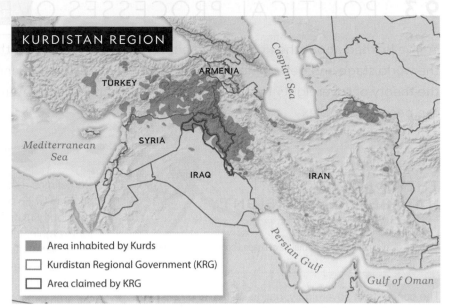

KURDISTAN REGION

■ Area inhabited by Kurds
☐ Kurdistan Regional Government (KRG)
☐ Area claimed by KRG

An estimated 25–30 million Kurds live throughout Southwest Asia in an area covering about 74,000 square miles.

BY THE NUMBERS

19%

Kurdish population of Turkey

10%

Kurdish population of Syria

15–20%

Kurdish population of Iraq

10%

Kurdish population of Iran

Source: CIA World Factbook

A DISTINCT ETHNIC GROUP OF PEOPLE called the Kurds lives in a region that covers parts of Iraq, Iran, Syria, and Turkey, unofficially called Kurdistan. However, the Kurds do not have their own state, despite having a history that dates back more than a thousand years, if not longer. The dream of an independent country was born in the late 19th century, and it came close to being realized after the breakup of the Ottoman Empire following World War I. At that time, a treaty was proposed that would define the borders of the region's new countries—including the option for a Kurdish state. However, the treaty was never ratified, and the one that replaced it did not include a provision to carve out a state for the Kurds. The treaty was negotiated between Turkey, Greece, and the Allied powers; the Kurds were not represented.

Since then, the Kurdish people have continued to work for a sovereign state, at the same time that their minority status in the four countries gives them minimal power and has led to persecution and worse. Under the rule of President Saddam Hussein in Iraq during the last decades of the 20th century, thousands of Kurdish men, women, and children were killed with poison gas.

Political obstacles have stalled any momentum toward a Kurdish state. To allow for the creation of a new state, the four countries where the Kurds reside would need to give up some of their territory. Not surprisingly, the countries' governments find this prospect very unappealing. Within Kurdish territory, infighting among leadership groups has proved to be another obstacle, as the lack of unity makes progress difficult. Pressure from external powers, such as the United States or European countries, in favor of an independent Kurdistan could build enough political will for a new country to be created. That pressure has not materialized, however, even though Kurdish fighters allied with U.S. forces in the complex conflict that engulfed Syria beginning in 2011. After the U.S. government hastily pulled most of its troops out of Syria in 2019, the Kurds found themselves under increasing pressure from both Turkey and Syria to abandon territories previously claimed for Kurdistan. At present, the Kurds can be described as a stateless nation, because they do not have an independent country to call their own, and a multination state, because they live in a region that spans multiple countries. ∎

GEOGRAPHIC THINKING

Describe what the map above illustrates about the Kurds' challenges as a stateless nation.

A later wave of imperialism hit Africa in the late 19th century, when European empires, looking to extend their economic, political, and social power, began to take African territories by force. In 1884, European leaders met at the Berlin Conference to arbitrarily define the boundaries between their conquered African possessions—boundaries that still exist between states today. Africans were not even present at the meeting, and no consideration was given for traditional ethnic boundaries or the governance structures that had existed for centuries.

Many believe the economic and social problems affecting Africa today can be traced back to imperialism and the Berlin Conference. By extracting wealth, establishing export-driven economies, and creating the conditions for conflict, European imperial powers laid the groundwork for events such as the Rwandan genocide of 1994, in which one ethnic group, the Hutus, slaughtered hundreds of thousands of Tutsis. Differences between the two groups had been profoundly exacerbated during colonial times, when the Belgian rulers had greatly favored the Tutsis over the Hutus, granting them better jobs and educational opportunities.

In countries or regions affected by imperialism, peoples have sought self-determination through independence movements. When World War II began in 1939, for example, much of Africa and Asia were still under European control, although independence movements were growing in numerous places. Following World War II, many countries fought for and gained independence from their colonial rulers. Among them was India, a British colony for 200 years that won its independence in 1947 and was split into the countries of India and Pakistan. The present-day boundary between Pakistan and India, which is still disputed in places, resulted from an agreement among leaders of the independence movement and the departing British authorities that the majority-Muslim and majority-Hindu regions should form separate states. In North Africa and Southeast Asia, the colonies of Morocco, Algeria, Vietnam, Cambodia, and Laos also exemplified the postwar movement to throw off colonial powers, gaining their independence from France during the 1950s after intense fighting. The contemporary political boundaries of all these countries are the result of their successful struggles to achieve independence from their former colonial rulers.

Sometimes related to independence movements, the process of **devolution** occurs when the central power in a state is broken up among regional authorities within its borders. Devolution tends to happen along national lines, allowing members of a nation to claim greater authority over their territory. In the case of the former Soviet Union, devolution led to the creation of 15 independent states. You will learn about devolution in greater detail in Chapter 11.

GEOGRAPHIC THINKING

1. Explain how the concept of self-determination might challenge the political structure of a multinational state.

2. Describe the cultural and economic aftereffects of imperialism.

9.4 THE NATURE AND FUNCTION OF BOUNDARIES

The states you've learned about would not exist without boundaries. Geographers recognize many different types of boundaries, but they all serve the same goal—to define political spaces and territories.

DEFINING POLITICAL BOUNDARIES

LEARNING OBJECTIVE
IMP-4.B Explain the nature and function of international and internal boundaries.

The amount of territory that falls within a state is defined by the boundaries that surround it. International boundaries, or borders, are the outcome of geopolitical relationships and expressions of territoriality—people's sense of connection to a place and their drive to control it. As such, boundaries are subject to change when relationships among countries change, or when people assert a claim to territory. As you have read, boundaries in Europe have been contested and redrawn many times as a result of conflicts, negotiations, and independence movements. Recall how the breakup of the Soviet Union resulted in the creation, or re-creation, of independent states such as Latvia, Lithuania, and Estonia. Each of these states had to establish its borders.

Even boundaries based on physical features can fluctuate. Features such as rivers, in fact, make notoriously poor borders because they often change course. This has repeatedly happened along the southern border of the United States, where the Rio Grande, which has changed its course more than once, was defined as the boundary with Mexico when the two countries signed a treaty in 1848.

Countries establish boundaries by defining, delimiting, demarcating, and defending them. When **defining** boundaries, countries explicitly state in legally binding documentation such as a treaty where their borders are located, using reference points such as natural features or lines of latitude and longitude. Definitional boundaries are typically straightforward and all interested parties agree on them, but there are sometimes exceptions, such as in the case of Belize and Guatemala. In 1859, Guatemala had achieved its independence from Spain, but Belize was still a British colony called British Honduras. That year, the British and Guatemalan governments signed a treaty establishing the boundary between the two states. In the 20th century, however, Guatemala declared the treaty was invalid and staked a claim to more than half of Belize's territory. The citizens of both countries have agreed to submit the border dispute to the UN's International Court of Justice, and both governments have agreed to abide by the court's decision, which may take several years to be concluded.

Countries **delimit** their boundaries by drawing them on a map in accordance with a legal agreement, as the United States did in its 1848 treaty with Mexico. Sometimes boundaries are **demarcated** with physical objects such as stones, pillars, walls, or fences. However, many long stretches of border between countries have no demarcation at all, because physical markers or barriers are thought to be impractical or unnecessary—or just too difficult to construct. In the 21st century, the United States government has been debating whether its entire border with Mexico can or should be fenced with a wall, and the difficulties of building such a physical barrier are very much part of the discussion. The border is more than 1,900 miles long, and much of it crosses rugged, isolated landscapes. Estimates for building the barrier have ranged from $17.3 million per mile to $36.3 million per mile. American citizens and lawmakers disagree over whether the potential benefits of a border wall would exceed the effort and expense of building it.

To defend their borders, countries must take steps to **administer** them, or manage the way they are maintained and how goods and people will cross them. Most of the world's borders are, to some extent, restricted, or closed. This means that people cannot freely cross the border from one country to the other. Instead, one must have official government permission to enter a country unless one is a citizen of that country, or the countries have agreements to allow entry to one another's citizens. Permission to enter a country typically comes in the form of documentation such as a visa. In rare cases, where borders are completely restricted, people are not permitted to cross at all. An example of this is the demilitarized zone between North Korea and South Korea. Some countries, such as the 26 found in the Schengen Area in Europe, which includes France, Germany, and Sweden, have decided to allow their borders to be largely open in certain circumstances. Citizens of participating countries are allowed to freely move about the Schengen Area in order to work, travel, and live. Tourists and other travelers are also able to freely cross borders within the Schengen Area.

While the United States government debates the building of a border wall with Mexico, large sections of wall or fence already exist in South Texas. Openings allow residents to access the land just south of the barrier. Notice that the Rio Grande—the river that forms the natural boundary between the United States and Mexico—lies just beyond the fence.

CASE STUDY

THE DMZ IN KOREA

THE ISSUE One of the most tightly closed borders in the world exists along the Demilitarized Zone (DMZ) on the Korean Peninsula, but glimmers of greater openness are appearing.

LEARNING OBJECTIVE
IMP-4.B Explain the nature and function of international and internal boundaries.

South Korean soldiers stand guard by the fence that marks the Demilitarized Zone between North Korea and South Korea. Even though the DMZ is heavily guarded, the two countries have worked to reconnect parts of the region in recent years.

BY THE NUMBERS

150 MILES

Length of Demilitarized Zone

51.8 MILLION

Population of South Korea

25.5 MILLION

Population of North Korea

Source: Encyclopedia Britannica; CIA World Factbook

BETWEEN 1950 AND 1953, North Korea and South Korea fought a war that ended with no victor when an armistice agreement was signed. The armistice ended the fighting and established a boundary called the Demilitarized Zone (DMZ) that divides the Korean Peninsula roughly in half. At 150 miles long and 2.5 miles wide, it's a buffer between the two countries that has kept hostilities mostly at bay for seven decades.

The war, fought between communist forces in the north and anti-communist capitalists in the south, was a fight that was part of the larger Cold War. The north received aid and training from China and the Soviet Union, while the south was supported by the United Nations and principally the United States. Because the two countries remain divided along democratic capitalist and authoritarian communist lines, South Korea is a strong ally of the United States while North Korea is an adversary.

Despite the differences between the two countries' economies and approach to governing, the north and south have found a way to coexist. The DMZ is heavily fortified with large numbers of troops from both countries on both sides, who are not allowed to cross the Military Demarcation Line that runs through the center of the DMZ. At the Joint Security Area in the village of Panmunjom, where the armistice agreement was signed, soldiers from North and South Korea stand face to face. The two countries still use the site for meetings and negotiations.

Although this boundary is seemingly impenetrable, North and South Korea do have some connectivity, and in recent years, more links have formed. The two countries have reconnected their railways and roads, and in late 2018, a train crossed the border for the first time in more than a decade. Other discussions about connecting the two countries have taken place, and there is some hope that they will host the 2032 Olympic Games together. ∎

GEOGRAPHIC THINKING

Explain why it is important that the border between South and North Korea is clearly demarcated.

Guttenfelder's photographs of everyday life in North Korea have made him a seven-time finalist for the Pulitzer Prize.

LEARNING OBJECTIVE
IMP-4.B Explain the nature and function of international and internal boundaries.

REVEALING MYSTERIES

One of the most mysterious places on the planet is North Korea. Since the country was established in 1948, the outside world has had little opportunity to see what happens inside its borders and how its people live. Recently, National Geographic photographer David Guttenfelder has helped to lift the veil of secrecy that shrouds North Korea.

In 2011, the Associated Press opened its first bureau in North Korea, and Guttenfelder became the first Western photographer to cover the rarely photographed country. His purpose, as he sees it, is to show the world how normal, everyday North Koreans live. "My job was really to get as far out there as I could go and as close and intimate as I could be with people and tell their story."

Guttenfelder's photographs add up to a picture that is larger than the sum of its parts. Although each individual shot might seem ordinary, when taken collectively they tell a relatable story of life in North Korea beyond the seemingly impenetrable boundary of the DMZ. These pictures of people going to work, waiting for the bus, hugging loved ones, or riding an escalator show that there's much more to North Korea than what we learn in the news about its government and its role in global politics.

"No one believes there's real people there," Guttenfelder says. "I find myself arguing with people who would say, 'Oh that's not true. There's not a father with his daughter in a supermarket. That's all just fake.' It was very surprising to me that I was having to defend that there was a real life and real people living lives in North Korea." ▮

CRITICAL VIEWING Shoppers go about their daily lives, comparing goods in a supermarket in Pyongyang, North Korea's capital. ▮ Describe how the images of North Korea and its cultural landscape at this particular scale alter your perspective on the country.

CRITICAL VIEWING   Top: Bicyclists ride past portraits of North Korean leaders Kim Il Sung and Kim Jong Il in Pyongyang. Portraits of the leaders are displayed prominently throughout the country. Bottom: Commuters in Pyongyang head home from work on the subway. ▮ What do these photographs suggest about how North Korea uses its leaders as a centripetal force?

TYPES OF BOUNDARIES

LEARNING OBJECTIVES
IMP-4.A Define types of political boundaries used by geographers.
IMP-4.B Explain the nature and function of international and internal boundaries.

Geographers define many different types of boundaries by considering not just their physical features but also how, when, and why they were created. **Antecedent boundaries** are established before many people settle into an area. An example of this is the boundary between the United States and Canada, established at the 49th parallel in 1846, before most European American settlers moved into the territories that became Minnesota, North Dakota, Montana, and Washington. The boundary between Malaysia and Indonesia on the island of Borneo is also considered to be antecedent because the Dutch and British colonists established it when the area was lightly inhabited. Like those drawn in Africa during the Berlin Conference, this boundary is also a legacy of imperialism.

Unlike antecedent boundaries, **subsequent boundaries** are drawn in areas that have been settled by people and where cultural landscapes already exist or are in the process of being established. These types of boundaries are the most common, since the process of establishing them is lengthy and related to territoriality. Many of the boundaries in Europe are subsequent, having evolved over centuries between neighboring states. France and Germany, for example, are delineated with subsequent boundaries.

A **consequent boundary** is a type of subsequent boundary. Consequent boundaries take into account the differences that exist within a cultural landscape, separating groups that have distinct languages, religions, ethnicities, or other traits. Recall what you have learned about the formation of new states in the Balkan region after the breakup of the Soviet Union and the devolution of Yugoslavia that followed. The borders between many of the newly formed countries in the former Yugoslavia may be called consequent boundaries because they follow ethnic and cultural divisions in the region. Serbia, for example, encompasses territory inhabited in large part by a single ethnic group, the Serbs. Croatia's boundaries enclose a population that is more than 90 percent Croat. When India gained its independence from Britain in 1947 and the territory was divided into modern-day India and Pakistan, the consequent boundary between the two states ran along religious lines: Pakistan's population is mostly Muslim, whereas Indians are largely Hindu.

While subsequent and consequent boundaries could be said to arise naturally from patterns of human settlement and the growth of cultures, other boundaries are **superimposed**, or drawn over existing accepted borders, by an outside or conquering force. This occurred in Africa when European colonial powers met at the Berlin Conference. The European empires drew up the boundaries of the new countries they conquered with no regard to the culture or ethnicity of the people who lived on the land. In many cases, ethnicities were split by the superimposed boundaries established by the Berlin Conference. When groups from a variety of cultural and ethnic backgrounds are forced to live alongside one another inside boundaries superimposed from the outside, the possibility of conflict within countries, or even civil wars, increases.

Looking at the "Africa: Political Boundaries and Cultural Groups, 2019" map, it's impossible not to notice that some boundaries feature many curves and squiggles, whereas others are perfectly straight. These **geometric boundaries** are mathematical and typically follow lines of latitude and longitude, or are straight-line arcs between two points, instead of following physical and cultural features. Many states in the western United States, such as Colorado, Wyoming, and Utah, have geometric boundaries. Geometric boundaries may be superimposed, as in Africa, or they may be antecedent.

Like boundaries based on physical features, geometric boundaries can be flawed and cause conflict when they are applied without thought for the people living on the lands being delimited. Consider the Kenya-Tanzania and Somalia-Ethiopia borders created by the Berlin Conference, both of which are straight-line borders that cut across ethnic lines. Ill-considered superimposed geometric boundaries are one reason armed conflict has occurred in parts of Africa.

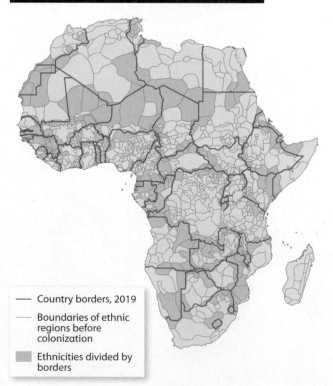

AFRICA: POLITICAL BOUNDARIES AND CULTURAL GROUPS, 2019

— Country borders, 2019

— Boundaries of ethnic regions before colonization

▓ Ethnicities divided by borders

This map highlights how the political boundaries created at the Berlin Conference were drawn with no regard to the diverse nations already living in Africa.

Former boundaries that once existed but no longer have an official function are considered to be **relics**. These borders illustrate how the control and management of geographic space changes over time as a result of different circumstances. The boundary between East and West Germany, for instance, is a relic whose presence continues to be felt. After its reunification in 1990, Germany became a single, unified country. Still, the impact of the former boundary lingers. The capitalist economy of West Germany created a very different physical and cultural landscape than the communist economy of East Germany during the 45 years they were separated. The drab, utilitarian housing of communist East Germany can still be seen in places like East Berlin, while West Germany generally has more varied and attractive housing that was designed to appeal to consumers.

In Asia, Vietnam also was divided into two countries as part of the proxy conflict between the United States and the Soviet Union. Unlike Korea, Vietnam was reunited under a single government in 1976, making the former border between North and South Vietnam a relic. Many hope the boundary between North and South Korea will also cease to exist someday. If that comes to pass, the former border will be a relic with a lasting and profound impact because of the enormous differences between South Korea, a capitalist democracy with a core economy, and North Korea, a totalitarian, peripheral state.

SEA BOUNDARIES Not all boundaries exist on land. In fact, many are miles out to sea. Also called maritime boundaries, sea boundaries allow countries access to offshore resources such as oil and coastal sites for wind farms.

This cement barrier is the longest surviving stretch of the Berlin Wall. After West Germany and East Germany were reunified, artists began painting colorful murals on the once-drab surface.

The "cod wars" were a series of clashes in the 1950s, 1960s, and 1970s over the rights of British fishers to fish in waters within Iceland's EEZ.

— Exclusive economic zone (EEZ)

With EEZs around Puerto Rico and other island territories, the United States controls a greater expanse of ocean than any other country.

Australia, Chile, and Argentina have tried to assert claims to land in Antarctica and EEZs extending from these territories.

READING MAPS The map shows the location of the world's exclusive economic zones (EEZs), which extend 200 nautical miles off the coasts of the countries that control them. ❚ Describe how maritime boundaries like the EEZs might influence foreign policy among the coastal states of the world.

Countries with sea boundaries are typically more economically developed than those that are landlocked because having maritime ports of entry makes it significantly easier to conduct trade with other countries. Bolivia is an example of a landlocked country that is poorer than its maritime neighbors, who have little incentive to help an economic rival reach their ports. Landlocked countries have also suffered from not receiving the flow of people and ideas that have made maritime countries with ports more dynamic through innovation.

The 1982 **United Nations Convention on the Law of the Sea** (UNCLOS) established the structure of maritime boundaries, stating that a country's territorial seas extend 12 nautical miles off its coast and that its **exclusive economic zone** (EEZ) extends 200 nautical miles from its coast. (A nautical mile is 1.1508 land miles, or 6,076 feet.) UNCLOS also specifies rules for determining how territorial seas and EEZs should be measured and delimited.

Countries exert different levels of control over their territorial seas and their EEZs. States have complete sovereignty

over their territorial seas, covering not only the surface but reaching down to the layers beneath the seabed and up into the airspace above the water. The principal restriction on this sovereignty is that countries must permit "innocent passage" of foreign ships through their territorial waters. Innocent passage is defined as nonstop direct travel through territorial waters between two points outside of a country's borders or from a point outside the country's borders to one of its ports. States do not have full sovereignty over their EEZ, but they do have sole access to resources found within the waters or beneath the sea floor of the EEZ, such as fish, oil, and natural gas. Countries also have the exclusive right to generate energy from the waves, wind, or currents inside their EEZ.

Along with the rights governing territorial waters and EEZs come certain responsibilities. For example UNCLOS specifies that within its EEZ, "the coastal State, taking into account the best scientific evidence available to it, shall ensure through proper conservation and management measures that the maintenance of the living resources in

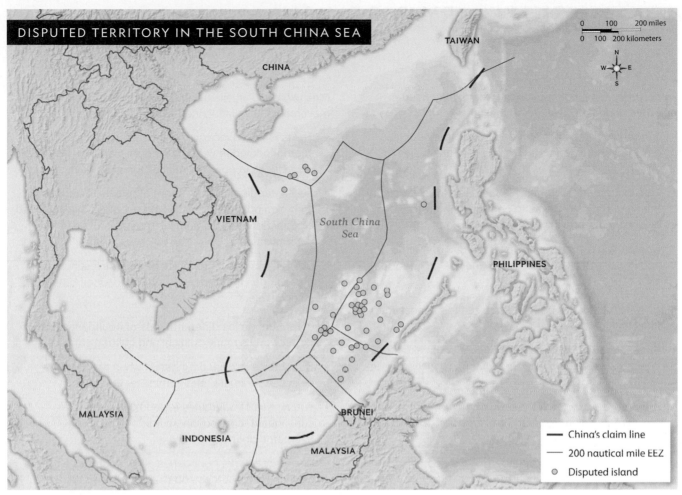

DISPUTED TERRITORY IN THE SOUTH CHINA SEA

CHINA

TAIWAN

VIETNAM

South China Sea

PHILIPPINES

MALAYSIA

INDONESIA

BRUNEI

MALAYSIA

—— China's claim line
—— 200 nautical mile EEZ
○ Disputed island

READING MAPS More than $3 trillion dollars in trade passes through the South China Sea every year. As tensions rise over the disputed ocean territory, countries including China, Vietnam, and the Philippines have increased military spending. ▮ Describe how the unresolved dispute over maritime territory in the South China Sea likely impacts each of the states that asserts claims to the region.

the exclusive economic zone is not endangered by over-exploitation." In other words, UNCLOS requires coastal countries to employ sound environmental practices in the waters they control, such as avoiding overfishing and depleting ocean species. In addition, states are required to make public any dangers to navigation that they know of within their territorial waters.

Disputes over maritime boundaries sometimes arise, as has happened in the strategically important South China Sea. There, China has laid claim to territory that, according to the 200-nautical-mile rule, falls within international waters. China argues that it has historical claims to the sea, dating back to naval expeditions in the 15th century, and after Japan was defeated in World War II, China laid claim to 90 percent of the sea. To solidify its claim, China is building artificial islands on top of reefs in the South China Sea, because the 200-mile line can be extended to include a country's islands. The dispute has not been resolved, and some are concerned that a military conflict could one day break out between China and others who assert claims to parts of the South China Sea, including Malaysia, Vietnam, and the Philippines.

WHY DO BOUNDARIES MATTER? Political boundaries are the result and the reflection of the ways humans divide space. As you have seen, some boundaries are products of balanced negotiation between groups, while others demonstrate the power imposed by one group over another. Sometimes boundaries follow ethnic or cultural lines in an attempt to delimit nation-states, and sometimes they divide nations among multiple countries. As sources of both conflict and harmony, change and permanence, boundaries shape the contemporary world.

GEOGRAPHIC THINKING

1. Compare subsequent and superimposed boundaries.

2. Describe how the nature of a country's boundaries is linked with its history and political situation.

3. Explain why countries find it necessary to delimit their boundaries.

4. Explain why coastal countries seek to expand and defend their maritime boundaries.

CHAPTER SUMMARY

Territoriality is the connection of people, their culture, and their economic systems to the land.

- Territoriality is the basis for the power that peoples assert over the geographic areas they call their own and the political spaces they create.

- The concept of territoriality is the basis for sovereignty, the right of governments to control their territory and decide what happens inside their borders.

- Coastal waters are considered part of a maritime country's territory and control of them is an important aspect of this sovereignty.

Maps reflect the ways people organize their spaces into political entities.

- States, or countries, are independent political units created by people to organize and manage themselves.

- Nations are cultural entities comprising people who have a shared identity through traits in common, such as language, religion, ethnicity, and heritage.

- Nation-states are countries with political boundaries that match the cultural boundaries of a people who consider themselves a nation.

The contemporary world has been shaped by a variety of factors, including the concepts of sovereignty and self-determination, and attempts to form nation-states.

Meanwhile, colonialism, imperialism, and independence movements have influenced political boundaries.

- The issue of sovereignty has been complicated by the interconnectedness of the modern world, as well as by imbalances in power in relationships between states.

- Self-determination is the right of people to choose their own political status. Some peoples have launched independence movements in the name of self-determination.

- Colonialism and imperialism have left a lasting mark on countries that have won independence from their colonial rulers.

Geographers define different types of boundaries that mark the world's many political and cultural entities.

- Countries establish boundaries when they define, delimit, demarcate, and administer them.

- The types of boundaries include antecedent, subsequent, consequent, superimposed, and geometric boundaries.

- Sea, or maritime, boundaries allow countries access to offshore resources and to exercise their sovereignty over offshore territories.

- Cultural boundaries differ from political boundaries and run along lines that separate people of different ethnicities or cultural backgrounds.

KEY TERMS AND CONCEPTS

Use complete sentences to answer the questions.

1. **APPLY CONCEPTUAL VOCABULARY** Consider the terms *political geography* and *nation-state*. Write a standard dictionary definition of each term. Then provide a conceptual definition—an explanation of how each term is used in the context of this chapter.

2. Provide an example of how a country uses its sovereignty to control what happens within its borders.

3. Why could the Panama Canal be considered a choke point?

4. Describe how a government might manipulate a map to tell a particular story.

5. Explain why the country of Bolivia is considered an independent state, while the Canadian province of Manitoba is not.

6. Identify a nation that does not have its own state.

7. Why is the surge of migrants into some European countries such as Germay and France causing discontent among some of the population?

8. Define the term *stateless nation*.

9. Explain why the Berlin Conference was so devastating to the continent of Africa.

10. Describe the difference between a delimited boundary and a demarcated boundary.

11. What type of boundary typically features straight lines?

12. How do the terms of the United Nations Convention on the Law of the Sea benefit countries with maritime boundaries?

■ INTERPRET MAPS

Study the map and then answer the following questions.

SOUTH AMERICA, 2020

13. **IDENTIFY DATA & INFORMATION** What types of information does this map give about the countries of South America? What information does it not include?

14. **ANALYZE MAPS** What feature defines the border between Chile and Argentina?

15. **EXPLAIN PATTERNS & TRENDS** What evidence of colonialism does this map show?

16. **ANALYZE GEOGRAPHIC CONCEPTS** In the early 1800s, Colombia, Ecuador, Panama, Venezuela, and parts of other countries all formed the state called Gran Colombia. For what reasons might Gran Colombia have broken up?

17. **ANALYZE MAPS** Why is Paraguay at a possible disadvantage compared to most of its neighbors? Explain your answer.

18. **EXPLAIN GEOGRAPHIC CONCEPTS** How does a map like this one illustrate the concepts of territoriality and sovereignty?

GEO-INQUIRY | LOCAL BOUNDARIES

Consider how to use Geo-Inquiry to answer questions about boundaries in your state and local community. Use the steps in the Geo-Inquiry Process below to create an actionable answer to your Geo-Inquiry question.

ASK Start with an authentic Geo-Inquiry question about the boundaries that exist in your state or community. It may be as simple as *How might we decide the best boundaries for a wildlife reserve in our community?* Additional need-to-know questions might include *What are the boundaries of existing protected areas in our community? Are there currently plans to protect lands, and if so where? What species might need protection?*

COLLECT Decide how you could learn answers to your Geo-Inquiry questions. Explore maps from a variety of sources and talk to friends, family, neighbors, and community leaders.

VISUALIZE Analyze and organize the information you collected on protected spaces in the community. Organize the information and use it to create a map that clearly defines the boundaries of the area you want to protect and will help others understand why you drew them.

CREATE Focus on ways to tell a Geo-Inquiry story in order to persuade others to implement your proposal. Be prepared to explain how the boundaries you have chosen for your protected space will affect the life of your community. Using the data you collected, outline or storyboard your plan to answer your Geo-inquiry question.

ACT Share your stories with others, including stakeholders and decision-makers. Consider how your project can inform and improve the quality of life in your community.

ASK   COLLECT   VISUALIZE   CREATE   ACT

SPATIAL PATTERNS OF POLITICAL POWER

CRITICAL VIEWING In 2019, protesters demonstrated in front of the U.S. Supreme Court against the controversial process of gerrymandering. The Court was hearing two cases that impacted legislative districts in Maryland and North Carolina. ▮ How do political boundaries affect people's lives?

GEOGRAPHIC THINKING What role do boundaries play as symbols of political power?

10.1
ORGANIZATION OF STATES

NATIONAL GEOGRAPHIC EXPLORER
Anna Antoniou

CASE STUDY: Political Control and Nunavut

10.2
ELECTORAL GEOGRAPHY

CASE STUDY: Gerrymandering and Race

10.1 ORGANIZATION OF STATES

States are divided into smaller regional units to make governance more efficient. (In this context, *state* means "country.") The ways in which a state's internal boundaries are set and its regional units administered reflect the balance of power between the central, or national, government and its internal political units.

UNITARY STATES

LEARNING OBJECTIVES
IMP-4.C Define federal and unitary states.
IMP-4.D Explain how federal and unitary states affect spatial organization.

Different forms of governance, or how a state is organized politically and spatially, affect a country's economic and social affairs. Most state governments are organized in one of two ways, either as a **federal state** or as a **unitary state**. Where power is held within a country affects the amount of authority governments have at national and regional levels. In federal states, power is held by regional units, such as the states of the United States or the provinces of Canada. These political units typically have their own governments that maintain some autonomy and hold substantial power. In unitary states, more power is held by a central government that maintains authority over all of the state's territory, its regional units, and its people.

A unitary state has a form of government that follows a top-down approach in which policies are conveyed by the central government and funneled down to regional units to be carried out. The central government creates its internal units, such as provinces, states, or other regional and local divisions, which are sometimes given a degree of power, perhaps even to make regional laws. But a unitary state always maintains supreme authority at the top.

The vast majority of the world's countries are unitary states. The United Kingdom is one example. The UK Parliament is the central governing authority over its four constituent units: England, Wales, Scotland, and Northern Ireland. Parliament controls a range of national affairs, including military defense, foreign relations with other countries, and immigration for the entire United Kingdom. To provide for each unit's own particular needs and concerns, the central government allows Scotland, Wales, and Northern Ireland to have their own national assemblies and to administer systems of local governments called districts, boroughs, and councils. (England does not have its own assembly.) Local governments oversee issues such as health services, housing, education, and the environment.

Other unitary states include Poland, France, Spain, China, Indonesia, Bangladesh, Algeria, the Scandinavian countries, and Japan. Japan's constitution establishes a central government while also giving power to local units.

The central government in Tokyo holds most of Japan's authority, with some autonomy given to a system of 47 local units called prefectures. While each prefecture has considerable administrative power within its territory, these local units are overseen by a central ministry and grouped into eight regions. Lower levels of government lie in each prefecture's cities, towns, and villages. In France's unitary system, the central government has supreme power over its major subunits, called provinces. The provinces do not have the power to act independently. France is also a republic; French citizens vote in democratic elections and choose a president, who then appoints a prime minister.

THE UNITED KINGDOM OF GREAT BRITAIN AND NORTHERN IRELAND, 2020

The United Kingdom is a unitary state with four constituent units: England, Wales, Scotland, and Northern Ireland. Though each unit has its own government (except for England) Parliament, the national legislature in London, holds central power over them.

UNDERSTANDING A DIVIDED CYPRUS

Anna Antoniou mixes archaeology and storytelling to discover more about the cultural heritage of communities around the world. Talking to residents during her exploration of Cyprus with other team members (above) led to a discovery that the long-segregated nation is not as divided as previously thought.

LEARNING OBJECTIVE

IMP-4.B Explain the nature and function of international and internal boundaries.

Anna Antoniou circumnavigated the Mediterranean island of Cyprus for 60 days to understand the effects of the internal boundaries that divide the landscape geographically, politically, and ethnically.

Cyprus is home to a majority ethnic Greek population and a small population of ethnic Turkish residents. An ongoing dispute between the two groups over settlement issues of the island has existed since the 19th century. Consequently, Cyprus has been partitioned since 1974, resulting in separate governments and territories. The southern two-thirds of the island form an independent country with majority Greek ethnic ties, called the Republic of Cyprus. The northern portion remains a Turkish-occupied territory called the Turkish Republic of Northern Cyprus.

Anna Antoniou, an anthropological archaeologist and Cypriot-American, set out to explore the cultural and political dynamics of Cyprus's division. She wanted to know, "What unites this divided island?" Antoniou talked to real people about their lives to hear if there was more commonality among the people of Cyprus beyond the issues of the political divisions that split the land.

From her discussions, Antoniou found that though the boundaries divide the economies and governments of the people of Cyprus, most residents feel like they are part of the same culture and community and desire to be a unified island again. Antoniou told National Geographic, "Although they do not share a language, a religion, and now a territory, Greek Cypriots and Turkish Cypriots believe they possess a single ethnic and cultural identity, with 'Greek' and 'Turkish' being a secondary affiliation. . . . Greek and Turkish Cypriots have a stronger bond with each other than they do with their mainland counterparts."

GEOGRAPHIC THINKING

Identify centripetal and centrifugal forces that impact Greek and Turkish Cypriots.

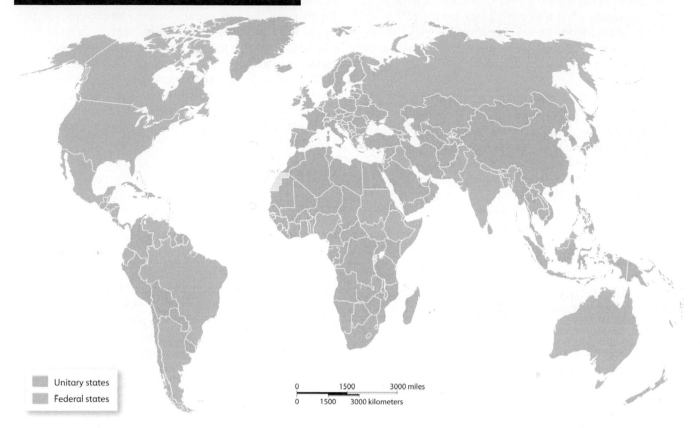

Unitary states

Federal states

0   1500   3000 miles

0   1500   3000 kilometers

READING MAPS Of the 192 countries that are United Nations members, the vast majority are unitary states. ▮ Explain one possible reason why there are so many unitary states in Africa.

Norway also has a unitary, top-down power structure. County and municipal authority is solely and totally granted by the national government. For instance, the central Norwegian government is in charge of devising health policy and establishing the budget for health services throughout the country. In the early 2000s, the Ministry of Health, which is part of the central government, coordinated efforts to tackle health inequity in Norway. Through comprehensive legislation and oversight by the central government, health policies were created and distributed to county and municipal governments who are each responsible for enacting different health services. This coordinated effort by the central government ensured coherence across the regional and local levels.

ADVANTAGES OF UNITARY STATES
The top-down nature of unitary systems gives them several advantages. One advantage is that unitary systems tend to have fewer government agencies, especially those dealing with taxation. States with unitary systems also tend to be less corrupt at the local level.

A major advantage of a unitary system is its efficiency: laws are implemented quickly, evenly, fairly, and with less duplication. For example, the efficiency of Singapore's highly regarded transportation system is credited to that city-state's unitary system of government. Since the 1970s,

spatial planning has been done according to the so-called Concept Plan, a nonstatutory framework by which all public transportation decisions are still made. In 1995, a governmental agency called the Land Transport Authority (LTA) was established to plan, regulate, and make policy for all urban transportation systems throughout Singapore. The LTA also builds and maintains the roads and transit infrastructures, both local and regional, providing a range of connected options for millions of daily commuters. Many take advantage of the extensive road-rail-bus network, or cycle and walk to destinations. The fact that one organization holds so many responsibilities related to transportation allows decisions and actions to be taken more deliberately. Further, because the LTA's decisions are always connected to the original Concept Plan, upgrades and expansions are implemented quickly and fairly.

Another example of unitary efficiency is found in the Netherlands, where decentralization has been applied to social policy. In 2011, the Dutch central government decided to shift certain tasks and responsibilities to regional and local units. Regional governments took on spatial planning, environmental concerns, regional economic issues, and transportation. Local authorities began to manage disabled and elder care and the youth. A law called the Child and Youth Act went into effect January 1, 2015. It empowered local municipalities to handle youth-related issues and tend to specific needs in a timely manner through the use of local social teams, which are groups of like-minded experts, in each municipality. While a federal agency, the Ministry of Interior Affairs, supports the municipalities' work and fosters good governance, the country's 42 youth care regions (and further subregions) do the actual work.

DISADVANTAGES OF UNITARY STATES

A unitary system of government often has negative characteristics. The overarching issue is that highly centralized governments can become disconnected from local areas and lose touch with the issues that concern people living there. Unitary systems tend to favor the politically or culturally dominant group, resulting in governments that issue one-sided policies that ignore the concerns of minority groups and local cultures. Also, the policies tend to serve the needs of the region adjacent to the capital or where the ruling elites reside. As a result, unitary governments can be slower than federal governments in responding to local issues. They may also fail to equitably distribute goods and services to peripheral areas or even have difficulty providing services to localities at all.

An incident in China illustrates how a unitary government must balance centrality and efficiency with the concerns of local areas. When a massive earthquake struck an area of Sichuan Province in 2008, the government quickly sent 130,000 workers to remote areas to help with relief efforts. Yet the event also exposed the need for stronger building codes and improved early warning systems in those places. The centralization of the government had actually been creating inefficiency: the responsibilities of several agencies and ministries overlapped to such a degree that the main issue—disaster management—was not properly tended to. In 2018, the central government in Beijing created an agency devoted entirely to improved emergency management.

FEDERAL STATES

LEARNING OBJECTIVES
IMP-4.C Define federal and unitary states.

IMP-4.D Explain how federal and unitary states affect spatial organization.

A federal state has a form of government in which the country's power is more broadly shared between a federal—sometimes called national—government and its regional units. These regional units, such as provinces or states, maintain greater autonomy, have their own governments, and have more authority to administer their regional territories to meet the needs of diverse groups. As a result, power is shared between central, regional, and

MEXICO'S STATE BOUNDARIES, 2020

READING MAPS Mexico is comprised of 31 states and a federal district in Mexico City. The geography, size, and population varies among each state. ▌ Based on what you observe in this map, what factors might impact the way internal state boundaries are drawn under a federal system?

THE SHARING OF POWERS

The federal system in the United States results in numerous concurrent, or shared, powers between the federal government, state governments, and local governments.
▌ Why do you think states decide school curricula?

FEDERALISM IN THE UNITED STATES

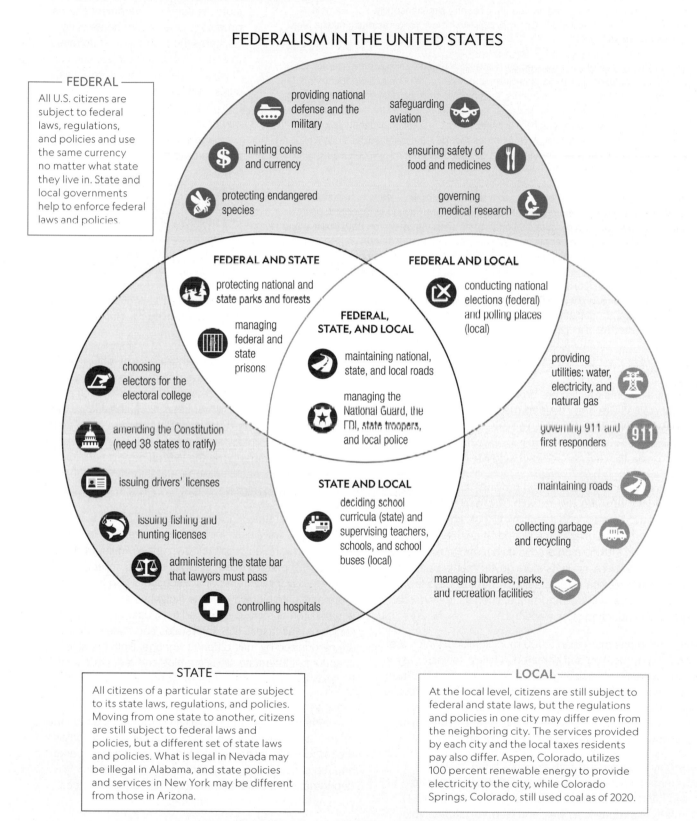

FEDERAL

All U.S. citizens are subject to federal laws, regulations, and policies and use the same currency no matter what state they live in. State and local governments help to enforce federal laws and policies.

providing national defense and the military

safeguarding aviation

minting coins and currency

ensuring safety of food and medicines

protecting endangered species

governing medical research

FEDERAL AND STATE

protecting national and state parks and forests

managing federal and state prisons

FEDERAL AND LOCAL

conducting national elections (federal) and polling places (local)

FEDERAL, STATE, AND LOCAL

maintaining national, state, and local roads

managing the National Guard, the FBI, state troopers, and local police

choosing electors for the electoral college

amending the Constitution (need 38 states to ratify)

issuing drivers' licenses

issuing fishing and hunting licenses

administering the state bar that lawyers must pass

controlling hospitals

STATE AND LOCAL

deciding school curricula (state) and supervising teachers, schools, and school buses (local)

providing utilities: water, electricity, and natural gas

governing 911 and first responders

maintaining roads

collecting garbage and recycling

managing libraries, parks, and recreation facilities

STATE

All citizens of a particular state are subject to its state laws, regulations, and policies. Moving from one state to another, citizens are still subject to federal laws and policies, but a different set of state laws and policies. What is legal in Nevada may be illegal in Alabama, and state policies and services in New York may be different from those in Arizona.

LOCAL

At the local level, citizens are still subject to federal and state laws, but the regulations and policies in one city may differ even from the neighboring city. The services provided by each city and the local taxes residents pay also differ. Aspen, Colorado, utilizes 100 percent renewable energy to provide electricity to the city, while Colorado Springs, Colorado, still used coal as of 2020.

PATRIOTISM AND NATIONALISM

Patriotism, the love that one feels for one's country, can be found in both unitary and federal systems. In a unitary system, patriotism is often bolstered by the sense of uniformity that results from the central system itself. In a federal system, patriotism tends to be more complex. It is not unusual for someone to feel a sense of belonging to both their local town or region and their country simultaneously. For example, a long-time resident of New York City may feel like a New Yorker as much as she feels like an American.

An increase in patriotism, however, can have both negative and positive results. On the positive side, patriotism causes citizens to have more pride in their country's history, culture, and accomplishments, leading to a stronger desire to find common good. Ruling governments may discover more popular support for their policy initiatives when patriotism is high. The development of a national identity also can help combat, or at least offset, certain forces that divide a state, such as political or economic inequality. These forces, called devolutionary forces, will be discussed in Chapter 11.

Patriotism is sometimes problematic, too, particularly when it leads to nationalism. When individuals feel greater devotion to the state than they do to other group interests, nationalism can occur. Nationalism as an ideology can be both positive and negative. The desire of a people to form their own nation and determine their own destiny drove the creation of the United States of America, for example. However, taken to an extreme, nationalist sentiments can lead to intolerance and exclusion of groups deemed outside of the national norm, such as racial, ethnic, or religious minorities. Indeed, history is littered with examples of toxic nationalism resulting in international and intranational tensions and conflicts, including the Holocaust and Japanese internment in the United States during World War II.

to elect representatives to the Bundestag, one of two legislative bodies. Members of the Bundestag, in turn, elect a chancellor who heads the government.

The United States also is a federal state. Its central government shares power with the governments of its 50 states (here, the term *state* refers to one of the United States, such as Ohio) and their numerous counties, cities, and towns. The federal structure has given state governments the sole power to conduct elections, issue marriage licenses, regulate intrastate commerce, administer driving regulations, and other activities. In fact, the Tenth Amendment to the U.S. Constitution "reserves to the States" any powers not explicitly "delegated to" the federal government. The federal government and state governments also have some **concurrent**, or shared, powers. Those include levying taxes, making and enforcing laws, establishing courts, and borrowing money.

The power structure of federal and state governments impacts groups of people across the United States in different ways. One area where this is exemplified is transportation, specifically the nation's highway system. The federal government initiated a national system of interstate highways, called the Interstate System, in the 1950s. While the federal government funded the entire system, each individual state constructed the actual highway (or highways) that ran through it.

Today, the Interstate highways are owned by the state in which they were built. Individual state transportation agencies set and enforce their own speed limits, fix the highways when they need repair, and some collect tolls that help pay for those repairs. Each state also has its own system of state highways. State highways are funded by a combination of state-determined tolls, user fees, and taxes (including gas taxes). U.S. Interstates and state highways are recognized by their differing signage. Both are shield-shaped, but Interstate signs are blue and red, while state highway signs vary from state to state.

local governments much more broadly than in unitary states. Federal states have often been formed where populations are very large, highly dispersed, or both. Examples of federal states include Russia, India, Brazil, Malaysia, the United States, Australia, Germany, Sudan, and Mexico.

The Mexican Federal Constitution provides for a central government that shares power with 31 organized political districts, called states, and a federal district, each with their own government. Similar to the United States, the federal government in Mexico (centered in its capital, Mexico City) has specific powers, while its state governments possess other powers. Mexican states hold the right to pass laws related to issues of state importance, such as raising local taxes and conducting state elections.

Mexico also has more than 2,000 municipalities, which are organized by location and centered in cities, towns, villages, and rural areas. Municipal governments enact local policies and oversee issues like public parks, public services, public safety and traffic, and urban planning. The municipalities manage the local concerns, while the central government focuses on issues affecting the entire country.

Germany has a federal system in which the central government shares its political power with its subunits, called Länder, but holds ultimate authority over them. Germany is a republic as well, and German citizens vote

State governments also have the power to establish local governments and distribute certain powers to them. In the United States, governments of counties and municipalities are responsible for decisions made regarding local parks and recreation, emergency services, police and fire departments, public transportation, and public services, such as sewers and snow removal.

ADVANTAGES OF FEDERAL STATES One positive result of decentralizing power in a federal system is the reduction of conflict between regions that differ on civil and political issues. A regional unit can pass a law that applies to it and not to the rest of the country. In this way, a federal state allows for the diversity of opinions, as reflected in its laws. A good example of this is the death penalty in the United States. The U.S. Supreme Court has ruled that the death penalty is constitutional, except in cases where the offender is mentally disabled or a juvenile. However, each of the U.S. states, like Pennsylvania or Texas, is permitted to ban the death penalty if it wishes.

Federalism also allows room for diversity. Multiple political parties can be in power in different areas of a country, and this pluralism, or coexistence of more than one party, helps keep oppression by one authority at bay. It also pushes against divisive forces that result from economic or cultural differences within a state. Attention to local issues within a federal system also boosts political participation among its citizens who want to make a difference in their local community. Some estimate that there are more than half a million elected officials in the United States, the vast majority of them in local offices, as in county, city, town, and village posts. In a federal system, government efficiency occurs when local governments can tend to local needs.

DISADVANTAGES OF FEDERAL STATES

A federal system is not perfect. Many disadvantages are the downsides of its perceived advantages. For example, a federal state's focus on regional and local issues allows regional and local leaders to stymie, or prevent, progress on issues that may impact the whole country. Policy areas like civil rights, energy, poverty, and pollution have all experienced roadblocks at the state or local level. Federalism can give undue, or improper, power to localized special interests. During the civil rights era in the United States, those in favor of racial segregation claimed

U.S. states' rights, which allowed them to dodge federal discrimination laws. In fact, decentralization contributed greatly to the spread of segregation. When civil rights for African Americans was mandated by Supreme Court rulings, including *Brown* v. *Board of Education* in the 1950s and 1960s, progress was made to protect voting rights for all.

Another negative aspect of federalism is that the costs and benefits of federal policy and aid are often distributed unevenly among the country's regional or local governments. Political motivations impact policies and affect where money is directed. Therefore, poorer communities can suffer in a federal system when they receive relatively fewer services in areas like health and welfare, police, and environmental protection because they aren't being represented as robustly as other constituents.

A good example of spatial inequality resulting from a wide disparity in tax revenue can be found in the funding of public education in the United States. Public schools in the United States are supported by a combination of federal, state, and local funds, with federal money accounting for only about 10 percent of the total figure. Money raised by property taxes at the local (and sometimes state) level is the major source of funds for a locality's school districts, and the monies are directed and supervised at the state level (in all but five states). As a result, a school district that is home to highly valued properties generates higher property taxes, and its schools are therefore more well-funded. By contrast, a less populated or poorer district would generate lower property taxes, and its schools would be more reliant on state funding, which is often scarce.

A federal state can also experience conflict within its constituent units. For example, the municipal government in Birmingham, Alabama, passed a local law in 2016 raising the city's minimum wage from $7.25 an hour to $10.10 an hour. Before the law could take effect, however, the Alabama state legislature intervened, passing a law preventing localities from setting their own minimum wage. A group of Birmingham citizens and state officials then sued the state to force it to comply with the local law. A series of federal court decisions culminated in the dismissal of the lawsuit. By the end of 2019, the state had won the battle over the minimum wage.

COMPARING TWO FORMS OF GOVERNANCE

Federal	Unitary
Power is divided between the national government and state and local governments.	Power is held in one central, national government.
Promotes diversity.	Promotes strong sense of national identity.
Power may be diffused.	Very little power is diffused.
State or provincial governments have some degree of self-rule and have their own legislatures.	Laws are standardized and implemented across the country.
Change can come slowly; conflicts between governments occur; abuse of power is prevented.	Change can come quickly; less intergovernmental conflict; abuse of power is more likely.

FEDERAL STATES VS. UNITARY STATES There are many distinctions between federal and unitary systems of government that can impact a state's unity. Sometimes tensions occur between different groups living within a state.

GEOGRAPHIC THINKING

1. Compare key spatial elements in unitary and federal systems.

2. Explain how the Chinese government's response to the Sichuan earthquake in 2008 highlights a disadvantage of unitary states.

3. Describe how the United States government is spatially organized and how power is distributed among its units.

POLITICAL CONTROL AND NUNAVUT

THE ISSUE Though federalism tends to support diversity—whether cultural or political—many countries with federal systems struggle to adequately serve their minority populations. Canada provides a good example of a federal system that accommodates multiple nationalities, ethnicities, and cultures.

LEARNING OBJECTIVE
IMP-4.C Define federal and unitary states.

BY THE NUMBERS

1,296 MILES

Distance from Ottawa to Iqaluit, capital of Nunavut

38,650

Population of Nunavut (2019)

37,512,000

Population of Canada (2019)

Sources: Google Maps, The Canadian Encyclopedia, Statistics Canada

Nunavut is homeland to the Inuit, an indigenous people of Canada who keep their traditions alive by wearing traditional clothes and engaging in activities like dog sledding. While Nunavut's government works to meet the needs of its majority Inuit population, the territory relies on Canada's federal government for monetary aid.

CANADA HAS A FEDERAL SYSTEM with a central government seated in Ottawa, its capital city. Canada's federal government holds authority over ten provinces and three large territories: Yukon, the Northwest Territories, and Nunavut. Each province has its own legislature, and the territories are governed by the federal government while also having their own territorial governments.

The Inuit, one of the First Nations peoples of Canada, make up four-fifths of Nunavut's population. Nunavut was part of the vast, remote Northwest Territories until the 1990s. The Inuit had pushed for independence at a time when their lifestyle was transitioning from one based on hunting, fishing, and fur trapping to one in which they were more permanently settled in small communities. Eventually, the Inuit wanted more control of their own local affairs, and they began to pressure the federal government to grant them more autonomy. In 1993, an act of Parliament recognized the Inuits' land rights and established Nunavut. The Nunavut Land Claims Agreement gave the Inuit political control over Nunavut, which became an official Canadian territory in 1999. The Inuit, who were once marginalized and largely ignored, had their status elevated through spatial reorganization.

The federal distribution of power has been beneficial for the Inuit because the territorial government, located in the capital city of Iqaluit, attends to their needs. For example, most of Nunavut's population speak the Inuktitut language. Accordingly, Inuktitut is used in the day-to-day running of the territorial government, and Inuktitut is officially recognized alongside English, French, and Inuinnaqtun (a dialect of Inuktitut). In fact, the territorial government is working to preserve the Inuktitut language in different ways, including ensuring Inuit schoolchildren are taught in their native language.

Canada's federal government has also played a role in helping the Inuit community by redistributing resources for the development of culturally sensitive policies and programs that benefit the Inuit. In 2019, the federal government and Inuit partners implemented an indigenous skills and job training program that provides more funding and improved training for the Inuit and other First Nations peoples. Nunavut provides a useful example of how the structure of political power can impact representation and recognition of groups. ∎

GEOGRAPHIC THINKING

Describe how Canada's federal system serves Nunavut.

10.2 ELECTORAL GEOGRAPHY

When geographers study electoral geography, they look at the spatial aspects of voting: how the boundaries of voting districts are set, how that process influences voting results, and what those outcomes mean for candidates and voters.

REPRESENTING THE PEOPLE

LEARNING OBJECTIVE
IMP-4.B Explain the nature and function of international and internal boundaries.

International boundaries are drawn to define and organize states. Boundaries are also drawn *within* states to divide areas into manageable spaces that are governed by different authorities. These internal boundaries define provinces (in Canada); prefectures (in Japan); states, counties, and county-equivalents (in the United States); and municipalities in many countries. Internal boundaries also form voting districts, the defining and drawing of which are sometimes manipulated to influence elections, and therefore political power. Congressional districts—voting districts in the United States—offer a prime example of the controversy that can surround the drawing of internal boundaries.

U.S. CONGRESSIONAL DISTRICTS In the United States, one measure of a state's political power is the number of members it has in the House of Representatives. Here, *state* refers to one of the United States, like Utah. A state's number of representatives depends on its population. A highly populated state like California, with 53 congresspeople, has more power in the House than a less populated state like Wyoming, with 1 congressperson.

Every 10 years in the United States, a census is conducted to determine the number of people living in each state. These numbers are used to reconfigure each state's congressional district map. Each congressional district elects one congressperson. The number of districts a state has equals the state's number of congresspeople. The total number of U.S. representatives is always 435, so the state's population growth and decline and migration rates are key pieces of data. When one state loses people and another gains or a state's population doesn't grow as fast as others, a process called **reapportionment** takes place, in which seats in the House of Representatives are reallocated to different states. The 2010 census revealed that Pennsylvania's population growth slowed, and as a result, it lost one congressional seat. Conversely, Florida and Texas saw high rates of population growth, and they each gained seats. Reapportionment ensures that a state's population is accurately represented in the House of Representatives.

A shift in population from one geographic region to another has implications for the whole country as well. The president of the United States is not elected directly by the people, but rather by the **electoral college**, a set of people—called electors—who are chosen to elect the president. The total number of available electors (and, therefore, electoral votes) is 538, which is the same as the total membership of Congress—435 members of the House of Representatives and 100 senators—plus 3 electoral votes for Washington, D.C., whose citizens vote in federal elections but who do

PROJECTED CONGRESSIONAL REAPPORTIONMENT, 2020

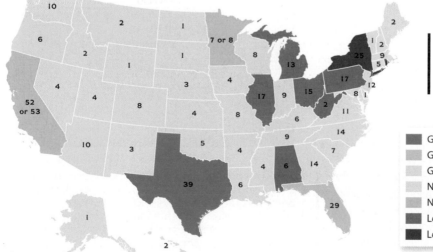

Based on projections of population changes that will occur as a result of the 2020 census, 7 states are likely to gain at least 1 seat in the House of Representatives, and 10 other states are projected to lose a seat.

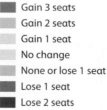

- Gain 3 seats
- Gain 2 seats
- Gain 1 seat
- No change
- None or lose 1 seat
- Lose 1 seat
- Lose 2 seats

not have a voting member of Congress. Consequently, to be elected president, a candidate must win a combination of states whose electoral votes add up to a minimum of 270. Therefore, when a state loses a congressional seat, it loses an electoral vote as well. The loss of an electoral vote is also a loss in electoral and political power for the state.

The U.S. Senate has its own representation issue—it represents states, not people. Every state has two U.S. senators in Congress, which does not result in proportional representation. North Dakota, with about 770,000 people, has the same number of senators as Florida, with more than 21.6 million people. The Senate has significant powers that the House does not, and some argue that gives small states unfair power. For example, it takes only 50 votes in the Senate to confirm a justice to a lifetime appointment on the U.S. Supreme Court. In 2018, Judge Brett Kavanaugh was confirmed receiving 50 votes that came from states holding only 45 percent of the U.S. population.

ELECTORAL DISTRICT BOUNDARIES

LEARNING OBJECTIVE
IMP-4.B Explain the nature and function of international and internal boundaries.

After each census is complete, reapportionment takes place along with a process called **redistricting**. During redistricting, a state's internal political boundaries that determine voting districts for the U.S. House of Representatives and the state's legislature are redrawn to accurately reflect the new census data. Redistricting is both a geographic and political process. It is a geographic process because the boundaries of districts must be redrawn to reflect any changes in population. It is a political process because those boundaries are drawn by the state's legislature—a political entity. Legislative districts within states are also redistricted after every census. Changing district boundaries can have a radical effect on who is elected to represent a geographic area.

GERRYMANDERING The party that controls a majority of seats in the state legislature typically draws legislative maps with a partisan advantage that favors their party over any other. This is called partisan **gerrymandering**, named for Governor Elbridge Gerry of Massachusetts, who in 1812 signed a law approving a map of state legislative districts that were drawn to favor his own political party. One of the districts resembled a lizard-like salamander, and a Boston newspaper coined the term "Gerry-mander."

Legislators can gerrymander a district by either "packing" the district or "cracking" the district. Packing a district is when local population data is used to draw a district that is full of the opposing party's voters. Concentrating opposition voters into a single district allows a greater number of the surrounding districts the opportunity to be won by the party that is in power. By contrast, cracking a district is the

practice of splitting up the opposition party's voters across many districts, thereby diluting their electoral strength. Either way, partisan gerrymandering is often used by majority parties to tip the electoral scales in their favor.

A crucial aspect of partisan gerrymandering is the role that race and ethnicity play in drawing the district's boundaries. The Voting Rights Act of 1965 was established to remedy the disenfranchisement of minorities attributed to the common practice of cracking, which spread African-American voters into multiple districts to diminish their impact on elections. The act created new **majority-minority districts**. These gerrymandered districts in which minorities made up the majority of voters, were designed to help ensure, for example, that African-American voters could elect their candidates of choice. Gerrymandered districts have resulted in an increase in the number of minority representatives in Congress.

In recent electoral history, African Americans—and to a lesser extent, Latinos—have favored Democratic candidates. So, Republican lawmakers in some states have packed African-American voters into a single district (or small number of districts), thereby creating majority Republican districts in the rest of the state. Consequently, the Voting Rights Act is now being manipulated to again disenfranchise minority voters. The distinction between partisan and racial gerrymandering is so slight that many who study the gerrymandering issue believe they have essentially become the same practice.

GERRYMANDERING TACTICS The top diagram shows what happens when one party (blue) packs voters from the opposite party (red) into one district. The bottom diagram shows cracking, when voters from an opposition party (blue) are spread into several districts. ▌ How do the graphics help you understand arguments against gerrymandering?

OPPOSITION AND REMEDIES Gerrymandering is considered by many to be unfair because voters who favor the opposition party in a gerrymandered district are essentially disenfranchised, which means they are prevented from having the right to vote. The argument is that their vote doesn't count because the district has been drawn so their party cannot win. Another argument points out that gerrymandering prevents an accurate representation of a state's partisan makeup. For example, in Ohio's 2018 congressional election, Democrats won about half of the state's popular vote, but the party won just 4 of the state's 16 congressional districts because the districts had been heavily gerrymandered to favor Republicans.

Legal challenges to gerrymandering have had mixed results. For Democrats, one bright spot was in Pennsylvania, when, in early 2018, the state Supreme Court ruled that the state's congressional map, drawn by the Republican-held state legislature in 2011, was a gerrymander in violation of the state's constitution. As a remedy, the court drew its own map and ordered both parties to comply with it. The effect was marked. Pennsylvania voters are pretty evenly divided between Democrats and Republicans, but in 2016, Democrats held just 5 of the state's 18 congressional districts. In late 2018 elections, with the court-ordered map, the two parties evenly divided the districts—nine seats each.

In 2019, two key judicial rulings on gerrymandering were handed down. First, the U.S. Supreme Court ruled that gerrymandering was a political issue, not a judicial one, and therefore not a matter for federal courts to decide. That ruling appeared to keep gerrymandering firmly in the hands of state legislatures. However, just a few months later, North Carolina's state court ruled that the Republican-drawn map of that state's 13 congressional districts was an "extreme partisan" gerrymander that violated not the U.S. Constitution but North Carolina's state constitution. That ruling raises the possibility that legal challenges may continue at the state level. By the end of 2019, a new Republican-drawn (and state court-approved) congressional map had somewhat eased the Republican gerrymander.

There are efforts to reform the gerrymandering process. One alternative is the use of a redistricting commission. More than 15 states have employed (or are planning to employ) commissions to draw their congressional and state legislative maps. Some of these commissions are bipartisan, meaning they are made up of members of both parties, and others are independent. For example, voters in Michigan approved a plan in 2018 to form a commission made up of 13 citizens—4 Republicans, 4 Democrats, and 5 independents. The districts the commission draws must avoid any partisan advantage and must, in an effort to avoid oddly-shaped districts, "reflect the state's diverse population and communities of interest." The state of Iowa has an even more straightforward remedy—a nonpartisan body called the Legislative Services Agency draws districts that must be made up of "convenient contiguous territory." In all cases, the goal is to reduce the acute partisanship of states' maps.

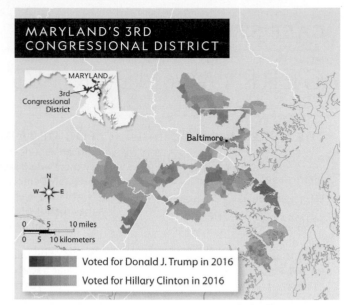

Maryland's 3rd Congressional District is an example of a packed district. Democratic state lawmakers drew the oddly shaped district so that it would be packed with Democratic voters. Democrats have consistently won this district by overwhelming margins. Darker shades on the map indicate higher vote totals.

AT-LARGE VS. SINGLE-MEMBER DISTRICTS Are the results of an election truly representative of a geographical area? The answer largely depends on the election method that area uses. In most local municipalities around the United States, for example, voters elect their representatives in one of three ways: by at-large elections, by district elections, or by a mixture of both. In an at-large election, the entire population of a geographical area, such as a city, town, or school district, elects someone to represent them as a whole. In a district election, a single individual is elected to represent the population of a smaller geographical area (in most local municipalities these sub-units are called wards). A good example of a mixed system is seen in the school board of Minneapolis, Minnesota. The board has nine members, three of whom are elected at large, and six represent certain individual school districts.

Political geographers debate which election type achieves better representation. Proponents of at-large districts argue that at-large representatives keep the interests of the entire community in mind and tend to be less partisan. Opponents argue that minority groups in at-large districts are underrepresented because those groups tend to be concentrated in certain areas. By contrast, single-member districts allow for greater representation of all groups and their representatives can be more attentive to the particular needs of a local community.

GEOGRAPHIC THINKING

1. Explain how reapportionment can impact the political power of a state.

2. Describe the arguments against gerrymandering.

GERRYMANDERING AND RACE

THE ISSUE Electoral districts are sometimes gerrymandered along racial lines, a practice that often triggers legal challenges.

LEARNING OBJECTIVE
IMP-4.B Explain the nature and function of international and internal boundaries.

BY THE NUMBERS

20%

of North Carolina's congressional districts are majority-minority (3 of 13 districts)

13%

of Wisconsin's congressional districts are majority-minority (1 of 8 districts)

28%

of U.S. congressional districts are majority-minority (122 of 435 districts)

Source: Ballotpedia

FOR DECADES, Republican lawmakers around the country have packed African-American voters into majority-minority districts in hopes that the remaining districts would lean in their favor. This is because African Americans have been a reliably Democratic-voting constituency. Racial gerrymandering has affected North Carolina for decades. After the 1990 census, population growth resulted in the creation of the 12th Congressional District. The then-Democratic-controlled state legislature packed the district with African Americans so that it became North Carolina's second majority-minority district. In 1993, the U.S. Supreme Court took notice of this majority-black district, and most of the justices objected to it, calling it a clear "racial gerrymander." District lines were later redrawn in North Carolina four more times as the constitutionality of majority-minority districts was examined.

By 2010, Republicans had secured control of North Carolina's state legislature. Lawmakers drew a map in which the state's 1st and 12th Congressional Districts were majority African American in order to favor the Republican Party, but in 2016, a federal court declared (and in 2017, the U.S. Supreme Court agreed) that the districts were unconstitutional gerrymanders. In response to the ruling, Republicans drew a new map that was used during the 2016 federal elections.

The challenge to North Carolina's 12th congressional district is a good illustration of how racial gerrymandering and partisan gerrymandering can be difficult to separate, a notion that you have already learned about. A similar instance occurred in Wisconsin in 2016, when a legal challenge to the state's legislative districts was treated as a partisan gerrymandering issue, but racial issues were also at play.

Beginning in 2011, the Republican party controlled both houses of the Wisconsin state legislature as well as the governor's mansion—a situation called a *trifecta*. The state legislature drew a state legislative map that favored their party. The map, called Act 43, was legally challenged in court by 12 Democratic voters who claimed Republicans had both packed and cracked districts to give their party an advantage.

There was a racial component as well, which was revealed in another court challenge to Act 43. In Milwaukee, Wisconsin's most populous and diverse city, arguments were made that one district had been cracked so that non-White voters, and especially Latino voters, were spread out. Milwaukee is infamous for having a stark divide between its largely non-White central city and its largely White suburbs. After redistricting, neighborhoods that were 60 percent non-White were tossed into a district that became 87 percent majority White. As a result, it was unlikely that a non-White representative would be elected.

In the larger legal challenge, a U.S. District Court panel agreed that Act 43 was a statewide partisan gerrymander. However, the state of Wisconsin appealed the decision to the U.S. Supreme Court, which essentially agreed with the state, saying that the 12 Democratic plaintiffs had no right to sue in the first place. The Supreme Court sent the case back to the district court for further proceedings. As a result of the precedent set by the Supreme Court's decision in 2019—that gerrymandering is a political issue and not a judicial one—it is likely that the original district map will remain in place. ▮

GEOGRAPHIC THINKING

Explain the role race played in the legal challenges to either North Carolina's or Wisconsin's gerrymandered congressional maps.

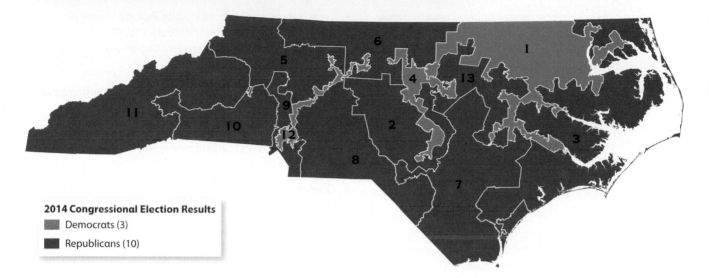

NORTH CAROLINA CONGRESSIONAL DISTRICTS, 2012-2014

2014 Congressional Election Results
- Democrats (3)
- Republicans (10)

After the 2010 census, Republican state lawmakers drew this map of North Carolina's congressional districts. Notice the unusual shape of the 1st, 4th, and 12th districts. Both a U.S. federal court and the U.S. Supreme Court ruled that the 1st and 12th districts were unconstitutional racial gerrymanders.

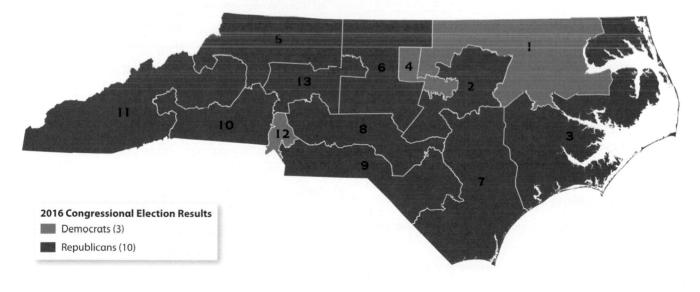

NORTH CAROLINA CONGRESSIONAL DISTRICTS, 2016-2018

2016 Congressional Election Results
- Democrats (3)
- Republicans (10)

This map of North Carolina's congressional districts was drawn by Republican state lawmakers in 2016 and was used in the 2016 and 2018 elections. ▌Describe how the boundaries of the 1st, 4th, and 12th districts changed between 2014 and 2016. How did this impact the congressional election results between the two years?

SUMMARY & REVIEW

■ CHAPTER SUMMARY

State governments—which represent country governments, in this context—are organized based on how political power is divided. There are two main approaches to organizing state governments: a unitary state or a federal state.

- In a unitary system of government, power is concentrated in the central government, which decides how much power to distribute to its regional units.

- Advantages of a unitary state include efficient implementation of laws and services across the state, less potential for corruption of local government, and fewer government agencies.

- Disadvantages of a unitary state include disconnection between the central government and local regions, favoritism for the dominant political or cultural group, and slowness to respond to local issues.

- In a federal system of government, power is shared between the central government and its regional units.

- Advantages of a federal state include reduced regional conflict, political diversity, and attention to local issues.

- Disadvantages of a federal state include undue power given to localized special interests that sometimes block national issues and uneven distribution of costs and benefits of government policies.

Electoral geography is the study of the spatial organization of voting districts.

- The United States' 435 congressional districts are reapportioned and redistricted every 10 years following the census.

- Changes due to reapportionment can result in shifts in political and electoral power.

- Gerrymandering is the process of drawing internal legislative districts to secure an advantage for one party or another by either "packing" or "cracking" the district.

- Gerrymandering can take place on the basis of partisanship or race and is therefore seen as an unfair practice by many.

■ KEY TERMS AND CONCEPTS

Use complete sentences to answer the questions.

1. **APPLY CONCEPTUAL VOCABULARY** Consider the terms *unitary* and *federal*. Write a standard dictionary definition of each term. Then provide a conceptual definition—an explanation of how *unitary state* and *federal state* are used in the context of the entire chapter.

2. Give an example of the efficiency that can result from the organization of government in a unitary state.

3. Explain how Norway's approach to public health exemplifies its unitary system.

4. Why is a federal system a good fit for a large, diverse country?

5. Explain how spatial inequality can occur in a federal state.

6. Summarize how federal and state governments share power by giving an example from the federal system of the United States.

7. Define *concurrent powers* and include an example of them in your response.

8. Describe the difference between patriotism and nationalism.

9. Explain how the term *reapportionment* is related to a census.

10. Describe the difference between reapportionment and redistricting.

11. Explain how the electoral college works, and identify who is elected using this process.

12. Define *gerrymandering* and give two examples of strategies used to gerrymander a district.

13. Identify and describe one remedy for gerrymandering.

14. Explain how majority-minority districts are related to gerrymandering.

15. Describe the difference between an at-large district and a single-member district.

INTERPRET MAPS

The 2011 map outlines Pennsylvania's 15th congressional district as it was drawn as part of a state-wide Republican gerrymander. The 2019 map shows the 7th congressional district that was drawn by the Pennsylvania State Supreme Court after it struck down the former gerrymandered map. The former 15th congressional district was broken up to form parts of other districts including the 7th congressional district. The map data showing Democratic and Republican voting behavior is based on the results of the 2016 presidential election between Hillary Clinton and Donald J. Trump. Study the maps and then answer the questions.

16. **ANALYZE MODELS & THEORIES** Identify aspects of the 2011 15th district that could be cited to argue that it was gerrymandered.

17. **ANALYZE GEOGRAPHIC CONCEPTS** What can be inferred about the Republicans' strategy in drawing the 2011 15th district by looking closely at the cities of Allentown and Easton?

18. **EXPLAIN GEOGRAPHIC CONCEPTS** The 2019 7th district appears to have more area that is red than is blue. Does that necessarily predict that the district will elect a Republican representative? Explain.

19. **IDENTIFY DATA & INFORMATION** Identify data that supports that districts in 2019 were less gerrymandered than districts in 2011.

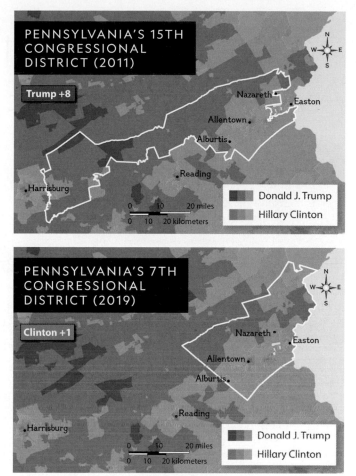

PENNSYLVANIA'S 15TH CONGRESSIONAL DISTRICT (2011)

Trump +8

Nazareth, Easton, Allentown, Alburtis, Reading, Harrisburg

0 10 20 miles
0 10 20 kilometers

Donald J. Trump
Hillary Clinton

PENNSYLVANIA'S 7TH CONGRESSIONAL DISTRICT (2019)

Clinton +1

Nazareth, Easton, Allentown, Alburtis, Reading, Harrisburg

0 10 20 miles
0 10 20 kilometers

Donald J. Trump
Hillary Clinton

GEO-INQUIRY | POLITICAL BOUNDARIES WHERE YOU LIVE

A Geo-Inquiry project begins with an overarching topic and Geo-Inquiry question, for example, *How were the political boundaries where I live determined?* Let's use this question to explore the components of the Geo-Inquiry Process.

ASK Start with an authentic Geo-Inquiry question about where you live. It may be as simple as *How can the political boundaries in my community best be drawn to reflect better representation in government?* Use the Geo-Inquiry Process to expand this question. Related questions could be *Are the political boundaries where I live fairly drawn? Are the voting sites accessible for all?*

COLLECT Decide how you will gather geographic information to answer your question. Explore online governmental sources to learn about the congressional district where you live, and investigate U.S. Census information for your area. Talk to local leaders who may

have shaped legislative boundaries. Explore local sources to learn more about how the boundaries are drawn and how they changed over time.

VISUALIZE Analyze the information you collected to draw conclusions. Organize it and use it to create a map, graph, or infographic that others can study. New maps proposing improvements to congressional districts may be in order.

CREATE Focus on ways to tell a Geo-Inquiry story, keeping your audience in mind. Create a list of the elements that you will use to tell your story, such as specific maps, images, videos, and clear charts and graphs. Outline or storyboard your Geo-Inquiry story, and then make sure all of your elements tell a consistent story.

ACT Share your Geo-Inquiry story with decision-makers. Consider how your project can inform people in your area about how they may be better represented.

ASK — COLLECT — VISUALIZE — CREATE — ACT

CHAPTER 11
POLITICAL CHALLENGES AND CHANGES

CRITICAL VIEWING Demonstrators in London gathered in March 2019 in support of Brexit, the United Kingdom's decision to leave the European Union. ▮ What cultural and economic impacts might these demonstrations have had on Europe?

GEOGRAPHIC THINKING What causes states to unify and to divide?

11.1
DEVOLUTION: CHALLENGES TO STATE SOVEREIGNTY

CASE STUDY: Irredentism in Ukraine

NATIONAL GEOGRAPHIC EXPLORER Michael Wesch

11.2
SUPRANATIONALISM: TRANSCENDING STATE BOUNDARIES

CASE STUDY: Brexit

11.3
FORCES THAT UNIFY AND FORCES THAT DIVIDE

11.1 DEVOLUTION: CHALLENGES TO STATE SOVEREIGNTY

A state's sovereignty is not absolute. Different processes and forces may place stress on a government's ability to control the land and people within its borders. Under certain conditions, these stresses can cause a state to destabilize or even disintegrate. Geographers study these processes to understand the causes and effects of shifts in political power at all scales, local to global.

THE PROCESS OF DEVOLUTION

LEARNING OBJECTIVES
SPS-4.A Define factors that lead to the devolution of states.
SPS-4.B Explain how political, economic, cultural, and technological changes challenge state sovereignty.

As you learned in Chapter 9, the world political map contains nearly 200 states of various sizes, population densities, and government structures. Each of these states, whether they're centuries old or nearly new, has experienced an evolution to arrive at its present situation. This may have involved a civil war, colonial rule, a revolution, conflict with other states, or more. But all states, even the oldest and strongest, face a range of divisive pressures that stress their existing structure. This process, termed devolution, can destabilize a state. Geographers study the forces that drive devolution, as well as the ways in which governments respond to this process.

A number of factors can challenge state sovereignty and may lead to the devolution of a state: the division of groups of people by physical geography, ethnic separatism, the practice of ethnic cleansing or terrorism, and the policy of irredentism, as well as economic and social problems. It is useful to look at each of these factors separately, but in many cases, there are multiple factors that lead to challenges to a state's sovereignty.

PHYSICAL GEOGRAPHY One factor that can pose great challenges to the sovereignty of a state is physical geography. Devolutionary forces are most often prompted by the distance that exists within a state from its center of power. As you know, friction of distance states that as distance increases between two locations, the quantity and quality of interaction between the two locations will decline. Although the challenges of physical geography are less of an issue in today's world due to advances in transportation and communications technologies, distance decay still plays a role. States with fragmented physical geography, such as a country that is spread out over a group of islands, or those disrupted by major topographic features such as mountain ranges, can have challenges with unity. It is more difficult to build a cohesive state when division—in the form of

mountains, deserts, or other physical impediments—is a factor in the state's physical geography.

Think about the difficulties involved in governing the Philippines, a country comprising more than 7,600 islands. The Philippines had the 13th largest population in the world in 2020, more than half of which lives in rural areas, in smaller villages in the rugged interior. To travel to cities and towns on the coastline, people use roads that for the most part are unpaved. The climate of the Philippines is tropical and monsoonal, which creates additional challenges with natural disasters such as typhoons, floods, and landslides.

In the 1960s, the Philippine government in Manila—located in the northern part of the country—made a decision that led to destabilization. The government attempted to develop the area of Mindanao in the south, more than 500 miles away from Manila. Mindanao was rich in natural resources and had fewer destructive typhoons than the northern islands. In order to encourage economic development there, the Philippine government resettled Christian people from other parts of the country in Mindanao, which was inhabited by indigenous peoples mostly of Muslim heritage. Part of this resettlement provided the Christian migrants with the best lands so they could prosper from the natural resources. They were also given government services that were not given to the Muslim population. Conflicts broke out between the new settlers and the Muslims. In turn, the Muslims started a movement to secede from the country, leading to violence and leaving the region one of the poorest in the country. The distance between the two areas proved to be too much for the Manila-based government to control.

ETHNIC SEPARATISM Another factor that can lead to devolution is **ethnic separatism**, which occurs when people of a particular ethnicity in a multinational state identify more strongly as members of their ethnic group than as citizens of the state. The Basques of Basque Country, a region in northern Spain, are a primary example. Basque nationalism is rooted in the region's history, culture, and language, cultivated and molded in its region separate from the rest of Spain. As Spain's efforts to control the region increased, and as Spanish immigrants were coming into the area at an alarming rate, the Basques wanted to salvage their autonomy and be recognized as their own nation. Basque Country was declared an autonomous region in 1979, which meant that it was given independence in some areas, but the push and pull between the Basques and the Spanish government continues.

The root of many cases of ethnic separatism is disparity, or difference, in how an ethnicity is treated, both culturally and by the laws of the state. The people of an ethnic group may feel like they do not have the power and autonomy that they deserve. This is especially common in the case of stateless nations. As you read in Chapter 9, a stateless nation is a group of people united by culture, language, history, and tradition but not possessing their own state. In extreme cases, the state government may attack the ethnic group and try to eliminate it through expulsion, imprisonment, or killing. This is known as **ethnic cleansing**.

Consider the discussion of the Rohingya people in Chapter 5. The Rohingya, a mostly Muslim group, have faced multiple military crackdowns in their homeland within Myanmar and many have been driven into neighboring countries such as Bangladesh. The Myanmar government's official stance on the Rohingya is that they are not an indigenous people, but rather are illegal immigrants in Myanmar. Another example is the National Socialist German Workers' Party, or the Nazi Party, led by Adolf Hitler. Its members believed in the supremacy of the Aryan people and blamed Jews and other groups for the economic and social problems in Germany. The Nazis had an ultimate plan for a systematic murder of all European Jews. These are just two examples that show that the goal of ethnic cleansing is to achieve ethnic homogeneity by eliminating those who are different.

Destabilization can also occur when a region shares ethnic, cultural, or historical traits with the people of a neighboring state. This can lead to irredentism, which was introduced in Chapter 9. Irredentism occurs when the majority ethnicity on one side of a boundary wants to claim territory from a neighboring state in order to bring in a minority group of the same ethnicity or other commonality who reside across the border. In the 1930s, for example, a region known as the Sudetenland in western Czechoslovakia was populated predominately by Germans who felt they were being discriminated against by the Czech government. The Nazi Party's anti-Semitic, anti-Czech propaganda drew these Germans to support annexation, and in 1938 the region was transferred to Germany until after World War II.

Advances in communication technology have greatly impacted ethnic identity, sometimes fueling separatist movements. The internet and smartphones have made it easier for groups to organize, advertise, and recruit for their causes. Social media can be used as a low-cost outlet for sharing and voicing concerns regarding treatment of the group. This in turn gives a group that has been disenfranchised, or deprived of rights, power that they wouldn't have had several decades ago. For example, in Afghanistan, despite its poor infrastructure connections and limited freedom of speech, more than 20 million people have telecommunications devices and in 2015, it was estimated that the country had 1.2 million social media users. The Taliban, a political and military organization that has long waged war within the country, once banned the internet because they thought it did not align with Islamic practices. But their perspective changed when they realized they could use it to promote their ethnic identity, spread their message, communicate with other members, and gather supporters.

ECONOMIC AND SOCIAL PROBLEMS Economic divisions within a state often work in tandem with ethnic and geographic pressures to cause devolutionary forces. These divisions can result from variations in economic productivity or development between regions within a state. Economic divisions may also arise because of the way funds are allocated by the government to different regions. The people of a given region might feel that the central government is misspending the taxes they pay or that the central government is not providing enough funds to the region.

The economy of the eastern Canadian provinces of Ontario and Quebec is driven mostly by manufacturing and white-collar jobs, while western Canada is supported by a different source: its natural resources. Farming, forestry, and mineral deposits bring in large amounts of revenue despite employing a small percentage of Canada's labor force. The Prairie Freedom Movement argues that the western provinces should have more control over this revenue, to invest it in the areas that generate the wealth, rather than using it to invest in the welfare of eastern Canada.

Economic issues fuel devolutionary forces in Catalonia, Spain, as well. Many citizens of the region feel they are victims of funding discrimination by the Spanish government. They believe the government takes too much of their tax money and unfairly redistributes it to the poorer regions of Spain. Governments often distribute revenue to reduce the gap between rich and poor regions, but Catalonians think the redistribution is dividing the country, as it provides more resources per capita to the poorer regions than what comes back to Catalonia for its essential services. They are also upset that the more autonomous Basque Country doesn't have to send all of its tax revenue to Madrid.

Social issues can also destabilize a state. Discrimination against a minority group, for instance, can cause rifts between people living within a state's borders that act as devolutionary forces. The small nation of Wales in the United Kingdom has a markedly different culture and language than the rest of Britain. And while the people of Wales—called the Welsh—are citizens of the United Kingdom every bit as much as the English, Scottish, and those of Northern Ireland, anti-Welsh sentiment is common throughout Britain. Examples of public officials and personalities insulting or making discriminatory jokes about Wales and its people are commonplace. This casual discrimination among groups living within a single country may prevent them from developing a feeling that they are all one people.

CASE STUDY

IRREDENTISM IN UKRAINE

THE ISSUE In 2014, Russian president Vladimir Putin incorporated Crimea into the Russian Federation, causing ongoing territorial disputes in eastern Ukraine.

LEARNING OBJECTIVE
SPS-4.A Define factors that lead to the devolution of states.

UKRAINE: DISPUTED TERRITORIES

0   100   200 miles
0   100   200 kilometers

RUSSIA

UKRAINE

Under control of the Ukrainian government

Russian Federation

Under control of pro-Russian and Russian forces

Sea of Azov

Crimea

Kerch Strait

Black Sea

The territories of Crimea and eastern Ukraine have had a long and tumultuous relationship with Russia. The region remains disputed to this day.

BY THE NUMBERS

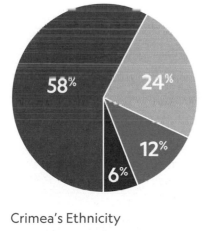

58%   24%   12%   6%

Crimea's Ethnicity

- Ethnic Russians
- Ukrainians
- Tatars
- Other

Source: Ukraine census, 2001

AN EXAMPLE OF IRREDENTISM occurred in Eastern Europe in March 2014, when Russia sent troops into Crimea, an autonomous republic in southern Ukraine. Russia annexed the region and connected it to the Russian Federation by a 12-mile bridge spanning the Kerch Strait.

Crimea is a peninsula on the Black Sea that became a part of Ukraine in 1954, when both Ukraine and Russia were part of the Soviet Union. Prior to this, Crimea's identity had flip-flopped. Joseph Stalin's regime suppressed many of Crimea's minorities (primarily the Tatars, a native Turkish-speaking people) and forcibly deported them. After World War II, Crimea was a part of the Ukrainian Soviet Socialist Republic.

In 1991, after the Soviet Union's collapse, Crimea was placed under the control of the newly independent state of Ukraine. The ethnic Russian majority in Crimea made for strained relations with Kiev (Kyiv), the capital of Ukraine. In addition, Moscow signed a lease agreement allowing it to base the Russian navy's Black Sea Fleet in the port at Sevastopol in Crimea, making the region strategically important to Russia.

Over the years, Ukraine tried to balance its ties between Europe (with which it hoped to connect) and Russia (with which it was historically tied). However, Crimea continued to lean toward pro-Moscow involvement. In 2013, the pro-Russian president of Ukraine, Viktor Yanukovych, backed out of a deal with the EU in favor of stronger ties with Russia. Protests erupted in Kiev. The Ukraine Parliament voted to remove the president from power and to ban Russian as the second official language, angering the Russian-speaking inhabitants of Crimea.

In 2014, Russian gunmen seized government buildings in Crimea's capital. The Crimean Parliament called a referendum and while the results have been disputed, voters decided to join Russia. Ukrainian troops pulled out of Crimea. Since then, Russia has supported Ukrainian separatists occupying key cities in eastern Ukraine. Fighting continued for more than five years, with more than 13,000 casualties. Desperate to keep Crimea out of Russian control, Western countries responded by imposing sanctions. In 2019, the United States' relationship with Ukraine was scrutinized because of the Trump administration's delay of financial aid to support Ukraine's military defense. Such aid had been provided regularly by the United States since 2014. The territories of Crimea and eastern Ukraine remain disputed. ∎

GEOGRAPHIC THINKING

Describe how Russia's annexation of Crimea is an example of irredentism.

RESPONSES TO DEVOLUTIONARY FORCES

LEARNING OBJECTIVE

SPS-4.B Explain how political, economic, cultural, and technological changes challenge state sovereignty.

Just as causes of devolutionary forces are varied, so are responses. States respond differently to processes of destabilization depending on their particular mixture of ethnic, cultural, economic, and internal territorial divisions. For instance, a state may address devolutionary forces by sharing more power with subnational units.

Canada has used this method to address various challenges to its state sovereignty. In response to demands by people in the Yukon Territory that a greater percentage of the money from mining and other resources be controlled within the territory, Canada shifted land- and resource-management responsibilities to the Yukon government. To appease French-speaking citizens in Quebec, Canada has decreed French to be the province's official language.

Devolutionary forces can also lead to sovereignty and self-determination for the people of a region within a country. For example, in the late 1970s, many people in Scotland pushed to form a Scottish Parliament within the United Kingdom that would allow the Scottish people to have greater control over their own affairs. It took 20 years, but after a series of referendums, the Scottish Parliament was formed in 1999. The Scots continued to push for more independence, and

a separatist movement gained traction. This movement is an example of a devolutionary force since it destabilized the United Kingdom through disagreement, disunity, and a desire for more autonomy. In 2016, the UK government gave Scotland more power as a compromise to counter the Scots' desire for complete independence.

Devolutionary forces may result in a shift in a state's form of governance. The European country of Belgium, for instance, transitioned from a unitary to a federal state. Belgium's citizenry consists of French-speaking people called the Walloons, concentrated in the southern provinces, and Flemish- or Dutch-speaking people called the Flemings, concentrated in the north. Until 1970 the country was a unitary state, but tensions between the two groups caused the Belgian Parliament to gradually shift to a federal government. Changes to the constitution created independent administrations within the Walloon and Flemish regions, giving each region control over economic, educational, and cultural decisions. A third region was created in the late 1980s that consists of the metropolitan area of Brussels, the country's bilingual capital.

The oil-rich country of Nigeria, in West Africa, responded to devolutionary forces by breaking the country up into subnational political units. In the 1960s, a different ethnic group dominated each of three regions of Nigeria, and conflict between the groups threatened to tear the country apart as leaders of each group fought for control. The government decided to break the country up into 12 states in order to lessen the power held by each of the three main

THE SOVIET UNION

ARCTIC OCEAN

Bering Sea

LATVIAN S.S.R.
LITHUANIAN S.S.R.
POLAND
ESTONIAN S.S.R.
BELORUSSIAN S.S.R.
MOLDAVIAN S.S.R.
UKRAINIAN S.S.R.
RUSSIAN S.F.S.R.
UNION OF SOVIET SOCIALIST REPUBLICS
GEORGIAN S.S.R.
ARMENIAN S.S.R.
AZERBAIJAN S.S.R.
KAZAKH S.S.R.
MONGOLIA
JAPAN
TURKMEN S.S.R.
UZBEK S.S.R.
KIRGIZ S.S.R.
IRAN
TADZHIK S.S.R.
CHINA

0 300 600 miles
0 300 600 kilometers

READING MAPS The collapse of the Soviet Union is an example of devolution. This map shows the many Soviet Socialist Republics (S.S.R.) that comprised the Union of Soviet Socialist Republics until 1991. ∎ Use the map to describe how friction of distance may have contributed to devolution in the U.S.S.R.

regions. The decision led to a bloody civil war as one region attempted to declare independence, but the government was able to hold the country together, partly with the help of money generated by an oil boom in the aftermath of the war. This response to devolution has continued, and there are now 36 Nigerian states.

Eritrea is a small African country on the Red Sea that was once a province of its more powerful neighbor, Ethiopia. The region's inhabitants are extremely diverse: they are Christian and Muslim, they come from as many as nine different ethnic groups, and they speak at least seven indigenous languages. This diversity resulted in tensions that acted as devolutionary forces that the Ethiopian government attempted to counteract by banning political parties and trade unions and weakening the Eritrean provincial government. As Eritreans started to lose their autonomy, their discontent with the Ethiopian government grew, eventually leading them to declare their independence. Eritrea became a sovereign state in 1993. The unrest did not end there, though. A series of border conflicts began in 1998 and tens of thousands of lives were lost, resulting in only minor border changes. In 2018 Ethiopia and Eritrea reopened trade and diplomatic relations, declaring an end to 20 years of war.

In Sudan, in North Africa, a civil war erupted in 1955. The attempts to form a democratic government failed, and military forces pushed Islamic ideals in the name of national unity. Years of fighting took place between the north and the south—civil strife that acted as a powerful devolutionary force on Sudan. In 2011, the people of the south voted for independence, and the country was split into two: Sudan and South Sudan. The split was a direct result of devolution.

When a state cannot resolve issues causing destabilization, these devolutionary forces may result in the disintegration of the state. The Soviet Union, for example, broke apart in 1991 as a result of stresses that challenged state sovereignty and led to devolution. Its republics faced many challenges, including physical geography—the country's vast size, the distance between regions, and the severe climate made unity difficult. Additional factors contributed to the destabilization: a failing economy, a weakened military, ethnic separatism among at least 100 groups, a series of unpopular social and political reforms, and public dissatisfaction with President Mikhail Gorbachev. These forces destabilized the state to such an extent that, one by one, its republics declared independence, and the Soviet Union dissolved.

GEOGRAPHIC THINKING

1. Describe how sovereignty is related to devolution.

2. Describe how the physical geography of the Philippines acts as a devolutionary force.

3. Identify devolutionary forces in Canada and the Soviet Union, and describe the results of each.

AFTER THE SOVIET UNION'S COLLAPSE

READING MAPS On December 31, 1991, the Soviet Union was formally dissolved. This map shows the independent states that were formed as a result. ▮ What challenges might the newly autonomous states that were part of the former Soviet Union face?

NATIONAL GEOGRAPHIC EXPLORER **MICHAEL WESCH**

TECHNOLOGY'S IMPACT ON SOCIETY

Wesch, an anthropology professor at Kansas State University, helps others understand the effects of the internet. Above: A long-exposure photograph reveals light trails from thousands of smartphones used by demonstrators in Hong Kong during a protest.

LEARNING OBJECTIVE
SPS-4.B Explain how political, economic, cultural, and technological changes challenge state sovereignty.

Advances in communication technology and social media continue to infiltrate societies all over the world. Geographers are working with other scientists who study culture—such as anthropologists and ethnographers—to examine the effects of the digital revolution. Michael Wesch is one of those scientists.

In 2005, there were just over one billion internet users. By 2019, that number had grown to over 4.3 billion users worldwide. This exponential growth has affected the world in ways we do not yet fully understand. Wesch studies these effects by examining how new digital technologies are altering human interaction. In one of his studies, he looks at the implications of an environment where information is available to us, anywhere, 24/7.

Among Wesch's most important work is his study of the effects of YouTube, the popular video-sharing website, on viewers. Wesch observed that when YouTube vloggers (video bloggers) share videos, "It's a gateway to anyone, anywhere, throughout all time. This inspires some to feel a profound connection with the entire world. But that's not the same connection felt with a close family member. It's a relationship without any real responsibility, one you can turn off at any moment."

The political ramifications of the constant connection that Wesch studies are widespread. Information and news stories are now broadcast across borders. People have access to knowledge and services from all over the world. They are able to communicate with large groups instantly, which has fueled devolutionary forces such as large-scale protest movements around the world in recent years. Propaganda and disinformation can be communicated just as quickly, and can be used to sow disunity within a state. And some governments restrict access to the internet, which allows them to control the information that their citizens have access to. Geographers are discovering that these effects are felt by both the governments that control states and the people who live within them. ▪

GEOGRAPHIC THINKING

Describe how technology could make devolutionary pressures increase or decrease.

11.2 SUPRANATIONALISM: TRANSCENDING STATE BOUNDARIES

Despite the importance of state sovereignty, sometimes the advantages of states working together outweigh the disadvantages. Geographers study how challenges that transcend—or reach across—states' boundaries may lead them to form cooperative alliances. These organizations can help member states, but they can also challenge state sovereignty by limiting the power of the individual states.

WHAT IS SUPRANATIONALISM?

LEARNING OBJECTIVE

SPS-4.B Explain how political, economic, cultural, and technological changes challenge state sovereignty.

A **supranational organization** is an alliance of three or more states that work together in pursuit of common goals or to address an issue or challenge that these countries share. The goals of supranational organizations might be economic, political, military, cultural, or a combination. Some of these organizations have formed under treaties, while others are considered general alliances. States join supranational organizations because they see an advantage in working with the other member countries, or they want to avoid the disadvantages of being left out of such a group.

The first example of supranationalism in modern history was the formation of the League of Nations. In 1920, at the end of World War I, the Allied Forces came together and, spurred by public demand for a lasting peace, formed an organization for international cooperation. The organization's guiding principle was the belief that war is a crime against more than just those who are attacked. Rather it is a crime against humanity, and it is the right and duty of all states to work together to prevent it.

The League was disbanded in 1946 and its powers were transferred to another newly formed group, the United Nations (UN). The UN was established in October 1945. The group's initial design was based on the concepts and guidelines of the League of Nations, but it developed into a more complex organization. The UN added a focus on respecting and protecting human rights; solving international economic, social, cultural, humanitarian, and environmental problems; and committing to promote economic and social development throughout the world.

Another supranational organization, the North Atlantic Treaty Organization (NATO), was established in 1949, primarily as a military collaboration in response to the occupation of parts of central and eastern Europe by the Soviet Union after World War II. NATO had 12 founding member states in 1949 (most of them in Europe), and 70 years later the organization had 29 members, with several more states being considered for membership. Each member state commits to the collective defense of the entire alliance, with Article 5 of the NATO agreement stating that "an attack against one Ally is considered as an attack against all Allies." Article 5 was invoked for the first time in NATO's history when its members joined the fight against terrorism after the attacks on the World Trade Center in New York City on September 11, 2001.

The European Union (EU) formed after a series of smaller organizations came together to build economic and security alliances in the wake of World War II. The EU was officially created in 1993 by the Maastricht Treaty. Its original intent was to address the economic, social, and security issues of Western Europe, but in the early 21st century it expanded into Central and Eastern Europe. The 27 members of the EU share common trade and foreign policies, citizenship rights, environmental rules, and judicial cooperation. A unified economic and monetary system is a goal of the EU, though only 19 of its member states use the euro as currency. The EU has seen ups and downs. Several countries have expressed concern about losing state sovereignty when joining the EU. Some of its prosperous members worry about struggling members hindering the EU's progress. Issues like immigration, asylum, and open borders have led to disagreements among EU members. In 2020, the United Kingdom made a high-profile and complicated withdrawal from the EU, known as "Brexit."

The Arab League, also known as the League of Arab States (LAS), formed in 1945 as a coalition of Arab countries in North Africa and Southwest Asia to strengthen and regulate political, cultural, economic, and social programs and to settle disputes among its members. There have been some political disagreements over time, and the Arab League has had to adjust and respond to social and political changes among its member states.

ASEAN, or the Association of Southeast Asian Nations, formed in 1967 by the governments of Indonesia, Malaysia, the Philippines, Singapore, and Thailand. Other countries have joined since then. The goals of ASEAN are to advance economic growth through trade in the region, encourage social progress, and bolster peace and security, which was extremely important through the Vietnam War and its

CHAPTER 9

CONFLICT OVER BORDERS

After about a century of domination by the British East India Company, India officially came under British rule in 1858. In 1947, Britain granted the territory's independence while at the same time dividing it into two separate states: Muslim-majority Pakistan and Hindu-majority India. Partition, as this act was called, did not result in peaceful borders, however. India and Pakistan have remained in conflict over the province of Kashmir since 1947, and each country claims the Siachen Glacier for its own. India and China also have border disagreements, with both claiming the regions of Aksai Chin and Arunchal Pradesh. ▮ Identify the effects of colonialism evident on the map of India.

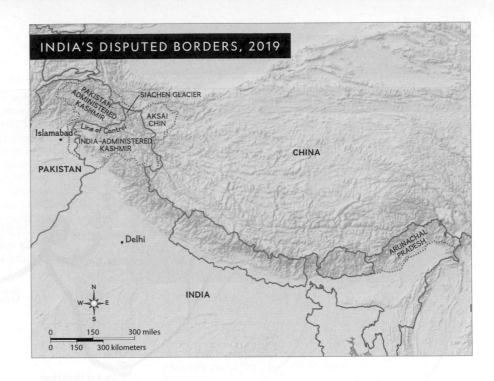

INDIA'S DISPUTED BORDERS, 2019

CHAPTER 9

NATIONS AND STATES

Catalonia is a semiautonomous region of Spain with a distinct culture and language—Catalan—as well as its own parliament. In recent years, Catalan separatist movements have gained strength and visibility. After a majority of Catalan people voted in favor of independence in a 2017 referendum, Spain revoked Catalonia's autonomy, only to restore it in 2018. Tensions between the Spanish and Catalan governments continue to be high. ▮ Compare the maps of the semiautonomous region of Catalonia and the extent of Catalan speakers. Explain whether or not an independent Catalonia would be a nation-state. Describe Spain in terms of nation-state, multistate nation, or multinational state.

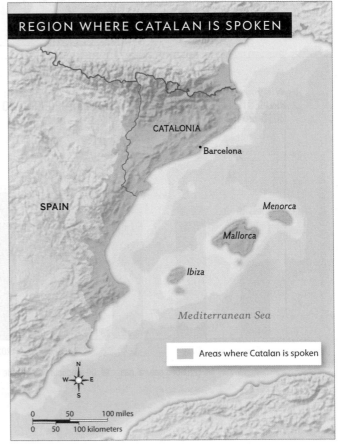

REGION WHERE CATALAN IS SPOKEN

CATALONIA, 2019

CHAPTER 10

ARE YOU SATISFIED WITH YOUR GOVERNMENT?

As part of its annual end-of-year survey for 2018, the polling organization Gallup International asked people in 58 countries to rate their satisfaction with their government. Respondents lived in countries with federal and unitarian governments, in democracies, republics, and dictatorships. ▌ Identify the scale of analysis depicted by this map and explain the value of studying people's attitudes toward government at this scale. Describe what perspectives you could gain on this topic using maps at different scales.

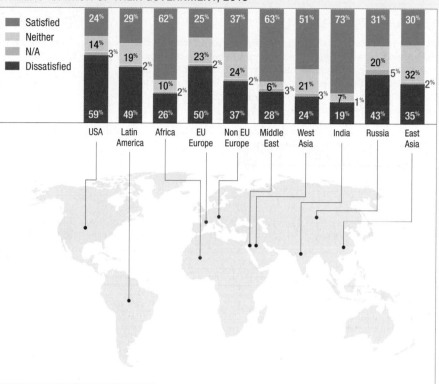

CITIZENS' OPINION OF THEIR GOVERNMENT, 2018

Legend:
- Satisfied
- Neither
- N/A
- Dissatisfied

	USA	Latin America	Africa	EU Europe	Non EU Europe	Middle East	West Asia	India	Russia	East Asia
Satisfied	24%	29%	62%	25%	37%	63%	51%	73%	31%	30%
Neither	14%	19%	10%	23%	24%	6%	21%	7%	20%	32%
N/A	3%	2%	2%	2%	2%	3%	3%	1%	5%	2%
Dissatisfied	59%	49%	26%	50%	37%	28%	24%	19%	43%	35%

Source: Gallup International

CHAPTER 10

WHO CREATES ELECTORAL BOUNDARIES?

In most states, the legislature is in charge of drawing congressional district borders, but increasing numbers of states have begun employing commissions. Not all commissions function in the same way, however. Advisory commissions participate with legislators in the process of drafting districting plans. Backup commissions step in to assist when a legislature does not successfully pass a districting plan. Politician commissions are smaller groups of elected officials who are in charge of drawing district boundaries. Independent commissions consist of members who are not state legislators. ▌ Identify who is in charge of congressional districts in the majority of states. Describe the possible effects, at the national scale and the state scale, if more states move to using independent commissions.

GROUPS RESPONSIBLE FOR DRAWING U.S. CONGRESSIONAL DISTRICTS

Legend:
- Legislature alone
- Advisory commission
- Backup commission
- Politician commission
- Independent commission
- States with only one district

0   200   400 miles
0   200   400 kilometers

LEAVING THE EU

In 2016, the citizens of the United Kingdom voted to leave the European Union—a political and economic coalition of European states. This map shows how the different districts voted in the referendum. ▌ Describe, in general, how the legislature of the United Kingdom might employ gerrymandering if it wanted to propose the referendum again and obtain a different result.

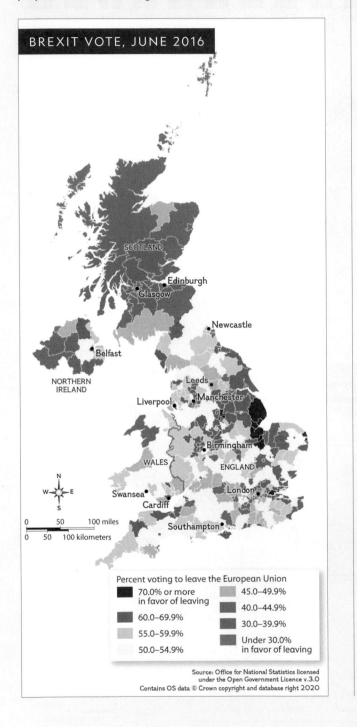

BREXIT VOTE, JUNE 2016

Percent voting to leave the European Union

- 70.0% or more in favor of leaving
- 60.0–69.9%
- 55.0–59.9%
- 50.0–54.9%
- 45.0–49.9%
- 40.0–44.9%
- 30.0–39.9%
- Under 30.0% in favor of leaving

Source: Office for National Statistics licensed under the Open Government Licence v.3.0
Contains OS data © Crown copyright and database right 2020

DISTANCE DECAY AND DEVOLUTION

The Philippines' capital city of Manila is on the island of Luzon at the north of the archipelago. It is separated from Mindanao, the second-largest population center, by a stretch of mountainous islands and ocean hundreds of miles long. At the same time, Mindanao is home to the majority of the country's Muslim population, as well as its largest concentration of ethnic minorities. ▌ Explain the degree to which the distance decay model could explain pressures on the Philippines' central government. Describe how distance decay could combine with cultural forces to push the Philippines toward devolution.

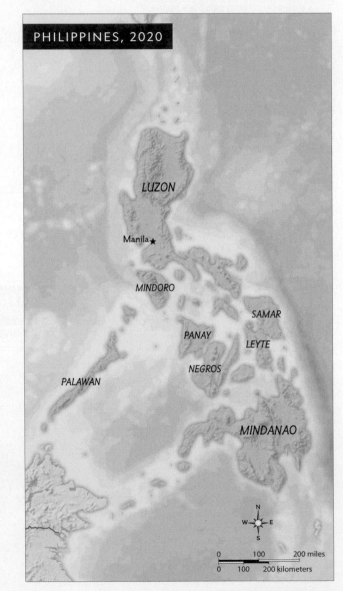

PHILIPPINES, 2020

CHAPTER 11

MEASURING GOVERNMENTAL STABILITY

The Fund for Peace (FFP), an international nongovernmental organization, publishes an annual report on fragile states, or countries in danger of becoming failed states. The map represents the report's findings for 2019. When determining each state's risk for failure, the FFP examines several centripetal and centrifugal forces such as infrastructure and public services, tensions among societal groups, a country's economic health, and the presence of refugees and IDPs. ▌Choose a country or region you have read about or that you know about from other sources. Identify its fragility status and describe the centripetal and centrifugal forces that explain the rating.

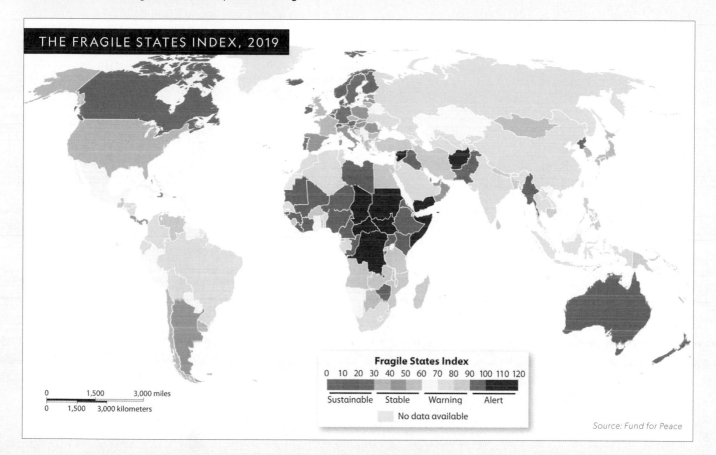

THE FRAGILE STATES INDEX, 2019

Fragile States Index

0 10 20 30 40 50 60 70 80 90 100 110 120

Sustainable   Stable   Warning   Alert

No data available

0   1,500   3,000 miles

0   1,500   3,000 kilometers

Source: Fund for Peace

STATE FRAGILITY TRENDS, 2009–2019

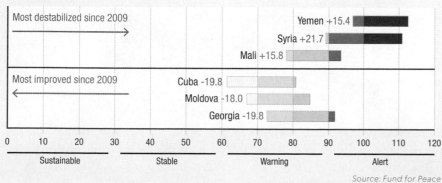

Most destabilized since 2009

Yemen +15.4

Syria +21.7

Mali +15.8

Most improved since 2009

Cuba -19.8

Moldova -18.0

Georgia -19.8

0   10   20   30   40   50   60   70   80   90   100   110   120

Sustainable   Stable   Warning   Alert

Source: Fund for Peace

▌Based on what you've learned about devolutionary forces, identify some factors that may have caused the six countries in the graph to become more fragile or more stable.

AGRICULTURE AND RURAL LAND-USE
PATTERNS AND PROCESSES

AGRICULTURE'S IMPACT

Zanskar Valley, northern India

Every person is affected by agriculture. It provides the food we eat and some of the fuel and products we trade and consume. The agricultural practices used to produce crops and livestock vary as widely as the physical geography of different regions, including Florida's flat, marshy land on which specific cattle (shown here) thrive.

Agriculture (commercial or subsistence) is impacted by geography, economics, politics, and technology. How people obtain and distribute food differs among regions and countries, creating many agricultural opportunities and challenges. Global networks of trade and transportation allow millions of people to access agricultural products that are grown in diverse climates across the planet. The challenge for agriculture lies in developing sustainable farming practices that feed a growing population.

CHAPTER 12
AGRICULTURE:
HUMAN-ENVIRONMENT INTERACTION

CHAPTER 13
PATTERNS AND PRACTICES OF
AGRICULTURAL PRODUCTION

CHAPTER 14
AGRICULTURAL SUSTAINABILITY
IN A GLOBAL MARKET

WRITING ACROSS UNITS, REGIONS
& SCALES

UNIT 5 MAPS & MODELS ARCHIVE

AGRICULTURE
FOR A HUNGRY FUTURE

AFRICA

MALAWI

Earth's most extensive type of land cover wasn't set by nature but by human activity. According to National Geographic Explorer Jerry Glover, agriculture takes up more acreage than any type of natural ecosystem. Glover is one of many researchers grappling with problems caused by farming practices that have replaced natural ecosystems and diminished biodiversity worldwide.

LEARNING OBJECTIVE
IMP-5.A Explain how agricultural practices have environmental and societal consequences.

PERENNIAL SOLUTIONS

As an agricultural ecologist studying farming systems around the world, Jerry Glover regularly sees the harmful consequences of farming techniques. "We've done more damage with agriculture in the past 50 years than I think were done in the previous thousands of years," he observes. In Glover's view, present-day farming practices are firmly tied to a 20th-century vision of agriculture, as farmers continue to plant the same crops that humans have been raising for centuries. These crops result in high rates of soil loss through erosion and require large amounts of fertilizers and pesticides to maintain them. Glover says, "Farmers have the thinnest and most nutrient depleted soil in history. Given the new challenges we face, we need a uniquely 21st-century vision for food security."

Glover advocates for innovative solutions to the problem of depleted soil, including a strategy called perenniation—the use of perennial plants in farm fields. Nearly all agricultural crops are annuals, or plants that must be replanted every year after harvesting. Perennial plants survive from year to year and are more resilient during droughts and other climate-related stresses. Glover works to expand the use of perenniation in regions of Africa where the soil is especially thin and starved for nutrients. In Malawi, for example, he studied how farmers greatly improve their yields of maize by planting "fertilizer trees" with roots that draw water and nutrients from deep within the soil. When the trees drop their leaves, they return the nutrients to the shallower layer of soil, where the maize has its roots. Glover also promotes the development of food crops that are perennials themselves, but while some promising strains of perennial wheat and rice have been created, none have entered large-scale cultivation as yet.

LOCAL CONVERSATIONS While some have claimed that Earth is capable of producing enough food for all its human citizens, Glover points out that the best farmlands are unequally distributed, explaining, "An adequate global food supply does not solve regional problems." At the same time, barriers to improving crop yields may arise from social and economic concerns, as well as from geographic challenges. For this reason, Glover strives to adapt agricultural solutions to a variety of local needs. This may mean breeding perennial crops that are adapted to specific soil and climate conditions, and it means working with farming communities and forming an understanding of their social structures. Glover has learned that women farmers in Malawi and elsewhere in Africa are best at identifying the most resilient and nutritious solutions for their families. To communicate effectively with women in some communities, however, scientists must consider cultural and family dynamics, because women's social position may affect the ways in which they can interact with them.

Glover envisions future generations feeding themselves with food sources that have been developed in only limited ways at present—such as seaweed and insects raised for protein. He also points to advanced technology that allows researchers to more directly manipulate GMOs (genetically-modified organisms) to better adapt them to local growing conditions. As the human population grows, Glover believes a new agricultural revolution is needed. "Farming is what we ultimately rely on to survive," he says. "You know we can't go back to low-yielding traditional practices. We can't go forward with . . . just pouring the chemicals onto the landscapes and hoping for the best."

GRAPHIC THINKING

Explain the long-term environmental and societal effects Glover's work might have on communities and regions.

Top: National Geographic Explorer Jerry Glover (left) learns about local farming practices as he talks with a family in Malawi that grows corn and tree crops, such as mangos. Bottom: Grains are harvested on the lands of the Agroscope research center in Switzerland in order to study GMOs and improve agricultural practices.

CHAPTER 12
AGRICULTURE: HUMAN-ENVIRONMENT INTERACTION

CRITICAL VIEWING The Chianti region of Italy is famous for its production of red wine, and its Mediterranean climate strongly influences its agricultural practices. Initially covered in dense forest, the land was transformed during the Middle Ages into a place where wine grapes could be cultivated. ❚ What interactions between people and the environment are evident in the photo?

GEOGRAPHIC THINKING How is agriculture a human-environment interaction?

12.1
AGRICULTURE AND THE ENVIRONMENT

12.2
AGRICULTURAL PRACTICES

FEATURE: Rural Survey Methods

FEATURE: Rural Settlement Patterns

NATIONAL GEOGRAPHIC PHOTOGRAPHER George Steinmetz

12.3
AGRICULTURAL ORIGINS AND DIFFUSIONS

12.4
ADVANCES IN AGRICULTURE

CASE STUDY: Women and Africa's Green Revolution

12.1 AGRICULTURE AND THE ENVIRONMENT

Agriculture is a major way of life around the world—and, of course, it feeds everyone across the globe. The ways in which agriculture is practiced, the number of people involved, and the resulting cultural landscapes all vary among Earth's environments.

INTRODUCTION TO AGRICULTURE

LEARNING OBJECTIVES

PSO-1.B Explain how major geographic concepts illustrate spatial relationships.

PSO-5.A Explain the connection between physical geography and agricultural practices.

Agriculture is the purposeful cultivation of plants or raising of animals to produce goods for survival. The first crops to be harvested through agriculture were food crops, such as fruits, vegetables, and grains, the most widespread being corn (or maize), wheat, and rice. Other crops, such as oats and alfalfa, are important for feeding livestock. Agriculture is more than growing food—though that is the primary purpose of farming and livestock-raising in many parts of the world. Fiber crops, such as cotton, are used for textile and paper products. And oil crops can be used for consumption or for industrial purposes. For example, olives, corn, and soybeans may be harvested and processed into oils used for cooking, for machinery lubrication, or as biofuel.

Geographers study agriculture to understand how humans have modified the environment to sustain themselves. The types and patterns of agricultural production and the processes that affect these patterns exist at a range of scales. Observing these global, regional, and local patterns informs geographers about the sustainability of agricultural practices, especially in food production.

ENVIRONMENTAL FACTORS Cultivating plants or raising animals requires adaptation to environmental limitations. Sunlight, water, and nutrients are all factors that affect plant growth. Agriculture is bound to the physical environment, and four factors have a profound effect on

GLOBAL CROPLAND, 2015

Cropland covers 18 percent of the United States, which contains 8.9 percent of the world's cropland.

India has the highest percentage of the world's cropland: 9.6 percent.

China has 8.8 percent of the world's cropland within its borders. Cropland covers 18 percent of the entire country.

Cropland

0   1500   3000 miles
0   1500   3000 kilometers

READING MAPS A recent study revised what geographers had previously thought about Earth's cropland. India, rather than China or the United States, ranks first, with 9.6 percent of the world's net cropland area. ▪ Describe the cropland percentages in the United States or in China.

the agriculture that can take place there: climate, which includes temperature and precipitation; elevation; soil; and topography.

You've read that climate is the long-term patterns of weather in a particular area. (Weather is what happens today: sunny or cloudy, rainy or snowy, hot or cold.) Climate is a major influencer of agricultural choices and practices because it provides precipitation and temperatures needed for seeds to germinate, plants to grow, or livestock to have the food needed to survive. Water, from natural precipitation or irrigation, critically provides the moisture plants and animals require. Temperature is the key factor in determining the growing season—the length of the year during which plant life can grow.

Generally, the greater the distance from the Equator, the shorter the growing season. At the Equator and in the tropics, the growing season can be year-round. In the temperate and subarctic zones, however, the colder temperatures of winter prevent plant growth for a varying number of weeks or months. In those regions, the growing season is measured in the number of frost-free days, as frost can kill plants.

Elevation also affects the growing season and what plants can be grown. Each increase of 1,000 feet above sea level means a corresponding decrease of about 3.6° F in average temperature. As a result, the higher the elevation, the shorter the growing season. Elevation can create different cultivation opportunities in all mountainous regions. For example, in tropical regions in Central America and South America, the hotter lowlands are used to grow tropical crops such as bananas and sugarcane. In the next highest zone, farmers can grow coffee, corn, and other vegetables. At higher elevations, crops must be hardier, like barley and potatoes. Higher still, the land can only be used for grazing livestock because only grasses can grow there.

Soil, a vital factor in determining the agricultural potential of a given area, is the biologically active coating of Earth's surface. This layer can range from a few inches to several feet in depth. It is formed by the weathering of rock by wind, water, and other factors, which break the rock into increasingly smaller pieces over an extremely long period. It can take thousands of years to form an inch of soil. Soil has four constituent parts: mineral particles, water, air, and organic matter like decaying plant material. The key characteristics of soil are its fertility, texture, and structure.

Topography, or an area's land features, includes the slope of that land, which affects the ability of the soil to stay in place and retain water. The steeper the slope, the more likely the soil will be affected by runoff. Slope can also be a factor in land productivity due to the position of the land toward or away from the sun, which affects how much of the sun's energy the land receives.

The most favorable land for growing crops has ideal temperatures, precipitation, soils, and slope. Sometimes landscapes are modified for better environmental factors. Terrace building for farming protects soil on steep slopes, while irrigation or drainage schemes influence water availability. (You will read about these agricultural practices in depth in Chapter 14.) Adding fertilizers enhances the soil fertility of cropland. In general, it is not feasible to modify the other environmental factors—soil texture, soil depth, soil mineral content, temperature, and terrain—at large scales.

ALTITUDINAL ZONATION Central America and South America both show how elevation can affect agriculture. ▮ Explain how climate is a factor in the elevation zones in the diagram.

Tierra Nevada		
	Snow line	15,000 feet
Tierra Helada (Punta)		Grazing (alpacas, llamas, sheep)
	Tree line	12,000 feet
Tierra Fría	Highest zone in Central America	Barley, potatoes. Grazing, dairy operations
		6,000 feet
Tierra Templada	Zone with largest human population	Sheep, cattle, dairy. Vegetables, coffee. Corn (maize), small grains
		2,500 feet
Tierra Caliente	Tropical rain forest	Bananas, sugarcane, rice. Other tropical crops, some livestock
		Sea Level

Agricultural practices are impacted by climatic conditions. For example, in the tropical climate of Malawi, tea fields are built along the contours of the sloping landscape to slow erosion. Terrace farming is another way to reduce soil erosion and water loss.

CLIMATE Climate varies greatly across the globe and is based on four key factors: distance from the Equator, wind and ocean currents, proximity to large bodies of water, and topography. These components interact with one another in different ways to create different climate regions.

Distance from the Equator determines the length of daylight and average temperatures. The Equator and the regions near it to the north and south, called the tropics, receive direct rays from the sun year-round. These regions have nearly equal periods of daylight and nighttime every day and are warm throughout the year. The northern and southern limits of these warmer regions are called the Tropic of Cancer and the Tropic of Capricorn, respectively.

Just to the north and south of the tropics are huge dry bands containing deserts including the Sahara, Kalahari, Sonora, and Atacama. Farther north and south of the desert bands are the temperate zones—large bands between the tropics and the frigid polar circles that have hot summers, cold or cool winters, and transitional springs and autumns.

Ocean and wind currents circulate cold or warm water and air masses over Earth's surface. The circulation of water and air masses in turn affects patterns of temperature and precipitation. Ocean currents that flow north and south transfer heat between lower latitudes (close to the Equator) and higher latitudes (farther from the Equator). When these currents flow away from the Equator, they bring warmth to temperate zones. For example, in January, the Gulf Stream carries warm water from the Gulf of Mexico into the Atlantic Ocean, where the current travels north along the eastern coast of North America before moving east toward Europe. Currents flowing from a temperate zone toward the Equator carry colder water in that direction. Winds also carry air at different temperatures from one region to another. Because warmer air tends to hold more moisture and colder air tends to be drier, these wind patterns affect precipitation patterns.

Location relative to large bodies of water affects climate in two ways. First, these bodies of water warm and cool more slowly than land. As a result, most coastal areas tend to have milder climates than regions farther inland. Second, coastal areas are cooled during the day by cool winds displaced by warmer air rising from the water. These regions are warmed at night by warm air blowing onshore as cooler night air pushes down toward the water. Location also affects precipitation, which tends to be heavier near coastlines and lighter farther inland, with some exceptions.

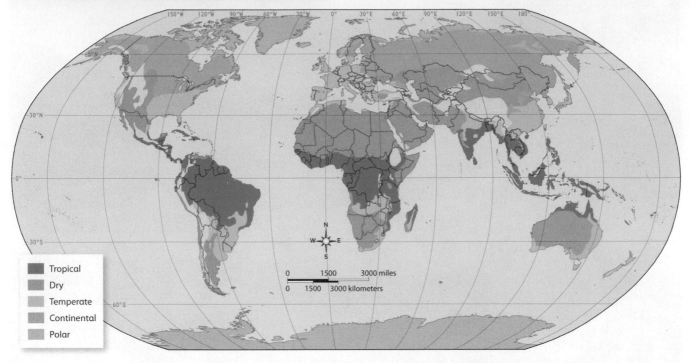

Tropical
Dry
Temperate
Continental
Polar

To classify the main climates on Earth, Vladimir Köppen considered global patterns of average temperatures, average precipitation, and natural vegetation. Climate in highland areas, represented by gray on the map, cannot be easily classified because both altitude and topography can vary wildly within these regions.

You read that elevation can affect temperature even in the tropical zone, but topography impacts climate in other ways. Coastal mountains have much heavier precipitation on the side facing the wind, and very light precipitation on the side away from the wind. This effect can be seen in the Pacific Northwest of the United States, which produces temperate rain forests along the Pacific Coast and dry conditions in areas such as the Yakima Valley of Washington State.

CLIMATE REGIONS

LEARNING OBJECTIVE
PSO-5.A Explain the connection between physical geography and agricultural practices.

The combination of temperature, precipitation, wind patterns, and topography produces different **climate regions**, or areas that have similar climate patterns generally based on their latitude and their location on coasts or continental interiors. Vladimir Köppen, a Russian-German scientist, developed a system for classifying the world's climates. He identified five broad climate types: tropical, dry, temperate, continental, and polar, which are represented in the "Köppen Climate Classifications, 2016" map in this lesson. Each of these broad climate types can then be subdivided into more specific climate types.

Areas with tropical climates all have warm temperatures year-round but vary in their amounts of precipitation. The wet tropical climate has plentiful precipitation, which fosters the growth of tropical rain forests. The tropical monsoon climate—found in South Asia and West Africa—has extremely heavy summer rains and dry winters. The tropical wet and dry climate also has distinct rainy seasons but less precipitation than the tropical monsoon climate. One example of the vegetation associated with this climate is the savanna grasslands in East Africa.

With some exceptions, dry climates are commonly found in continental interiors and are either arid (very dry) or semiarid (minimal precipitation). Semiarid climates receive enough precipitation to allow the growth of grasslands.

There are three basic types of temperate climates, or climates with moderate temperatures and adequate precipitation amounts. All three tend to have long, warm summers and short winters. Humid temperate climates, typically found on the eastern sides of continents, have colder winters and year-round precipitation. The marine west coast climate (on the west coast of continents at higher latitudes) has cooler winters and plentiful rain, supporting the growth of temperate rain forests. Mediterranean climates are commonly found on the west coasts of continents near deserts and around the Mediterranean Sea in countries such as Italy, Greece, and Tunisia.

The milder, wet winters of the Mediterranean climate are conducive to agriculture, as you will read about in detail in 12.2, and the hot, dry summers are ideal for cultivating

The province of Khövsgöl in northern Mongolia is a mix of tundra and taiga, which are evergreen forests found in the far Northern Hemisphere. Because temperatures are so cold there, little farming occurs. Instead, the Tsaatan (or Dhukha), a local people, herd reindeer.

certain vines and trees. **Mediterranean agriculture** consists of growing hardy trees (such as olive, fruit, and nut trees) and shrubs (like grape vines) and raising sheep and goats. These animals forage in the sparse, scrubby summer growth and maneuver around the region's steep landscape.

The two polar climate types, tundra and ice cap, are found near the North and South Poles and are both extremely cold. The tundra climate has a short, mild summer but is too cold to allow farming, although some of the Sami people of northern Europe engage in reindeer herding. Continental climates are found in the interior of continents in the Northern Hemisphere, and are characterized by distinct seasons that include cold winters and snow. The temperatures in the ice cap climates of the Arctic and Antarctic rarely rise above freezing.

The warm temperatures of the tropics allow for year-round agriculture, which can also permit multiple harvests of crops, like rice, in a year. The type of tropical climate limits that potential, however. Areas with a tropical wet and dry climate may not receive sufficient precipitation in the dry months to allow crop production. Even the plentiful precipitation of the tropical wet climate poses challenges. The heavy year-round rains allow for the flourishing growth of rain forests, but the soils in these areas tend to be poor. The main source of nutrients needed to produce crops in rain forests is plant matter.

The temperate zones, with their long growing seasons, are home to major grain-producing regions. Hardier grains like wheat, which can thrive in shorter growing seasons and drier conditions, grow well toward the north of the temperate zones. Corn, which requires a higher average temperature to germinate than wheat, generally grows farther south. Rice, which needs an even longer growing season, grows in the southernmost parts of the temperate zone, near the tropics. Rice requires more water than wheat and corn and is grown along the warm, wet southern portion of the Mississippi. The humid tropical and subtropical climates on Earth are well suited to wet-rice farming. And in some other areas, such as California, rice growing needs irrigation.

GEOGRAPHIC THINKING

1. Identify the four elements that make land favorable for growing crops.

2. Describe how the agricultural practices of certain regions are influenced by the Mediterranean climate.

3. Explain why areas on different continents—such as Western Europe and coastal East Asia—have similar climates at different latitudes.

12.2 AGRICULTURAL PRACTICES

The physical geography, available resources, and cultural practices in an area influence rural land-use patterns and agricultural practices such as the choice of crops to grow and livestock to raise. Such farming practices fall into two overall categories: subsistence agriculture and commercial agriculture.

SUBSISTENCE AGRICULTURE AND COMMERCIAL AGRICULTURE

LEARNING OBJECTIVES

PSO-1.B Explain how major geographic concepts illustrate spatial relationships.

PSO-5.C Explain how economic forces influence agricultural practices.

For some farmers, growing food is a matter of survival. They grow and raise a diverse range of crops and livestock for their family's consumption. This form of farming is called **subsistence agriculture**, which you briefly read about in Chapter 3. Occasionally, subsistence farmers enjoy a plentiful harvest and produce more than meets their needs. They may barter or sell their excess products for cash. Ultimately however, subsistence farming is about obtaining enough yield to feed one's family and close community using fewer mechanical resources and more hand labor to care for the crops and livestock.

Other farmers grow crops and raise livestock for profit to sell to customers, who buy these goods in a form of agriculture known as **commercial agriculture**. The goods commercial farmers produce depend on a range of geographic and economic factors, including the comparative advantages

of their farmland and environment, market demands for particular products, and their agricultural practices. Subsistence and commercial agricultural practices help define the agricultural production regions across the world, as conveyed in the "Agricultural Regions Around the World" map later in 12.2.

Both subsistence and commercial agriculture are practiced at different scales known as intensive and extensive scales. The **bid-rent theory** explains how land value determines how a farmer will use the land—either intensively or extensively. Where land value is high, farmers will buy less land and use it *intensively* to produce the most agricultural yield per unit of land. Where land has a lower value or is farther from the market, farmers will buy more land and use it less intensively, or *extensively*. You will learn more about intensive and extensive agriculture later in this lesson.

According to this theory, dairy and produce farmers, concerned with issues of freshness, perishability, and transportation, for example, are willing to pay higher costs—or "rent"—for land close to the market. However, farmers growing grains and cereal crops, which are easily stored and transported, will not pay as much.

MODEL: BID-RENT THEORY

The bid-rent theory, which is used to describe how land costs are determined, was developed in 1964 by American economic geographer William Alonso. This theory explains the relationships between land value, commercial location, and transportation (primarily in urban areas) using a bid-rent gradient, or slope. The gradient is based on the practice of land users bidding against one another for land. The most desirable land, which is also the most accessible, receives the highest bids. The majority of consumer services are located in the center of a city because the accessibility of the location attracts these services. This central location is called the **central business district (CBD)**. The demand for central locations is translated into high land values. As the distance away from the CBD increases, land value decreases. The bid-rent theory assumes there is one CBD.

In terms of agriculture, the bid-rent theory explains how land costs determine how intensively the land is farmed.

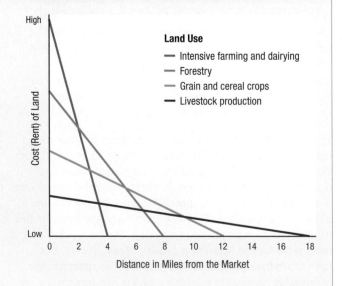

RURAL SURVEY METHODS

LEARNING OBJECTIVE
PSO-5.B Identify different rural settlement patterns and methods of surveying rural settlements.

Land ownership requires owning a title to the land, but for clear title to exist, the boundaries of one owner's land must be clearly differentiated from those of another's land. The scientific technique called land surveying is used to determine a property's three-dimensional position of points and the distances and angles between them. Land boundaries are drawn according to land survey methods, and the North American landscape is shaped by the use of three different methods.

In the 17th century, a system called *metes and bounds* spread from Great Britain to its North American colonies through relocation diffusion. This system describes property boundaries in terms of lines drawn in a certain direction for a specific distance from clear points of reference. Those points of reference were typically a natural feature, such as the crest of a hill or even a particular tree. This process resulted in unusually shaped land parcels that can still be seen in aerial photographs of land in the mid-Atlantic region.

French and Spanish colonies from the same period used the *long-lot survey system*. Property was divided into a series of adjacent long strips of land stretching back from frontage along a river or lake. Land divisions like these can still be seen in Louisiana, parts of Missouri, some Great Lakes states, French Canada, and along the Río Grande. This system allowed equal access to the waterway and a mix of soils: richer soils near the river to the woodlands and less fertile areas farther away. Over time, lots became narrower when property was divided, per French tradition, equally among all children at the owner's death. That issue did not arise in British colonies, where an entire estate went to the eldest male child.

With the arrival of improved scientific surveying practices in the 18th century, people began to use rectangular grid systems to divide land. Some areas of the original 13 colonies as well as parts of Ohio that were surveyed by private land companies followed this system. When the U.S. government organized the Old Northwest—the area from Ohio to Minnesota—it adopted a cadastral system that created rectangular land lots. This survey system is called the *township and range system*, and it was designed to create survey townships of 6 miles x 6 miles, giving a total of 36 square miles. Each square mile contains 640 acres. Land was sold by the full, half, or quarter section. This system was used to survey and sell land controlled by the U.S. government as the country acquired new territories. Most land west of the Mississippi is surveyed using this system, which can be seen in the largely rectangular agricultural landscape visible when flying over areas like the Great Plains.

Exceptions to this rule show the results of sequent occupance—the cultural imprint left behind by successive societies. Parts of modern Missouri settled by the French have property lines that reflect the long-lot system. Areas controlled by Spain, such as present-day Florida and the region from Texas to California, show a mix of the metes and bounds and long-lot systems. But areas of these states that had not been surveyed under those systems divide land according to the township and range system, creating a mix of property types that demonstrates historical changes written on the land. ∎

GEOGRAPHIC THINKING

Explain how geographic features would affect the grid pattern of the township and range system.

Farmland along the Richelieu River in central Quebec, Canada (left), shows the influence of the long-lot system. By contrast, farmland along the Pacific coast of California (right) shows a rectangular agricultural landscape, a result of the township and range system.

INTENSIVE AGRICULTURE

LEARNING OBJECTIVES

PSO-1.B Explain how major geographic concepts illustrate spatial relationships.

PSO-5.A Explain the connection between physical geography and agricultural practices.

PSO-5.C Explain how economic forces influence agricultural practices.

With **intensive agriculture**, farmers expend a great deal of effort to produce as much yield as possible from an area of land. To achieve high productivity, they rely on high levels of "inputs" and energy. In some regions, commonly used inputs include chemical fertilizers, pesticides, and growth regulators. In other regions, the inputs may be human or animal labor, natural fertilizers, and thoughtful care of the soil. Regardless of the inputs, large amounts of energy are always needed in intensive agriculture—to run machines, to work the land by hand, and to utilize various degrees of technology. Technology and energy speed up the essential steps of farming—plowing, planting, and harvesting. These inputs and expenditures of energy maximize crop yields in intensive agriculture.

Women farmers plant rice by hand in a field in Mandalay, Myanmar. This wet-rice intensive subsistence agriculture is labor-intensive and supports large populations with its high yields.

INTENSIVE SUBSISTENCE AGRICULTURE

When people work the land intensively, putting forth a large amount of human labor to generate high crop yields on small plots of land to support their family and local community, they are practicing intensive subsistence agriculture. This type of farming feeds more than half the people living in densely populated semi-peripheral and peripheral countries. In addition to heavy human labor, intensive subsistence agriculture relies upon careful land stewardship practices and sometimes fertilizers—mainly animal manure—to maintain soil productivity.

As with any type of agriculture, the yields from intensive subsistence farms are impacted by weather, seed quality, and the use or lack of fertilizers and pesticides. Yet when farms are primarily being used to feed a family or community (the definition of subsistence agriculture), yields reduced by weather, disease, or pests can be devastating and can lead to undernutrition or even widespread starvation in a community versus a reduction in profits, as with commercial agriculture. In 2019, for example, Cyclone Idai hit southern Africa with heavy rains, flooding, and damaging winds that destroyed crops throughout the region, greatly reducing crop yields and contributing to widespread hunger. Fortunately, new technology is helping intensive subsistence farmers by providing weather information and data that will help them to better strategize on fertilizer use and harvest times, and by improving seed quality and farming tools.

As populations increase in intensive subsistence agriculture regions, many farmers maximize food production by modifying their local environment. One such example of intensive subsistence farming is the wet-rice agriculture of Asia. In South, East, and Southeast Asia, growers make large investments in productive seed types and fertilizer and use human labor rather than mechanized equipment to carry out the planting, weeding, and harvesting. Rice farmers in India modify their environment by leveling and flooding rice paddies, creating additional suitable land for growing a grain they depend on. In the mountainous terrain of China and Southeast Asia, farmers terrace the fields to effectively grow wet-rice crops. In dry-climate regions, farmers build irrigation systems to provide water to their crops as well as manage environmental degradation. These practices are indicative of intensive agriculture because of their reliance on heavy labor and the high crop yields they aim to generate.

INTENSIVE COMMERCIAL AGRICULTURE

Farmers in some core countries engage in intensive commercial agriculture, which involves heavy investments in labor and capital and results in high yields for profit—its products are commodities intended for sale at market. Intensive commercial agriculture often incorporates chemical fertilizers and machines, instead of relying mainly upon human and animal labor. It can be carried out close to or far from the market, or the place where the products are sold, processed, or consumed. For example, dairy farms in northern Europe are relatively close to their urban-dwelling consumers. However, the palm oil plantations of Malaysia and Indonesia are far from the factories that turn their product into cosmetics, soaps, ice cream, and chocolate bars. Regardless of the proximity to market, what all intensive commercial producers have in common is the use of intensive methods, whether these are capital- or labor-intensive, and a high yield.

The characteristics of intensive commercial agriculture can be observed in several specific types of farming including monoculture systems, plantation agriculture, market gardening, Mediterranean agriculture, and mixed

RURAL SETTLEMENT PATTERNS

In general, people all over the world tend to cluster together in villages, towns, and communities. Collective living is the norm, and isolated living is rare. Rural settlement patterns can take several forms, each with advantages and disadvantages.

The most common form of settlement is a **clustered settlement** (also known as a nucleated settlement), in which residents live in close proximity. Houses and farm buildings are near one another, with farmland and pasture land surrounding the settlement. This settlement pattern promotes social unity. Its physical closeness also allows residents to share common resources and expand their land outward. However, this immediacy can be too much of a good thing, and may lead to social friction or to a family's fields extending too far away from the settlement.

In **dispersed settlements**, houses and buildings are isolated from one another, and all the homes in a settlement are distributed over a relatively large area.

Dispersed settlements often exist in areas with difficult terrain, such as places where resources like water and fertile land are scarce. These settlements promote independence and self-sufficiency but lack social interaction; access to shared institutions, such as schools; and the ability to easily defend their residents.

In a **linear settlement** pattern, houses and buildings extend in a long line that usually follows a land feature, such as a riverfront, coast, or hill, or aligns along a transportation route. The linear features—including railroads and roads—generally predate the settlement, and people settle along these features because they provide access to water or transportation. Fields stretch out from the line of settlement, making the far end of those fields distant from homes. ∎

GEOGRAPHIC THINKING

Compare the advantages and disadvantages of clustered, dispersed, and linear settlements.

Clustered   Dispersed   Linear

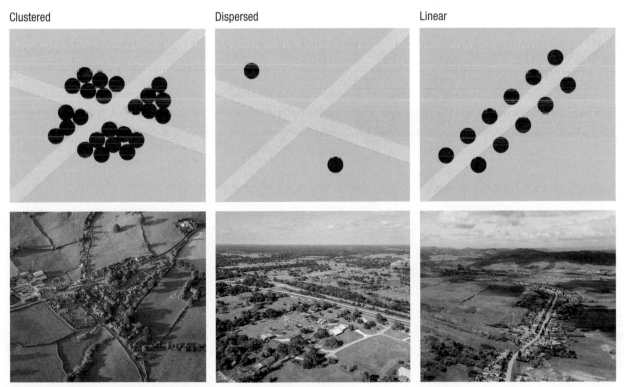

Most settlements are clustered, such as this one outside Usk, Wales (left). The town of Somerville, Texas (middle), is a dispersed settlement. This community in Hungary (right) is a linear settlement.

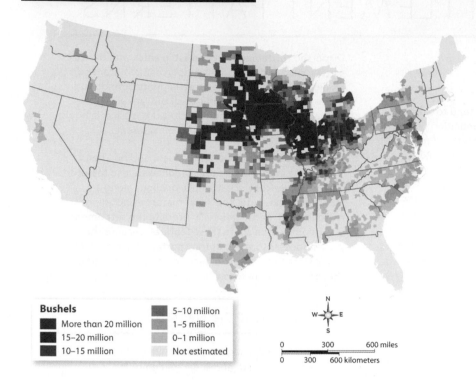

U.S. CORN PRODUCTION, 2018

Bushels

- More than 20 million
- 15–20 million
- 10–15 million
- 5–10 million
- 1–5 million
- 0–1 million
- Not estimated

0 300 600 miles
0 300 600 kilometers

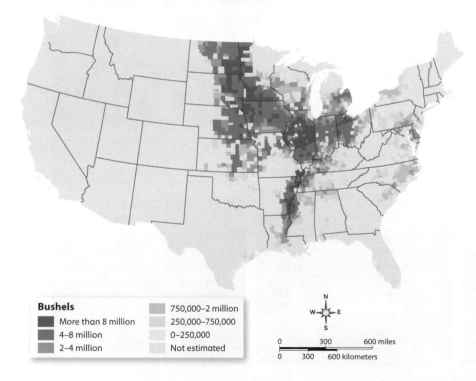

U.S. SOYBEAN PRODUCTION, 2018

Bushels

- More than 8 million
- 4–8 million
- 2–4 million
- 750,000–2 million
- 250,000–750,000
- 0–250,000
- Not estimated

0 300 600 miles
0 300 600 kilometers

READING MAPS In 2018, farmers in the Corn Belt of the Midwest planted close to 90 million acres each of corn and soybeans. Commercial farmers sometimes rotate what they plant—one year corn fills their fields and the next year soybeans. Rotating crops strips fewer nutrients from the soil. ▌ Use the maps to describe the agricultural production regions of the midwestern United States.

crops and livestock systems. Many people who participate in intensive commercial agriculture in the United States focus on **monocropping**, the cultivation of one or two crops that are rotated seasonally—commonly corn, soybeans, wheat, or cotton. These crops are usually what the market demands and therefore can be very profitable for plantations as well as large corporate farms.

Similarly, **monoculture** refers to the agricultural system of planting one crop or raising one type of animal annually. In the years following World War II, farmers in the American Midwest shifted from farming many crops to focus on one or two crops—typically corn and soybeans, depending on market prices—or on raising hogs or cattle.

Monocropping allows for specialization, simplifies cultivation, and maximizes efficiency. Farmers can purchase bulk seeds, as well as fertilizers and pesticides specific to a single crop, and they don't need a variety of equipment or other inputs that may be necessary to cultivate several different crops. Growers choose a crop that is especially conducive to the environment available, which also increases efficiency. For example, the soil and average climate conditions in the midwestern United States are suitable for growing corn and soybeans, and therefore farmers invest in fewer inputs to establish a favorable environment. Monocropping also leads to high yields, which means increased sales and a strong return on investment.

However, monocropping can strip nutrients from the soil; for instance, intensive cotton production leads to soil exhaustion. One way to prevent this depletion of nutrients is through **crop rotation**, the varying of crops from year to year to allow for the restoration of valuable nutrients and the continuing productivity of the soil.

The shift to monoculture also raises the stakes for farmers. As yields go up, crop prices can decrease. Falling prices can force many farmers out of business and may encourage successful operators to purchase the land of failing farms. To compete, farmers must invest heavily in high-yield seeds, fertilizers, and pesticides to maintain the soil and maximize plant growth. Fertilizers, while helping plants temporarily, can harm the soil long-term, and pesticides can contaminate water supplies and hurt air quality.

Plantation agriculture involves large-scale commercial farming of one particular crop grown for markets often distant from the plantation. This type of intensive commercial agriculture typically takes place in peripheral and semi-peripheral economies in the tropical regions of Asia, Africa, and the Americas. Major plantation crops include cotton, tobacco, tea, coffee, sugarcane, bananas, palm oil, and rubber.

Plantation agriculture is one of the oldest forms of intensive commercial agriculture, with its roots going back to the European colonization of the Caribbean and Central and South America as well as Asia and Africa. As tropical countries like Jamaica, Brazil, and Sri Lanka cut ties from European rule, they continued to take advantage of their plantation culture and have become well-known for certain goods—Sri Lanka for tea, for instance. These former colonies continue to rely on their production of specialty crops, and their economies depend upon these neocolonial relationships.

However, many larger plantations are owned by European or American individuals and multinational corporations. These businesses wish to ensure a steady stream of revenues and profits, so they invest heavily in such inputs as pesticides and fertilizers. Brazil—a leading producer of crops like sugarcane and coffee—is one of the world's leading consumers of pesticides. Plantations tend to be labor-intensive operations, although since many are located in peripheral countries, the cost of that labor is relatively low.

Market gardening is farming that produces fruits, vegetables, and flowers and typically serves a specific market, or urban area, where farmers can conveniently sell to local grocery stores, restaurants, farmers' markets, and road stands. The practice of market gardening is driven by the perishability of the products, or their likeliness to spoil, and the demand by local consumers for fresh fruits and vegetables. Market gardens can be found near most large cities in the United States, from the Northeast to Texas to California. The farm-to-table movement, which emphasizes fresh, locally grown ingredients, is giving a new momentum to market gardening. Still, in the winter months, most fruit and vegetables consumed in the United States are grown in Chile or Mexico.

Operators of market gardens often need to invest in technology such as greenhouses—which also entail high energy costs—to germinate seeds before the growing season so that the operators can stagger or spread out crop production to provide a constant supply of products throughout the year. They also need to use costly high-quality seeds and fertilizers and pesticides to ensure

harvests. Some market garden operators practice organic farming, which involves using natural methods to fertilize the land and prevent pest infestations.

Successful market gardens cultivate relatively high yields on small tracts of land using intensive production methods. Selling directly to public markets, including community farmers' markets, increases a farmer's profits by eliminating the need to bring in another company to sell the produce. In 2019, the U.S. Department of Agriculture listed approximately 8,700 farmers' markets in the United States. They are popular with consumers who, for the most part, value locally produced food over processed and packaged items from grocery retailers.

Truck farming, once synonymous with market gardening, now serves markets that are very distant from the farm. Large commercial farms in Mexico and the western and southern United States, where the climate is conducive to locally growing seasonal produce in high quantity, transport specialty crops to distant markets using large-capacity refrigerated trucks. The demand in markets like the upper Midwest and northeastern states is high because the cultivation in these areas is limited by climate. Truck farms produce crops such as tomatoes, lettuce, melons, beets, broccoli, celery, radishes, onions, citrus, and strawberries.

As you have read, agriculture thrives in the Mediterranean climate of southern Europe, southwest Asia, South Africa, Australia, and California. In some Mediterranean agriculture regions, subsistence farmers may cultivate beans, lentils, onions, tomatoes, carrots, and leafy vegetables year-round for their family's consumption. Just down the road might be commercial orchards and vineyards producing citrus fruits, olives, figs, and grapes, which are mostly exported for market. Much of the land in these climate regions is used for this type of intensive commercial agriculture.

Another type of intensive commercial agriculture practiced frequently is **mixed crop and livestock systems**, in which both crops and livestock are raised for profit. There are two types of mixed farming: on-farm and between-farm. In on-farm mixed farming, the crops and livestock are raised on the same farm. In between-farm mixing, two farmers share resources, with one growing crops and the other raising livestock. One example of this is livestock ranchers in the United States who buy feed from grain-producing farms. This practice is also carried out in such areas as West Africa and India, where crop producers exchange their crops with livestock raisers for manure to fertilize the land or for milk.

On-farm mixing effectively combines a farm's focus on one or two crops, such as corn and soybeans, with the raising of animals to meet the demand for high-quality meat. Mixing provides a farmer with certain advantages: part of the crop can be fed to the livestock, and the animals' waste can be used to fertilize the crops. This type of farming boosts labor needs, which makes it a form of intensive commercial agriculture. The diversity of mixing also may provide some protection from a bad crop year or low market value.

EXTENSIVE AGRICULTURE

LEARNING OBJECTIVES

PSO-1.B Explain how major geographic concepts illustrate spatial relationships.

PSO-5.A Explain the connection between physical geography and agricultural practices.

PSO-5.C Explain how economic forces influence agricultural practices.

With relatively few inputs and little investment in labor and capital, farmers who participate in **extensive agriculture** typically have lower outputs than farmers who employ intensive practices. Like intensive agriculture, extensive agriculture can be practiced in subsistence agricultural regions as well as in commercial agricultural regions. Extensive agriculture is found in countries in the periphery and semi-periphery, as well as in ranching enterprises in core countries.

EXTENSIVE SUBSISTENCE AGRICULTURE

Extensive subsistence agriculture is often found in regions in which intensive subsistence agriculture is not feasible because the environment is marginal—that is, too wet, too dry, or too cold—and thus, the carrying capacity (the maximum population size an environment can sustain) is low. One type of extensive subsistence agriculture that uses relatively simple technology requiring little capital investment is shifting cultivation. **Shifting cultivation** is the practice of growing crops or grazing animals on a piece of land for a year or two, then abandoning that land when the nutrients have been depleted from the soil and moving to a new piece of land where the process is repeated. Although the size of the piece of land being used short-term is not large, shifting cultivation requires a relatively large area in which to operate over time. This type of agriculture is practiced worldwide in marginal agricultural areas of the tropics, particularly in areas with high rainfall, such as in the rain forests of South America, Central and West Africa, and Southeast Asia.

Some farmers, including those in Colombia and Brazil in South America and Papua New Guinea in Oceania, use traditional subsistence farming techniques, such as **slash and burn** —a type of shifting cultivation—to maintain the land. They clear the land by cutting down the trees and brush, and after the vegetation dries, burning this "slash," resulting in a nutrient-rich ash fertilizer. The cleared land is then cultivated for several years until the soil becomes infertile. The process is then repeated on a new patch of land. While slash and burn has long been practiced, it is becoming unsustainable as more farmers engage in this practice. The cleared land can become severely degraded and open to erosion. In slash and burn agriculture—and in all agricultural methods—clearing forests for cropland leads to loss of habitat for local species, and increases air pollution and the amount of carbon released into the atmosphere, contributing to global climate change.

Another example of extensive subsistence farming is **nomadic herding**, also called **pastoral nomadism**. People who practice this type of agriculture move their animals seasonally or as needed to allow the best grazing. It requires far-reaching areas of land to prevent overgrazing—the destruction of feed plants that results from livestock overpopulation or overfeeding.

Some nomads engage in **transhumance**, the movement of herds between pastures at cooler, higher elevations during the summer months and lower elevations during the winter. For example, the Kohistani people of eastern Afghanistan are nomads who move their herds of livestock among five different altitude levels from 2,000 to 14,000 feet above sea level over the course of a year. Families have five different homes—one at each level—to provide shelter during the seasonal stay at each level. Transhumance may be practiced by non-nomads, too, who move their herds upslope or downslope but live in only one home.

EXTENSIVE COMMERCIAL AGRICULTURE

Ranching is an extensive commercial farming practice. It takes place in semiarid grassland areas around the world in which crop production is difficult or impossible, including in the American and Canadian West; Brazil, Argentina, and Uruguay in South America; Australia and New Zealand in Oceania; and Botswana and South Africa in Africa. Ranching is not as labor-intensive as other forms of agriculture. A rancher can rely on as little labor investment as one cowhand for every 800 to 1,200 head of cattle.

In the United States, livestock ranching is mostly found in the western states, where there are large, open tracts of land for livestock such as cattle and sheep to roam and graze. The arid grasslands of this region are suitable only for extensive agriculture, and therefore the price of this marginal land is low. Ranchers take advantage of the low land costs, the availability of federal lands, and the fact that less labor and capital is required to prepare the land for grazing. Ranching is typically carried out in sparsely populated areas farther away from markets or city centers, and ranchers must transport their livestock to markets for sale.

Extensive commercial ranching, while a common agricultural practice of the western United States, is in direct contrast to the increasingly common intensive commercial practice of Concentrated Animal Feeding Operations, or CAFOs. With CAFOs, farmers on small tracts of land rear pigs, cows, or other livestock in limited spaces called feedlots so that they can maximize the potential of their land. This practice makes it easier to manage the animals, and there are fewer costs involved in the operation, though some concerns have been raised over animal welfare. Some cattle raised on the range may also be "finished" in feed lots.

GEOGRAPHIC THINKING

1. Identify the environmental impacts of slash-and-burn farming techniques.

2. Explain why nomadic herding is the most extensive type of agriculture.

National Geographic photographer John Stanmeyer photographs a child playing in an irrigation water tank on a rice farm in Punjab, India. Intensive subsistence farmers rely on inputs such as this rudimentary irrigation system to make dry soils more productive for farming.

COMPARING INTENSIVE AND EXTENSIVE AGRICULTURE

A society's agricultural practices depend on several factors, including climate, culture, the availability of capital, the quality of the land, the supply of labor, global markets, and the societal needs and demands for agricultural output. Many countries will participate in a mix of practices. Kenya, for example, has both coffee and tea plantations—which reflect intensive commercial agriculture—and nomadic herding, a type of extensive subsistence agriculture.

Physical geography is a major determinant of the agricultural practices used. Large expanses of land with less nutrient-rich soil available for growing crops, such as in the rain forests of the Amazon Basin or in the semiarid grasslands of Central Asia and the American West, call for the use of extensive agricultural practices. The only way to make up for the low yields that such land produces is to work a more extensive expanse of land. In contrast, rich soils—such as those in eastern China and the American Midwest—are better suited to intensive agricultural practices because they can produce high yields.

Of course, inputs such as fertilizer or irrigation can be used to make deficient land more productive. However, there are limits to what inputs can achieve. The heavy rains of the tropical rain forest decompose organic matter quickly and leach nutrients from the soil. Even if fertilizers are added, they can also be washed away in the region's regular rains.

Areas with marginal agricultural potential are generally only able to support small populations. In contrast, areas with highly productive agriculture are able to support large populations. And a populous society needs intensive agriculture. This situation generates a continued cycle. Intensive agriculture generates high crop yields, which can support a large population. A large population, in turn, requires high yields, which means emphasizing intensive agriculture.

GEOGRAPHIC THINKING

3. Compare the similarities and differences between subsistence and commercial farming practices.

4. Describe how intensive and extensive farming practices are determined in part by the bid-rent theory..

5. Identify an example where an agricultural practice is influenced by the availability of natural resources and the climate.

AGRICULTURAL REGIONS AROUND THE WORLD

Agriculture takes many forms. In the late 1930s, an American geographer named Derwent S. Whittlesey developed a world agriculture map that identified 11 separate agricultural regions (as well as areas where agriculture is not practiced).

The large map shows the global distribution of agriculture today. For example, the intensive commercial agriculture practices of dairy farming and grain farming—represented by the colors brown and yellow, respectively—can be found in North America, South America, Europe, Asia, and Australia. Rice, produced through intensive subsistence farming practices and represented as dark green, mainly grows in Asia.

The text annotations on the large map provide geographic context for many of the types of farming, rural survey methods, and settlement patterns that have been represented in this chapter.

The smaller topographical map shows the elevation of global lands. Land topography plays a major role in the kind of agriculture that can take place in a specific location. Some regions cannot sustain certain crops or animals—even with human intervention.

LONG-LOT SYSTEM, QUEBEC

TOWNSHIP AND RANGE SYSTEM, CALIFORNIA

DISPERSED SETTLEMENT, TEXAS

BANANA PLANTATION, ECUADOR

ATLANTIC OCEAN

PACIFIC OCEAN

0   500   1000 miles
0   500   1000 kilometers

TOPOGRAPHY OF THE WORLD

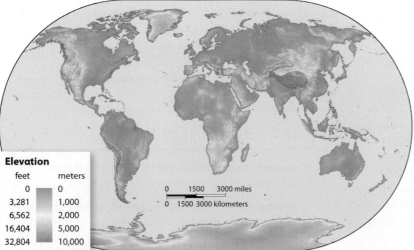

Elevation

feet	meters
0	0
3,281	1,000
6,562	2,000
16,404	5,000
32,804	10,000

0   1500   3000 miles
0   1500   3000 kilometers

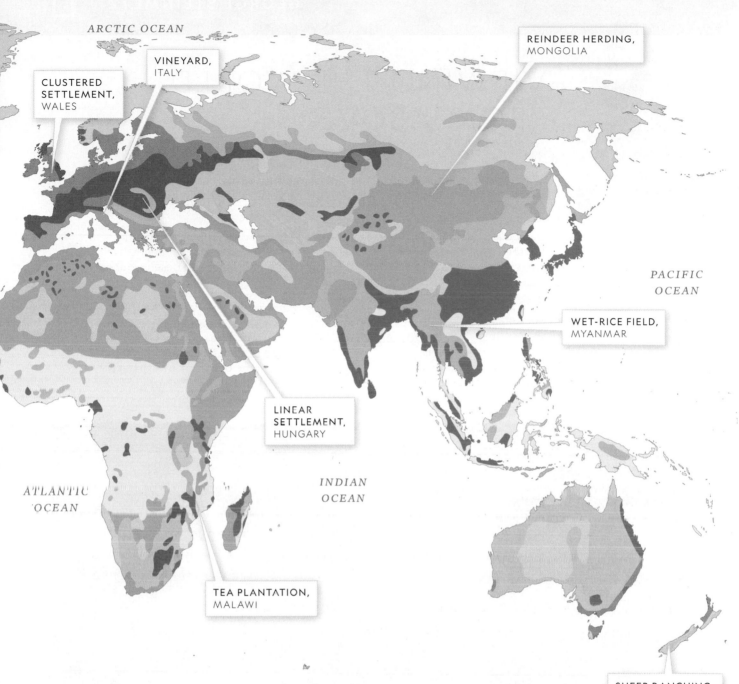

ARCTIC OCEAN

CLUSTERED SETTLEMENT, WALES

VINEYARD, ITALY

REINDEER HERDING, MONGOLIA

PACIFIC OCEAN

WET-RICE FIELD, MYANMAR

LINEAR SETTLEMENT, HUNGARY

ATLANTIC OCEAN

INDIAN OCEAN

TEA PLANTATION, MALAWI

SHEEP RANCHING, NEW ZEALAND

Legend:
- Dairy farming
- Grain farming
- Intensive subsistence farming—mainly rice
- Intensive subsistence farming—mainly not rice
- Mediterranean agriculture
- Market gardening
- Plantation agriculture
- Mixed crop and livestock systems
- Shifting cultivation
- Nomadic herding
- Livestock ranching
- Little or no agriculture

GEOGRAPHIC THINKING

6. Identify which continent likely produces the most diverse array of agricultural exports and explain your reasoning.

7. Explain what the areas that cultivate grain have in common.

8. Identify the highest elevations of North and South America using the "Topography of the World" map, then describe the types of agriculture that take place in those regions.

9. Compare the agricultural practices of New Zealand and Australia to those of North America.

VIEWING THE WORLD FROM ABOVE

George Steinmetz specializes in remote deserts, little-known cultures, and new developments in science and technology.

LEARNING OBJECTIVE

IMP-1.B Identify different methods of geographic data collection.

National Geographic Photographer George Steinmetz seems to think that a bird's-eye view of Earth is the best way to see the planet. This belief might explain why he's willing to strap himself into a motorized paraglider and soar into the air with his legs dangling below to photograph a lettuce farm in California. He calls his aerial photos "street photography from the sky."

Trained as a geophysicist, Steinmetz took up photography during a hitchhiking trip through Africa when he was in his 20s. He has returned to that continent many times to capture its land and people. Steinmetz has photographed deserts, dunes, cityscapes, and farmland—including the growing of crops in countries such as Brazil, Japan, and the United States.

While he has flown as high as 6,000 feet to take his photos, Steinmetz prefers a much lower altitude—around 100 to 500 feet. "You are seeing [the land] more obliquely, so you see the 3-D relationship," he explains. "It's the perfect mix where I can see the gross pattern—the infinite skyline or the mountains in the distance but also people and what they are doing."

CRITICAL VIEWING The Naxi (also called Nakhi or Nasi), an ethnic group in China, use terrace farming to cultivate millets, cabbage, corn, and wheat. Steinmetz's photo of a Naxi farm shows piles of manure dotting the landscape. The manure is mixed with straw before being folded into the soil.
▌ Identify human-environment interactions that are easily seen in the aerial photo.

CRITICAL VIEWING Top: The Adjder oasis in Algeria features small family gardens nestled into scalloped depressions created by the powerful Harmattan winds. Bottom: Organic lettuce is farmed near Hollister, California, by a machine that can harvest 10,000 pounds of lettuce per hour. ▮ Explain how farmers could use aerial photographs like Steinmetz's in their work.

12.3 AGRICULTURAL ORIGINS AND DIFFUSIONS

When you eat pizza, you're enjoying an intercontinental food. Wheat and cattle—which provide grain for the crust and the milk that goes into the cheese—were first grown and raised in ancient Southwest Asia. South America was the ancient home of tomatoes. If you like onions on your pizza, thank Central Asia. And don't forget the people of Naples, who first put the ingredients together to make pizza and who then brought it to the United States when they migrated from Italy. The story of many foods is the story of the spread of plants and animals from their original homes.

AGRICULTURAL HEARTHS

LEARNING OBJECTIVE
SPS-5.A Identify major centers of domestication of plants and animals.

Answering when, where, and why agriculture started is tricky. Unfortunately, no one at the time could post social media messages. In fact, people weren't even recording the event on cave walls, clay tablets, or papyrus scrolls. Finding answers to these questions might be more difficult than figuring out when dinosaurs lived. The fossils of seeds and pollen are much smaller than most dinosaur fossils. To compound the difficulty, modern plants don't look exactly like their ancient ancestors. Still, people have discovered fossils of ancient plants and early domesticated animals, and some conclusions have been drawn. Those answers can be summarized in this statement: People living in many different places domesticated different plants and animals at different times from about 11,000 to 1000 B.C.E. **Domestication** is the deliberate effort to grow plants and raise animals, making plants and animals adapt to human demands, and using selective breeding to develop desirable characteristics.

FROM FORAGING TO FARMING Why did domestication take place? For thousands of years, humans lived as **foragers**, small nomadic groups who had primarily plant-based diets and ate small animals or fish for protein. Plant foods included fruits and vegetables, seeds and nuts, tubers, and other plants. Foragers fished in rivers and lakes or gathered shellfish and used traps, stones, or projectile weapons to hunt small game. Small bands sometimes formed within the group to hunt for larger animals. These humans lived by ranging over the land to exploit the food resources that were in season, often returning to the same areas each year.

Between 12,000 and 11,000 years ago, Earth entered a period of increased warming. The impact on the environment was substantial; this warming melted almost all the massive glaciers that had covered much of the Northern Hemisphere. Sea levels rose as a result, and climate regions changed, with more extreme changes in temperate regions than in the tropics. About 11,000 years ago, average rainfall in Southwest Asia dropped significantly for an extended time—perhaps as long as 1,000 years. People there adapted to this environmental stress by domesticating animals and plants to ensure a steady food supply, making them the first humans to do so. People also began migrating to and settling in warmer environments where more foods were available for foraging. Population growth increased pressure on the environment, and wild foods became scarce, which required the cultivation of a stable surplus.

The first animals to be domesticated were sheep and goats, which supplied hides, milk, and meat. With the changing climate, people in Southwest Asia began to plant seeds to secure a plant food supply in the new climate conditions. They selected plants such as cereal grains that produced plentiful seeds that could be ground or boiled to be eaten. In the switch to cultivation, people collected wild seeds and planted them in areas with sufficient sunlight. They tended the crops by ensuring that the plants had enough water and by removing weeds. Through selective breeding—accomplished by cultivating the plants that produced the most seeds—people gradually improved the plants to increase both their yields and nutrition.

ANCIENT HEARTHS Each area where different groups began to domesticate plants and animals is called an **agricultural hearth**. Scientists have identified several major agricultural hearths of domestication, and they continue to adjust their understanding of the timing of the emergence of these hearths as archaeologists and other experts unearth new information.

Domestication first took place in Southwest Asia. This hearth is called the **Fertile Crescent** because it forms an arc from the eastern Mediterranean coast up into what is now western Turkey and then south and east along the Tigris and Euphrates rivers through present-day Syria and Iraq to western parts of modern Iran. The people of this region grew wheat, barley, rye, and legumes (peas or beans) and domesticated sheep, goats, cattle, and pigs.

Maize (right), an early form of corn, originated in the Central American agricultural hearth, which began about 8000 B.C.E. It was domesticated 8,700 years ago from a Mexican wild grass called *Balsas teosinte* (left).

Another agricultural hearth arose in Southeast Asia, where people raised pigs and grew sugarcane and root vegetables. Domestication began there about 7000 B.C.E. Ancient North Central China had two hearths with distinct crop types, both developing between 8000 and 7000 B.C.E. To the north, in the somewhat dry valley of the Huang He, people used the river's fertile soil to grow millets, hemp, Chinese cabbage, and wheat. In the warmer, wetter south, they grew rice.

In South Asia, an agricultural civilization thrived in the Indus River Valley from 2500 to 1700 B.C.E. This group, known as the Harappan civilization, was based primarily in two large cities—Harappa and Mohenjo-Daro—as well as in other towns and villages. These people took advantage of the fertile valley and farmed wheat, barley, peas, sesame, and possibly cotton. Their domesticated animals included cattle, fowl, pigs, camels, and buffalo.

In northern Central America and into southern Mexico, an agricultural hearth began about 8000 B.C.E. People there grew sweet potatoes, beans, and other crops. They also domesticated the turkey. Maize (corn) later became the staple, or basic crop, of the region. About the same time, another agricultural hearth in the Andean highlands of South America began. Its chief crops were beans, tomatoes, and potatoes. The people there also domesticated llamas, alpaca, and guinea pigs.

Hearths were also located in Africa. In East Africa, crops like coffee, olives, peas, and sesame originated around 8000 B.C.E. Sorghum, a type of grain, was likely domesticated in Ethiopia around 4000 to 3000 B.C.E. In West Africa, people raised millets and sorghum.

Scientists distinguish such hearths as the Fertile Crescent from other ancient areas that adopted agriculture later through diffusion, which as you know is the spread of an idea or cultural trait from one place to another over time. For example, the ancient Nile River Valley—home to the Egyptian civilization that lasted for several thousand years and that was a hearth for other innovations—adopted farming and raising animals from Southwest Asia. The people who lived in the Nile River Valley did not develop these practices on their own. Sometimes it is difficult to know if a region was a hearth itself or if it was along a pathway of diffusion from that hearth. For example, rice may have been domesticated independently in the Ganges River Valley of India, or it may have been introduced by travelers from its home in China.

SHARED CHARACTERISTICS While ancient hearths have different physical characteristics, they share some features. Agriculture flourished in these regions because of fertile soil, the availability of water, moderate climates, and the organizational skills of the residents. These agricultural hearths were areas of independent innovations that people were able to develop over time, through trial and error, and with luck.

Because rains in these regions were not uniform throughout the year, the people in some areas developed methods of irrigation. In the valley of the Tigris and Euphrates rivers, for example, snow in the mountains that fed water to rivers melted in the spring, causing flooding. The floodwaters deposited rich soil that helped make the valleys fertile. By using low dams and reservoirs, the people made catch basins to hold the water to irrigate during dry months.

Many of the societies that developed in these hearths relied on the collective work of most of their members to tend the fields and harvest crops. This cooperation helped ensure success and encouraged settled life—and also put more pressure on the farmers to produce bountiful crop yields. Good harvests promoted population growth, which supplied more workers. Another factor that promoted agriculture was the development of efficient methods of storing seeds and harvests using gourds, baskets, and pottery.

THE DIFFUSION OF AGRICULTURE

LEARNING OBJECTIVES

PSO-2.D Explain how population distribution and density affect society and the environment.

SPS-5.B Explain how plants and animals diffused globally.

Agriculture depends on the land, but like all human activities, it is mobile because people are mobile. Diffusion of agricultural practices has produced patterns of flow throughout history, from ancient times to the present.

HEARTHS, CIVILIZATIONS, AND DOMESTICATION

AGRICULTURAL HEARTHS

0   1500   3000 miles
0   1500   3000 kilometers

1 CENTRAL AMERICA
Cassava, chiles and peppers, cocoa beans, cottonseed oil, maize, palm oil, sweet potatoes

2 ANDEAN HIGHLANDS
Beans, potatoes, tomatoes

3 WEST AFRICA
Coffee, cowpeas, millets, palm oil, rice, sorghum, yams

4 EAST AFRICA
Bambara beans, coffee, cottonseed oil, cowpeas, millets, olives, peas, sesame, sorghum

5 FERTILE CRESCENT
Barley, beans, peas, rye, wheat

6 INDUS RIVER VALLEY
Barley, cotton, peas, sesame, wheat

7 NORTH CENTRAL CHINA
Apples, grapefruit, grapes, lemons and limes, millets, oranges and mandarins, rice, soybeans, tea

8 SOUTHEAST ASIA
Bananas, cloves, coconuts, grapefruit, rice, sugarcane, taro, tea, yams

Source: International Center for Tropical Agriculture (CIAT)

Agriculture developed in several early hearths of domestication. The first map shows eight regional hearths and their major crops. Some hearths raised the same animals and cultivated the same crops; for example, palm oil was produced in both Central America and West Africa.

The second map shows the spread of domesticated animals and farming methods from Southwest Asia. Farming enclaves, or groups, developed along the Mediterranean Sea more than 11,000 years ago. The information in the time line is based on archaeological remains. ▮ What crops and animals do you think the farmers in western Europe most likely cultivated? Explain using details from the visuals.

FIRST GLOBAL DIFFUSIONS In ancient times, agriculture evolved independently and separately in several hearths. People migrated for various reasons, including population pressures, different opportunities, or conflict. These travelers introduced agriculture to new areas by relocation diffusion, which, as you know, is the spread of culture traits through the movement of people. As people migrated to different regions, the distribution of their crops and animals expanded. One study of archaeological sites in Southwest Asia and Europe suggests that agriculture spread steadily from the former region to the latter at a rate of about 0.6 miles a year over a period of about 3,000 years. Of course, the seeds these people brought did not flourish in all of the new areas. But through stimulus diffusion, humans could use their cultivation knowledge to adapt the practice to other, more resilient plants. In addition, some people already living in these areas recognized the value of the migrants' successful innovations and adopted them.

Over hundreds of years, many important crops diffused throughout Asia, Europe, and Africa as a result of relocation diffusion or through trade. The spread of crops and domesticated animals was limited by the climate and resources that each plant or animal needed. By the time of the Roman Empire, in the first centuries of the common era, Egypt and other areas of North Africa were a major source

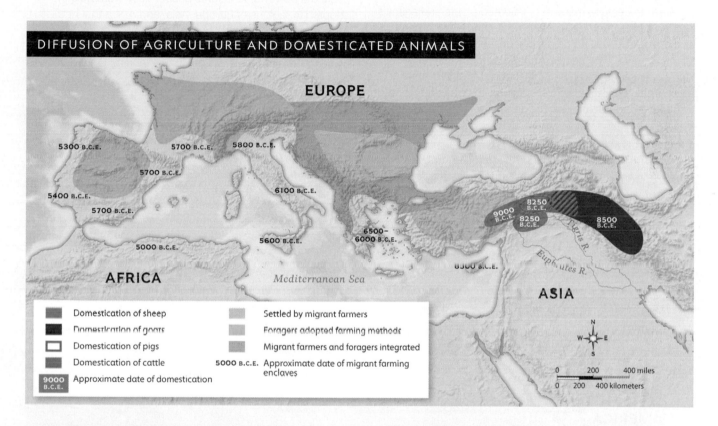

DIFFUSION OF AGRICULTURE AND DOMESTICATED ANIMALS

EUROPE

5300 B.C.E. 5700 B.C.E. 5800 B.C.E.

5700 B.C.E.

5400 B.C.E. 6100 B.C.E.

5700 B.C.E. 9000 B.C.E. 8250 B.C.E. 8500 B.C.E.
8250 B.C.E.

6500–
5000 B.C.E. 5600 B.C.E. 6000 B.C.E. *Tigris R.*

8300 B.C.E. *Euphrates R.*

AFRICA *Mediterranean Sea* ASIA

Legend:
- Domestication of sheep
- Domestication of goats
- Domestication of pigs
- Domestication of cattle
- **9000 B.C.E.** Approximate date of domestication
- Settled by migrant farmers
- Foragers adopted farming methods
- Migrant farmers and foragers integrated
- **5000 B.C.E.** Approximate date of migrant farming enclaves

0   200   400 miles
0   200   400 kilometers

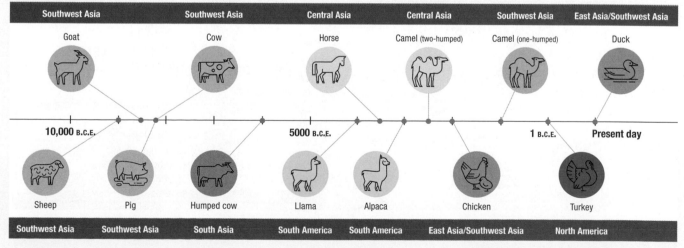

DOMESTICATION OF ANIMALS

Southwest Asia	Southwest Asia	Central Asia	Central Asia	Southwest Asia	East Asia/Southwest Asia
Goat	Cow	Horse	Camel (two-humped)	Camel (one-humped)	Duck

10,000 B.C.E.   5000 B.C.E.   1 B.C.E.   Present day

Sheep	Pig	Humped cow	Llama	Alpaca	Chicken	Turkey
Southwest Asia	Southwest Asia	South Asia	South America	South America	East Asia/Southwest Asia	North America

Source: Science News

of wheat. Rye, which can grow in cooler climates than wheat, spread to northern and Eastern Europe from its origin in Southwest Asia. Oranges spread from their native habitat in Malaysia to India to East Africa and then to the eastern Mediterranean. Bananas also reached Africa from their original home in Southeast Asia. Millets and sorghum, on the other hand, diffused from Central Africa to South Asia.

In some cases, diffusion simply introduced new crops—and the knowledge of their specific needs—rather than the practice of agriculture itself. The indigenous peoples of eastern North America already knew how to farm when maize was introduced to the region in its diffusion from Central America. Similarly, tomatoes and quinoa diffused to Central America from South America.

By the 15th century, many domesticated plants and animals had spread throughout Africa, Europe, and Asia. Other crops and animals had diffused widely between North and South America. The peoples of the Eastern and Western Hemispheres, however, had minimal contact with each other. That separation set the stage for the transformation that marked the Columbian Exchange.

THE COLUMBIAN EXCHANGE The exchange of goods and ideas between the Americas, Europe, and Africa, known as the **Columbian Exchange**, began after Christopher Columbus landed in the Americas in 1492. It had an huge impact on people, plants, and animals around the world and offers many examples of agricultural diffusion.

Columbus's arrival directly affected the human population. Isolation proved disastrous for the indigenous peoples of the Americas, as they had no immunities to diseases from the Eastern Hemisphere, including smallpox and malaria. These diseases devastated the Americas' native populations. And while not considered part of the Columbian Exchange, the global diffusion of millions of people—including the forced migration of enslaved people from Africa to provide labor for sugarcane and cotton production—throughout the Americas, along with their interactions with American Indian populations, gave rise to new cultures.

In terms of agriculture, the Columbian Exchange had other momentous consequences on both sides of the Atlantic Ocean. Crops from the Americas like maize and potatoes packed a powerful nutritional punch. They were quickly adopted in regions of Europe, Asia, and Africa that had climate conditions similar to areas where the crops grew in the Americas. Significantly, these crops often thrived in places where native plants could not flourish. One result was population explosions in Europe and Asia.

Over time, some crops from the Americas dominated the diets of many people in the Eastern Hemisphere. The results can still be seen today. Seven of the 10 countries that rely most on maize for daily caloric intake are in Africa and Asia. People who live in European, Asian, and African countries are the top 10 consumers of cassava and potatoes, and 8 out of the top 10 for sweet potatoes. The Columbian Exchange also transformed the Americas, with European crops and animals spreading widely throughout the Western

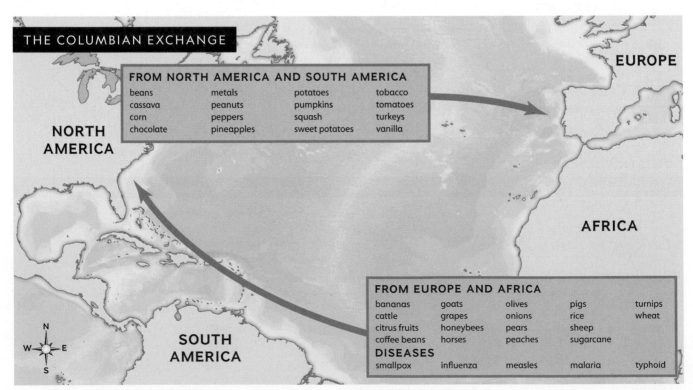

THE COLUMBIAN EXCHANGE

EUROPE

FROM NORTH AMERICA AND SOUTH AMERICA

beans	metals	potatoes	tobacco
cassava	peanuts	pumpkins	tomatoes
corn	peppers	squash	turkeys
chocolate	pineapples	sweet potatoes	vanilla

NORTH AMERICA

AFRICA

FROM EUROPE AND AFRICA

bananas	goats	olives	pigs	turnips
cattle	grapes	onions	rice	wheat
citrus fruits	honeybees	pears	sheep	
coffee beans	horses	peaches	sugarcane	

DISEASES

| smallpox | influenza | measles | malaria | typhoid |

SOUTH AMERICA

READING MAPS The Columbian Exchange was a massive global event. A wide variety of animals, plants, and diseases moved between Europe, Africa, and the Americas. ▪ Explain how the Columbian Exchange contributed to the global diffusion of agricultural products and practices.

Hemisphere. The fields of wheat covering much of the Great Plains in the present-day United States replaced native grasses. The ranches of the American West and the South American Pampas are home to cattle and sheep introduced by Europeans. Sugarcane from the Southeast Asian agricultural hearth replaced native plants to become a plantation crop in the islands of the Caribbean and in Brazil. Coffee, which originated in the East African highlands of Ethiopia, became a dominant cash crop in some temperate highland areas of both Central and South America.

DIFFUSION IN MODERN TIMES Agricultural diffusion continues today. People have developed a worldwide system of agriculture with global markets and expanding tastes due to scientific advances and focused marketing. Producers seek new consumers for their products year-round. One recent example is the kiwi fruit. Native to China, it was transplanted to New Zealand in the early 20th century, where it grew well and became a popular food. During World War II, members of the U.S. armed forces stationed in New Zealand enjoyed the fruit and introduced it to the United States after the war. Today's top producers of kiwi fruit include countries as diverse—and far from China—as Italy, Chile, Turkey, and the United States.

There are other examples as well. Ostrich farms were first established in what is now South Africa in the mid-19th century to supply the market for the bird's exotic feathers. In the late 20th century, ostrich farming became popular in the United States and Europe, mostly for meat. Tilapia—freshwater fish from Africa—have become a major food in the 21st century because they are easy to raise and feed and mature fairly quickly. Tilapia are raised in more than 80 countries, and China produces half the world's output.

GEOGRAPHIC THINKING

1. Describe how environmental changes contributed to the development of agriculture.

2. Identify a physical characteristic the ancient agricultural hearths in the Fertile Crescent and North Central China have in common, and explain how it likely influenced the development of both hearths.

3. Identify the earliest animals to be domesticated and explain when and where the domestication occurred.

4. Compare agricultural diffusion today with diffusion during the Columbian Exchange.

12.4 ADVANCES IN AGRICULTURE

Over millennia, humans have invented new technologies and practices that have had far-reaching impacts on life, society, and cultures. Geographers call these sweeping changes *revolutions* because they cause such radical transformations. There have been three—and some experts would say four—such revolutions in agriculture.

THE FIRST AGRICULTURAL REVOLUTION

LEARNING OBJECTIVE
SPS-5.B Explain how plants and animals diffused globally.

The **first agricultural revolution**, which occurred about 11,000 years ago and lasted for several thousand more, was the shift from foraging—or searching for food—to farming, which marked the beginning of agriculture. You read that this revolution occurred independently in several different hearths across five continents. In other words, it did not occur simultaneously. Rather, the revolution occurred in different hearths at different times. From those points of origin, the first agricultural revolution diffused into other areas as groups of people transitioned from foraging to

agriculture. Some advancements were independently developed, while others may have been borrowed from other hearths.

By some estimates, more than 80 percent of the world's diet comes from a dozen or so staple crops, such as rice, wheat, and maize. These staples were originally cultivated in the first agricultural revolution. In addition, this revolution included domestication of the most common animals that humans raise today, including sheep, goats, cattle, pigs, chickens, horses, and camels.

The first agricultural revolution is sometimes called the Neolithic Revolution because it took place during a time in history now known as the Neolithic Age, or New Stone Age. In this period, people used tools made of stone or bone.

Çatalhöyük was a Neolithic settlement in what is now Turkey. An excavation begun in the 1960s revealed that Çatalhöyük was an early agricultural society; seeds, nuts, and edible grains were cultivated there. This reconstruction of Çatalhöyük shows what typical homes may have looked like.

SOCIETAL CHANGES The first agricultural revolution profoundly changed the lives of the people who experienced it. For one thing, they went from being nomadic to being sedentary or semisedentary. *Sedentary* means settling in one place and making that place a permanent home. People built more durable housing and possessed goods that didn't have to be light enough to transport to a new area.

Living a settled life also meant increased reliance on one place rather than the variety of places exploited by foragers. While farming and herding promised a steadier food supply, these activities also decreased the variety of foods consumed. The focus of the human diet became the multiple staple crops that people produced. People often supplemented those crops with nuts, berries, and other foods gathered near the settlement when those resources were in season. Still, the overall diet was less diverse.

Farming practices in agricultural societies improved over time. Farmers learned to plant seeds from their strongest plants to generate more productive crops. New tools and

practices made farming tasks easier. For example, some societies began to use domesticated oxen to pull plows, which made farming more efficient and improved yields. People in some areas began to practice irrigation, expanding the areas that could be farmed and ensuring a ready supply of water during the growing season.

Increased efficiency meant more food. Having more food supported a growing population, which provided more workers. Another impact of having more food was the need to store the surpluses for future use. People began making clay pots and other containers for carrying and setting aside food. These methods of storage could not have been created without skilled artisans to make them, which presents another feature of the first agricultural revolution— the development of specialization of labor.

As farm fields became more productive, some members of society were not needed to cultivate food. They could live off the surplus produced by the farmers. Instead of food production, they focused on skills such as pottery-making or woodworking. Eventually, people began to work with metals, and skilled metal workers produced stronger tools and weapons or made luxury goods like jewelry.

In addition, farmers produced some nonfood crops. Cotton was grown in the Nile River Valley in Egypt, which also produced flax that was used to make linen. Cotton grew in the Indus River Valley as well. Sheep and goats were not kept solely for their meat; their wool could be sheared each year. Fibers such as cotton, flax, and wool could be woven into clothing, blankets, and other goods, so weaving became another specialized task.

As societies became more productive, they also became more complex. Larger settlements led to new forms of social organization. Ruling classes arose in many societies, as certain individuals or groups took charge of making laws, organizing productive activities, distributing resources, and settling disputes. Food surpluses created new dangers—they became potential targets for raids by other groups. The need to defend a society and its resources led to the development of a fighting class, which was typically under the control of the rulers. Some experts argue that members of certain societies established the idea that certain ritual practices could ensure good harvests. Some individuals assumed the role of priests to conduct these rituals and thereby gained higher status in the society.

Population growth meant larger and larger villages. Eventually, the first cities developed. Nearby settlements traded with one another and with distant communities as well, which provided locally available raw materials such as metals and luxury goods. Over time, the first ancient civilizations developed. They were characterized by large urban centers, complex societies, and advances in knowledge and the arts. You'll learn more about cities and their origins in Unit 6.

Mohenjo-Daro was one of the two main city centers of ancient Harappa, a civilization that developed in the Indus River Valley in the third millennium B.C.E. The Indus River Valley was extremely fertile, and barley, field peas, and sesame were some of the crops cultivated there. Harappa was also known for its terra-cotta pottery, which was used for cooking and storage.

THE SECOND AGRICULTURAL REVOLUTION

LEARNING OBJECTIVE
SPS-5.C Explain the advances and impacts of the second agricultural revolution.

For the next several millennia, people around the world continued to make breakthroughs that made agriculture more productive. The ancient Romans were systematic about improvements, taking notes on farming practices they saw in the lands they conquered and using methods that could be applied in other parts of their empire. In the 11th century C.E., farmers in southern China planted a faster-growing rice native to Vietnam. The new variety allowed Chinese farmers to produce two crops of rice a year. Farmers in northern Europe in the Middle Ages developed a wheeled plow that improved cultivation. These advances increased productivity but fell short of the widespread, deep impact of the Neolithic Revolution. Essentially, societies continued to grow food largely for themselves.

That changed in the early 1700s, when new practices and tools launched the **second agricultural revolution**, which began in Britain and the Low Countries (Belgium, Luxembourg, and the Netherlands) and diffused from those regions. This revolution saw dramatic improvements in crop yields, innovations like more effective yokes for oxen, and later the replacement of oxen by horses, as well as advancements in fertilizers and field drainage systems.

A change in the way farms were organized was a major driver of the revolution. Whereas most agriculture was previously done by peasants who were, for the most part, growing food for themselves on communal, or shared land, Britain gradually switched to an **enclosure system**. In this system, communal lands—lands owned by a community rather than by an individual—were replaced by farms owned by individuals, and use of the land was restricted to the owner or tenants who rented the land from the owner. This change gave owners more control over their farms and therefore led to more effective farming practices. However, it also pushed peasants off the land and created a labor surplus—a factor that contributed to the Industrial Revolution, which began in Britain in the 1700s and spread to Western Europe and the United States in the 1800s. The second agricultural revolution continued into the late 1800s, and much of it coincided with the Industrial Revolution.

One of the most important new technologies of the second agricultural revolution was a horse-drawn seed drill invented by Jethro Tull in England around 1701. Tull's machine meant that farmers no longer had to scatter seeds by hand, a time-consuming process that was potentially wasteful if seeds did not land in the plowed furrows or were not evenly distributed. Tull's drill was widely adopted across Europe.

New tools of this agricultural revolution were invented in the United States, too. Cyrus McCormick designed and produced a mechanical reaper in the 1830s that

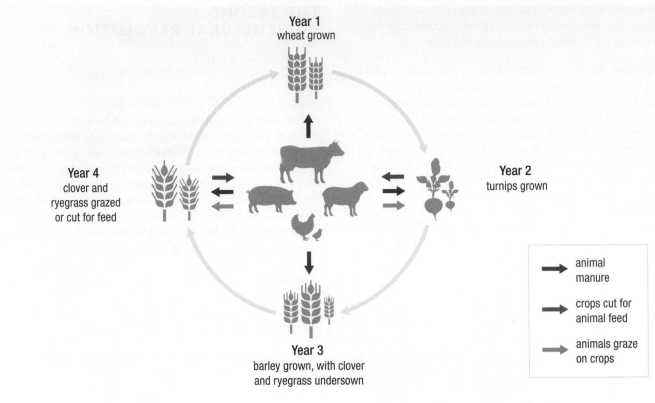

Year 1
wheat grown

Year 4
clover and
ryegrass grazed
or cut for feed

Year 2
turnips grown

Year 3
barley grown, with clover
and ryegrass undersown

→ animal
manure

→ crops cut for
animal feed

→ animals graze
on crops

NORFOLK FOUR-FIELD SYSTEM The Norfolk four-field system was a key innovation of the second agricultural revolution. Soil benefited from richer manure because animals were better fed with crops produced by the improved soil. ▌Describe what happens during the fourth year of this field system.

mechanized harvesting grain. John Deere invented a steel plow that by 1838 made it easier to plow in deep, tough soil, such as that found in the American Midwest. The steel plow made it possible to farm new areas that had not been arable—or able to grow crops—with earlier technology.

Farmers also adopted new methods of crop rotation that prevented soil exhaustion and increased yields. One system developed in England called for the rotation of several crops from year to year. Called the Norfolk four-field system, it involved the yearly rotation of several crops, including wheat, turnips, barley, clover, and ryegrass. The rotating of crops added nutrients to the soil, making it unnecessary to leave a field fallow—or unplowed—for a year, which had been the earlier practice. Crop rotation also fed livestock and promoted greater yields.

These changes resulted in another population boom, similar to the one that had accompanied the first agricultural revolution. People had more food, more nutritious diets, and longer life expectancies. As farms became more productive through mechanization and pushed peasant farmers off the land, these former laborers—and the overall growth of the population—provided a ready workforce for the new factories of the Industrial Revolution. These events all coincided with advancements in transportation made during the Industrial Revolution. The railroad allowed food to be transported greater distances, creating a larger market for the higher yields of the second agricultural revolution.

THE THIRD AGRICULTURAL REVOLUTION

LEARNING OBJECTIVE

IMP-1.C Explain the geographical effects of decisions made using geographical information.

IMP-5.B Explain challenges and debates related to the changing nature of contemporary agriculture and food-production practices.

SPS-5.D Explain the consequences of the Green Revolution on food supply and the environment in the developing world.

The **third agricultural revolution** began in the early 20th century and continues to the present day. It features further mechanization and the development of new technology, changes brought about by scientific and technological advances outside agriculture. The first shift was the move to mechanical and then electrical power, breaking away from the millennia-old reliance on animal power. Scientists also developed synthetic, or human-made rather than natural, fertilizers and pesticides. The third agricultural revolution occurred in core countries such as the United States before mid-20th-century scientists brought some of the revolution's advancements to the countries in the periphery.

Late in the 20th century into the early 21st, scientists added two more tools to improve agriculture. First, they applied advances in scientific understanding to manipulate the genetic makeup of plants and animals. The resulting **genetically modified organisms (GMOs)** can enhance the ability of the new strains to resist disease or drought or to have more nutritional impact or consumer appeal. For example, scientists added a gene from a bacterium that is a natural pesticide to such crops as potatoes, cotton, and corn. By making these plants genetically resistant to pests, the scientists reduced the need for growers to use pesticides. Another innovation was to add a daffodil gene to rice to boost the amount of beta-carotene—needed for human consumption of vitamin A—in the grain. Producers are also using information technology to monitor their fields for water and nutrient levels, allowing targeted delivery to meet crops' needs.

Some scientists refer to this use of information technology and data analytics as a fourth agricultural revolution. This revolution involves intensive data collection and manipulation that relies on global positioning system (GPS) technology, smart technology farm equipment with sensors and wireless connections (precision agriculture), computer databases, and information-processing power. This recent period has been characterized by efficiency driven by data. For example, producers now use drones to deliver fertilizer and pesticide in measured quantities along precisely controlled routes to fields that were difficult to reach in the past.

PRODUCTIVITY THROUGH TECHNOLOGY

The increased mechanization of farming initially took the form of the invention and use of motorized tractors. These multipurpose pieces of equipment had attachments that could be used for plowing, harvesting, and other functions. Tractors replaced horses, oxen, and other beasts of burden, speeding a farmer's work and facilitating cultivation of larger plots of land. Later, inventors developed special machines that were larger and more suited to the huge farms that came to typify commercial agriculture in many core countries. Mechanical combines cut grain and separate the seed from the stalk, expediting the harvest. Similarly, corn picker-shellers pick ears of corn and strip them of kernels in one operation.

Adopting electricity greatly aided crop storage and preservation and enhanced livestock raising and dairy farming. Electric-powered livestock facilities allowed for the efficient rationing of feed and the maintenance of controlled growing conditions. Electric-powered milking and storage facilities radically changed dairy operations.

Another 20th-century innovation was the development and widespread use of synthetic fertilizers and pesticides. The former helped make fields more productive. The latter combated the potentially destructive effects of insects, other pests, and diseases and boosted yields by preventing damage to crops. Crop dusting, in which airplanes spray pesticides over fields, made the delivery of these products more efficient.

THE GREEN REVOLUTION

During the 1950s and 1960s, scientists used increased knowledge of genetics to develop new high-yield strains of grain crops, particularly wheat and rice. This movement, known as the **Green Revolution**, was an offshoot of the third agricultural revolution. The new crop strains—already in use in the United States—were introduced in areas with low yields and large populations, including Mexico, India, and Indonesia.

Spearheading this movement was Norman Borlaug, an American scientist from Iowa who was dedicated to the idea of transferring the advances of the third agricultural revolution to peripheral and semi-peripheral areas. Borlaug first became involved in this work in Mexico in the 1940s, where he found a population of subsistence farmers plagued by chronically poor harvests. He worked for more than a decade to develop a disease-resistant strain of wheat and to convince Mexican farmers to plant these seeds. By the mid-1950s, Mexican farmers were able to produce enough wheat to meet their country's demand.

Borlaug turned next to South Asia, where his improved seeds and methods helped increase wheat harvests in both India and Pakistan fourfold. A crucial part of his vision of the Green Revolution was to train local agricultural scientists so that they could continue to make advances. For his work, Borlaug was awarded the 1970 Nobel Peace Prize and has been called the "father of the Green Revolution."

In the early 21st century, several groups began work on spreading the Green Revolution to Africa. A key to some of these efforts was the goal—set by former United Nations secretary-general Kofi Annan, of Ghana—to make the next part of the revolution environmentally friendly.

IMPACT AND RESPONSE

While it saved many lives and nourished millions, the third agricultural revolution came at a steep cost as well. First, increased mechanization reduced the need for human labor. Agricultural workers became displaced—a continuation of the trend begun in the second agricultural revolution. When human labor was required, growers came to rely increasingly on migrant workers. Second, some technology of this revolution is dominated by multinational corporations, making producers vulnerable to the companies' marketing and sales practices.

For example, one multinational company sells crop seeds that resist one of its pesticides. That encourages farmers to buy the seeds and the pesticide, which can be used to kill weeds. However, the corporation does not allow farmers to preserve seeds from one year's crop for the next year's planting—the growers must purchase new seeds each year. The expense of some of these practices forced many individual farmers out of business, leading to the replacement of small family farms with large-scale commercial agricultural operations. However, large corporations in the United States contributed only 11 percent of total agriculture production in 2015.

The third agricultural revolution has also had environmental impacts. Green Revolution crops have increased growers' demand for water, causing regional inequities and the need for more water development projects. Some of those projects have had disastrous consequences. In the 1960s, the Soviet Union enacted an agricultural policy that diverted water from two rivers to irrigate cotton fields in Central Asia. As a result, the water no longer reached the Aral Sea, which shrank dramatically in size due to the semiarid climate of the region. Fish populations were devastated. The former seabed also had high amounts of salt, which resulted in health problems among the people of the surrounding area.

Widespread use of synthetic pesticides consisting of powerful chemicals can harm both pests as well as helpful insects and animals. The buildup of chemicals can pollute water supplies and cause human health problems. The concentration of livestock production in huge facilities can lead to difficulties related to the great amounts of waste products the animals generate. The spread of livestock production means diversion of more crop output to animal feed, which some critics view as a high-cost way of meeting nutritional needs.

Larger facilities run by corporations often require large amounts of energy and other natural resources. Another cost is the loss of biodiversity as producers focus on heavily marketed, high-yield seed strains. Industrial-scale, market-oriented agriculture has also led to monocropping, which, as you know, is when a farmer or company produces the same crop year after year. This practice has contributed to a decline in soil fertility and biodiversity as well.

Many producers have reacted against these various drawbacks by focusing on alternative approaches to farming. One such method is sustainable agriculture, which you read about earlier in this chapter. Sustainable agriculture is partially based on protecting the environment, ensuring profitability, and promoting greater social equality. Producers work toward ensuring the health of soils by avoiding the use of synthetic fertilizers and minimizing water use, among other practices.

Some people interested in sustainable agriculture practice organic farming. This method of growing crops completely eliminates the use of chemical fertilizers and pesticides, relying instead on natural products, like animal manure, and simple-but-proven farming practices, like crop rotation. These methods produce crops that are better for the environment but have lower yields.

GEOGRAPHIC THINKING

1. Describe how the three agricultural revolutions were similar and how they were different.

2. Explain the advances and impacts of the second agricultural revolution.

3. Compare advantages and disadvantages of the Green Revolution for the food supply and environment in the periphery.

4. Explain how the changes that some call the fourth agricultural revolution use geographic principles, skills, and technologies and have geographic consequences.

CRITICAL VIEWING A crop dusting plane sprays fungicide, a type of pesticide, to protect the crops on a banana plantation in Tagum in Davao del Norte province, which is located in Mindanaoa, a southern island in the Philippines. ❚ Describe some of the possible negative impacts caused by the use of these types of chemicals.

CASE STUDY

WOMEN AND AFRICA'S GREEN REVOLUTION

THE ISSUE Women are important crop producers in sub-Saharan Africa, but they suffer discriminatory barriers that impair their ability to benefit from their labor.

LEARNING OBJECTIVE
SPS-5.D Explain the consequences of the Green Revolution on food supply and the environment in the developing world.

FACTORS FOR CHANGE

The Pathways program focuses on five "change levers" that help women gain success and increase agricultural output:

- Capacity—building skills, relationships, and self-confidence
- Access—technical advice, inputs such as seeds, and markets
- Productivity—improving output and crop diversification
- Household Influence—women having more control over household decisions and assets
- Enabling environment—working to change attitudes toward women's roles

Source: CARE.org

Women work in a field in a rural farming community in Nkwandu, Arusha, Tanzania. Tanzania is one of four sub-Saharan countries in Africa where a program has been developed to help women farmers gain success and improve agricultural output.

FOR MILLENNIA, women have worked in sub-Saharan farm fields. However, they have not benefited from their crucial position in the agricultural workforce. Historically, women were barred from owning property and denied access to financial backing, better seeds, water, tools, and agricultural extension services such as training or business planning. Patriarchal attitudes, which place greater importance on men's role in society than women's, left women as second-class citizens.

In recent years, international food agencies have developed programs to encourage women practicing agriculture. Pathways to Empowerment is a program for women in South Asia and sub-Saharan Africa developed by nongovernmental organizations (NGOs) like CARE and the Bill and Melinda Gates Foundation.

The Pathways program was implemented in more than 400 villages in 4 African countries—Ghana, Malawi, Mali, and Tanzania—with more than 34,000 women receiving support. Special schools were set up to improve women's skills and help them believe they could succeed. The program encouraged greater connections to extension services and used innovative approaches to improve access to seeds and other inputs. Coaching helped women gain more access to markets, which not only allowed them to sell more of their output but to secure better prices as well.

Pathways participants in Malawi saw increased yields at a time when national output was falling by 30 to 50 percent due to adverse weather patterns. In Mali, the women growers produced nearly 4,500 more metric tons of millets and more than 2,120 metric tons of rice than in the past, which was enough to feed 31,000 more families in that country for a year. Improvements to women's income were seen as well, including a 50 percent increase in Malawi villages over a few years.

While the gains are impressive, equally important is the societal change. Increasing numbers of women are more involved with their husbands in making decisions involving farmwork. In Ghana, the number of communities with laws that protected a woman's right to own and work land doubled. Attitudes about violence against women also changed, which substantially improved women's lives. ∎

GEOGRAPHIC THINKING

Explain how the Pathways program has changed both agriculture and society in the four target African countries.

CHAPTER 13

PATTERNS AND PRACTICES OF AGRICULTURAL PRODUCTION

CRITICAL VIEWING On a large pineapple plantation in Oahu, Hawaii, workers use machinery to move pineapples from the fields onto a conveyor. Compare how advanced machinery and technology might affect agricultural production on small-scale and large-scale farms.

GEOGRAPHIC THINKING What factors influence agricultural practices?

13.1
AGRICULTURAL PRODUCTION REGIONS

FEATURE: The Changing Dairying and Ranching Industries

13.2
THE SPATIAL ORGANIZATION OF AGRICULTURE

NATIONAL GEOGRAPHIC EXPLORER Tristram Stuart

13.3
THE VON THÜNEN MODEL

13.4
AGRICULTURE AS A GLOBAL SYSTEM

CASE STUDY: Coffee Production and Consumption

13.1 AGRICULTURAL PRODUCTION REGIONS

Agricultural practices help define the agricultural production regions around the world. Distinguishing regions of agriculture allows geographers to determine how economics, politics, culture, and the environmental characteristics of an area impact farming.

ECONOMIC FORCES AND AGRICULTURE

LEARNING OBJECTIVE
PSO-5.C Explain how economic forces influence agricultural practices.

In addition to environmental and cultural factors, why people farm, where people farm, and how people farm are also affected by the availability of resources and economic forces. Agricultural practices are influenced by such economic forces as the costs of materials, land, and labor; the availability of capital (money or other assets); the impacts of government policies; and ultimately, consumer preferences or what people want to eat or consume, also known as market demands.

Economic forces help to distinguish subsistence agriculture from commercial agriculture. Most subsistence agriculture occurs in rural Africa and parts of Asia and Latin America, where connections to the global market are limited and farmers have less access to credit and financial capital. Many subsistence farmers live in poverty and do not have the economic resources to pay for labor or expensive machinery. Most often labor costs, either the farmer's own time spent tending to the land or wages for hired workers, are low relative to the costs of machinery.

Most commercial farming takes place in core and semi-peripheral countries with the **infrastructure** in place to access and supply the global market. Modern farm equipment, advanced technologies, and large plots of land are all characteristic of commercial agriculture. Commercial farmers maximize their income by purchasing a high level of external inputs. The impact of all of these costs can make commercial agriculture an expensive business. Therefore, it is important to have access to capital, which is easier to obtain in core countries than peripheral countries.

A **dual agricultural economy** refers to two agricultural sectors in the same country or region that have different levels of technology and different patterns of demand. In these areas, subsistence farms where food is grown for farmers to consume exist next to commercial operations that cultivate a crop to sell and often export to core countries where demand for the crop is high. South Africa and Zimbabwe are examples of dual agricultural economies. South Africa has both subsistence farms and well-developed commercial operations. Farmers who have the resources to invest in equipment, land, and materials participate in

commercial agriculture. Farmers with fewer resources tend to be limited to providing food for their families.

In most instances, the costs of materials and labor are relative to the size of the farm. However, large-scale farming can be more cost-effective when fixed costs are spread over a greater area and lower bulk prices are negotiated for inputs, like seed or fertilzer. For example, farmers often receive a bulk discount when buying a large quantity of pesticides to spread over several hundred acres of land. As a result, the cost of the pesticide per acre is reduced. When production increases, expenses are lower per unit of output. This is an example of economies of scale, which have always existed in farming, but have increased considerably since the introduction of modern farming technology and the innovations of the third agricultural revolution that helped to make agriculture a business.

The term **agribusiness** refers to the large-scale system that includes the production, processing, and distribution of agricultural products and equipment. Commercial farmers, large and small, are just one part of the agribusiness system, which has grown substantially over the last century. This growth has caused a major change in the nature of farming. Before the 20th century, farmers were typically self-sufficient small businesses, but as farm machinery, fertilizers, pesticides, genetically modified organisms, and smart technologies have made agriculture more efficient and specialized, farmers have become much more dependent on food manufacturers, distributors, and marketers. In fact, many farms are controlled by the producers, processors, and retailers who are part of the agribusiness system, which will be described in more detail later in this chapter.

TECHNOLOGY AND INCREASED PRODUCTION
Modern equipment, improved fertilizers and pesticides, and new types of seeds all allow farmers to create higher yields. In fact, farmers today produce 262 percent more food with 2 percent fewer inputs than farmers in 1950. Technology has changed the growing season for many crops and improved production. For instance, scientists have taken the natural process of hybridization to intentionally create **hybrid** grains, fruits, and vegetables, in which different varieties of plants are bred to enhance desired characteristics and improve disease resistance. Some hybrids can grow in extreme temperatures or wet or dry conditions. For instance, seed technologies have helped corn and wheat become more frost tolerant, allowing growers to plant seeds sooner

in cooler temperatures and harvest crops later. Additionally, farmers have new tillage practices, used to prepare the land for planting crops, that allow them to grow corn in areas that have historically not successfully produced corn.

One problem farmers all over the world continuously face is the reduction of crop yields due to pests. Weeds and other unwanted plants compete for resources and crowd out desired crops, and insects can destroy an entire field if not controlled properly. Since the 1960s, the use of pesticides, including herbicides and insecticides, around the world has increased considerably and led to higher crop yields. Herbicides are chemicals that are toxic to weeds and unwanted plants. Insecticides are chemicals that are toxic to insects. In the last six decades, the average yield of wheat and rice has more than doubled due in large part to the use of pesticides. While pesticides can harm human and environmental health, without them crop production would drop and could result in soaring food prices.

Advanced farm machinery also increases production by improving efficiency. Farmers can plant and harvest several more acres of land in a shorter period of time with modern tractors and combines, for example. Advances in irrigation have also provided better agricultural conditions, which increases yields.

It is more difficult for subsistence farmers and small, family-operated commercial farms to adopt expensive technologies, like machinery. They generally don't have the capital input needed that large commercial farms have. Some smaller farms benefit from jointly owning machinery with neighboring farms or by joining cooperatives, but the economies of scale are much greater for large corporate-owned farms. A cooperative is a system in which farmers pool their resources to produce, market, and sell their crops.

The amount of capital farmers have impacts their ability to operate and expand their farms. Capital, in turn, can impact a farm's productivity. Capital includes not only the money to purchase materials and equipment to make improvements but also a farmer's buildings, equipment, and animals. Farmers who can afford better (often expensive) machinery, fertilizers, and pesticides will increase their output and profitability. Large-scale farms often have more cash capital than small-scale farms, whose capital is found in their equipment, land, buildings, and for some, livestock.

POLICIES AND PREFERENCES Government policies and consumer demand both greatly impact agricultural practices. Most governments around the world intervene in agricultural markets in a few ways. They provide payments to farmers for growing certain crops or for not growing others, place regulations on agricultural imports and exports, or establish price supports in the form of crop purchases made by the government at a guaranteed price. All of these actions have been utilized by the U.S. government over the last century to protect farmers who have struggled at various times, including during the Dust

Bowl of the 1930s, the farm debt crisis of the 1980s, and the volatile agricultural landscape of the 21st century.

In the mid-1930s, farmers limited their production and began receiving government payments in order to stabilize agricultural prices. This lasted until the late 1970s, when attitudes in the government changed. Farmers were no longer paid to produce "nothing," as some argued, but instead were incentivized to produce as much as possible, resulting in surplus grains and low prices. Today excess corn, in particular, is used as feed for animals, for ethanol fuel, and for producing high fructose corn syrup—an inexpensive sweetener made from corn found in most processed foods. As a result, processed foods have become less expensive than fresh fruits and vegetables, directly impacting the food choices available to consumers.

Governments continue to control the supply of certain crops by enacting quotas, or the amount farmers can produce and sell. For instance, quotas are used in Canada in the dairy and poultry industries to keep prices of these goods stable and guarantee farmers a steady income. All of these policies impact pricing and therefore the quantity of crops farmers grow and harvest. In the United States, a farm bill is passed by the U.S. Congress about every five years to authorize policies regarding commodity programs and crop insurance, conservation, agricultural trade, nutrition, farm credit, rural economic development, and organic agriculture. These policies set guidelines for participating in agricultural and food programs such as the standards required to farm organically or the actions farmers must take to receive payments from the government.

Dietary preference and the kinds of agricultural products consumers choose to purchase also affect agriculture. Farmers will produce more of the products that are in demand. For instance, ahead of annual Super Bowl viewing parties across the United States, demand for avocados jumps. In 2020, almost 75 million pounds of avocados crossed the border from Mexico the week before America's largest sporting and television event. Farmers in Mexico employ methods to increase yields to meet the booming demand for avocados that has increased not just in the United States but around the world.

While government incentives and price controls help farmers, it is ultimately consumers who drive the market in commercial agriculture. In general, farmers will look to the market to determine what and how much to plant of the most sought after crops each season.

GEOGRAPHIC THINKING

1. Compare the influence of economic factors among subsistence and commercial farming practices.

2. Explain how government policies have impacted farm practices and the foods available to consumers.

This farm near Goodland, Kansas, uses multiple combines to harvest wheat. Large-scale farming operations take advantage of economies of scale and technology to increase the amount of crops they produce. The number of farms larger than 2,000 acres continues to rise, as they are poised to take advantage of the latest machinery and agricultural practices.

The owner of an 800-acre ranch tends to her cattle in Woodland Park, Colorado. Changes in agriculture have impacted U.S. family farms and ranches such as this one for years.

THE CHANGING DAIRYING AND RANCHING INDUSTRIES

LEARNING OBJECTIVE

PSO-5.C Explain how economic forces influence agricultural practices.

Commercial dairying is the production and selling of milk and related food products. In the United States, dairy farms are most prevalent in the upper Midwest and Northeast, and primarily run by families, but dairying is changing. Family-owned commercial operations are going out of business or changing their practices. In 2018, nearly 3,000 dairy farms closed in the United States. Many are selling their dairies to larger operations who have the capital to withstand a volatile market in which prices for milk fluctuate. Others are specializing in organic dairy products that are sold for a higher price than conventional ones. Some farmers are participating in cooperatives in which they pool their money together to purchase supplies and services. Making purchases collectively keeps down costs for farmers.

Several factors affect the dairy market. Pricing is one of them. The price of milk is determined partly by market demand and partly by government pricing regulations. The price of milk has been generally falling since 2014. The market for cow's milk has declined as alternative milk products made from soy or nuts have become popular.

Meat production has also experienced change in recent decades, as the demand for meat has increased in some places around the world. Ranching operations have grown in regions where the land is open and plentiful for cattle to graze, like in the United States and South America. As the cattle mature, most are sent to feedlots where they are fed corn in order to fatten them up before being processed into meat. The number of feedlots has increased in order to reduce costs and maximize profits. Animals are confined to smaller spaces than they have on the ranch and are fattened in a short period of time, increasing the number of animals that can be processed. As of 2017, 97 percent of U.S. beef was grain-fed feedlot beef and only 3 percent grass-fed beef.

Still, the number of organic meat producers who provide their animals access to open pastures has grown despite the fact that the price of organic beef is higher than conventionally raised beef. In 2016, there were more than 2.3 million acres of organic-certified land on which animals could graze and more than 46,000 organically certified beef cows in the United States. The number of beef cows is expected to increase at an annual 7 percent rate between 2019 and 2026. ▮

GEOGRAPHIC THINKING

Describe the factors that impact commercial dairying and ranching.

13.2 THE SPATIAL ORGANIZATION OF AGRICULTURE

The rising demand for food and our changing appetites are fueling growth and change in agribusiness. Large-scale corporate operations are replacing more and more small family farms. Such changes impact all who are part of the complex global food supply system that includes not just farmers, but governments, businesses, and consumers.

FAMILY VS. CORPORATE CONTROL

LEARNING OBJECTIVE
PSO-5.C Explain how economic forces influence agricultural practices.

Family farms represent the vast majority of farms worldwide. However, these small family-owned enterprises account for less of the share of the world's total farmland. According to the Food and Agriculture Organization of the United Nations (FAO), approximately 84 percent of farms worldwide are smaller than five acres, and these small farms operate about 12 percent of the total farmland. Meanwhile, approximately 16 percent of farms worldwide are larger than five acres and represent 88 percent of the world's farmland. The vast majority of the share of farmland controlled by larger farms is in core countries, such as the United States, Canada, Australia, and countries in Europe where commercial agriculture is more prevalent. Most family subsistence farms are located in the periphery including countries in Asia and Africa; while they are small, collectively they produce food for a large portion of the world's population.

There are limitations to the estimated data gathered about agriculture worldwide, especially at the regional and local levels. These limitations include the number of participants in the agricultural census and variations in the manner in which the data is collected. The latest information available from the FAO reported that globally, between the years 1960 and 2010, the total number of farms increased to about 608 million. The average farm size decreased between the years 1960 and 2000 and remained about the same between the years 2000 and 2010. Of course, the figures vary country by country, and the difference is striking between countries in the core and those in the periphery.

Data gathered strictly about U.S. agriculture differs in some respects from the global data. Since the 1960s, the number of farms in the United States has decreased—from

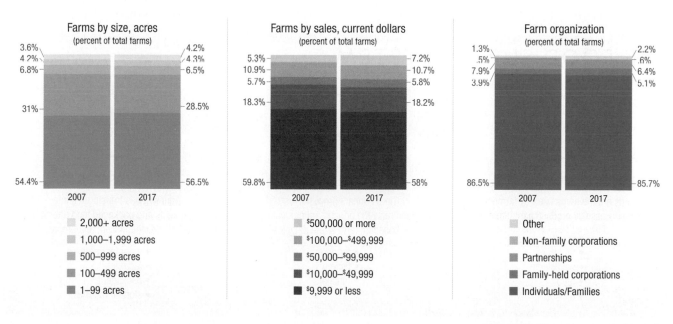

U.S. AGRICULTURAL PRODUCTION, 2007 AND 2017 Today, farming in the United States is still comprised of mainly family farms, but the number of family farms has decreased since 2007. The graphs give a closer look at the distribution of farms according to size, sales in dollars, and ownership.

Source: United States Department of Agriculture

approximately 3.7 million farms to just over 2 million, a number that has held steady for the last few decades. Of these 2 million farms, more than 90 percent are classified as small, and are mostly family-owned and operated.

Recent trends are hurting the family farm and causing a shift in the spatial organization of agriculture. The overall population across the world is shifting away from rural areas and into urban areas. Many from younger generations see the amount of time and hard work established farmers devote to rural agriculture just to earn a very small profit. Therefore, fewer people are interested in or willing to take on the challenges that come with farming. Additionally, the farming population is aging. Farmers who were once prosperous are retiring or dying without successors in place.

Another challenge some farmers face is rising costs. When farming costs are greater than the income generated for many years in a row, farmers struggle to remain in agriculture. At times, a supply-heavy market causes the price of goods to fall. For example, when corn production is high, the price of corn decreases. Farmers make little, if any, profit when agricultural prices fall drastically. If another farmer or a corporation offers a struggling farm owner a tremendous amount of money for the land, it might be an offer that is hard to resist. Over time, such offers reduce the number of individual farm operations. The result is a shift from small family-operated farms to large corporate-controlled, vertically integrated agribusiness operations.

Vertical integration occurs when a company controls more than one stage of the production process. When a company manages all aspects of their business operations, from production to processing to shipping and then to selling, it helps reduce costs, improve efficiencies, and increase profits. It is difficult for small, family-owned-and-operated farms to practice vertical integration, but large, corporate agribusinesses have the capital and systems in place to do so. Examples of vertically integrated agribusinesses include orange juice, chickens, cereal, and French fries. Some fast-food restaurant companies use vertical integration, which has allowed them to offer products at prices lower than the competition. McDonald's has complete control over its agricultural sources, its own processing facilities, distribution centers, transportation systems, and the land that the restaurants occupy.

COMMODITY CHAINS

LEARNING OBJECTIVE
PSO-5.C Explain how economic forces influence agricultural practices.

The rise of agribusiness has led to the establishment of a complex network that connects places of production with distribution to consumers. This network is called a **commodity chain**. Numerous people in many regions have a hand in producing and distributing agricultural products. Agricultural commodity chains begin with inputs such as land, seeds, fertilizers, and animals all tended to by farmers to produce a crop. After cultivation and harvest, the crop is processed, packaged, and then transported to wholesalers and retailers. Eventually, the end result is a finished commodity that is marketed to consumers.

THE FOOD SUPPLY SYSTEM

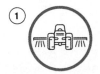

① AGRICULTURAL INPUTS

Inputs are the items used by farmers to successfully produce agriculture.

- seeds
- fertilizers
- pesticides
- feed
- utilities

② PRODUCERS

The producers grow, harvest, and raise the agricultural products based on farm size and type.

- farmers
- fishers
- ranchers

③ PROCESSORS

Agriculture is transformed into ingredients and packaged food after it is sorted, cleaned, milled, and prepared.

- manufacturers
- factories
- packagers
- storage facilities

CRITICAL VIEWING The production of food, from farm to consumer, is a highly complex system that goes through many exchanges. ▌How might external factors, such as physical environment and financial markets, impact agricultural products as they move through the food supply system?

Successfully delivering a product from the farm to the consumer involves many exchanges that must be considered and planned. Factors that influence the agricultural process include the weather, the physical environment, financial markets, labor relations, government policies, and trade. Businesses sign labor contracts and create marketing plans, while governments negotiate trade agreements, both establishing relationships and policies to ensure the successful delivery of an orange from the grove, for example, to a consumer's table.

The commodity chain for orange juice reveals that the product changes hands several times during the process. The citrus industry operates on long-term contracts and the futures market (an obligation for a buyer to purchase—and the seller to sell—a crop at a set price at a future time). This creates an arrangement where parties in the production chain work together but remain independent entities.

First, orange growers manage, harvest, and sell the fruit. Some growers are small farms that sell their fruit to a fruit handler or a cooperative, where farmers pool their resources to produce, market, and sell their produce. Other growers are part of a larger fruit processing company. Fruit processors take the fruit and produce either packaged juice or concentrate. Processors that produce packaged juice then market and sell it. Bulk processors that produce frozen concentrated orange juice work on distributing it and marketing it to stores and consumers at the end of the commodity chain. Consumers often have a choice among multiple, competing orange juice products.

PRICING AND POLICIES

LEARNING OBJECTIVE
PSO-5.C Explain how economic forces influence agricultural practices.

The dramatic growth in the production of crops due to technology leads to a greater supply. When supply is high, prices go down—this is the function of the law of supply and demand. At times of high production success, prices can drop so low that production costs are higher than the value of the product. This can be catastrophic for farmers. If coupled with a devastating loss of crops due to weather events, farmers can go bankrupt and lose their farms.

SUBSIDIES Some solutions to rising costs of production have been for the U.S. federal government to provide low-cost loans, insurance, and payments called **farm subsidies** to some farmers and agribusinesses. Farm subsidies originally started during the Great Depression of the 1930s to help struggling farmers and to make sure there was enough food being produced for American consumption.

In theory, subsidies continue to this day to protect all farmers and owners of farmland. But studies have shown that this isn't the case. Small family operations, the ones that need the help perhaps more than large farms, aren't seeing the money. Instead, the highest quantity producers of commodities like corn, soybeans, wheat, cotton, rice, and sugar are benefiting the most. In fact, one study revealed that the largest 15 percent of farm operations receive 85 percent of the subsidies. The benefits of the farm subsidies are debatable. There are many proponents on both sides

DISTRIBUTORS

Food and ingredients are distributed locally, regionally, and globally.

- importers
- exporters
- wholesalers

RETAILERS AND FOOD SERVICES

Retailers make food available for consumers.

- restaurants
- supermarkets
- convenience stores
- food banks

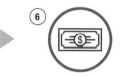

CONSUMERS

Consumers cook and/or eat the food.

- individuals
- families

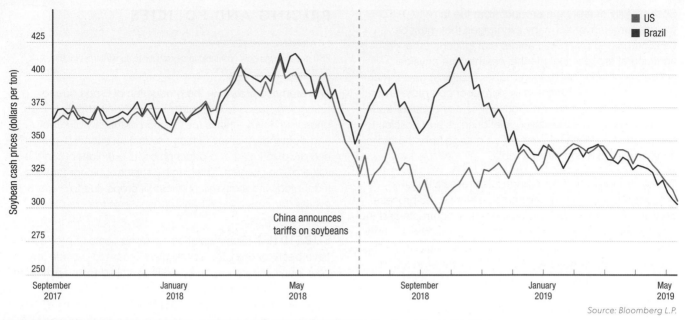

IMPACT OF TRADE WAR ON U.S. AND BRAZIL SOYBEAN PRICES Brazil and the United States are the top exporters of soybeans in the world. China is the top importer. After China implemented tariffs on U.S. products in response to President Trump's 2018 tariffs, there was less demand for U.S. soybeans. The U.S. price fell lower than the price of Brazilian soybeans, which fluctuated at a higher price. Prices converged in early 2019 when a limited number of soybean exports to China from the United States resumed and U.S. soybean exports reached additional countries.

of the argument. Many believe that the subsidies help the agricultural economy of the United States, even though they are directed to large producers. Others believe that the money is just a bonus to operations that are already successful and don't need the assistance.

The United States government currently pays out about $20 billion each year in farm subsidies. Congress legislates this complex process. About every five years, with the help of the United States Department of Agriculture (USDA), Congress evaluates and approves a farm bill that allocates the subsidies among other important regulations for farmers.

TARIFFS Another factor affecting prices of crops is the use of government **tariffs**. A tariff is a tax or duty to be paid on a particular import or export. Tariffs can affect trade between countries and can bring about a trade war, in which countries try to negatively impact each other's trade. Tariffs are used to raise government revenue, or income, but they are also used to protect domestic industries against foreign competition. Tariffs raise the price of imported goods, making them more expensive to purchase than goods made within the country. Therefore, domestic producers of soy, for example, are given a price advantage, making soy imports less competitive. Consumers, however, face higher prices for products that contain soy as a result of the tariffs.

One example of tariffs leading to a trade war and impacting U.S. agriculture is when President Donald Trump, in 2018, imposed a 25 percent tariff on foreign steel and a 10 percent tariff on aluminum imports. This tariff affected more than 800 types of products—worth $34 billion—entering the United States from China. These products included

industrial machinery, medical devices, and auto parts. Trump imposed the tariff for multiple reasons: to raise revenue for the federal government, to raise the price of Chinese products so Americans would not buy them, to promote steel and aluminum products made in the United States so Americans would buy those instead, and to force China to stop participating in unfair business practices. China responded by imposing its own tariff on U.S. products worth $34 billion. These products included many American manufactured goods, as well as agricultural products like soybeans, beef, and pork. This was especially challenging for hog farmers, as the Chinese are the world's top consumers of pork. Imposing tariffs and engaging in such a trade war can greatly disrupt established commodity chains, lower the price of farm products, and cause farmers to lose business.

GEOGRAPHIC THINKING

1. Explain why the number of small farms is decreasing and the number of large commercial farms is increasing.

2. Describe how the closure of several food processing plants would disrupt agriculture commodity chains.

3. Explain how farm subsidies combat the issue of rising costs of production.

4. Identify an impact of the trade war between the United States and China on agriculture.

EATING UGLY

Stuart works to combat issues of food waste, including throwing away vegetables that are cosmetically imperfect but entirely edible.

LEARNING OBJECTIVE

PSO-5.E Explain the interdependence among regions of agricultural production and consumption.

Every year some 2.9 trillion pounds of food—nearly a third of all that the world produces—is discarded. National Geographic Explorer Tristram Stuart is on a crusade to reduce waste in the food supply system by encouraging the consumption of "ugly food" that is often thrown out only for aesthetic reasons.

Stuart's campaign started when he was young, collecting unconsumed food from his school kitchens and a bakery to feed hogs he was raising in the English countryside. He realized that the food many people waste is in fact fit for human consumption. Stuart then began studying the issue of food waste on a global scale. To support his research, he looked at quantitative data about the food supply of every single country and compared it to what was actually, likely, being consumed. His study considered obesity levels, diet intake surveys, and other factors that determine what people eat.

The study resulted in a chart with a line that shows the normal level of consumption that a country should have assuming every resident has a stable, secure, and nutritious diet. Countries above the line represent those with an unnecessary surplus of food, meaning food availability in its communities is much larger than consumption. So, what happens to the surplus food? Simply, food is being wasted, thrown in dumpsters or given to animals, often because the produce is considered subpar. Stuart notes, shocked, "Potatoes that are cosmetically imperfect, all going for pigs. Parsnips that are too small for supermarket specifications, tomatoes in Tenerife [an island in Spain], oranges in Florida, bananas in Ecuador, all being discarded . . . perfectly edible, because they're the wrong shape or size."

Stuart's goal is to confront the business community, raise public awareness, and find solutions to these wasteful practices. "If we make noise about it, tell corporations about it, tell governments we want to see an end to food waste, we do have the power to bring about that change."

GEOGRAPHIC THINKING

Describe the impact Stuart's research could have on food consumption patterns.

13.3 THE VON THÜNEN MODEL

Commercial agriculture is the large-scale production of crops and livestock to sell at market. The market may be either a wholesaler (which then sells the products to retailers) or the retail store itself. The distance and transportation costs to market can influence what the farmer grows or raises and create specific patterns of land use.

RURAL LAND USE PATTERNS

LEARNING OBJECTIVE
PSO-5.D Describe how the von Thünen model is used to explain patterns of agricultural production at various scales.

Johann Heinrich von Thünen was a German farm owner with an interest in the geography and economics of farming. In 1826, he wrote a book about observations he had made regarding the spatial patterns of farming practices in his community. He found that specific types of agriculture took place in different locations surrounding the market, or center where business took place in a city or town. A pattern of intensive rural practices close to the market and extensive rural practices farther from the market emerged. In his book, von Thünen suggested that a farmer decides to cultivate certain crops or raise certain animals depending on the distance between the farm and the market. Based on this principle, the **von Thünen model** hypothesizes that perishability of the product and transportation costs to

the market each factor into a farmer's decisions regarding agricultural practices.

The model has four distinct concentric rings representing different agricultural practices. In the center is a core representing the market. The first ring outside the core represents intensive farming and dairying. The perishability of milk products and produce, like berries, lettuce, or tomatoes, makes it critical that they are produced close to the market and transported and sold within a limited time frame. These products cost more to transport, so having them produced closer to the market is a cost-saving measure. And even though this land is more expensive (remember bid-rent theory from Chapter 12), the products have a greater value and consumers will pay a higher price for them. For example, a farmer with land close to the market might choose to raise chickens and produce eggs for sale, because the transportation costs would be low and the fragile, perishable eggs would arrive at the market in a shorter amount of time while still fresh.

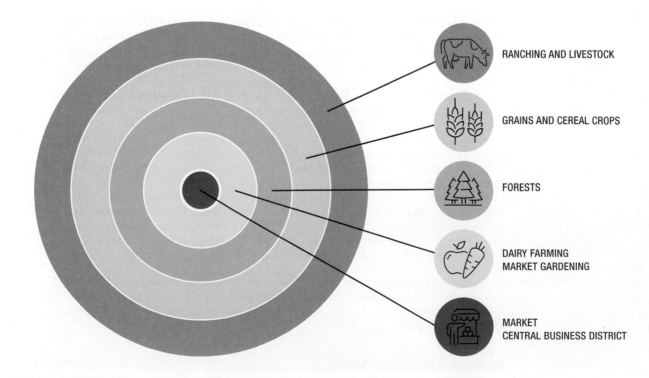

RANCHING AND LIVESTOCK

GRAINS AND CEREAL CROPS

FORESTS

DAIRY FARMING
MARKET GARDENING

MARKET
CENTRAL BUSINESS DISTRICT

CRITICAL VIEWING The von Thünen model suggests that farmers make decisions about which crops and animals to raise based on their proximity to markets. The model was created before industrialization. Why was dairy farming placed so close to the market city in the early 1800s? Explain.

The von Thünen model is based on an ideal environment that he specified back in 1826. These assumptions, when present, make this model work. They include:

- The market is located in an isolated, self-sufficient state without external influences.
- A commercial agricultural system exists where farmers will seek to maximize profits.
- A single, centrally located market is the destination of a farmer's produce.
- The land is *isotropic*, or flat and featureless, not containing mountains or rivers.
- There is only one means of transportation (oxen pulling a wooden cart over land).

The next ring represents forests. In the 19th century, timber and firewood were important commodities used for heating, cooking, and building. Wood is heavy and bulky, so its weight would make it expensive to transport. Producing wood close to the market reduces transportation costs.

The third ring is devoted to grains and cereal crops like rye, wheat, and barley—favored grains in 19th-century Germany. These crops are less perishable and not too bulky or heavy, so they can be grown farther from the market. The grain or cereal farmer could profitably raise and transport these crops to market. The land here, farther from the market, is less expensive and allows for less intensive agriculture.

Finally, the ring farthest away from the market in the von Thünen model is where livestock production occurs. Land is less desirable here and therefore less expensive. Farmers can buy or rent large pieces of land for extensive agricultural activities such as ranching. In the early 1800s, animals were walked to the market for sale, so transportation costs were not high.

APPLYING VON THÜNEN TODAY

LEARNING OBJECTIVE
PSO-5.D Describe how the von Thünen model is used to explain patterns of agricultural production at various scales.

All models are based on assumptions, and no model accounts for every exception or deviation that takes place in real-life situations. Von Thünen made assumptions (listed in the box) based on the realities of the early 19th century. Most of his assumptions don't apply to today's world. Many cities have multiple centers of business, not just one. An isolated state that has not been influenced by outside cultures or events no longer exists. In fact, the influence of modern industrialization, technology, and government policies has dramatically altered agricultural systems around the world. Some governments have introduced policies that favor the growing of certain crops over others, which influences what farmers grow. However, despite the enormous changes over time, the model can still be loosely applied to contemporary agricultural production, especially when it comes to the role of transportation influencing patterns of production.

Perhaps the most innovative technology that has improved transportation of agricultural products is the refrigerated container that can be transported on trucks, trains, ships, and cargo planes. The development of this technology has permitted perishable items like eggs and dairy to be produced much farther from markets. At even greater distances, fruits and vegetables that are only grown in certain parts of the world can be flown to grocery stores in another hemisphere. Von Thünen could never have imagined the movement of produce over thousands of miles—like blueberries from Chile to stores in the United States.

Time-space compression—the ability to quickly exchange goods across distances, as a result of more efficient transportation systems—as well as growing demands for food worldwide have expanded the markets available to most producers. Whereas in the past, farmers sold all or nearly all of their goods at the nearest market, today's farmers can reach an abundance of hungry markets hundreds and thousands of miles away thanks to technology, including refrigerated containers, and a complex network of roads, rails, shipping channels, and air routes.

In today's global agricultural system, specialty farming thrives in regions with particular climates and soil types, unlike von Thünen's assumption that the land was all the same. Truck farming is common in regions like South Florida and California's Central Valley, where farmers ship produce nationwide and internationally. "Out of season" produce is essentially a thing of the past, as growers in tropical Central Mexico ship avocados and Chilean vineyards airfreight their Southern Hemisphere summer grapes all winter long to markets in the United States and northern destinations.

GEOGRAPHIC THINKING

1. Explain the spatial relationship between land-use and market areas, based on the von Thünen model.

2. Explain the von Thünen model assumptions that are no longer present in agriculture today.

3. Use the "Agricultural Regions Around the World" map in Chapter 12 to describe how the von Thünen model could be used to generally describe agricultural production across the continental United States.

13.4 AGRICULTURE AS A GLOBAL SYSTEM

Importing and exporting agricultural products has been important to countries for centuries, but never before have so many regions been integrated into the global agricultural system. To manage the flow of food around the world, a large, complex network exists. Political relationships, trade patterns, and transportation networks all affect the distribution of food, which consequently impacts what appears on your plate.

AGRICULTURAL INTERDEPENDENCE

LEARNING OBJECTIVE
PSO-5.E Explain the interdependence among regions of agricultural production and consumption.

In today's global economy, consumers purchase foods from all over the world—including bananas from Costa Rica and teas from China. Agriculture, like other economic activities, has become globally integrated and organized, often connecting peripheral countries with core countries. No one country produces all of the food that its population consumes. Either a country's climate isn't conducive to growing certain foods, like bananas that require a tropical climate, or it is less expensive to import foods from a country that specializes in growing certain foods efficiently and in a high-quality manner. **Global supply chains**, which are the same as commodity chains but on a global scale, enable the delivery of a product between two different countries. For example, consumers in a store in Canada who purchase vegetables that originated from a farm in the Netherlands are each part of the global supply chain. As these networks have grown more complex, many regions of agricultural production and consumption have become increasingly interdependent.

Commodity agricultural products, including wheat, corn, soybeans, and cotton along with coffee, tea, cacao, and vanilla, are traded through global supply chains. Commodities are highly sought after in global markets. The supply chains for some agricultural commodities start with production in a peripheral country where crops are grown and harvested using low-cost, local labor, allowing for reduced overall production costs. Other commodities, like wheat or cotton, might start in the United States. Processing and packaging the product, the next step in the supply chain, may occur in the same country or a different one. Finally, the finished commodity is distributed to markets usually in core locations of the world.

Consider, for example, the commodity chain of cacao. Cacao beans come from trees grown in tropical environments near the Equator. The largest concentration of cacao farms are in peripheral countries like Ghana and Côte d'Ivoire. Many farmers work tirelessly cultivating cacao—a crop that requires much of the work to be done by hand. After beans are picked and dried, they are sent to processing and manufacturing plants throughout the world. At the plants, the beans are turned into cocoa powder, which then is used to make baking chocolate, chocolate bars, and other products transported to retailers.

The final leg of this global chain is the consumer. The cacao bean travels from the tropics to consumers all around the world, but most chocolate products end up in the United States and Europe. European countries such as Germany, the UK, Belgium, the Netherlands, and France import large amounts of chocolate.

COMMODITY DEPENDENCY International trade can be vital to a country's economy, and many rely on exports for financial stability. Some peripheral countries struggle with developing and maintaining export economies and end up becoming dependent on a single export **cash crop**, a crop that is produced for its commercial value. This dependency on one export can have negative consequences. Alternatively, though, if supply of a cash crop is limited, countries specializing in the crop can reap profitable rewards.

The vanilla industry is one example. The island of Madagascar, off the coast of Africa, has three-quarters of the world's vanilla fields. The vanilla bean is Madagascar's cash crop. It takes three years for beans to mature for harvest. Between 2016 and 2019, Madagascar has experienced small crop yields and devastating storms that have impacted vanilla production. Supply became limited, demand for vanilla remained the same, and prices went up.

Comoros, an archipelago (group of islands) located between the coast of Africa and Madagascar, also produces vanilla. The economy of Comoros is primarily agricultural. Some studies show that close to 70 percent of the working population of Comoros is involved in vanilla production. With very few other industries in Comoros, it relies on this single commodity and the resulting trade relationship with countries such as France, India, and Germany to keep its economy going. In 2017, 74 percent of Comoros's exports came from spices, including vanilla.

The specialization of one product creates a reputation and a demand for production. However, the reliance on a single commodity is risky, and it's unhealthy for an economy. Changes in world markets due to supply and demand

Workers at a vanilla processing center in Madagascar spread the vanilla pods on mats to dry in the sun. In 2017, Madagascar exported $894 million in vanilla to countries including the United States, France, and Germany.

issues can disrupt a country's economy that relies on one export. If demand for that one commodity dramatically falls, the revenue the commodity generates for the country declines. Not only can storms, droughts, and extreme temperatures cause crop failure and lead to a decline in a country's exports and revenue, but a trade war can erupt between trade partners, causing the costs of trading goods to fluctuate. Each of these scenarios can bring uncertainty to a country's economy. In fact, any disturbance in the supply chain can impact the financial stability of a country or region. Infrastructure, political relationships, and world trade patterns all impact the complex food distribution network.

INFRASTRUCTURE

LEARNING OBJECTIVE
PSO-5.E Explain the interdependence among regions of agricultural production and consumption.

Participating in the global agricultural system means having the infrastructure, or networks and facilities, in place to efficiently produce and distribute crops and livestock.

Infrastructure includes communication systems; sewage, water, and electric systems; and most importantly roads and transportation for exporting goods. Take, for example, the vegetables grown in the rural Netherlands. In order to get them to a city in Canada, the proper roads, seaports, ships, and all the communication systems necessary to hand off the vegetables to each party in the chain must be in place and function accordingly. Countries need to build main routes from agricultural, manufacturing, and production centers to airports and seaports to easily move and process imports and exports. Sometimes core countries provide financial support to peripheral countries to improve their infrastructure, which is mutually beneficial.

Railroads and waterways are efficient ways to transport agricultural commodities. Most products traded internationally move by sea. Many countries use trains and railways to move goods within their country and to neighboring countries on shared rail systems. On the massive Eurasian landmass that includes the continents of both Europe and Asia, there are four major interconnecting rail systems, along with a number of smaller rail systems. In North America, the countries of Canada, the United States,

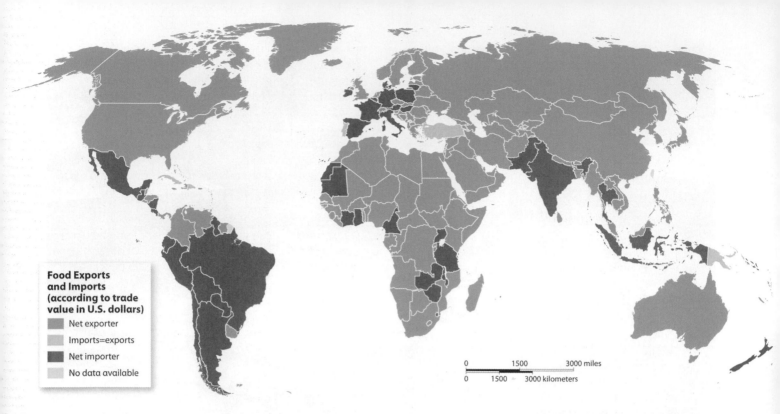

Food Exports and Imports (according to trade value in U.S. dollars)

- Net exporter
- Imports=exports
- Net importer
- No data available

0   1500   3000 miles
0   1500   3000 kilometers

WORLDWIDE AGRICULTURAL TRADE

The volume of agricultural trade has grown steadily over the past three decades, driven by a growing population and technological advances. Countries export and import agricultural goods depending on growing conditions and food preferences. The food net exporters ship out is greater in value than the food they import, and the food net importers bring in is greater in value than the food they export.

WORLD AGRICULTURAL TRADE GROWTH, 1995–2018

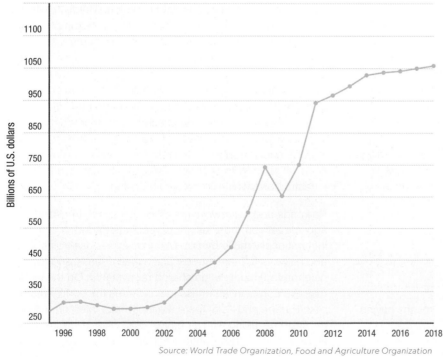

Billions of U.S. dollars

1100
1050
950
850
750
650
550
450
350
250

1996 1998 2000 2002 2004 2006 2008 2010 2012 2014 2016 2018

Source: World Trade Organization, Food and Agriculture Organization

LEADING EXPORTERS, 2017

European Union	$647 Billion
wheat, corn, barley	

United States	$170 Billion
soybeans, corn, wheat	

Brazil	$88 Billion
soybeans, sugar, chicken	

China	$79 Billion
garlic, vegetables, fruit	

Canada	$67 Billion
wheat, rapeseed, pork	

LEADING IMPORTERS, 2017

European Union	$649 Billion
wheat, corn, soybeans	

China	$183 Billion
soybeans, beef, palm oil	

United States	$161 Billion
coffee, beef, fruit	

Japan	$79 Billion
pork, beef, corn	

Canada	$39 Billion
chocolate, beef, fruit	

Source: World Trade Organization, Food and Agriculture Organization

and Mexico are connected by an extensive rail network. Brazil is a huge semi-peripheral country and exports many agricultural products across the globe. It also has a large network that enables it to transport commodities from its interior agricultural regions to its seaports on the Amazon River and the Atlantic Ocean.

POLITICAL RELATIONSHIPS

LEARNING OBJECTIVE
PSO-5.E Explain the interdependence among regions of agricultural production and consumption.

Supply chains work best when trade partnerships are stable, reciprocal, and understood by all parties. Any kind of instability can rock the trade boat, but perhaps the biggest threat to a supply chain is political instability. Political instability can affect global supply chains with varying degrees of damage to countries and their economies. For example, Brexit, set to be finalized by 2021, in which the United Kingdom left the European Union (EU) on January 31, 2020, could have major implications for Britain's agricultural supply chain. Brits import a lot of what they eat, especially during the winter months. They import fresh fruits and vegetables from southern European countries, like Italy, and other countries around the world. With the EU's border system, imports travel seamlessly between member states. However, with Brexit, the supply chain could become broken. New safety and document checks required at borders may cause delays. In addition, concerns over Brexit have already created a weaker currency, and experts fear that food prices in the United Kingdom will soar with these new import concerns.

Another example of how politics impacts a country's supply chain is the trade war between China and the United States that started in 2018 and was discussed earlier in this chapter. U.S. President Donald Trump imposed increased tariffs and other trade barriers on China, and China retaliated with tariffs of its own. This affects both importing and exporting supply chains, as they have to adjust for shifts in costs, supply, and demand. For U.S. businesses, some may be able to continue to manufacture in China, even with the tariffs calculated into their costs. On the other hand, some will shift manufacturing to other nontariffed countries or may manufacture in the United States. Because of the extra taxes on U.S. exports, the U.S. agriculture export supply chains face the most risk. Many Chinese companies are not buying the tariffed products, which is resulting in a surplus for U.S. farmers and lower prices.

PATTERNS FROM THE PAST Global supply chains can trace their roots back to European colonial and imperial networks between the 16th and 18th centuries. European cities became markets for exotic foods from every corner of the world. While building new colonies across the globe, European powers dictated which crops would be grown on their newly acquired lands, often growing agricultural products that had become popular in the markets back home. This resulted in patterns of monocropping. Monocropping was also a way that a controlling country could monopolize, or have exclusive control over, the dependent country's economy. Egypt, under British occupation, grew massive quantities of cotton; in West Africa, it was cocoa; and in South Asia, it was tea. With the development of refrigeration and faster shipping, these relationships between producer and market deepened.

Some former colonies today are still economically tied to the country that once colonized the area. Often, the former colony (now usually a peripheral country) receives aid from a former colonizer (a core country) that is in a position to continue the same unequal trade relationships of the past that once benefited the colonizer. The peripheral country is economically dependent on the core country that uses its natural resources and labor to inexpensively produce an export commodity. When a colony received independence, it often did not have the economy or the workforce to compete in the global market. Consequently, it became reliant on its former colonial power for trade, financial aid, and other support—an example of neocolonialism.

PATTERNS OF WORLD TRADE

LEARNING OBJECTIVE
PSO-5.E Explain the interdependence among regions of agricultural production and consumption.

The amount of agricultural trade is both growing and changing every year. Trade in food alone has nearly doubled since 1995 (in real terms adjusted for inflation). This is largely a result of economic growth in peripheral and semi-peripheral countries that have become more engaged with global markets, resulting in greater demand for agricultural products globally. While core countries, including the United States and those comprising the European Union, remain leading agricultural exporters and importers, the increasing relevance of emerging economies such as Brazil, China, India, Indonesia, and Russia is a growing trend in global food trade. Population growth and income changes are directly related to the growth in agricultural trade. According to the FAO, China's share of world imports increased from 2.3 percent in 2000 to 8.2 percent in 2016 while a substantial number of people living in poverty declined—the poverty headcount ratio declined in China from 31.9 percent in 2002 to 1.8 percent in 2013.

Another area of growth for agricultural trade is between peripheral and semi-peripheral countries. The share of imports by peripheral and semi-peripheral countries from other peripheral and semi-peripheral countries increased from 41.9 percent in the year 2000 to 54.4 percent in 2015, due primarily to population growth in the periphery and semi-periphery. Exports followed a similar growth trend in peripheral countries.

PREFERENCES As global agricultural trade increases, consumers gain access to a variety of foods. New foods are introduced to regions, and information about different foods spreads. This can influence food preferences and alter the patterns of production and consumption. The popularity of a food dictates increased importation of it. Recent trends, including food that is not only good for consumers but good for the environment as well, are changing what farmers plant and their agricultural practices around the world.

The rising interest in plant-based foods is creating new demands for the production of vegetable proteins. Types of vegetable proteins include soybeans, lentils, hemp seeds, pumpkin seeds, seitan (made from wheat), nuts, green peas, and beans. These are used to make tofu and other alternatives to common meat products. Even though tofu has been produced for 2,000 years, its popularity has grown in recent decades due to its nutritional value, low cost, and availability from soybeans. As a result of the trend in some countries to eat less meat for health reasons and to lesson climate change, many farms are shifting to cultivate these agricultural products. In Montana, farmers who traditionally raised wheat are giving pulses a try. Pulses include dried beans, lentils, chickpeas, and cowpeas. In 2018 the state led the nation in pulse crop production. Food manufacturers are also investing in infrastructure needed to support emerging commodities like pulses and a variety of seeds and nuts. Modifications in crop production will continue to evolve as trends change.

FAIR TRADE The wages paid to laborers who produce commodity crops and other crops are often low. The palm oil industry in Indonesia and tea producers in India are just two instances where investigations have uncovered unfair wage practices on plantations of commodity crops.

The **fair trade** movement is a global campaign to fix unfair wage practices and protect the ability of farmers to earn a living. Fair trade is meant to improve the lives of farmers and workers in peripheral and semi-peripheral countries by providing more equitable working and trading conditions. The movement works to increase incomes paid directly to the farmers by paying an above-market fair price provided they meet certain standards and regulations. Fair trade also provides price guarantees that limit damages if farmers face devastating challenges due to environmental or social issues, and it helps farmers access global markets.

Early in the fair trade movement countries talked about the idea of "Trade not aid." Together, they realized that establishing equitable trade relationships between core and peripheral countries would have a stronger impact than continuing to send aid money to countries with economic challenges. To ensure the success of the movement, a labeling system was created to raise consumer awareness. To place the fair trade label on a product, the producers must be a small farm that engages in a democratically operated cooperative, and they must follow basic health, environmental, safety, labor, and human rights regulations.

Products are priced higher both as a result of this certification and because they are often higher quality or organic. Consumers pay more money for products that are fair trade certified, supporting the belief that the producers have a basic right to fair wages and living conditions. Retailers, such as Whole Foods Market, Target, Starbucks, and Caribou Coffee, specifically market fair trade products to those consumers, which is helping to expand the industry and increase access to European, Asian, and North American markets.

As of 2019, more than 1 million small-scale producers are part of the fair trade movement. Fair trade products are available everywhere, but in limited quantities. Products range from tea, cocoa, and sugar to wine, nuts, and spices. The most widespread and well-known fair trade product is coffee. Hundreds of thousands of coffee farmers have benefited from fair trade. But is the program doing enough?

Studies are measuring the actual impact of fair trade. Reports show that fair trade relationships are benefiting farmers. Cooperatives are improving land management practices, investing in better seedlings, and exploring advanced production technologies. Fair trade has also helped farmers and workers get out of debt and better assist the communities they live in economically. A community development premium, included in the price of the good, provides extra money to the farm cooperative to be used for community projects including school and infrastructure improvements.

However, there are reports that even though cooperatives are benefiting, the workers they hire may not be seeing the same level of aid, and poverty still exists in many areas. Some critics argue that fair trade practices artificially inflate market prices. They also argue that the focus on cooperatives ignores the small, individual farmers that may need the most assistance. Moreover, peripheral countries are seeing the emergence of corporate controlled plantations and agribusinesses—many moving in to compete with small farming cooperatives, even right next door—creating unequal competition that will ultimately hurt those benefiting from the efforts of the movement.

GEOGRAPHIC THINKING

1. Explain the economic impact of commodity dependency on a region.

2. Explain how political relationships affect global food distribution.

3. Consider the supply and demand for a cash crop such as vanilla. Describe the impact the global supply chain has on supply and demand.

4. Describe how the fair trade movement affects the interdependence between core and peripheral countries.

CASE STUDY

COFFEE PRODUCTION AND CONSUMPTION

THE ISSUE The coffee industry's global supply chain is based on a system of unequal power relations.

LEARNING OBJECTIVE

PSO-5.E Explain the interdependence among regions of agricultural production and consumption.

BY THE NUMBERS

$0.40/LB
Farmers sell for

$0.60/LB
Brokers sell to processors

$0.70/LB
Processors sell to exporters

$0.85/LB
Exporters sell to importers

$1.05/LB
Importers sell for

$4–$6/LB
Distributors sell to retailers

$7–$12/LB
Retailers sell to consumers

Source: Food and Agriculture Organization

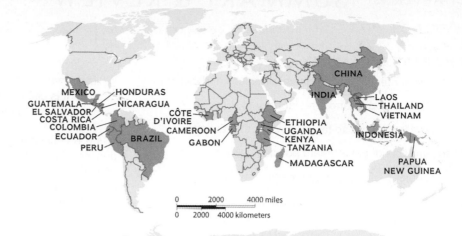

TOP COFFEE-PRODUCING COUNTRIES, 2019 Brazil tops the list, producing 5.7 billion pounds of coffee per year that is shipped to places around the world.

GLOBAL SUPPLY CHAINS HAVE MANY BENEFITS, but they are not shared equally among the people who produce and distribute agricultural products. In the case of coffee, the supply chain takes the crop from countries that have proper conditions for coffee-growing—namely, mountainous regions with humid, tropical climates—to core countries that can afford the highly popular bean. Countries where coffee is a major export tend to be semi-periphery countries that depend on the income that coffee generates.

The global distribution of coffee involves many people, starting with farmers, brokers who handle the transaction between farmers and processing plants, the processors at the plant, exporters, importers, distributors, and retailers. Each person adds value to the commodity, even though the coffee beans themselves undergo little, if any, physical change as they exchange hands.

Having access to the coffee supply chain increases the otherwise limited business opportunities of small farmers and helps them reach new customers. However, the people who actually produce the coffee beans for export often receive the smallest share of wealth that is generated by the global coffee trade. A typical example is a farmer selling his or her coffee beans for $.40 a pound while the end consumer pays between $7 and $12 a pound. Each person playing a role in the supply chain receives a share of the total income, with the largest shares going to the companies who import and distribute the coffee. These are often large corporations that take advantage of economies of scale and vertical integration by controlling the processing, or roasting, of the coffee bean in the country of origin, as well as the distribution networks in the consuming country, including the packaging, branding, and marketing of the coffee to consumers at retail stores and coffee shops.

When conditions are right, coffee-producing farmers benefit, but the market for the bean is not stable. As a globally traded commodity, the price of coffee can change from minute to minute. Its price is determined by a host of variables such as changing weather, political uncertainty, transportation costs, and crop disease. All of these issues affect the profits of every person in the supply chain, and sometimes result in a price hike for consumers. When farmers, who are at the start of the supply chain, receive the smallest share of the profits generated from the sale of coffee, any fall in market price can be devastating to their livelihoods.

GEOGRAPHIC THINKING

Explain the degree to which the production of coffee increases the interdependence between semi-periphery countries and core countries.

CHAPTER SUMMARY

Economic forces drive agricultural practices and include:

- cost of materials, land, and labor

- the availability of capital (money or other assets)

- the impacts of government policies

- consumer preferences and market demands

Economies of scale explain how production costs are reduced as the quantity of production increases.

Agribusiness refers to the large-scale system that includes the production, processing, and distribution of agricultural products and equipment. While family farms still make up the majority of farms worldwide, large corporate-controlled agribusiness operations are replacing small family farms.

Technology, including modern equipment, improved fertilizers and pesticides, and new types of seeds allow farmers to increase production and create higher yields.

High-yield crop growth can lead to lower commodity prices, which can have a negative impact on commodity crop growers. Government policies to protect pricing and the livelihood of farmers influence trade practices. These policies include:

- Farm subsidies, government payments to farmers and agribusinesses

- Tariffs, which affect pricing on imports and exports

While government incentives and price controls help farmers, it is ultimately consumers who drive the market in commercial agriculture.

The von Thünen model, based on certain assumptions, describes the ideal pattern for agricultural practices outside of a city center, with the production of perishable goods closest to the city, then wood, then grains and cereal crops, and finally livestock and ranching.

Agriculture is globally integrated and organized. Countries in the core, periphery, and semi-periphery depend on each other for agricultural production and consumption.

Global food distribution networks are affected by political relationships, infrastructure, and patterns of world trade.

- Agriculture is a part of the global supply chain, including the production and export of commodity crops to consumers in markets such as the United States, Europe, and China.

- Improved infrastructure and the fair trade movement are helping equalize trade among core and peripheral countries.

KEY TERMS AND CONCEPTS

■ Use complete sentences to answer the questions.

1. **APPLY CONCEPTUAL VOCABULARY** Consider the term *hybrid*. Write a standard dictionary definition of it. Then provide a conceptual definition—an explanation of how it is used in the context of this chapter.

2. Provide an example of a dual agricultural economy.

3. Explain how hybrids are impacting agriculture.

4. How are the terms *cash crop* and *agribusiness* related?

5. Provide an example of infrastructure in terms of the global supply chain.

6. Provide an example of how farm subsidies might help a farmer.

7. Define the term *fair trade* in relation to the global supply chain.

8. Describe the von Thünen model. Give one example of a way in which the model could be used on a local level today.

9. Explain how tariffs affect commodity pricing.

10. Define the term *cooperative* in relation to a commodity chain.

11. Why would a commercial agriculture operation favor vertical integration?

12. Give an example of something that can increase economies of scale. Explain why.

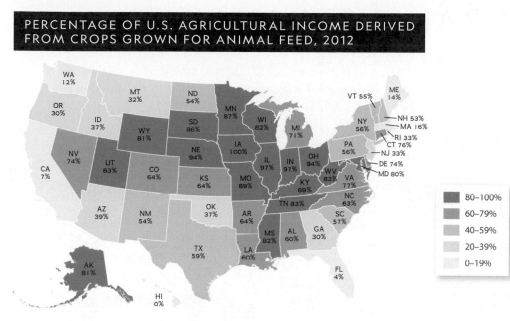

PERCENTAGE OF U.S. AGRICULTURAL INCOME DERIVED FROM CROPS GROWN FOR ANIMAL FEED, 2012

- 80–100%
- 60–79%
- 40–59%
- 20–39%
- 0–19%

13. **IDENTIFY DATA & INFORMATION** Which state earns the highest percentage of its agricultural income from crops grown primarily for animal consumption, and which state earns the lowest?

14. **DESCRIBE SPATIAL RELATIONSHIPS** Describe the connection among the states that earn more of their agricultural income from animal feed.

15. **DESCRIBE PATTERNS & PROCESSES** Describe the pattern among states that earn less than 50 percent of their agricultural income from animal feed.

16. **SYNTHESIZE** Based on what you know about monocropping, do you think the dark green states or the light green states practice monocropping? Explain your answer.

GEO-INQUIRY | REDUCING FOOD WASTE

Consider how to use Geo-Inquiry to answer questions about issues regarding food waste in your community. Use the steps in the Geo-Inquiry Process to identify, research, and propose solutions to a food waste issue in your region.

ASK Start with an authentic question. It might be as simple as: *How might we reduce food waste and solve hunger issues in our community?* Use the Geo-Inquiry Process to expand this question and ask need-to-know questions such as: *What is the largest producer of food waste in the community? What groups or organizations would benefit from food donations?*

COLLECT Decide how you could gather geographic information to answer your original question. Explore local sources for data and statistics. Interview people, including those with important roles in your community's activities.

VISUALIZE Analyze the information you collected on food waste in your region to draw conclusions, identify patterns, and formulate a possible solution. Synthesize and organize the information in order to create visuals that show the issue and represent a positive outcome.

CREATE Focus on ways to tell a Geo-Inquiry story that will support a proposal for the reduction of food waste. Keep your audience in mind. *How can you use images, videos, and charts and graphs to help tell your story?* Tie your elements together using a storytelling tool.

ACT Share your Geo-Inquiry story with decision-makers. Consider how your project can inform decision-makers about how they may reduce food waste and improve lives.

ASK — COLLECT — VISUALIZE — CREATE — ACT

CHAPTER 14

AGRICULTURAL SUSTAINABILITY IN A GLOBAL MARKET

CRITICAL VIEWING These giant Japanese scallops are farmed off Vancouver Island in Canada. They consume fish waste. How might fish farming like this be considered a form of sustainable agriculture?

GEOGRAPHIC THINKING Why is sustainable agriculture a goal for the future?

14.1
CONSEQUENCES
OF AGRICULTURAL
PRACTICES

NATIONAL GEOGRAPHIC
EXPLORER Hindou
Oumarou Ibrahim

CASE STUDY: Building Africa's
Great Green Wall

14.2
CHALLENGES OF
CONTEMPORARY
AGRICULTURE

FEATURE: Precision Agriculture

14.3
FEEDING THE
WORLD

CASE STUDY: Food Deserts

NATIONAL GEOGRAPHIC
EXPLORER Jennifer Burney

14.4
WOMEN IN
AGRICULTURE

14.1 CONSEQUENCES OF AGRICULTURAL PRACTICES

Agricultural practices have profound effects on the environment, and they play an important role in shaping cultural practices. As food production expands to meet the needs and tastes of a growing global population, the environmental and societal impacts of agriculture are also increasing.

ALTERING THE ENVIRONMENT

LEARNING OBJECTIVE

IMP-5.A Explain how agricultural practices have environmental and societal consequences.

The agricultural practices you've learned about alter the land in different ways to create a variety of **agricultural landscapes**, or landscapes resulting from the interactions between farming activities and a location's natural environment. Some agricultural landscapes have endured for centuries, while others are constantly changing.

SHIFTING CULTIVATION As you have learned, the practice of shifting cultivation involves farming a piece of land until the soil becomes infertile and then leaving it or using it for a different purpose. This form of subsistence agriculture is predominantly practiced in peripheral and semi-peripheral countries in South America, Central and West Africa, and Southeast Asia. Shifting cultivation differs from crop rotation: instead of rotating crops on a regular basis to maintain soil fertility, farmers using shifting cultivation set aside fields or plots once the soil is no longer suitable for farming. The idea is to let the land recover before using it again, but shifting cultivation systems can fail if fields are not given enough time to recover. When the land does not have an adequate fallow (uncultivated) period, the result is soil degradation. In areas where shifting cultivation is practiced, the landscape becomes an ever-changing mosaic of planted crop fields, abandoned plots, and plots in various stages of regeneration.

Shifting cultivation is commonly practiced on a small scale by indigenous peoples. In northern Vietnam, for example, the people of Ban Tat simultaneously manage shifting fields on the hillsides, permanent rice paddies in the valleys, and wild resources in the forest. Shifting cultivation is one integral component within a complex **agroecosystem** — an ecosystem modified for agricultural use. Because of its diverse agriculture, the Ban Tat community can ensure a varied and sustainable food supply while preserving the ecological value of the landscape. Village committees ensure that the agroecosystem is effectively managed and cultivated. The argument can be made that if shifting cultivation is replaced by intensive commercial agriculture,

such as palm oil or rubber plantations, the negative environmental impact is much greater.

SLASH AND BURN Slash and burn farming is considered to be a type of shifting agriculture. However, slash and burn often alters landscapes permanently, while fields under other types of shifting cultivation return regularly to cropland. People most often practice slash and burn agriculture in tropical wet climates where dense vegetation covers the land. As you learned, this method involves cutting and burning forests to create fields for crops. The burn removes weeds, disease, and pests, and the ash layer provides the newly cleared land with a nutrient-rich layer that helps fertilize crops. Within a few years, the nutrients are used up and the weeds return. Having lost fertility, the soil is no longer suitable for farming, and as a result, the field is abandoned, and farmers move on to a new plot of land to repeat the process. Sometimes the forest regenerates on abandoned fields.

Slash and burn farmers generally live on marginal land in the tropical rain forests of Latin America, Africa, and Asia. Tribal communities historically have used this technique to survive and still do so in the present day. As you learned in Chapter 12, slash and burn contributes to numerous environmental problems, including massive **deforestation** (loss of forest lands) and soil erosion—the wearing away of topsoil by wind, rain, and other phenomena. On the other hand, some observers argue that about seven percent of worldwide agriculture is based on the slash and burn technique and that this method can be sustainable if it is practiced by small populations in large forested areas and if the land is given adequate time to recover before the burn is repeated. In Thailand, for example, farmers in the agricultural village of Hin Lad Nai have practiced slash and burn cycles to plant dry upland rice for 400 years. Hin Lad Nai's commitment to proper rest times for the soil and deliberate crop rotation has resulted in resilient, sustainable farmland.

TERRACING Terracing, which is commonly practiced by subsistence farmers, is the process of carving parts of a hill or mountainside into small, level growing plots. This method is used in mountainous areas in various climates, including tropical wet climates. Farmers can cultivate crops in these rugged regions by building "steps" or terraces into

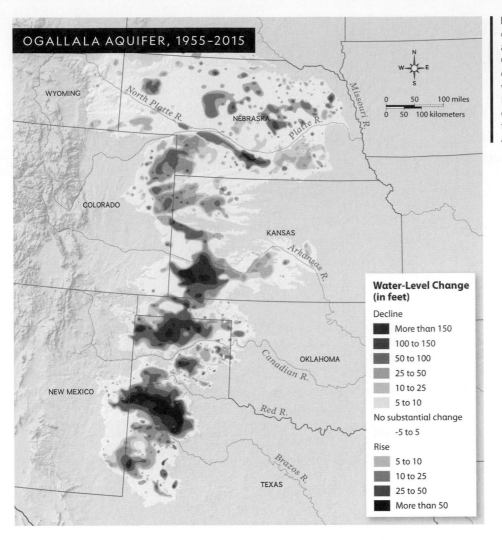

OGALLALA AQUIFER, 1955–2015

WYOMING

North Platte R.

NEBRASKA

Platte R.

Missouri R.

COLORADO

KANSAS

Arkansas R.

OKLAHOMA

Canadian R.

NEW MEXICO

Red R.

Brazos R.

TEXAS

N
W E
S

0   50   100 miles
0   50   100 kilometers

Water-Level Change (in feet)

Decline
- More than 150
- 100 to 150
- 50 to 100
- 25 to 50
- 10 to 25
- 5 to 10

No substantial change
- -5 to 5

Rise
- 5 to 10
- 10 to 25
- 25 to 50
- More than 50

READING MAPS Thirty percent of all water used to irrigate U.S. agriculture is pumped from the Ogallala Aquifer. This map shows degrees of change in the aquifer's water level between 1955 and 2015. ▮ Identify a small area on the map, circle it, and then write a sentence to explain what has changed in that area over time.

the steep slopes and creating paddies for cultivating water-intensive crops such as rice. During rainfall, the paddies flood and water flows through small channels from terrace to terrace without carrying soil down the slope. Preservation of the soil nutrients leads to the growth of healthy crops, and the terraces slow heavy rain flows so plants and soil are not carried away. Through terracing, hilly or mountainous land that would otherwise be unusable becomes productive. Although terracing is labor intensive, it is often part of a cultural heritage and an undertaking that everyone in a community participates in to ensure that the entire system is well managed. Maintaining the terraces is critical in preventing dangerous runoff and mudslides. In the case of the Ifugao Rice Terraces in the Philippines, knowledge is passed down through generations to preserve this traditional and effective method of farming that is a vital part of the community's survival and culture.

IRRIGATION Humans have been using irrigation for millennia, most commonly in areas without dependable precipitation, to supplement rainfall by bringing water from its natural sources to farm fields through canals and other means. Irrigation can affect surface landscapes in many ways. Using irrigation, humans have transformed arid or

semiarid landscapes into green fields. Especially striking are the landscapes created by center-pivot systems that use enormous sprinklers that rotate around a central point, creating expansive green circles in otherwise dry regions.

Irrigation supports both small subsistence farms and major commercial agriculture operations. **Reservoirs** are one common source of irrigation for crops in the United States. These artifical lakes are created by building dams across streams and rivers. Canals carry water from the reservoirs to the fields and orchards where it is needed. People have also rerouted natural water paths to aid irrigation.

The Aral Sea in Central Asia is an inland water body with no outlet to the ocean. It was fed by two rivers that were diverted in the 1960s to irrigate the desert regions surrounding the sea for cotton production. As a result, water levels dropped, salinity rose, and fish populations dwindled. As of 2019, the Aral Sea was one-tenth of its original size.

The Colorado River is one example of a river that has been dammed and is heavily used for irrigation. It is the American West's most vital water resource, supplying water to 40 million people and 5.5 million acres of farmland across seven states and Mexico. To preserve this important

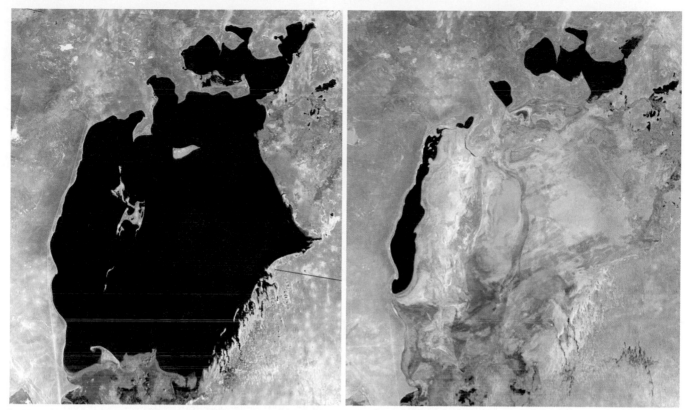

CRITICAL VIEWING Satellite images show the Aral Sea, which spans Kazahkstan and Uzbekistan, in 1977 (left) and 2019 (right) after its rivers were diverted for irrigation. The turquoise color in the 2019 image shows sediment deposits in shallow waters that result from seasonal rainfall. ▌ Identify the changes in the 2019 photo and describe their possible societal and environmental consequences.

Over the past 60 years, the Aral Sea steadily dried up due to irrigation practices. These rusted ships used to be docked in the seaport of Mo'ynoq, Uzbekistan. Today, they are part of a "ship graveyard" in an area renamed the Aralkum Desert. The sea's drastic retreat obliterated the local fishing industry, but recent restoration efforts, including repairing dikes and constructing a dam, have partially revived it.

water resource, the United States Bureau of Reclamation (USBR), state representatives, Native American nations, and the Mexican government have developed and signed plans of action in case of drought affecting the Colorado River. Despite these plans, the water supply from the river is threatened by increasing agricultural demands, and many researchers have expressed concern about the dams' negative effects on species that rely on that water.

Some water sources tapped for irrigation lie below the land's surface. Layers of underground sand, gravel, and rocks that contain and can release a usable amount of water are called **aquifers**. People tap into aquifers to access fresh water for both agriculture and household uses. If not recharged or replenished by drainage through the soil, groundwater levels in aquifers can fall or even become completely depleted. North America's largest aquifer, the Ogallala Aquifer beneath the Great Plains of the United States, formed millions of years ago and is fed by meltwater flowing from the Rocky Mountains. In recent decades, it has been overdrawn and is not receiving enough water to replenish itself. Farmers in the Great Plains, a region dominated by agriculture, are no longer able to pump enough water from the aquifer to sustain their crops, which are mostly wheat. Large aquifers in Asia, Africa, and Southwest Asia are facing similar declines.

China practices groundwater irrigation and the moving of surface water on a massive scale. Chinese farmers use groundwater to irrigate crops with pumping systems reaching down more than 200 feet. One advantage of groundwater is that the energy it requires is inexpensive and new technology makes it efficient. On the other hand, the pumps emit more than 30 million metric tons of carbon dioxide in one year—a damaging level of atmospheric pollution. In April 2018, China launched its South-to-North Water Diversion Project, which is anticipated to move 44.8 billion cubic meters of fresh water annually from the Yangtze River to the northern provinces using three canal systems. Critics argue that improved water conservation practices by the agricultural sector—which accounts for 60 to 70 percent of the water taken from groundwater sources—would be far less expensive and far more effective.

The United Nations estimates that within the next few decades, the world will need to increase food production by 60 percent to support its growing population. This demand will put pressure on aquifers and surface water sources. If a water crisis is to be avoided, therefore, farmers will need to better manage how much water they draw for irrigation. Today, some farmers are using technology to help them measure and gauge their water use, which allows them to slow the rate of water depletion.

DRAINING WETLANDS Areas of land that are covered by or saturated with water—such as swamps, marshes, and bogs—are called **wetlands**. Draining wetlands and converting them into farmland has historically been viewed as an acceptable practice because these areas were considered wastelands: the soil does not support construction or development, and wetlands provide a habitat for pests such as mosquitos. The Netherlands stands out among countries that have used wetland reclamation to increase land for farming and habitation. Around 17 percent of the country's present land area was once under the sea or coastal wetland.

Drained wetlands can be converted into agricultural land, but this results in a significant loss of habitat for fish, waterfowl, and mammals. Broader environmental issues have also resulted from the loss of wetlands, which help reduce storm and flood damage, improve water quality, and trap carbon dioxide that might otherwise be released into the atmosphere. For example, the conversion of wetlands into large-scale palm oil plantations in Malaysia is predicted to cause extreme flooding in the coming decades.

More than half the original wetlands in the United States have been lost, largely due to drainage for agricultural purposes. In Australia, the government is working with commercial farmers to adopt sustainable agricultural practices to protect wetlands, such as planting drought-resistant crops to make the most of lands already under cultivation and reusing wastewater so the amount of water needed from wetlands is reduced.

PASTORAL NOMADISM Like shifting cultivation, pastoral nomadism, also caled nomadic herding, is an extensive practice and generally a form of subsistence agriculture. Pastoral nomads are herders who move their animals seasonally or as needed to allow the best grazing. Nomads and their herds range in dry climates in Southwest Asia, North Africa, the Arctic, and other regions where crop cultivation is difficult or impossible. Traditionally, pastoral nomadism includes practices to preserve the resources upon which nomadic families depend, such as rotating grazing zones, limiting excess concentrations of people or animals, and protecting dry season resources. Pastoral lands have degraded in areas where these practices have collapsed due to war, nationalization of resources, agricultural expansion, and societal change.

When disrupted or poorly executed, pastoral nomadism can have serious consequences for the landscape and the environment. Overgrazing can cause land degradation, which is long-term damage to the soil's ability to support life. **Desertification**—a form of land degradation that occurs when soil deteriorates to a desert-like condition—can be the result of poor pastoral nomadism practices in arid or semiarid lands. Herds may favor certain plants over others, which can impact **biodiversity**—the variety of organisms living in a location—and reduce plant cover. When grazing is concentrated on mountain slopes, soil erosion can result. Livestock compact the soil with their hooves, which leads to wind and water erosion.

As with other traditional agricultural practices that have been pressured by modernization and urbanization,

The Tuareg, who live and roam in North Africa, are pastoral nomads. Life for the cattle-dependent Tuareg has changed dramatically in recent years as rainfall has declined during wet seasons, affecting their pasturelands. As one Tuareg nomad put it, "When the animals die, the Tuareg dies."

pastoral nomadism has evolved and, in some places, is under threat. In Mongolia, nomadic families have migrated between high and low pastures with their horses, goats, and sheep for thousands of years. Though herders now rely on motorcycles as well as horses to get around, the migration patterns remain the same.

The Tuareg, nomads who live in the Sahara Desert in North Africa, numbered just over two million in the 2010s. Their economy has revolved around cattle and trans-Saharan trade for thousands of years. However, lack of adequate rainfall over the past few decades has made it difficult for nomadic Tuareg families to support their herds. They depend on the animals for milk, clothing, tents, trade, and societal power. In the Sahel area on the southern fringe of the Sahara Desert, deep narrow wells have provided water for the Tuaregs' livestock, but access to the wells often leads to overgrazing, which increases the risk of soil erosion.

GEOGRAPHIC THINKING

1. Explain why agricultural practices and landscapes vary so widely across regions.

2. Identify a positive and a negative effect of irrigation.

ENVIRONMENTAL CONSEQUENCES

LEARNING OBJECTIVE
IMP-5.A Explain how agricultural practices have environmental and societal consequences.

All agricultural practices have an impact on the environment. When farmlands and water resources are overused, negative consequences often result. Effects of agriculture on the landscape and soil include pollution, land cover change, soil salinization, and land degradation such as desertification.

POLLUTION Whether fields receive their water from rainfall or irrigation, water running off farmland has environmental consequences for habitats well outside the agroecosystem. Runoff from fields may contain chemicals and nutrients from pesticides and fertilizers, as well as bacteria and disease-carrying organisms. All of these can pollute and damage ecosystems. High concentrations of nitrate from fertilizer, for example, promote uncontrolled plant growth and low oxygen levels in bodies of water, damaging habitats in lakes, ponds, and even oceans. The Gulf of Mexico "dead zone" is an area about the size of Massachusetts where most marine life has been killed by oxygen deprivation due to human-caused nutrient pollution.

LAND COVER CHANGE Geographers refer to land cover change to describe how the surface of land is altered by different land uses—especially by the way humans use the land. In terms of agriculture, humans transform Earth's surface for the purpose of growing food. No matter for what purpose, the environmental consequences of land cover change can be difficult to remedy.

As you learned earlier, terraced farming creates a dramatic agricultural landscape on slopes that are too steep for other farming practices. A frequent problem associated with terracing is groundwater saturation, which hinders the land's ability to absorb more water during heavy rains. Massive labor is required to properly maintain terraces, and if they are allowed to deteriorate, soil erosion down the slope can be severe and even cause catastrophic mudslides during rainy seasons or strong storms.

Deforestation caused by slash and burn agriculture is also a land cover change. While it is true that logging is by far the greater culprit when it comes to deforestation, poor farming practices have been responsible for environmental damage in some locations, especially when farmers clear and replant a patch of forest land before it has had sufficient chance to recover. This tends to happen when farmers intensify their efforts as a result of increasing populations coupled with more competition for scarce land. As deforested areas expand, they may diminish wildlife habitat, which over the long term can lead to endangered species or extinction.

In the summer of 2019, timber cutting and slash and burn operations in Brazil caused record-breaking forest fires in the Amazon region that are likely to leave massive tracts of land uncovered. The consequences of these fires may reach well beyond land cover change. The Amazon Rain Forest absorbs millions of tons of carbon emissions every year, and environmental scientists are convinced that intact rain forests are instrumental in helping to slow climate change.

SOIL SALINIZATION Irrigation, too, can lead to short-term and long-term environmental damage such as **salinization**, the process by which water-soluble salts build up in the soil. Salinization occurs in arid and semiarid regions when water evaporates from the ground more rapidly than it is replenished by rain or irrigation, causing a concentration of salts in the soil. When salts accumulate in the root zone of a crop, the plants can no longer extract adequate water, which can in turn result in crop yield reductions. Excessively saline irrigation water can contribute to the problem. Egypt, for example, has struggled with soil salinity issues for years because of extensive irrigation and the highly saline drainage water from the Nile Delta that is used to water the fields.

DESERTIFICATION When water consumption significantly exceeds the rate at which it is replenished—think of the Aral Sea and the Ogallala Aquifer—the result can be desertification, which is a permanent form of land degradation. Poor pastoral nomadism practices such as overgrazing can contribute to desertification, but other human causes include overgrazing by stationary herds, deforestation, and the clearing of land for expanding human habitation. The areas most vulnerable to desertification are those with low or variable rainfall. One-third of farmland in India is now affected by desertification. In 2019, the UN reported that desertification is occurring at 30 to 35 times the historical rate. Desertification not only harms food supplies but also may endanger the health of those who breathe the dust carried on the wind from dried-out soil.

In 2019, tens of thousands of individual fires burned through the Amazon region in Brazil. The fires moved especially quickly through areas that had been deforested. This aerial view reveals the scale of the fires; even from a great height, the flames are evident.

CONSERVATION AND SUSTAINABILITY EFFORTS

LEARNING OBJECTIVE

IMP-5.A Explain how agricultural practices have environmental and societal consequences.

Governments and organizations worldwide are addressing the negative environmental effects of agriculture through a variety of policies and sustainability efforts. Many focus on conservation, which involves managing and protecting natural resources to prevent their depletion. Conservation initiatives often use laws or education to encourage farmers to modify their practices. Given the diversity not only of agriculture types but also of ecosystems and political systems, these plans and policies vary tremendously from place to place. For example, the effort to conserve water has led the government of Zambia, in southern Africa, to charge fees on groundwater use. The idea is to increase awareness of water usage that extends beyond household consumption by attaching a cost to it. The money collected from water consumption for farming and industry will be used to implement solutions to the growing problem of water pollution in Zambia.

Nongovernmental groups also help with with these efforts. One example is EcoLogic, which partners with rural and indigenous peoples in Central America and Mexico to help communities trying to achieve sustainability, preserve natural resources, and restore ecosystems. EcoLogic's efforts include replacing slash and burn agriculture with alternative methods such as planting food crops alongside trees and diversifying crops.

Some efforts have met with mixed success. For instance, international lending agencies such as the World Bank have established **debt-for-nature swaps** with peripheral countries that borrow money. In exchange for local investment in conservation measures, the banks agree to forgive a portion of a country's debt. While some conservation agencies and debtor countries consider debt-for-nature swaps to be a useful strategy because they generate money for conservation efforts, the United States, for example, has not reauthorized funding for its debt-for-nature programs since 2014.

COMMERCIAL FARMING

In areas of the world where large, commercial agribusiness corporations dominate agricultural practices, conservation efforts set goals such as reducing air pollution from heavy machinery, encouraging better stewardship of water resources, and seeking to minimize the amount of toxins seeping into groundwater from chemical fertilizers and pesticides. The United States Department of Agriculture Farm Service Agency (FSA) has an array of conservation programs ranging from setting aside land for threatened or endangered wildlife to water management practices and air quality initiatives. Often, these plans use financial incentives for farmers to incorporate more sustainable practices into farm operations.

For example, the Conservation Reserve Program offers annual payments to farmers who are willing to avoid using environmentally sensitive land for agricultural purposes and to plant crops on their fields that improve the quality and health of the environment. The FSA also works with the National Rural Water Association (NRWA) to establish protection plans for local communities to prevent water pollution. These plans, which the communities help create, outline voluntary steps that ranchers and farmers can take to prevent water pollution.

In some parts of the world, small-scale commercial farming is also benefiting from targeted conservation efforts. For example, the Food and Agriculture Organization of the United Nations (FAO) works globally to help countries develop sustainable agricultural practices based on each country's unique opportunities and challenges. To preserve forests and biodiversity in and around the Amazon River, for example, the FAO has collaborated with other organizations to help agricultural communities understand how to manage the Amazon's ecosystem while protecting their livelihoods and respecting their cultural values. Also in the Amazon, some international companies have established fair-trade relationships with indigenous communities that sustainably grow guayusa leaves, which are used to make a traditional tea that is gaining popularity as a healthy drink. The Amazon provides food, water, and livelihood to 33 million people, including approximately 420 indigenous communities.

SUBSISTENCE FARMING

Policy makers in areas of the world where subsistence farming is common are recognizing the critical need to preserve soil fertility and prevent soil erosion while simultaneously increasing yields by intensifying land use. In areas that practice shifting cultivation, for example, farmers can replenish the soil and achieve higher yields by rotating fields systematically to include cover crops—plants that protect and nourish the soil. Other techniques exist to help subsistence farmers improve thin or depleted soils. In some cases, the solutions lie in intensifying inputs (such as fertilizers and pesticides) in land that is already productive while setting aside less fertile land for nature conservation rather than farming.

Many of the same sustainable practices applied to commercial farming can also be used in subsistence agriculture, but it is important to distinguish that while large-scale commercial farmers may be motivated by higher yields leading to increased profits, subsistence farmers are more focused on survival and generally have lesser financial means and access to information. Thus, they may need different types of support in terms of education and resources necessary for implementing new techniques.

In Bangladesh, the agricultural sector—which is largely composed of subsistence farms—has been instrumental in reducing poverty, partly through the assistance of the World Bank and other nongovernmental organizations. Bangladesh's agricultural system faces significant risks. Nearly half of its workforce is directly employed in agriculture, and the country is among the most vulnerable to climate change, with much rural land threatened by flooding, drought, or salinization. The World Bank has helped Bangladeshi farmers adapt to climate challenges by introducing soil management techniques and crops that tolerate drought and high levels of salt. The bank also promotes education initiatives and programs to help increase Bangladeshi farmers' access to markets.

In China, policies affecting pastoral nomads have changed as understanding of the herds' impact on the environment has evolved. At first, Chinese policies toward Tibetan nomads were based on the assumption that the herders were primarily responsible for the degradation of China's grasslands. In recent years, these policies have begun to change as scientists have acknowledged that the grasslands of Tibet actually benefit from moderate and intermittent grazing of herds. Past governmental polices have included the limitation of herd sizes, closing pastures to convert them to grasslands, and forcing nomads to live in settlement homes. These and similar policies still in force ignore the role Tibetan nomads have had in sustaining regional wildlife,

ecosystems, and water resources—a role recognized and honored by the UNESCO World Heritage Committee as well as the International Union for the Conservation of Nature.

Some private organizations have also been active in promoting the health of subsistence farms through resource conservation and other measures. The Bill and Melinda Gates Foundation, for example, founded the Alliance for a Green Revolution in Africa (AGRA) in partnership with the Rockefeller Foundation to address some of the continent's challenges. AGRA has invested funds and supported projects to help African farmers improve their farm yields. The organization also advocates for policies at the national level that will benefit smallholder farmers. Its primary purpose is to capitalize on the production of crops in areas with reliable rainfall, decent soil quality, and a dependable infrastructure. AGRA then works to apply successful solutions elsewhere on the continent. As Africa faces the twin challenges of climate change and rapidly growing populations south of the Sahara, the ability to greatly improve crop yields on subsistence farms may be key to providing sufficient food for future generations.

CRITICAL VIEWING In Burkina Faso, in Africa, AGRA has partnered with a local organization to develop seeds that are designed to produce higher crop yields. This worker is collecting vegetables grown in fields outside the city of Bobo-Dioulasso. ▌ Identify an environmental consequence of introducing new types of seeds to subsistence farms.

NATIONAL GEOGRAPHIC EXPLORER **HINDOU OUMAROU IBRAHIM**

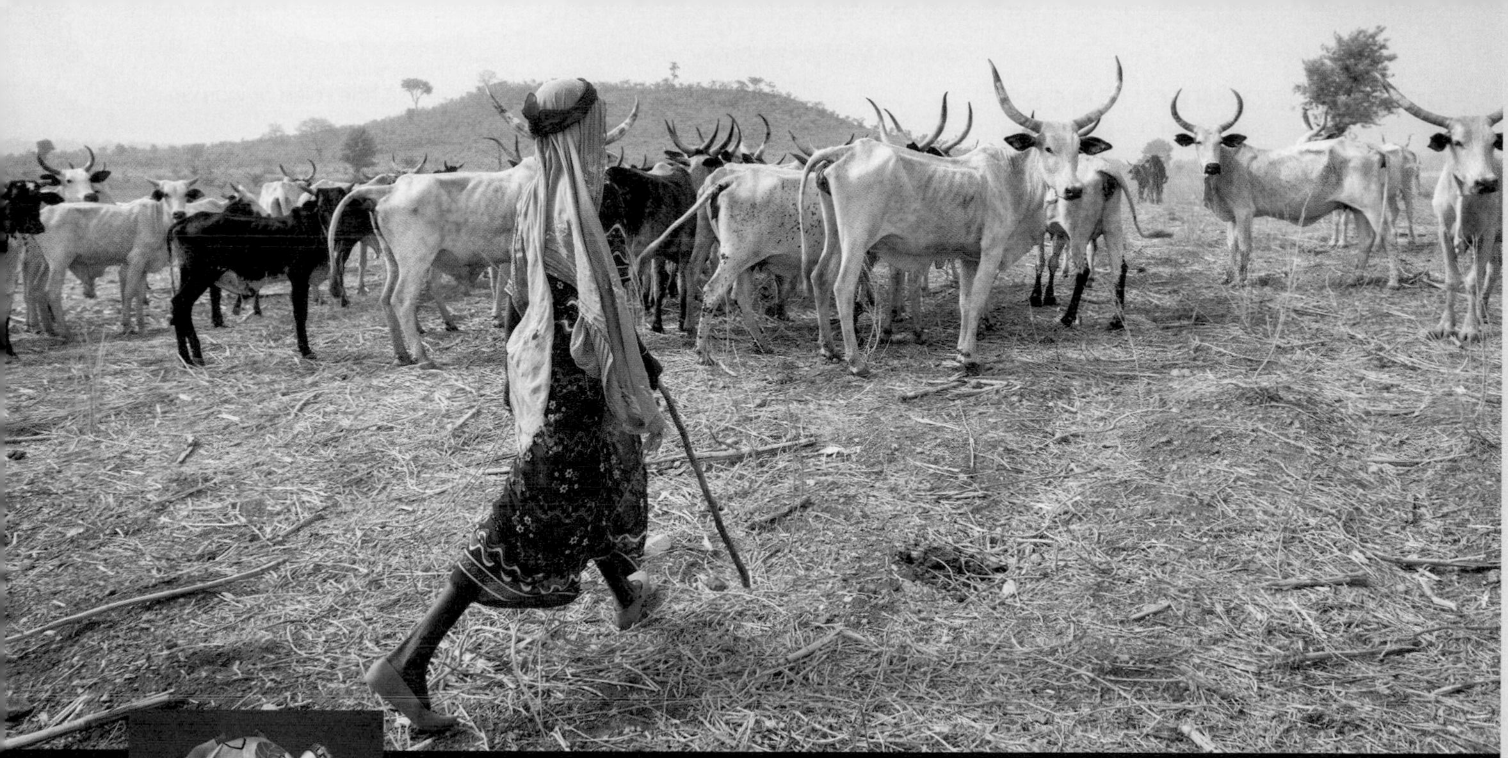

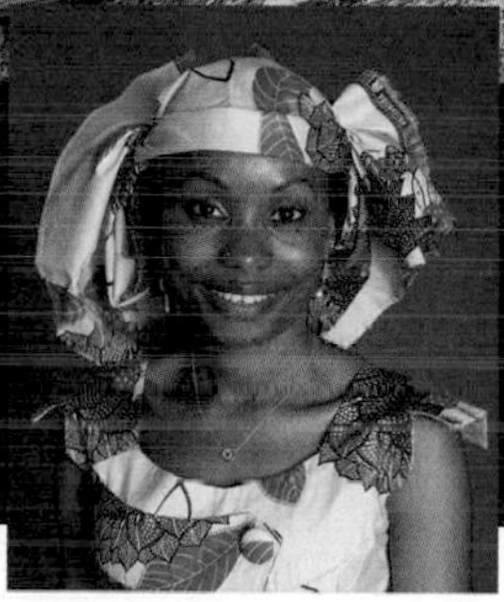

MAPPING INDIGENOUS CLIMATE KNOWLEDGE

In the desert region of Chad, 250,000 nomadic Mbororo depend on herding (shown above) and subsistence farming to survive. Hindou Oumarou Ibrahim has used the Mbororos' intimate knowledge of their land to help advocate for the rights of the environment.

LEARNING OBJECTIVE

IMP-5.A Explain how agricultural practices have environmental and societal consequences.

Hindou Oumarou Ibrahim's quest to give indigenous people a voice in environmental activism began at an early age. When she was a child, she spent part of her year in the Mbororo nomadic community where her parents grew up, and part of the year living in N'Djamena, the capital of Chad, where she went to school.

Chad is a country in the Sahel, a semiarid region of Africa that extends from Senegal eastward to Sudan. Like the rest of the world, the Sahel is experiencing the effects of climate change.

In collaboration with local elders, herders, UNESCO, the government of Chad, and other organizations, Ibrahim has conducted a 3D mapping project designed to help indigenous communities adapt to climate and weather changes. 3D maps profile objects in three dimensions to show how they appear in the real world. Ibrahim's 3D maps of Chad's desert region incorporate indigenous knowledge about the land and its natural resources. They document how climate change affects the landscape, seasons, weather, and flora and fauna, and they are continually updated.

When asked how the data gathered in 3D mapping helped empower her community while at the same time promoting environmental protection, Ibrahim explained that the mapping helps guide the community in making decisions about when to move to a new location, what is the best time to collect certain food, and which species are dwindling and in need of protection. It also gives the Mbororo community tools to make informed decisions about participating in projects that will affect their natural resources.

GEOGRAPHIC THINKING

Describe some possible environmental consequences of the Mbororo community's use of Ibrahim's 3D maps.

SOCIETAL CONSEQUENCES

LEARNING OBJECTIVE

IMP-5.A Explain how agricultural practices have environmental and societal consequences.

Societal consequences of agricultural practices are broad and varied, affecting diets, the roles of women in farming, the economic purpose of both farmers and consumers, and the lives of communities.

Consumers in many countries have altered their diet and lifestyle choices in reaction to recent innovations in agriculture. These individuals are concerned about the potential environmental harm of crops that require large amounts of inputs such as fertilizers and pesticides. Some people, particularly in Europe, also worry that crops consisting of genetically modified organisms (GMOs) could carry as-yet-undiscovered health risks.

These consumers are purchasing organically grown foods they believe are better for the environment and for their own bodies. Organic farming centers around an agricultural system that refrains from using artificial chemical inputs, and it has received much attention from movements toward sustainable food production. You will learn more about organic farming and other food choice movements later in the chapter.

In many countries, however, longstanding agricultural practices and traditions have profoundly influenced both diets and social customs, and consumers strongly resist change. For example, beef production has been part of Argentina's agricultural history and food traditions since the 16th century. Argentina has long ranked as a country with one of the highest levels of beef consumption in the world; generations have grown up on farms and ranches and have participated in barbecues called "grills."

In the face of an economic recession in 2019, Argentines cut back on their weekly beef consumption, but because this food choice is deeply rooted in tradition and social gatherings, beef sales persisted. The same holds true even as new information emerges about possible links between the consumption of red meat and the risk of certain types of cancer and concerns about agrochemicals and antibiotics potentially impacting the safety of beef. Argentines consider the risk but continue to make beef a part of their regular diets because it is central to their culture.

The roles of women in farming vary tremendously across regions and agriculture types. Women who are pastoral nomads, for example, share responsibility for the care of animals with men, but they are more likely to be in charge of dairy animals or animals such as poultry that are kept near the home. In aquaculture, women work both as entrepreneurs and as laborers. In some parts of Southeast Asia, women form the majority of the aquaculture workforce. In most countries, women in agriculture face obstacles due to gender discrimination. With changes in both agricultural practices and available opportunities, the roles of women in many types of farming are changing rapidly.

Since the time of the Industrial Revolution, the changing economic purpose of many farms has also had societal consequences. Chapter 13 described agribusiness and the shift from small, family-owned farms to larger corporate operations in the United States and elsewhere—principally in core countries. In the United States, these changes have meant a loss of small and midsize farms, which were once the backbone of American agriculture. At present, large-scale commercial farming dominates most American farmland, and farm families often sell their land to agribusiness corporations when they encounter financial struggles. It has been noted that the loss of small farms can harm the social and economic fabric of rural communities. Family farms tend to employ more workers per acre of land, and when these farms go out of business or are sold to large commercial firms, rural towns lose population. As a result, nonfarm businesses in these communities are often forced to close. Critics of agribusiness point to both the financial consequences and the loss of community in rural towns when small and midsize farms close down.

The rise of monocropping has also had societal consequences in the United States. As you learned, monocropping can be very profitable because it is an efficient way to grow corn, soybeans, and other crops. At the same time, however, it poses risks to the livelihoods of both farmers and consumers. The lack of diversity in crops can cause prices to be turbulent, because any single disrupter such as disease or natural disaster can have a major impact on the entire system. In the face of a drought, for example, the prices of corn and all the products made from corn are driven up due to shortages.

In some cases, it is consumers who make their choices with an economic purpose. These choices are related to the socially conscious diet changes mentioned earlier, and they often have benefits for small and midsize farmers. Consumers in core countries concerned about avoiding GMOs, eating organic, or supporting small, local farms may choose to shop at farmers markets or eat at restaurants that buy local organic produce. These diet choices encourage small farmers to consider switching to organic production. Consumers of fair-trade products, which you also read about in Chapter 13, hope to benefit farmers and workers in peripheral countries through their purchasing choices.

GEOGRAPHIC THINKING

3. Identify possible negative land cover changes associated with terrace farming.

4. Explain factors that may cause a country to have strict sustainability policies. Give examples.

5. Describe a societal consequence resulting from changes in farm ownership structures.

BUILDING AFRICA'S GREAT GREEN WALL

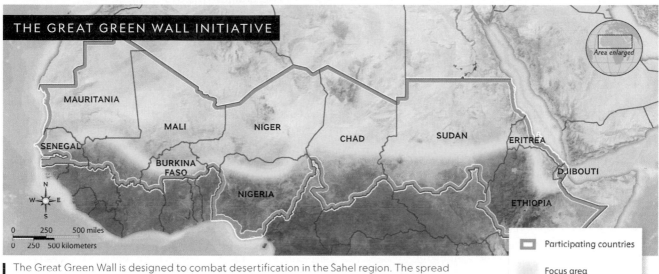

THE GREAT GREEN WALL INITIATIVE

MAURITANIA

MALI

NIGER

CHAD

SUDAN

ERITREA

SENEGAL

DJIBOUTI

BURKINA
FASO

NIGERIA

ETHIOPIA

Area enlarged

0   250   500 miles
0   250   500 kilometers

Participating countries

Focus area

The Great Green Wall is designed to combat desertification in the Sahel region. The spread of desert lands puts populations at risk of starvation, thirst, respiratory disease caused by dusty air, and diseases stemming from a lack of clean water.

THE ISSUE Desertification due to overgrazing and other causes combined with climate change means the Sahara is encroaching deeper into the farmlands of sub-Saharan Africa.

LEARNING OBJECTIVE
IMP-5.A Explain how agricultural practices have environmental and societal consequences.

BY THE NUMBERS

15% of the wall completed as of 2020

4,350 MILES of tree belt when the Great Green Wall is completed

OVER 70 MILLION acres of land restored by 2018

Sources: greatgreenwall.org, Smithsonian.org, Landscape News

WORLDWIDE, DESERTIFICATION IS ACCELERATING.

According to the European Commission's Joint Research Centre, every year an area half the size of the European Union is degraded globally, and Africa is particularly affected. In Africa's Sahel region, population growth has led to increases in wood harvesting, illegal farming, and land clearing for housing, all of which help drive desertification. Droughts exacerbated by climate change also play a major role.

To restore degraded land, national and regional leaders in Africa launched the Great Green Wall initiative in 2007. The goal was to plant a barrier of trees across Africa along the edge of the Sahara to prevent creeping desertification. Indigenous land-use techniques have been at the core of the initiative. For example, farmers in Burkina Faso use grids of deep planting pits that help retain water during dry periods, while in Niger, farmers take steps to protect trees that grow up naturally among their fields. As a result, the Great Green Wall has been described as a mosaic of land practices that will ultimately act in a similar way to a physical wall.

The project has many facets in addition to trees and is successfully addressing environmental and societal issues at both local and global levels. Planting the forest may create millions of jobs, which will help fight poverty. The improved soil quality produces a higher crop yield and directly impacts communities' food security. In addition to planting and regeneration, the Green Wall initiative incorporates the establishment of sustainable agricultural and energy practices, climate change reduction and adaptation, and the preservation of biodiversity.

Scientists were skeptical at first, but the success of the Great Green Wall continues to inspire and compel change across the continent. Smallholder farmers are now viewed as part of the solution to land degradation, simple and affordable interventions have proven that change is possible, and food security is increasing. As the wall and sustainability efforts continue to progress, each patch of trees connects to the next, forming a green chain and extending the reach of sustainability. ∎

GEOGRAPHIC THINKING

Explain why the Great Green Wall initiative extends beyond planting trees.

14.2 CHALLENGES OF CONTEMPORARY AGRICULTURE

Contemporary agriculture and food production practices are constantly changing in response to new technologies, consumers' food choices, and the challenges of feeding growing populations. But much debate surrounds farming innovations that may have negative or unknown consequences for human health and the environment.

DEBATES OVER INNOVATIONS

LEARNING OBJECTIVES
IMP-5.A Explain how agricultural practices have environmental and societal consequences.

IMP-5.B Explain challenges and debates related to the changing nature of contemporary agriculture and food-production practices.

Biotechnology, genetically modified organisms, and aquaculture are among the techniques at the forefront of efforts to expand food production. These innovations have benefits that include better quality and higher production. At the same time, they remain at the center of political and scientific controversy, largely due to their unknown future consequences to both humans and the environment.

One key concern is sustainability. Sustainable agriculture encompasses environmental, economic, and social practices designed for the long term. Farmers must manage the environment in a way that minimizes pollution of the air, soil, and water, in order to ensure continued productivity well into the future. At the same time, agriculture must also

be economically viable—farmers need to make a profit to stay in business. A healthy farm economy, in turn, can help maintain a good quality of life for farmers, farm families, and farming communities, as well as supporting fair and reliable incomes and healthy working conditions for farm laborers. Supporters of recent innovations in agriculture believe they represent progress toward sustainability, while critics fear that some of the latest technologies and practices actually create less sustainable systems. As the debate continues, it's clear that a balance needs to be reached between environmentally sustainable farming and the development of agricultural innovations to help feed a global population that will likely exceed ten billion people by the end of the century.

BIOTECHNOLOGY AND GMOS As you have read, a genetically modified organism (GMO) is a living organism with a genetic code that has been manipulated to produce certain desirable qualities. The use of genetic modification (GM) in agriculture is not a new concept: farmers have been improving plants and animals by selecting and breeding optimal characteristics for thousands of years. High-yield

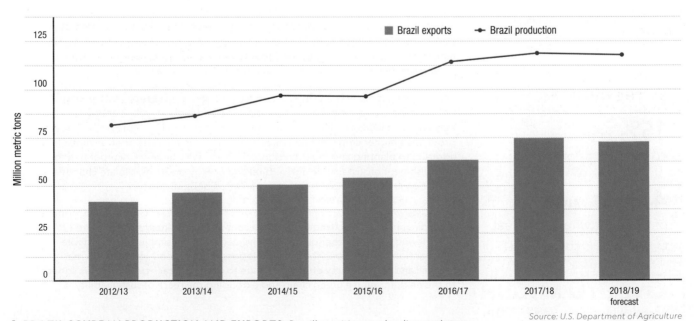

Source: U.S. Department of Agriculture

BRAZIL SOYBEAN PRODUCTION AND EXPORTS Brazil's position as a leading soybean producer and exporter demonstrates how it has benefited from recent technological advances: 97 percent of its soybeans are cultivated using biotechnology.

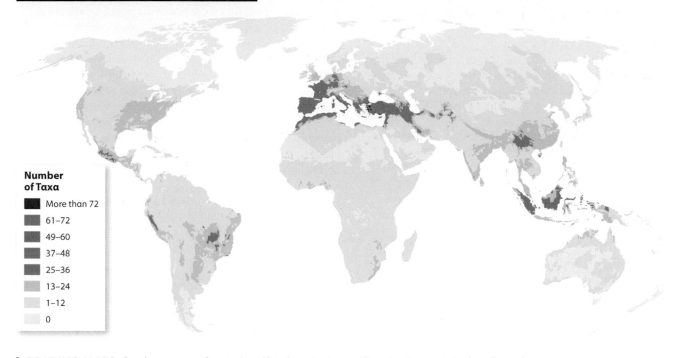

Number of Taxa

- More than 72
- 61–72
- 49–60
- 37–48
- 25–36
- 13–24
- 1–12
- 0

READING MAPS One key aspect of agricultural biodiversity is crop diversity. A recent study collected data on 81 important crops and about 1,100 species of their wild relatives. The map shows how many taxa—which are groups of similar organisms, in this case, the crops' relatives—were found in each region.
▌ Identify the richest global areas of crop diversity.

seeds introduced during the Green Revolution in the mid-20th century, for example, were the result of this type of breeding. **Biotechnology** is the science of altering living organisms, often through genetic manipulation, to create new products for specific purposes, such as crops that resist certain pests. Genetic modification is a broader category that includes all types of genetic manipulation of foods. Modern biotechnology supports genetic engineering (GE), a type of GM in which scientists transfer specific genes from one organism to another.

Supporters argue that the unfolding revolution in biotechnology will be needed to solve world hunger problems. Biotechnology can result in improvements such as increased crop yields; resistance to drought, disease, and pests; and improved nutritional values. But these practices raise the question: How much modification is too much?

Brazil's agricultural sector can be considered one example of a biotechnology success story. With soybeans, rice, and corn leading its list of important crops, Brazil benefited from the Green Revolution of the mid-20th century and more recently has been at the forefront of biotechnology applications. Brazil is a world agricultural leader. Since 1961, its grain production has increased by 574 percent, while its population has increased 175 percent. More significantly, high-yield seeds have allowed Brazil to nearly triple its grain production since the early 1980s even as the amount of land under cultivation has remained largely unchanged. Brazil has benefited economically as it has grown to become one

of the world's largest food exporters. The country is now the second largest producer of biotech crops.

One potential global benefit of genetic engineering is a reduction in the cost of food production, which could lead to an increased supply of food—making food more affordable at worldwide, national, regional, and local scales. One 2010 study by University of Iowa scientists concluded that without biotechnology, the prices of corn, soybeans, and canola (a type of seed grown for cooking oil) would all be higher, as would the prices of many products made from these crops.

On the other hand, those who question the advantages of biotechnology feel that its environmental impacts have not been thoroughly investigated. Additionally, the long-term consequences of genetic alteration are still unknown. Foods modified through GE have been banned in much of Europe because their safety has not been proven, and there are concerns about their effects on the species that consume them, including humans.

Another debate on contemporary agriculture centers around biodiversity, with experts disagreeing over whether biotechnology decreases or increases agriculture's impact on the diversity of species. The term **agricultural biodiversity** describes the variety and variability of plants, animals, and microorganisms that are used directly or indirectly for food and agriculture. Agricultural biodiversity is integral to environmentally sustainable agriculture. It plays an important role in enabling agriculture to achieve productivity gains, improve sustainability, and manage changing conditions, such as climate change. Critics claim that genetic engineering poses a threat to agricultural biodiversity. For example, a common type of genetic engineering is the insertion of bacterial genes into a crop. The bacteria functions like an insecticide: when insects consume the crop, they are infected by the bacteria and die. A new plant is introduced into the field ecosystem, but a species of insect is eliminated from that space.

Critics also point out that innovations intended to minimize chemical inputs may actually lead to intensified uses of pesticides, herbicides, and fertilizers. For instance, one common type of genetic engineering involves inserting herbicide-resistant genes into crops. When herbicides are sprayed on these crops, the weeds die, but the crops survive because of the resistant genes. Pests that are constantly exposed to these inputs can develop their own genetic resistance, meaning either the genetically modified crops eventually become obsolete, or more chemicals are needed to eliminate the pests. Another risk is that genetically modified crops may transfer genetic material into unmodified plants. An herbicide-resistant crop may transfer traits to a weed that makes it herbicide-resistant also, creating a new problem that again requires more herbicides and pesticides to treat. Genetically modified organisms that escape the fields where they are planted may also threaten biodiversity in the wider ecosystem by becoming invasive and crowding out wild species.

Soil fertility, too, can be a concern. In general, soil fertility has declined with the intensification of food production, which means that land's productivity is lessened or threatened. This leads to farmers applying more synthetic fertilizers to keep up with the growing demand for key food crops. Between 30 and 50 percent of agricultural crops are grown with the use of fertilizers, and more than 50 percent of people consume crops that are grown using synthetic fertilizers containing chemicals and minerals such as nitrogen, sulfur, and magnesium—all of which impact the ecosystem. Synthetic fertilizers build up in the soil, decreasing the soil's fertility and affecting surrounding organisms and their natural life cycles. Rain and sewage can carry fertilizers into bodies of water, which can create a toxic environment by increasing the growth of algae and decreasing oxygen levels. As you have learned, marine animals struggle or die in these damaged environments.

Supporters and opponents also disagree on the use of GE crops to conserve water. Proponents of GE crops argue that they conserve water because herbicide-tolerant biotech crops don't require tilling, or breaking up the soil, which can lessen its moisture content. Such crops have been successful in Brazil for more than two decades. Another argument is that biotech seeds are drought tolerant and water efficient, and produce higher yields. Such seeds are being tested in several countries in sub-Saharan Africa, including Kenya and Mozambique, where drought is a concern.

Arguments against using biotech crops to solve water usage problems are similar to those raised in the case of herbicide-resistant crops: concerns about possible unintended biological effects on local plant communities and the danger of plant species expandng into areas where they are not wanted. Potential risks include the development of undesirable traits in the GE plants, such as invasiveness or weed-like attributes. Some scientists also argue that plants that are modified to more efficiently extract water still require the same amount of water to grow. Others believe there have not been enough comprehensive studies of biotech crops that include detailed attention to their effects on plants and animals in nearby ecosystems.

Economically, the monetary costs of using new agricultural technologies result in many farmers taking on tremendous debt loads to purchase fertilizers, high-yield seed varieties, and machinery. If crop prices fall on global markets, this debt can be crippling. Overall, biotechnology is expensive, and its use is often limited to agribusinesses that can afford to invest in it. At the same time, governmental policies, especially in peripheral countries, are aimed at keeping food prices low and affordable. This reduces incentives for commercial farmers to produce food, and food crops such as corn or millet are often replaced with cash crops such as cotton or tobacco.

AQUACULTURE Aquaculture is another innovative branch of agriculture that has demonstrated advantages on several fronts. This type of fish farming is less space- and care-intensive than other types of agriculture and represents one of the fastest growing food production sectors in the world. Aquaculture, an alternative to natural fisheries, can provide enormous and consistent amounts of fish and seafood—supplementing wild harvests and increasing the global food supply. Artificially raised salmon and oyster stocks have helped meet current seafood demands, and aquaculture has provided thousands of jobs. Outside of food production, algae fuel is being developed that could potentially replace fossil fuels such as gasoline and reduce energy costs.

Aside from these economic benefits, aquaculture offers environmental advantages as well. For example, the farming of shellfish can improve water quality because the shellfish filter water as part of their feeding process. At the same time, shellfish farms decrease pressure on wild stocks of the same species.

Aquaculture, however, is not without its disadvantages. Concerns include water pollution from chemicals used in fish farming and excess nutrients such as fish waste. Aquaculture farmers use antibiotics to prevent disease among farmed fish, and these antibiotics can have a negative impact on the ecosystem. Another possible consequence involves the compromise of native gene pools if farmed fish and native fish interbreed. Farmers of wild fisheries also argue that aquaculture amplifies and transfers disease and parasites to wild fish populations.

These field workers in China's Hebei Province are using drones for farm work. Drones have numerous applications for precision agriculture, including gathering detailed data about fields.

PRECISION AGRICULTURE

LEARNING OBJECTIVES

IMP-5.A Explain how agricultural practices have environmental and societal consequences.

IMP-5.B Explain challenges and debates related to the changing nature of contemporary agriculture and food-production practices.

Precision agriculture—also known as precision ag or precision farming—is part of the movement that some see as a fourth agricultural revolution. It uses a variety of cutting-edge technologies to apply inputs such as water and fertilizer with pinpoint accuracy to specific parts of fields in order to maximize crop yields, reduce waste, and preserve the environment.

By using drones or other remote sensing technologies to acquire data, farmers can employ GIS software to map their fields and develop a micro-level analysis of each field's physical characteristics. This helps them target their watering, fertilizing, and herbicide and pesticide application strategies. Remote sensing devices can perform a multitude of tasks such as managing irrigation, detecting disease early enough for a grower to intervene, and estimating crop yields. These computer-based applications result in reduced expenses and higher yields. They also support environmentally friendly improvements such as water conservation and reductions in the amount of fertilizer applied to a field. Using precision agriculture can reap similar benefits for both the small-scale vegetable farmer and the commercial grain farmer managing multiple fields and huge acreages.

GPS guidance, robotics, and information technology are the tools of precision agriculture. Million-dollar combines—farm machines that both harvest and process crops—have control stations that tractor drivers use to set coordinates and avoid costly overlaps on fields.

By deploying these tools, today's farmers are acting as scientists, geographers, and marketing specialists in addition to food producers. Most farmers are not software engineers, however, and precision farming does pose technological as well as financial challenges. Software systems can have poor user interfaces or produce information that is hard for farmers to interpret. Systems can also overproduce data, forcing farmers to sort through intimidating quantities of information to make decisions. Farmers may be compelled to hire consulting firms to take the data and help them turn it into a plan of action. Some precision agriculture methods are affordable for large agribusiness operations but too costly for family farmers, and other technologies involving seed and fertilizers have experienced slow adoption rates due to complexities such as weather variables. Nevertheless, precision agriculture has opened new possibilities for farmers to maximize yields while minimizing costs and environmental impact. ▮

GEOGRAPHIC THINKING

Describe the benefits and drawbacks presented by precision agriculture to both large and small farmers.

FOOD CHOICES

LEARNING OBJECTIVE

IMP-5.B Explain challenges and debates related to the changing nature of contemporary agriculture and food-production practices.

As you have learned, food preferences and dietary shifts are important motivators of changes in contemporary agriculture and food-production practices. Individuals' food choices influence general patterns of consumption. In turn, food producers choose crops and methods to meet consumer demands. The goals of food choice movements include eating healthier foods, encouraging sustainable farming practices, and supporting independent farmers. Participants in food choice movements are enthusiastic about their benefits, but debate exists over whether they are effective in bringing about large-scale changes.

LOCAL FOOD MOVEMENTS In the United States, some consumers are employing new and different ways to acquire fresh foods for their tables. Urban farming, for example, converts vacant lots, rooftops, or abandoned buildings into spaces to grow produce. In many inner-city areas of the United States, communities are banding together to collectively work these small plots as a way to provide fresh fruits and vegetables in areas where such foods are scarce.

Borough Market in London has been in existence since the year 1014. Then, as now, it sold local vegetables and fruits; today it is a bustling marketplace of foods from all over the world. In the early 1990s, Borough Market became a destination for lovers of artisanal, or handmade, foods. Since then, demand for specialty foods has expanded the international market for fair trade and value-added crops.

Consumers who participate in Community Supported Agriculture (CSA) purchase shares in the output of a local farm. During the growing season, they receive a weekly box or bushel of freshly harvested produce from the farm. In return, farmers who operate CSAs receive a guaranteed income from the sale of shares. In addition to providing fresh produce, urban farms and CSAs strengthen the relationships between those who grow the food and those who eat it, and they allow the public to be more aware of where their food comes from. However, the impact of these food choice movements is limited—not all CSAs are profitable, and urban farms typically do not reach large populations.

Similar to CSAs, local food movements aim to connect food producers and food consumers in the same geographic region. Both farmers markets and farm-to-table restaurants, for example, provide connections between producers and consumers. Shoppers choose to buy locally to support the local economy, to have access to fresh food, and to know where the food on their table is coming from.

ORGANIC FARMING As you've learned, organic farming has seen a rise in popularity in some areas, in part as a response to concerns about chemical inputs and GMOs. Organic farming practices are more expensive than traditional farming, but wealthier consumers in the United States and elsewhere have shown they are willing to pay higher prices for organic food. Instead of using chemicals or genetic engineering, organic farmers use natural fertilizers such as plant-based products or animal manure to promote long-term soil health and prevent harmful runoff and water contamination. They also use crop rotation to manage weeds, insects, and diseases, and they focus on maintaining biodiversity within their agricultural systems and the surrounding environment. Organic farmers attempt to reduce or eliminate external agricultural inputs and strive for sustainability. Europe has the largest percentage of land given over to organic practices, and land percentages dedicated to organic farming will continue to grow in food-secure, developed countries in North America and Europe, where there is a demonstrated demand for organic food.

Not everyone agrees that avoiding GMOs by buying organic or through other means is a healthier option. Many scientists insist that genetically modified foods pose no danger to consumers and are essentially the same as non-GMO foods in terms of nutrition and health benefits. Whether or not organic foods are more healthful, their higher price means that the demand for them will likely remain among a smaller but relatively influential share of consumers.

FAIR TRADE AND VALUE-ADDED CROPS
Another type of production driven by consumer choice is fair trade, described in Chapter 13. In the interest of supporting agricultural sustainability and a better quality of life for growers, many consumers—especially Americans in the millennial generation—are willing to switch brands and pay more money.

Food choice often extends to value-added specialty crops—organic or other specialty crops that are transformed from their original state to a more valuable state, such as converting milk into cheese and yogurt. Coffee is another popular value-added crop. You have read about the global coffee supply chain, at the end of which the beans are roasted and converted into ground coffee for home consumption or brewed coffee sold in cafes and restaurants. Other high-value crops in this category include tea and chocolate.

Consumer demand for value-added products can be driven by the desire to eat healthy, nutritious food, the need for convenience, or both. For example, many consumers buy yogurt because they enjoy the taste and believe it has health benefits. These same consumers would not consider taking the time and trouble to make yogurt at home, even if they found that making their own yogurt in bulk quantities might cost less.

As food producers have found ways to become more productive and discovered technological advances that help them efficiently produce consumer-specific products, the possibilities of value-added agriculture have increased, each with pros and cons. Being able to meet specific consumer demands can lead to producers capturing a larger share of the food dollar, but that comes at a cost. While consumer demand may entice farmers into producing value-added crops, farmers must also consider the capital required as well as the necessary production and business skills that may be different from those required to produce traditional crops. They have to become adept at marketing to the end user in areas such as packaging and variety and be willing to invest in innovation and research while continuously working to minimize costs.

DIETARY SHIFTS Broader global trends in diets may exert the strongest influence on agriculture related to food choice. The global demand for all meats is growing, for example, and so the need for grains to feed the livestock is expanding. According to the UN, meat production in 2017 was almost five times higher than in the early 1960s. In Southeast Asia, countries such as the Philippines and Malaysia have experienced increases in income and urbanization that have resulted in an increased demand for diversified diets focused on higher levels of meat and dairy consumption. According to the World Health Organization (WHO), there is a direct link between the level of income and the consumption of animal protein.

The influence of urbanization on meat consumption is obvious in rapidly growing countries like China and Brazil, both of which have experienced large rises in meat consumption in recent decades. In the United States, meanwhile, the total per capita consumption of meat has grown over a period of five decades, but the consumption of beef has declined by approximately one-third, while chicken consumption has doubled. These data points matter because different types of meat production have different costs in terms of the land needed to grow feed crops. It takes more feed to produce beef than chicken or pork. Precise statistics for beef are problematic, however, because the entire animal is not used for food. That said, about five pounds of feed produces one pound of beef. In contrast, one pound of pork takes less than four pounds of feed, and one pound of chicken takes less than three pounds of feed. These numbers are reflected in the amount of farmland dedicated to growing grains for animals instead of humans.

A growing international appetite for processed food products also impacts growers' choices of crops. For example, around five percent of the U.S. corn harvest is used to produce sweeteners including high-fructose corn syrup, which is used to sweeten soft drinks, candy, salad dressings, and yogurt. The demand for foods that are easy and quick to use, packaged well, nutritious, and offer a variety of choices is often driven by busy lifestyles and aging populations. In India and other emerging countries, an increased number of women in the workforce combined with a rise in disposable income has spurred the demand for packaged foods among middle-income families.

AGRICULTURE AND DIET

LEARNING OBJECTIVE
IMP-5.A Explain how agricultural practices have environmental and societal consequences.

Food choices affect agriculture, but the reverse is also true. Contemporary agricultural practices have transformed diets around the world, with agricultural improvements resulting in the possibility of consumers having access to more and varied foods. Chapter 12 described the diffusion of foods, a process that began even before the Columbian Exchange and continues at a rapid pace today, thanks to globalization and modern technologies. You've also learned about global supply chains. Crops such as corn and sweet potatoes, which are indigenous to the Americas, can be exported across the globe thanks to expanded transportation methods and advanced storage systems. Refrigerated transport has allowed farmers to ship perishable food over long distances, overcoming the limitations of what can be grown in the local climate and terrain. As a result, shoppers in the United States can choose from a year-round variety of fresh produce that was unthinkable for earlier generations. For example, Chile, located in the Southern Hemisphere, has a growing season that is the opposite of that of the United States. With refrigerated transportation, Chile can provide American consumers with fresh fruit throughout the winter. Consumers in other core countries benefit equally from global food supply chains across climate regions.

Improvements in aquaculture, meanwhile, have allowed sushi to remain an international favorite, and the UN reported that in 2019 aquaculture produced almost as much fish as wild fisheries. Farmed fish require around 1.1 pounds of feed to produce one pound of body mass.

CRITICAL VIEWING Mexico exports more than 800,000 tons of avocados to the United States every year. In recent years, Mexico has also exported avocados to China, where few avocados are grown locally. ▌How has Mexico's exporting of avocados affected society in the United States and Mexico?

Trade policies, too, may help change diets and individual tastes. In one instance, the North American Free Trade Agreement (NAFTA) of 1994 resulted in a boom of avocado exports from Mexico to the United States. Mexico has produced avocados for thousands of years but exported very few—a situation that changed drastically with the enactment of NAFTA. Now Mexico produces approximately one-third of all avocados in the world, and avocados are the United States's most valuable fruit import, in addition to being a regular feature of many Americans' diets. In 2018, NAFTA was replaced by a revised trade agreement, the United States-Mexico-Canada agreement (USMCA), which provides similar trade protections. Together, trade policies, technology, and contemporary agriculture have boosted the process of diffusion to provide people around the world with a diverse, globalized diet.

GEOGRAPHIC THINKING

1. Describe some environmental limitations of biotechnology.

2. Explain how the concept of biodiversity helps geographers analyze the impacts of modern-day farming practices.

3. Identify and describe factors that could cause more farmers to embrace agricultural innovations.

4. Compare the commercial approach to agriculture with the sustainable approach.

14.3 FEEDING THE WORLD

Food production is just the first step in providing for a hungry world. Establishing reliable access to nutritious food for all people means facing challenges such as uneven distribution systems, severe weather, and the loss of farmland to expanding urban areas.

FOOD INSECURITY

LEARNING OBJECTIVE
IMP-5.B Explain challenges and debates related to the changing nature of contemporary agriculture and food-production practices.

Food security is reliable access to safe, nutritious food that can support a healthy and active lifestyle. The opposing concept, **food insecurity**, is the disruption of a household's food intake or eating patterns because of poor access to food. According to the United States Department of Agriculture (USDA), the most commonly reported cause of food insecurity is lack of money or other resources.

The Food and Agriculture Organization of the United Nations (FAO) reports that in 2018, more than 700 million people suffered from severe food insecurity, and 1.3 billion people experienced moderate food insecurity, for a combined total that represents about 26 percent of the world's population. In the United States, food insecurity affects 40 million people. The FAO further states that more than 820 million people do not have access to enough food to lead a healthy, active life even though the planet produces enough to feed everyone. If the world can grow enough food now, why does evidence show that so many continue to suffer from hunger? Recall what National Geographic Explorer Jerry Glover said at the beginning of this unit: "A good global food supply does not solve regional problems."

GLOBAL FOOD INSECURITY Scientists and researchers have found that much food insecurity is the result of distribution issues and economic decisions about what to do with the crops that are produced. According to a 2019 study by the FAO, only 55 percent of the world's overall crop calories (corn and other grains) feed people, with approximately 36 percent going to livestock and about 9 percent being used to make biofuels such as ethanol and other industrial products. Decreasing the amount of food crops used to feed livestock and make biofuels could in turn help decrease food insecurity. Growing meat more efficiently and shifting to diets that are less meat-intensive could also release significant amounts of food crops—large percentages of which are currently feeding livestock—for human consumption. A portion of the crop calories consumed by livestock do reach humans in the form of meat, dairy, and eggs, but the caloric value of these products is a fraction of the original value of what is fed to the animals.

Another serious ongoing threat to Earth's ability to continue producing sufficient food is adverse weather—including severe storms, drought, and extreme temperatures—caused or intensified by climate change. More than 80 percent of food-insecure people in the world live in areas susceptible to such extreme weather events, but even relatively food-secure regions are vulnerable to weather-related shocks. In France in 2019, severe storms did so much damage to the food-growing region known as the "orchard of France" that the government declared a state of emergency. Some farmers lost 80 to 100 percent of their crops. At the same time, the Caribbean is in the midst of a decades-long drying trend punctuated by several multi-year droughts, including one so severe in 2015 that half of Haiti's crops were lost and millions of people in the region experienced food shortages. Brazil, Ethiopia, and Indonesia have experienced extreme maximum temperatures for periods of three or more years, another result of climate change that may stress crops.

On the national level, instability and chronic poverty also contribute to food insecurity. The Democratic Republic of the Congo (DRC), for example, is ranked as one of the least food-secure countries in the world on the Global Food Security Index. Severe food insecurity in the DRC nearly doubled between 2017 and 2018. Most of the country's families are subsistence farmers, and they produce about 42 percent of the food they consume. However, due to years of unstable and corrupt governments and outright civil war in parts of the country, these farmers are vulnerable to displacement.

Loss of agricultural land to growing urban areas is another threat to global food production. Beginning in the 20th century, **suburbanization**, the shifting of population from cities into surrounding suburbs, has accelerated as increasing numbers of city dwellers seek advantages such as cheaper housing, more space, and lower crime rates. At the same time, cities in many parts of the world are growing rapidly. One 2016 study estimated that globally, urban areas will triple in size by 2030, and 60 percent of the planet's farmlands are located near cities. Expanding cities and suburbs can encroach on productive farmlands.

The impact of urban growth on agriculture has been highly debated at national and local levels. Some argue it has had a negative effect, claiming the reduction in the amount of land available for food production contributes to the declining ratio of food producers to food consumers. Growing urban populations demand more agricultural

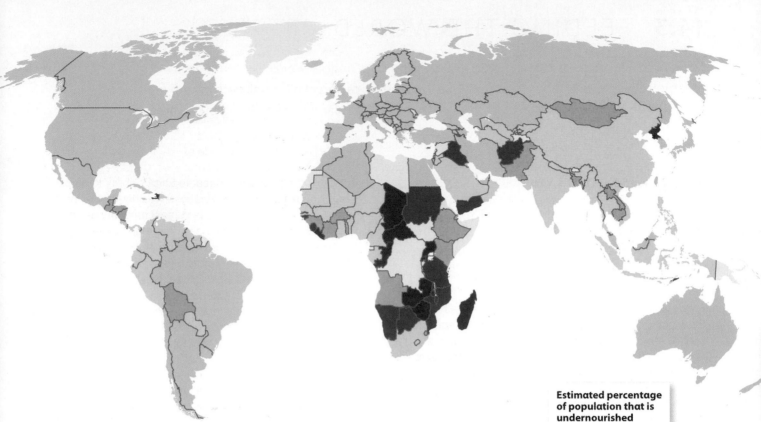

WORLD HUNGER, 2015–2017

READING MAPS An organization called the World Food Programme (WFP) creates a world hunger map every year. The map classifies every country in the world based on its level of undernourishment, which is defined as "the condition in which an individual's habitual food consumption is insufficient to provide the amount of dietary energy required to maintain a normal, active, healthy life." ■ Identify the world regions that are suffering the greatest rates of undernourishment.

Estimated percentage of population that is undernourished

- 35% or more
- 25%–34.9%
- 15%–24.9%
- 5%–14.9%
- Less than 5%
- Missing or insufficient data

11%

OF THE WORLD POPULATION DOES NOT HAVE ENOUGH TO EAT

821

MILLION PEOPLE

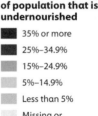

1 IN 4 CHILDREN SUFFER FROM STUNTING

THAT MEANS 150 MILLION CHILDREN UNDER 5 ARE PHYSICALLY TOO SMALL FOR THEIR AGE DUE TO UNDERNOURISHMENT.

GLOBAL HUNGER and malnutrition are the number one risks to health—greater than AIDS, malaria, and tuberculosis combined.

ONE IN THREE women of childbearing age suffer from anemia (low red blood cell count or insufficient hemoglobin) as a result of poor diets.

Among the key drivers of world hunger are **CLIMATE EXTREMES** and **POVERTY**.

Source: World Food Programme

products, and as cropland is replaced by housing and other urban developments, the question of whether local farming communities can sustain demand and remain profitable becomes more compelling. Opposing viewpoints argue that because of food globalization and commercialization, urban growth has little impact on the ability of agriculture to meet overall food demands in cities and elsewhere.

FOOD ISSUES IN THE UNITED STATES Like other countries, the United States is losing farmland to urban development. As suburbs have grown up around cities in the United States, land that was once cultivated by small-scale family farms has been bought by developers to build suburban neighborhoods. According to the USDA, between 1980 and 2018, the amount of land being farmed or grazed was reduced by 13 percent.

In many low-income areas of the United States—urban, rural, and suburban alike—food insecurity is an ongoing concern. In 2017, 12.3 percent of households in the country suffered from food insecurity, and nearly 13 million children were food insecure. Single women with children represent almost one-third of Americans reporting food insecurity.

Although poverty in the United States is strongly linked to food insecurity, the two problems are not always perfectly connected. Not all people living in poverty experience food insecurity, and not all people living above the poverty line are exempt from it. The cost of living compared to wages earned and other factors, such as medical expenses, can affect food security. Families with children and low wages may not have adequate incomes to purchase enough food, but their incomes may be high enough to disqualify them from receiving social services. For example, in some New York City boroughs such as the Bronx, where nearly half the children are food insecure, the families who participate in food assistance programs are headed by people with

jobs. Contrary to some perceptions, most food-insecure Americans are employed or live in a household where someone works at least part time.

HUNGER AND CONFLICT About 60 percent of the world's hungry—490 million people—live in countries affected by war, and the UN reports that conflict is one of the key factors affecting food security and nutrition. In 2018, the number of people experiencing acute (severe and life-threatening) food insecurity rose by 11 percent globally, an increase attributed to conflict in countries including the Democratic Republic of Congo, Myanmar, and Yemen. Afghanistan, Sudan, South Sudan, and Nigeria, also war-torn, are suffering the most serious hunger crises in the world. In South Sudan, civil war has caused a mass displacement of citizens, which has left crops untended, resulting in crop failure and leaving more than 6 million people food insecure.

In some instances, warring parties have used food as a weapon by deliberately denying access to it for people associated with the opposition. In many cases, food distribution is inadequate or unequal in conflict zones because political systems are poorly managed, corrupt, or in disarray. People living in areas torn by fighting have few food options, and humanitarian workers attempting to provide food relief often face violence themselves.

GEOGRAPHIC THINKING

1. Compare food insecurity in the United States and food insecurity in other parts of the world. How does the problem manifest itself across different regions?

2. Explain the argument that food insecurity has more to do with distribution issues than production issues.

Mobile food trucks are one way of reaching people living in areas where little fresh food is available. An old city bus in Chicago, Illinois, has been converted into a single-aisle grocery store serving city dwellers who have no such stores in their neighborhoods.

FOOD DESERTS

THE ISSUE In the absence of mapping, food deserts in the United States are invisible contributors to the food insecurity problem—and invisible problems are not easy to solve.

LEARNING OBJECTIVE

IMP-5.B Explain challenges and debates related to the changing nature of contemporary agriculture and food-production practices.

BY THE NUMBERS

23.5 MILLION

Americans live
in food deserts

6.5 MILLION

are children

43,000

households in Houston, Texas, are located in a food desert

Source: United States Department of Agriculture; National Geographic, August 2014

HOUSTON'S FOOD DESERT

0   3   6 miles
0   3   6 kilometers

Number of Households

100   250   500

■ Without a car and more than 0.5 miles from a supermarket...

■ ...and in neighborhoods with the greatest poverty

Houston, Texas, provides an example of what is happening in many American cities: Food insecurity extends beyond areas of greatest poverty. Fourteen percent of the people living in Harris County, where Houston is located, receive SNAP (Supplemental Nutrition Assistance Program) support in the form of food stamps.

TWENTY-THREE AND A HALF MILLION AMERICANS

live in **food deserts**, areas where residents lack access to healthy, nutritious foods because stores selling these foods are too far away. The USDA defines "low-access communities" as places where at least 33 percent of the population live more than one mile from a supermarket or large grocery store. For rural areas, the distance is more than 10 miles. Food deserts, whether rural or urban, are often characterized by a low median income, higher unemployment, and higher poverty rates.

Food deserts occur in every major urban area in the United States. Large cities, such as Milwaukee and Baltimore, may appear to have plentiful grocery stores, but because stores and bus lines are unequally distributed, many residents find that healthful food is out of easy reach. Indeed, nearly 40 percent of residents in Milwaukee County live in a food desert.

Convenience stores and small independent stores are more common in food deserts than full-service supermarkets or grocery stores. These shops may have higher food prices, lower-quality foods, and a smaller variety of offerings. The result is that food consumed in food deserts is typically high in cholesterol, sugar, and fat. To help combat this problem, Milwaukee's Hunger Task Force created the Mobile Market in partnership with the grocery chain Pick 'n Save. The market makes stops in food desert communities to ensure that people have access to quality fresh foods.

Geographers map food deserts to better understand the challenge to obtaining fresh, healthy food. In Baltimore, approximately 25 percent of residents live in a food desert, but a recent partnership between the city of Baltimore and the Johns Hopkins Center for a Livable Future (CLF) is working to change that. CLF researchers developed 14 district maps showing food deserts and grocery store locations. The maps compelled city officials to create solutions. Today, food retailers who open or renovate establishments in or near food deserts can receive tax credits. The city also lifted building restrictions on temporary greenhouses known as hoop houses so residents can raise their own produce. The partnership project was so successful that CLF researchers have expanded their mapping tool to the state level. The hope is that other states will adopt similar tools and use them to reshape policies and solutions to America's food desert problem. ∎

GEOGRAPHIC THINKING

Explain how food deserts present both an opportunity and a challenge.

ECONOMIC IMPACTS ON FOOD PRODUCTION

LEARNING OBJECTIVE
IMP-5.B Explain challenges and debates related to the changing nature of contemporary agriculture and food-production practices.

One of the factors that contributes to food insecurity is poor distribution. Effective food distribution systems connect producers to consumers and allocate the food to meet local needs. However, there are challenges in deciding how food will be distributed among people, who has the authority to make decisions about food distribution, and what methods should be used. Complex social and economic factors often prevent the consumers who need food the most from receiving it. Low-income consumers may not have transportation or the financial means to obtain adequate food, or they may live in areas where government subsidies and services are not available or accessible. Rising prices can also prevent people from buying enough food or healthy food, whether they are employed or not.

STORAGE AND TRANSPORTATION ISSUES

Farms, food-processing facilities, and the markets where foods are sold are often located at considerable distances from one another. Recall the example in the previous lesson of produce imported from Chile to U.S. grocery stores. In some places, supply chains are much shorter than the distance between continents, existing within a single country or region. Because of poor storage, processing, transportation, or infrastructure, however, even short supply chains may break down, leading to food insecurity. Many regions of Africa and Latin America, in particular, are seeing a rise in severe food insecurity due at least in part to transportation and storage issues.

Inadequate infrastructure in many peripheral countries means that food grown elsewhere often cannot be transported to those who need it. According to the FAO, approximately 25 percent of the world's food calories are lost or wasted before they are consumed, and in peripheral countries food is typically lost between the time the farmer harvests it and when it arrives at the market. Farmers in these countries have limited access to reliable storage and transportation. They may have crops but no way to get them to market. Sometimes basic storage problems claim crops before they can be transported: Milk spoils before it can be pasteurized or pests ruin grain because there are no adequate storage facilities. Even in core countries, small farmers with lower incomes may lack the capital to invest in ways to overcome transportation and storage challenges.

By improving rural infrastructure (roads, storage, electrification), governments can strengthen the ability of farmers to develop sustainable businesses, reducing waste and increasing food access. In some instances, nongovernmental agencies and private companies are contributing knowledge and resources to help resolve local infrastructure-related problems. For example, a group of volunteers from several large U.S. agribusiness firms has formed a nonprofit group called Partners in Food Solutions to help entrepreneurs in food commodity supply chains in African countries. The group assisted the owner of a milling business in reducing waste and implementing quality control measures to ensure that she had more milled grain to sell. They also enabled Soy Afric, a food processing company, to acquire a large cooler designed by engineers in the United States and assembled in Nairobi, Kenya. Other nonprofits are targeting Africa's dependence on imported food. At present, African countries import approximately $40 billion a year in food. Producing and processing more food on the continent shortens the commodity supply chain between producers and consumers and may open doors to greater food accessibility.

ECONOMY OF SCALE

Economy of scale is the reduced cost of producing food items as the quantity of production increases. For example, if fixed costs such as tractors or combines are spread out over many units of production (for example, tons of wheat harvested), the return on investment is greater because the fixed costs remain the same. In agriculture, the concept of economy of scale shows that farming on a larger scale is more efficient than farming on a smaller scale: The average cost of production decreases as the farm size increases.

Economy of scale offers a good way to think about how to best use available resources to meet agricultural needs. Think of a production unit as a gallon of milk or a bushel of apples. The cost to produce each unit is lower on large farms due largely to technology and mechanization. Precision agriculture, biotechnology, and large machines are more productive per unit when used on areas larger than the average small farm. Almost every aspect of modern agriculture favors the large-scale farm over the small-scale because as the quantity of units produced increases, the cost per unit goes down.

Economy of scale also indirectly affects the way food is distributed. To make the best use of specialized technology, larger farms are less diversified as farmers focus on one or two crops to maximize profits. Often these are field crops such as corn or soybeans. These farms also have access to more far-reaching distribution networks. Small farms, with a higher cost per unit, may struggle more than larger ones when prices are low. Many small-scale farmers choose to grow organic or specialty crops and distribute them locally in the hopes that the premium they can charge for organic produce will cover their costs and produce a profit.

GOVERNMENT POLICIES

In the United States, the rise of large-scale farming has led to sizable corporate landholders controlling most of the land used for agriculture. In 2017, the USDA reported that the largest farms (those with sales of $5 million or more) accounted for less than one percent of all farms but 35 percent of all sales. The largest commercial farms receive the majority of the approximately

$20 billion in annual farm subsidies. In 2019, when the government delivered a massive farm aid package to offset losses due to Chinese trade tariffs, most of the $19 billion paid out that year went to large commercial farms.

The three largest government subsidy programs go to farms that produce corn, soybeans, and wheat. Such subsidies have the power to distort the decisions made by farm businesses by encouraging overproduction and discouraging diversification. From a business standpoint, farmers often feel they must choose to grow the crops that are the most cost-effective. These same commodity crops lend themselves to large-scale production, easy storage, and long-distance shipping. With soybeans and corn at the top of the list of exported U.S. products, government policies may encourage farm businesses to produce crops that enhance agricultural exports rather than bolstering food security.

In India, where a rapidly growing population contributes to widespread poverty and hunger, government policies regarding agriculture have struggled to improve the country's food security. India ranks high in production volume for both rice and wheat; those two crops, along with aquaculture, account for more than half of total farm exports. But despite being one of the largest grain-producing countries in the world, India still accounts for one-fourth of the world's hungry people. Critics of India's governmental policies argue that agricultural subsidies bypass small farmers, and instead are given to large-scale farms.

In hopes of improving farmers' incomes and remedying unequal food distribution, the Indian government has recently implemented a program through which state governments buy food grains from local farmers at a guaranteed price that protects farmers from price fluctuations. On the consumer side, qualifying households can purchase food through the program at subsidized prices. Supporters of this government policy argue that it has helped India make significant progress in delivering food grains to the poor, but critics claim that the program is unable to identify and reach the country's poor and that the guaranteed price is inadequate for farmers.

FIGHTING THE PROBLEM In many core economies, globally conscious diets are gaining followers as one way to help solve the problem of feeding everyone. Some consumers are making food choices, such as reducing

The Food and Agriculture Organization of the United Nations believes that edible insects can be a way to combat scarcities of land and water while relieving pressures on the environment. Edible insects are rich in protein, need little feed, and emit few greenhouse gases. The burgers in the photo are made from buffalo worms, which are larvae of the darkling beetle.

their intake of meat, with global as well as personal consequences in mind. As more land goes under cultivation to grow feed for livestock, edible grains become too expensive for people in peripheral countries to purchase. A large-scale shift to less meat-intensive diets could have considerable impact on the availability of food. By cutting their intake of meat and other crop-intensive foods—while simultaneously increasing the market for locally produced fruits and vegetables—the wealthiest billion could significantly alter the global pattern of food production, distribution, and consumption.

Changing diets in wealthier countries has the potential to free up more croplands to grow food; the next step is creating transportation systems and infrastructure to ensure that the food reaches those who need it most. Much relies on the decisions of governments, businesses, and organizations, but economically stable consumers, too, can use their purchasing power to help transform the global food system and encourage sustainable farming practices.

GEOGRAPHIC THINKING

3. Explain how agricultural policies in the United States could be modified to strengthen the agricultural system's ability to perform as a sustainable food production system.

4. Describe the types of geographic data that might be useful in helping meet the demand of food security.

5. Explain how economy of scale can be used to support an argument that favors large-scale farming over small-scale farming.

6. Explain the degree to which food production can be impacted by violent conflict and extreme weather.

LOCAL CHANGES, GLOBAL CONSEQUENCES

Jennifer Burney's fascination with physics has led her to explore how energy and climate affect food security, water availability, and agriculture.

LEARNING OBJECTIVE
IMP-5.B Explain challenges and debates related to the changing nature of contemporary agriculture and food-production practices.

Environmental scientist Jennifer Burney has made global sustainability her goal. She's determined to "chart a realistic pathway for greening the global food system."

Jennifer Burney is a professor at the University of California San Diego School of Global Policy and Strategy, where her research focuses on improving global food security while reducing climate change. At present, she is working to understand how global climate changes affect people locally. While carbon dioxide is the largest contributor to climate change globally, she hopes this project will help shed light on other compounds that harm local air quality and cause health problems such as asthma.

Burney has spent many years working toward hunger and climate solutions in the field as well as in the lab. In Benin, West Africa, where agricultural production is the main livelihood and residents spend 50 to 80 percent of their income on food, Burney cooperated with a women's farm collective that implemented solar irrigation in local farm fields. The irrigation system was powered by solar panels, and it succeeded in both conserving water and extending the growing season, allowing farmers to increase yields and supplement household income and nutritional intake. Burney was also involved with a project in northern India that helped several communities replace traditional cook stoves with better combusting eco-stoves. The traditional stoves emitted excessive black carbon, or soot. Inside homes, these emissions caused respiratory infections; outside, the emissions contributed to the air pollution that altered monsoon cycles. The new stoves drastically limit black carbon emissions and reduce fuel use.

Burney believes community-scale innovations can make a global difference in agriculture-related climate change. "People care about the local stuff," she says, "and they mobilize resources and make politics happen to solve problems."

GEOGRAPHIC THINKING

Explain the challenges that Jennifer Burney helped the women farmers in Benin overcome.

14.4 WOMEN IN AGRICULTURE

Women have always played key roles in agriculture, whether as landowners or workers, pastoral nomads or settled farmers. These roles have changed over time and continue to do so, as social, political, and environmental circumstances evolve. Geographers take a keen interest in female farmers because strong connections exist between the empowerment of women, agricultural productivity, and food security.

A VARIETY OF ROLES

LEARNING OBJECTIVE

IMP-5.C Explain geographic variations in female roles in food production and consumption.

Women produce more than 50 percent of the world's food and make up 43 percent of the agricultural labor force. Most working women in peripheral countries labor in agriculture, and about a third of farmers in the United States are female. Women's roles in agriculture vary widely across the world, from region to region, and locally. Women throughout the world are involved in both crop and livestock production in subsistence and commercial settings. They manage mixed agricultural operations that may include crops, livestock, and fish farming, and they produce both cash crops and food for their families. Women are also deeply involved in the distribution of agricultural products and decisions about how these products are consumed. As agriculture changes because of technology, science, and economic and social pressures, the role of women within the sector changes too.

In peripheral countries, women are largely limited to participation in subsistence agriculture. Malawi, in southern Africa, serves as a good example of this phenomenon. In Malawi, 11 million people—the majority of the population—participate in smallholder subsistence farming. Opportunities to transition to commercial farming can be limited by gender bias in educational and other opportunities. When sustainable techniques for growing sweet potatoes, a major part of Malawi's farm production, were taught, the men

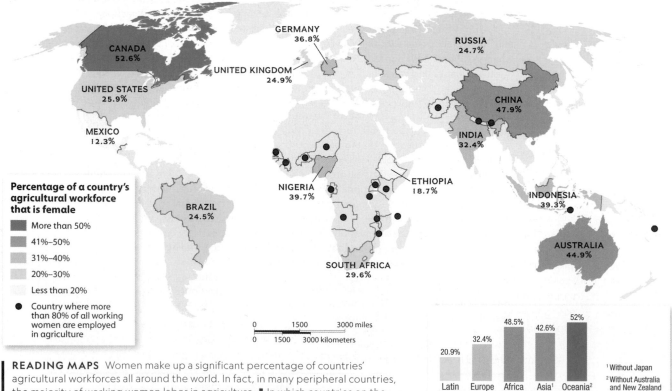

FEMALE AGRICULTURE WORKERS IN SELECTED COUNTRIES, 2010

GERMANY 36.8%
CANADA 52.6%
RUSSIA 24.7%
UNITED KINGDOM 24.9%
UNITED STATES 25.9%
CHINA 47.9%
MEXICO 12.3%
INDIA 32.4%
NIGERIA 39.7%
ETHIOPIA 18.7%
INDONESIA 39.3%
BRAZIL 24.5%
AUSTRALIA 44.9%
SOUTH AFRICA 29.6%

Percentage of a country's agricultural workforce that is female

- More than 50%
- 41%–50%
- 31%–40%
- 20%–30%
- Less than 20%
- ● Country where more than 80% of all working women are employed in agriculture

0   1500   3000 miles
0   1500   3000 kilometers

Latin America 20.9%
Europe 32.4%
Africa 48.5%
Asia¹ 42.6%
Oceania² 52%

¹ Without Japan
² Without Australia and New Zealand

READING MAPS Women make up a significant percentage of countries' agricultural workforces all around the world. In fact, in many peripheral countries, the majority of working women labor in agriculture. ▮ In which countries on the map do women make up more than half the agricultural workforce? What spatial patterns do you notice about working women who work mostly in agriculture?

Sources: Soil Atlas 2015, Institute for Advanced Sustainability Studies

received training related to market-oriented production, while the women received training related to subsistence farming and how to use the sweet potato crops in their roles as care providers of the household. Women in Malawi tend to be viewed as inexpensive labor and not as actively involved in significant decision-making. This marginalization of women resulted in their exclusion from education on important topics such as how to manage crop disease and pests, as well as other sustainable farming techniques.

The most difficult gender-specific challenge that women working in agriculture face is the lack of land rights. For example, in the Republic of Congo, most of the agricultural workers are the women who produce approximately 75 percent of the food in rural areas but have no ownership rights because they are female. Only 10 to 20 percent of landholders in peripheral countries are women. If a female farmer has no legal right to own or control land, she also doesn't have the legal backing to make decisions about the land or negotiate farm agreements. These limitations restrict the amount and reliability of income. In some areas, legal rights exist on paper but are disregarded in practice.

Women in agriculture also face obstacles when attempting to conduct the business of farming. In some peripheral countries, even unspoken gender roles can be rigid and keep women from taking their crops to market. Female subsistence farmers with small land holdings in these countries often face technical problems and cultural biases that block them from borrowing money. In some countries, laws require a woman to obtain her husband's signature before she can receive a loan. Even in the United States, before federal legislation overruled the practice in 1988, some states required women to provide a signature from a male relative in order to obtain a business loan. Without access to loans, women farmers cannot purchase fertilizer, seeds, or advanced farming tools and equipment.

In many places, women in agriculture experience difficult working conditions and a poor quality of life. Worldwide, family farms are central to global food security and sustainable productivity, but at the same time, they are the main institutions where women work as unpaid and unrecognized laborers. In India, for instance, rural-to-urban migration by men and steady growth in the production of labor-intensive cash crops has led to women performing significant farm tasks. However, these tasks are simply viewed as an extension of their household responsibilities. A typical expectation of a female farmer in a peripheral country is that she takes care of all household responsibilities—such as preparing food, caring for the children, and collecting fuel and water—and maintains her agricultural labor contribution as well. Similar challenges exist for women in other regions of the world. The Food and Agriculture Organization of the United Nations (FAO) reported in 2017 that in Latin America and the Caribbean, 40 percent of working women over age 15 did not have a personal income. Eight out of ten of these women worked in the agricultural sector, and not necessarily as subsistence farmers.

The United States provides examples of the varied and changing roles women play in agriculture. In 2017, the United States Department of Agriculture reported that 36 percent of the country's 3.4 million producers involved in daily decision-making were female. According to the Bureau of Labor Statistics, women farmers, ranchers, and agricultural managers exceeded the earnings of their male counterparts in 2017. Female ranchers are also leading the way in practicing sustainable ranching. One rancher, Kelsey Ducheneaux, raises sustainable beef on 7,500 acres of tribally leased land in South Dakota. A member of the Lakota Nation, Ducheneaux points out that generations of Lakota worked the same land before her, and Native American women being involved in ranching is not a new concept.

While American female farmers may not face the same hardships and challenges as those in other countries, obstacles still exist to their equal participation in agriculture. Despite progress, female farmers and ranchers in the United States encounter resistance from male counterparts. Though an equal partner in her family's dairy farm in Minnesota, Tara Meyer finds she is often referred to as a "farm wife," when she is in reality a farmer with a master's degree in agriculture.

In Europe, women farmers are actively involved in food distribution in roles that extend beyond production and often surpass the participation of men. They take their produce to farmers markets, distribute it through catering companies, and hold leadership roles in social movements working toward food sovereignty, which is defined by the U.S. Food Sovereignty Alliance as "the right of peoples to healthy and culturally appropriate food produced through ecologically sound and sustainable methods, and their right to define their own food and agriculture systems."

According to Euractiv France, in 2019 women represented one-fourth of all French farmers, with 41 percent of agricultural businesses being established by women. French women are increasingly involved in agricultural distribution as well, taking on roles in the agricultural supply chain. In Italy one-third of farms are run by women, and women manage almost 40 percent of the companies in the emerging agritourism industry. Agritourism provides a creative alternative to standard food distribution models by bringing in tourists to stay—and sometimes work—on farms and enjoy meals made from local products.

Along with changing roles in food production and distribution, women's roles in food consumption have also changed. In cultures throughout the world, women have traditionally been—and often still are—in charge of selecting, cooking, and serving food to their families. New economic realities, however, are altering that vision. In Singapore, a country that has experienced extensive economic growth, large numbers of women continue to enter the workforce. Fewer women cook on a regular basis, families eat out more frequently, and domestic workers within the home may be left to make food purchasing and consumption decisions.

In other smaller countries, such as Cyprus, women are active in the workforce, but grandparents remain in the home, and food purchasing and consumption decisions are often left to the grandmother.

Research conducted by the FAO in Asia, Africa, and Latin America found that in general, women who earn an income spend a much higher proportion of their money on food for their families than men do. These expenditures may include food for direct consumption or resources needed for food crops. In areas of India, more women are choosing to engage in poultry production, an agricultural sector that is typically controlled and managed by women. Poultry production allows women to provide nutritious food for their families and contribute to the household income by selling eggs and birds at local markets.

EMPOWERING RURAL WOMEN

LEARNING OBJECTIVE
IMP-5.C Explain geographic variations in female roles in food production and consumption.

In the context of farming, empowerment means having the ability to make decisions about factors such as land, livestock, seeds, fertilizer, and machinery, as well as control over finances and one's own time. Empowering women in the agricultural sector has the potential to bring significant benefits at the individual, community, national, and global scales. At the household level, children receive better nutrition and education when their mothers' incomes increase. Communities also benefit when women have money to spend on schooling and other resources. At the regional and national scales, empowering female farmers may help improve food security for millions. According to a report issued by the FAO in 2017, if women in rural areas had the same access as men to agricultural resources (land, technology, markets, financial services), agricultural productivity would increase by 20 to 30 percent—enough to reduce the number of hungry people by 100 to 150 million.

In some regions of the world, rural women face fewer economic and cultural barriers to empowerment. According to a 2011 United Nations study, women in Southeast Asia have more equal access to land than do women in South Asia. Women in Southeast Asia also tend to exert more control over household income than men. In some areas of sub-Saharan Africa, such as Angola, Ghana, and Uganda, women are encouraged to strive for economic self-reliance and traditionally are given significant responsibilities in agricultural production. Some countries hit hard by male emigration, deaths from HIV/AIDS, and conflict have given large percentages of the agricultural labor force over to women. Many women in peripheral countries function as the head of household and primary caregivers, which makes

EMPOWERING WOMEN FARMERS

In many parts of the world, female farmers are making progress toward empowerment, even in areas such as the Punjab region of Pakistan that place high hurdles in front of women. Against all odds, for example, 28-year-old Almas Parveen became the only woman farmer in Punjab who trains other farmers. Parveen manages 23 acres of family farmland in a village where agriculture is male-dominated. Parveen's status as a single woman and a farm manager and trainer is exceptional. One of the few women farmers who goes to the market to sell, Parveen has the experience to bargain for the best market rate and is also trusted by her family to manage all the farm's finances.

She received formal agricultural training in 2017, which opened her eyes to the critical importance of water conservation. The new sustainable agricultural methods Parveen implemented resulted in a higher crop yield, and other farmers followed in adopting the same practices. As a certified field facilitator with the nonprofit organization Rural Education and Economic Development Society, she has taught more than 400 farmers—both males and females—how to implement sustainable practices. Parveen is also an advocate for fair wages for women and pays female farmhands at a higher rate than is customary. Of her journey to empowerment she says, "It has not been easy, but it is not impossible either."

Almas Parveen teaches both male and female farmers in Pakistan about sustainable agricultural practices.

Caitlyn Taussig is an American rancher in Kremmling, Colorado. She helps run the family operation along with her mother, sister, and other female ranchers.

them the link between farms and tables; they are the ones making decisions about food consumption and nutrition for their families and communities.

The steps to empowering female farmers include education, technical support, access to capital, and government policies that promote gender equality. Several nongovernmental organizations are implementing programs that target all these facets of empowerment. The Global Forum on Agricultural Research (GFAR), for example, manages a women's collective called Gender in Agricultural Partnership (GAP). GAP is made up of more than 150 institutions that work together to provide education, land, and credit—the ability to borrow money—to female farmers. They also address gender discrimination in the agricultural sector and lobby for policy change to empower women in agriculture at the global, national, and local levels.

Working with a network of institutions in Africa, the Americas, and Asia, the Grameen Foundation extends microfinancing, or loans in very small amounts, to the world's poorest people, including female farmers. These small loans enable small farmers to invest in new equipment or expand their businesses. Grameen's agricultural program uses technology and a large network of resources to help women access microloans, agricultural supplies and tools, information, and technical assistance.

Governments and supranational organizations, too, are implementing measures to advance women's empowerment in agriculture. In the United States, the U.S. Department of

Agriculture Farm Service Agency reserves a portion of its loan funding for underserved farmers and ranchers, which includes women. The U.S. government program Feed the Future has also worked with more than 2.4 million women around the world to apply new agricultural technologies and practices. UN Women promotes connectivity as a means to integrate rural areas with global financial and payment systems in order to provide financial access for female farmers and ranchers who are starting out in business.

Whatever their particular focus, all agencies working to empower female farmers recognize that women's basic right to equality and control over their lives is closely linked with the health of the agricultural system in general. Given the opportunity to increase their incomes and develop a consistent and reliable livelihood, female farmers will play an important role in ensuring food security for their families and communities—and in confronting the complex challenge of feeding the world.

GEOGRAPHIC THINKING

1. Explain why working in the agricultural sector is more difficult for female farmers than for male farmers.

2. Describe how women's changing roles in food distribution and consumption affect their communities.

3. Explain the degree to which a region's economy and culture affect the empowerment of its female farmers.

■ CHAPTER SUMMARY

Agricultural landscapes result from the interactions between farming practices and physical geography.

Agricultural techniques have environmental consequences.

- Pollution results from chemicals that run off farmland.

- Land cover change caused by agriculture can result in erosion or land degradation.

- Soil salinization is a result of irrigation.

- Desertification is a type of land degradation in which arid and semiarid lands become deserts.

- Numerous governments and organizations are promoting conservation and sustainable practices.

Agricultural practices have societal consequences.

- The growth of agribusiness has led to fewer small and midsize farms in the United States.

- Some people have changed their diets in response to concerns about agricultural practices.

Debates exist over the pros and cons of GMOs.

- Supporters believe GMO crops can feed more people more efficiently.

- Opponents believe GMOs threaten biodiversity and could have negative health effects on humans.

Consumer food choices have an effect on food production.

- Buying local, organic, or fair-trade crops helps create markets for certain types of agriculture.

- Dietary shifts such as greater meat consumption also strongly affect the agricultural sector.

Global food insecurity results from a number of causes, including loss of agricultural lands, climate change, conflict, and croplands devoted to biofuels.

Food production and distribution are affected by several economic factors.

- Storage and transportation issues can lead to food waste.

- Government policies can affect farmers' decisions and help or harm food consumers.

Women in agriculture face a variety of challenges, including cultural bias and legal obstacles to land ownership.

Empowering women in agriculture leads to numerous benefits, including better nutrition for families and greater food production overall.

KEY TERMS AND CONCEPTS

■ Use complete sentences to answer the questions.

1. **APPLY CONCEPTUAL VOCABULARY** Consider the term *agricultural landscape*. Develop a dictionary definition of the term. Then provide a conceptual definition—an explanation of how the term is used in the context of this chapter.

2. How are the terms *pastoral nomadism* and *desertification* related?

3. Describe three agricultural techniques from around the world. Provide examples of the environmental consequences of each one.

4. Identify an example that explains how an agricultural technique can have positive environmental consequences.

5. How can dams and reservoirs impact farming?

6. Define and provide an example of an aquifer. Include a possible environmental consequence of using aquifers for irrigation.

7. Describe the characteristics of a wetland and explain its environmental vulnerability because of agriculture.

8. Identify and explain three causes of food insecurity.

9. Define the term *debt-for-nature swap*. Explain how the term relates to agricultural sustainability and conservation efforts.

10. What is the difference between biotechnology and biodiversity?

11. Describe how precision agriculture can help the environment.

12. Explain how the decisions of wealthy consumers may lead to food insecurity.

13. Explain how food trends in core countries affect producers in other parts of the world.

14. Describe how the role of women in agriculture has changed, specific to food distribution.

■ INTERPRET GRAPHS

Study the graph and then answer the questions.

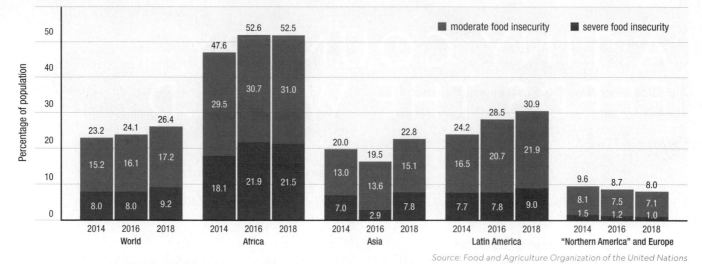

■ FOOD INSECURITY; 2014, 2016, 2018

Source: Food and Agriculture Organization of the United Nations

15. **IDENTIFY DATA & INFORMATION** What was the average percentage of severe food insecurity in Asia for this period?

16. **ANALYZE DATA** Which area had the greatest percentage increase in food insecurity and in what year did that increase occur?

17. **COMPARE PATTERNS & TRENDS** Compare the food insecurity percentages in Asia with those of North America and Europe.

18. **SYNTHESIZE** How do the percentages represented by Africa support what you learned about global food insecurity in the text?

GEO-INQUIRY | FOOD DESERTS IN YOUR AREA

Consider how you can use Geo-Inquiry to solve an issue concerning food deserts in your community. Use the steps in the Geo-Inquiry Process below to explore the availability of healthy food on a local level.

ASK Start with an authentic Geo-Inquiry question about your community. It may be as simple as: *How might we remove barriers that exist in our community to accessing healthy foods?* Use the Geo-Inquiry Process to expand this question and ask need-to-know questions such as: *Are there food deserts in my community? How can we work together to ensure access to healthy foods?*

COLLECT Decide how you could gather geographic information to answer your questions. Explore community and online organizations that study food availability. You can also use your own methods to collect data, such as using an online map to identify the locations of grocery stores in your community and cross reference them with public transportation and housing density.

VISUALIZE Analyze the information you collected on food deserts in your community. Use the information to identify gaps, draw conclusions, and outline actions that are needed. Organize the information and think about how you can present it in a visual format, such as a map, to share with others. Create drafts to help you plan.

CREATE Focus on ways to tell a Geo-Inquiry story, such as a multimedia presentation that provides scientific data, research, and visuals. Keep your audience in mind and choose elements that will inspire them to take action. Create a list of the elements that you will use, such as specific images, videos, maps, and clear charts and graphs. Outline or storyboard your story, then tie all your elements together using a storytelling tool.

ACT Share your Geo-Inquiry story with decision makers and other community members. Consider how your project can help them take action to improve access to healthy food in the community.

ASK — COLLECT — VISUALIZE — CREATE — ACT

A TINY COUNTRY FEEDS THE WORLD

BY FRANK VIVIANO

Technology helps farmers create the perfect conditions for tomatoes to grow abundantly inside this greenhouse in the Netherlands.

In a potato field near the Netherlands' border with Belgium, Dutch farmer Jacob van den Borne is seated in the cabin of an immense harvester before an instrument panel worthy of the starship *Enterprise*. From his perch 10 feet above the ground he's monitoring two drones—a driverless tractor roaming the fields and a quadcopter in the air—that provide detailed readings on soil chemistry, water content, nutrients, and growth, measuring the progress of every plant down to the individual potato. Van den Borne's production numbers testify to the power of this "precision farming," as it's known. The global average yield of potatoes per acre is about nine tons. Van den Borne's fields reliably produce more than 20 tons.

One more reason to marvel: The Netherlands is a small, densely populated country, with more than 1,300 inhabitants per square mile. It's bereft of, or lacking, almost every resource long thought to be necessary for large-scale agriculture. Yet it's the world's number two exporter of food as measured by value, second only to the United States, which has more than 235 times the landmass of the Netherlands. How on earth have the Dutch done it?

MORE TOMATOES, FEWER RESOURCES

At every turn in the Netherlands, the future of sustainable agriculture is taking shape—not in the boardrooms of big corporations but on thousands of modest family farms. You see it vividly in the terrestrial paradise owned by Ted Duijvestijn and his brothers Peter, Ronald, and Remco. The Duijvestijns have constructed a self-contained food system in which a near-perfect balance prevails between human ingenuity and nature's potential.

At the Duijvestijns' 36-acre greenhouse complex near the old city of Delft, visitors stroll among ranks of deep green tomato vines, 20 feet tall. Rooted not in soil but in fibers spun from basalt and chalk, the plants are heavy with tomatoes—15 varieties in all—to suit the taste of the most demanding palate. In 2015, an international jury of horticultural experts named the Duijvestijns the world's most innovative tomato growers.

Since relocating and restructuring their 70-year-old farm in 2004, the Duijvestijns have declared resource independence on every front. The farm produces almost all of its own energy and fertilizer and even some of the packaging materials necessary for the crop's distribution and sale. The growing environment is kept at optimal temperatures year-round by heat generated from geothermal aquifers that simmer under at least half of the Netherlands.

The only irrigation source is rainwater, says Ted, who manages the cultivation program. Each kilogram of tomatoes from his fiber-rooted plants requires less than 4 gallons of water, compared with 16 gallons for plants in open fields. Once each year, the entire crop is regrown from seeds, and the old vines are processed to make packaging crates. The few pests that manage to enter the Duijvestijn greenhouses are greeted by a ravenous army of defenders such as the fierce *Phytoseiulus persimilis*, a predatory mite that shows no interest in tomatoes but gorges itself on hundreds of destructive spider mites.

A few days before I visited the Duijvestijns' operation, Ted had attended a meeting of farmers and researchers. "This is how we come up with innovative ways to move ahead, to keep improving," he told me. "People from all over Holland get together to discuss different perspectives and common goals. No one knows all the answers on their own."

EXPORTING KNOWLEDGE Dutch firms are among the world leaders in the seed business, with close to $1.7 billion worth of exports in 2016. The sales catalog of Rijk Zwann, a Dutch seed breeder, offers high-yield seeds in more than 25 broad groups of vegetables, many that defend themselves naturally against major pests. Heleen Bos is responsible for the company's organic accounts and international development projects. Like many of the entrepreneurs at Dutch firms, Bos has worked in the fields and cities of peripheral countries. With lengthy postings to Mozambique, Nicaragua, and Bangladesh over the past 30 years, she knows that hunger and devastating famine are not abstract threats.

"Of course, we can't immediately implement the kind of ultrahigh-tech agriculture over there that you see in the Netherlands," she says. "But we are well into introducing medium-tech solutions that can make a huge difference." She cites the proliferation of relatively inexpensive plastic greenhouses that have tripled some crop yields compared with those of open fields, where crops are more subject to pests and drought.

Some 4,000 miles south of the Netherlands, in a family-owned bean field in Africa's Eastern Rift Valley, a team from SoilCares, a Dutch agricultural technology firm, explains the functions of a small handheld device. In conjunction with a cell phone app, the device analyzes the soil's chemistry, organic matter, and other properties, then uploads the results to a database in the Netherlands and returns a detailed report on optimal fertilizer use and nutrient needs—all in less than 10 minutes. At the cost of a few dollars, the report provides input that can help reduce crop losses by enormous margins to farmers who have never had access to soil sampling of any kind.

Less than 5 percent of the world's estimated 570 million farms have access to a soil lab. That's the kind of number the Dutch see as a challenge. ▪

Adapted from "This Tiny Country Feeds the World," Frank Viviano, *National Geographic*, September 2017

WRITE ACROSS UNITS

Unit 5 examined agriculture from a geographer's perspective. In Chapter 14, you read about precision agriculture—one way technology might help meet humanity's needs in the future. This article focuses on some of the world's most advanced practitioners of precision farming. Use information from the article and this unit to write a response to the following questions.

LOOKING BACK

1. How are farmers using geographic tools to practice precision farming? UNIT 1

2. What effect do you think implementing Dutch farming methods might have on populations in other countries? UNIT 2

3. How might adopting Dutch farming methods affect the cultural landscape in countries such as Mozambique, Nicaragua, and Bangladesh? UNIT 3

4. How might countries with a history of colonialism react to Dutch companies or the Dutch government offering agricultural solutions? UNIT 4

5. How do the farming techniques described in the article compare with innovations of the Second Agricultural Revolution and the Green Revolution? UNIT 5

LOOKING FORWARD

6. How might adopting the Dutch pattern of agriculture affect the growth of cities in a region? UNIT 6

7. How might international trade agreements and the world economy affect a farmer's decisions about trying precision farming? UNIT 7

WRITE ACROSS REGIONS & SCALES

Research a country or place outside Europe that has worked with Rijk Zwann or another Dutch entity to implement farming techniques like those described in the article. Write an essay comparing the results with those obtained in the Netherlands. Drawing on your research, this unit, and the article, address the following topic:

How well do some of the Dutch innovations work outside the Netherlands? Why might the results differ in other countries and locations?

THINK ABOUT

- cultural and economic conditions that affect agriculture in each country

- soil, climate, and other conditions in the Netherlands and in the other country

WHERE CROPS ARE MOST LIKELY TO THRIVE

USDA PLANT HARDINESS ZONES, CONTIGUOUS UNITED STATES, 2012

Zone 3
Zone 4
Zone 5
Zone 6
Zone 7
Zone 8
Zone 9
Zone 10

Climate is one of the key determinants of crops that will grow in a region. For this reason, the United States Department of Agriculture has created detailed climate maps of the United States and updates them occasionally. The most recent update was in 2012. These plant hardiness zone maps help farmers and gardeners alike understand which plants are suitable for their location, based on average extreme minimum temperature, or the average of lowest winter temperatures for a location. All plants are assigned a zone or zones in which they will grow. ▮ Identify the scales of the two maps, and explain the degree to which they indicate the conditions of an agricultural region. Identify factors, in addition to climate, that growers need to consider before planting crops.

USDA PLANT HARDINESS ZONES, ARIZONA, 2012

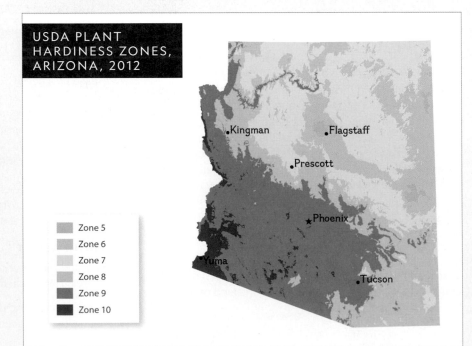

Zone 5
Zone 6
Zone 7
Zone 8
Zone 9
Zone 10

CHAPTER 12

MALTHUS AND THE GREEN REVOLUTION

As you know, Thomas Malthus theorized an eventual worldwide famine, resulting from exponential population growth that he anticipated would far outpace the world's capacity for food production. Events such as the Green Revolution, however, have shown that food production can be increased at rates Malthus had no way of imagining. ▌ Compare Malthus's theory to the actual results of the Green Revolution in India, China, and Mexico. Using what you learned in Chapters 4 and 12, explain how a Neo-Malthusian thinker would describe the results.

MALTHUS'S THEORY

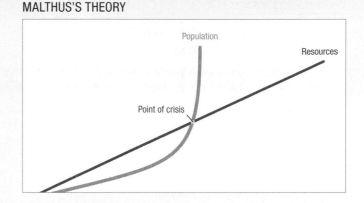

INDEX OF CEREAL PRODUCTION AND LAND USE, 1961–1985

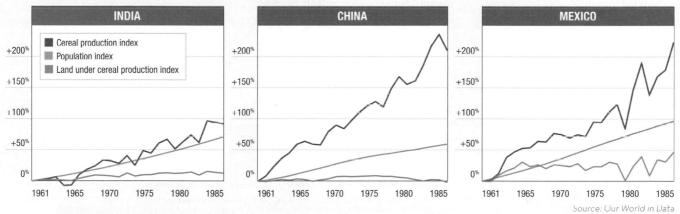

Source: Our World in Data

CHAPTER 12

CATTLE STATIONS

In 2016, the Kidman family of Australia sold its cattle stations, or ranches, to a new owner. These ranches cover a reported 1.6 percent of Australia's territory. The largest station, Anna Creek, spreads out over 9,142 square miles, an area larger than the country of Israel. ▌ Identify the three largest cattle stations on the map, and explain whether the map shows a pattern of intensive or extensive agriculture. Identify information from other sources that may help explain Australia's agricultural patterns.

KIDMAN CATTLE RANCHES, AUSTRALIA, 2016

Ruby Plains
3,076 sq mi

Helen Springs
3,937 sq mi

Glengyle
2,139 sq mi

Durrie
2,548 sq mi

Morney Plains
2,405 sq mi

Macumba
4,271 sq mi

Rockybank
56 sq mi

Anna Creek
9,142 sq mi

Durham Downs
3,440 sq mi

Naryilco
2,899 sq mi

Innamincka
5,232 sq mi

Tungali
7 sq mi

BID-RENT THEORY AND THE VON THÜNEN MODEL

The bid-rent theory and the von Thünen model use different visualizations to explain aspects of the same phenomenon: how land is used in relation to a market, or central business district. The two ideas can be considered independently or in a combined fashion to analyze spatial patterns in agriculture.

▌ Describe how the von Thünen model supports the bid-rent theory and how both account for the distribution of agriculture.

BID-RENT THEORY AND THE VON THÜNEN MODEL

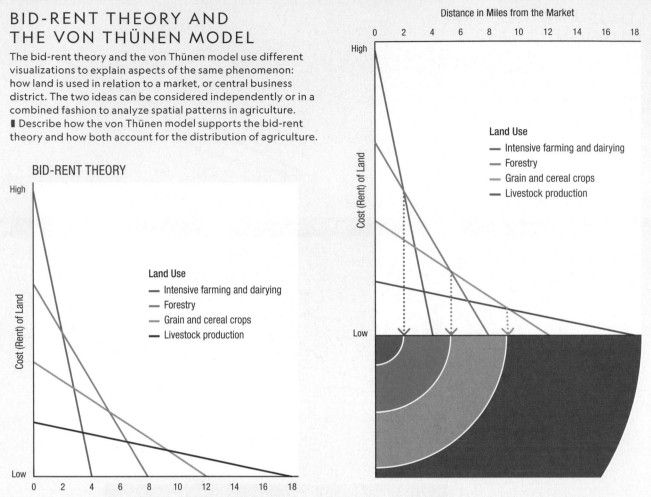

Distance in Miles from the Market

Cost (Rent) of Land

Land Use
— Intensive farming and dairying
— Forestry
— Grain and cereal crops
— Livestock production

BID-RENT THEORY

Cost (Rent) of Land

Distance in Miles from the Market

Land Use
— Intensive farming and dairying
— Forestry
— Grain and cereal crops
— Livestock production

THE VON THÜNEN MODEL

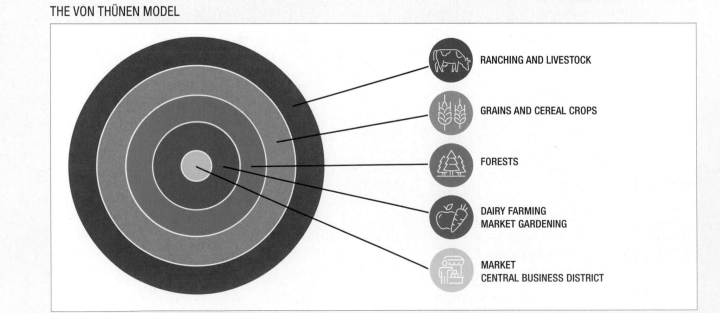

RANCHING AND LIVESTOCK

GRAINS AND CEREAL CROPS

FORESTS

DAIRY FARMING
MARKET GARDENING

MARKET
CENTRAL BUSINESS DISTRICT

CHAPTER 13

BANANAS: A GLOBAL COMMODITY

Bananas are a global commodity, with exports totaling $13.7 billion in 2017. Since the 1990s, banana crops have been threatened by a fungus that can destroy entire plantations and, at present, has no cure. This map shows the percentage share of the banana market claimed by the top five importing and exporting countries in 2017. ▌ Identify the patterns in the global banana trade shown on this map. Explain the possible effect of the banana disease on both importing and exporting countries.

GLOBAL BANANA TRADE, 2017

CHAPTER 13

SMALL AND LARGE FARMS

Worldwide, the distribution of small farms versus the distribution of larger entities varies a great deal across continents. In 2014, the Food and Agriculture Organization of the United Nations estimated that of the 570 million farms on the planet, approximately 84 percent were 5 acres or smaller, and 97 percent were smaller than 25 acres. ▌ Compare the patterns of agriculture shown in these pie charts. What conclusion can you draw about the distribution of farms around the world?

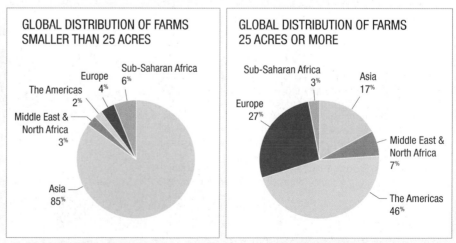

GLOBAL DISTRIBUTION OF FARMS SMALLER THAN 25 ACRES

GLOBAL DISTRIBUTION OF FARMS 25 ACRES OR MORE

Source: Food and Agriculture Organization of the United Nations

HOW CROPS ARE USED

In 2014, National Geographic created a map highlighting the percentage of crops used for animal feed and fuel versus those destined for direct human consumption. Researchers found that 55 percent of food-crop calories directly nourished people, while meat, dairy, and eggs from animals raised on feed supplied another 4 percent.

▌ Identify which regions grow more crops for feed and fuel. Explain the degree to which this map explains issues that surround the global food supply.

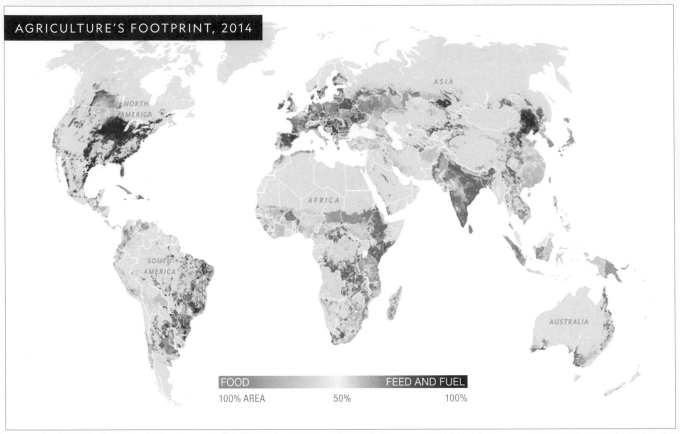

AGRICULTURE'S FOOTPRINT, 2014

FOOD — FEED AND FUEL
100% AREA   50%   100%

Source: National Geographic

LAND USE AND NUTRITION

One solution that has been suggested to fight global hunger is a large-scale switch to eating more plant-based foods. Proponents of this idea point to the amount of land required to feed animals that in turn feed humans. If more crops were directly consumed by humans, supporters argue, there would be more food for everyone. This graph reflects a calculation of the average amount of land needed to produce an ounce of protein in different animal and plant-based food sources. ▌ Describe what the data in this graph reveals about agricultural production and consumption.

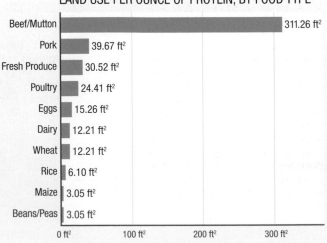

LAND USE PER OUNCE OF PROTEIN, BY FOOD TYPE

Food Type	Land Use
Beef/Mutton	311.26 ft²
Pork	39.67 ft²
Fresh Produce	30.52 ft²
Poultry	24.41 ft²
Eggs	15.26 ft²
Dairy	12.21 ft²
Wheat	12.21 ft²
Rice	6.10 ft²
Maize	3.05 ft²
Beans/Peas	3.05 ft²

0 ft²   100 ft²   200 ft²   300 ft²

Source: Our World in Data

CHAPTER 14

WHERE FOOD IS LOST

Eliminating food waste is one possible path toward improving global food security and supporting farmers who struggle to make a living. This chart shows food lost or waste at different points along the global supply chain. ▮ Describe where the most food waste occurred in 2017, according to the charts. Explain why food might be wasted at the different stages of the process from production to consumption.

GLOBAL FOOD WASTE ACROSS THE SUPPLY CHAIN

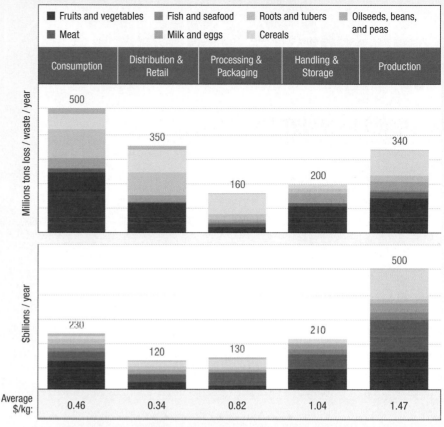

Source: Food and Agriculture Organization of the United Nations

CHAPTER 14

THREATS TO BIODIVERSITY

Globally, biodiversity is threatened by expanding agriculture and a number of other human causes, including climate change, the expansion of cities and suburbs into natural areas, and the breaking up of natural habitats into smaller sections. This projection predicts the pressures on biodiversity from several agricultural and other human-related causes. ▮ Identify the projected trends in pressure on biodiversity from different forms of agriculture. Using the information about population projections that you learned in Unit 2, provide a possible explanation why the threat from crops and pasture does not increase a great deal between 2030 and 2050.

PRESSURES ON BIODIVERSITY BY YEAR

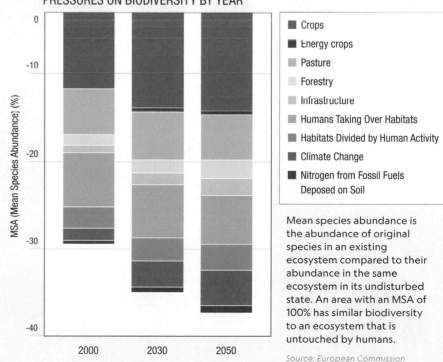

Mean species abundance is the abundance of original species in an existing ecosystem compared to their abundance in the same ecosystem in its undisturbed state. An area with an MSA of 100% has similar biodiversity to an ecosystem that is untouched by humans.

Source: European Commission Joint Research Center

397

CITIES AND
URBAN LAND-USE
PATTERNS AND PROCESSES

AN URBAN WORLD

Housing development in Ixtapaluca, Mexico

Well over half of humanity lives in cities, and that proportion is growing. Many cities, too, are expanding—to such an extent that new words, such as *megacity*, have been invented to describe them. With the growth of megacities like Delhi, India (shown here), which has 29 million inhabitants, come challenges in areas like food supplies, transportation, education, housing, employment, and migration. The ways in which governments handle these issues will affect the lives of the majority of humans on Earth.

Although cities differ vastly in terms of their locations and inhabitants, they have many patterns and trends in common relating to their origins and the ways they grow and change. Geographers study data from myriad sources about the people, cultures, and economies of cities in order to gain a deeper understanding of these vibrant, complex, present and future homes to billions of humans.

CHAPTER 15
URBAN SETTLEMENTS

CHAPTER 16
THE URBAN LANDSCAPE

CHAPTER 17
URBAN LIVING

UNIT 6 WRITING ACROSS UNITS, REGIONS & SCALES

UNIT 6 MAPS & MODELS ARCHIVE

UNITED
KINGDOM

EUROPE

GEOGRAPHY
FOR THE PEOPLE

Daniel Raven-Ellison's definition of geography is more expansive than most. The 2012 National Geographic Explorer says, "Geography is anything that happens somewhere, which means that everything has a geographic place." Following his singular vision, Raven-Ellison has created original ways to teach geography to children, pioneered the genre he calls guerrilla geography, and turned London into the first National Park City.

LEARNING OBJECTIVE

IMP-6.C Identify the different urban design initiatives and practices.

GUERRILLA GEOGRAPHER According to Daniel Raven-Ellison, "Guerrilla geography is about encouraging people to see the world differently." Along with fellow members of an organization called the Geography Collective, he has been putting that philosophy into tangible action. One of Raven-Ellison's acts of guerrilla geography, for instance, was a series of urban walks in which he crossed several cities—such as Mexico City and London—on foot, passing through the most disadvantaged neighborhoods and taking a forward-facing photograph every eight steps. The result was a group of films that illuminated the cities from a completely new perspective. In another eye-opening geographical demonstration, Raven-Ellison and a group of students spread out bedsheets over an extensive outdoor field to explore the idea of an ecological footprint—the quantity of productive land that is used to support the lifestyle of a young person in the United Kingdom. Raven-Ellison describes guerrilla geography as "creative, alternative, radical, strange, exceptional," and he makes it clear that it can—and should—be practiced by everyone.

NATIONAL PARK CITY In 2014, Raven-Ellison started a campaign that engaged London's residents and leaders in a novel vision of the city's geography. Why, he asked, shouldn't urban nature be protected in the same way that governments protect the ecosystems found in national parks? "A city park or garden can be more ecologically diverse and rich, and provide more pleasure to a community, than a much wider area of land somewhere more remote," he says. "What is it about our prejudice that means we value that space less, despite the fact we know it is even more important because of the benefits to

our health and productivity, as well as the economy and business?" Raven-Ellison's campaign came to fruition in July 2019, as Mayor Sadiq Khan officially declared London a National Park City.

In fact, the city of London is greener than many might imagine, harboring about 15,000 species and with green space covering around 47 percent of its surface. One of the goals of the National Park City movement is to help Londoners appreciate these natural areas, which are a blind spot for many on their daily rush through the city. Another goal is to expand London's green footprint by taking advantage of the city's vertical geography and adding more green roofs and wall gardens. In this way, the National Park City exemplifies a key facet of guerrilla geography: educating the public about humans' role as geographic place makers. Raven-Ellison explains, "Wherever you are, you are shaping and making places, and whenever you buy or consume something you help to shape or make a place elsewhere." Although the National Park City is not a governmental body with the legal ability to create rules or legislation, Raven-Ellison and his supporters believe it will influence policy through public forums and dialogues with stakeholders.

Raven-Ellison likes to imagine how children will learn to connect with nature in the National Park City of London. "Imagine them in 20 years," he says, "as they grow up to become architects or designers or planners. What ideas and solutions might they have to make us even healthier, even happier, and make this city even better?" ▮

GEOGRAPHIC THINKING

Describe how the National Park City designation might influence future urban design initiatives in London.

Top: Greenwich Park, which has existed since 1433, covers 183 acres on the south bank of the River Thames. Bottom left: The red fox is a common sight in London. Its strong stomach and immune system make it well-suited for the urban environment. Bottom right: National Geographic Explorer Daniel Raven-Ellison.

URBAN SETTLEMENTS

CRITICAL VIEWING The Buddha Tooth Relic Temple stands in the center of the Chinatown district of Singapore, a city-state of more than 5.8 million people. ▌ What factors might have influenced the growth of Singapore?

GEOGRAPHIC THINKING   What factors initiate and drive the growth of cities?

15.1
THE ORIGIN AND INFLUENCES OF URBANIZATION

NATIONAL GEOGRAPHIC EXPLORER Michael Frachetti

15.2
FACTORS THAT INFLUENCE URBAN GROWTH

CASE STUDY: Re-urbanizing Liverpool

15.3
THE SIZE AND DISTRIBUTION OF CITIES

NATIONAL GEOGRAPHIC FEATURE: City of the Future

15.4
CITIES AND GLOBALIZATION

CASE STUDY: How Shanghai Grew

NATIONAL GEOGRAPHIC FEATURE: The Shape of Cities

15.1 THE ORIGIN AND INFLUENCES OF URBANIZATION

Many factors attract people to cities. Some are drawn by economic opportunities. Others come for the excitement of life in the city. A city often serves as a region's political, economic, cultural, and educational center. Many cities are also cosmopolitan centers, home to a variety of ethnicities and vibrant cultures.

THE GROWTH OF CITIES

LEARNING OBJECTIVE
PSO-6.A Explain the processes that initiate and drive urbanization and suburbanization.

For most of human history, the vast majority of people lived in rural areas. During the Neolithic Period (about 10,000 B.C.E.), agricultural advances allowed more people to live in permanent or semipermanent settlements, which eventually grew into cities. They settled in these early cities for a variety of purposes, including trade, defense, and religion. The city of Uruk, for instance, was founded around 4500 B.C.E. along the banks of the Euphrates River, a critical waterway for transportation. Uruk's location facilitated its rise as a trading center to become the largest and most important city in ancient Mesopotamia.

Urbanization—the process of the development of dense concentrations of people into settlements—also led to the rise of cities in places such as the Nile River Valley, the Indus River Valley, and the Wei River Valley in China, but for thousands of years only a small minority of the world's population was made up of urban dwellers. Urbanization increased rapidly during the Industrial Revolution, as factories sprang up in cities and attracted people in search of jobs. Since that time, new cities have developed around the world, and many existing cities have grown in area and population. Today, according to the United Nations, 55 percent of the world's population lives in urban areas.

That number will continue to grow. The UN projects that by 2050, 68 percent of the world population will be urban. The growth of cities has occurred quickly, rising from 751 million urban dwellers in 1950 to 4.2 billion in 2018. Depending on how a country defines what an urban center is, the numbers might be even higher. In fact, after analyzing satellite images of Earth's inhabited regions, some researchers estimate the world's urban population to be significantly higher—as high as 85 percent. In short, cities are an important part of how humans live as well as an important topic in the study of human geography.

An **urban area** is defined as a city and its surrounding suburbs. Beyond this basic definition, the concept of what is urban varies considerably. The United States Census Bureau, an agency responsible for gathering and producing data about the American people, defines urban as "densely developed territory" and recognizes two types of urban areas: (1) an urbanized area, which has a population of 50,000 or greater, and (2) an urban cluster, which has a population between 2,500 and 49,999.

Other countries use different criteria to define an urban area. According to the European Commission, 85 percent of countries define an urban area as having a population of 5,000 or more, but Mali sets the minimum threshold at 30,000, Japan at 50,000, and China at 100,000. India is among the countries that doesn't set a minimum number. Instead, it classifies as urban any place in which fewer than 25 percent of working men are employed in agriculture. Only a few countries consider population density as a measure of urbanization. Rural areas are generally characterized as open swaths of land with few buildings or other structures and a low population density. In most rural areas, agriculture is the primary industry.

Cities and towns provide for their residents in many different ways, including political, medical, financial, and educational services as well as infrastructure such as transportation and communication services. While a city has set boundaries, its area of influence often extends beyond those boundaries. You may have heard people talk about the Greater New York area, or the Los Angeles metropolitan area. A **metropolitan area** includes a city and the surrounding areas that are influenced economically and culturally by the city. The suburbs of a city are the less densely populated residential and commercial areas surrounding a city. Many people who live in suburbs commute into the city to work and to enjoy the city's culture.

GEOGRAPHIC THINKING

1. Explain some of the challenges geographers face when comparing the size of cities or urban areas in different parts of the world.

2. Compare a metropolitan area to a city.

SITE AND SITUATION

The origin, functions, and growth of a city depend in varying degrees on its site and situation. Recall that a city's site is the actual place or location of the settlement and the land on which the city was built. Site factors include the landforms, climate, availability of water, soil quality, and natural resources of the land. A city's situation, on the other hand, refers to the connections between its site and other sites. A city with a favorable situation has easy access to trading partners, resources, and other connections, which fuels growth and economic development.

SITE Certain sites in the landscape are more likely than others to attract settlements. Features such as favorable topography, natural resources, location on a trade route, and land that is easy to defend draw people to a site. Generally, people favor flat topography for building, but if defense is an issue, they may choose a site at an elevated location. In ancient Greece, for instance, Athens was built on hills, which gave the city a view into the distance—useful for detecting advancing armies—as well as a strategic advantage in the event of an attack, because a location is easier to defend when a foe must climb upslope.

Key natural resources, such as iron and coal deposits, a water supply, and waterpower, fuel the growth of settlements. San Francisco, California, for instance, grew up seemingly overnight when gold was discovered in the area in the mid-1800s. Kimberley, South Africa, grew on the site of some of Africa's richest diamond mines.

Sites located on transportation systems attract settlements as well. Early settlements often developed on islands and natural harbors. Islands offer access to water routes and are defensible, as armies have to travel across an open sea, lake, or river to attack. Harbors provide boats and ships a safe haven from the waves of the open ocean, making them a good base for trade. New York City, Rio de Janeiro, Brazil, and Sydney, Australia, are all located on natural harbors. Other cities are located along a river's bend or where it narrows. In Quebec, Canada, two cities are located where the St. Lawrence River narrows—Quebec City on the north bank and Lévis on the south. Likewise, London, England, is located where the Thames River narrows. Because bridges are more easily constructed on the narrow part of a river, this enables people to settle on both banks.

Trade routes also played a significant role in the sites where cities are located. Rivers are historically important avenues for trade, and cities often grew up where two or more rivers meet. Pittsburgh, for instance, is located where the Allegheny and Monongahela Rivers meet to form the Ohio River. Cities also grew where routes converge, such as the mouths of rivers, where they pour into a lake or sea.

With the advent of the railroad, railway junctions became influential factors in dictating the sites of new communities. Businesses wanted to be strategically located along trade routes, as this decreased the time and cost of transporting goods. Cities also arose where goods had to be moved from one mode of transport to another. People were needed to provide the labor, and warehouses were built to house goods until the next leg of the journey.

Factors that make for a quality site can change as technology advances. The development of waterpower resulted in settlements developing along fall lines where waterfalls and rapids provided power for factories. A fall line is the narrow strip of land that marks the geological boundary between an upland region and a plain. The flow of water in rivers and streams speeds up as it descends across the fall line, resulting in falls and rapids. Waterwheels placed in this rapidly flowing water could be used to generate power for mills and factories. At the beginning of the Industrial Revolution, factories took advantage of the power provided by rivers along the Atlantic fall line, a 900-mile ribbon of land between the Piedmont and the Atlantic Coastal Plain, giving rise to some of the largest U.S. cities of this time.

SITUATION A city's situation is equally important to its origins, functions, and growth—or decline. The relative location of a city often dictates its functions. Given the importance of trade throughout human history, it is not surprising to find urban areas along major trade networks. Aleppo, in present-day Syria, is one of the world's oldest continuously inhabited cities, due in large part to its strategic position at the crossroads of trade routes, including the legendary Silk Road. The cities of Samarkand, Uzbekistan, and Ki'an, China, also grew as a result of the Silk Road.

Many cities were built along the Atlantic fall line, where mills and factories could take advantage of the power made possible by fast-flowing rivers.

Mexico City stands on the site of the ancient Aztec city of Tenochtitlán. The ruins of Templo Mayor, the main Aztec temple, are still visible today.

The advantages of a city's situation might change over time as new technologies lessen the impact of old connections. Before the Erie Canal was completed in 1825, for instance, the port cities of New Orleans, Philadelphia, and Baltimore were more influential than New York City. The canal connected New York to the Great Lakes, giving the city access to the Midwest and making it the commercial capital of the country.

As trade networks have changed, new cities have grown to take advantage of new connections. In the United States, the Transcontinental Railroad gave rise to the city of Omaha. In Russia, the Trans-Siberian Railroad similarly led to the development of Novosibirsk. Today, as globalization fuels the transport of goods across the ocean, growth occurs in cities that have ports, where goods and people depart and arrive from numerous points of origin. Indeed, most of the world's largest cities are port cities, located on or near the sea.

The city of Tenochtitlán provides a striking example of the role that site and situation play in the life of a city. In the mid-1300s, the Aztecs moved their capital from a hill in the Valley of Mexico to a marshy island near the western shore of Lake Texcoco. The city they built there, Tenochtitlán, served as the capital of the Aztec civilization until European conquest in 1521. Boasting a population of over 200,000, it was the largest city in pre-Columbian America. Building the city on the site the Aztecs chose required significant technological ingenuity. Three causeways connected the city to the mainland, with bridges that could be removed to allow boats to pass or in case of attack. Canals were built to transport goods from one part of the city to another. Waterways facilitated transportation and trade within the city and with communities lying beyond it. Today Mexico City, with almost 22 million inhabitants in its metropolitan area, thrives on and around the site where the Aztecs built their capital.

GEOGRAPHIC THINKING

3. Compare site and situation and describe factors related to each.

4. Describe the role that both site and situation played in the location of Tenochtitlán.

UNEARTHING SECRETS OF A SILK ROAD CITY

Frachetti (top) collaborates with co-director Farhod Maksudov (bottom) to better understand sites like Tashbulak in present-day Uzbekistan.

LEARNING OBJECTIVE
PSO-6.A Explain the processes that initiate and drive urbanization and suburbanization.

Some of the same factors that drive urbanization today, such as site, situation, and the connections between settlements, influenced the origin and growth of cities in the ancient world. Archaeologist Michael Frachetti and his collaborator Farhod Maksudov have spent years using high-resolution satellite imagery, 3-D models, and computer simulations to predict, discover, and document ancient cities found in Central Asia.

In 2011, Frachetti and Masudov made a startling discovery on a plateau 7,000 feet above sea level in present-day Uzbekistan. Buried under 20 inches of topsoil were the remains of Tashbulak, a vast, ancient city (shown above). The find raised questions relating to site and situation, including who lived there and why they built a city so high in the mountains. Over several years, Frachetti and his team set about excavating the site. They used remote sensing to conduct meticulous surveys of the site, hoping to use a better understanding of the city's layout to direct the dig and provide insights into life in Tashbulak.

Tashbulak was built more than 1,000 years ago by a nomadic civilization called the Qarakhanids. The city's site provided rolling green hills where the Qarakhanids could graze livestock and iron deposits they could mine for tools. And its situation provided connections to the wider world—Tashbulak was located along the Silk Road, a network of trade routes that contributed to the exchange of ideas among diverse cultures in Europe and Asia for more than 1,500 years. At the site, the archaeologists unearthed clues about the city's culture: fragments of tools, ceramics, glass beads, coins dating to about 975 c.e., and a peach pit—evidence that food traveled along the Silk Road from East Asia.

GEOGRAPHIC THINKING

Identify and describe the site and situation factors that likely influenced the location of Tashbulak.

15.2 FACTORS THAT INFLUENCE URBAN GROWTH

Cities grow, change, and evolve. Some changes occur rapidly, while others happen gradually. Changes in transportation and communication networks, population, economic development, and government policies all influence how cities grow—or sometimes decline. A city's growth can blur boundaries as it expands into surrounding areas.

TRANSPORTATION AND COMMUNICATION NETWORKS

LEARNING OBJECTIVE
PSO-6.A Explain the processes that initiate and drive urbanization and suburbanization.

One of the most influential factors in urban growth is transportation. Waterways, railroads, and highways provide a means for raw materials to get to factories, for goods to get to market, and for workers to access jobs. Ongoing advancements in transportation and communication technologies continue to influence urban growth. Transportation systems often make it possible for manufacturing facilities, as well as retail and office environments, to relocate to suburbs where residential areas are plentiful.

Advances in transportation had a profound impact on settlement patterns in the United States. During the colonial period, the earliest cities—such as Boston, New York, and Savannah—developed on the Atlantic Coast or along rivers in order to facilitate trade. As the economy developed and settlement expanded, interior cities grew up on rivers with good access to the coast. Philadelphia, which was the largest city of the colonial era, benefited from its location at the mouth of the Schuykill River. It grew in large part from its thriving trade with the West Indies. Following the American Revolution and the Louisiana Purchase of 1803, New Orleans also rose in prominence due to its great strategic situation at the mouth of the Mississippi River along the Gulf of Mexico. (See the Case Study on site versus situation in New Orleans in Chapter 1, as well as the video in Unit 1.)

The site of present-day Chicago, Illinois, was chosen for its defensive position; Fort Dearborn was built there in the late 18th century. Chicago was an inconsequential settlement until the Erie Canal, completed in 1825, connected the Great Lakes to the Hudson River, and thus the Atlantic Ocean. This route gave Chicago, located on the southwest shores of Lake Michigan, access to the East Coast and transatlantic shipping routes. The advent of the railroad sealed Chicago's destiny as a transportation hub. Chicago was the meeting point of railroads stretching to the east and the west, and the city became the central connecting point between the farms and ranches of the west and markets in the

eastern United States and Europe. Grain processing plants, warehouses, stockyards, and meatpacking plants sprang up, and Chicago's population grew from just a few thousand to more than a half million in less than five decades. Today, 50 percent of rail freight in the United States continues to pass through Chicago. The city is an example of how an urban area can thrive with unexceptional site factors but an advantageous situation.

Communication advances have also influenced the growth of cities. For centuries, the main communication networks were the trade networks, as information traveled along with goods. This changed in the 19th century, with the advent of the telegraph and, later, the telephone. These and later advances in telecommunications technologies revolutionized business and how people lived and worked.

The telephone made business more efficient. Factories located in cities began to take phone orders directly from customers located far from the city. This increased production, which in turn required more workers. More recently, similar changes have taken place due to communication and computer technologies. Today, high-speed internet and wi-fi services allow businesses to instantly communicate, both internally and with their customers. Like advances in transportation, these advances significantly reduced the cost of transmitting and communicating information over long and short distances.

Like any change, advances in communications do not affect all areas equally. Because there are more customers in an urban area, communication companies provide service to these areas first. Meanwhile, new businesses look for locations where there are strong communication networks. Access to the internet is as important to future growth as access to rivers and highways had been in the past.

The telecommunications industry itself also fuels urban growth—the industry is big business with huge corporations that employ tens of thousands of people. Like other high-tech and computer companies, telecommunication companies tend to locate where there is access to an educated workforce. Today's technological hubs draw workers from other areas in the same way factories did a century ago, contributing to urbanization.

POPULATION GROWTH AND MIGRATION

LEARNING OBJECTIVE
PSO-6.A Explain the processes that initiate and drive urbanization and suburbanization.

Rural-to-urban migration is a driver of urbanization, due to a combination of push and pull factors. As the population of a rural area grows, there are often fewer opportunities to make a living there, which pushes people to move away from the area. For farmers, drought or other environmental or economic push factors may cause them to move. For many reasons, these migrants are often drawn to cities. As you learned in Chapter 5, cities offer jobs—or at least the perception of better work opportunities—to potential migrants. For some newcomers, cities offer greater freedom, safety, schools, health care, and more. Beginning with the Industrial Revolution in Europe and North America, as countries have developed economically, urbanization has followed. Today rural-to-urban migration drives urbanization mainly in peripheral and semi-peripheral countries.

Throughout the United States in the 1800s, settlements developed at railroad terminals and grew in size and density to eventually become cities. New towns emerged at regular intervals along the railroad as layover points for passengers and goods. Kansas City, Missouri, for instance, experienced a population explosion following the completion of a railroad line from St. Louis in 1865 and the construction of a bridge across the Missouri River that linked it with the Hannibal and St. Joseph Railroad.

More recently, the region south of San Francisco known as Silicon Valley has experienced massive population growth. Computer manufacturers flocked to the area beginning in the 1950s and, in fact, the region got its name from the silicon used in computer chips. Over the past several decades, the economy of Silicon Valley has gradually shifted from computer manufacturing to high-tech research and development. The population of San Jose, Silicon Valley's largest city, grew from roughly 200,000 in 1960 to over three million by 2020. Like other post-industrial centers, Silicon Valley has struggled with its rapid growth. The influx of highly educated—and highly paid—tech workers has caused rents to skyrocket and put housing in short supply. Many people who don't work in the tech industry can no longer afford to live in the area, and homelessness is a growing issue.

Sometimes called the "Silicon Valley of India," Bengaluru (formerly Bangalore), India, is another example of a post-industrial city with a strong information technology presence. The city is situated along a major national highway and a regional rail hub. In 1998, an industrial park opened near the city's center, attracting hundreds of technology, software, and telecommunication companies. The rapid growth has contributed to a housing shortage. Experts estimate that one-quarter of the city's residents, or some 2.2 million people, live in substandard housing.

Shenzhen, China, a coastal city just north of Hong Kong, had a population of 30,000 in 1979, when the government of China reduced restrictions on foreign investment. From that point, the city grew at an extremely fast rate. Workers and professionals flocked to Shenzhen to take advantage of opportunities in pharmaceutical and textile factories. The high-tech industry has also become an increasingly important part of the economy. Among those drawn to Shenzhen in search of work are migrant workers. Historically, these were farmers who worked in the city only part of the year, but the city's growth has engulfed surrounding farmland, and many now live in the city year-round. Their temporary residency status prohibits them from receiving equal access to government resources.

ECONOMIC DEVELOPMENT AND GOVERNMENT POLICIES

LEARNING OBJECTIVE
PSO-6.A Explain the processes that initiate and drive urbanization and suburbanization.

Although the economies of cities vary considerably, all cities serve important economic functions. A city's functions depend largely on its location and its history. The largest, most influential cities tend to be centers of diversified business services and government or public-service centers. Other cities serve more specific functions. The main function of a capital city like Washington, D.C., is government. Some cities are military centers, some are processing sites for mines, and some are known for manufacturing. Detroit, Michigan, serves as the center of automobile manufacturing in the United States. Houston, Texas, functions as a center of the oil and energy industry.

A city's economic function can change over time. Bruges, Belgium, for example, began as a manufacturing center in the 1200s. Today, the city's striking historical architecture is the basis for its current function—tourism.

Some cities are consumer-oriented centers. These include cities that attract retirees, as well as resort communities such as Cancún, Mexico.

The economy of Pittsburgh, Pennsylvania, revolved around one main industry—the iron and steel industry—in the 19th and 20th centuries. This foundational economic activity, sometimes referred to as a *basic industry*, gives rise to secondary industries that support the basic industry. These secondary industries meet people's needs for housing, food, transportation, and other goods and services. Together, they contribute to a city's economic development.

The functions of a city tend to change over time as a result of technological advances or changes in economic or population trends. Bruges, Belgium, for instance, developed as an important port and wool manufacturing center in the 13th century. Today, it has become one of the most visited tourist destinations in Europe.

While most cities have expanded as the world's population has grown and become increasingly urban, some cities experience a decline when their economic or other functions are no longer relevant. The population of Detroit, for instance, has declined as automobile manufacturing has expanded to other parts of the United States and other countries that offer less expensive labor. Other rust belt cities, like Cleveland, Ohio, and Allentown, Pennsylvania, thrived during the U.S. manufacturing boom in the first half of the 20th century but then fell into economic and population decline as industry moved to the southern United States or to other countries. Some cities that have experienced a decline in manufacturing or other industry have transitioned to service industries. When they attract new businesses and professionals, these economic changes can reverse a city's decline.

Government policies can also influence urbanization. Governments at all levels seek to attract businesses and boost the economy. At the regional level, city governments may compete with one another by offering tax incentives or financial incentives for businesses to relocate. Or local governments may join together in regional alliances to market a region's advantages for economic development. Local governments may create industrial parks or zone huge tracts of land for industrial or other commercial uses. Governments also enact land-use plans and zoning ordinances to separate heavy industry from residential areas, while also providing transportation linkages for workers, such as roads or rail lines. Together, these policies can draw businesses to a city.

Anything that makes a city more attractive will contribute to its growth. Safety and security are important to businesses and residents alike. Cities with adequate policing, public safety, and judicial services may grow faster than comparable cities with higher levels of crime or instability. City governments also seek to draw business and residents with policies that encourage livability—the combination of factors that make one place a better place to live than another. A city's livability factors include housing, transportation, the environment, health and public services, civic life, and economic opportunities. Governments seek to improve livability by providing access to public transportation, quality education, and reliable and efficient city services and assuring the availability of affordable housing.

SUBURBANIZATION, SPRAWL, AND DECENTRALIZATION

LEARNING OBJECTIVE
PSO-6.A Explain the processes that initiate and drive urbanization and suburbanization.

In the United States, changes in urban transportation during the 19th and 20th centuries led cities to grow as people moved outward from the city center. With the development of networks of trolleys, or streetcars, workers no longer needed to live within walking distance of work. This decentralization caused new areas, sometimes called "streetcar suburbs," to develop outside of the core areas of cities. Commuter rail lines gave cities more access to surrounding areas, resulting in "railroad suburbs." New highway development connecting central cities with outlying areas resulted in the growth and expansion of more suburbs.

The process of suburbanization causes the land area that a metropolitan area takes up to expand, but the population of the central city does not necessarily grow. As cities grow outward into surrounding areas, the amount of land per person increases. The relatively inexpensive land that surrounded cities allowed developers to build neighborhoods of single-family homes. These developments often featured tract housing, multiple homes that are similar in design and building materials, that could be built quickly. Upper- and middle-class families were drawn to the suburbs by the promise of low crime, good schools, and more land for larger homes and yards.

Sometimes urban areas expand in an unplanned and uncontrolled way, covering large expanses of land in housing, commercial development, and roads. This process is called **urban sprawl**. While the central cities of metropolitan areas are generally compact, densely settled places with well-planned land uses, street networks, and infrastructure systems, sprawl is a result of chaotic urban growth. As land is developed at the edges of the urban area, often with no overall plan, infrastructure may not keep up.

Urban sprawl has become common in U.S. metropolitan areas, particularly in cities that grew up with the automobile and freeway expansion, such as Atlanta, Los Angeles, and Dallas. While suburbanization has been occurring in the United States since the 19th century, it was only after World War II that urban sprawl became an issue. The growing popularity and affordability of the automobile meant that

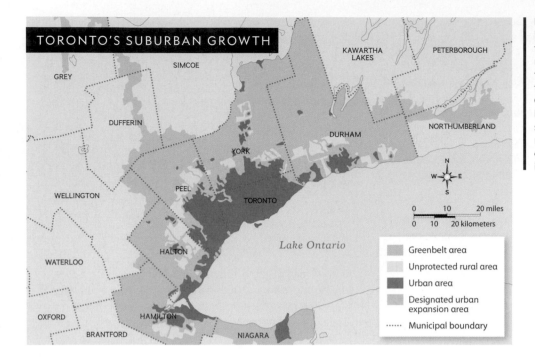

TORONTO'S SUBURBAN GROWTH

Greenbelt area
Unprotected rural area
Urban area
Designated urban expansion area
Municipal boundary

READING MAPS The map highlights the enormous growth taking place in the suburbs north of Toronto and the ways the Canadian government has tried to regulate this growth. The Greenbelt area, for example, has been protected by legislation since 2017. ∎ Explain how the map helps you understand the decentralization of urban areas in and around Toronto.

residential areas were not limited to locations near streetcar or rail lines, and the postwar baby boom meant that many families were looking for single-family homes with a yard.

The expansion of cities has given rise to new land-use forms. The term **edge city** describes a type of community located on the outskirts of a larger city. Edge cities are commercial centers with office space, retail complexes, and other amenities typical of an urban center. Over the years, developers have built residential housing in edge cities as well. Thus, edge cities are perceived as destinations for work, shopping, entertainment, and housing. Tysons Corner, Virginia, located at the intersection of several highways outside of Washington, D.C., is an example of an edge city. What began as a small commercial center today offers more than 25 million square feet of office space and one of the largest retail malls on the East Coast.

A **boomburb** is a suburb that has grown rapidly into a large and sprawling city with more than 100,000 residents. The population of boomburbs often exceeds that of nearby big cities. While edge cities are largely occupied by office and retail space, boomburbs are often made up of many planned communities that have begun to merge together. Anaheim, California; Mesa, Arizona; and Plano, Texas, are examples of boomburbs. An **exurb** is a typically fast-growing community outside of or on the edge of a metropolitan area where the residents and community are closely connected to the central city and suburbs. Exurbs are often low-density residential communities that may include wealthy estates or small rural towns.

Critics attribute a number of negative effects to suburbanization, contending that suburban communities lack identity or a sense of place. The dependence on automobiles contributes to traffic congestion, air pollution, and other environmental issues. In many cases, the people who remain in the city are those who are too poor to move out. This leaves a lower tax base in the city and can contribute to economic decline and urban decay.

REDUCING SPRAWL Urban planners have undertaken efforts to address urban sprawl. In many places, revitalization and redevelopment of decaying areas have helped to lure people back inside city limits. Revitalization focuses on instilling new life into a community by reusing or renovating buildings and beautifying an area through landscaping. Redevelopment focuses on converting an existing property to another, more desirable use. Redevelopment can help address sprawl by creating new mixed-use neighborhoods where people can walk to public transportation, retail, and entertainment venues.

Planners also use **infill** to address and counter sprawl. Infill is redevelopment that identifies and develops vacant parcels of land within previously built areas. Infill helps to counter sprawl because it focuses on areas already served by transportation and other public infrastructure. You'll learn more about infill in Chapter 16.

GEOGRAPHIC THINKING

1. Explain why many U.S. cities developed along rivers in the 19th century. Would you predict these cities to experience future growth?

2. Compare the ways in which economic development and government policies drive urbanization.

3. Explain how the automobile has transformed modern American cities. How are American cities that evolved after the automobile different from earlier cities?

4. Describe how suburbanization relates to urban sprawl.

CASE STUDY

RE-URBANIZING LIVERPOOL

THE ISSUE Once a thriving industrial city, Liverpool experienced several decades of decline until the 1980s, when urban renewal advocates began a concerted effort to turn the tide.

LEARNING OBJECTIVE
PSO-6.A Explain the processes that initiate and drive urbanization and suburbanization.

BY THE NUMBERS

Population of Liverpool

286,487
Population in 1841

846,101
Population in 1931

439,428
Population in 2001

494,800
Population in 2018

Sources: Office for National Statistics, United Kingdom

Today, the waterfront in Liverpool is a mix of old and new. Many older buildings, such as the Albert Dock, have been repurposed by developers in recent years.

OVER THE PAST TWO CENTURIES, LIVERPOOL, a city in northwestern England, has experienced periods of wealth followed by decline and decay. Its initial prosperity was due largely to its site on a natural harbor where the River Mersey meets the Irish Sea. By the end of the 18th century, Liverpool's port had more dock space than London. Industry was further fueled by the 1830 completion of the Liverpool and Manchester Railway, which gave Liverpool access to key industrial areas within Britain. Irish immigrants helped the city's population grow, particularly during the Irish Potato Famine of the 1840s. During the Industrial Revolution, the port provided access for England to markets worldwide.

Liverpool's population peaked at 870,000 in the 1930s, when it began to experience a decline in both prosperity and population that coincided with the collapse of Britain's manufacturing base. By the 1980s, Liverpool's population had dropped to less than 500,000, and its unemployment rate rose from 10.6 percent in 1971 to 21.6 percent in 1991—exceeding 40 percent in some neighborhoods.

At this time, the national government initiated a renewal—or "regeneration"—effort of the central business district. This included the revitalization of the waterfront for leisure use, the development of mixed-use buildings and downtown apartments, and the construction of a new waterfront area, conference center, and public spaces. Liverpool ONE, for instance, involved the redevelopment of 42 acres in the city's central district. Today, it is a mixed-use neighborhood with shopping, a cinema, an adventure golf center, apartments, offices, and outdoor public space. The Royal Albert Dock, which was opened in 1846, has become a major tourist attraction and houses the Merseyside Maritime Museum, the Beatles Story, and the Tate Liverpool art gallery and museum. In 2011, the city also opened the Museum of Liverpool, which is the largest national museum to open in the United Kingdom in over a century. These efforts have achieved their goal of increasing the number of visitors to the city. Liverpool is among the top tourist destinations in the United Kingdom.

Liverpool's renewal efforts have also provided a boost to the economy. The population of the city's center quadrupled in just 20 years. Yet critics contend that the prosperity has not benefited all segments of the population equally. There remain significant pockets of poverty in the city. Liverpool's experiences mirror those of most industrial-era cities worldwide. ∎

GEOGRAPHIC THINKING

Explain how government policies influenced urbanization in Liverpool.

CITY OF THE FUTURE

Adapted from **National Geographic**, *April 2019*

Cities aren't built from scratch. They grow and evolve over time. It's a useful exercise, though, to imagine what an ideal city of the future might look like if urban planners were able to design one from the ground up. Knowing what an ideal city looks like in the future can help those who make decisions about actual cities to make improvements today. The design shown on these pages was imagined for a city of 2050, when the world's population will be 9.8 billion, with 68 percent living in urban areas. ▌ Explain how the future city is more efficient and sustainable than a present-day city.

COMPACT, MIXED-USE NEIGHBORHOODS
Mixed-use districts with housing for different income levels provide all services within walking distance of homes and workplaces.

SPONGE CITY
Parks and infrastructure allow water to percolate through soil to recharge the water table.

AUTOMATED RECYCLING
Waste collection and recycling are fully automated for more efficient reuse of waste.

PRINCIPLES OF CITY DESIGN

 SUSTAINABILITY The future city is designed around natural features, protecting wildlife habitat and natural resources. The city is compact and dense to limit impacts on the ecosystem.

 INFRASTRUCTURE Buildings are constructed more efficiently and include technology that can improve the quality of natural resources such as water, soil, and air. Infrastructure is designed for pedestrian access with limited roads for cars.

RAINWATER CLEANSING
In place of gutters, long rainwater gardens collect and filter rainwater for reuse.

SOCIAL TRANSIT
Regional high-speed rail stations become centers of business and social activities.

FAMILY LIFE
Open and green spaces, community venues, and buildings with larger units foster happier and healthier families.

URBAN FARMS
New communities and developments take advantage of advanced technology for urban farming.

GREEN ROOFS
Solar panels and roof gardens are common atop buildings, encouraging sustainable energy and small-scale farming.

BACKYARD AND SCHOOL GARDENS
Local, organic, and sustainable farming is taught in future city schools.

WATER Protecting upland water systems and rigorous collection and cleansing of stormwater improve water quality. Wetland restoration and sponge-city measures revive habitats and protect against flooding and sea-level rise.

URBAN LIVING The way in which people live in a city is built into the future city's design. Professional, social, and family life becomes more efficient and healthier as small, diverse neighborhoods conveniently provide for the needs of inhabitants.

LOCAL FARMING
Sustainable agriculture is located close to city hubs to limit transportation.

OUTDOOR RECREATION
Wilderness parks nearby provide wildlife habitats, clean air, and opportunities for recreation.

HALF WILD
50 percent of the ecosystem and its waters are protected.

RESILIENCY ZONES
Development is limited in areas likely to flood. Only absorbent surfaces and structures that collect water are allowed.

CONNECTED EMPLOYMENT
Compact city centers connected by high-speed rail knit together employment hubs and reduce urban sprawl.

TRANSIT EQUITY
Affordable and widely available public transit systems give people easy access to regional workplaces.

PROTECTED
WILDERNESS
AREA

AGRICULTURAL
AREA

CITY
WILDERNESS
PARKS

URBAN
HUB 4

URBAN
HUB 3

URBAN
HUB 5

URBAN
HUB 2

PROTECTED
WILDERNESS
AREA

AREAS

HIGH-SPEED RAIL

Dense
urban
center

URBAN
HUB 1

Airport

PROTECTED COAST

Urban
area

Major
rail station

Local
transit

Local
rail station

PRINCIPLES OF CITY DESIGN

SUSTAINABILITY The future city is designed around natural features, protecting wildlife habitat and natural resources. The city is compact and dense to limit impacts on the ecosystem.

INFRASTRUCTURE Buildings are constructed more efficiently and include technology that can improve the quality of natural resources such as water, soil, and air. Infrastructure is designed for pedestrian access with limited roads for cars.

URBAN HUB 7

PROTECTED WILDERNESS AREA

SUSTAINABLE FISHING
Marine ecological areas next to cities are protected and regulated, resulting in sustainable fish habitats.

PROTECTED COASTAL AREAS

TRANSPORTATION
The region is connected by local rail, bus lines, and high-speed trains capable of reaching 600 miles per hour.

URBAN HUB 6

COASTAL PROTECTION
To protect against sea-level rise and flooding, development is barred in coastal areas.

TERRITORIAL WATERS

MARINE CONSERVATION AREA

PROTECTED ISLANDS
Development is banned on protected islands to preserve marine habitats and prevent coastal erosion.

CRITICAL VIEWING The city of the future is designed as a series of urban hubs: dense developments connected by high-speed rail. The regional environment dictates where and how hubs grow. City centers move inland, away from rising seas. ■ Compare the layout of the future city to a present-day city you have studied.

WATER Protecting upland water systems and rigorous collection and cleansing of stormwater improve water quality. Wetland restoration and sponge-city measures revive habitats and protect against flooding and sea-level rise.

URBAN LIVING The way in which people live in a city is built into the future city's design. Professional, social, and family life becomes more efficient and healthier as small, diverse neighborhoods conveniently provide for the needs of inhabitants.

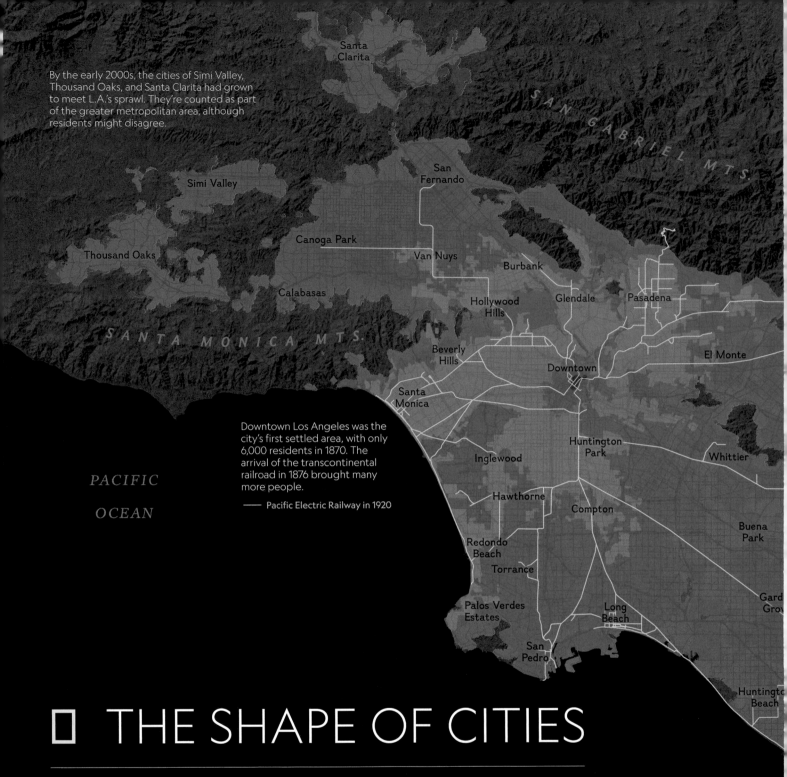

By the early 2000s, the cities of Simi Valley, Thousand Oaks, and Santa Clarita had grown to meet L.A.'s sprawl. They're counted as part of the greater metropolitan area, although residents might disagree.

Downtown Los Angeles was the city's first settled area, with only 6,000 residents in 1870. The arrival of the transcontinental railroad in 1876 brought many more people.

—— Pacific Electric Railway in 1920

⬚ THE SHAPE OF CITIES

A TALE OF FIVE CITIES AND HOW THEY GREW
BY CLARE TRAINOR, JASON TREAT, AND KELSEY NOWAKOWSKI
Adapted from **National Geographic**, *April 2019*

LOS ANGELES, UNITED STATES

Real estate developer Henry Huntington bought up land on the outskirts of Los Angeles in the late 1890s. Then he established the Pacific Electric Railway to link the scattered suburbs. The interurban rail system, which operated from 1901 to 1961, propelled the city's expansion and for a time was the world's largest electric-powered system. Eventually it was dismantled and replaced by bus lines and cars, making sprawl the norm.

**Urban extent
by year**

2014
2000
1990
1980

1950

1920

1890

Fontana

San Bernardino

Ontario

Redlands

Pomona

Chino

In the years after World War II, a new
freeway system and assembly-line
housing construction hastened the
exodus to the suburbs.

Riverside

Moreno
Valley

Yorba
Linda

Corona

SANTA ANA MTS.

Santa
Ana

Irvine

CRITICAL VIEWING Geographers at New York University used
historical maps and satellite imagery to track how metropolitan
regions around the world have developed, using colors to
illustrate how each city has expanded over time. The shape of
a city is determined by many factors. Rail lines, roads, and real
estate play a role. Importantly, so does physical geography. The
boundaries of the Los Angeles metropolitan area, for instance,
are determined by the Pacific Ocean and surrounding mountain
ranges. Cities without such geographic barriers tend to grow more
uniformly into a circle. | Using elements from the map, describe
how Los Angeles spread outward from downtown over time.

Mission
Viejo

San
Clemente

Sources: Shlomo Angel and ALEJANDRO BLEI, Atlas of Urban Expansion, New York University; Pacific Electric Railway;
Los Angeles Railroad Heritage Foundation; COPYRIGHT OPENSTREETMAP CONTRIBUTORS, AVAILABLE UNDER
OPEN DATABASE LICENSE, OPENSTREETMAP.ORG/copyright

LONDON, UNITED KINGDOM

With the opening of the London Underground in 1863, the city spread outward. The Cheap Trains Act of 1883 allowed working-class people to move from grim tenement blocks to railway suburbs. London added the bulk of its population between 1800 and 1900, growing from 1.1 million people to 6.5 million.

Thames

SHANGHAI, CHINA

What had been a relatively compact industrial city of 12 million people in 1982 has now doubled. The city rapidly spread in the 1980s when the government began opening the country to foreign investment. Shanghai's physical footprint has swelled so quickly that population density has declined since the 1990s.

Yangtze River

Huangpu

Urban extent by year (approximate)

2014

2000
1990
1980

1950

1920

1890

0 mi   5
0 km   5

MANILA, PHILIPPINES

Situated between the sea and a lake, the city expanded on a north-south axis. Since 1950, nearly 50 percent of the Philippines' urban population growth has been in the Manila area. That intensified from 1980 to 2000, when almost all the urban growth took place in the city's suburbs.

Manila Bay

Laguna Lake

LAGOS, NIGERIA

After Nigeria gained independence from the British Empire in 1960, oil production soared, bringing people and money to the capital. Now coastal wetlands are being drained to meet development demands from foreign investors and rural Nigerians migrating to the city.

Lagos Lagoon

Gulf of Guinea

INNOVATIONS THAT SHAPED CITIES

RESISTING ATTACK

Walls long protected cities from invaders. Cannons became a threat—until residents developed thick, sloped walls able to withstand blasts. Once countries made the walls unnecessary, cities could spread out.

FACILITATING TRADE

Port cities flourished as global centers of industry. To move cargo inland, rail lines extended out from the cities into the country in all directions. This led to tentacle-shaped development patterns.

MOVING PEOPLE

When the elevator was introduced in the 1850s, cities grew denser and taller. Cities were able to stretch farther into the suburbs when cars and buses filled in the transportation gaps left by rail lines.

CRITICAL VIEWING Some cities grow steadily over time while others, like Shanghai, grow quickly to cover a much bigger area based on changes in government policies or other political, economic, or social factors. ▌Compare the shape, size, and time frames of the cities depicted in the maps.

CHAPTER 15 SUMMARY & REVIEW

■ CHAPTER SUMMARY

Cities often serve as a region's political, economic, and cultural center.

- The number and size of cities continue to increase. Today 55 percent of the world's population lives in urban areas.

- Site and situation factors influence the origin, functions, and growth of a city. Early cities developed close to water for drinking and transportation, had fertile land, and were defensible. Many of the fastest growing cities have been along trade routes. Industrial cities are often located near key natural resources.

Post-industrial urbanization is characterized by rapid change, increasing size, large metropolitan areas, and urban sprawl.

- Cities grow and change—or decline—as a result of changes in transportation and communication networks, population growth and migration, economic development, and government policies.

- As cities grow, populations push outward, contributing to suburbanization, urban sprawl, edge cities, boomburbs, and exurbs.

- Policies to address sprawl include urban growth boundaries, infill development, and other planning efforts.

Geographers have developed a variety of ways to describe, categorize, and understand varied urban environments.

- The gravity model states that the level of spatial interaction between two cities depends on the size of the cities' population and the distance between them.

- Rank-size rule states that the largest city in a country will have a population twice as large as the second largest city. The third largest will be one-third the size of the largest, and so on.

- A primate city is one in which the population far exceeds the next city in size and is significantly more important.

- Central place theory states that size and spatial patterns of settlements are determined by consumer behavior.

Cities have grown exponentially in recent decades. They are sometimes ranked according to their influence.

- Megacities have populations of more than 10 million; metacities have populations of more than 20 million.

- Economic opportunity in urban areas and rural-to-urban migration contribute to the growth of cities.

- World cities influence and are influenced by the economic, political, and cultural processes of globalization.

- World cities are linked within a global hierarchy, and each works to increase its influence on the world stage.

■ KEY TERMS AND CONCEPTS

Use complete sentences to answer the questions.

1. **APPLY CONCEPTUAL VOCABULARY** Consider the terms *suburbanization* and *urban sprawl*. Write a standard dictionary definition of each term. Then provide a conceptual definition—an explanation of how each term is used in the context of this chapter.

2. Identify and differentiate between the two types of urban areas defined by the U.S. Census Bureau.

3. Why is it important for a country to define what it considers to be an urban area?

4. What is a metropolitan area?

5. Differentiate between the terms *site* and *situation*.

6. What is a fall line? How did fall lines influence human settlement?

7. What challenges are associated with post-industrial urbanization?

8. Compare edge cities, boomburbs, and exurbs.

9. Explain how urban planners attempt to reduce urban sprawl.

10. Explain whether infill is an example of revitalization, redevelopment, or both.

11. Describe how the gravity model helps to explain interactions between cities.

12. Explain how the rank-size rule is related to primate cities.

13. Explain central place theory using the terms *threshold* and *range*.

14. Describe the characteristics of world cities.

INTERPRET MAPS

Study the map and then answer the following questions.

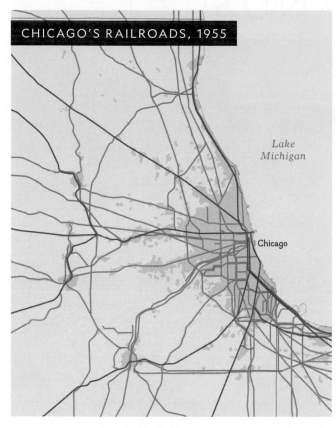

CHICAGO'S RAILROADS, 1955

Lake Michigan

Chicago

— Built 1848–1855
— Built 1856–1875
— Built 1876–1895
— Built after 1895

— Interurban railroads (built after 1895)
▨ Built-up area in 1955

15. **DESCRIBE SPATIAL RELATIONSHIPS** Based on the map, what site and situation features likely influenced where Chicago was located?

16. **EXPLAIN GEOGRAPHIC CONCEPTS** How did railroads affect urban growth in Chicago?

17. **DESCRIBE SPATIAL PATTERNS** Describe how the railroads affected the shape of the area of Chicago that had been built up by 1955.

18. **ASK QUESTIONS** What geographic questions could you ask to learn more about the growth of Chicago between the dates shown in the map key?

GEO-INQUIRY | URBANIZATION IN YOUR COMMUNITY

Consider how you can use Geo-Inquiry to solve an issue about urbanization or suburbanization in your community. Use the steps in the Geo-Inquiry Process below to explore urbanization in your town or city.

ASK Start with an authentic Geo-Inquiry question about urbanization in your community, perhaps something like: *How might we improve an area of decay in our community?* Use the Geo-Inquiry Process to expand this question and ask need-to-know questions such as: *Where and why had urban decay occurred? What efforts, if any, has the local government taken to address these problems? What are other communities doing to revitalize areas of urban decay?*

COLLECT Decide how you could gather geographic information to answer your first question. Explore local government and news sources to learn more about issues of decay, such as homelessness or abandoned buildings in your city, town, or suburb.

VISUALIZE Analyze the information you collected to draw conclusions. Organize the information and use it to create a map, graph, or infographic that others can study and learn from. Using GIS software to create layers of information that can be visualized on a map will aid in finding geographic patterns and possible solutions.

CREATE Focus on ways to tell a Geo-Inquiry story, such as a multimedia presentation that provides scientific data, research, and visuals. Keep your audience in mind and choose elements that will inspire them to take action. Create a list of the elements that you will use, such as specific images, videos, maps, and clear charts and graphs. Outline or storyboard your story, then tie all your elements together using a storytelling tool.

ACT Share your Geo-Inquiry story with decision-makers. Consider how your project can inform them about how they might revitalize areas of decay in the community.

ASK   COLLECT   VISUALIZE   CREATE   ACT

THE URBAN LANDSCAPE

GEOGRAPHIC THINKING How do land-use patterns influence a city?

16.1
THE INTERNAL STRUCTURE OF CITIES

CASE STUDY: Informal Housing in Cape Town

16.2
URBAN HOUSING

CASE STUDY: Land-Use Change in Beijing

16.3
URBAN INFRASTRUCTURE

NATIONAL GEOGRAPHIC EXPLORER T.H. Culhane

16.1 THE INTERNAL STRUCTURE OF CITIES

Although cities vary across the world—partially due to physical geographic factors and available natural resources—they typically have similarities in their patterns of land use. Experts have devised models and theories to help explain the internal structures of cities.

URBAN LAND USE

LEARNING OBJECTIVE
PSO-6.D Explain the internal structure of cities using various models and theories.

Social, economic, and spatial processes determine the land-use structure of cities. Market forces propel dynamic changes at a range of scales, from individual decision-makers to large scale projects such as public roads or housing initiatives. People want to maximize their access to jobs, homes, goods, and services. The most accessible part of a city is its central business district, or CBD, which you learned about in the context of the bid-rent theory in Unit 5. When applied to urban land-use patterns, the bid-rent theory explains the relationships between land value, commercial location, and transportation using a bid-rent gradient, or slope. The gradient is based on land users bidding against one another to purchase land, which means that the cost of land is highest near a central business district and decreases as distance from the CBD increases.

Competition for accessible sites near the city center is an important determinant of land-use patterns. The more accessible a location, the greater the demand for it, which is reflected in the distribution of land value. The CBD is the commercial center of a city and contains offices and public, business, and consumer services. Public services in the CBD include libraries, government offices, and museums. Consumer services are offered at retail stores, restaurants, movie theaters, and concert venues. The accessibility of the city center and the high value of its land attract these services. CBDs are often found in the historic hearts of cities, the original site of settlement.

Bidders are prepared to pay different costs of land for locations at various distances from the city center. For example, a business that generates a significant amount of profit, such as an investment firm, will be better able to afford property near the CBD than a business specializing in selling second-hand clothing.

One shortcoming of the bid-rent theory is its assumption that a city exists on a flat, featureless plane, with all employment opportunities found in a single CBD. Another limitation is the suggestion of consistent city transportation. Finally, in the bid-rent theory, values decrease equally in all directions, which is not reflected in real-life applications.

But the central business district is only one part of an urban area. Cities include different zones, or areas with distinct land uses and purposes. Residential and industrial zones are typical examples of urban areas with specific characteristics and types of activities.

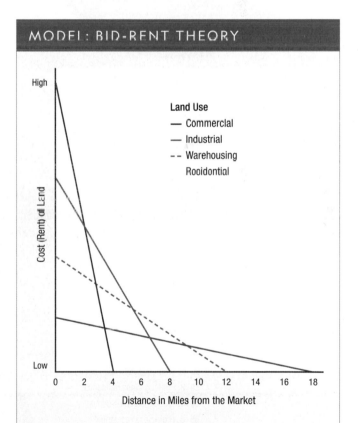

MODEL: BID-RENT THEORY

Land Use
— Commercial
— Industrial
-- Warehousing
Residential

Cost (Rent) of Land (vertical axis, High to Low)

Distance in Miles from the Market (horizontal axis, 0 to 18)

This diagram of the bid-rent theory illustrates that land costs drop as distance from the CBD grows. It also shows that business offices and retail stores tend to be located closer to the CBD, followed by manufacturing activities, warehouses, and residences.

MODEL: BURGESS CONCENTRIC ZONE

The strength of Ernest Burgess's concentric-zone model lies in its usefulness in explaining the basic arrangement of cities such as Chicago and Philadelphia.

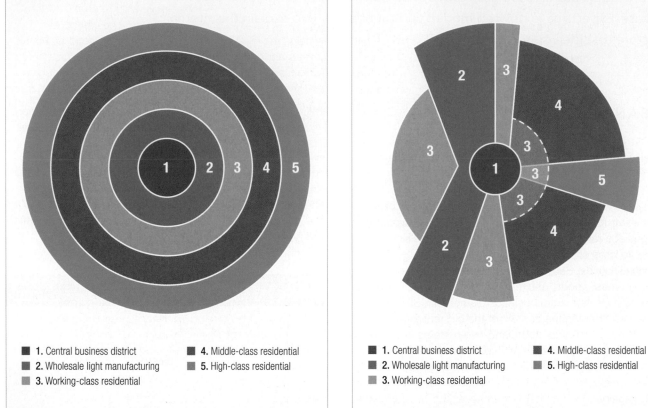

1. Central business district
2. Wholesale light manufacturing
3. Working-class residential
4. Middle-class residential
5. High-class residential

MODEL: HOYT SECTOR

The irregular-shaped segments of the Hoyt sector model develop along transportation routes. Access to transportation and distance from central business district help form the particular shape of each segment.

1. Central business district
2. Wholesale light manufacturing
3. Working-class residential
4. Middle-class residential
5. High-class residential

MODEL: HARRIS AND ULLMAN MULTIPLE NUCLEI

In the Harris and Ullman multiple-nuclei model, different kinds of economic activities cluster together in nodes. Commerce and business nodes tend to be separate from clusters of manufacturing and warehousing.

1. Central business district
2. Wholesale light manufacturing
3. Working-class residential
4. Middle-class residential
5. High-class residential
6. Heavy manufacturing
7. Outlying business district
8. Residential suburb
9. Industrial suburb

MODELS OF URBAN STRUCTURE

LEARNING OBJECTIVE

PSO-6.D Explain the internal structure of cities using various models and theories.

Recall that a model is a generalized representation of reality that helps geographers analyze spatial features, processes, and relationships. Geographers and other experts have developed various models to clarify and describe the spatial and social processes that explain the internal structure of cities. As you read about different city models, consider their strengths, weaknesses, and limitations and how they might be useful in better understanding urban landscapes.

BURGESS CONCENTRIC-ZONE MODEL

Ernest Burgess devised the **concentric-zone model** by studying Chicago in the 1920s. This model observes that a city grows outward from its CBD in a series of concentric rings. Most economic activity occurs in the center (1), the place where you will most likely find a major transportation hub, main offices of businesses and financial institutions, and headquarters of civic and political organizations. As you have read, the central business district is the most accessible area of the city.

The ring (2) adjacent to the CBD is the zone in transition and an area of mixed-land use, moving from industry, factory production, and wholesale light manufacturing to older, densely populated, and typically declining neighborhoods. This transitional zone also generally includes the segment of the urban population earning the lowest incomes, with many people living in poor conditions: crammed into apartment buildings, residing in public housing, or settling in run-down housing previously inhabited by wealthy tenants. Residents in the transition zone are often first-generation immigrants or the elderly.

The third zone (3) is home to the working class and offers the benefit of being located near factory jobs in the CBD and the zone of transition. Population density decreases, and people live in closely spaced single-family homes, apartments, and duplexes. The next ring in the model (4) includes higher-value residences, largely for the middle class, such as private homes and larger apartments. Its overall population density is lower than the third zone.

The zone farthest from the CBD (5) is the commuter zone. This outer ring contains more expensive, single-family detached housing in more spacious suburban settings, with the lowest population density. The impact of the bid-rent curve is apparent in the model: as one moves away from the CBD, land values decline and land use—and population—becomes less dense.

HOYT SECTOR MODEL

In 1939, Homer Hoyt sought to improve the limitations of Burgess's concentric-zone model by adding the concept of direction to the concept of distance from the central business district. After Hoyt conducted research mapping of the average residential rent values for every block in 142 U.S. cities, he concluded that the general spatial arrangement was characterized better by sectors than concentric zones.

His **sector model** illustrates that as cities develop, wedge-shaped sectors and divisions emanate from the CBD and emerge generally along transit routes. The city center remains the location of many commercial functions. As the city expands, each division will extend outward in a sector. The sector model assumes that working-class residential wedges will develop alongside wholesale light manufacturing around the CBD. High-class neighborhoods follow a definite path along transportation routes, on high ground free from flooding, toward open country, or along riverfronts or lakefronts not used by industry. And new middle-class housing built on the city periphery attracts people who want to move away from the city center. In this filtering process, lower-income groups then move into those vacated urban residences. Sectors grow and change over time, with better quality homes at the periphery and older, deteriorating housing closer to the CBD.

HARRIS AND ULLMAN MULTIPLE-NUCLEI MODEL

In their **multiple-nuclei model**, proposed in 1945, Chauncey Harris and Edward Ullman observed that most large U.S. cities don't grow in rings or in sectors but are formed by the progressive integration of multiple focal points of a functional region, or **nodes**. While the Burgess concentric-zone model and the Hoyt sector model suggest predictable patterns, Harris and Ullman claimed that land use varies depending on local context.

The location and growth of the nodes rely on four factors. First, highly specialized activities involve specific sites. Industry, for example, requires transportation facilities and is often located close to railway lines, major roads, airports, or port facilities. In Philadelphia, one node related to the shipping industry has formed along the Delaware River. That location includes import-export companies, rail yards for freight trains, warehouses, and other facilities necessary for the shipping industry to function well.

Second, in certain areas of a city or region, related companies find it economically beneficial to arrange themselves together, leading to specialized areas such as financial quarters, legal districts, and groups of health-related facilities. By clustering together, these concentrations of economic activities all have access to the same pool of expertise and workers, suppliers, and information channels. A cluster of medical and surgical experts can be found on Harley Street in central London. A similar phenomenon happens when health-related facilities like nursing homes, florists, medical supply stores, and pharmacies cluster around hospitals.

Third, negative consequences of commerce and industry, such as pollution, can contribute to the formation of nodes.

MODEL: GALACTIC CITY

The galactic city model is a modification of the multiple-nuclei model and describes a place where economic activity moves away from the CBD toward the urban fringe or surrounding suburbs.

- ■ Central city
- ■ Suburban residential area
- ■ Shopping mall
- ■ Industrial district
- ■ Office park
- ■ Service center
- ■ Airport complex
- ■ Combined employment and shopping center

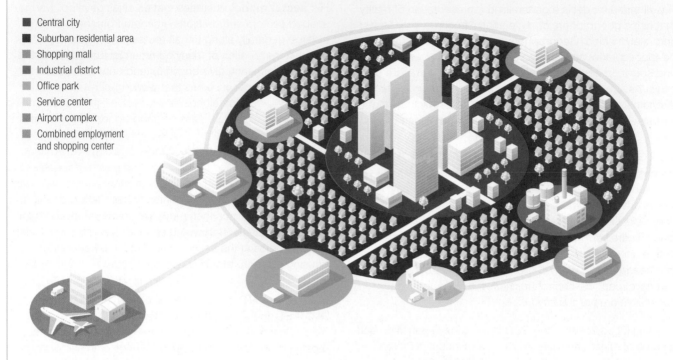

CRITICAL VIEWING Most of Detroit's decentralization took place during the 1950s, when the "Big Three" automobile makers—Ford, Chrysler, and General Motors—built auto plants in suburbs outside of the central city. ∎ What characteristic parts of the galactic city model can be identified in this photograph of Detroit?

Some activities don't coexist well together and repel one another. For example, affluent people choose to live away from areas of industry.

Fourth, economic considerations influence the formation of other kinds of nodes. Because areas closer to central business districts tend to have expensive real estate, large warehouses or grocery wholesaling that require a significant amount of land are typically located farther from city centers. Amazon, for example, has a warehouse closer to Houston's outskirts than the city's downtown, where land is more costly. Warehousing or grocery wholesaling are examples of activities that could benefit from a central location in or near the CBD but cannot afford the affiliated high rents, and therefore must locate farther away from the center.

GALACTIC CITY MODEL Proposed by Pierce Lewis in the early 1980s, the **galactic city model**, also called the peripheral model, explains cities that have a traditional downtown and loose coalitions of other urban areas. This model helps explain what occurred in metropolitan areas that became decentralized and formed suburbs after automobile use became more widespread. The galactic city model includes newer business centers, internal edge cities, external edge cities located along transportation routes, edge city complexes for back offices and research and development (R&D) centers, and specialized subcenters for education, entertainment, sports, and convention centers. Airports in this model are located outside city limits but are connected to the city by radial highways or peripheral highways that are a standard part of galactic cities.

Detroit has highways that radiate from the city center and peripheral highways that circle the boundary of the city. New City, a historic district in uptown Detroit, is considered by some historians to be the original edge city. (Recall that edge cities are commercial centers with office space, retail complexes, and other amenities typical of urban centers but are located on the outskirts of a larger city.) With its numerous edge cities, including Century City, Los Angeles is considered by many to be a galactic city.

ASSUMPTIONS AND LIMITATIONS OF GEOGRAPHIC MODELS It should be noted that many cities have aspects of more than one of these models. And although city models help geographers better understand the internal structure of cities, they are based on assumptions. The concentric-zone model, which was developed nearly 100 years ago, assumes the rapid physical and economic expansion of a city with a diverse, growing population and cheap public transportation in every direction. Property is privately owned and the city's economy is based on commerce and industry. The central business district is the center of employment.

But the concentric-zone model doesn't account for conditions that have prevailed since it was devised, including deindustrialization, suburban flight, widespread automobile use and the highway development that accompanied it, and the declining use of public transportation in many cities in the second half of the 20th century.

The other city models have shortcomings as well. One limitation of the sector model is that its major focus is residential land use. Another is that it doesn't account for multiple business centers. Weaknesses of the multiple-nuclei model include its failure to consider the impact of government policies, and it doesn't represent cities well. And all three of these "classic" models share an economic bias and ignore important factors, such as how race and ethnicity influence urban land-use change.

The galactic city model assumes that there is enough space to contain the ever-expanding sprawl of suburbs and edge cities. This model is also heavily dependent on the use of automobiles.

LATIN AMERICAN CITY MODEL After careful observation and data gathering, geographers Ernest Griffin and Larry Ford developed the **Latin American city model** in 1980. Also known as the Griffin-Ford model, it shares some similarities with the concentric-zone model and sector model. The traditional central market shares the CBD with a modern business center plus important religious and governmental buildings. A high-end commercial sector, or spine, extends outward from the CBD, generally along a boulevard brimming with shops, offices, restaurants, and clubs. Wealthy residents live in the blocks adjoining both sides of the spine, which typically ends at what might be considered an edge city (shown as a mall on the model). A radial road—or a *periferico*—likely circles the city, connecting the mall with an industrial park or parks.

Outside the elite residential sector, as distance from the CBD increases, residential areas of decreasing wealth and quality are found. The zone of maturity, near the CBD, contains older but good quality residences. The area between the zone of maturity and the zone of peripheral squatter settlements, called the zone of in-situ accretion, has mixed-quality housing, but renovations and improvements associated with gentrification can occur.

Other areas of mixed-quality housing in the Latin American city model are called **disamenity zones**—high-poverty urban areas in disadvantaged locations containing steep slopes, flood-prone ground, rail lines, landfills, or industry. Disamenity zones often include informal housing areas known as **squatter settlements**, which are beset with overcrowding and poverty. Sometimes called shantytowns, squatter settlements feature temporary homes often made of wood scraps or metal sheeting. Squatter settlements lack basic infrastructure and services such as fresh water, sanitation, and electricity. The people who live in these settlements aren't legally permitted to be there.

Shortcomings of the Latin American city model include concerns that it fails to differentiate between commercial and industrial uses and that the model is overly influenced by the physical appearance of Latin American cities.

CRITICAL VIEWING Hong Kong is one of the most densely populated regions in the world, with a population density of 17,311 people per square mile. As a comparison, the United States has a population density of 96.2 people per square mile. ▌ If you did not know that Hong Kong had a high population density, what clues from this photo might suggest that it does?

HOUSING DENSITY AND DEVELOPMENT

LEARNING OBJECTIVE

IMP-6.A Explain how low-, medium-, and high-density housing characteristics represent different patterns of residential land use.

Density of housing is usually described as high, medium, or low. Because some areas are generally denser than others, these terms are relative and can take on different meanings in different places. But broadly speaking, in high-density areas, a large number of people live on a small amount of land; in medium-density areas, a moderate number of people live on an intermediate amount of land; and in low-density areas, a small number of people live on a large amount of land. You'll recall that the bid-rent theory shows that housing density is influenced by land values—higher-value land generally leads to higher density housing.

As you read, Manhattan in New York City has high-density housing, with its high-rise luxury towers and mid-rise apartment buildings. An abundance of medium-density housing can be found in Boston and some of its neighboring cities in the form of triple-deckers, which are three-story homes with three separate living quarters. Many other older U.S. cities have variously configured and named medium-density housing: brownstone apartments in New York City, cities in New Jersey, and other urban areas on the East Coast; narrow, multistoried townhouses or row houses in New Orleans, Charleston, Baltimore, Philadelphia, and Washington, D.C.; and two- or three-story, multifamily residences called "flats" in cities like Chicago and Milwaukee.

Low-density housing is common in many suburban areas, which include mostly detached single-family homes. Within cities, certain sections can seem high density simply because other sections of the city are low density in comparison. In Houston, for example, all housing is low density compared to a place like Mumbai, India. But in Houston, the areas with townhouses, apartment buildings, duplexes, or small single-family homes located in close proximity to one another feel high density in relationship to the places with large single-family houses on large lots.

City and regional governments use various legislative tools to permit or prohibit certain land uses as well as to limit density and to guide the direction of growth within their borders. In the United States, one of the most powerful tools is **zoning**—the process of dividing a city or urban area into zones within which only certain land uses are permitted. For example, manufacturing would only be permitted in areas zoned for industrial use. Other areas are zoned for residential, commercial, or mixed use. Zones can be further subdivided so that a residential area might be zoned strictly for single-family homes, or the area might permit medium- or high-density housing such as apartment buildings. Note that zones enforced by municipal governments are not the same as the zones depicted in the city models you learned about earlier in this chapter. Cities set their zoning according

to their present and perceived future needs, which may or may not create zones that reflect patterns like those in the various city models.

Through changes in land-use planning and zoning laws, housing density can increase. Until 2019, most areas in Minneapolis were zoned so that only single-family detached houses could be built. A change in the law allowed the construction of up to three dwellings on one piece of land in all parts of the city. Allowing more homes to be built on each parcel of land makes it more likely for people to be able to find homes at an affordable price. Another way to increase density and create additional housing opportunities in a city is infilling, which you learned is redevelopment that identifies and develops vacant parcels of land within previously built areas. Underused parcels such as parking lots or abandoned industrial land can also serve as sites for new residential or commercial buildings. Infill development often targets key transportation nodes, such as subway or commuter rail stations, or takes place along transportation routes that are connected by bus service.

Some urban areas have embraced increased development, infilling, and changes in land use more than other cities. For example, demand for housing is high in both Seattle and San Francisco due to the presence of high-technology industries. Seattle has rezoned parts of the city to allow for more infill as well as an increase in the height and density of housing. Because of this more pro-development attitude, Seattle, while expensive, doesn't suffer from the exorbitantly high cost of housing that San Francisco does. Currently, just one unit of housing is available for every 10 existing jobs in the San Francisco Bay area. Advocates for solving San Francisco's housing problem with more infill argue that the city core is currently realizing only 57 percent of its infill housing potential.

Increased density offers other benefits, including making it easier for governments and businesses to provide high-quality services. Effective public transportation relies on a certain amount of density because people won't use buses or trains if they have to walk a long distance to reach a station or stop. A mass-transit system also needs enough riders to sustain it financially. In a similar way, businesses need enough customers to provide strong services. For example, cell phone providers are able to supply better service in dense urban areas because the large number of customers leads to a significant amount of revenue. This density also motivates cellular service businesses to launch new technological capabilities in urban regions.

GEOGRAPHIC THINKING

4. Compare low-, medium-, and high-density housing in the United States in terms of what it is and where it can be found.

5. Explain the relationship between housing density and city services. Give examples as part of your answer.

16.3 URBAN INFRASTRUCTURE

Every individual benefits from streets and roads, electric power lines, water supply and sewer systems, railroads, and communications supports like cell phone towers and fiber-optic cables. These features are all examples of infrastructure and are essential elements of a modern society.

WHY IS INFRASTRUCTURE IMPORTANT?

LEARNING OBJECTIVE
IMP-6.B Explain how a city's infrastructure relates to local politics, society, and the environment.

A well-functioning society relies on strong infrastructure, a framework that helps ensure that people have a high quality of life and can move from place to place. Some experts consider infrastructure—in a broader context—to include all services and institutions that help maintain the health, safety, economic, and social aspects of a country: police and fire protection, hospitals, schools, emergency services, and government.

Infrastructure includes mass-transit systems such as subways, buses, and light rail; energy-generating facilities such as power stations, wind farms, and hydroelectric plants; power lines; telephone cables; ports, airports, waterways, and canals; roads; and water supply systems, sewage systems, and wastewater treatment facilities. Without highly operational infrastructure, disease would be more likely to spread, performing basic everyday tasks would be nearly impossible, and going to work or visiting friends and family would be more difficult.

Airports, an essential infrastructure element, allow cargo and passengers to travel both short and long distances at great speed and are typically located near cities with large population centers. The busiest airport in the world, in Atlanta, Georgia, carries more than 100 million passengers annually. However, the Istanbul airport in Turkey, which opened in 2018, is expected to carry nearly twice as many travelers. Jets can fly nonstop to about 60 countries from Istanbul, which is in a critical geographic area between Asia and Europe in Southwest Asia, not far from Africa.

INFRASTRUCTURE AND DEVELOPMENT

LEARNING OBJECTIVE
IMP-6.B Explain how a city's infrastructure relates to local politics, society, and the environment.

Core countries with powerful economies have the best infrastructure. Their wealth and expertise make it possible to build strong and efficient electrical grids, highways, sanitation systems, and other important frameworks. Peripheral countries and many semi-peripheral countries don't have the money to build high levels of infrastructure, and as a result, many people who live in these regions are unable to improve their standards of living. To some extent, this disparity also exists between the core and peripheral areas within a single country. In a city like Philadelphia, which suffers from extreme wealth inequality, areas with lower incomes suffer from unsafe roads, while areas with wealthier residents are much less likely to have roads that put motorists, cyclists, and pedestrians at risk. This imbalance makes it harder to escape poverty. In cities in India, inadequate security on public transportation discourages people from working because commuting to a job could put them in danger. This issue especially affects women, who disproportionately depend on mass transit to get to work.

Places with the strongest infrastructure experience the most economic and social development. For example, well-regulated sanitation systems reduce the spread of disease, efficient rail and highway systems increase people's mobility, and quality education improves knowledge, problem-solving skills, and other key abilities for success. According to a World Bank study, infrastructure improvements in African cities accounted for more than half the economic growth the continent experienced between 2001 and 2005.

Infrastructure helps businesses succeed because it allows them to effectively and confidently transport goods and share information while enjoying a capable labor pool from which they can hire. Infrastructure is one reason businesses and workers may relocate from one place to another. If companies and people are located in a place where it's difficult to get around and communicate, they may instead look for a place with good airports, speedy public transportation, and reliable telecommunications systems. If infrastructure begins to fail, economic activity can be reduced and quality of life diminished.

Solid infrastructure is especially important to the economic vitality of a city. In Nigeria, poor infrastructure in cities such as Lagos and Abuja have contributed to the country's economy performing below its potential. In Lagos, just 6 percent of households have a flushing toilet connected to a piped sewer system. Poor transportation infrastructure has contributed to high costs for residents of Lagos.

T.H. Culhane works all over the world helping communities with few resources achieve energy sustainability. In Nepal, he helped install solar panels on the roofs of buildings.

LEARNING OBJECTIVE
IMP-6.B Explain how a city's infrastructure relates to local politics, society, and the environment.

NATIONAL GEOGRAPHIC EXPLORER **T.H. CULHANE**

EMPOWERING PEOPLE WITH CLEAN ENERGY

T.H. Culhane didn't set out to save the world. He only wanted to help people. But he just might wind up doing both.

Culhane is the founder of an organization called Solar C.I.T.I.E.S., a non-governmental organization that assists individuals and small groups living in impoverished areas in learning how to generate clean, renewable energy that they can use to power their basic needs. Poorer sections of cities such as Cairo, Nairobi, and Rio de Janeiro are extremely dense and have poor infrastructure. Culhane helps people in these places heat water and generate two hours of cooking gas per day, without fossil fuels. "If people don't have access to enough hot water, if people can't boil water, it becomes a serious health issue," he points out. "And when women spend all their time collecting firewood or charcoal and tending stoves to cook and heat water, then how can they go to school or get ahead?"

Culhane began his work in poverty-stricken areas by helping residents build solar water-heating systems, but he realized that not all homes have access to sunlight. To harness the energy that exists in food waste and human waste, he developed a simple open-source biodigester made from containers that anyone can build themselves, which produces fertilizer and creates gaseous fuel called biogas. This fuel—which is methane, or natural gas—can then be used to heat water, cook food, and run electric generators.

At the Zaatari refugee camp in Jordan, Culhane and his organization installed biodigesters while also educating technicians and farmers. In time, these people will become experts and eventually increase their incomes by selling the fertilizer and biogas they produce.

Culhane's hope is that by providing people with these tools, they will be able to thrive. "The poor don't need our pity; they need a chance to help themselves," he says. "I categorically do not believe in categories. The poor aren't a class of weak victims; they're millions of creative individuals."

GEOGRAPHIC THINKING

Explain how the communities using Culhane's tools will benefit in the future.

CRITICAL VIEWING In Copenhagen, Denmark, the DSB—the commuter rail system—includes rail cars set aside for travelers with bicycles and baby carriages. ▌Based on evidence in the photo, draw some conclusions about the economic and social health of Copenhagen.

One recent report estimates that more than 60 percent of low- and medium-income earners in Lagos spend more than half their income on transportation. This problem has contributed to a decrease in Nigeria's economic growth.

Infrastructure can be used not only to improve the economy but also to make lives better for people and create more equality. Cities around the world, including Bogota, Colombia, have created dedicated bus lanes so that buses carrying dozens of passengers will not be forced to sit in the same traffic that cars do. These dedicated lanes help bus riders, some of whom cannot afford their own car, move from place to place more quickly than the slowly moving automobiles. More road and sidewalk space is also being set aside in Bogota and other cities for pedestrians and cyclists. All these measures improve mobility for people with fewer financial resources and can help them lift themselves out of poverty by getting them to and from work faster.

In European cities, high densities, the lack of space, and cultures that are comfortable with using mass transit have led to the creation of bike-friendly infrastructure. This is particularly evident in Copenhagen, Denmark. In Copenhagen, bicycles outnumber cars by more than five to one, nearly one-third of all trips across the city are done by pedal, and more than 40 percent of work- or school-related trips are done on the two-wheelers. The number of miles traveled by bicycle in Copenhagen has increased steadily over the past 25 years, as the government has invested more money into infrastructure that makes cyclists feel safe. This change has provided multiple benefits to the city, including more economic growth and reduced greenhouse gas emissions.

Amsterdam is another city with some of the best bicycle infrastructure in the world. Amsterdam had long been a city where cycling was popular, but after World War II, city planners built roads to accommodate more cars, leading to fewer cycling trips. But a backlash from activists who were angry about traffic deaths forced a reversal starting in the 1970s. Today, nearly 40 percent of all trips in Amsterdam are made on bicycles. Other cities in Europe have also embraced this bike-friendly infrastructure.

GEOGRAPHIC THINKING

1. Describe what might happen to a core country whose infrastructure has started to crumble and become less reliable.

2. Explain why, from a spatial perspective, it makes sense to dedicate lanes for buses only.

THE POLITICAL ORGANIZATION OF CITIES

LEARNING OBJECTIVES

IMP-6.B Explain how a city's infrastructure relates to local politics, society, and the environment.

SPS-6.A Explain causes and effects of geographic change within urban areas.

Like countries, states, or provinces, cities are political entities with governments whose job it is to respond to the needs of their residents. Municipal—or city—governments are responsible for performing a variety of services, such as building and maintaining infrastructure, including roads, sidewalks, sewer lines, and water mains. Cities often also deliver services, most significantly schools but parks and libraries too. They work to ensure public safety by providing police departments and fire departments as well as emergency medical service (EMS) professionals.

Issues with municipal governance arise when an urban area consists of many different local governments that are unable to collaborate because they aren't integrated. For example, if a recently paved road suddenly becomes rough, its repair may involve multiple municipalities that aren't necessarily used to working together. A lack of collaboration can arise at the regional level as well. A large number of separated municipalities can struggle to agree on how to solve region-wide problems. They also tend to operate inefficiently due to offering the same or similar services.

Fragmented governments can face difficulties when the interests of each municipality collide with the interests of the larger region. This is evident in areas with a housing shortage. Local governments often have a desire to limit the growth of their communities because they are concerned about the pressure more development might put on their infrastructure, such as schools. Residents of a community also influence their local government because they want to maintain their quality of life and limit changes perceived as problematic. If enough municipalities work to stop the development of housing, it becomes difficult for the housing sector in a region to provide enough homes.

Issues also arise when government bureaucracies are dispersed between the city, the county, and the state, and they don't cooperate. Lines of accountability become unclear as the actions of different agencies and institutions are influenced by different motivations. The subway system in New York City is often beset with problems because the agency that runs public transportation in the city and its surrounding areas, the Metropolitan Transit Authority (MTA), is not a government organization. As an independent corporation run by a board of directors, the MTA is not controlled by the state government or the government of New York City. It has the power to make spending decisions but not the power to tax the region's residents. The MTA's collected fares have not reduced its large amount of debt, which makes it increasingly difficult for the MTA to spend the money necessary to make the subway operate well.

QUALITATIVE URBAN DATA

LEARNING OBJECTIVE

IMP-6.E Explain how qualitative and quantitative data are used to show the causes and effects of geographic change within urban areas.

Cities are dynamic, and responsible governments analyze these changes and prepare for their impacts. Collecting data—both qualitatively and quantitatively—is one way these governments and others build an understanding of the evolution of their cities and plan for the future. Qualitative research is based on descriptions and rich narratives; quantitative research is based on collecting data about observable phenomena. Researchers gather and record qualitative data through field studies—research conducted in the field—through actions such as interviews, focus groups, surveys, and observations about both the past and present. City employees might stand on a street corner and talk to passersby about their experiences in the neighborhood. Questions focus on what the interviewees think the city is doing well, what they think the city is doing poorly, and what other services they think the city should be providing.

Qualitative researchers document their own observations as well. In a city, they might observe and document how bicyclists and motorists interact with one another, or what activities appear to be popular in a park. Qualitative and quantitative techniques provide a trade-off between breadth and depth. Many people recommend using both or a mixed-method approach, especially considering the nature of the research questions.

CRITICAL VIEWING Municipal governments provide a number of services, including public libraries, many of which are architectural wonders. The Vennesla Library and Culture House in Norway was completed in 2011 and has won several architectural prizes. ∎ Describe some of the effects the library may have on the local area.

CHAPTER SUMMARY

The way land is used in urban areas depends on variables ranging from the desirability of land to historical factors and technological changes. Models help geographers understand how land is used.

- The bid-rent theory explains that land is most expensive near a central business district (CBD) and falls as distance from the CBD grows.

- The concentric-zone model illustrates how a city grows outward from its CBD in a series of concentric rings. The sector model shows wedge-shaped divisions emanating from the CBD.

- The multiple-nuclei model illustrates an urban area where activities have clustered as a result of their unique needs. The galactic city model also depicts an urban area where economic activity isn't centralized but moves outward to the urban fringe or suburbs.

- The Latin American city model incorporates elements from the concentric-zone and sector models but includes other features, such as a spine and an outermost ring where impoverished communities live.

- The African city model shows how African cities tend to have three CBDs: a colonial central business district, a traditional central business district, and a market zone.

- The Southeast Asian city model illustrates cities that grow around ports and lack a central business district.

Urban areas feature high-, medium-, and low-density areas, with density generally decreasing as distance increases from a city's urban core.

- Areas with the greatest density are typically found closest to a city's central business district.

- Available space, history, culture, geography, and different housing types all contribute to why some cities are more densely populated than others.

- Zoning is the division of a city or urban area into zones within which only certain land uses are permitted.

- U.S. cities have typically used redevelopment, infilling, and zoning and land-use changes to address demand for housing.

A well-functioning society requires strong infrastructure.

- The benefits of strong infrastructure are critically important to the economy, health, and overall standard of living of a society.

- Governments face difficulties in responding to the needs of a region when the needs of local municipalities clash and do not match the overall need of the region.

- Cities gather qualitative data, which is based on descriptions and rich narratives, and quantitative data—numerical data with definite quantities—to plan for beneficial geographic change.

KEY TERMS AND CONCEPTS

1. **APPLY CONCEPTUAL VOCABULARY** Consider the term *node*. Write a standard dictionary definition for the term. Then provide a conceptual definition—an explanation of how the term is used in the context of the chapter.

2. Provide an example of an urban area that fits the galactic city model.

3. Why does Hoyt's sector model explain the way cities are arranged better than Burgess's concentric-zone model does?

4. Describe the criticisms of the bid-rent theory when applied to accessibility in cities.

5. Compare the differences between the three central business districts in the African city model.

6. Define the term *infilling* and explain where it can take place in a city.

7. How can zoning influence the shape of a city?

8. Describe the living conditions in squatter settlements.

9. How do the types of housing in a city affect its population density?

10. Describe how Minneapolis and Seattle changed their land-use policies to meet the increased demand for housing.

11. Why do countries with strong economies have stronger infrastructures?

12. How can better bus and bike infrastructure address economic inequality within an urban area?

13. What issues do urban areas with fragmented governments have?

14. Identify an example of qualitative data and explain what it reveals about its topic.

15. Identify an example of quantitative data and explain what it reveals about its topic.

■ INTERPRET GRAPHS

Study the graph and then answer the following questions.

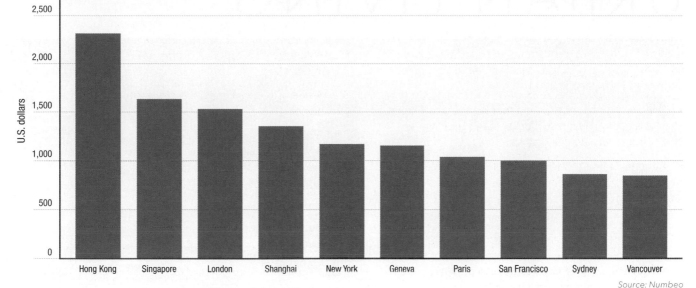

■ PRICE OF DOWNTOWN APARTMENTS PER SQUARE FOOT, 2018

Source: Numbeo

16. IDENTIFY DATA & INFORMATION Which North American city has the most expensive housing measured in price per square foot?

17. MAKE CONNECTIONS How can population density affect the prices of downtown apartments?

18. APPLY MODELS & THEORIES What additional data would you need for each city to assess the validity of the bid-rent theory?

19. DRAW CONCLUSIONS Why do you think most of the cities on the graph are located in core countries?

GEO-INQUIRY | LOCAL INFRASTRUCTURE

Consider how you can use Geo-Inquiry to solve issues about infrastructure in your city or town. Use the steps in the Geo-Inquiry Process below to explore the adequacy of the infrastructure near your home.

ASK Start with an authentic Geo-Inquiry question about the infrastructure in your community. It may be as simple as: *How could I propose a solution to a local community infrastructure issue such as improving recycling?* Use the Geo-Inquiry Process to expand this question and ask need-to-know questions such as: *What is the existing recycling system? Are there items that should be recycled but are not? What existing barriers prevent recycling?*

COLLECT Describe how you could collect qualitative and quantitative data to answer your questions. Explore maps, go to city hall, and talk to friends, family, and neighbors.

VISUALIZE Analyze and organize the information you collected on recycling in your community to draw conclusions. Organize the information and create visuals that will help others understand the issue.

CREATE Focus on ways to tell your Geo-Inquiry story, such as a multimedia presentation that provides scientific data, research, and visuals. Keep your audience in mind and choose elements that will inspire them to take action. Create a list of the elements to use in your Geo-Inquiry story, including images, videos, or compelling storylines. Outline or storyboard your story, then tie all of your elements together using a storytelling tool.

ACT Share your Geo-Inquiry stories with other decision-makers in your community. Consider how your project can inform decision-makers about the infrastructure needs in your community.

ASK   COLLECT   VISUALIZE   CREATE   ACT

URBAN LIVING

CRITICAL VIEWING Between 1998 and 2004, Millennium Park, in downtown Chicago, was transformed from an industrial area of railroad tracks and parking lots into a vibrant public space, including the Jay Pritzker Pavilion with its trellis of steel pipes that contain a sound system. How might this urban park affect Chicago residents and visitors?

GEOGRAPHIC THINKING How can we create sustainable cities for the future?

17.1
DESIGNING FOR
URBAN LIFE

17.2
CAUSES AND IMPACTS
OF URBAN CHANGES

CASE STUDY: The Effects
of Redlining in Cleveland

FEATURE: New York City's
High Line

17.3
CREATING SUSTAINABLE
URBAN PLACES

NATIONAL GEOGRAPHIC EXPLORERS
Zachary Damato and Maria Silvina Fenoglio

CASE STUDY: Milan and Urban
Sustainability

NATIONAL GEOGRAPHIC FEATURE:
Designing to Scale Smart Buildings

17.1 DESIGNING FOR URBAN LIFE

Cities grow in response to a variety of human decisions, both conscious and unconscious, voluntary and forced. How can understanding these geographic processes help in designing and planning livable, sustainable cities?

PLANNING FOR SUSTAINABLE CITIES

Cities worldwide are confronting the challenge of sustainability in the face of growth and population changes. The concept of urban sustainability includes controlling pollution and reducing a city's **ecological footprint**, or its impact on the environment expressed as the amount of land required to sustain its use of natural resources. Sustainable cities are also livable. Livability is the sum of the factors that add up to a community's quality of life, including the built and natural environments, economic prosperity, social stability and equity, and educational, cultural, and entertainment opportunities. People in highly livable cities have few reasons to move away.

Today's urban planners are employing a number of sustainable design initiatives in the effort to make cities both environmentally friendly and welcoming to diverse communities. These strategies include mixed land use, walkability, transportation-oriented development, and smart-growth initiatives such as New Urbanism, greenbelts, and slow growth cities.

As you learned, urban sprawl leads to environmental consequences such as the loss of rural land and pollution due to the excessive use of cars in areas with insufficient public transportation. Meanwhile, time spent commuting to work and school—whether by car or by public transportation—is a drag on sprawl dwellers' quality of life. **Mixed-use development** (MUD) is one way to limit sprawl and design livable urban spaces. A mixed-use development is a single planned development designed to include multiple uses, such as residential, retail, educational, recreational, industrial, and office spaces.

MUDs can range in scale, but all are intended to increase residential densities and minimize the need for travel outside the development, thus reducing transport and commute distances and costs. A MUD may be a single building or a group of multistory buildings that incorporate, for example, retail and commercial uses on the ground floors with apartments and office spaces on the upper floors (vertical mixed-use development). Some MUDs consist of one or more city blocks, and some are even larger, covering 1–2 square miles, with varied types of housing plus schools, businesses, shopping, services, dining, and cultural and recreational opportunities.

Mixed-use development is characterized by continuous pedestrian and bicycle-friendly connections that form a walkable community; **walkability** refers to how safe, convenient, and efficient it is to walk in an urban environment. Measures of walkability may also include the ratio of people who walk or bike to destinations within the community versus those who drive, as well as the availability of locations such as stores or workplaces that are within walking distance of people's homes. Walkable communities must combine land uses within a compact area while also offering safe and inviting spaces for those traveling on foot. Some cities are engaging in revitalization and redevelopment to improve walkability in existing spaces.

Access to transportation options is another goal of sustainable city design. By reducing the number of cars on the road, thoughtful transit planning minimizes the use of fossil fuels and can reduce urban pollution. Better bicycle infrastructure has been listed as one of several reasons that European countries produce fewer greenhouse gas emissions than the United States, which produces 16.5 metric tons of carbon dioxide per capita. In comparison, France produces 4.6 metric tons; Denmark, 5.9 tons; and Germany 8.9 metric tons. Integrated transportation includes biking and walking infrastructures, high-quality public transportation, and well-maintained bridges and roads—all of which come together in an interconnected streetscape.

Transportation-oriented development is the creation of dense, walkable, pedestrian-oriented, mixed-use communities centered around or located near a transit station. Arlington County, Virginia, has created just such an environment in the Rosslyn-Ballston corridor, a development built along one of the major Metro lines running into nearby Washington, D.C. (Metro is the name of Washington's subway system.) Arlington County has seven walkable and bike-friendly Metro transit villages with two Metro corridors that together accommodate 36 million square feet of office space and more than 47,000 residential units. About 40 percent of the residents take public transportation to work and 6 percent walk to work. Major streets have seen a decrease in automobile traffic, while Metro ridership has risen. Walkability and access to transportation have attracted many residents to Arlington County.

for public infrastructure. These lot sizes also encourage the construction of higher-priced homes, which benefit a community financially through property taxes. In addition, states like California have set growth limits by establishing annual quotas for building permits and regulating the rate of development so that it does not outpace what the community's infrastructure can support.

Critics of growth management argue that it increases the cost of housing, contributes to rapidly changing real estate prices, and can even harm the national economy by slowing the building industry. Large-lot zoning, too, can encourage sprawl because each lot takes so much space, and it can push lower-income people out of neighborhoods where they cannot afford the larger, more expensive properties.

Successful growth management plans, however, succeed in balancing the needs of residents with diverse incomes and concerns. In Lancaster County, Pennsylvania, county commissioners developed a growth management plan to protect farmland and nature preserves for public use and constrain growth to designated areas. Lancaster's plan included designing new communities and revitalizing existing communities to be higher density, so that agricultural and conservation areas could be left untouched. The county also took into consideration the importance of preserving historic areas as well as the open lands that are home to long-standing Amish and Mennonite communities. The plan permanently protects approximately 82,000 acres of farmland, as well as 6,000 acres of parks and natural lands.

DIVERSE HOUSING OPTIONS Zoning also plays a role in encouraging housing diversity—a mix of housing types in a neighborhood or community—which is another component of many smart-growth initiatives. Housing diversity is normally encouraged through planning codes that promote low-cost housing such as townhouses, multi-family dwellings, and live-work spaces—units that provide both a place to live and a workspace such as a shop or an art studio. Diverse housing promotes mixed-income neighborhoods, as more affordable units and higher-priced housing can be found side by side. Income diversity helps build the economic base needed to support services and transportation, helps create higher-quality housing, and results in wider access to affordable housing. Other benefits of housing diversity include economic stability and commuting advantages. A shortage of affordable housing in a city can force young professionals, as well as middle-class and working poor families, to live in outlying areas, requiring lengthy commutes to and from their jobs. The results of this migration include traffic congestion and a diminished tax base for the city.

Tucson, Arizona, created a neighborhood with diverse housing when it completely renovated the Connie Chambers Public Housing Project. The former community eyesore was transformed into 180 units of mixed-income housing and renamed Posadas Sentinel. Half of the new units were set aside for families who earn at least 60 percent of the area's median income; the other half are public

LONDON'S GREEN BELT, 2019

0   5   10 miles
0   5   10 kilometers

▢ Green Belt

Greater London

LONDON

Thames R.

The Green Belt of London is a ring of open space created in the 1930s to prevent urban sprawl. Today, it is home to golf courses, farms, and parks—along with some rundown buildings. Whether or not to allow parts of the nearly 2,000 square miles of protected land to be developed for new housing has been a subject of debate.

housing—affordable units owned and administered by the government. Posadas Sentinel was designed to be walkable, energy efficient, and integrated into the larger community. Rather than building on unoccupied land and expanding the city, Tucson recycled the former housing project into usable and lively urban space.

URBAN GREENBELTS At a city's edge, greenbelts sometimes feature in New Urbanist or smart-growth plans. A **greenbelt** is a ring of parkland, agricultural land, or other type of open space maintained around an urban area to limit sprawl. Greenbelt areas can serve as urban growth boundaries, because converting rural land to urban land use is strictly prohibited within them. Greenbelts contribute to the ecological health of a region by limiting pollution, promoting plant growth, and protecting wildlife habitats. Additionally, these areas give city dwellers a chance to connect with nature and enhance their quality of life.

The idea of urban greenbelts is not new: the Green Belt of London, England, was first established in the 1930s, and it still rings the city. In California's Bay Area, the Greenbelt Alliance is a nonprofit organization that actively lobbies to protect the greenbelt spanning four counties surrounding the city of San Francisco. With the Bay Area growing at a rate almost double that of the United States as a whole, natural landscapes in the region are at increasing risk from urban sprawl.

Other urban areas have created political bodies that, while not specifically designed to create greenbelts, serve to protect natural lands in cities and suburbs. For example, Cook County, Illinois, which contains Chicago, established the first forest preserve district in the early 20th century. As stated by its founders, the district's goal was "to acquire, restore and manage lands for the purpose of protecting and preserving public open space with its natural wonders . . . in a natural state for the education, pleasure, and recreation of the public now and in the future." Many counties and municipalities have established forest preserve districts since then, but Cook County's remains the largest, with nearly 70,000 acres.

PROS AND CONS OF URBAN DESIGN

LEARNING OBJECTIVE
IMP-6.D Explain the effects of different urban design initiatives and practices.

Purposeful urban planning, integrated with sustainability, is challenging because it can be difficult to anticipate and understand the real needs of a city's future residents. For this reason, it is important to engage citizens early in the planning stages. In the case of Lancaster County, the planning commission involved farmers, residents, and the Mennonite and Amish communities, as well as other organizations in the area to integrate as many views and ideas as possible into the completed plan. Even as they take into account current needs and concerns, urban planners must also be open to refining their designs as needs change and unforeseen circumstances arise. In addition, urban residents and experts frequently disagree on which planning strategies, methods, and outcomes are best.

So far, the strategies advocated by the smart-growth movement have received both praise and criticism. Supporters point to a significant reduction in the negative environmental impact of cities—largely due to the slowing of urban sprawl, a more efficient use of space, and the promotion of sustainable options. The focus on density, mixed-use developments, and preserving open land is thought to reduce a smart city's ecological footprint. The greater variety of transportation options, including biking, walking, and public transportation, also decreases auto traffic, fuel consumption, and air pollution.

Many also argue that smart growth cities enhance residents' quality of life. For example, transportation-oriented development reduces commute times and the costs associated with daily travel, thus increasing personal time and money available for spending. Mixed-use developments allow residents convenient access to shopping, recreation, services, and jobs. Additionally, measures to manage and slow growth (as in the example of Boulder, Colorado) reduce the strain on a city's infrastructure and ensure that residents have the services they need to ensure an appropriate quality of life.

GREENBELT TOWNS

Greenbelt towns are not precisely the same as greenbelts. Founded by the U.S. government during the Great Depression, they were experiments in urban design intended to provide affordable housing, jobs for the unemployed, and a model for future city developers. The aptly named Greenbelt, Maryland, predates New Urbanism but incorporates many New Urbanist features, including natural open spaces, mixed urban development, and features to enhance walkability. The aim was to create a wholesome, community-focused culture for lower-income workers. To be admitted as residents of Greenbelt, people had to apply and be approved by the government. Greenhills, Ohio, and Greendale, Wisconsin, were the other New Deal Greenbelt towns. Like Greenbelt, they were built as suburbs of larger cities.

Critics contrast the original Greenbelt towns with more recent New Urbanist developments that are often geared for the needs of wealthier residents and feature less affordable housing. At the same time, it is worth noting that the original Greenbelt communities were not perfect models of inclusivity. In Greenbelt, applicants for homes had to be married couples, the husband had to be employed, and at first, African Americans were not considered.

CRITICAL VIEWING The Flame Towers in Baku, the capital of Azerbaijan, rise above the Old City walls. Each of the three towers (one is not pictured) is designed for a different function, including a residential tower, a hotel, and an office building. ▮ Explain how the Flame Towers are examples of smart-growth urban design.

The social benefits of smart-growth urban design initiatives include more diversified housing options within neighborhoods and communities, which encourage social interactions across groups. Such day-to-day communications may help lower barriers between people of different income groups, age ranges, or ethnicities. Personal connections also help create a sense of community and strengthen social identity. The Noji Gardens neighborhood in Seattle, Washington, was designed to encourage just such interactions. State-level growth management requirements for affordable housing led the nonprofit developer to construct the mostly two-story manufactured homes within Seattle city limits near schools, playgrounds, public transportation, and the Columbia City commercial core.

Using space efficiently and creatively through revitalization and redevelopment can lead to fewer building vacancies and reduced crime—another powerful social benefit. In 1999, the city of Richmond, Virginia, launched the Neighborhoods in Bloom revitalization initiative, targeting for improvement vacant and unsafe city lots across six neighborhoods. The city worked with community groups to identify and rehabilitate abandoned and substandard buildings using smart-growth strategies. The program has been successful in turning areas of blight into areas that are economically viable by attracting new businesses.

Critics of smart growth and New Urbanism claim that the promises of communities with mixed income levels and diverse ethnic groups are not often realized. Smart-growth design creates desirable neighborhoods, where real estate prices rise to the point that homes are not affordable for poor or working-class families. Lower-income residents are then displaced to the suburbs or lower quality housing in surrounding areas. At best, say the critics, the result of this process is lack of income diversity in neighborhoods. In some cases, **de facto segregation** (segregation that results from residential settlement patterns rather than from prejudicial laws) occurs when lower-income people of color are unable to afford to live in desirable new smart-growth developments, which then become populated by wealthier White residents.

The United States provides several examples of New Urbanist designs that have failed to create economic or racial diversity. Baxter Village in Fort Mill, South Carolina, represents a mix of new and renovated buildings and a community within which people can work, recreate, go to school, and live. The problem is that it is also, by vast majority, White and middle class—not at all reflective of South Carolina's racial or economic diversity. Beginning in the 1990s, Providence, Rhode Island, began re-imagining its downtown, including launching several mixed-use developments with a goal of attracting financially diverse residents. However, research has shown that the desired mix of income levels has remained stubbornly out of reach. Cases like those of Baxter Village and Providence imply that smart-growth design, regardless of its benefits, does not guarantee affordability. In some cases, urban design initiatives risk promoting homogenous living spaces and ethnic and economic segregation.

Another criticism of urban design initiatives is they apply similar design concepts across many different urban areas. This can result in a sense of placelessness or a loss of historical character. Some commentators argue that multi-use areas can even begin to develop artificial-feeling atmospheres. Standardized designs that may involve the removal or transformation of historic buildings are said to result in sterile and bland-looking places that detract from the character of a neighborhood. New Urbanists claim that suburban architecture is "cookie cutter" and repetitive. In turn, New Urbanist architecture itself is criticized as lacking in the unique qualities or diversity that help give a place its own individual character.

For example, Celebration, Florida, is a community that was built by the Walt Disney Company beginning in 1995 and designed around New Urbanist principles such as walkability, mixed-use development, and abundant public spaces. Homes in Celebration follow strict design rules meant to create the nostalgic look of a classic American small town. Thousands of potential purchasers loved what they saw in Celebration and flocked to buy homes. Many critics, however, have called Celebration's architecture "inauthentic" and find that the community resembles a film set rather than a real town.

Both sides of the smart-growth debate can point to successes and failures of urban design to support their arguments. At present, smart growth, slow growth, New Urbanism, and associated movements are experiments in progress. It remains to be seen how successfully people form neighborhoods and communities within the spaces created by urban designers. The ultimate verdict on the value of different smart growth initiatives may lie many years in the future.

GEOGRAPHIC THINKING

1. Explain the difference between mixed-use development and traditional zoning practices.

2. Describe how mixed-use development supports urban sustainability.

3. Explain whether smart-growth policies are successful in achieving affordable and accessible housing.

4. Identify possible benefits and drawbacks of building on urban greenbelt sites.

5. Describe some of the urban design principles illustrated in the "Cities of the Future" feature in Chapter 15.

17.2 CAUSES AND IMPACTS OF URBAN CHANGES

Urban areas can be hubs of opportunity, but each city faces unique economic, political, cultural, and environmental challenges. The one thing all cities have in common is that they are changing. As urban areas continue to evolve, with some growing and some declining, it is crucial for planners and government officials to understand both the causes and impacts of urban changes.

URBAN CHALLENGES

LEARNING OBJECTIVE
SPS-6.A Explain causes and effects of geographic change within urban areas.

The urban areas of core countries, for all their wealth, power, and opportunity, have serious challenges. In the United States, cities face three major interconnected problems: a declining tax base in the central city, infrastructure costs, and patterns of poverty and neighborhood decay.

The central cities of most U.S. urban areas, especially those that grew in population and wealth during the industrial era, depend (as do all municipalities of any size) on tax revenue—primarily from property owners and businesses. As you've learned, these tax dollars support a city's infrastructure and services: streets, water supply and sanitation systems, police and fire protection, parks, and a broad range of social services. Over the past half century, with economic restructuring and deindustrialization occurring in American cities, tax revenues have declined, sometimes dramatically, as businesses, jobs, and people have moved out of the central city to the suburbs or other regions and countries. Additionally, properties in many older central city neighborhoods have not retained their value, and thus less tax is generated from these homes and buildings.

At the same time that the tax base of most central cities has diminished, the costs of maintaining aging infrastructure and providing urban services to older, often decaying neighborhoods have increased. Old water and sewer lines cost more to maintain, and breaks in these systems are both common and expensive to repair. Transportation systems and schools also have high maintenance costs. Inner-city neighborhoods typically have more elderly, low-income, and immigrant populations, and these groups have greater need for a city's social services. Institutions such as museums and parks, which are enjoyed by residents of the entire urban area, are also the responsibility of the central city's government.

As middle-class and wealthier populations, along with many businesses and jobs of all kinds, have moved away to the suburbs and beyond, the low-income populations left in many older central city neighborhoods face multiple challenges. For many, renting an apartment or house is the only option, and these rental properties are often poorly maintained. These patterns of poverty extend to the businesses in central city neighborhoods as well: restaurants, stores, and service shops often struggle or move away, and failures may result in vacant or even abandoned buildings. Less funding for schools may lead to poorer-quality education. Difficulties with city transportation may prevent some people from taking or keeping jobs in the suburbs. Lack of employment opportunities may cause some to turn to crime, while at the same time, declining tax revenues mean less funding for police departments. The combination of factors that leads to neighborhood decay is difficult to combat, and one result is often concentrated, multigenerational poverty in the central city.

HOUSING DISCRIMINATION
In the United States, discrimination has long been a driver of urban population movements and racial segregation, and it still exists. Housing discrimination is an attempt to prevent a person from buying or renting a property because of that person's race, social class, ethnicity, sexuality, religion, or other characteristic. Discriminatory practices by landlords, owners, real estate agents, or lenders may favor one population group over another, or a certain group may be excluded from a particular neighborhood. These practices have included deed restrictions, redlining, and blockbusting.

For at least the first half of the 20th century in the United States, many property deeds—documents that prove ownership—included statements stipulating that the property could not be sold or rented to someone belonging to a certain racial or ethnic group. In many cities and suburbs, these deed restrictions prevented African Americans from moving into more desirable neighborhoods, where houses could only be sold to Whites.

Housing discrimination also happens through a process called **redlining**, when a lending institution such as a bank refuses to offer home loans on the basis of a neighborhood's racial or ethnic makeup. In the 1930s, as part of a plan to encourage investment and homeownership, the U.S. government created maps that indicated areas considered poor investments for lending institutions. These areas, delineated in red, were predominantly neighborhoods with high African-American populations. Properties in redlined areas fell into disrepair or were sometimes abandoned because residents could not get loans to purchase homes or to improve homes they already owned. The Fair Housing Act of 1968 made redlining illegal, yet recent studies have found that African Americans in many cities such as Atlanta, Detroit, St. Louis, and San Antonio still are approved for mortgages and other loans at lower rates than Whites.

Blockbusting was practiced for decades by real estate agents who would stir up concern that African-American families would soon move into a neighborhood. These unscrupulous agents would convince White property owners to sell their houses at below-market prices. Blockbusting promoted fear of minorities and the discriminatory belief that houses in diverse or African-American neighborhoods were not as valuable as those in other areas. In the resulting outmigration of White homeowners, real estate agents profited through property sales: White sellers sold at a loss and Black buyers paid too much, while the racial makeup of residential blocks changed rapidly. Like redlining, blockbusting was outlawed in 1968, but it has been found that some real estate agents may still guide potential home buyers to particular neighborhoods and away from others.

As a result of these discriminatory practices and other factors, studies have shown that African-American families in the United States, on average, have much less wealth than White families. In cities and elsewhere, the largest investment that most Americans have is in homeownership. Not being able to buy a home or relocate to a better neighborhood with higher home values makes it difficult for a family to build wealth. This reinforces the urban reality that multigenerational poverty is all too common in inner-city neighborhoods surrounding central business districts, where urban minority populations are concentrated.

Another urban challenge at least partially associated with segregation is crime. When people are economically and racially segregated and isolated in urban neighborhoods, crime rates increase. Cities with integrated neighborhoods are among the safest. Other connected factors, such as poverty, also influence urban crime rates. According to the U.S. Census Bureau, urban areas often have higher rates of income disparity than rural areas because a greater range of jobs and educational levels are typically found in cities. Unemployment rates, as well, are generally higher in urban areas. Rural areas tend to have less industry, attract fewer professionals, and have a larger population of retirees—factors that contribute to a more constant and moderate median income. The U.S. Census Bureau reports that while American rural areas have lower median incomes, people living there have lower poverty rates than their urban counterparts.

GEOGRAPHIC THINKING

1. Explain how declining tax revenue is linked to infrastructure problems and patterns of urban poverty.

2. Compare the practices of redlining and blockbusting.

In Levittown, New York, one of the earliest versions of the modern suburb, Long Island's potato fields were transformed into a community of more than 17,000 houses between 1946 and 1951. The original lease agreement for Levittown houses stated that they could not "be used or occupied by any person other than members of the Caucasian race."

THE EFFECTS OF REDLINING IN CLEVELAND

THE ISSUE Though the 1968 Fair Housing Act banned redlining because it promoted racial and economic segregation in many U.S. cities, housing discrimination and segregation persist in Cleveland today.

LEARNING OBJECTIVE
SPS-6.A Explain causes and effects of geographic change within urban areas.

▌ BY THE NUMBERS

8,500
Cleveland's African-American population in 1910

72,000
Cleveland's African-American population in 1930

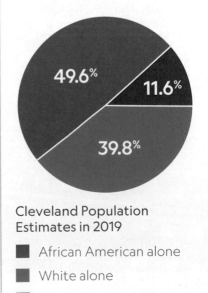

49.6%

11.6%

39.8%

Cleveland Population Estimates in 2019

■ African American alone

■ White alone

■ Mixed-race and other

Source: US Census Bureau

PATTERNS OF RESIDENTIAL SEGREGATION in the United States persist more than 50 years after redlining and blockbusting were declared illegal. Maps produced by the Anti-Discrimination Center, a civil rights organization, provide evidence that not only is residential segregation in the United States alive and well—in cities like Cleveland, Ohio, it is a persistent long-term effect of redlining.

Recall that during the Great Migration, African Americans from the rural South migrated to cities in the Midwest and West. The city of Cleveland's population increased by 60 percent between 1910 and 1930 to more than 900,000 people. During the same period, the African-American population in Cleveland grew by about 40 percent. Although segregation was not enforced by law in the North, many African Americans and immigrants were pushed into low-income, often poor-quality housing in the inner city. These challenges grew as the cities became increasingly crowded and Whites who were biased against African Americans saw the newcomers as competition for jobs and a threat to their neighborhoods. In Cleveland, segregation was further encouraged by redlining and by officials who refused to issue deeds for land owned by African Americans.

Even after the Great Migration ended, fair housing opportunities continued to be a challenge for African Americans in Cleveland. In some instances, policies intended to promote integration deepened the problem instead. From the 1970s to the mid-1990s, for example, the city attempted to use busing to overcome segregation in schools. This move had the effect of deepening housing segregation because it motivated Whites to move out to the suburbs in greater numbers to avoid having their children bused to integrated schools.

A 2019 analysis found that the vacancy rates in some Cleveland neighborhoods were greater than three times the state average. The resulting **zones of abandonment** are areas that have been largely deserted due to lack of jobs, declines in land values, and falling demand. **Filtering** is the process of neighborhood change in which housing vacated by more affluent groups passes down the income scale to lower-income groups. Zones of abandonment are the result of years of redlining, blockbusting, and filtering. They are not merely unattractive; they have a negative effect on the city's tax revenues due to low property values. Zones of abandonment are also havens for crime, as businesses close and buildings are vandalized or even set on fire.

Many of the same neighborhoods that were redlined almost 100 years ago have Cleveland's highest poverty and crime rates today. In 2018, the U.S. Department of Housing and Urban Development awarded more than $2.4 million in grants to fair housing organizations across Ohio with one goal: to fight housing discrimination.

Faced with the lingering effects of redlining, city dwellers often choose to leave. According to a 2019 census finding, Cuyahoga County, where Cleveland is located, had the ninth greatest population loss in the United States. Leaving the city, however, does not guarantee an escape from zones of abandonment. If the problems of discrimination are not addressed in the central city, too often these unfair practices follow residents to the surrounding suburbs. ▌

GEOGRAPHIC THINKING

Describe how zones of abandonment contribute to the economic and social challenges in urban areas.

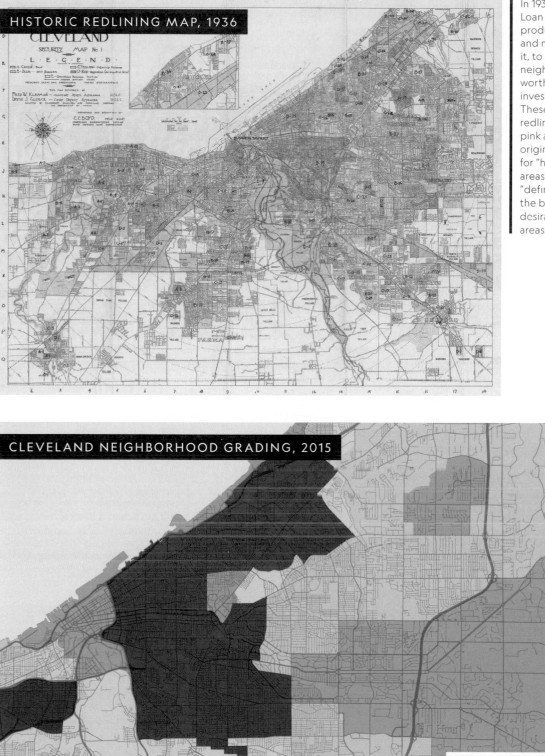

HISTORIC REDLINING MAP, 1936

In 1936, the Home Owners Loan Corporation (HOLC) produced this map, and many others like it, to demarcate which neighborhoods were worthy of property investment in Cleveland. These became known as redlining maps. The faded pink areas of the map were originally red, which stood for "hazardous." The yellow areas were considered "definitely declining," the blue areas were "still desirable," and the green areas were "best."

CLEVELAND NEIGHBORHOOD GRADING, 2015

Neighborhoods receiving an "A" grade
Neighborhoods receiving a "B" grade
Neighborhoods receiving a "C" grade
Neighborhoods receiving a "D or F" grade

READING MAPS In 2015, a real estate agent in Cleveland created this map, in which Cleveland's neighborhoods were grouped into color-coded categories. Those deemed the best investment for real estate investors were given an "A" grade, and so forth. ▌Compare the two maps and explain how they illustrate the legacy of redlining in Cleveland.

CHALLENGES OF RAPID URBANIZATION

LEARNING OBJECTIVE
SPS-6.A Explain causes and effects of geographic change within urban areas.

As you have learned, some of the most rapidly developing cities are located in countries of the periphery or semi-periphery. People in these countries migrate internally from rural areas to cities in search of better economic opportunities, an improved quality of life, or an escape from worsening environmental or security conditions in their villages. Often, the new arrivals are crowded together with previous rural-to-urban migrants in squatter settlements. As you learned, squatter settlements are informal settlements where residents do not have legal ownership of their land and where they usually lack adequate housing and basic infrastructure services such as fresh water, sanitation, and electricity. These cities are simply overwhelmed with the massive inflow of often-desperate immigrants, yet the crowded, difficult conditions do not slow the pace of immigration. Delhi, India, and Jakarta, Indonesia, provide good illustrations of some issues these cities face.

Based on 2018 rural-to-urban migration numbers, the urban population of India is projected to reach nearly 600 million by 2030. The urban area of Delhi, India, has been experiencing some of the most rapid growth in the world. Delhi forms part of India's National Capital Region, along with nearby cities including New Delhi, the capital. The National Capital Region is the country's largest employment center and is receiving record numbers of arrivals. To deal with this inflow of people, the government of India launched the Delhi-Mumbai Industrial Corridor (DMIC) Development Project, with plans to develop 24 new industrial cities between Delhi and Mumbai. Other efforts include improved drinking water distribution, better electricity supply, a high-capacity transportation network, and job skills training.

Jakarta, the capital of Indonesia and largest metropolitan area in Southeast Asia, with about 10 million people, has long been beset with urban problems. At the close of Ramadan, a monthlong Muslim religious observance, the city's population commonly balloons as thousands of Indonesians from rural areas come to attend festivities and then remain in the city to pursue employment and a better quality of life. In response, government officials have revived a program informally named "Return to Village." The government offers villages funding to develop economic growth and stability, which in theory should translate to new and more opportunities for villagers that will motivate them to stay. The Indonesian government is willing to invest in staving off rural-to-urban migration because rapid urbanization is causing significant problems in Jakarta, including traffic congestion caused by insufficient public transportation. Jakarta also experiences flooding due to its location in a lowland area with 13 rivers, a problem that has been exacerbated by unchecked urban growth. As industrialization has increased around the edges of Jakarta, water containment areas have been bulldozed, leading to more severe flooding throughout the megacity.

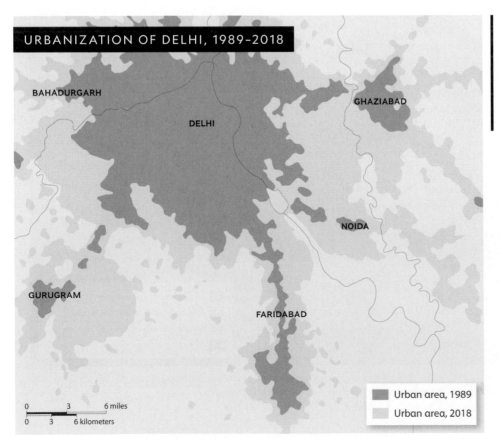

URBANIZATION OF DELHI, 1989–2018

BAHADURGARH

DELHI

GHAZIABAD

NOIDA

GURUGRAM

FARIDABAD

| 0 | 3 | 6 miles |
| 0 | 3 | 6 kilometers |

■ Urban area, 1989
■ Urban area, 2018

The colors on the map illustrate the rapid urbanization of Delhi, India, and its surrounding areas over the past 30 years. The number of urban households in Delhi doubled between 1991 and 2011 as croplands and grasslands were turned into streets, housing, and other city structures.

Though they can be areas of high crime, favelas are also dynamic places where people live, work, and play. The colorful Santa Marta favela in Rio de Janeiro was the first favela in Brazil to receive a Police Pacification Unit as part of the city's attempts to reduce gang-related crime.

INCREASED CRIME RATES In all parts of the world, concentrations of poverty, often caused or exacerbated by rapid urbanization, lead to desperation, social isolation, and often subsequently higher crime rates. Since educational and formal economic opportunities are sparse in poverty-stricken areas, some residents resort to illegal activities such as drug dealing, which then generally leads to other crimes including robbery, prostitution, and murder. In some regions, areas of extreme poverty have developed into disamenity zones—areas composed of shantytowns or other informal housing. Often located on the periphery of large cities, disamenity zones do not receive city services and are controlled by gangs and drug lords.

The favelas of Brazil are one example of disamenity zones with corresponding high crime rates. As you learned, favelas are illegal housing settlements, usually made up of temporary shelters. Some older favelas have more permanent structures, a few of which have electricity. Favelas also have large homeless populations. According to the 2010 census of Brazil, those living in favelas represent 6 percent of the country's total population. Law enforcement has a small presence, if any, within these communities, and drug lords represent an informal ruling body, often battling one another for dominance. Crime in the favelas pushes up Brazil's overall crime rates. According to the Brazilian Forum of Public Security, in 2017, 175 people were murdered per day in the country, which equates to an annual rate of 30.8 murders per 100,000 people. To put these numbers in perspective, in the same year, the United States had 5 intentional homicides per 100,000 people.

AFFORDABLE HOUSING Changing urban populations result in challenges to affordable housing in cities all across the planet, although the specific difficulties vary among cities of the core, periphery, and semi-pheriphery. In core countries, affordable housing is a top urban challenge for a variety of reasons. In the United States, as you have learned, practices such as redlining have created barriers to homeownership for members of minority groups. Many core cities are seeing other challenges to affordable housing as well. Increasing labor and material costs have made it more difficult to build affordable housing units. In addition, as rents and home prices rise in desirable areas close to successful business districts, people with lower incomes are forced to move farther from their workplaces, adding the higher cost of transportation to the cost of housing.

Governments in both core and semi-peripheral countries have attempted a variety of policy solutions such as rent control and public housing developments. Some local governments offer rent subsidies, tax credits, or reduced property taxes to help long-term, low-income residents remain in neighborhoods with rising housing costs. Successful transportation-oriented developments such as Arlington's Rosslyn-Ballston corridor can offer another solution by helping residents reduce both the money and time they spend commuting to work.

Municipalities in the United States have also used zoning to address issues of affordable housing. Inclusionary zoning is a strategy first developed in the 1970s to counter the effects of exclusionary and racially segregated zoning. **Inclusionary zoning laws** create affordable housing by offering incentives for developers to set aside a minimum percentage of new housing construction to be allocated for low-income renters or buyers. The practice has been the subject of debate. Those in favor argue that it requires fewer government subsidies than other affordable housing policies and promotes economic, racial, and cultural integration in urban neighborhoods. Those against maintain that it may result in an overall increase to the cost of housing for a large segment of the population, as consumers who pay market-rate prices for housing are asked to subsidize lower-cost housing. Critics also believe inclusionary zoning is a disincentive for developers and a burden for buyers, claiming that it reduces the overall supply of housing units, which negatively impacts the homebuilding industry.

In 2016, the Lincoln Institute of Land Policy found that 886 cities and counties in 25 U.S. states and the District of Columbia had inclusionary housing programs. Most inclusionary zoning laws are mandatory, while others instead provide government-sponsored incentives for developers to voluntarily include affordable units in their projects. In Boulder, Colorado, developers of rental properties are required to provide affordable rental units, which are purchased by the city of Boulder. The city then sells or gives the units to its Housing Authority or a similar agent. These measures ensure that housing options exist within city limits for low-income residents and working people. In their absence, more expensive housing would be built, which can result in a rise for all home prices within a community.

The United Kingdom has established affordable housing programs that are similar in practice to mandatory inclusionary zoning. Under the Town and Country Planning Act, agreements between local authorities and for-profit builders created more than half of the affordable housing in England. The UK has experienced significant success with this strategy because the law grants local authorities the power to devise their own inclusionary housing policies. The Greater London Authority reported that between 2000 and 2017, London produced more than 11,000 affordable homes per year on average, and as of 2018 more than 20 percent of London households lived in subsidized rental housing. London's inclusionary housing program is one of the largest and most successful in the world.

Cities in the periphery and semi-periphery face particular challenges to affordable housing because of ongoing rural-to-urban migration. These urban areas have insufficient affordable housing and resources to accommodate the rapid increase in their populations. The lack of adequate affordable housing leads to the development of squatter settlements like Brazil's favelas outside of many cities. These informal settlements are often overcrowded, lack basic services (water, electricity, sanitation), and are not officially part of the city, leaving residents to develop their own systems for administration.

LAND TENURE People living in squatter settlements in rapidly growing cities are especially vulnerable because they do not have an official claim or title to the land they live on. They lack **land tenure**, or the legal rights, as defined by a society, associated with owning land. The concept of land tenure encompasses who can use the land, for how long, and under what conditions.

In 2018, Lagos, Nigeria, was ranked the 35th largest urban area in the world with a population estimated by the United Nations at more than 14 million people, 7 million of whom moved into the city between 1990 and 2004. The Lagos state government estimates its population to be closer to 21 million. Many of the tens of thousands of people who arrive in Lagos each week end up living in waterfront settlements, where they have no formal claim to the spaces they inhabit. In fact, Lagos is home to the world's biggest floating informal settlement, Makoko, with population estimates that range from 40,000 to 300,000. In the 19th century, Makoko was a small fishing village that has since evolved into a community of shacks on stilts and boats after the exploding population in Lagos left the poor with very few housing options. Located under the most traveled bridge in the megacity, Makoko has been repeatedly targeted by the government in an effort to erase it from such public view, though the authorities term these forced evictions as "urban regeneration." In July 2012, demolition workers wielded machetes and set fire to the settlement, leaving 30,000 people homeless.

Critics of the Lagos authorities, and of other governments attempting to clear squatter settlements by force, claim that eviction will not eliminate their existence. As Samuel Akinrolabu of the Nigerian Slum and Informal Settlement Federation says, "The moment you demolish a slum, naturally two or more slums will spring up because people need somewhere to sleep."

Rapid urbanization challenges structures of land tenure because it brings about abrupt, large-scale changes in land use, which in turn causes land values to change quickly. These sudden shifts can profoundly affect those living in squatter settlements. Often, local governments cannot keep up with registrations of new land developments. Paperwork delays, coupled with the substantial increase in land value in areas set aside for housing, result in both permanent development and squatter settlement in areas declared

Top: Two women stand in the doorway of a waterside hair salon in Makoko, an informal community built over the Lagos Lagoon in Lagos, Nigeria. Bottom: Workers tend to timber that is waiting to be milled in the neighborhood next to Makoko, which can be seen in the distance.

Some cities, like Mexico City and Beijing, are surrounded by mountains, which further exacerbate air pollution issues by trapping the contaminated air. Mexico City strengthened its restrictions on the number of polluting vehicles allowed in the city in 2019. Other temporary recent measures included residents wearing face masks and school closures.

Climate change remains a rising global problem and a formidable challenge to sustainable cities. Urban areas are both causes and victims of climate change. They consume massive amounts of energy, making them a key source of greenhouse gases. According to the UN in 2016, cities accounted for between 60 and 80 percent of the world's energy consumption and generated up to 75 percent of greenhouse gas emissions from transportation and buildings. At the same time, many of the world's largest cities are threatened by the effects of climate change. London, Mumbai, Cairo, Rio de Janeiro, and New York City are all in low-lying coastal areas vulnerable to rising seas, for example. According to the Global Covenant of Mayors for Climate Change and Energy, cities such as Lima, Cairo, and Tehran also face the possibility of more frequent heat waves with extreme high temperatures.

Through climate action planning, cities such as Vancouver, Copenhagen, and Boston are taking the lead on both combatting climate change and mitigating its impacts, as national governments sometimes lag in their responses.

But experts warn that the problem cannot be solved at the local scale. The UN predicts that the most effective efforts to overcome the challenges of climate change will be coordinated at the "global, regional, national, and local levels." Cities must be a center of solutions to mitigate the effects of climate change, but municipal governments will achieve much less if they act in isolation. For example, while mayors exert partial control over emissions sources within city limits, national governments can complement these efforts by eliminating fossil fuel subsidies and by providing financial support for local initiatives. To this end, China's central government bolstered its national support of cities in 2014 when it launched its National Plan for Urbanization, which will assist cities in their efforts toward sustainable growth.

Funding is a key issue for cities striving to limit the causes and effects of climate change. The UN reports that in 2016, international financial institutions gave a creditworthy rating to just 4 percent of the 500 largest cities in countries of the periphery and semi-periphery. Cities need opportunities to collaborate with financial institutions and establish credit ratings that will allow them to borrow the money necessary for taking meaningful steps toward reducing carbon and other greenhouse gas emissions. Lima, Peru, for example, was able to gain financial support from international organizations to invest in a low-carbon mass transit system.

A wildfire burns close to Canberra, Australia's capital city, in January 2020 (summer in Australia). Extreme heat and drought, two effects of climate change, were blamed for brushfires that scorched one-fifth of Australia's forests that summer. Cities like Canberra and Sydney experienced smoke that impaired visibility and taxed residents' lungs.

Maria Silvina Fenoglio researches the effects of urban green spaces on the habitats of insects such as bees.

LEARNING OBJECTIVE

SPS-6.B Describe the effectiveness of different attempts to address urban sustainability challenges.

NATIONAL GEOGRAPHIC EXPLORER **MARIA SILVINA FENOGLIO**

TRANSFORMING URBAN ROOFTOPS

Biologist and ecologist Maria Silvina Fenoglio is fascinated with a subject that many people would prefer to avoid—bugs in the city. One of her lines of research is urban ecology, studying the impact of urbanization on herbivorous insects and their natural enemies.

National Geographic Explorer Maria Silvina Fenoglio says she is passionate about insects because "although they are extremely tiny, they are amazing organisms performing many valuable ecological processes." She believes that research on insect diversity in urban green spaces could ultimately contribute to the design of more sustainable cities—for example, by helping to maintain green roofs. As the name implies, green roofs transform the tops of buildings into spaces covered with vegetation. Green roofs improve buildings' energy efficiency, retain rainwater, help decrease air pollution, and can lower the temperature in a city by lessening the amount of surface that reflects sunlight.

Fenoglio's research takes a new direction by investigating how roofs can function in an ecological role as a habitat provider for plants and animals, including beneficial insects such as pollinators, natural enemies to pests, and decomposers. In Córdoba, the second most populous city in her home country of Argentina, Fenoglio is examining the possibility of using urban green spaces as biodiversity shelters that allow insect ecosystems to thrive and perform beneficial services. She and other researchers have established field experiments consisting of small green roofs installed on several buildings. In addition to enhancing biodiversity, the insects on these roofs serve as indicators to help scientists measure the effects of urbanization.

Fenoglio's group hopes their findings will convince decision-makers in urban areas to incorporate green roofs as part of urban planning and development. She explains that her ultimate goal is to find evidence that contributes to the development of more sustainable cities and helps bring nature into the lives of city dwellers. ▊

GEOGRAPHIC THINKING

Explain how green roofs can make cities more sustainable.

RESPONSES TO THE CHALLENGES

LEARNING OBJECTIVE

SPS-6.B Describe the effectiveness of different attempts to address urban sustainability challenges.

The spread of urban influences into surrounding rural areas and the physical growth of cities have created urban regions—large areas of interconnected cities, suburbs, edge cities, and boomburbs. To address sustainability, planning must take place at the regional scale to coordinate efforts across all parts of the metropolitan area. Coalitions of governments may work together to establish urban growth boundaries and enact laws that protect farmlands from sprawl.

Regional planning is planning conducted at a regional scale that seeks to coordinate the development of housing, transportation, urban infrastructure, and economic activities. A group of municipalities, such as the central city of a metropolitan region and its suburbs, may cooperatively share a variety of services such as infrastructure, parks and recreation, and public transit. By sharing in the costs of planning, building, and maintaining services such as sewage, regions can achieve economies of scale. Well-executed regional planning can overcome many of the barriers posed by fragmented local governments, and the coordinated efforts of multiple political bodies can be more effective than those of individual governments working independently. Lancaster County, Pennsylvania, which was discussed in 17.1, provides one example of an effective regional planning effort.

The Twin Cities region in Minnesota is one of the most successful examples of regional planning over multiple jurisdictions in the United States. In 2010, under Minnesota state law, the council that oversees planning for the Minneapolis-St. Paul area developed a 30-year project plan called MSP 2040 for its metropolitan region. This long-term plan provides direction and guidelines for the region's future development, including a comprehensive land-use policy. For example, new developments are located and designed to reduce pressures on the environment and natural resources. Growth is promoted in areas that are already urbanized rather than encroaching on agricultural land or open areas. The regional groundwater system is protected from land use changes that could harm its quality, and a regional inventory of natural resources is maintained. MSP 2040 recognizes that issues may transcend any single unit of space: neighborhood, city, or county. The region uses its investments and resources to foster urban sustainability.

Farmland protection policies and urban growth boundaries are often associated with regional planning. Farmland protection means enacting laws that prevent agricultural lands from being converted to nonagricultural uses. MSP 2040, for example, incorporates a farmland protection policy to preserve the half-million acres of agricultural land in the region. Urban growth boundaries also support sustainable cities, as they limit sprawl and protect farmland and other undeveloped lands. Planners in Portland, Oregon, combined an urban growth boundary with infilling to promote efficient and sustainable land use. The city's plans also include affordable housing to address the needs of low-income residents. Nine counties around Denver, Colorado, also established an urban growth boundary in 1997 as part of their regional planning.

The oldest urban growth boundary in the United States may be the greenbelt around Lexington, Kentucky, established within Fayette County in 1958. Originally designed to protect the region's horse breeding industry, the greenbelt has also helped contain the city's sprawl. However, both Denver and Lexington are facing issues with growing populations pushing against the city limits. It has become challenging to maintain affordable housing for all residents without infringing on the urban growth boundaries.

Within cities, cleaning up and developing old industrial sites can lead to the creation of new, more sustainable land uses. Brownfield remediation and redevelopment processes can offer innovative responses to multiple urban sustainability challenges. **Brownfields** are abandoned and polluted industrial sites in central cities and suburbs. Remediation means removing the contaminants in these sites, which reduces health and safety risks to nearby residents and opens the land up for new development. Brownfield remediation and redevelopment can promote growth within a neighborhood and reduce the number of zones of abandonment in a city.

London's King's Cross district is one of Europe's largest city center brownfield remediation sites. Begun in 2007, the project will eventually create eight million square feet of mixed-use development, which will include both high-end and affordable housing, an educational campus, parks, and offices. King's Cross had been plagued by the buried and entangled infrastructure of an abandoned gasworks (an industrial plant that produces flammable gas for lighting and other purposes), along with contaminated soil and groundwater. Remediation of the site created the foundation for projects such as the transformation of the nearby King's Cross and St. Pancras train stations. The King's Cross station in its original state had become a magnet for crime, but it has since been given a dramatic update that includes new, airy open spaces and more efficient connections between the many rail lines that pass through it.

GEOGRAPHIC THINKING

1. Compare the types of urban sustainability challenges faced by different countries.

2. Explain the degree to which urban areas contribute to climate change.

3. Describe why you think regional planning is an effective way to overcome urban sustainability challenges.

Giant cast iron frames, called gas holders, were built in the 1860s as part of Pancras Gasworks in London. They once held tanks of gas that was used to provide heat and light to the local area. Today, new luxury apartments have been built within the former gas holders, dramatically transforming the neighborhood.

DESIGNING TO SCALE
SMART BUILDINGS

Adapted from National Geographic,
April 2019

In the ideal city of the future, buildings incorporate natural elements, generate energy, and produce less waste. Spaces can quickly transform to meet changing housing, industrial, or business needs. ▮ Which of these elements seems most important to you?

SKY GARDENS
Interspersed green spaces promote natural airflow in buildings while providing shade and social areas.

SOLAR WALLS AND WINDOWS
Solar panels incorporated into all surfaces of the building's facade during construction capture the sun's energy.

ENERGY ENHANCEMENT
Data-collection devices are embedded in all new developments to monitor and boost energy performance.

AUTONOMOUS VEHICLES
Most future vehicles are self-driving and electric, especially those used for business purposes.

HONORING HERITAGE
New uses are found for historic buildings, primarily to encourage cultural diversity and continuity.

NATURAL LIGHTING
Bioluminescent materials capture sunlight and illuminate infrastructure and buildings.

GREEN STREETS
Water filtration, environmental monitoring, and native landscaping are part of the streetscape.

THE LOW GLOW
Low-rise buildings allow more light and air to reach the ground, promoting health and well-being.

Source: © Jason Treat / National Geographic Image Collection

PRINCIPLES OF CITY DESIGN

ENERGY In the city of the future, energy is 100 percent renewable. Enough power is produced within or close to the city for it to be self-sufficient. Area buildings share energy resources, generating as much energy as they consume.

LIVABILITY The city of the future is designed for accessibility and safety as more people populate urban areas. Residents have healthier lives with more streamlined access to nature, services, and automated technology.

CASE STUDY

MILAN AND URBAN SUSTAIN-ABILITY

THE ISSUE The Porta Nuova district in Milan was in need of redevelopment, largely in response to the growing challenges of climate change and air pollution. The solution was one of the largest urban regeneration projects in Europe.

LEARNING OBJECTIVE
SPS-6.B Describe the effectiveness of different attempts to address urban sustainability challenges.

BY THE NUMBERS

215,278 SQ FT
of vertical forest

23
tree species in the vertical forest

94
plant and shrub species in the vertical forest

40
average number of plants per inhabitant

Source: Greenroofs.com

The Bosco Verticale (Vertical Forest) towers, supporting nearly 20,000 shrubs and plants, stand within a park called Biblioteca degli Alberi (Library of Trees).

THE CITY OF MILAN, ITALY, has struggled for years with environmental challenges, including one of Europe's most serious smog situations. Seeking to remediate these problems and create a model of urban sustainability, Milan has focused intently on improving its ecological footprint, transportation systems, walkability, and livability.

A milestone was reached in 2014 when Bosco Verticale opened, a pair of residential high rises that by 2019 appeared to be transforming into literal vertical forests. Part of a massive urban redevelopment project of the Porta Nuova district, the towers feature almost 20,000 shrubs and plants in addition to 800 trees. This living insulation moderates the temperature in summer and winter and converts 30 tons of carbon dioxide into oxygen annually. If that weren't impressive enough, the plant life also filters noise and dust and creates a microhabitat for insects and birds. Twenty bird species nest in the towers, along with bumblebees and hermit bees. The buildings are equipped with solar panels, geothermal heating, and a system that recycles water used for washing to irrigate the external greenery.

Weaving throughout Porta Nuova is a connected pedestrian system with green areas, gathering places, and bridges. A huge public park resembling a modern botanical garden is in the center of the pedestrian system and connects the three surrounding neighborhoods. The total redevelopment area for Porta Nuova is 3.2 million square feet.

The city of Milan has received worldwide attention as it continues to take its green projects seriously. Local authorities announced in 2019 that they will plant three million trees in Milan by 2030 to enhance livability, improve air quality, and support the health of residents. A tree covering of this magnitude could absorb five million tons of carbon dioxide annually, helping to reduce air pollution, respiratory disease, and the risk of cancer. The trees will also help lower Milan's temperature, which is hot and humid during the summer. In addition to planting trees in schoolyards, urban parks, and private gardens, the city will also plant them on rooftops. ∎

GEOGRAPHIC THINKING

Explain whether the construction of "vertical forests" can solve the challenges of urban sustainability in other cities.

CHAPTER 17 SUMMARY & REVIEW

■ CHAPTER SUMMARY

Urban design and construction initiatives attempt to control the effects of rapid urbanization, including urban sprawl.

- Smart-growth policies aim to create sustainable communities by placing development in convenient locations and designing it to be more efficient and environmentally responsible.

- New Urbanism is a philosophy that includes designing growth to limit urban sprawl, preserve open spaces, and create spaces that promote interaction.

- Mixed-use zoning permits multiple land uses in the same space or building.

- A mixed-use development (MUD) is a planned development that includes multiple uses, such as residential, retail, educational, recreational, industrial, and office. MUDs exist at many scales, from a single building to a neighborhood of 1 or 2 square miles.

- Transportation-oriented developments are dense, walkable, pedestrian-oriented, mixed-use communities centered around or located near a transit station.

- A greenbelt is a ring of land maintained as parks, agricultural land, or other types of open space to limit the sprawl of an urban area.

- An urban growth boundary separates urban areas from other spaces by limiting how far a city can expand.

Urban design initiatives have positive and negative effects.

- Positive effects include mitigation of urban sprawl, reduced environmental impact and ecological footprint, decreased pollution, reduced strain on the infrastructure, creation of affordable housing options, reduced commute time, and enhanced livability.

- Negative effects include displacement of lower-income families, de facto segregation, neighborhoods with little diversity, and increased placelessness.

Urban challenges are influenced by a country's population and demographics and include housing discrimination, rapid urbanization, crime rates, affordable housing, land tenure, and environmental injustice.

Gentrification has benefits and drawbacks.

- The benefits are increased property values, increased tax base, new businesses, attractive landscapes, and upgrades to infrastructure.

- The drawbacks are decreased affordability, compromised historical integrity, displaced residents, loss of community, and placelessness.

Air and water pollution, climate change, decreases in healthy lifestyle, and threats to the environment present challenges to sustainability. Responses to these challenges include regional planning and brownfield remediation.

■ KEY TERMS AND CONCEPTS

Use complete sentences to answer the questions.

1. **APPLY CONCEPTUAL VOCABULARY** Consider the terms *blockbusting* and *filtering*. Write a standard dictionary definition of each term. Then provide a conceptual definition—an explanation of how each term is used in the context of this chapter.

2. How are the terms *smart-growth policies* and *slow-growth cities* related?

3. Explain walkability and describe how it has been implemented in a specific city.

4. Describe the possible effects of transportation-oriented development on a city or neighborhood.

5. Explain how some urban design approaches might lead to de facto segregation.

6. Define and provide an example of a greenbelt. Include social and environmental considerations with your response.

7. What is a zone of abandonment? Explain why it represents an urban challenge.

8. Explain the significance of restricted property deeds within the context of housing discrimination.

9. Define the term *redlining*. Explain how the term relates to zones of abandonment.

10. Compare the land tenure challenges faced by men and women.

11. How do inclusionary zoning laws help with affordable housing?

12. Explain how brownfield remediation and redevelopment attempt to address urban sustainability challenges.

13. How does regional planning enhance urban sustainability?

■ INTERPRET MAPS

Study the map and then answer the following questions.

TEMPERATURES IN WASHINGTON, D.C., AUGUST 28, 2018

14. **IDENTIFY DATA & INFORMATION** Which area experiences the highest summer temperatures?

15. **ANALYZE DATA** Which types of areas have the lowest temperatures? Why do you think this is the case?

16. **CONNECT VISUALS & IDEAS** Select one area and describe how you could transform it by applying smart-growth policies and New Urbanism. Explain how your ideas would help mitigate urban climate change.

17. **ASK QUESTIONS** If you were contracted for the urban design and development of this area, what questions would you ask?

101.9°F

93.5°F

85.4°F

GEO-INQUIRY | LIVABILITY IN YOUR COMMUNITY

Consider how you can use Geo-Inquiry to solve issues of livability in your city or town. Use the steps in the Geo-Inquiry Process below to explore an area where livability could be improved.

ASK Start with an authentic Geo-Inquiry question about your community. It may be as simple as: *How walkable is my town?* Use the Geo-Inquiry Process to expand this question and ask need-to-know questions such as: *Does my city or town have footpaths and bicycle infrastructure? How do most people get around in the community?*

COLLECT Explore resources to gather geographic information and answer your questions. Find city and neighborhood maps, and ask local government offices about future development plans for your community.

VISUALIZE Analyze the information you collected. Organize the information and create visuals that will help others understand the issue and possible solutions.

CREATE Focus on ways to tell a Geo-Inquiry story, such as a multimedia presentation that provides geographic data, research, and visuals. Choose elements that will inform and inspire your audience to take action. Create a list of the elements you will use to tell your Geo-Inquiry story, such as specific images, videos, maps, and clear charts and graphs. Outline or storyboard your story, then tie all your elements together using a storytelling tool.

ACT Share your Geo-Inquiry story with residents and decision-makers. Consider how your project can prompt community leaders to take action on a livability issue.

ASK   COLLECT   VISUALIZE   CREATE   ACT

WALKING TOKYO

BY NEIL SHEA

Located beneath a train line in a narrow strip of Tokyo, Japan, the Yurakucho neighborhood offers city dwellers one of the joys of urban life—a walkable area densely packed with restaurants and cafés.

If you agree with Harvard urban researcher Edward Glaeser that cities are humanity's greatest invention, then Tokyo is perhaps our greatest example: a stunning metropolis, home to more than 37 million people and one of the world's wealthiest, safest, most creative urban centers. Even if you're not particularly interested in how megacities shape human behavior, Tokyo is unavoidable—it has already changed your life. The city is the ultimate social influencer, the node through which the world connects to Japanese culture.

The author Jane Jacobs, a major influence on urban planning, said that the best way to know a city, to feel its mashed-up power, is to walk it. So photographer David Guttenfelder and I did. For weeks we crossed and recrossed Tokyo, sometimes together, often apart; sometimes in a straight line, often leapfrogging from one area to another. We couldn't be comprehensive. But we could try to see more deeply, linking the city to the people who through their lives give it power.

A SPIRITED SENIOR NEIGHBORHOOD
In the northern neighborhood of Sugamo, clerks were wrestling tables and clothing racks out onto the pavement along the shopping street Jizo-dori, hoping to lure customers from a stream of mostly elderly, female pedestrians.

Older women in twos and threes strolled along, pulling through the racks, pausing here and there. Younger people flitted past the stands or slipped into a nearby coffee shop, but the crowd was mostly elderly, *oji-sans* and *obaa-sans*, grandfathers and grandmothers.

Cities often talk about themselves in terms of life, growth, youth—but old age and death are always there too, even when they're largely ignored or treated as a matter of dull housekeeping. Harvard anthropologist Ted Bestor had pointed me toward Sugamo because the neighborhood reveals a defining feature of Tokyo: its enormous, rapidly increasing elderly population.

"In Tokyo they don't try to hide the old people away," Bestor said. "There are just too many of them. So the old folks have their own district; they make their own fun."

A NEW TYPE OF URBAN DESIGN
A few weeks later, in the Asakusa neighborhood on the other side of the city, I met with Kengo Kuma, the architect who designed the new national stadium for the Summer Olympics (rescheduled from 2020 to 2021 due to COVID-19). We sat in a room on the third floor of the Asakusa Culture Tourist Information Center, which, like nearly all the buildings Kuma has designed, is both hypermodern and surfaced in natural materials, in this case wood—a combination intended to lend warmth and presence while also paying homage to traditional Japanese craftsmanship. Kuma is sometimes taken for an anti-urbanist—opposed to the hardness of cities—but he was quick to reject that label.

"People say I'm a critic of cities," he said, shaking his head. "I want to reshape the city. I want to break space up and return things to a smaller scale." That smaller scale, he said, was once a defining feature of Japanese life, and would allow for more trees, gardens, parks—and more human connections.

Of course the massive oval stadium will likely define him to future generations. But even that wears Kuma's vision—a future in which structures are all built for multiple uses over their lifetime and sit lightly on the landscape. After the Olympics his stadium will be converted for use as a soccer arena. It will sit in a grove of trees, and its several floors will be ringed with more greenery, planted around open-air walkways. The stadium's roof is also open, allowing natural light to flood its interior.

"Our urban design up until now was to find land and put a huge building on it," Kuma said. "Destroying everything to make way for skyscrapers and shopping centers—that has been the method in Asia." Kuma was animated, sketching with his hands as he described Tokyo. Many ideas he supports, from environmental sustainability to programs aimed at "returning nature to the city," have slowly gained ground. Kuma described Japan as a "mature society"—wealthy, technologically advanced, and aging. Ready, in other words, to grow more responsibly. "The best thing we can do," he said, "is set an example. . . . We can show how to do things differently."

IN THE CITY'S HEART, A CALL FOR DIVERSITY
Yuriko Koike, Tokyo's first female governor, attended university in another massive metropolis—Cairo. "What's attractive about Cairo is that it's chaotic," she said, smiling at memories of hectic streets. "But of course what's attractive about Tokyo is that everything is controlled."

We were walking down a shaded gravel path in the central Hama-rikyu Gardens, a calm refuge of manicured lawns and flower beds with stands of black pines, crape myrtles, and cherry trees flush against the Sumida River.

"What's missing now in Tokyo is diversity," she said. Arriving from Brooklyn, I found Tokyo's lack of diversity a regular, striking feature of my journey. Sizable populations of Koreans and Chinese live in Tokyo, and the number of "international residents" has also increased over time—in 2018, one in 10 Tokyoites in their 20s were non-Japanese. But in a city so vast, those groups faded quickly.

Koike herself has been criticized for talking diversity without doing much to enable it. But her election itself was seismic and may yet prove part of a broader shift. And she understands that Tokyo's composition will soon change no matter what. If nothing else, old age guarantees it. ▌

Adapted from "Walking Tokyo," Neil Shea, *National Geographic*, April 2019

GRAVITY MODEL

The gravity model is used to explain the interactions among cities based on the size of the cities' populations and the distance between them. According to the model, New York City, which is a massive population center, draws more traffic in terms of trade, visitors, migrants, and communication than smaller cities do. Because the gravity model does not take geographic features such as political, cultural, or physical barriers into account, its predictions do not perfectly reflect real-world interactions. ▮ Think about where you live. Use the gravity model to describe interactions of trade, tourism, and communication between your community and the cities shown on the map.

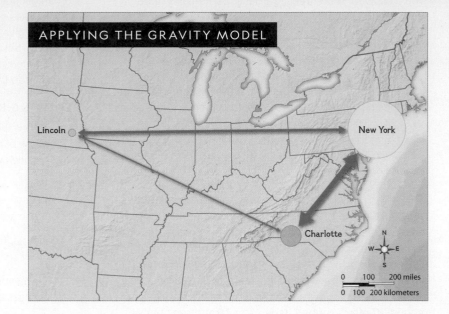

APPLYING THE GRAVITY MODEL

RANK-SIZE RULE

The rank-size rule states that the second-largest city in a country will be approximately one-half the size of the largest; the third-largest city will be approximately one-third the size of the largest city; and so on. This graph depicts the populations of the five largest cities in Australia. ▮ Explain the degree to which Australia's most populous cities follow the rank-size rule.

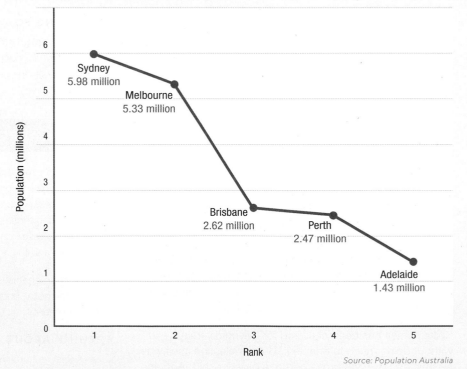

LARGEST CITIES IN AUSTRALIA, 2020

Source: Population Australia

CHAPTER 15

CENTRAL PLACE THEORY

Central place theory describes the distribution of cities, towns, villages, and hamlets in a given region, not taking into account physical geographic barriers such as mountains or bodies of water. According to the theory, large cities produce higher-order goods and services, thus drawing trade and population from surrounding towns and villages.

▍ Use central place theory to explain the distribution of cities, towns, and villages surrounding Nairobi, Kenya.

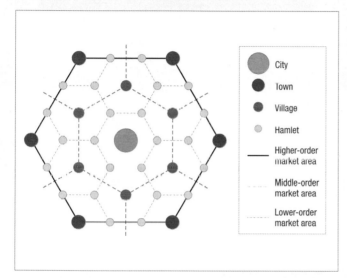

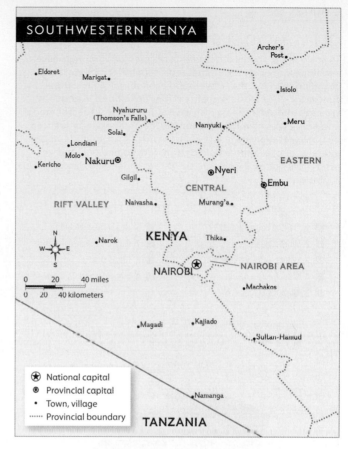

CHAPTER 16

BID-RENT THEORY

The bid-rent theory explains that the cost of land determines how it will be used. In agricultural settings, the theory portrays types of farming that take place at different distances from the central business district (CBD). Within cities, it may help explain the spatial organization of different sectors. ▍ Choose one of the city models from Chapter 16 and use bid-rent theory to explain the locations of the different economic sectors in the model. Describe other factors influencing the location of sectors.

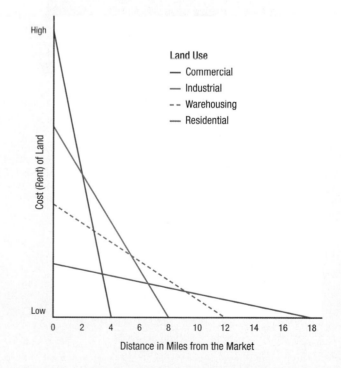

CHAPTER 16

CITY MODELS

To analyze the spatial organization of cities, geographers have developed several models that represent how cities are laid out, based on the ways they developed economically. The Burgess concentric-zone model visualizes cities developed in rings around a central business district, or CBD. The Hoyt sector model envisions cities developed around a CBD and heavily influenced by transportation routes. The Harris and Ullman multiple-nuclei model proposes a more fluid design, with commercial and residential nodes. ▌Compare the three models and describe their limitations.

1. Central business district
2. Wholesale light manufacturing
3. Working-class residential
4. Middle-class residential
5. High-class residential
6. Heavy manufacturing
7. Outlying business district
8. Residential suburb
9. Industrial suburb

BURGESS CONCENTRIC-ZONE

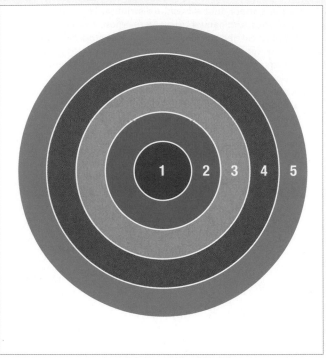

HOYT SECTOR

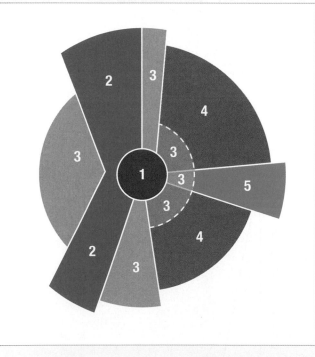

HARRIS AND ULLMAN MULTIPLE-NUCLEI

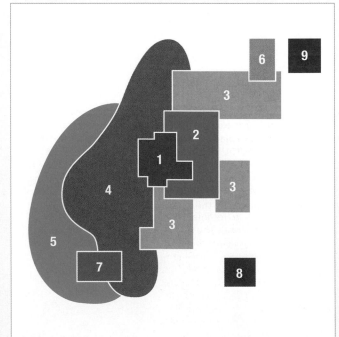

CHAPTER 16

THE GALACTIC CITY MODEL

The galactic city model evolved from the multiple-nuclei model and represents a break from the traditional view of cities in which land values and economic activities are strongly or almost exclusively linked to the location of the CBD. Galactic cities are ringed by smaller urban centers and hubs for commerce and manufacturing. ▌ Explain how the invention of the automobile supported the development of galactic cities.

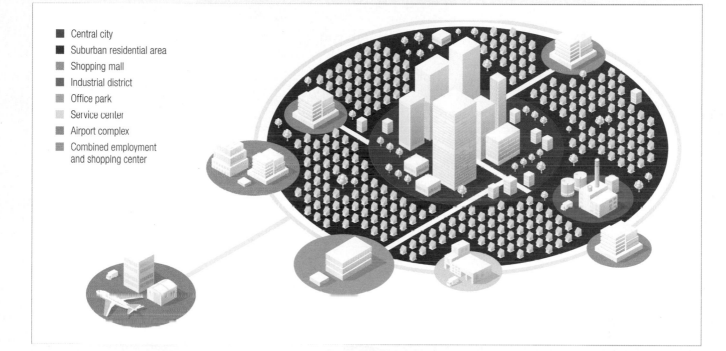

- ■ Central city
- ■ Suburban residential area
- ■ Shopping mall
- ■ Industrial district
- ■ Office park
- ■ Service center
- ■ Airport complex
- ■ Combined employment and shopping center

CHAPTER 16

LATIN AMERICAN CITY MODEL

The cities on which the Latin American city model is based date to the Age of Exploration, when the Spanish colonialists built towns and cities placing the church, government, and businesses at the center. The spine is a high-end commercial center around which wealthy residents live. High-poverty areas called disamenity zones are located on inconvenient land like steep slopes or flood-prone ground and are usually overcrowded. ▌ Explain the degree to which the Latin American city model reflects the effects of colonialism on urban development.

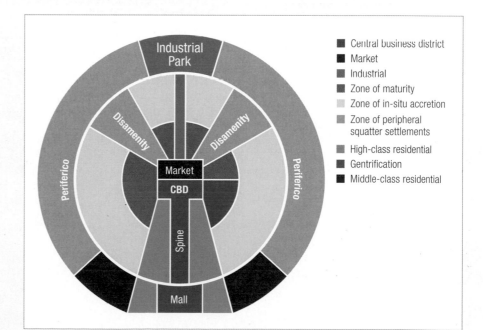

- ■ Central business district
- ■ Market
- ■ Industrial
- ■ Zone of maturity
- ■ Zone of in-situ accretion
- ■ Zone of peripheral squatter settlements
- ■ High-class residential
- ■ Gentrification
- ■ Middle-class residential

AFRICAN CITY MODEL

Many African cities have three CBDs. The first, created by colonial powers, is often built in a grid pattern for power and control. The second CBD is more traditional, with retail stores and curbside commerce. The third is a zone for open-air markets. Higher income neighborhoods are located within the CBDs, and wealth and services decrease the further out you get in the rings surrounding the CBDs. ▌ Compare the African city model and the concentric-zone model.

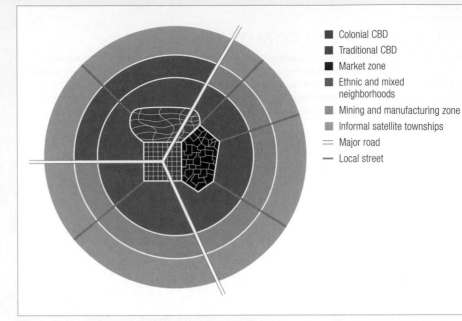

- Colonial CBD
- Traditional CBD
- Market zone
- Ethnic and mixed neighborhoods
- Mining and manufacturing zone
- Informal satellite townships
- Major road
- Local street

SOUTHEAST ASIAN CITY MODEL

The Southeast Asian city model reflects the fact that many cities in the region are located on ports. According to the model, port cities lack a clearly defined CBD. They have two formal zones—the port zone and the market gardening zone on the periphery. In addition to these two zones, Southeast Asian cities that follow the model consist of a variety of zones in concentric arcs around the port, such as the Western and alien commercial zones, suburbs, and squatter settlements, as well as industrial parks on the cities' outskirts. ▌ Identify and explain a limitation of the Southeast Asian city model.

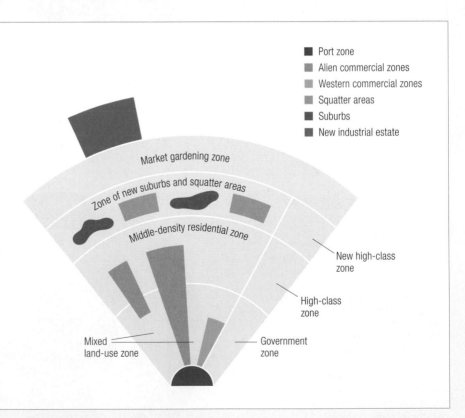

- Port zone
- Alien commercial zones
- Western commercial zones
- Squatter areas
- Suburbs
- New industrial estate

Market gardening zone

Zone of new suburbs and squatter areas

Middle-density residential zone

New high-class zone

High-class zone

Government zone

Mixed land-use zone

CHAPTER 17

ZONING MAP

Zoning is an important tool for cities planning for sustainability, economic development, and the well-being of residents. City governments work with planners to develop zoning maps such as this one to plot the land use for each street, block, or area. ▌Identify the spatial patterns you see in the zoning map concerning the locations of the CBD, residential areas, and commercial areas.

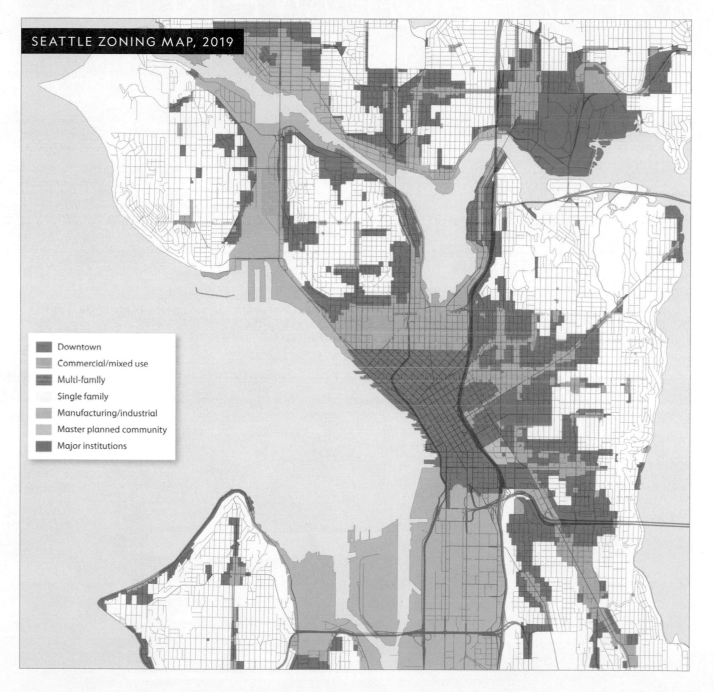

SEATTLE ZONING MAP, 2019

- Downtown
- Commercial/mixed use
- Multi-family
- Single family
- Manufacturing/industrial
- Master planned community
- Major institutions

INDUSTRIAL AND ECONOMIC DEVELOPMENT
PATTERNS AND PROCESSES

An employee at the BMW plant in Cowley, Oxford, England, watches as automated robots on the production line work on Mini automobile parts.

GLOBAL CONNECTIONS

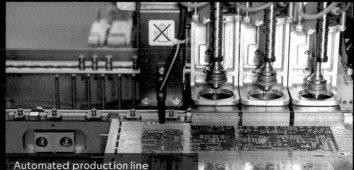

Automated production line

Originating in 18th-century Britain, the Industrial Revolution released an unstoppable wave of innovation that transformed the world. Advanced forms of industry and manufacturing remade the economies of entire countries. As new global networks of trade, transportation, and communication evolved, people's livelihoods were linked to a worldwide economy.

Core countries have vibrant, postindustrial economies and high standards of living. Some peripheral and semi-peripheral countries are rapidly industrializing, while some are not—but all of these countries are adapting to changes of uneven development. Understanding both the history and present course of industrial development is crucial to building economies that are sustainable for the long term and can support and benefit people across the globe.

CHAPTER 18
THE GROWTH AND DIFFUSION OF INDUSTRIALIZATION

CHAPTER 19
MEASURING HUMAN DEVELOPMENT

CHAPTER 20
GLOBALIZATION, INTERDEPENDENCE, AND SUSTAINABILITY

UNIT 7 WRITING ACROSS UNITS, REGIONS & SCALES

UNIT 7 MAPS & MODELS ARCHIVE

EDUCATING
AFGHAN GIRLS

ASIA
AFRICA **AFGHANISTAN**
AUS.

Shabana Basij-Rasikh became a criminal at the age of six. That year, the extremist group known as the Taliban took power in Afghanistan, where she lived, and imposed its strict interpretation of Muslim laws—including a provision that made it illegal to educate girls. For five years, Basij-Rasikh disguised herself as a boy so that she could study in secret. Today, the National Geographic Explorer works to ensure that girls in Afghanistan receive the educational opportunities once denied them so that her students will be empowered to strengthen their country's economy as they build their own futures.

LEARNING OBJECTIVE
SPS-7.D Explain how and to what extent changes in economic development have contributed to gender parity.

RISKING HER LIFE TO LEARN Basij-Rasikh knew that the penalty for her illicit schooling could be death. "We'd hear horrible stories about how some neighboring school was discovered, and they beheaded the teacher in front of the students," she recalls. "Even at that young age, we knew the risks we were taking every day."

When Basij-Rasikh was 11, the Taliban was ousted from power, and she resumed her education in a public school—dressed as a girl. In high school, she spent a year as an exchange student in Wisconsin, and she later attended college in the United States. She credits her academic success to her parents' exceptional determination that their daughters receive an education, even in the most harrowing of circumstances.

SOLA While she was still in college, Basij-Rasikh co-founded the School of Leadership, Afghanistan (SOLA)—a nonprofit organization with the goal of giving young Afghans access to quality education abroad and employment back home. At first, SOLA's mission was to obtain scholarships for Afghan students to study outside of their home country, but eventually the organization established a boarding school for girls in the capital city of Kabul.

Basij-Rasikh chose the boarding school model because in parts of Afghanistan, it still isn't safe for females to pursue an education. Some girls are verbally harassed or physically attacked on their way to school. One father and his daughter narrowly missed an assassination attempt by roadside bomb as they traveled from SOLA. "In some parts of the country, there are traditional practices where, once girls reach puberty, they don't leave the house," Basij-Rasikh notes. "She is either married off, or she is the babysitter for younger siblings. If you take that girl from that household and put her in a boarding school, all of a sudden you buy several hours of her day that she can use to focus on herself and her personal development."

INVESTING IN EDUCATION By educating Afghan girls, Basij-Rasikh hopes to address several social and economic issues that confront Afghanistan. The national economy is struggling, and Afghans cope daily with shortages of housing, clean water, electricity, medical care, and jobs. The situation for women looks especially bleak; Basij-Rasikh shares statistics from Human Rights Watch, a nongovernmental organization, showing that 63 percent of girls in Afghanistan are illiterate and one-third marry before they turn 18. She claims that "investment in girls' education comes with an enormous rate of return: girls who are educated marry later, have fewer and healthier children, and invest as much as 90 percent of their income back into their families," so society as a whole benefits.

Currently, Afghanistan's economy relies extensively on foreign aid, but Basij-Rasikh sees the country's future in the generation of Afghan girls who are currently studying at SOLA. "The best way for Afghanistan to experience sustainable development," she argues, "is for the people who know the problems, but also the opportunities, to come up with creative solutions."

GEOGRAPHIC THINKING

How might overcoming barriers to gender parity in Afghanistan affect the country's economic development?

Top: Shabana Basij-Rasikh—National Geographic Explorer and cofounder and president of the all-girls School of Leadership, Afghanistan (SOLA)—shows students how to ride a bicycle in a car park because it is not possible for the girls to ride outside. Bottom: Students decorate head scarves to celebrate the International Day of the Girl.

CHAPTER 18

THE GROWTH AND DIFFUSION OF INDUSTRIALIZATION

CRITICAL VIEWING The EUROGATE Container Terminal in Hamburg, Germany, is one of the main transport hubs in northern Europe. Shipping containers are prepared there and then transported via road and rail to locations all over Europe and Russia. ▌ Explain how this photo helps you understand the role that transportation costs play in determining where industries locate.

GEOGRAPHIC THINKING What drives patterns of industrialization?

18.1
PROCESSES OF INDUSTRIALIZATION

CASE STUDY: The Fourth Industrial Revolution

18.2
HOW ECONOMIES ARE STRUCTURED

CASE STUDY: Damming the Xingu River

NATIONAL GEOGRAPHIC PHOTOGRAPHER
Aaron Vincent Elkaim

18.3
PATTERNS OF INDUSTRIAL LOCATION

18.1 PROCESSES OF INDUSTRIALIZATION

Beginning in the 18th century, new, mechanized ways of making goods led to mass production. This change transformed human life by raising the standard of living for many people. However, the economic development has been spatially uneven, with advantages spreading disproportionately to the core rather than the periphery.

WHAT IS INDUSTRIALIZATION?

LEARNING OBJECTIVE
SPS-7.A Explain how the Industrial Revolution facilitated the growth and diffusion of industrialization.

Industry is any economic activity that uses machinery on a large scale to process raw materials into finished goods. Raw materials can include metals, wood, plant products, animal products, or other substances that are used to make goods intended for sale to customers. Crude oil, for instance, is a raw material that can be converted into a number of different products, including gasoline, heating oil, kerosene, and asphalt. Metals begin as metallic ores that must be extracted from the earth. Then they are processed before being made into finished goods. Metals are used to make machines that make finished goods. Trees can be cut down into lumber and then converted into building materials like boards and plywood, finished goods like furniture, or pulp that is made into paper.

Industry can also refer to a collection of productive organizations that work with the same materials or produce similar products. The manufacturing industry is generally divided into two broad categories—heavy industry and light industry. Heavy industry requires huge production facilities that produce goods on a massive scale and generally employ skilled workers. The goods produced by heavy industry include machinery and equipment, ships, railroad equipment, airplanes, and motor vehicles. Light industry requires less investment in production facilities and equipment, and produces finished goods that can be made on a massive scale or a small, custom scale. Workers can be either highly skilled or relatively unskilled. Light industries produce a wide range of products, including clothing, processed foods, gemstones, and electronics.

Manufacturing takes place at different scales. Production of manufactured goods through most of human history was small scale, meaning goods were made in relatively small quantities using hand tools or basic machines. Large-scale manufacturing arrived with the shift to industrial production, using specially purposed machinery in factories for mass production. Because heavy industry produces large goods like commercial jetliners or construction cranes, and produces goods in massive quantities, such as petroleum

refining or steel production, it requires a greater investment of capital, which is wealth in the form of money or assets, than light industry.

The scale of facilities and production varies dramatically within light industries. For instance, goods like soaps and candles can be crafted on a small scale by a tiny workforce working out of a single shop or even a home, or they can be mass-produced in a huge processing plant. Smaller-scale operations like craft furniture makers or local bakeries tend to emphasize quality of output over quantity. Large-scale processors are interested in mass-producing identical goods and often competing on the basis of price. As you will see, it was the appeal to consumers of the availability of low-cost, mass-produced goods that helped fuel the shift to large-scale manufacturing.

Industrialization is the process by which the interaction of social and economic factors leads to the development of industries across a community, region, or country. The process began with the Industrial Revolution in Britain in the 18th century and spread to other countries in western Europe and North America in the 19th century. Still more countries industrialized in the 20th century, and some are still industrializing today. While not all countries have experienced large-scale industrialization, the goods produced by industrial processes are found throughout the world.

THE INDUSTRIAL REVOLUTION

LEARNING OBJECTIVE
SPS-7.A Explain how the Industrial Revolution facilitated the growth and diffusion of industrialization.

A revolution involves rapid, massive, and transformative change. The Industrial Revolution was no exception. It marked the shift from small-scale, hand-crafted production to power-driven mass production. New technologies increased the quantity and variety of goods that could be produced, expanded the market for these goods through new modes of transportation, and increased the quantities of natural resources needed for production. This revolution changed people's lives and societies in profound ways, with both positive and negative results.

CRITICAL VIEWING Modern manufacturing operates at different scales. At left is a candy and ice cream factory in Bakersfield, California, where ice cream cones are mass-produced by machines. At right, a worker at a small chocolate factory in Toronto, Canada, produces chocolates by hand. ▍What different costs are evident in the photos of the two factories?

BEFORE THE INDUSTRIAL REVOLUTION

Prior to the Industrial Revolution, the production of goods took longer, and transportation was slow. With industrialization, both production and transport got faster. Manufactured goods followed several different patterns, depending on what was being produced.

High-quality craft goods were made in isolated, independent, small-scale operations run under the guild system that had begun in the Middle Ages. Guilds were trade associations made up of the master craftsmen in a given industry, such as shoemakers, leatherworkers, armorers, weavers, and bakers. Each guild operated in a town or city, capitalized on local resources or specialized skills, set standards for quality, and worked to control production, price, and output.

Large products like ships were produced in selected settings based on geographic factors and employed many workers. Shipyards dotted the Mediterranean and Atlantic coasts of Europe. Skilled craft workers focused on producing particular components, such as decking, masts, and sails, while unskilled laborers assembled the pieces under the supervisors' close scrutiny. Goods needed in large quantities, like textiles or shoes, were produced by **cottage industries**. In a cottage industry, members of families, spread out through rural areas, worked in their homes to make goods. Their production was funneled to urban-dwelling entrepreneurs who controlled distribution of the finished products.

Regardless of the location of pre-industrial manufacturing— whether urban workshop, port city shipyard, or rural cottage—they shared certain features. First was scale:

production was done locally, on a small scale. Second was the general reliance on hand-operated tools and equipment. Third was the dependence on muscle power, whether human or animal. Raw materials and finished products were chiefly transported by people or vehicles pulled by strong animals like oxen or horses, unless they could be moved over waterways or seas by ship. These constraints limited the amount of goods that could be produced.

INDUSTRIALIZATION BEGINS The Industrial Revolution began as a result of technological innovations and inventions, and it occurred where it did largely because of the availability of natural resources, specifically coal, iron ore, and water. In the years before the Industrial Revolution began, expansion of agricultural fields in Britain depleted the country's forests, leaving iron makers without a steady supply of charcoal (which is made from wood) to power their furnaces. Seeking new sources of energy, they turned to coal, but as coal miners dug deeper into the earth, mine shafts often filled with water, creating a need for more powerful pumps. The need was met by iron maker and inventor Thomas Newcomen, who developed the first commercially successful steam engine in 1712. In the 1760s, inventor James Watt vastly improved the steam engine's efficiency. The steam engine would play a major role in powering the Industrial Revolution.

The first industry affected by industrialization was textiles. A series of inventions introduced in the 1760s and 1770s— the spinning jenny, water frame, and spinning mule— mechanized the spinning of thread, significantly increasing the output of high-quality thread. Next, inventors turned to mechanizing weaving, which was achieved with the invention of the power loom in the 1780s. The water frame

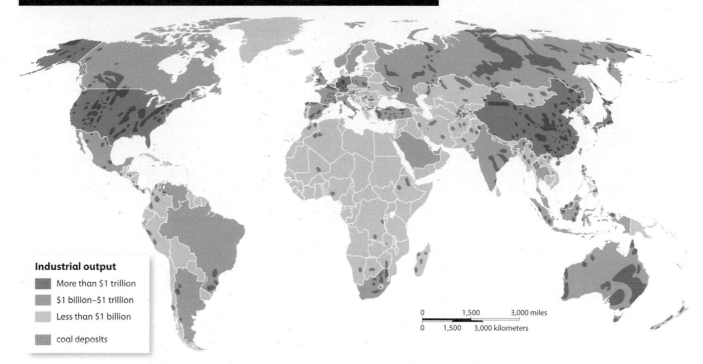

Industrial output

■ More than $1 trillion

■ $1 billion–$1 trillion

■ Less than $1 billion

▨ coal deposits

0   1,500   3,000 miles
0   1,500   3,000 kilometers

READING MAPS As of 2020, the United States has the largest economy in the world. However, it ranks second in industrial output, behind China. Japan, Germany, and India round out the top five countries with the highest industrial outputs. ■ Use the map to help you describe the relationship between the countries with the highest industrial outputs and the locations of the world's major coal deposits and then explain how this reveals an advantage for the United States and China.

and power loom originally relied on waterpower. By the 1780s, though, Watts's improved steam engine was put to the task, and suddenly manufacturing processes were no longer dependent on either muscle power or water. Coal-fired steam engines enabled machines to produce vast amounts of fabric far faster than was possible under the old cottage industry system.

The spatial patterns of early industrialization were determined by several factors. The high capital cost of equipment and the need to maintain the machinery made it important to focus operations in one location. From this need, the factory system of industrial production developed. Textile production had been focused in Britain's Midlands region, a broad stretch of counties in the middle part of England. That area became the center of the industrialized textile industry as well, for several geographic reasons. First was the ready availability of coal in or near the region, making it cheaper and easier to transport the power source to the rising factories. Second, the Midlands was near the port of Liverpool, which became a hub for the import of raw cotton from India and, later, the United States. Third, merchants had developed a system of canals in the Midlands in the early 18th century to transport coal and textiles. These waterways could be employed to move the increased output of textiles generated by the new factories.

By the mid-19th century, canals were replaced by overland transportation employing another feature of industrial power.

Constant tinkering with steam engines led to the invention of a mobile steam engine—the locomotive. Geography helped the Midlands here too, as the region's flat landscape made it relatively easy to build a rail network across the area to speed the shipment of coal and textiles.

Increased use of coal power also transformed the iron industry. While iron had long been an important metal, its production was a small-scale enterprise carried out by craftsmen in the pre-industrial age. Coal power and the steam engine made it possible for iron makers to generate more heat, which in turn created new processes for fashioning iron. These processes required expensive machinery, which meant that iron production, like textiles, became a large-scale industrial enterprise. One important use of iron was to build the new locomotives that were now needed, as well as the rails themselves.

GEOGRAPHIC THINKING

1. Explain how the availability of natural resources facilitates industrialization.

2. Describe the essential changes that took place during the Industrial Revolution.

3. Describe the geographic factors that led to the Industrial Revolution emerging in the Midlands region of Great Britain.

THE SPREAD OF INDUSTRIALIZATION

LEARNING OBJECTIVE

SPS-7.A Explain how the Industrial Revolution facilitated the growth and
diffusion of industrialization.

The success of industrialization made it likely to diffuse
to other locations. But Britain recognized that there were
economic advantages to being the only industrialized
country and took steps to stop the diffusion of
industrialization. The country passed laws that made it
illegal to export new machines, manufacturing methods, and
even skilled workers. Seeing the rapid growth of the British
economy, however, other countries sought the know-how
that would provide the foundation for similar expansion.

When industrialization finally did diffuse beyond Britain's
borders, it did so through expansion diffusion and relocation
diffusion. As you've read, expansion diffusion occurs when
an idea or innovation—or in the case of industrialization,
a series of innovations and processes—spreads outward
while still remaining strong in its place of origin. Relocation
diffusion is the spread of ideas or innovations through the
movement of people.

CONTINENTAL EUROPE AND NORTH
AMERICA In the first decade of the 19th century,
Belgium became the first country in continental Europe to
industrialize. It had plentiful supplies of coal and iron ore
that facilitated its industrialization, in the same way that the
availability of these resources had promoted industrialization
in the British Midlands. Belgium also had a tradition of
textile production, which meant its business leaders were
eager to embrace Britain's new advances in order to stay
competitive. Belgium also had a king willing to invest his own
resources in new industrial enterprises.

In an example of relocation diffusion, the revolution spread
to the United States when a British textile manufacturer
immigrated there in 1789. Settling in Rhode Island, he
constructed spinning machines and established textile mills
run by waterpower. This technology was adopted by others
in New England, which became the first center of industrial
production in the United States.

The diffusion of the Industrial Revolution was delayed in
the rest of Europe by political and economic conditions
as well as the availability of needed resources. In France,
for instance, political upheaval, the larger size of the
country, and the lack of developed waterways to move its
isolated coal and iron deposits all delayed industrialization.
Germany had plentiful supplies of coal but for decades was
not a single country but a collection of separate, fiercely
independent states. Industrialization there lagged until the
latter part of the 19th century, enabled by unification in 1871.
Some Eastern European countries, Poland in particular,
had plentiful supplies of coal, and Russia was rich in many
resources, but industrialization did not diffuse to these areas
until the late 19th century as well.

When industrialization did take root in Europe, the United
States, and Japan, the same criteria that determined the
spatial patterns of industrial regions in Britain determined the
site of the new industrial zones. The leading factor was close
proximity to natural resources, particularly the coal needed
in large quantities to power industrial processes.

The coal-rich Ruhr Valley became the industrial heart of
Germany and by the end of the 19th century was one of the
leading industrial regions in the world. It benefited from the
Ruhr and Rhine rivers, which facilitated the import of iron. In
the United States, the textile mills that dotted New England
relied on waterpower to drive their machinery, so the earliest
American factory towns were those built on the Atlantic fall
line, where rivers and streams flow down from the upland
region to the coastal plain, producing rapids and falls used
for power. These locations also facilitated the transportation
of raw materials to the factories and the shipment of finished
products from them.

By the middle of the 19th century, location on waterways
was less important as industrializing countries began to
build canal systems and, later, extensive rail networks.
These networks could reach deep into the interior of
countries, and railroads could more easily transport heavy
raw materials like coal and iron and finished products like
steel. Nevertheless, the core industrial areas often remained
the center of industrial production, as new industries, like
the chemical and automobile industries, developed where
industry had originally arisen.

SECOND AND THIRD INDUSTRIAL
REVOLUTIONS The Industrial Revolution that
began in Britain in the 18th century is called the First
Industrial Revolution; however, it was not the last. While
industrialization continued in Europe and North America—
and later in other regions—it entered new phases called
the Second and Third Industrial Revolutions. Each of
these revolutions was built on a system of interrelated
technologies. The First Industrial Revolution was powered
by steam, coal, and waterpower and was focused on the
textile, iron, and coal industries.

The steel and petroleum industries that became so
important late in the 19th century paved the way for the
Second Industrial Revolution, which was powered by
electricity and the internal combustion engine. Factories
were reconfigured to use the assembly line, in which
individual workers perform a narrow range of repetitive
tasks on products that are carried from one workstation
to the next mechanically. The assembly line and the use
of interchangeable parts—pioneered by the American
innovator Eli Whitney early in the 19th century—allowed
industry to engage in mass production, a process by which
large numbers of identical products that meet certain quality
standards are manufactured. Another key feature of this
revolution was the invention and increasing sophistication of
machine tools—the use of machines to make parts or pieces
out of metal for use in other machines.

The Second Industrial Revolution saw the growth of the steel, automobile, and airplane industries, as well as the chemical industry and the development of consumer appliances. Since steel was a major manufacturing material, factories were often located in regions with access to coal and iron ore. Places located near coalfields or sources of iron ore, like Pittsburgh, Pennsylvania, and Chicago, Illinois, became centers of the steel industry in the United States. Detroit, Michigan, and other cities in the Midwest, along with some cities in the South like Birmingham, Alabama, took advantage of their location near steel production centers to become manufacturing centers, converting the steel into automobiles and other manufactured goods. Concentration of factories in these areas promoted the growth of related businesses, such as tool-and-die shops that produced parts.

The Third Industrial Revolution began after the end of World War II and was marked by reliance on electronics and information technology systems and by automation of production processes. Made possible by advances in computerization and miniaturization, this revolution brought in new industries like computer manufacturing, software engineering, and telecommunications. During the Third Industrial Revolution, computers changed drastically, from room-sized units affordable only by governments and the largest enterprises to handheld devices that provide ordinary people with opportunities for productivity, information access, communication, and entertainment.

Industrialization in all its phases also promoted the rise of service industries like banking and insurance to promote the formation and ongoing operations of industrial firms. Increased productive output relied on the rise of transportation and wholesale and retail trade to facilitate the distribution of the industrial output.

While the Industrial Revolutions are distinguished by certain patterns and trends and can be placed roughly on a historical time line, it is important to keep in mind that they were not specific events, but rather large-scale developments that took place over time and had the effect of changing human society through technology.

COLONIALISM AND IMPERIALISM

In the 19th century, industrialization became interlinked with colonialism and the two processes helped to fuel one another. Britain was Europe's leading imperial power in the late 18th century. It had colonies in North America, Australia, and the Caribbean and was in the process of asserting control over India. The wealth that poured in from Britain's role in the slave trade and the sugar trade helped provide the capital needed for industrial expansion.

As industrialization spread in the 19th century, control of colonial areas became attractive both to provide sources of raw materials and to guarantee exclusive access to new markets. The expansion of European influence that had begun in the 15th century increased with Britain's enhanced industrial power. Improvements in transportation—specifically steamships and railroads—opened the colonies' interiors, making

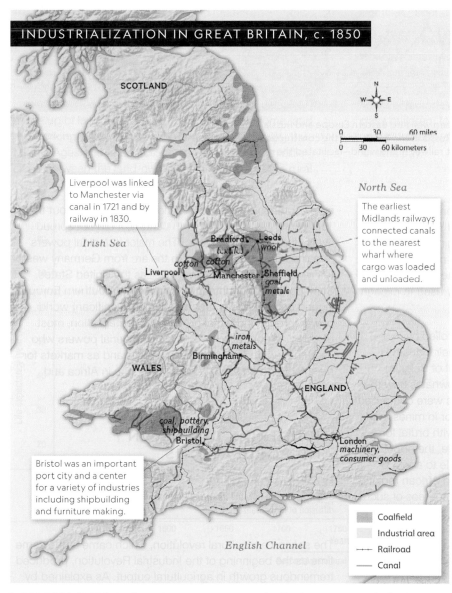

INDUSTRIALIZATION IN GREAT BRITAIN, c. 1850

SCOTLAND

Liverpool was linked to Manchester via canal in 1721 and by railway in 1830.

Irish Sea

North Sea

The earliest Midlands railways connected canals to the nearest wharf where cargo was loaded and unloaded.

Bradford

Leeds
wool

cotton cotton

Liverpool
Manchester

Sheffield
coal,
metals

iron,
metals

Birmingham

WALES

ENGLAND

coal, pottery,
shipbuilding
Bristol

London
machinery,
consumer goods

Bristol was an important port city and a center for a variety of industries including shipbuilding and furniture making.

English Channel

- Coalfield
- Industrial area
- Railroad
- Canal

READING MAPS By the mid-1800s, Great Britain had built a vast network of rail lines and canals through which the raw materials and finished goods of the country's rapidly growing industries could be transported. ▮ Use details from the map to explain how Bristol's site and situation were advantageous during the Industrial Revolution.

CRITICAL VIEWING In 1881, New York City created a Department of Street Cleaning, a precursor to today's Department of Sanitation. The photo shows workers in the late 1890s clearing garbage from a city street. ▌Explain how the photo is evidence of New York City's developing urban infrastructure.

Many of the features of modern urban life arose in the wake of the Industrial Revolution. City growth created serious public health challenges such as disposing of waste, providing adequate water, and controlling contagious diseases. In response, city officials developed new systems such as public water and sewage systems. Cities built hospitals to care for the ill and schools to teach the children.

Concern over a perceived rise in crime—for which the working class and poor were blamed—led officials to organize professional police forces. Concern over fire hazards led to the creation of units of firefighters. By the end of the 19th century, cities were adopting electric lights, creating an atmosphere in which the facets of daily life, from work to leisure activities, could continue into the night.

By this time Europe was experiencing the results of industrial development, marked by rising wages, better health, higher levels of schooling, and more comfortable lives for many. The populations of industrial regions followed the demographic transition model—better nutrition, medical advances, and public health measures meant declining

death rates and longer lives. Declining infant mortality rates, combined with the costs of raising children in the city, meant that couples decided to have smaller families, slowing the population growth rate.

As literacy became important for more and more jobs, the core countries began to institute public education systems. The middle class and even working class grew more literate, and subsequently their members began to demand a political voice. Several of the industrialized societies expanded voting rights to all men and, eventually, to women.

GEOGRAPHIC THINKING

4. Explain the relationship of industrialization to the location of coal resources.

5. Explain how world system theory can be used to explain the spread of industrialization.

6. Describe how industrialization expanded the middle class.

CASE STUDY

THE FOURTH INDUSTRIAL REVOLUTION

THE ISSUE The Fourth Industrial Revolution is upon us. How will humanity handle the changes to come?

LEARNING OBJECTIVE
SPS-7.B Explain the spatial patterns of industrial production and development.

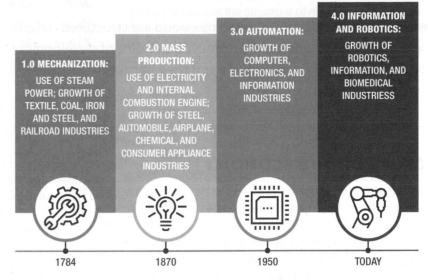

INDUSTRIAL REVOLUTIONS OVER TIME The First Industrial Revolution is sometimes called the revolution of mechanization. The second is the revolution of mass production, and the third of automation. The world is now experiencing a Fourth Industrial Revolution, the revolution of information and robotics.

BY THE NUMBERS

51.7%

of the world's population is online (2017)

MORE THAN
293 BILLION

emails sent and received per day (2019)

MORE THAN
20 MILLION

manufacturing jobs lost to automation by 2030 (2019 est.)

Sources: Nodegraph, The Radicati Group, Oxford Economics

ADVANCES IN TECHNOLOGY, such as artificial intelligence, augmented reality, genome editing, robotics, nanotechnology, and 3-D printing, characterize the Fourth Industrial Revolution. This revolution takes advantage of the trend toward digitizing information that developed in the Third Industrial Revolution and of advances in basic sciences from biology to physics. The fourth revolution may result in new cyber systems that blend biological and computerized elements in ways certain to transform people's lives. Given the rapid pace of technological change, it is not clear how quickly this phase of production will morph into yet a fifth industrial revolution.

One feature that makes this particular revolution distinct from the earlier ones is the fact that it is global. Modern communications technology, the deep interconnectedness of the world's economics, and the proliferation of scientific and technical expertise to all regions of the world mean that new developments made anywhere can spread rapidly. As in the earlier revolutions, social change resulted in the development of distinct groups of "haves" and "have nots." The nature of those distinctions in the Fourth Industrial Revolution—and the extent and success of efforts to minimize them—will be important questions humanity will have to address.

Another key feature of the Fourth Industrial Revolution is the idea of sustainability— the development of economic processes that can be self-perpetuating and promote the long-term maintenance of communities and the environment. One particular concern of the push for sustainability is the environmental cost of unchecked industrial growth and the intensive exploitation of natural resources. Climate scientists have increasingly warned of the accelerating processes of climate change resulting from mounting levels of greenhouse gases in the atmosphere. Those greenhouse gases are generated by burning fossil fuels, industrial processes, and changing patterns of land use and land cover. Biologists warn of the impact on plant and animal populations, including increasing rates of extinction and decreased biodiversity. The goal of sustainable development is to adopt methods of production that minimize the environmental harm and can thus be perpetuated for the benefit of future generations. ∎

GEOGRAPHIC THINKING

Describe how the Fourth Industrial Revolution has differed from the previous three industrial revolutions.

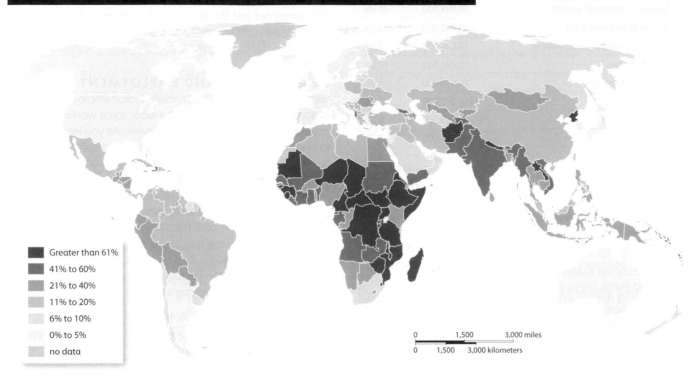

Greater than 61%
41% to 60%
21% to 40%
11% to 20%
6% to 10%
0% to 5%
no data

0   1,500   3,000 miles
0   1,500   3,000 kilometers

READING MAPS In countries with little industrialization, it is common for more than half of the workforce to be employed in agriculture. ▮ Considering what you have learned about Africa, why is it not surprising that so many African countries have large shares of their labor force working in agriculture?

factories and ship finished goods to markets. Wholesale and retail workers distribute industrial output to corporate purchasers or consumers.

PATTERNS OF ECONOMIC ACTIVITY Economic activities occur in spatially uneven patterns across a range of scales, from global-scale differences among countries to places and regions within countries. As you've just learned, countries of the periphery have many workers in the primary sector, generally practicing subsistence agriculture.

The shift to the secondary sector that comes with industrialization typically results in a population concentrated in urban areas, as evidenced by the urbanization of the First and Second Industrial Revolutions in the core areas of Europe and North America. In those periods, the concentration resulted from the desire to locate industrial facilities near sources of raw materials, energy sources, and labor. This concentration is also a function of the high capital cost needed to erect industrial facilities. It makes more economic sense to focus capital investment in fewer rather than many locations.

This pattern of urbanization is occurring today in countries that are in the process of industrializing. Industrial facilities are generally located in urban areas, especially at ports or along rail networks. Urban areas provide the potential workforce as well as a potential market. Locating industries in urban areas with ports and transportation hubs facilitates

the movement of raw materials to and finished products from the industrial facilities.

Tertiary industries vary widely in their spatial distribution because they represent many different economic activities. While banking and finance services tend to concentrate in urban areas, retail stores, restaurants, and a wide range of services from insurance to health care and education are distributed throughout a country. These tertiary activities are needed wherever there are people—though the density of these services will vary according to population.

Information industries of the quaternary sector tend to cluster near institutions of higher learning that provide the educated workforce they need. In the United States, for instance, major centers of the computer science industry are found in or near the universities of the San Francisco Bay Area in California; in Boston, Massachusetts, Austin, Texas, and Denver, Colorado; and in the Research Triangle region of North Carolina. The quinary sector is found in captial cities and other political centers of countries.

THE POSTINDUSTRIAL ECONOMY Industrializing countries tend to follow a pattern in which the share of agricultural employment declines over time and the share of tertiary employment rises. Secondary sector employment grows for a time as a country industrializes. Eventually, that share may also decline if a country develops a **postindustrial economy**. This economic pattern is

marked by extremely low primary sector employment, relatively low secondary sector employment, and predominant tertiary sector employment with a rising share of quaternary and quinary jobs. The United States is a country with a postindustrial economy, as are Japan, Australia, and Singapore.

Postindustrial countries share several features. The emphasis in their economies has shifted from the production of goods to the production of services. The share of blue-collar secondary sector workers has lowered, and the share of tertiary, quaternary, and quinary sector workers has risen. Information technology and related fields, such as artificial intelligence, have developed to evaluate new technologies and social issues. And postindustrial economies place a strong emphasis on institutions of higher learning as resources in developing and using the new technologies.

Any transition from one economic phase or technology to another is jolting for certain segments of a society. During the Industrial Revolution, farm laborers found it increasingly difficult to make a living in their chosen field. To survive, many had to move to cities, even if it meant leaving home for an uncertain future, because that's where the jobs were. The shift to the postindustrial economy has, for the past several decades, been a major challenge to manufacturing workers in the United States and other core countries. As manufacturing jobs move out of these postindustrial countries to peripheral and semi-peripheral countries, workers must learn new skills in other fields and, often, other sectors of the economy where they are usually less qualified, due to lack of experience and training.

The breakdown of U.S. employment by sector shows that almost 80 percent of all people in the labor force work in the tertiary sector—far more than the 19 percent employed

in the secondary sector—with an increasingly significant portion employed in the quaternary and quinary sectors.

Employment is not the only way to think of the impact of each sector on the economy. It is also useful to consider what each sector contributes to the **Gross Domestic Product (GDP)** —the total value of all goods and services produced by a country's citizens and companies within the country in a year.

Another feature of postindustrial economies is the growing role of women in jobs outside the home. Of course, women have always worked, taking primary responsibility for raising children, caring for family members, tending to the home, and cooking. Women have traditionally done other kinds

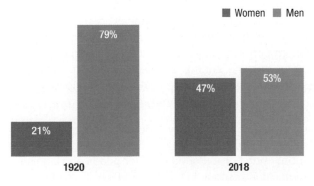

Source: U.S. Bureau of Labor Statistics

▌ **U.S. WORKFORCE BY GENDER** The percentage of women in the U.S. workforce has risen significantly since 1920, but by 2018, women still made up less than half of the total. Gender-based employment disparities endure in the United States: women earn about 81 cents for every dollar a man earns, and women (particularly single women and women of color) are more likely than men to live in poverty.

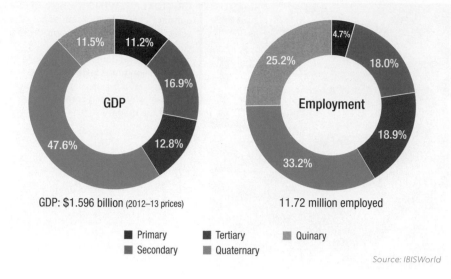

GDP

11.5% 11.2%

16.9%

47.6% 12.8%

GDP: $1.596 billion (2012–13 prices)

Employment

4.7%

25.2% 18.0%

18.9%

33.2%

11.72 million employed

■ Primary ■ Tertiary ■ Quinary
■ Secondary ■ Quaternary

Source: IBISWorld

AUSTRALIA'S ECONOMIC SECTORS, 2014–2015 With more than 75 percent of its workforce employed in the tertiary, quaternary, or quinary sectors, Australia is clearly a country with a postindustrial economy. These same sectors account for about 72 percent of Australia's GDP. ▮ Based on what you've learned about postindustrial economies, describe three trends that are likely occurring in Australia.

of labor as well, taking part—or playing the lead role in some countries—in farming, family businesses, or their own businesses. In addition, from the earliest days of the First Industrial Revolution, women were recruited to work in manufacturing jobs.

Later, traditions developed that discouraged women from working outside of the home. That narrowing of women's life choices started to change in the 20th century, and the acceptance of women taking jobs outside the home is generally widespread in industrial and postindustrial societies. Women are also receiving more advanced educations, enabling them to fill a significant number of quaternary and quinary jobs. Yet barriers to professional advancement and inequalities in pay and promotions persist.

DUAL ECONOMIES Development does not take place uniformly within a country. In fact, industrialization often leads to geographically uneven development. Geographers have found that some peripheral and semi-peripheral countries have what are called **dual economies**, or two distinct divisions of economic activity across the economic sectors. In these countries, much of the population may work in the traditional primary-sector economy, often depending on subsistence agriculture. At the same time, another substantial share of workers participates in a more varied market-based economy with a heavy emphasis on secondary sector jobs.

One example of a country with dual economies is Vietnam, where the country's leaders tried to find a way to combat rising consumer demand for goods and lagging manufacturing output. In the mid-1980s, with the help of foreign investors, these officials worked to expand the manufacturing base, developing such industries as textiles, electronics, and automobiles. The result has been a long period of substantial economic growth. Fully two-fifths of the country's workers still labor in the agricultural sector,

but that is barely half the share of farmworkers in 1991. Meanwhile, the share of workers in the secondary sector has risen to 25 percent; they generate nearly a third of the country's GDP and the majority of its top exports.

Geographers differ on why dual economies develop and why the agricultural workforce seems to be resistant to change. Some think that the resistance is due simply to tradition. Other observers think that the agricultural workers do not see enough benefit in shifting to the secondary sector. Still others see this uneven development as a manifestation of a core-periphery dynamic within a country. In this view, the core area that industrializes has more easily maintainable ties to the global economy and its market forces. This usually includes urban and coastal areas where ports are located, as these areas are often connected to global transportation routes and telecommunications networks. The agricultural workforce, meanwhile, labors in the interior hinterland, a peripheral area with little contact with that global economy.

GEOGRAPHIC THINKING

1. Explain how the five economic sectors are related to one another.

2. Explain the degree to which the core-periphery model applies to industrialization.

3. Identify the factors that will decide whether Vietnam, with its dual economy, will become fully developed or remain with a two-tiered economy. Explain how each factor would contribute to Vietnam's development.

DAMMING THE XINGU RIVER

THE ISSUE A massive hydroelectric project in the Amazon Basin promises to provide Brazil with clean energy, but critics assert the dams will have more negative than positive effects on the environment.

LEARNING OBJECTIVE
SPS-7.B Explain the spatial patterns of industrial production and development.

BY THE NUMBERS

80%
of the Xingu River's flow to be diverted through the Belo Monte Dam

MORE THAN 20,000
indigenous people will lose their way of life

16%
of world's energy output provided by hydroelectric power

25,000
Approximate number of workers needed to build the dam

Sources: NASA, Yale University, Forbes

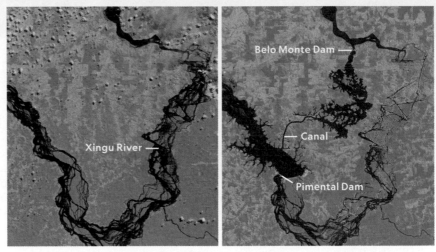

These satellite images from 2000 (left) and 2017 (right) show the Xingu River, a major tributary of the Amazon River, before and after the construction of the Belo Monte Dam. The tan and orange areas in the second image show resulting dry areas that are impacting aquatic life and indigenous peoples in the region.

IN 2011, BRAZIL BEGAN CONSTRUCTION on the Belo Monte Dam, a massive project along the Xingu River, a major tributary of the Amazon. The government approved the effort despite opposition from environmentalists and the indigenous peoples living along the waterway. With this huge development project, the government hopes to foster economic growth to raise people's standard of living, and—perhaps to a larger degree—to cater to powerful economic interests looking to profit from that growth.

Brazil, a newly industrializing, semi-peripheral country, has a large landmass—the fifth largest in the world—that is rich in natural resources. The country is a world leader in mining, agriculture, and manufacturing. Its service sector is growing quickly. All of this economic activity requires a strong energy industry, and Brazil has long looked to the gigantic Amazon River system to provide needed power. In fact, 90 percent of the country's electricity is provided by hydroelectric power.

The Belo Monte Dam project actually consists of two dams, which will form two reservoirs that will flood the homelands of thousands of indigenous peoples. The dams will have the capacity to generate more than 11,000 megawatts of electricity, which is enough to provide electricity for 60 million people, but are expected to operate at less than half that capacity most of the time. Worse, in the three- to four-month dry season, when the river's flow is substantially reduced, the dams will only generate about a tenth of the peak capacity. At an estimated cost of $18 billion, this limited output seems like a waste of money to critics.

Critics also point to the environmental havoc the dams will cause. The project will result in damage to more than 370,000 acres of rain forest. They fear the reduced water flow will convince Brazil's government to build more dams upstream to allow for the controlled release of water and a steady flow of electricity throughout the year. Such construction will extend the damage to more of the Amazon rain forest.

Growing concerns about the environmental impact of dams like Belo Monte have led to questions about whether to dismantle some existing dams. In response to these concerns, over a thousand dams are being taken down across the United States. Deconstruction is even more extensive in Europe, which has seen 5,000 such projects come down over the past two and a half decades. ∎

GEOGRAPHIC THINKING

Explain how changes to a country's economic structure might affect a government's decision about whether to build a controversial construction project.

cheated out spacing throughout BYN's to make this fit

Aaron Vincent Elkaim is committed to documenting the impact of economic development on the lives of indigenous peoples.

LEARNING OBJECTIVE

SPS-7.B Explain the spatial patterns of industrial production and development.

DOCUMENTING IMPACTS OF THE BELO MONTE DAM

When National Geographic photographer Aaron Vincent Elkaim came across the story of the Belo Monte Dam project, he was not just interested in its environmental impact, he was also taken with the challenges it thrust upon indigenous groups. "There is much we can learn from indigenous and traditional peoples," he says. "For them, the natural world is intertwined with the sacred, and they understand the importance of creating balance and harmony with it. This perspective is increasingly important to spread in today's world."

The Juruna, the Munduruku, and other peoples have lived in the region for thousands of years, hunting, fishing, farming, and gathering food. But many have been displaced by the Monte Belo Dam project. The company building the dam and the Brazilian government have paid to relocate many traditional people. While they have built new housing developments for the displaced people, there have been few jobs available in the area, resulting in communities with high crime rates and drug and alcohol abuse.

Elkaim sees the dam as an outdated approach to the use of natural resources. "Dams are one of our most ancient technologies for producing power, but we now have the technology to do better," he says. Giant dams do "permanent and drastic damage to vital and unique ecosystems," he argues. ❚

CRITICAL VIEWING By altering the natural environment, the Belo Monte Dam complex is damaging the land and disrupting the way of life of indigenous groups. One group, the Juruna, gathers at a public meeting to protest the building of the dam. ❚ What are some ways that indigenous people's way of life might be disrupted by the damming of the Xingu River?

CRITICAL VIEWING A large portion of the Brazilian city of Altamira was flooded when the reservoirs of the Belo Monte Dam were filled at the end of 2015. The boys in the photo climb a tree above a flooded area where mostly poor neighborhoods once stood. ▮ Use details from the photo to describe how economic decisions made by a country's government can affect people living in a specific region.

18.3 PATTERNS OF INDUSTRIAL LOCATION

The First Industrial Revolution began in Britain's Midlands region because it was located near natural resources and linked to the major port of Liverpool. But why did Pittsburgh, Pennsylvania, become "Steel City" and Detroit, Michigan, the "Motor City"? What geographic principles explain why industries are located where they are?

Workers assemble vehicles at a Ford factory just outside of Detroit, Michigan. The area was the world's center of auto manufacturing for most of the 20th century. However, by the 1990s, the city had experienced a massive loss of auto manufacturing jobs. Today, Detroit is still home to the so-called "Detroit Three" auto companies (General Motors, Ford, and Fiat Chrysler).

LEAST-COST THEORY

LEARNING OBJECTIVE
SPS-7.B Explain the spatial patterns of industrial production and development.

As you know, geographers are concerned with the "why of where." As it relates to industrialization, they might examine why one location for a factory is more suitable than another, or why a particular industry took hold in the region that it did. Is there a city or town nearby that could provide a workforce or a market for the goods produced? Or are there reasons related to physical geography and the availability of natural resources that make the choice a smart one?

In a capitalist system, location decisions are based on the profit motive. Companies invest capital, which is wealth in the form of money or assets, with the goal of generating profits. A profit is the money that remains after costs are subtracted from revenues. Capitalists seek to minimize costs so they can maximize profits. That aim influences where industries are located. To explain these decisions, German economist Alfred Weber first devised the **least-cost theory**, a model that geographers use to analyze spatial patterns in the secondary economic sector. The theory considers the factors that influence where enterprises locate manufacturing production. It proposes that businesses locate their facilities in a particular place because that location minimizes the costs of production. A firm chooses a location where the cost of moving raw materials to the manufacturing site, and finished products to the markets, will be as low as possible.

FACTORS THAT INFLUENCE LOCATION

Least-cost theory focuses on three factors that influence the decision of where to locate—transportation, labor, and degree of **agglomeration**. Agglomeration is a term that describes the advantage for companies in the same or similar industries in locating near each other in order to take advantage of specialized labor, materials, and services.

Weber considered transportation costs to be the determining factor in where an industry is located. Production is drawn to its most advantageous location relative to the cost of transport, and that site is one where those costs are lowest both in terms of bringing raw materials to the production site and distributing the final products to consumers.

Later scholars refined Weber's theory to include other factors, including labor and agglomeration. If labor costs are high in an area, profit margins are reduced. In that case, it makes sense to locate the manufacturing site farther away from the raw materials and markets as long as cheap labor compensates for the added transportation costs.

The decline of the textile industry in the American South and the rise of garment manufacturing in such locations as Vietnam and Bangladesh reflect these decisions. Of course, the American South had textile mills because textile manufacture relocated to that region from higher-cost facilities in the Northeast early in the 20th century.

Agglomeration is an interesting factor in patterns of location, because it means that competitors often locate near one another. Geographers observe that enterprises in the same industry tend to cluster together because it provides benefits to each enterprise. They can assist each other in controlling costs through shared talents, services, and facilities. With several enterprises located in close proximity, each has access to the same pool of people from which to hire workers and the same natural resources and transportation networks. Also, companies that support the industry will be drawn to an area of agglomeration. All of these factors reduce costs, making a location more attractive when new firms are thinking of establishing a plant or factory in an area. Agglomeration can offer enough of a cost advantage that it sometimes distorts the basic spatial pattern established by transportation costs and modified by labor.

For example, the concentration of the auto industry in the Detroit area in the early 20th century demonstrated agglomeration. Henry Ford, founder of the Ford Motor

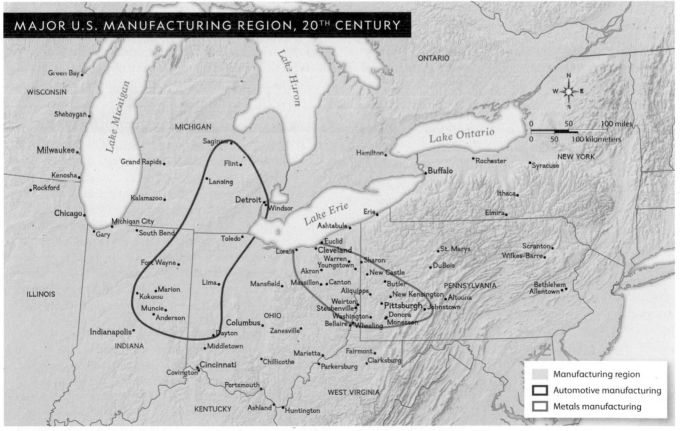

MAJOR U.S. MANUFACTURING REGION, 20TH CENTURY

Legend:
Manufacturing region
Automotive manufacturing
Metals manufacturing

READING MAPS For much of the 20th century, the core of U.S. manufacturing was located in a swath of land along the Great Lakes. Many cities became synonymous with their major industry, such as Detroit for cars and Pittsburgh for steel. ▮ Explain how the map demonstrates agglomeration.

Company and innovator of the assembly line process, grew up outside Detroit and opened his company there. Ford and Oldsmobile, another successful car company located in Detroit, drew skilled labor and parts manufacturers to the city, and soon it made good economic sense for other car companies to set up shop in the "Motor City." The prevalence of car manufacturers drew companies that produced related products as well, such as tire companies and parts manufacturers.

The first and most important factor in the least-cost theory—transportation—plays a key role in where agglomeration occurs. It often occurs at **break-of-bulk points**, which are locations where it is more economical to break raw materials into smaller units before shipping them farther. Break-of-bulk points are often located at places where the mode of transportation changes, for instance, where materials that have come in on a ship are being moved to rail cars. Thus, ports that receive shipments of raw materials from elsewhere and then distribute the materials to interior regions by rail or highway networks are often break-of-bulk points. Because they may receive vast quantities of raw materials that cannot be distributed all at once, these locations often develop storage facilities. The raw materials may need to be processed in some way to facilitate transportation to production sites, so these locations may become processing centers as well. For instance, many port cities develop petroleum storage and refining industries because they handle, store, process, and distribute large amounts of crude oil delivered to them by tankers.

There are several assumptions in the least-cost theory. One is that it ignores the influence of economic or political systems. A second assumption is that there are fixed sources of raw materials. A third is that the workers who make up a labor force will not move. A final assumption is that there is a uniform cost of transportation from any one point to any other.

RAW MATERIALS According to the least-cost theory, there are two significant features of raw materials. The first is related to where raw materials are found. With raw materials that are ubiquitous, or found in many places, factories can be located anywhere. The ideal location for factories that use ubiquitous raw materials is near the market. In that case, transportation costs are minimal because there are limited expenses involved in bringing the readily available raw material to the plant and in shipping the finished good to the market. Localized raw materials—those found in a particular place—tend to limit the location of processing plants to places that have that raw material. Industries that rely on raw materials that are mined from the earth, such as iron ore, coal, and bauxite, tend to locate processing plants near where those materials are found.

The second significant feature is the cost of transporting raw materials. This cost is often related to whether raw materials gain or lose weight during processing. Fuel and shipping costs make it expensive to transport heavy material

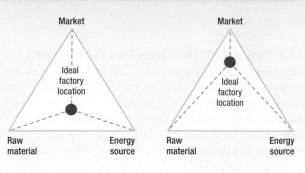

MODEL: LEAST-COST THEORY

Bulk-reducing industry

Market / Raw material / Energy source / Ideal factory location

Bulk-gaining industry

Market / Raw material / Energy source / Ideal factory location

According to the least-cost theory, companies should minimize transportation and labor costs and maximize the money that can be saved through agglomeration. Of these factors, according to the theory, transportation costs are most important. While real-world manufacturing processes are often more complex, Weber devised his theory based on a product made using one raw material and one source of energy (to power the processing plant), and having a single market. The ideal processing location is found at the intersection of lines from each corner and depends on whether the industry is bulk-reducing or bulk-gaining.

over long distances. Generally, raw materials either gain or lose weight in processing, and this weight change affects the ideal location of processing plants. If there is no weight change during manufacturing, transportation costs from the source of raw materials to market will be consistent and the company can take other factors into account when deciding where to locate a factory.

In **bulk-reducing industries**, raw materials cost more to transport than finished goods. With raw materials that lose weight through the manufacturing process, the best location for the factory is near the source of the raw materials. Coal-burning power plants rely on a raw material that loses weight in processing—the coal is burned and emitted as smoke and carbon dioxide. Locating power plants near coalfields minimizes the cost of transporting heavy coal. It is relatively inexpensive to transmit electricity from the plant to markets along electric lines. The lumber industry is a bulk-reducing industry, because the boards produced at a sawmill weigh less than the massive tree trunks brought in for processing.

In **bulk-gaining industries**, raw materials cost less to transport than finished goods. If manufacturing results in a product that weighs more than the sum of its raw materials, then the best location for the factory is near the market because it costs more to ship the finished product than it does the raw materials. In automobile manufacturing, for instance, the component parts of a car weigh less than the weight of the finished product. Factors besides weight play a role as well. Bread, for instance, is more perishable than

TIMBER is the name for trees and the wood before it has been processed.

LUMBER is the name for the wood once it has been sawn into planks or boards.

FROM RAW MATERIAL TO MARKET

THE LUMBER INDUSTRY

Lumber is a bulk-reducing industry, which means that lumberyards are typically located close to forests, where the raw material (wood) is located. However, there are other factors to consider. ▌ Using what you have already learned, describe factors involved in deciding where to locate a lumberyard.

① ### Growth & Harvesting

Timber is harvested from forests that are naturally occurring or planted by humans.

Felling: Mature trees are cut down and saplings are planted to maintain the forest.

Trimming: Trees are delimbed and cut into uniform, manageable pieces at the felling site.

Storing: The logs are stored near the felling site to allow water stored in the wood to evaporate, which decreases the weight—and therefore the transportation costs—of the logs.

② ### Transportation

The timber is transported to a processing site. Because lumber is a bulk-reducing industry, processing plants tend to be located close to forests where the wood is harvested.

③ ### Processing

At the processing site—in this case, a lumberyard—the logs are cut into specific lengths and the bark is removed. The pieces are then cut into boards. This process causes the wood to lose most of its water, further reducing the weight and making it less likely to warp.

④ ### Manufacturing

The lumber is purchased by manufacturers and made into various products.

⑤ ### Market

The products are sold in stores or to other industries.

Bulk-Reducing Industry

If raw materials cost more to transport than finished goods, then processing plants will be located near the source of the raw materials.

Examples: copper smelting, furniture manufacturing

Bulk-Gaining Industry

If raw materials cost less to transport than finished goods, then processing plants will be located near the market.

Examples: car manufacturing, bread production, construction equipment

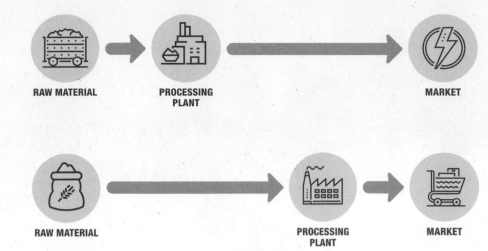

RAW MATERIAL   PROCESSING PLANT   MARKET

RAW MATERIAL   PROCESSING PLANT   MARKET

WHERE TO LOCATE? According to the least-cost theory, certain characteristics of raw materials, such as whether they lose or gain weight during processing, determine where manufacturing will take place.
❚ Explain why construction equipment manufacturing is an example of a bulk-gaining industry.

the wheat that acts as a raw material, so bread is more expensive to transport. The best location for bread factories, therefore, is near the market.

LIMITATIONS OF LEAST-COST THEORY

LEARNING OBJECTIVE
SPS-7.B Explain the spatial patterns of industrial production and development.

Like all theories, the least-cost theory does not line up perfectly with conditions in the real world. For instance, the theory ignores the influences of political or economic systems. Of course, political and economic systems are not uniform, and the differences can strongly influence decisions about locations. Tariffs or quotas, for instance, can cause the leaders of a business to avoid a certain market or to build a production plant where they otherwise would not have located. Japanese automakers began building cars in the United States in the 1980s not because of transportation costs but rather to avoid quotas placed on their auto exports to the United States. Countries and regions also compete with one another by offering tax breaks to companies willing to open new factories in their territory. Additionally, the theory works in capitalist societies where profit is the primary business motive. In communist systems, industry was often located for social reasons, not based on the cost of manufacturing.

In addition, markets are usually not located at a single point. Markets for consumer goods are found wherever consumers live. Markets for goods needed by an industry are found wherever companies within that industry are located.

LOCATION DECISIONS TODAY

LEARNING OBJECTIVE
SPS-7.B Explain the spatial patterns of industrial production and development.

Beyond these limitations, there are other critiques of least-cost theory as Weber proposed it in 1909. Because of changes in manufacturing, raw materials, shipping costs and methods, and labor costs and characteristics, transportation costs play a less significant role in location decisions today than they did in Weber's time.

The use of airplanes, ships, and supertankers have greatly reduced transportation costs. Shipping containers, like those seen in vast numbers in the chapter introduction image, have done much to increase shipping speed and efficiency. Their standardized size makes the containers intermodal, meaning they can be shipped by different modes of transportation, such as ships, trains, and trucks.

Shipping costs are also less significant than in the past because many of the goods being produced weigh less than they used to, when the products of heavy industry formed a larger share of the goods and materials being transported. It is less costly to ship a day's production of smartphones than a day's production of wrought iron. In addition, materials like plastics are lighter than steel and wood. These lighter materials have made their way into the products of heavy industry. In the average car produced in North America, about 8 percent of the total weight—more than 300 pounds—comes from plastic components. Use of this material reduces the costs of both transporting raw materials and of shipping finished cars.

While transportation costs have fallen, the relative cost of labor has become more significant. Two competing trends are at work. First, for sophisticated, high-tech products, labor expertise is in high demand. This limits production to those areas that have highly educated, highly skilled workers. Second, for many other mass-produced goods, semiskilled workers can do the work. In these cases, manufacturing companies have an incentive to seek out the least expensive productive workers. In the drive to lower labor costs, companies have located factories in peripheral countries with relatively low wages—and no labor unions.

For example, in the 20th century the U.S. textile industry moved from New England to the lower-wage, non-unionized South as factory owners sought to hold down labor costs. Decades later, after wages in that region rose, manufacturers shifted their production to other countries with low-wage workers. Today, the top ten countries for apparel exports include such low-wage countries as China, Bangladesh, Vietnam, India, Indonesia, and Cambodia. The auto industry has seen a similar shift. U.S. automakers, once concentrated in the high-wage, unionized Midwest, began

Ningbo Bird, a Chinese mobile phone manufacturer, uses a vast, single, open floor plan in its factory. It is a good example of the type of facility that characterizes today's modern factories.

opening factories in the South, where they were later joined by European and Japanese automakers wishing to establish a U.S.-based manufacturing presence. In more recent years, automakers have opened factories in Mexico and other lower-wage countries. In a sense, the least-cost theory still holds—businesses locate factories to minimize costs. The original formula of the least-cost theory, however, with its emphasis on raw materials and energy costs, does not play as large a factor when labor costs are more significant.

With changes in products and materials, the configuration of factories has also changed. Modern factories are far more likely to be long, wide, single-story structures rather than multistory buildings. This change in factory design has contributed to the flow of manufacturing out from urban centers to **industrial parks**. An industrial park is a collection of manufacturing facilities. Industrial parks are typically found in suburbs and located close to highways to facilitate movement of raw materials and finished products. Several factors contributed to the rise of industrial parks. The high cost and low availability of land in cities versus the lower cost and greater availability of land in suburbs plays a role. Since most workers—especially in the suburbs—rely on cars to get around, facilities can be built away from mass transit systems. Also, industrial parks have room for loading docks from which to load and unload trucks.

Finally, the availability of customers on a global scale has led producers to locate plants in all corners of the world, as exemplified by the sportswear manufacturer Nike. The company employs more than one million workers in 41 countries located on five of the world's seven continents. Toyota has 51 manufacturing plants in 28 countries on five continents, where more than 370,000 workers produce nearly 9 million vehicles a year. Though these and other global companies have complicated networks of production, they will still consider least-cost theory factors in their decisions about where to locate manufacturing plants.

GEOGRAPHIC THINKING

1. Explain how agglomeration benefits companies that are in the same industry.

2. Compare the three factors that influence the location of industry, according to the least-cost theory.

3. Describe what has changed in manufacturing since the least-cost theory was first proposed.

GNI PER CAPITA IN U.S. DOLLARS (2018)		
1	Switzerland	$84,410
2	Norway	$80,610
3	Luxembourg	$70,870
4	Iceland	$67,960
5	United States	$63,080
6	Qatar	$61,390
7	Denmark	$61,150
8	Ireland	$60,140
9	Singapore	$58,770
10	Sweden	$55,490
11	Australia	$53,230
12	Netherlands	$51,260
13	Austria	$49,310
14	Finland	$48,280
15	Germany	$47,090
16	Belgium	$45,910
17	Canada	$44,940
18	Japan	$41,770
19	United Kingdom	$41,310
20	France	$41,080
21	United Arab Emirates	$40,920
22	Israel	$40,880
23	New Zealand	$40,640
24	Kuwait	$34,290
25	Italy	$33,730

One way to measure the economic welfare of a country is Gross National Income (GNI) per capita. GNI per capita is the total value of goods and services produced by a country in a year divided by the country's population.
Source: World Bank

same amount of wealth as the poorest 50 percent of the population (around 100 million people). About 16 million Brazilians live below the country's poverty line. Countries with a more even income distribution have less poverty and a greater sense of equity within the population, which often equals political stability and a healthier populace.

ECONOMIC STRUCTURE The structure of an economy is another measure of development. Economic structure is connected to economic prosperity, and the level of development of a country can be predicted by examining the country's economic structure. Most diversified economies result from populations who work in every economic sector, which you learned about in Chapter 18. As countries develop, the percentage of the population operating in different sectors of the economy often shifts; for instance, more workers move from the primary sector (agriculture) to the secondary sector (manufacturing). This shift increases productivity, which in turn strengthens a country's economic success. More development enhances jobs in the tertiary sector (services), which also adds to a country's economic

prosperity. As countries flourish, the quaternary and quinary sectors (knowledge sectors) bloom. Information technology expands, scientific research is promoted, and media extends to the farthest reaches of the country.

In addition to classifying economic sectors, the structure of an economy can also be broken into two categories: the formal sector and the informal sector. The **formal sector** includes businesses, enterprises, and other economic activities that have government supervision, monitoring, and protection, and are taxed. The taxes collected from businesses and workers most often are used by a country to finance a variety of public services.

In the United States, money collected by the government funds Social Security (a federal system that provides retirement, disability, and survivors' benefits), health insurance programs such as Medicare and Medicaid, defense and international security systems, safety net programs that provide aid, and interest on money the U.S. government has borrowed from banks. A small portion of these funds goes to public services like education, environmental programs, food and drug safety, and infrastructure. Workers in this sector have a formal contract with their employer, predefined job responsibilities, a guarantee of safe work conditions, a fixed duration of work time, wages or a salary, and coverage by Social Security for health and life risks, such as becoming disabled and not being able to work.

The **informal sector**, sometimes called the informal economy, is any part of a country's economy that is outside of government monitoring or regulation and is not taxed. Individuals and businesses in the informal sector typically deal in cash and include a wide range of money-making activities: street vendors hawking flowers or candies, unlicensed and unregulated food or beverage stands, cleaning or moving services, and more. In contrast, some street vendors—such as food trucks in the United States and certain taco stands in Mexico—are in the formal sector because they are licensed and pay location fees and sales taxes. But workers in the informal sector do not have formal employment contracts, regulated work conditions, or fixed hours of work. They may not be paid regularly or evenly, and are not covered by any worker health and safety protections or social security system. These workers are sometimes in less-than-safe working situations and are especially vulnerable to downturns in business.

It's difficult to accurately measure the financial or social impact of informal sector activities. Without government interaction, many of these economic activities aren't documented and can't be traced. Likewise, the informal sector is not included in the GDP or GNI of a country. As a result, many countries surely have greater income than their official statistics suggest. Informal economies are active all over the globe. In core countries, the informal sector represents anywhere from 10 to 20 percent of a country's income. Phrases such as "under the table" and "off the books" reflect this untaxed, cash economy. In peripheral

The back of a pick-up truck serves as a fruit stand on the street in the historic center of Mexico City. Street vendors are often part of the informal economic sector.

countries, the informal sector is much larger, representing as much as 50 percent of a country's income. Although critics claim that the informal sector is unmanageable and can hinder a growing economy, other experts argue that it provides financial opportunities for people at the bottom of the socioeconomic ladder, and most say that it is growing.

FOSSIL FUELS AND RENEWABLE ENERGY

Measuring the use of fossil fuels (hydrocarbon-containing material of biological origin that can be burned for energy) or of renewable energy (energy from a source that is not depleted when used) can indicate a country's level of development. Fossil fuels, like coal, oil, and gas, were introduced during the Industrial Revolution. These fuels powered plants, factories, and homes. In the approximately 250 years since the Industrial Revolution began, the world has come to rely on fossil fuels for its main energy supply.

All countries use fossil fuels for electricity, transportation, heat, and fuel for automobiles. More than 29 countries depend on fossil fuels for at least 90 percent of their energy, and 5 countries—Brunei, Kuwait, Oman, Qatar, and Saudi Arabia—are 100 percent reliant. These countries have large deposits of fossil fuels, which gives them primary access to these sources that drive their economies. When making energy decisions, countries utilize their natural resources or what they can purchase to generate the power they need. But countries also explore ways to use renewable energy and alternative fuel sources. China is the biggest generator of global wind power and also produces the most

solar energy in the world. Considering that fossil fuels are nonrenewable and could eventually become depleted, and the fact that burning fossil fuels harms the environment, planning for and implementing renewable energy programs improves a country's energy infrastructure and development.

SOCIAL INDICATORS

LEARNING OBJECTIVE
SPS-7.C Describe social and economic measures of development.

Geographers also use noneconomic factors, such as fertility rates, infant mortality rates, literacy rates, life expectancy data, access to health care, and measures of democracy, to help complete the analysis of a country's level of development. These social, cultural, and political factors may not directly affect the level of national income and output, but they are the cause and the effect of a population's well-being.

As you have read, the total fertility rate (TFR) is the average number of children one woman in a given region or country will have during her child-bearing years. Social factors that affect a country's TFR include level of health care and level of education for women. The total fertility rate is high in most peripheral countries, and although it has been trending down in recent years, the TFR still remains higher than the rates in core and semi-peripheral countries. In the 1990s, Afghanistan's TFR was about 7.5, one of the highest in the

Workers in Iran assemble panels at a solar power farm. Some countries like Iran that have historically been heavily dependent on fossil fuels have, in recent years, increased their use of renewable energy.

world at the time. The country's fertility rate in 2017 was 4.5. Improvements in health care, sanitation, and diet—along with better access to hospitals and medicine—generally cause a decline in the number of births. But when access to health care and education is limited, fertility rates skyrocket. In 2017, the countries with the highest TFRs were Niger (7.0), Somalia (6.2), and the Democratic Republic of Congo (6.0). All three countries in the periphery had fewer than 0.2 doctors per 1,000 people. In contrast, there were 4.0 doctors per 1,000 people in Argentina—a semi-peripheral country—the same year, and its TFR was 2.3.

Cultural factors, such as the status of women and religions or traditions that encourage couples to have large families, affect total fertility rates as well. Women with higher levels of education and those who pursue careers generally have fewer children. In countries with fewer formal employment opportunities or where women face barriers to work outside the home, women are likely to have more children. Political factors, such as government-sponsored family-planning efforts, can impact the TFR and population growth, too.

You learned that the infant mortality rate (IMR) is the number of deaths of children under the age of 1 per 1,000 live births. The IMR is a good indicator of maternal and infant health, which itself is a reliable gauge of quality of health care. Globally, the leading causes of infant deaths are preterm birth complications, birth defects, and diseases such as pneumonia, diarrhea, and malaria. Leading causes of infant deaths in the United States include birth defects, preterm births, and low birth weights. Like total fertility rate, the infant mortality rate is higher in peripheral countries and lower

in core countries; Chad's IMR was 73.1 in 2017, while the United States had an infant mortality rate of 5.8 that same year. High IMRs are connected to higher percentages of people who live in poverty.

Life expectancy, the average number of years a person is expected to live, is a powerful indicator of health from prenatal to elderly care. And access to comprehensive, quality health care is a dependable measure of a country's standard of living. When a population can maintain good health, prevent and manage diseases, and reduce disabilities and premature death through attainable health care, its citizens can work, produce, and create income, which in turn creates a healthy economy. In peripheral and semi-peripheral countries with low per capita income and often-fractured governments, health care for many of their residents is difficult to obtain. Countries in which people do not have access to immunizations, medications, antibiotics, and sanitary water are often economically underdeveloped.

Literacy rates and education standards are important measures of development as well. Literacy provides people with a set of skills required to function effectively in contemporary societies, and it also empowers them intellectually. Higher levels of literacy can drive the successful economic development of a country, especially in today's rapidly changing, technology-driven world. But while global literacy rates are higher than ever, challenges remain. Many marginalized children who are poor or live in rural areas do not have access to educational opportunities. For example, in sub-Saharan Africa, countries such as Niger and South Sudan struggle with literacy rates below 30 percent.

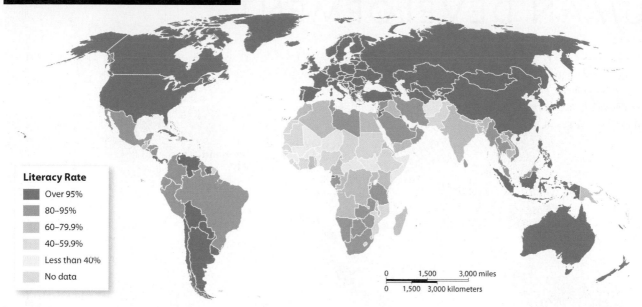

Literacy Rate

- Over 95%
- 80–95%
- 60–79.9%
- 40–59.9%
- Less than 40%
- No data

0   1,500   3,000 miles
0   1,500   3,000 kilometers

READING MAPS This map reveals percentages that measure the number of people 14 years or older in each country who are able to read and write. Though more recent data for some countries exist, the map contains the most comprehensive global information for literacy rates. ▮ Choose a country and explain how its literacy rate might impact the economic development of that country.

HUMAN DEVELOPMENT INDEX

LEARNING OBJECTIVE
SPS-7.C Describe social and economic measures of development.

The United Nations uses the **Human Development Index (HDI)** to determine overall levels of development of countries. This measure incorporates three key dimensions of human development: life expectancy at birth (health dimension), access to education measured in expected and mean years of schooling (education dimension), and standard of living measured by GNI per capita (economic dimension). In short, the HDI is a summary measure—scaled from 0.0 to 1.0—of basic achievement levels reached through an average of each examined dimension.

When determining HDI, health and education indicators are just as important as economic indicators. In 2018, the United States had a GNI per capita of $63,080, and its HDI ranking was 15 out of 189 countries and territories. Countries such as Ireland and Germany both had lower GNI per capita. But since these countries have higher life expectancies than the United States, both Ireland and Germany had a higher HDI. Qatar had the highest GNI per capita at $124,410, but its HDI was ranked 41 because of fewer years of schooling. Cyprus's GNI per capita was only $39,880, but Cyprus's HDI rank was 31 because of relatively high life expectancy rates.

When looking at these rankings, it's important to understand the theory of purchasing power parity (PPP). This concept measures economic variables in different countries so that exchange rates don't distort across-the-board comparisons. In essence, PPP is synonymous with "international dollars."

Although the HDI score is an important measure of spatial variation in levels of development among states, it has limitations. The HDI is a simplified calculation and doesn't capture every aspect of human development. It doesn't reflect other quality-of-life factors, such as poverty, gender equality, environmental quality, sustainability, or an overall feeling of security or even of happiness. The HDI also doesn't take into account that in many countries, some groups—perhaps ethnic minorities, followers of a minority religion, or speakers of a minority language—don't have access to the same opportunities for income, education, or health care. Additionally, the HDI does not consider the political dimensions of human development.

The UN and other organizations also collect and share other data—such as a country's rate of economic growth, expansion of employment opportunities, and the success of initiatives undertaken—to help leaders and policy makers evaluate and work to improve quality of life within a country.

GEOGRAPHIC THINKING

1. Define each of the following measures and its importance: GDP, GNP, and GNI per capita.

2. Describe the formal and informal sectors of an economy, and explain the connection between the structure of an economy and economic prosperity.

3. Explain why a country might have conflicting GDP and HDI measures.

HUMAN DEVELOPMENT INDEX, 2017

The HDI combines data about life expectancy, expected and average years of school, and GNI per capita, resulting in a score that ranges from 0.0 to 1.0. Higher HDI values are considered better. ▮ Identify the health, education, and economic dimensions of the HDI.

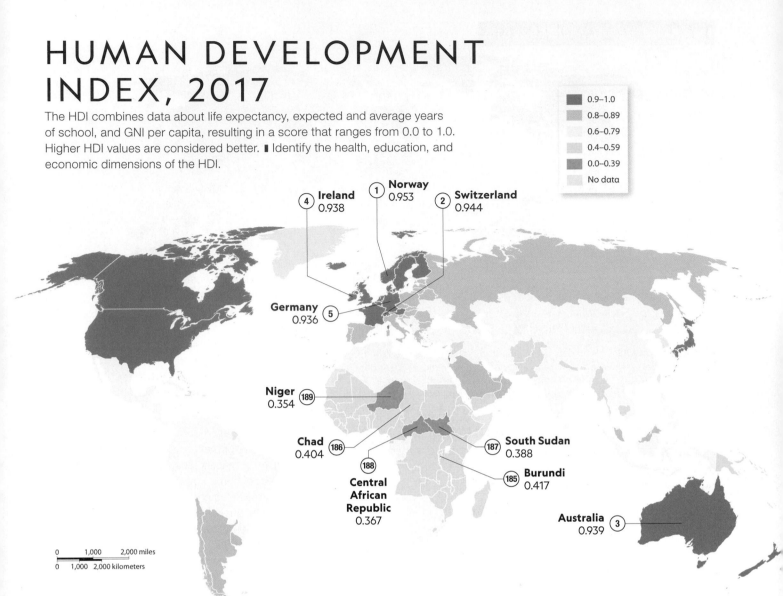

	0.9–1.0
	0.8–0.89
	0.6–0.79
	0.4–0.59
	0.0–0.39
	No data

Ireland ④ 0.938
Norway ① 0.953
Switzerland ② 0.944
Germany ⑤ 0.936

Niger ⑱⑨ 0.354
Chad ⑱⑥ 0.404
South Sudan ⑱⑦ 0.388
Central African Republic ⑱⑧ 0.367
Burundi ⑱⑤ 0.417
Australia ③ 0.939

0   1,000   2,000 miles
0   1,000   2,000 kilometers

		Life expectancy at birth (years)	Expected years of schooling (years)	Mean years of schooling (years)	GNI per capita (2011 PPP $)
COUNTRIES WITH HIGHEST HDIs	① Norway	82.3	17.9	12.6	68,012
	② Switzerland	83.5	16.2	13.4	57,625
	③ Australia	83.1	22.9	12.9	43,560
	④ Ireland	81.6	19.6	12.5	53,754
	⑤ Germany	81.2	17.0	14.1	46,136
COUNTRIES WITH LOWEST HDIs	⑱⑤ Burundi	57.9	11.7	3.0	702
	⑱⑥ Chad	53.2	8.0	2.3	1,750
	⑱⑦ South Sudan	57.3	4.9	4.8	963
	⑱⑧ Central African Republic	52.9	7.2	4.3	663
	⑱⑨ Niger	60.4	5.4	2.0	906

Source: United Nations Development Programme

19.2 MEASURING GENDER INEQUALITY

Gender inequality is based on distinctions between men and women on an assortment of variables, including education, politics, and income. These differences can have a negative impact on human development, especially for women, girls, and families.

GENDER DISPARITIES

LEARNING OBJECTIVES

SPS-7.C Describe social and economic measures of development.

SPS-7.D Explain how and to what extent changes in economic development have contributed to gender parity.

Although the words *parity, equality,* and *equity* are related terms, they are not synonyms. *Parity* is a balance between two groups. *Equality* refers to the same level of resources and opportunities for everyone, no matter the location or situation. *Equity,* however, is about fairness, and it acknowledges how the lack of access to opportunities and certain resources affects underserved people, groups, or communities.

Assuring equity means providing additional aid to make sure everyone is treated fairly in all circumstances, according to their needs. So an indicator that compares gender parity between males and females is not equivalent, or similar in value, to one that compares gender equality, which ensures that men and women have equal access to opportunities and resources. And according to the United Nations Educational, Scientific and Cultural Organization (UNESCO),

gender equity is "fairness of treatment for both women and men, according to their respective needs."

The level of gender equality can be a measure of a country's overall level of development. Groups such as the United Nations assess gender parity by looking at wages, educational opportunities, and gender rights—including civil liberties and access to voting. The UN uses two measures to track gender inequality. The first is the **Gender Development Index (GDI)**, which calculates gender disparity in the three basic dimensions of human development: health, knowledge, and standard of living. It measures the female Human Development Index (HDI) as a percentage of the male HDI. Current GDI calculations show factors in which a difference between women and men exists as well as where near equity is achieved.

The second measure of gender inequality is the **Gender Inequality Index (GII)**, which calculates inequality based on three categories: reproductive health, empowerment, and labor-market participation. The GII ranges from 0.0 to 1.0; 0.0 shows that men and women share equal roles, and 1.0 shows that women have little equality. In 2017, Afghanistan had a GII score of 0.653, whereas Belgium scored 0.048.

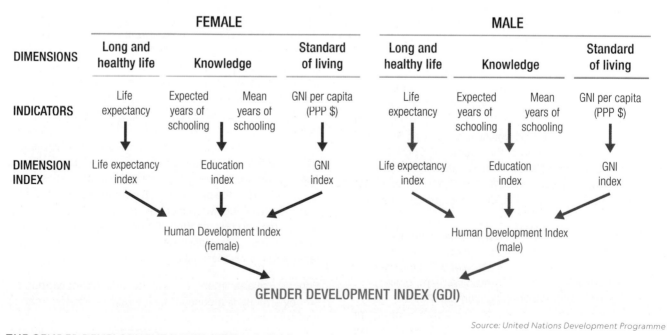

Source: United Nations Development Programme

THE GENDER DEVELOPMENT INDEX (GDI) includes the same key dimensions as the Human Development Index (HDI). By comparing these measures between women and men, the GDI reveals gender gaps in human development.

Mexico came in at 0.343, Canada was 0.092, and the United States was 0.189.

The World Bank and other international entities determined that gender equality contributes to the overall development or growth of an economy and is beneficial to every country. Several countries have introduced policies to promote gender parity. In 2018, Iceland became the first nation to make pay inequality illegal and currently imposes a fine on companies that don't comply. Rwanda, too, made recent moves toward gender parity by creating inclusive economic policies. However, Rwanda is an exception to most economically disadvantaged countries. Countries that dedicate the least amount of attention toward gender parity are usually peripheral, such as Chad, Syria, and Pakistan.

REPRODUCTIVE HEALTH The GII is the first major index to include reproductive health indicators as a measure of gender inequality. It uses two barometers related to women's reproductive health: one measures maternal deaths related to childbirth and the other measures births among adolescent mothers.

The maternal mortality ratio (MMR) is the number of maternal deaths per 100,000 live births. The MMR is considered a good indicator of women's access to health care because maternal deaths usually result from a lack of adequate care before, during, and just after childbirth. According to a 2019 report compiled by the World Health Organization, UNICEF, the UN Population Fund, and the World Bank, the worldwide MMR fell by 38 percent between 2000 and 2017, from 342 deaths to 211 deaths per 100,000 live births. During that time period, South Asia and sub-Saharan Africa had substantial ratio reductions of 59 percent and 39 percent, respectively. While these improvements are impressive, these two regions accounted for 86 percent of maternal deaths around the world, with sub-Saharan Africa suffering an MMR of 533.

The adolescent birth rate (ABR) is the number of births per 1,000 women aged 15 to 19. Early childbearing is associated with increased health risks for mothers and infants as well as keeping young mothers from accessing higher education. In 2018, the global average was 44 per 1,000 15- to 19-year-old women. The countries with the highest ABRs were Niger (184), Mali (167), and Chad (158), all sub-Saharan African countries. On the other end of the spectrum, South Korea's ABR was 1, Switzerland's was 3, and Singapore, Slovenia, Japan, the Netherlands, Denmark, and Cyprus each had an ABR of 4. The United States' adolescent birth rate was 19.

EMPOWERMENT **Women's empowerment** includes women's options and access to participate fully in the social and economic spheres of a society. The GII uses two indicators to measure women's empowerment: political representation and educational attainment. Political representation, which concerns women's civic involvement, is measured by the ratio of women with seats in government compared with men. The Inter-Parliamentary Union (IPU) tracks this information.

Women have traditionally been greatly outnumbered by men at every level of government. Gender inequality in the political sphere has improved over the last 25 years, but women are still underrepresented in decision-making political roles. Progress is occurring, albeit slowly. In 1995, 57 women held seats in the U.S. Congress, but by 2018, the number more than doubled to 127 women. However, that total is only 20 percent of all seats. Globally, the number of women in national legislatures increased from 11 percent in 1995 to 24.3 percent in 2019. However, 27 countries have less than 10 percent female participation in their parliaments. The majority of these countries are peripheral countries in Africa and Asia.

The countries that do have higher numbers of women in important political seats are a compelling mix. Core countries top the list, illustrated by the Scandinavian countries that have consistently had women hold around two-fifths of its seats in the legislatures since 2000. Interestingly, around 30 percent of the top 30 countries with the highest percentage of women in government are countries that have recently ended wars.

Rwanda is a strong example of this. Every year since 2004, Rwanda has had more women in its parliament than any other country in the world. Rwanda is not economically strong, but it experienced a social upheaval in the 1990s that caused this gender shift. In the devastating genocide of 1994, approximately 800,000 Rwandans were killed, many of them men. The president at the time decided that women would be the key to rebuilding the country, and in 2003, he added a decree to the constitution stating that at least 30 percent of political seats would be filled by women. Clearly, the roles of women changed in Rwanda as the country redeveloped after a crippling tragedy. Having women in decision-making roles tends to help a country improve its social and economic inequalities.

By 2019, underrepresentation of women remained an issue in every region and country of the world, though some countries saw progress in closing the gender gap in political representation. The only three countries that have reached or surpassed gender parity in their governments are Rwanda, Cuba, and Bolivia. According to the Pew Research Center, seats held by women in Nordic countries average around 40 percent, with Sweden at the high end (47 percent) and Denmark on the low end (37 percent). These countries score well on gender equality indices. At the other end of the spectrum, 28 countries throughout the world still fall short when it comes to political equality, with women making up less than 10 percent of their legislatures. Yemen, Oman, and Haiti have less than 3 percent female representation in their national parliaments.

Educational attainment, the second indicator of women's empowerment, is measured by the ratio of adult women and adult men (ages 25 and older) with some secondary education. Studies show that women's access to education affects their social and economic opportunities as well

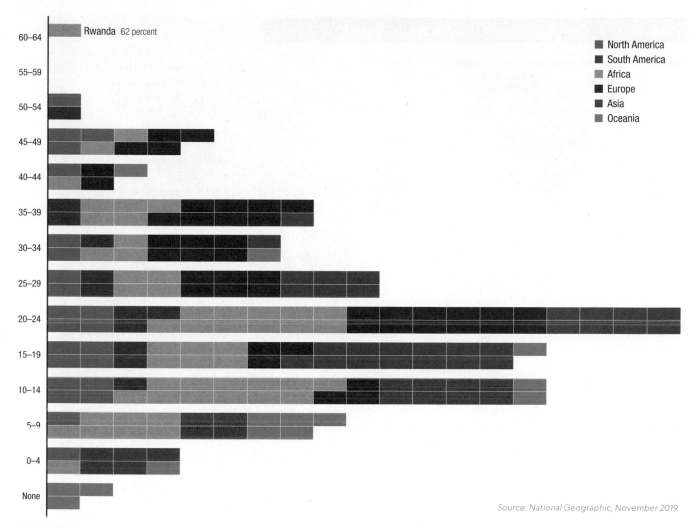

Source: National Geographic, November 2019

PERCENTAGE OF WOMEN IN NATIONAL LEGISLATURES, 2019 The percentage of women in government has risen in recent decades, but women continue to lag significantly behind men in the political sphere in most countries. Each rectangle in this chart represents an individual country from one of the six world regions.

as their health outcomes. UNESCO tracks this data by country and region. Although there are some advances in educational achievement, UNESCO points out that it still sees disparities. More girls than boys remain out of school; according to UNESCO's Institute for Statistics, 16 million girls will never set foot in a classroom. An alarming 9 million of these girls are in sub-Saharan Africa.

In addition, women account for two-thirds of all adults who lack basic literacy skills. In 2013, the majority of illiterate women ages 15 to 24 came from nine countries: India, Pakistan, Nigeria, Ethiopia, Bangladesh, Democratic Republic of Congo, United Republic of Tanzania, Egypt, and Burkina Faso. UNESCO reports that the many obstacles preventing women and girls from participating in education include poverty, geographic isolation, minority status, disability, early marriage and pregnancy, gender-based violence, and traditional attitudes about the status and role of women. Women who are able to complete a higher level of education see an expansion of their freedom because

their education strengthens their capacity to question, to reflect and act on their condition, and to enter the workforce with more skills.

LABOR-MARKET PARTICIPATION The **labor-market participation (LMP)** rate measures an economy's active labor force and is calculated by taking the sum of all employed workers and dividing that number by the working-age population. (The LMP is also known as labor-force participation, or LFP rate.) Identifying participation in formal and informal sectors allows geographers to make generalized assumptions about other important social indicators, such as the availability of education and health care, infant mortality, and gender equality. The conclusion that a high labor-force participation rate equals a highly economically developed country is not necessarily true. For example, Mozambique has one of the highest LMP rates in the world, but it doesn't have a strong economy. Also, the rates of LMP vary between genders in many countries. Male LMP tends to be high while female LMP tends to be

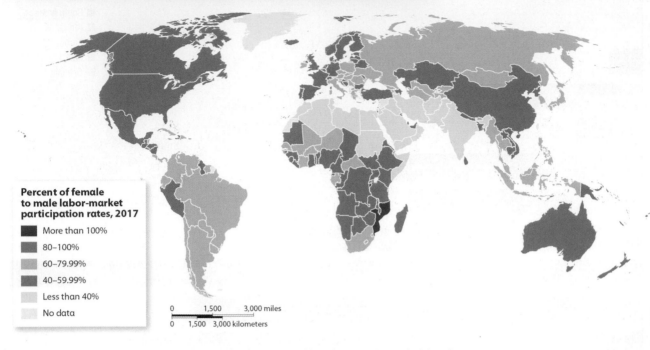

RATIO OF WOMEN TO MEN IN THE LABOR MARKET, 2017

Percent of female to male labor-market participation rates, 2017

- More than 100%
- 80–100%
- 60–79.99%
- 40–59.99%
- Less than 40%
- No data

0   1,500   3,000 miles
0   1,500 3,000 kilometers

READING MAPS Percentages on the map show the ratio of females to males in the labor force. The labor-market participation (LMP) rate is measured as the proportion of members of the population who are more than 15 years or older who are economically active. ▌In which regions of the world are female LMP rates highest? Choose one country and explain whether its LMP reflects that country's level of economic development.

low, and the variation between these two rates is even more pronounced in countries that practice distinct gender roles.

The roles that women play in a country's workforce often reflect that country's level of economic development. Core countries usually have more women working full-time jobs outside the home. Women in core countries are able to pursue careers in the tertiary sector that require a college education. Women in peripheral and semi-peripheral countries participate mainly in the primary and secondary sectors, do work just to provide food for the family, or perform unpaid work, often in the informal sector. These same groups of women also have high birth rates. Both the labor-intensive jobs and high birth rates are factors that inhibit women's ability to participate fully in economic and social spaces—which in turn holds back a country's development.

At the same time, female labor-market participation does not solely describe a country's economic development, as seen in some African countries in the periphery and semi-periphery. In Mozambique, Rwanda, Malawi, and Togo, the LMP is close to, or even slightly above, 100 percent. How can more than 100 percent of women be in a country's workforce? This data reflects gender parity in labor-force participation or the fact that more women than men are participating in the labor market in that country. At the same time, female labor-market participation is also high in some

of the richest countries in the world. Interestingly, the female LMP is lowest in countries that are right in the middle with average national incomes.

GEOGRAPHIC THINKING

1. Define the following terms: gender parity, gender equality, gender equity.

2. Identify what the Gender Development Index measures.

3. Describe what the Gender Inequality Index measures.

4. Explain the similarities between the maternal mortality ratio and the adolescent birth rate.

5. Compare the Gender Inequality Index with the Gender Development Index.

6. Explain how female labor-market participation can affect a country's economic development.

"WOMEN-ONLY" CITIES

THE ISSUE The Kingdom of Saudi Arabia's conservative rules about what women can and cannot do have recently changed, and Saudi women are taking advantage of these opportunities.

LEARNING OBJECTIVE

SPS-7.D Explain how and to what extent changes in economic development have contributed to gender parity.

BY THE NUMBERS

100:98

ratio of men to women who participated in the health sector in Saudi Arabia in 2019

100:92

ratio of men to women who participated in the education sector in Saudi Arabia in 2019

100:42

ratio of men to women who participated in the economic sector in Saudi Arabia in 2019

100:13

ratio of men to women who participated in the legislation and regulation sector in Saudi Arabia in 2019

Source: General Authority for Statistics, Kingdom of Saudi Arabia, 2019

Women work at a company in Riyadh that, in partnership with the Ministry of Labor, places women in jobs both virtually and in offices around the country.

IN THE LATE 20TH CENTURY, some people in Saudi Arabia started to question the social restrictions its women faced in their everyday lives. They expressed interest in ratifying a UN-created international bill of rights for women, called the Convention on the Elimination of All Forms of Discrimination Against Women (CEDAW). By 2005, a new king came to power who agreed to begin reforming the role of women in Saudi society.

Until 2013, Saudi women couldn't acquire an ID card for themselves without getting permission from a man. They had a few basic rights—some of which, like education, had just recently been granted. The country opened the first school for girls in 1955 and the first university for women in 1970. Other restrictions on Saudi women started dissolving, however, and women began achieving more and more firsts.

By 2009, the first woman was appointed as a minister in government. Female athletes first competed on the Saudi Arabian team in the 2012 Olympics. Women were allowed to ride bikes and motorcycles in recreational areas—with male chaperones—in 2013. Women gained the right to vote in 2015. And in 2018, women were finally allowed to get a driver's license without attaining permission from a male guardian and were also permitted to drive without a male chaperone.

By 2012, Saudi women made up almost 60 percent of the country's university students but only 15 percent of its workforce; more than 78 percent of Saudi Arabia's female college graduates were unemployed. To improve the overall productivity of the country, authorities approved a plan initially introduced by businesswomen in 2003: to build a string of "women-only" industrial cities where women can work in jobs that would otherwise be considered unsuitable for them in an environment shared with men. The first of these industrial cities—built in the eastern province city of Hofuf—created between 3,000 and 5,000 of these jobs.

While these women-only cities clearly benefit both Saudi women and the country, they haven't resolved the larger national segregation issues. Saudi Arabia is still the world's most gender-segregated country. Women can't eat at restaurants that don't have a separate designated family section, and they must use a separate entrance from men. The legal position of women in Saudi Arabia is not equal to men, so women can't receive a fair trial because they don't have equal representation in court. Additionally, Saudi law still prohibits women from jobs considered "detrimental to health" or "likely to expose women to specific risks." ▮

GEOGRAPHIC THINKING

Explain how women-only cities can impact Saudi women.

Toensing has been publicizing the difficulties of widows worldwide since she first shot a story in India in 2005.

LEARNING OBJECTIVE
SPS-7.C Describe social and economic measures of development.

WIDOW WARRIORS

Photojournalist, filmmaker, and National Geographic Photographer Amy Toensing shares intimate stories of everyday individuals. "For myself as a storyteller," she says, "the deeper the connections I make with my subjects, the deeper my audience is going to connect with my story." Her projects include photographs documenting Muslim women in the United States, the aftermath of Hurricane Katrina, the last cave-dwelling tribe of Papua New Guinea, and urban refugee children in Nairobi, Kenya. For one assignment, Toensing spent four years recording daily life in Aboriginal Australia. She also teaches photography to children and young adults in underserved communities to help them develop their voices.

In 2017, *National Geographic* magazine published Toensing's work as part of a feature that examines widowhood in three regions of the world. Sponsored in part by the Pulitzer Center for Crisis Reporting, the article highlights—and her photographs document—the cruel treatment that many widows face. "In many regions of the world widowhood marks a 'social death' for a woman—casting her and her children out to the margins of society," Toensing explains. These shunning acts can have huge negative effects on economic development. When women are isolated, ignored, or treated like property, they don't participate in the economy, and the community, state, or country suffers. Thankfully, some organizations have recently begun to protect and empower these women by helping them navigate existing laws. ▌

CRITICAL VIEWING Widows in Uttar Pradesh, India, learn how to sew. This valuable skill will allow the women to earn their own income. ▌ Describe how Toensing's photographs illustrate the changing roles of Indian widows in society.

Top: Women line up to receive food donations at the Nabadwip Bhajan Ashram in West Bengal, India. Widows often live in extreme poverty and depend on aid from nonprofit organizations to sustain themselves. Bottom: Widows enjoy the Holi celebration at the Gopinath Temple in Uttar Pradesh. Until recently, many people considered it inappropriate for widows to participate in this Hindu spring festival.

19.3 CHANGING ROLES OF WOMEN

The status of women in society—and the rate and categories of change—vary over time and across the world. Today, efforts to secure gender parity are occurring faster and in more places than ever before. As countries develop economically, opportunities for women evolve. Yet in most countries, women have not achieved parity, socially and economically, with men.

EVOLVING OPPORTUNITIES

LEARNING OBJECTIVE
SPS-7.D Explain how and to what extent changes in economic development have contributed to gender parity

Gender roles are generalized "normal" roles that men and women are expected to perform in their everyday lives, bounded by social and behavioral norms as practiced in a society. In most societies across the world, people who support these gender roles believe that a man's role is breadwinner and head of the household, while a woman's role is primary caretaker in the home, handling domestic duties and raising children. As you read in Chapter 6, traditional gender roles often keep women from playing a part in certain aspects of society and push women to fulfill cultural expectations that can be limiting. However, with economic development, societies change—and so do the roles of women, men, and even children.

Industrialization brought working-class women into the workforce with factory jobs, and postindustrial economies have offered women greater opportunities in both education and employment. As countries became more economically developed, the disparity in gender roles diminished. But this imbalance hasn't been eliminated. While education has become more equal—more than half of U.S. college students are women—men still make more money overall: on average, women earn roughly 80 percent of what men do. Other economic disparities exist as well. Globally, women don't share the benefits of development equally with men. Women in the United States are less likely to hold supervisory and managerial roles, and when they do, they tend to carry less authority. Even so, economic and social restructuring changes how people live, earn their livelihoods, and practice their gender roles.

RURAL AND URBAN OPPORTUNITIES Gender parity begins with equal opportunities. Economic changes often result in gender equity changes, and vice versa. For example, in rural areas in peripheral countries, women are starting to find opportunities outside the home in factories and in the service sector, which add to the household income. This, in turn, creates economic growth. One example of all-female entrepreneurship is occurring in Guatemala, in the tiny village of Urlanta. The initiative started with 29 village women, all with different knowledge and skill sets. They decided to try beekeeping. After some struggles, the women were able to extract and bottle honey and sell it at a profit. In Urlanta, the community mindset shifted. Before the beekeeping enterprise, the village women were expected only to stay home and raise children. They are now welcome participants in village meetings, sharing their experiences and offering advice to others.

It may be easy to think that urban areas have more economic opportunities for women. Generally, urban areas offer a greater array of services and infrastructure, opportunities for education and employment, and fewer social and cultural restrictions. But access to opportunities really depends on the location. In some regions—particularly North Africa, Southwest Asia, and South Asia—urban areas present a greater number of challenges, inequities, and insecurities for women. Women struggle with finding decent well-paying jobs, increasing workloads while juggling jobs and care at home, accessing financial assets, interacting with city and area authorities, and having housing security and personal security. The biggest challenge is dealing with traditional behaviors toward women's roles; many men in these urban areas don't allow women to easily participate in the job market. In many countries, strong attitudes about gender roles continue to make it difficult for women to break away from child-rearing and home life.

ECONOMIC OPPORTUNITIES Despite the overall trend of a continued gender gap, attitudes about women in the workforce are changing, and women are playing a larger part in the global economy. As women start to contribute to household incomes, roles are shifting; men and families see how two incomes can benefit a household. Much of the industrialization in countries in the periphery now relies on women working outside the home (because of the lower wage rates, which remains an issue). In addition, women in peripheral and semi-peripheral regions are edging into the service industry, and this trend is happening in core regions as well, thanks to huge growth in the tertiary sector.

The cultures of some countries are beginning to realize the value of women in economic roles. For example, women in Japan have not traditionally played a role in the workforce. However, since Japan's economy has been hindered over the past several decades by its aging and dwindling

The disciplines of science, technology, engineering, and math (STEM) have long been dominated by men. Recent efforts promote equity in education as well as career opportunities for young women. At the International Science and Engineering Fair, three teammates who attend school in Hong Kong display the prosthetic hand they created.

population, circumstances have changed. The government implemented an economic plan that focuses on eliminating the employment gender gap: it expects to see an increase of 13 percent in the country's Gross Domestic Product as a result of this initiative. Saudi Arabia is also focusing on a shift in women's roles in the economy. With recent drops in oil prices, government officials are looking at ways to diversify its economy by investing in human capital—including that of women.

In the United States, roles for women have expanded, and the number of women working outside the home is rising. In 2017, there were more than 74 million female workers in the workforce, comprising 47 percent of workers. The range of occupations has expanded; in many occupations, such as speech-language pathologists, dental assistants, social workers, physical therapists, and pharmacists, more than 50 percent are women. Women are making notable gains in professional and managerial occupations as well. In 1974, only 1 in 10 lawyers were women; in 2016, 1 in 3 are women. In 2017, well over half of human resources managers and education administrators were women.

But in some instances, the roles of women remain little changed. In higher-level managerial positions, only 27 percent of chief executives are women, and just 7 percent of construction managers are women. A Morgan Stanley report in 2017 stated, "More gender diversity, particularly in corporate settings, can translate to increased productivity, greater innovation, better decision-making, and higher employee retention and satisfaction." The number of opportunities has increased, but an obvious need for more women at this level persists.

EDUCATIONAL OPPORTUNITIES Until recently, women in many parts of the world have been denied access to education. This situation can severely limit all connections and opportunities a woman has during her lifetime. Women's health, limited future prospects, lower income, and increased vulnerability to exploitation and trafficking severely inhibit female growth. This hindrance, in turn, can cripple the economic advancement of a country.

As countries evolve and make strides in their economic and social development, women have greater access to educational opportunities, which leads to positive progress toward gender parity. Exposure to educational opportunities also encourages women to explore specialized careers, which can increase income possibilities, provide empowerment, lower birth rates, and create a variety of fulfilling activities for women outside the home. All these factors can help raise households and communities out of poverty and support national development.

An interesting correlation exists between education and fertility rates. A 2015 study in Ethiopia reported that 61 percent of women with no schooling have a baby before they turn 20, compared with 16 percent of women with eight years of schooling. Recall that the education dimension of the Human Development Index (HDI) is access to education. In most cases, women with more education tend to marry later and have fewer, healthier children. It's important to note, though, that studies show that other factors besides education can lower the total fertility rate, such as access to health care, additional work opportunities, and reduced child mortality. But education certainly plays a role.

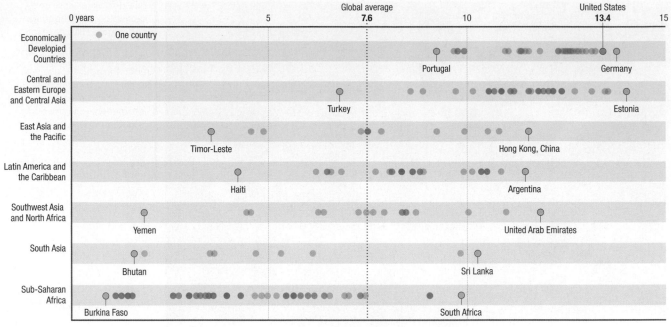

GIRLS' EDUCATION LEVELS AROUND THE WORLD, 2019 Many countries have high rates of girls finishing primary school, but they often fall short in graduation rates and quality of secondary schools; the global average in 2019 was 7.6 years of schooling. Each circle on the graph represents the average number of years of schooling for girls for one country. For example, the average for the United States was 13.4 years of schooling. The countries with the lowest and the highest averages in their regions—such as Bhutan and Sri Lanka in South Asia—are labeled as well.

Source: National Geographic, November 2019

Many public and private organizations—at local, national, and international levels—provide educational opportunities to break down the barriers that limit education access for women and girls around the world. Some obstructions are harder to crack, such as cultural traditions and religious restrictions, but others can be chipped away. Groups working to help women and girls contribute scholarships and loans, build schools to decrease the distances girls have to travel to get to school, create gender-sensitive curricula, ensure safe and inclusive learning environments, and invite men to join gender equality discussions.

In many places, girls struggle with social norms and economic challenges that threaten their ability to attend and remain in school. An organization in southern Africa created an innovative program that uses mobile-based technology to build digital skills to help empower girls and encourage them to continue their education. And a group called the Asia Foundation is working to increase literacy across the continent, with a huge focus in Afghanistan. The organization provides study kits to schools for girls to help these students pass entrance exams and gain entry to four-year national universities.

WAGES More educational opportunities for women have emerged over time, which means that women now have a better chance at earning higher wages. However, a wage gap between men and women still exists, even in core countries—although this is where the greatest strides to decrease the wage gap have been taken. In 2018, women

in Iceland protested against unfair pay. At the time, Icelandic women were paid 74 percent of the average wage of Icelandic men. In response, demonstrators declared that women should work 74 percent of the eight-hour workday. The protest worked. The following year, Iceland created a law requiring employers with 25 or more workers—in both the government and the private sector—to prove that they pay men and women equally for the same work.

In June 2019, women in Switzerland made a similar objection. Although Switzerland is one of the world's richest countries, women there were also frustrated by unequal pay. Thousands demonstrated by skipping work, ignoring household responsibilities, and marching in the streets. The 2019 protest marked the 28th anniversary of the first protest women made in Switzerland regarding unequal pay.

In the United States in 2017, women on average made 81 cents for every dollar a man makes. Studies show that education does not determine wage equality. According to a 2012 study, women who graduated with a business degree earned on average $38,000 their first year out of college, whereas men earned $45,000. Additionally, wage disparity can be tied to women pursuing professions commonly filled by women, taking time off to care for children, and choosing lower-paying jobs that allow for more flexibility.

Wage disparity exists unevenly throughout the United States. In 2019, the worst states for equality were Wyoming, West Virginia, Alabama, North Dakota, and Louisiana, where women earned just 69 cents for every dollar earned by

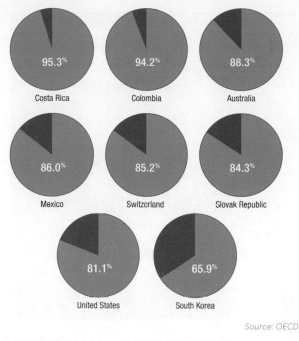

Source: OECD

GENDER PAY GAP COMPARISON, 2018 These pie graphs show the percentages of what women earn compared with men in selected countries in the Organization for Economic Cooperation and Development (OECD).

men. In contrast, California had the narrowest difference in the country, with women earning 88 cents for every dollar earned by men. The other states in the top five were New York, Maryland, and Nevada; Washington, D.C., also made the top five. Wage inequality also occurs along racial lines. White women and Asian American women, on average, make more than Hispanic, African-American, or Native American women.

Even workplaces in the spotlight have wage inequality. The U.S. women's soccer team won an historic fourth World Cup victory in 2019. Their record-breaking triumphs were undeniably impressive, yet female team members were paid just 38 percent of what their male counterparts earned. The women's team sued U.S. Soccer in federal court for gender discrimination and violations of the Equal Pay Act and Title VII of the Civil Rights Act of 1964. The result of the lawsuit could affect wage disparities for other female professional athletes in the United States and around the world.

EMPOWERING WOMEN

LEARNING OBJECTIVE

SPS-7.D Explain how and to what extent changes in economic development have contributed to gender parity.

In addition to providing more economic and educational opportunities for women, other endeavors seek to empower women. In places across the globe, women are still subject to violence, social injustice, and a lack of health care. Many women have been conditioned to believe that they are not

worthy of the right to food and shelter, to be educated, to work, or to be free. They may not realize that they are robbed of basic human rights. Some countries make it legally impossible for women to accept higher-paying jobs, and in others, a husband can legally deny his wife the opportunity to work outside the home.

Several initiatives aim to provide independence and choices for women and continue to make strides toward equality. In coordination with African governments and regional organizations, the United Nations has written several protocols and decrees for human rights and inclusion, with an emphasis on gender equality and the empowerment of women in Africa. As African countries continue to develop economically, they turn their focus to women. The result is a stronger presence in the workforce across the African continent. While women still work longer hours and earn less money than men, African women overall are highly entrepreneurial. In some countries, such as Rwanda and Ghana, women run nearly one-half of all businesses in the country.

MICROLOANS In recent years, women in peripheral and semi-peripheral countries have started applying for loans to start small businesses. For them, being an entrepreneur is the answer to breaking away from poverty and improving financial security for their family and children. **Microloans** are very small short-term loans with low interest intended to help people in need. Microloans became one option for women wanting to take a risk on their own enterprises. Most of the women obtaining the loans would not qualify for loans from a traditional bank, so nongovernment organizations searched for ways to make loans available.

The microloan industry was started by a Bangladeshi professor who eventually opened the Grameen Bank, a microloan institution. Other microloan institutions followed, and the industry has flourished. In 2015, market analysts determined that an estimated 125 million people worldwide—about 80 percent of whom were women— received a total of about $100 billion (U.S.) in microloans from the key microfinance institutions.

Microloans range in size depending on location, from a low of about $200 in South Asia to a high of nearly $3,000 in Eastern Europe and Central Asia. The amounts are based on the borrower, the entrepreneurial opportunity, the location, and the income variation. Microloans cover startup costs for a variety of businesses, such as the cost of nail polish for setting up a home-based nail salon or an individual purchasing chickens to sell the eggs. Many of the loans also cover education costs. Numerous microloan institutions offer business training and other resources. This small amount of financial help greatly contributes to leveling the playing field.

Many women have succeeded in business thanks to getting their start from a microloan. Take the example of Oiness, a single mother of three in Zambia, who lives in a remote rural village with few employment opportunities. She realized she

WOMEN IN LEADERSHIP

Diverse women—from teenagers to adults and from rural regions to urban centers—have risen to leadership roles in the fields of government, business, activism, and education. By speaking up and blazing trails, they inspire people around the world. Clockwise from top left: Michelle Bachelet, first woman president of Chile • Tracy Chou, Taiwanese-American proponent for women in technology • Emma González, Cuban-American advocate for gun control • Jane Goodall, British primatologist and environmental activist • Malala Yousafzai, Pakistani advocate for female education • Greta Thunberg, Swedish leader of global youth movement demanding action on climate change • Autumn Peltier, Indigenous Canadian clean water activist • Kakenya Ntaiya, Kenyan educator and champion for women's rights.

could start a business selling small, portable cooking stoves to people in her community. Thanks to a microloan, she was able to buy the materials she needed to make the stoves. When she started earning money, she reinvested those funds into her business, so it grew. She now earns enough money to send all of her children to school.

Obtaining a microloan in and of itself does not ensure success. Starting, running, and maintaining a business is tough. However, as more women become successful business owners in poorer countries, gender inequality continues to narrow in those areas.

INVESTING IN GIRLS AND WOMEN As countries develop, more attention and money can be invested in issues relevant to women. According to the Organization for Economic Cooperation and Development (OECD), four key strategies need increased investment: (1) Ensure that financial assets are in the hands of women. (2) Keep girls in school. (3) Improve reproductive health and access to family planning. (4) Support women's leadership.

These strategies coincide with the goals in the UN's 2030 Agenda. To reach these goals, the United Nations thinks that every country must make public services available for women, confront and overcome the cultural and social norms that hold back women and girls, put voluntary family planning back on the development agenda, gather evidence about which methods in the agenda work, and accurately track the proportion and coverage of aid focused on achieving gender equality and women's empowerment.

GEOGRAPHIC THINKING

1. Identify and explain the relationship between economic development and gender parity.

2. Compare global wage equality using the content in 12.3 and the "Gender Pay Gap Comparison, 2018" pie graphs.

3. Describe how microloans can help get women out of poverty.

THE DEVELOPMENT OF THE GRAMEEN BANK

THE ISSUE For many people without economic resources, starting a business is the only way to escape poverty. And these people don't have the collateral (capital or property) needed to acquire a traditional bank loan.

LEARNING OBJECTIVE
SPS-7.D Explain how and to what extent changes in economic development have contributed to gender parity.

BY THE NUMBERS

97%

of Grameen Bank borrowers are women, and nearly 99 percent of the loans have been paid back as of 2018.

9.08 MILLION

Grameen Bank members in Bangladesh as of 2018

100+

countries have Grameen Bank–backed projects as of 2018

Source: Grameen Bank, 2018

A woman conducts business at a weekly meeting held for borrowers at the Grameen Bank in Bangladesh.

IN 1983, MUHAMMAD YUNUS STARTED THE GRAMEEN BANK, which means "rural" or "village" bank in Bengali. He reasoned that if financial resources could be made available to poverty-stricken people through reasonable and appropriate terms and conditions, then "these millions of small people with their millions of small pursuits can add up to create the biggest development wonder."

Yunus got the idea for the bank when he was an economics professor in Bangladesh. One day he took his students on a field trip to a small rural village in India. They interviewed a woman who was making bamboo stools to sell. After paying for the bamboo, she barely made a profit from her sales. Yunus loaned her money, and she was able to buy her raw material at a cheaper price because she was able to buy it in volume. The result: she made a larger profit. Yunus and his students studied her continuing business, and they realized the key to survival and economic growth for this woman—and many others like her—was just a little bit of money: a small loan.

The Grameen Bank offers microloans, or microcredit, with no collateral required, no legal contracts, low interest, and comfortable repayment plans. The bank provides loans to pay for raw materials, livestock, agriculture, grocery shops, and cell phones. Products made from these loans go to local markets, the main market in the capital city, and markets all over the world.

Borrowers repay monthly installments to bank representatives who visit them, listen to their stories, and discuss business successes and challenges. Money earned by women borrowers has a huge impact on their families, and these women tend to save their money or invest it, rather than spend it. In 2006, the Grameen Bank and its founder were awarded the Nobel Peace Prize "for their efforts to create economic and social development from below."

The success of Grameen Bank has led to the creation of many other microloan institutions, and borrowers are found in every corner of the world. Yunus is proud of what he started and the women he has helped. "There are roughly 160 million people all over the world in microcredit, mostly women," he said in 2017. "And they have proven one very important thing: that we are all entrepreneurs." ∎

GEOGRAPHIC THINKING

Describe how Grameen Bank can be an example for societal change.

19.4 THEORIES OF DEVELOPMENT

Economic growth results in lower unemployment rates, higher tax revenues, improved living standards, and a reduction in poverty. Additionally, governments of growing economies can afford to invest in infrastructure and social services. Theories that explain spatial variations in development include Rostow's stages of economic growth, Wallerstein's world system theory, dependency theory, and commodity dependence.

ROSTOW'S STAGES OF ECONOMIC GROWTH

LEARNING OBJECTIVE
SPS-7.E Describe different theories of economic and social development.

In the 1960s, after much of Africa and Asia gained independence, Walt W. Rostow developed his **stages of economic growth** model. He studied countries that had success in developing economically and asked: How were these countries able to achieve this modernization, and could poorer countries follow a similar path? At the time, it was assumed that every country wanted to achieve modernization, that is, the social, political, economic, and technological changes associated with becoming industrialized and moving away from traditional ways of life. Rostow suggested that all countries could be categorized on a spectrum from traditional to modern and that to become modern, countries needed to pass through distinct stages of economic growth in succession. He also assumed that all countries practiced a form of market-oriented capitalism.

Stage 1: Traditional Society In the simplest and most primitive form of organization, political power is local, regional, or based on land ownership. Family plays a dominant role, and social structures limit economic mobility. Rostow described traditional society as one that is primarily rural, centered on subsistence farming by family labor and using primitive technology. Modern science and technology are nonexistent in this stage.

Stage 2: Preconditions for Takeoff Progressive elements begin to form, and people start to seek knowledge and break free from the traditional mindset. New types of enterprises emerge with long-term goals, investment increases, and output rises. As industry accelerates, improved infrastructure becomes essential. The workforce shifts from agriculture to manufacturing, and credit institutions are developed to make investments more accessible.

Stage 3: Takeoff Political, social, and institutional frameworks in society change. Urbanization increases, infrastructure continues to improve, and productive capacity surges in some manufacturing industries, with technological advances as well.

Stage 4: Drive to Maturity The economy keeps progressing in a period of self-sustained growth. In this respect, "maturity" is the state in which a country's successes become the norm, or habit. Industries function at maximum effectiveness, and electric power generation and consumption are high. Consumption patterns shift thanks to increased income. Entrepreneurial leadership changes from individual industrialists to managerial bureaucracy.

Stage 5: High Mass Consumption Modern societies are urban, centered on wage labor, and organized into states. Production shifts from industrial manufacturing to consumer goods and services. Problems of production change to problems of consumption, and trade expands.

Rostow envisioned that each country could be categorized in one of these stages, and that all countries could follow these principles to achieve economic growth and success. Various factors influence the speed of progression according to Rostow's model. They include natural resource availability, productivity, and political and social decision-making.

The earliest country to reach maturity was Great Britain. Its production of textiles placed it in takeoff stage in the early 18th century. The Industrial Revolution, with the introduction of the water frame, the power loom, and the use of steam power, propelled the country to its drive to maturity stage around 1850. The next major country to hit maturity was the United States around 1900. Canada and Russia both hit maturity around 1950, but Canada has been able to reach stage 5. Russia remains in stage 4 because it has oligarchs and widespread corruption instead of leadership that follows the rule of law.

Singapore illustrates Rostow's model. With a population of around 5.8 million in 2019, Singapore had a successful, linear path of economic growth. After its independence in 1965, it focused on industrialization and developed profitable manufacturing and high-tech industries. It hit its maturity not long after it passed its takeoff stage. Singapore is now highly modernized, quite wealthy, and a leading trade partner in the global market, placing it securely in Rostow's stage five.

LIMITATIONS OF THE STAGES OF ECONOMIC GROWTH MODEL Since Rostow's model was based on the United States and Europe in the 1960s, critics argue

Rostow created his model of the stages of economic growth in 1960 to answer questions such as *What causes traditional societies to begin the process of modernization?* and *What forces drive this process of growth?*

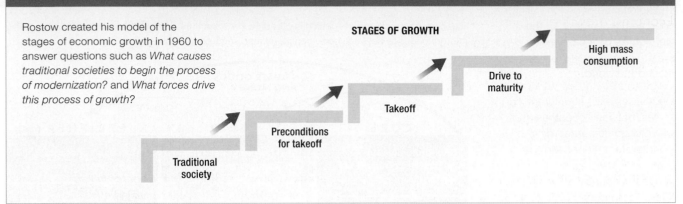

STAGES OF GROWTH

- Traditional society
- Preconditions for takeoff
- Takeoff
- Drive to maturity
- High mass consumption

that it can't be applied to every country. According to the model, the result of the sequence of growth stages is an industrialized, capitalist, democratic country; the assumption is that all countries will wish to have these characteristics.

A further limitation of the model is that the stages of growth in some countries differ by region. For example, India is difficult to categorize using Rostow's model. The country as a whole might be placed in stage 3 or stage 4, but some regions remain in stage 2.

In addition, Rostow's model does not take into account geographic influences and challenges. One country may make the leap from being a rural, agrarian state to an industrialized one, but that breakthrough does not mean other countries will follow suit in exactly the same way, following the same ordered stages of growth.

Moreover, Rostow's stages of economic growth assume that all countries follow a progression of development in which they will become mass consumers, but they don't allow for Earth's carrying capacity and new ecological limits—information that was unavailable to Rostow in the 1960s. Mass consumerism creates a "the more, the better" attitude, and Rostow did not consider that consumers at the final stage would use and demand more than they actually should. Sustainability becomes an issue as consumers deplete resources and create environmental degradation.

Another criticism of Rostow's model is that it doesn't consider how countries influence one another and how these impacts can affect the progression of development. Countries in this time of globalization are interconnected and interdependent. The road to maturity was much different for the "early starters"—the countries that matured sooner—like Great Britain and the United States. Their path was much clearer: They had less competition and fewer obstacles. The "late starters" in today's peripheral regions have much bigger barriers to overcome that in many cases are a direct result of the success of the early starters, such as colonial legacies or lack of access to the latest technologies.

WALLERSTEIN'S WORLD SYSTEM THEORY

LEARNING OBJECTIVE
SPS-7.E Describe different theories of economic and social development.

In response to Rostow's stages of economic growth model, Immanuel Wallerstein published his world system theory (which you learned about in Chapter 1) in 1974. This theory describes the spatial and functional relationships between countries and helps explain the history of uneven economic development in the world economy.

According to Wallerstein, countries are dependent on one another and don't develop in isolation: Some countries dominate and some are exploited. His theory illustrates global inequality through a social structure, dividing the world into a three-tiered structure consisting of core, peripheral, and semi-peripheral regions. As you've read throughout the text, core countries dominate and take advantage of peripheral countries for labor and raw materials, and peripheral countries are dependent on core countries for capital. Semi-peripheral countries have qualities of both core countries and peripheral countries.

World system theory includes both political and economic elements and can be viewed as either a political or economic theory with geographic effects. Wallerstein examined the world economy and how it developed due to capitalism. Capitalism became a global system with stronger, interdependent economic ties between regions and countries, gradually encompassing all countries in the world in some way. Today's core countries are able to accumulate capital internally through taxation, government purchasing, funding of infrastructure, and sponsorship of research and development. Core countries are also able to accumulate capital through control of the world economy. They use their power—economic, political, social, and military—to pay low prices for raw materials, to employ cheap labor in peripheral regions, and to install trade barriers and quotas. It is possible for countries to move from the periphery to the semi-periphery, and from the semi-periphery to the core as they develop economically.

However, since the prosperity of core countries depends on exploitation of peripheral countries, movement up the hierarchy is difficult, and the system produces imbalances around the world.

Inequalities exist at different scales: between countries and within countries. According to world system theory, Mexico is an industrializing, semi-peripheral country. Why? Within Mexico's borders are large peripheral areas, such as its southern states of Chiapas and Oaxaca, in the rural highlands of the country where economic opportunities are limited and poverty rates are high.

The World Bank found that in 2018, 42 percent, or more than 52 million, of Mexico's people lived below its poverty line, and that 7 of 10 people living in poverty resided in just 6 of Mexico's 32 states, mostly in the country's south. In Mexico City and in most of Mexico's northern states, poverty rates are much lower. This high rate of income inequality—along with related factors such as less access to education, health care, and basic infrastructure—illustrate the continuum of poverty that keeps Mexico in the semi-periphery. Its 2018 GNI per capita was U.S. $9,180.

Compare this data to those of a less economically developed country like Angola, whose poverty headcount ratio jumped from 30.1 percent in 2010 to 47.6 percent in 2018 and whose GNI per capita was U.S. $3,370. The United Nations notes that many people do not have "food security, access to basic services such as healthcare, transportation and education," or live "in peaceful, stable societies." In world system theory, the cycle of interaction between the core and the periphery often keeps those living in poverty from being able to improve their situation.

LIMITATIONS OF WORLD SYSTEM THEORY

The biggest criticism of world system theory is that the model is too focused on economics. Categorizing countries based on a global economy isn't comprehensive. Experts claim that there are more determinants for the economic development or connection to the world system than capitalism. Critics also argue that a study of core-peripheral relationships must take into account other measures of integration or dominance, such as cultural influence.

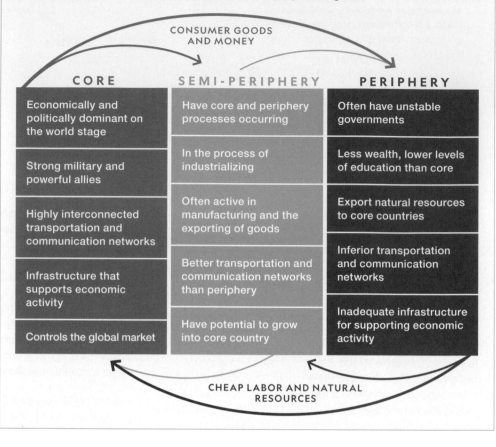

MODEL: CORE-PERIPHERY

The core-periphery model—which is part of world system theory—illustrates the interdependence between core, peripheral, and semi-peripheral regions.

CONSUMER GOODS AND MONEY

CORE	SEMI-PERIPHERY	PERIPHERY
Economically and politically dominant on the world stage	Have core and periphery processes occurring	Often have unstable governments
Strong military and powerful allies	In the process of industrializing	Less wealth, lower levels of education than core
Highly interconnected transportation and communication networks	Often active in manufacturing and the exporting of goods	Export natural resources to core countries
Infrastructure that supports economic activity	Better transportation and communication networks than periphery	Inferior transportation and communication networks
Controls the global market	Have potential to grow into core country	Inadequate infrastructure for supporting economic activity

CHEAP LABOR AND NATURAL RESOURCES

A further limitation is that the theory may work as an historical analysis but may not be the best measure of modern development. Another weakness is that the theory states that countries can change their status but gives no explanation as to how that can happen. Detractors argue that a theory explaining an event should also include supporting material when making a claim.

DEPENDENCY THEORY

LEARNING OBJECTIVE
SPS-7.E Describe different theories of economic and social development.

In the late 1950s, experts at the United Nations tried to explain why economic growth in industrialized countries did not lead to economic growth in nonindustrialized countries. They identified a financial dependency among countries with widely diverse economies. This reliance explained the failure of less economically developed countries to experience financial growth despite investments from more economically developed countries. **Dependency theory** describes the development challenges and limitations faced by poorer countries and the political and economic relationships poorer countries have with richer countries.

According to dependency theory, peripheral countries offer cheap labor and raw materials to the global market. Core countries buy the raw materials and hire the cheap labor. They use these two economic factors to produce goods and sell them at high prices. Peripheral countries have a demand for these goods, so they buy them at the increased prices, which depletes the funds they might have used to upgrade their own production structures. So to produce capital, peripheral countries continue to sell their raw materials and offer their labor. It's a vicious process that explains the huge gap between the rich core and the poor periphery: The needs of the core keep the periphery in a state of underdevelopment. One leading dependency theorist suggests that a lack of development prevails in some countries because core countries have deliberately kept some peripheral countries from developing. This plight reflects the underlying cause of dependency: imperialism.

Both world system theory and dependency theory aim to explain global economic inequality. Both include the concept of core, peripheral, and semi-peripheral world structure. The key difference between the two is based on the focus of the inequality. In world system theory, global economic inequality exists because core countries thrive through economic exploitation of peripheral countries. Supporters of dependency theory argue that the global economy has been unequally structured since Europeans began colonizing the world in the 16th century. Although the form of the dominance of core over periphery has changed from colonialism and imperialism to neocolonialism, an overall transfer of wealth from periphery to core continues to fuel growth in some places at the expense of others.

As with all models and theories, dependency theory has limitations. Critics point out that dependency theorists fail to define critical terms, including *dependence* and *underdevelopment*. Additionally, there is no standard to distinguish between dependent and nondependent countries. Other detractors note that the theory fails to take into account other factors that cause underdevelopment. According to these critics, the nature of underdevelopment in Latin America is different than in Asia. Finally, critics argue that the theory doesn't reflect that underdevelopment can be a product of leaders making bad decisions.

COMMODITY DEPENDENCE One aspect of dependency theory is **commodity dependence**, when more than 60 percent of a country's exports and economic health are tied to one or two resources such as oil, timber, or plantation crops. This dependency is indicative of the narrow economic base that peripheral and some semi-peripheral countries depend upon, unlike the broad, diversified, and healthy economies that core countries enjoy. These countries in the periphery have not had the opportunities to add value to their resources through manufacturing, so they are often trapped in neocolonial economic relationships, exporting raw materials and importing manufactured goods.

Unfortunately, export earnings for dependent countries are at the mercy of commodity pricing. Commodity markets set prices based on supply and demand, so commodity trade is never a stable environment. When the commodity price of its major export increases, such a country sees economic growth. But when supply is high, demand drops and so do prices. If a country is commodity dependent (or has "all its eggs in one basket"), it suffers. Employment decreases, exports diminish, and government revenues slump. These conditions are why many economists find a connection between commodity dependency, poverty, and financial turmoil.

Consider oil, which can be a volatile market. In June 2014, the price of oil was at an all-time high of $115 a barrel. After global demand decreased, the price fell below $50 a barrel in January 2015. Several countries were devastated when oil prices dropped. Venezuela had assumed that the price of oil would remain stable and started funding welfare programs from its oil revenues. When prices fell, Venezuela could not meet its debt obligations. Saudi Arabia is another country dependent on oil. Fortunately, it had ample financial reserves to weather the price drop. Since then, the kingdom has tried to diversify its economy to become less dependent on oil.

Geographers have found another link to commodity dependency. For countries with a single commodity, there is extreme interest in who controls that commodity. This situation can cause governments and political factions to clash, creating political instability. This relationship between commodity dependence and political instability can be seen in countries like Sierra Leone, with its single commodity of diamonds. Mercenaries and criminals run rampant in the African country as they try to control the diamond trade and profit from it. As such, commodity dependency can be described as a "resource curse." Such commodity-dependent countries, rich in a specific resource but lacking economic diversity, are often trapped in volatile situations.

Commodity dependency can have a negative impact on a country's development. Because the welfare of commodity-dependent countries can be critical to the global economy, these countries are closely monitored. The UN issues a State of Commodity Dependence Report every two years to summarize and analyze the state of commodity-dependent countries. In 2019, the report looked at 189 countries, of which 102 were commodity-dependent, including 89 percent of sub-Saharan countries in Africa and 50 percent of Latin American countries. These numbers are stark proof of the uneven geography of economic development.

GEOGRAPHIC THINKING

1. Compare Rostow's stages of economic growth, world system theory, and dependency theory.

2. Explain the degree to which commodity dependence slows and fuels economic development.

CHAPTER 19

SUMMARY & REVIEW

■ CHAPTER SUMMARY

Geographers classify countries as core, periphery, and semi-periphery, but all countries fall on a continuum.

Indicators used to measure economic conditions include:

- Gross Domestic Product (GDP)—the total value of goods and services produced by a country in a year; limited to what is produced within the country

- Gross National Product (GNP)—the total value of the goods and services produced by a country in a year, including those produced internationally

- Gross National Income (GNI) per capita—a country's total annual income divided by the country's population

The structure of an economy can be divided into formal and informal sectors. Social indicators used to measure growth include fertility rates, infant mortality rates, access to health care, and literacy rates.

The Human Development Index (HDI) looks at three indicators to determine overall levels of development: life expectancy, access to education, and standard of living.

The UN uses two measurements to track gender inequality:

- The Gender Development Index (GDI) measures the gender gap in health, knowledge, and living standards.

- The Gender Inequality Index (GII) measures gender inequalities in three categories:

   1. reproductive health (maternal mortality ratio and adolescent birth rate)

   2. empowerment (political representation and educational attainment)

   3. labor-market participation (the role of women in the workforce)

As countries experience economic changes, the roles of women and gender equity change as well. Attitudes about women in the workforce have evolved, and women are playing a larger part in the global economy. Women have more access to education, and women's wages have increased, although most women still make less than men.

Countries and individual organizations are focused on empowering women. Financial institutions offer microloans to women living in poverty to start small businesses.

Theories of development include:

- Rostow's stages of economic growth, a model that shows how countries progress from traditional to modern through a sequential set of stages

- Wallerstein's world system theory, a theory that states that peripheral countries are dependent on core countries, and core countries often exploit countries in the periphery

- dependency theory, a theory that describes how non-industrialized countries are financially dependent on industrialized countries

- commodity dependency, which occurs when more than 60 percent of a country's exports are made up of primary commodities

■ KEY TERMS AND CONCEPTS

Use complete sentences to answer the questions.

1. **APPLY CONCEPTUAL VOCABULARY** Consider the term *development*. Write a standard dictionary definition of it. Then provide a conceptual definition for the term—an explanation of how it is used in the context of this chapter.

2. What is a semi-peripheral country, and how is it different from a core country or a peripheral country?

3. Differentiate between the terms *GDP* and *GNI*.

4. How does the HDI show spatial variation among states in levels of development?

5. Explain the relationship between core countries and peripheral countries using world system theory.

6. Use an example to show how distribution of income is an important measure of development.

7. Explain how political representation is an indicator of gender equality.

8. Why might a critic argue that Rostow's stages of economic growth model is not as linear as a graph would suggest?

9. Explain how reproductive health affects a country's Gender Inequality Index.

10. How does price volatility affect commodity dependency?

11. Why is it difficult to measure informal sectors of the economy accurately?

12. Explain how measuring GNI per capita reveals a better understanding of a country's overall well-being.

■ INTERPRET GRAPHS

Study the graph and then answer the following questions.

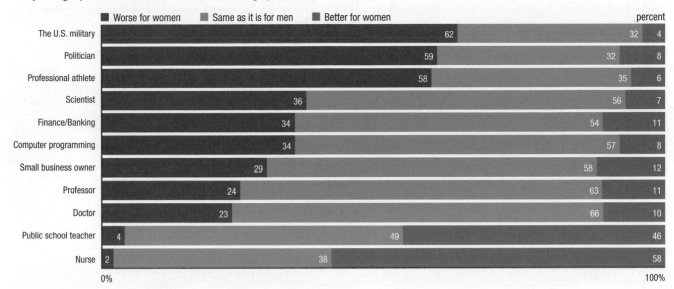

■ Worse for women   ■ Same as it is for men   ■ Better for women

Profession	Worse for women	Same as it is for men	Better for women
The U.S. military	62	32	4
Politician	59	32	8
Professional athlete	58	35	6
Scientist	36	56	7
Finance/Banking	34	54	11
Computer programming	34	57	8
Small business owner	29	58	12
Professor	24	63	11
Doctor	23	66	10
Public school teacher	4	49	46
Nurse	2	38	58

0% — 100%

PROFESSIONAL OPPORTUNITIES POLL, 2019 This bar graph displays the results from more than 1,000 women in the United States who were asked whether the opportunity for women to advance in the listed professions is better, worse, or about the same as it is for men.

13. IDENTIFY DATA & INFORMATION Based on the bar graph, which two professions had the best advancement opportunities for women?

14. ANALYZE VISUALS What generalizations can you make about the professions of professor and doctor?

15. DRAW CONCLUSIONS What conclusions can you draw about how women might feel about professional opportunities and the workplace in the United States? Use information from the graph to support your answer.

GEO-INQUIRY | MEASURE DEVELOPMENT IN YOUR COMMUNITY

Consider how you can use Geo-Inquiry to analyze human development for your community in order to propose a solution for improvement. Use the steps in the Geo-Inquiry Process below to explore the best way to measure how economically and socially developed your community is and offer a proposal for improvement.

ASK Start with an authentic question about your community. It may be as simple as: *How might we increase gender equality in the community?* Use the Geo-Inquiry Process to expand this question and ask related questions, such as: *What economic indicators can identify and measure the issue? What social indicators can be used? Is there a gender gap in my community? Are educational opportunities available equally to everyone?*

COLLECT Decide how you could gather geographic information to answer your original question. Explore local sources of information for data and statistics. Interview people, including those with important roles in your community's economic and social spheres. Visit schools and health-care facilities.

VISUALIZE Analyze the information you collected to draw conclusions. Organize the information and use it to illustrate the community situation and the proposed solution.

CREATE Focus on ways to tell a Geo-Inquiry story that will describe the issue and your proposed solution. Keep your audience in mind. Will you be sharing your story with community leaders? How can you use images, videos, charts, and graphs to help tell your story? Tie your elements together using a storytelling tool.

ACT Share your story with decision-makers. Show how your project can increase awareness in gender inequalities and offer a proposed solution.

ASK — COLLECT — VISUALIZE — CREATE — ACT

CHAPTER 20

GLOBALIZATION, INTERDEPENDENCE, AND SUSTAINABILITY

CRITICAL VIEWING Every year, Las Vegas, Nevada, hosts the Consumer Electronics Show, a trade show where more than 4,500 electronics companies from all over the world display their latest products to consumers. LG Electronics, a company based in South Korea, displayed its newest video screens at the 2019 event. ▌ How does the photo demonstrate globalization?

GEOGRAPHIC THINKING How has globalization affected spatial relationships?

20.1
TRADE RELATIONS AND GLOBAL CORPORATIONS

20.2
CONNECTED ECONOMIES

CASE STUDY: The Financial Crisis of 2007–2008

20.3
DEVELOPING A SUSTAINABLE WORLD

CASE STUDY: Reducing Waste in Fisheries

NATIONAL GEOGRAPHIC EXPLORER Andrés Ruzo

20.1 TRADE RELATIONS AND GLOBAL CORPORATIONS

Technology and free trade (trade without restrictions) have expanded people's awareness of resources and available products for consumption and allowed goods to be shipped quickly and inexpensively from thousands of miles away. These are two key factors that have helped to increase international trade and interdependence in the world economy.

INTERDEPENDENCE OF CORE, PERIPHERY, AND SEMI-PERIPHERY

LEARNING OBJECTIVE
PSO-7.A Explain causes and geographic consequences of recent economic changes such as the increase in international trade, deindustrialization, and growing interdependence in the world economy.

The world is linked through complex economic systems in which free trade agreements invite participation in market economies that connect regions and countries more than ever before. As a result, international trade has skyrocketed in the last century. In 2018, about 60 percent of the world's gross domestic product (GDP) was made up of international trade, as compared to about 25 percent in 1960. Countries engage in trade when it is mutually beneficial. One country lacks a resource, and another country provides the resource in exchange for money. However, the benefits to both trading partners are not always equal. Globalization is expanding the gap between the core and the periphery and within countries with widening income disparities. Two factors are the basis for trade and impact its benefits: **comparative advantage** and **complementarity**.

Assuming free trade exists, comparative advantage refers to the relative cost advantages of producing certain goods and services for trade. For example, if two countries can both produce corn and computers, it may not make economic sense for both of them to produce these goods for their domestic markets. It may be more cost effective for one to specialize in corn and the other in computers and trade them. From an economic standpoint, it would be advantageous for countries to produce and export a select range of goods and not make everything themselves. However, countries must consider their available resources, technology, and capital, as well as labor costs, all of which affect comparative advantage.

Complementarity refers to the mutually beneficial trade relationship between two countries that results when they have different comparative advantages. There must be demand in one place and supply that matches in another. Factors that affect complementarity include variation in the distribution of resources; the relationships between core and peripheral or semi-peripheral countries, in which the periphery supplies raw materials and the core supplies

manufactured goods; and the economic advantages of specializing in certain goods. In general, countries export goods that they have a relative advantage in producing in exchange for goods that are less expensive to import than to produce internally. For example, Mexico imports specialty apples from the United States, and the United States imports avocados from Mexico because it is more expensive to grow them in their own countries than to import them.

New trade relationships are fueled by economic development. Countries need raw materials for production, and in general, core countries import natural resources from peripheral countries. The result is an interdependence of countries as part of an interconnected global economy.

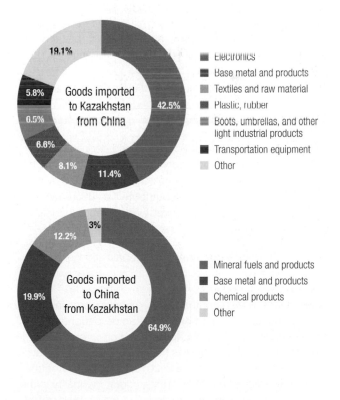

COMPLEMENTARITY: CHINA AND KAZAKHSTAN
Complementarity exists between China and Kazakhstan because each country has its own comparative advantage. Kazakhstan is rich in natural resources like oil, natural gas, minerals, and metals; China has a comparative advantage in making electronics and industrial equipment. ■ Explain how the two graphs demonstrate complementarity between China and Kazakhstan.

In many countries of the periphery, globalization leads to commodity dependence, in which the economy is reliant on the export of agricultural products, metals, ores, minerals, oil, or other commodities. Some geographers worry that commodity dependence negatively impacts a country's economy and can lead to a fixed state of underdevelopment.

NEOLIBERAL POLICIES **Neoliberalism** is the belief that open markets and free trade (two key characteristics of capitalism) across the globe will lead to economic development everywhere, lessen tensions between countries by fostering support for common values, and spread democracy and human rights. Neoliberal policies encourage free markets and discourage political interference with economic systems. The interdependence of countries in a global economy has led to neoliberal policies that free private enterprise from government involvement and are associated with deregulation and privatization. When the U.S. airline industry was deregulated in 1978, airlines had more freedom to set their own fares and routes. Some countries have privatized their utilities, transferring government control over energy to private companies.

Free trade agreements are neoliberal policies that are restructuring the world into new, economics-based regions. Groups of countries, referred to as trading blocs, agree to a common set of trading rules in order to encourage trade and reduce trade barriers between the countries in the group. The North American Free Trade Agreement (NAFTA), which took effect in 1994, was an example of a neoliberal regional free trade agreement. NAFTA eliminated tariffs (a tax on imports to make them more expensive) on almost all trade between the United States, Canada, and Mexico, and dramatically increased imports and exports among these countries. The agreement was renegotiated in 2018 and renamed the United States-Mexico-Canada Agreement.

Globalization and trade benefit the world economy by increasing efficiency and opening new markets. These have contributed to unprecedented global economic growth. Globalization and trade also contribute to a decrease in worldwide poverty and an overall higher standard of living, and bring technology, jobs, and ideas to new places.

However, this does not mean that globalization is good for all people everywhere. Globalization hurts economic development in countries with a high commodity dependence. It also contributes to global income inequality; core countries gain more benefits than do peripheral countries, and the flow of capital from rich to poor countries has not occurred as much as neoliberal proponents have anticipated. In Latin America in 2019, many protested the neoliberal policies that have created great inequality in the region. Countries with less-skilled workforces tend not to gain advantages through globalization and are motivated to keep their competitive advantage in providing low-skilled labor. In addition, the absence of environmental and labor standards contributes to pollution and the exploitation of workers in countries vying for a competitive advantage.

For example, garment workers in Bangladesh earn less in one month than the average U.S. worker does in one day.

SUPRANATIONAL ORGANIZATIONS

LEARNING OBJECTIVE
PSO-7.A Explain causes and geographic consequences of recent economic changes such as the increase in international trade, deindustrialization, and growing interdependence in the world economy.

Supranationalism, as you learned in Chapter 11, is when three or more countries come together to establish collective policies in response to an international challenge. Many supranational organizations have formed to address challenges associated with international trade and the growing interdependence in the world economy.

Some supranational organizations have been formed specifically to support neoliberal policies and foster greater globalization through regional trade networks. These trade networks facilitate free trade and open markets, and enhance the competitiveness of the region. To this end, the Southern African Development Community (SADC) was formed in 1979 to foster economic cooperation and integration among its 16 member states. Another organization similar to NAFTA, known as Mercosur (a Spanish acronym for Southern Common Market), was established to create a South American trade bloc. The European Union (EU) likewise was formed to focus on strengthening the economic development of countries within this prominent economic region by eliminating trade barriers (such as tariffs or quotas) between member countries. The EU took efforts a step further, creating a new standard currency shared by 19 member countries that make up the eurozone. In each of these examples, eliminating trade barriers and encouraging free trade facilitate the exchange of goods across international borders. The growing exchange of goods and ideas fosters greater globalization.

Founded in 1995, the World Trade Organization (WTO) is a supranational organization with 164 member countries from around the world. The goal of the WTO is to provide governments with a forum to negotiate trade agreements, settle disputes, and oversee trade rules. The overriding purpose is to help trade flow as freely as possible. WTO agreements, negotiated and signed by most of the world's trading countries, are designed to remove obstacles to trade and to ensure that rules are transparent and predictable. Another worldwide supranational organization is the International Monetary Fund (IMF), an organization of 189 countries. Created in 1945, the IMF's primary mission is to ensure the stability of the international monetary system that enables countries and their citizens to conduct business with each other. Other goals include facilitating international trade, promoting sustainable economic growth, and reducing poverty. It is important to note that the WTO and IMF are controversial. Proponents of free trade point out that these organizations are unnecessary and actually interfere

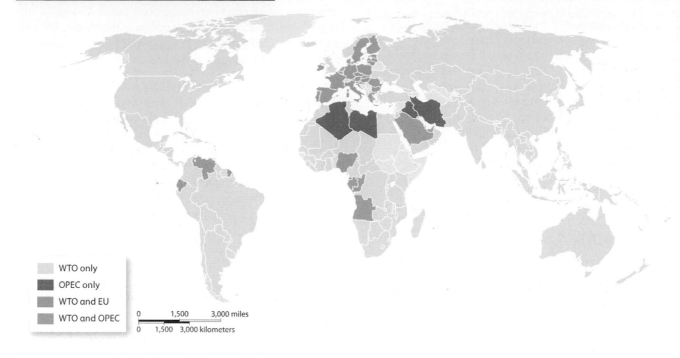

Legend:
- WTO only
- OPEC only
- WTO and EU
- WTO and OPEC

0   1,500   3,000 miles
0   1,500   3,000 kilometers

READING MAPS The WTO, EU, and OPEC are all examples of supranational organizations. Tensions can arise within and among them. For example, in 2019, Indonesia filed a lawsuit at the WTO against the entire EU over a dispute about biofuels. ▌ Draw a conclusion about Europe based on the map.

with natural market forces like supply and demand that regulate prices and the amount of goods in a market.

In theory, members of the WTO operate on equal terms, but the WTO allows some countries to protect industries if the removal of tariffs would result in the loss of vital domestic industries. Food production, steel production, and auto production have all fallen under these protections. In addition, core countries have argued that the loss of jobs should be added to the list of justified tariffs. Critics argue that the WTO's practices involve politics and that more powerful countries tend to win in such political battles.

The IMF, too, has fallen under criticism. The IMF makes loans to countries on the condition that specific economic policies are put into action. Advocates point out that the intent of such policies is to reduce corruption and ensure that the funds are used as intended, as well as help to ensure that the country will be able to pay back the loan. Critics contend that the policies interfere with the autonomy of the borrowing country. They also note that the IMF's policies sometimes make economic situations worse. In 1997, for instance, the IMF required Indonesia, Malaysia, and Thailand to increase interest rates to reduce their budget deficits. The tight fiscal policies caused a serious economic recession and high unemployment in these countries.

Some supranational organizations are focused on one industry or commodity. Most influential of these is likely the Organization of the Petroleum Exporting Countries,

or OPEC. Initially formed by 5 oil-producing countries in 1960, the coalition has expanded to include 13 member countries across Southwest Asia, Latin America, and Africa, which together control 75 percent of the world's crude oil reserves. OPEC's stated mission is to coordinate and unify the policies of member countries to ensure an efficient supply of petroleum to customers. However, one criticism of OPEC is that the organization's main goal is to make money for its member countries. OPEC's actions impact the world's economy because so many industries across the globe rely on oil production. OPEC influences the price and supply of oil that is shipped around the world.

DEINDUSTRIALIZATION In the last century, globalization has led to **deindustrialization** in many core countries with aging infrastructure and manufacturing processes. These countries could not compete with newly emerging industrial states, like South Korea and China that built new state-of-the-art steel plants and shipbuilding yards. Deindustrialization is the change that occurs with the decline in the percent of workers employed in the secondary sector and a reduction of a region's industrial capacity or activity, particularly heavy industry and manufacturing. As discussed in Chapter 15, the eventual result is post-industrial cities and regions in which the service industry becomes more important than the manufacturing industry. Deindustrialization has led to more tertiary service-sector jobs with generally lower salaries and fewer benefits in core countries. It has also increased the interdependence between core countries and peripheral or semi-peripheral countries by creating global supply chains.

Like industrialization, deindustrialization has ripple effects that can have long-term and often unintended consequences for local areas in both the core and the periphery. Deindustrialization leads to the loss of jobs in the industrial sector and contributes to rising unemployment rates. When a plant closes, businesses across the community suffer. In addition to the businesses that once directly supported the plant, stores and restaurants also lose customers and close. Central business districts may decline, and the population may drop, causing a loss of tax dollars.

GOVERNMENT TRADE POLICIES

LEARNING OBJECTIVE
PSO-7.A Explain causes and geographic consequences of recent economic changes such as the increase in international trade, deindustrialization, and growing interdependence in the world economy.

The public and private sectors both play critical roles in national, regional, and local economies. Private-sector organizations—corporations and businesses—are the drivers of economic growth. They determine where they will locate and establish business relationships with suppliers and customers. They also operate within the parameters established by government. Governments make laws to ensure that the economy is stable, and, ideally, that all players within it are treated fairly. Governments also regulate the banking industry and establish trade and monetary policies to provide corporations with an environment that is conducive to doing business. The Federal Reserve, which is the central bank of the United States and part of the public sector, lowers and raises interest rates to either stimulate economic growth or to prevent an unsustainable rise in the price of goods. Interest rates affect lending to businesses and consumers and impact job creation.

Governments at all scales—national, regional, local—implement policies to spur economic development. At the national level, countries may seek to enhance development in less economically stable areas. China has created special economic zones, using tax and business incentives to attract foreign investment. These zones are discussed in more detail later in the chapter.

Businesses often choose to locate where there are similar types of businesses in order to take advantage of economies of scale in the workforce. This agglomeration explains the spatial distribution of some industries, such as the location of computer and high-tech manufacturing in Silicon Valley, California, and Bengaluru, India.

Governments today also try to develop **growth poles** — places of economic activity clustered around one or more high-growth industries that stimulate economic growth by capitalizing on some special asset. Highly innovative and technically advanced industries, such as research and development, biotech firms, and computer software and hardware development, stimulate opportunities for regional economic development in related businesses. These businesses include suppliers of goods and services, as well as those fulfilling the needs of employees living and working in the area, such as restaurants and banks.

State and local governments also may seek to attract new business by lowering corporate taxes or offering special tax incentives or cash grants for businesses that are willing to relocate. As an example, in 2017 the state of Wisconsin offered infrastructure improvements and a multibillion-dollar subsidy to convince Foxconn, a large Taiwanese multinational tech company, to build a manufacturing plant in the southeastern part of the state. The plant is expected to produce liquid crystal display screens (LCDs) for phones, televisions, and other products. Similarly, about 30 years ago, South Carolina lured German automaker BMW to build a plant in Spartanburg by offering some $100 million in incentives, including funding to extend a runway at the airport and to improve roads and sewers.

Providing financial incentives is just one tool that governments use to fuel economic development. Governments may provide workforce training programs, particularly if the economy is in transition from one type of industry to another. In addition, governments seek to provide an environment that is conducive to doing business. This means providing political and economic stability, as well as reliable infrastructure, including transportation and communication networks that require regional and local governments to work together.

National governments encourage economic development through the use of tariffs. The goal of tariffs is to give domestic businesses an advantage by taxing foreign competitors' imported products and making them more expensive. The cost of the tariff is included in the resource or product price, which may enable a domestic company to offer goods at a lower price than foreign competitors. This helps domestic businesses create more jobs and possibly pay workers more. But while tariffs protect a country's industries, including agriculture or mining, they can have a negative impact on the economy. Tariffs limit free trade and reduce competition, which usually results in higher prices for consumers. Quality and innovation also may suffer when there is less competition in the market.

Imposing tariffs can prompt other countries to respond with their own tariffs. When U.S. President Donald Trump imposed additional tariffs on a wide range of goods imported from China in late 2018, China retaliated with tariffs on U.S. agricultural products. The trade war affected the economies of both countries. As one example, Shanghai General Sports, one of the biggest bicycle manufacturers in China, had to lay off almost one-third of its employees. In South Carolina, Kent Bikes, which imports Shanghai General Sports' parts, had to raise its prices on bikes to cover the cost of the tariffs on the parts. This contributed to a significant drop in sales and resulted in the layoff of about

Apple Park, the corporate headquarters of Apple, is located in Cupertino, California. In 1997, the city made a deal to pay 35 percent of local sales taxes to the company so long as it agreed to remain in Cupertino and build a campus there. It is estimated that Apple has collected almost $70 million in sales taxes since the deal was struck; in return, Cupertino reaps rewards from being Apple's home town, including the 65 percent of sales taxes it keeps for itself.

one-fourth of Kent Bikes' employees. Ripples of the trade war were felt throughout the world and contributed to an economic slowdown worldwide.

Free trade agreements among governments eliminate tariffs and often boost trade between the countries involved. Peripheral countries gain manufacturing jobs and core countries gain access to low-cost labor. The United States has trade agreements with more than 20 countries. Since no tariffs are paid on exports to those bound by the agreements, U.S. businesses target their exports to these countries.

GEOGRAPHIC THINKING

1. Explain deindustrialization and how it impacts regions going through this process as well as other regions.

2. Explain how spatial patterns of globalization relate to economic development.

3. Describe the advantages and disadvantages for countries establishing trade relations with one another.

20.2 CONNECTED ECONOMIES

The economies of countries are interdependent. Changes in industry are one cause of this interconnectedness. Industries apply international strategies that affect jobs and manufacturing practices, and countries institute policies in order to spur local, regional, and national economic development.

IMPACTS OF THE GLOBAL ECONOMY

LEARNING OBJECTIVE

PSO-7.A Explain causes and geographic consequences of recent economic changes such as the increase in international trade, deindustrialization, and growing interdependence in the world economy.

Businesses in market economies naturally seek cheaper ways to do things. Labor tends to be far less expensive in countries in the periphery than in core countries. In the 1970s, U.S. and European corporations increasingly decentralized their manufacturing processes to take advantage of inexpensive sources of labor (and the lack of unionized labor and environmental regulations) in other countries. Some companies built production facilities abroad; others looked for existing suppliers to integrate into their production process. Corporations also built offices around the world to oversee and facilitate an increasingly complex supply chain and to extend their reach to new markets. The proliferation of multinational corporations operating at a global scale was followed by the globalization of banking and financial services. By the 1990s, global companies provided business services throughout the world, facilitating the global flow of money, goods and services, and information. National and regional economies became increasingly interconnected and were influenced by global forces more than ever.

Today, the widening economic development gap among core and peripheral countries is evident when comparing global incomes, a common measure of global wealth. According to the World Bank, the gross national income (GNI) per capita for the United States in 2018 was more than $62,000. For Bangladesh, the GNI was $1,750 for the same year. The imbalanced distribution of wealth across the globe impacts development. Peripheral countries lack the funds for development, so investors from the core provide financial support through direct investment and loans.

Multinational corporations that operate in countries other than the ones in which they are headquartered are large sources of funds for peripheral and semi-peripheral countries. Corporations such as Apple, Microsoft, Nike, and Coca-Cola all have investments and operations in developing economies. The facilities that these companies build in the periphery and semi-periphery increase the local productive capacity. The influx of capital can also help the economy develop. In 2019, Taiwan's GDP grew almost 3 percent mainly due to exports in the electronics sector, including smartphones. These corporations provide local employment opportunities. The wages may be low compared to wages in the core, but they are typically much higher than other alternatives in the area. A factory or production facility also helps to diversify the local economy, providing an important alternative to agriculture. Multinationals may also invest in infrastructure, such as road improvements, workforce education, and health initiatives.

Financial institutions have also contributed to an increasingly interrelated global economic system. In addition to microlending, deregulation (the removal of restrictions) of the banking industry in many countries has brought new funding to businesses operating in the periphery and semi-periphery. Global financial institutions like Goldman Sachs, Deutsche Bank, Credit Suisse, HSBC, and Citigroup have expanded their reach and helped increase the number of businesses in new parts of the world. These businesses and startups in turn help the global economy as a whole.

The International Monetary Fund (IMF) and the World Bank also foster economic development. The IMF provides no-interest loans to low-income countries and offers financial assistance to member countries to help stabilize the world economy. The World Bank, which has 189 member countries, similarly focuses on encouraging a global economy to reduce poverty, increase shared prosperity, and promote sustainable development worldwide. It provides funding and technical assistance to countries in the periphery to develop infrastructure, including systems for safe drinking water, improved sanitation, new schools, and expanded transportation and communications networks. Some countries use the money to repay other loans, provide emergency relief, or expand health care. The establishment of these international lending agencies demonstrates how widely varying economies are now more closely connected.

The global economy has contributed to integrated financial markets like the European Union. Members of the EU conduct commerce and trade free from barriers that could hinder investment in another EU country. While financial integration helps facilitate the flow of capital across national borders, the risks of interconnectedness to global markets became evident during the 2007–2008 worldwide recession and the COVID-19 global pandemic that began in 2019.

THE FINANCIAL CRISIS OF 2007–2008

THE ISSUE The financial crisis of 2007–2008 resulted in widespread unemployment and a worldwide recession. What is the obligation of countries to closely regulate their financial institutions?

LEARNING OBJECTIVE
PSO-7.A Explain causes and geographic consequences of recent economic changes such as the increase in international trade, deindustrialization, and growing interdependence in the world economy.

BY THE NUMBERS

$12.8 TRILLION
Cost of the crisis to the U.S. economy based on GDP loss

5 YEARS
for the British economy to return to its prerecession size

$586 BILLION
Cost of China's stimulus plan to address downturn in its economy

Sources: U.S. Government Accountability Office, UK Office for National Statistics, the World Bank

During the financial crisis of 2007–2008, widespread homelessness in the United States resulted from people losing their homes due to foreclosure. Foreclosure occurs when homeowners who cannot afford their house payments are forced to sell their homes. As a result, many people had to live in tent cities like this one in Sacramento, California.

IN 2008, THE WORLD ECONOMY PLUNGED, contributing to the worst financial crisis since the Great Depression of the 1930s. The crisis began in the United States when home prices started to fall at an alarming rate. Monitored by loose regulatory laws, U.S. mortgage dealers had issued high-risk mortgages to homebuyers who could not qualify for traditional loans because of low credit scores or low incomes. These mortgages offered low initial interest rates that increased, or even doubled, after a few years. They also often included steep penalties for missed payments. Many homeowners borrowed against the equity in their homes to pay the loans. Equity is the difference between the value of the property and what is still owed. Using equity became a problem when housing prices fell, however; many people found themselves owing more than their houses were worth. Numerous homeowners were unable to make their mortgage payments, and either sold their homes at a loss or simply abandoned them.

U.S. banks and other financial institutions that made these home loans were not being repaid by the borrowers; some could not recover and went out of business. Because banks could no longer afford to loan money, the crisis expanded to companies that usually operated on credit, including the American auto industry. The federal government bailed out both the banks and the auto industry by offering hundreds of billions of dollars in loans, payouts, or investments in each industry.

The crisis spread to major trading partners and countries that had significant investments in American real estate. Export-oriented countries struggled as demand in American and European markets plunged. By the end of 2008, Germany, Japan, and China were all struggling with a recession. Peripheral and semi-peripheral countries suffered as foreign investment dried up. Unemployment increased in the United States and in countries that provided manufacturing labor for U.S. companies.

The recession changed the world of international finance. Governments were forced to make huge investments to strengthen their banks and guarantee their loans. The U.K. government, for instance, provided more than $500 billion in financial assistance to its banking industry. While the economies of most core countries have largely recovered, many peripheral countries are still feeling the repercussions. The crisis revealed the potential risks of a global economy and an interconnected world. ∎

GEOGRAPHIC THINKING

Explain how the financial crisis of 2007–2008 was an indication of globalization.

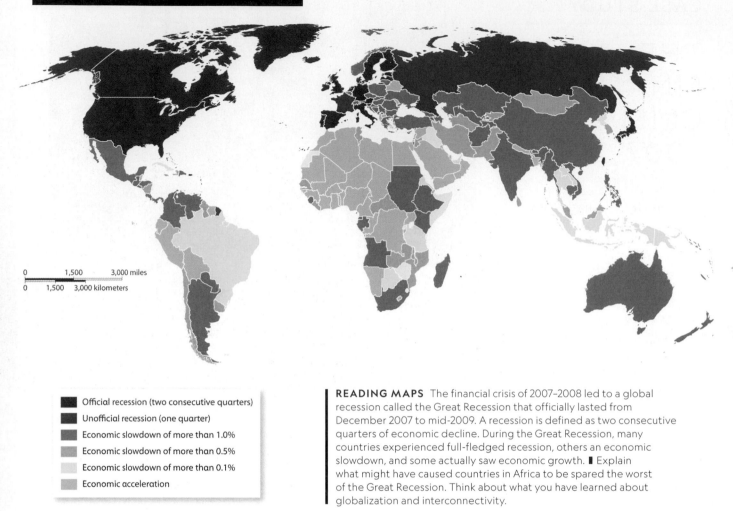

THE GREAT RECESSION, 2007–2009

Legend:
- Official recession (two consecutive quarters)
- Unofficial recession (one quarter)
- Economic slowdown of more than 1.0%
- Economic slowdown of more than 0.5%
- Economic slowdown of more than 0.1%
- Economic acceleration

READING MAPS The financial crisis of 2007–2008 led to a global recession called the Great Recession that officially lasted from December 2007 to mid-2009. A recession is defined as two consecutive quarters of economic decline. During the Great Recession, many countries experienced full-fledged recession, others an economic slowdown, and some actually saw economic growth. ▌ Explain what might have caused countries in Africa to be spared the worst of the Great Recession. Think about what you have learned about globalization and interconnectivity.

AUSTERITY MEASURES

In the years following the Great Recession, numerous policies were enacted around the world in hopes of lessening the long-term impact of the crisis and to prevent it from happening again. With an eye on cutting countries' deficits, the IMF urged the passing of austerity measures. A country's deficit—or the amount that its spending exceeds its revenues—rises and falls as its economy contracts and expands. In a period of economic growth, tax revenues increase, and unemployment benefits decrease, which reduces the deficit. Austerity policies aim to reduce a government's structural deficit, which is debt that is persistent for some time and that is not affected by market forces. Austerity measures usually include tax increases, spending cuts, or both.

Britain imposed austerity policies following the crisis. In 2010, Parliament imposed tight spending controls in an attempt to reduce the deficit. It also raised taxes to increase revenues. As a result, Britain experienced another recession before its economy rebounded, causing economists to disagree on the impact and effectiveness of the austerity measures.

Another country to enact austerity measures was Greece, which by 2009 had a very high deficit. In 2010, a series of severe budget cuts and tax increases were passed; however, concern with the country's overall economic health and its impact on the Euro, which is the currency of most of the European Union, did not decrease. As a result, the EU and the IMF were compelled to loan Greece large amounts of money to prevent its economy from collapsing. Cycles of spending cuts and bailout loans continued until 2018, when its GDP grew at 1.9 percent.

Austerity policies are controversial. Many economists believe that they can do more harm than good because they counteract the natural forces of an economy. Failing to invest in a weak economy may cause tax revenues to fall further while spending on benefits goes up. The contrasting viewpoint holds that in recommending austerity, the IMF was conscientiously looking for a global response to a global crisis. The IMF pointed out that financial support (including loans and bailouts) for troubled countries must consider cross-border effects, including on emerging economies. In other words, any solution must take into account the forces of globalization.

CHANGES IN THE ECONOMIC LANDSCAPE

LEARNING OBJECTIVE

PSO-7.A Explain causes and geographic consequences of recent economic changes such as the increase in international trade, deindustrialization, and growing interdependence in the world economy.

The contemporary economic landscape has been transformed by many factors. Computerized logistics systems facilitate **just-in-time delivery** of raw materials and manufactured parts. Logistics is the handling of the details of an operation, such as the movement of supplies between regions. Entire systems are devoted to determining how to efficiently transport supplies and products to and from factories and stores. Just-in-time delivery means that materials are delivered when they are needed for short-term production, so that companies can avoid paying to store extra inventory at their facilities. Improved logistics and efficient transportation streamline operations and enable companies to be located farther from raw materials, which has fueled growth and contributed to lower labor costs.

Changes in industry have helped to fuel global interconnectedness. Before the 18th and 19th centuries, goods were produced in people's homes. Then the Industrial Revolution transformed industry with the growth of factories, leading to the advent of the assembly line. Each event has been another step toward greater interdependence among countries. In the 1920s, Henry Ford's assembly line revolutionized the way businesses operated and enabled mass production of complex goods such as automobiles. Mass production and rising affluence allowed the broad masses to expand their use of goods, termed mass consumption. The ultimate goal of factories was to make products for mass consumption faster and more efficiently. This system of manufacturing, known as **Fordism**, focused on automation, standardization, economies of scale, and a division of labor in which each worker has just one task. Machines replaced several workers in the secondary sector, enabling large-scale mass production.

Today, globalization and deindustrialization have changed the decision-making criteria for businesses and industries. In recent decades, an increasing number of companies have begun to turn away from mass production, which requires huge capital investments, to instead focus on specialization. The term **post-Fordism** is used to describe the system of production that relies on automation through the use of robots and computer systems and is centered on low-volume manufacturing and flexible systems that allow for quick responses to changes in the market.

Post-Fordist companies either are much smaller than traditional manufacturers, or contract work to smaller firms that oversee different parts of production, including fabricating or marketing a product, and are therefore better able to respond to changes in demand. Often the bureaucracy of a single, large corporation can slow decision-making and hinder timely changes in production.

Post-Fordist organizations also tend to be less top-down than Fordist organizations; rather than imposing a strict division of labor, post-Fordism encourages the use of multidisciplinary teams with different types of knowledge and skills that work together on a project from start to finish.

Post-Fordism is made possible by advances in computer and information technology, which provide new tools that emphasize knowledge and creativity over physical labor.

CRITICAL VIEWING A culinary robotics company in San Francisco, California, has devised a machine that cooks and assembles burgers. The machine contains 20 computers, 350 sensors, and numerous other mechanisms. ▌Explain why this machine is an example of post-Fordism.

In the post-Fordist environment, rather than an entire car being manufactured and assembled in one plant, each part is made in a different location by a company that specializes in that one part. Automobile companies then purchase parts from a range of suppliers across the world. Post-Fordist industry may also focus on a specialized product for the end consumer and create a smaller amount of the product at one time in order to accommodate product changes as technology advances. Several global chains of clothing store including Benetton, Zara, H&M, and Superdry vary their product lines frequently and regularly use different suppliers of materials to accommodate changing clothing preferences.

Post-Fordism has changed the manufacturing landscape. When Ford made its mass-produced cars, there was a joke that consumers could have any color—as long as it was black. In the post-Fordist world, companies provide consumers with far more choice. Post-Fordism has also made it possible for many companies to start small. As a student at the University of Texas, Michael Dell started Dell Computers by providing customized upgrades for personal computers, or PCs. The company grew by continuing to create and sell custom-built PCs directly to consumers through advertisements and mail-order catalogues. Today, many computer software programs and phone applications are created by small, independent companies that target a niche or specialty market. The app YogaGlo, for instance, focuses on online yoga, meditation, and Pilates classes. Its small size enables it to target specific products to accommodate changes in preferences and technologies.

OUTSOURCING Advances in technology and communications have allowed companies more flexibility in the locations they choose to conduct business. As the service industry grows, many jobs like accounting, customer service, and research and design are each being performed in separate locations or in multiple locations. Many corporations outsource aspects of production or information services, turning the work over to a third-party provider to cut costs. Outsourcing can take place within a country, but companies are increasingly moving production to places outside the country in which they are headquartered—a process referred to as **offshore outsourcing**. Some large companies in the United States and the United Kingdom, for example, have established customer service call centers in the Philippines and India, respectively, where lower wages and English-language use make this outsourcing effective.

Internal communication across the geographically dispersed workforces of a multinational corporation is facilitated when the workforce speaks a common language. Even among organizations based across Europe or Japan, English has become the lingua franca, or language of choice, for business. As a result, English proficiency of a potential workforce is an important criterion for companies deciding where to build a new plant or outsource production, or when choosing a supplier. This puts some countries at significant advantage over others. The high level of English proficiency among educated workers in the Philippines and India is one

OUTSOURCING

Effects on Outsourcing Countries	Effects on Countries Providing Outsourced Labor
Loss of jobs	Gain jobs
Domino effect leading to other similar businesses or suppliers also outsourcing	May stifle economic development; workers may be stuck in lower-paying jobs
Competition threatens to drive down labor standards and wages	Possible access to higher than average wages depending on the skills required
Companies can operate more efficiently, increasing profits	Multiplier effects
Goods available at lower prices	Technology transfer

Outsourcing impacts both the country using the labor and the country providing it. A good example of the latter is India, where IT outsourcing employed 3.7 million workers. The IT industry generated more than $175 billion for India in 2019, largely driven by providing outsourcing to core countries.

reason that many companies have chosen to relocate their customer service operations offshore to these places.

Core countries have taken advantage of cheap labor sources by moving production facilities to newly industrialized countries (NICs). This offshore outsourcing has led to a decline of traditional manufacturing jobs in core regions and increased the number of such jobs in NICs. Vietnam is among the countries that have benefited. Nike, an American sportswear and shoe company headquartered in Oregon, employs almost four times more workers in Vietnam than in the United States. In the early 21st century, Vietnam became known for low-end manufacturing industries, but its reputation soon grew to attract more technologically advanced manufacturers as well. In 2013, Microsoft built a factory in Bac Ninh, Vietnam, to serve as the main production center for its Nokia cell phones. South Korean manufacturer Samsung similarly has moved offshore the production of many of its phones, as well as appliances, flat-screen TVs, and other consumer electronics, to Vietnam.

DIVISION OF LABOR In the late 1800s, wealthy and powerful countries of the core instituted an **international division of labor** through imperialism. Colonies or other countries in peripheral regions specialized in producing the raw materials required by more developed economies, and then served as markets for the manufactured goods produced by core countries. The result was a spatial pattern of production and labor based on geographic comparative advantage. Specialization of production and labor continued after countries gained their political independence. Less-skilled workers in the periphery and semi-periphery produced raw materials for trade with core countries who specialized in manufacturing by more-skilled labor.

Since the 1970s, the international division of labor has evolved, as core countries began to deindustrialize. Corporations sought lower-wage labor locations for their

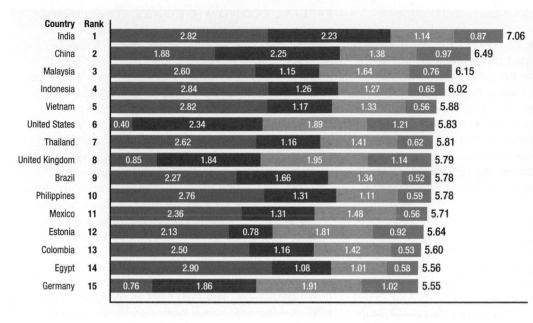

Country	Rank								Financial attractiveness (35%)
India	1	2.82	2.23	1.14	0.87	7.06			
China	2	1.88	2.25	1.38	0.97	6.49			
Malaysia	3	2.60	1.15	1.64	0.76	6.15			
Indonesia	4	2.84	1.26	1.27	0.65	6.02			
Vietnam	5	2.82	1.17	1.33	0.56	5.88			
United States	6	0.40	2.34	1.89	1.21	5.83			
Thailand	7	2.62	1.16	1.41	0.62	5.81			
United Kingdom	8	0.85	1.84	1.95	1.14	5.79			
Brazil	9	2.27	1.66	1.34	0.52	5.78			
Philippines	10	2.76	1.31	1.11	0.59	5.78			
Mexico	11	2.36	1.31	1.48	0.56	5.71			
Estonia	12	2.13	0.78	1.81	0.92	5.64			
Colombia	13	2.50	1.16	1.42	0.53	5.60			
Egypt	14	2.90	1.08	1.01	0.58	5.56			
Germany	15	0.76	1.86	1.91	1.02	5.55			

35% Financial attractiveness
Compensation costs
Infrastructure costs
Tax and regulatory costs

25% People skills and availability
ITO/BPO experience and skills
Labor force availability
Educational skills
Language skills

25% Business environment
Country environment
Country infrastructure
Cultural adaptability
Security of IP

15% Digital resonance
Digital skills
Legal and cybersecurity
Corporate activity
Outputs

Source: A.T. Kearney

GLOBAL SERVICES LOCATION INDEX, 2019 Every year, a firm called A.T. Kearney releases its Global Services Location Index, a ranking of countries based on their desirability as an outsourcing destination. Countries are evaluated in four areas: financial attractiveness (which is most heavily weighted), people skills and availability (with ITO standing for "information technology outsourcing" and BPO meaning "business process outsourcing"), business environment (with IP meaning "internet protocol"), and digital resonance (which is weighted the least). ▌ Explain why, based on what you have already learned, the United States, the United Kingdom, and Germany likely get such low scores in financial attractiveness.

manufacturing and decentralized their operations, both within their own country and to peripheral and semi-peripheral countries. New regions and countries across the globe have developed new specializations. As noted, the footwear industry has exploded in Vietnam. There were 800 businesses in Vietnam that produced more than 1.1 billion pairs of shoes, making it the world's second largest exporter of footwear in 2017. China, meanwhile, has specialized in the manufacturing of high tech goods, such as flat-screen televisions and computer parts. More than 80 percent of rare earth materials—which are used in the production of batteries and other electronics—are mined in China. The country also makes nearly all of the world's circuit boards, fundamental building blocks for computers. A state-led industrial policy called "Made in China 2025" calls for even further development in high-tech fields ranging from robotics to aerospace engineering. The program aims to use government funding to advance the use of emerging technologies in manufacturing and infrastructure.

Other economic activities have also decentralized from core countries. Financial services, like those provided by credit card and accountancy companies, have moved to peripheral and semi-peripheral countries, aided by technological innovations. Transportation and communications advances have internationalized production and trade, accelerating globalization. More and more peripheral and semi-peripheral countries are becoming integrated into the global economic system as both producers and consumers, and incomes are rising for many. It is important to note that these processes work both between and within countries. For example, in the last decade, some manufacturers have left China for still

lower labor wages in other countries of Southeast Asia, like Thailand and Vietnam. Some manufacturing in Mexico has been moving from higher labor-cost areas along the United States border to lower-wage regions much farther south.

Spatially, today's new international division of labor is represented by the North-South divide: Countries of the Global North, with just one-quarter of the world's population, control four-fifths of the world's income, and countries of the Global South, with three-quarters of the population, have acquired just one-fifth of the world's income.

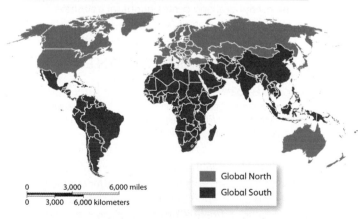

INTERNATIONAL DIVISION OF LABOR

0 3,000 6,000 miles	■ Global North
0 3,000 6,000 kilometers	■ Global South

READING MAPS The international division of labor is best expressed by a map of the so-called North-South Divide. ▌ Identify what the map shows about countries that primarily speak English and then draw a conclusion about the North-South Divide today and in the future.

One factor driving down wages in the Global South is competition to provide cheap labor. As a result, many factory workers in NICs work long hours for little pay. More than a billion people worldwide earn less than $2 per day working in factories. Critics argue that people should be paid a fair wage regardless of where they live. On the other hand, many multinational corporations pay more than local companies because they can afford higher wages. Advocates of offshore outsourcing further argue that people in peripheral countries often are in desperate need of jobs and opportunities, and that the **multiplier effects** will help the local economy grow. Multiplier effects are opportunities that can potentially develop from an economic change. For instance, when a corporation chooses to build a new manufacturing plant, it brings jobs to the area. In addition, the plant and its workers need support services, including office supplies, lunch, and gasoline to travel to and from work. The money spent on these local goods and services sometimes results in the area businesses adding staff. Multiplier effects can provide a significant boost to the local economy. The business and workers also pay taxes on their earnings. Combined with the taxes on the goods that are sold, this can fuel the national economy as well.

The economies of countries across the globe look very different from one another but are nonetheless interdependent. Today, economically dominant core countries and less wealthy peripheral and semi-peripheral countries rely on each other for economic growth—though the economic gains are often unequal.

GEOGRAPHIC THINKING

1. Describe the factors that contributed to the rise of post-Fordism.

2. Compare the goals of Fordism and post-Fordism.

3. Explain why companies in core countries outsource manufacturing operations to countries in the periphery.

4. Explain the degree to which outsourcing helps and hinders peripheral and semi-peripheral countries.

NEW MANUFACTURING ZONES

LEARNING OBJECTIVE

PSO-7.A Explain causes and geographic consequences of recent economic changes such as the increase in international trade, deindustrialization, and growing interdependence in the world economy.

In many countries outside the core, the growth of industry has resulted in the creation of new manufacturing zones. These zones are established by many governments to attract foreign investment. Corporations are offered incentives to bring manufacturing jobs to the zone and in return the country gains expanded trade, the transfer of technology and management expertise, and new employment opportunities for its residents.

SPECIAL ECONOMIC ZONES Some countries have attempted to facilitate economic growth by creating **special economic zones** (SEZs). A special economic zone is an area within a country that is subject to different and more beneficial economic regulations than other areas. Companies doing business in a SEZ usually receive tax incentives and are subject to lower or no tariffs. Governments tend to provide SEZs with more accessible and reliable infrastructure (including land and utilities). The goals of creating SEZs is to bring foreign business and investment to generate economic development. However, economists and government officials debate their economic benefits. One aspect that has drawn criticism is their tendency to operate as isolated groups with few benefits spilling over to the country's local suppliers.

SEZs were initially used in industrialized countries, but since the 1980s, they have proliferated in peripheral and semi-peripheral countries in East Asia and Latin America. More recently, countries in Central and Eastern Europe, Central Asia, Southwest Asia, and North Africa have begun implementing SEZ programs to compete for the growing interest in international production.

China is among the most successful countries using SEZs. Beginning with the Shenzhen Special Economic Zone in 1979, China based its initial SEZs along the southeastern coast of the country, including the cities of Shenzhen, Zhuhai, Shantou, and Xiamen. The economic success of these four zones prompted the Chinese government to add 14 cities plus the province of Hainan to the list of SEZs. In 2017, SEZs contributed more than $1 trillion to China's GDP, and they have generated millions of jobs. China continues to allow its SEZs to offer tax incentives and develop local infrastructure without central government approval.

Other countries, especially throughout Asia, have followed China's example with varying degrees of success. The Philippines and India have each established hundreds of SEZs. Some SEZs, such as in South Korea, seek to address uneven development within the country. Cambodia created SEZs to establish links between urban and rural areas. Other countries have used SEZs to try to diversify their economy. Specific SEZs specialize in services, innovation, or natural resource processing. SEZs are found in almost all countries in Central and South America. As of 2019, the region has almost 500 SEZs that collectively employ about 1 million people. Sometimes, however, the cost of investment in maintenance of the zone outweighs the benefits.

EXPORT PROCESSING ZONES The purpose of **export processing zones** (EPZs) is to attract multinational organizations to invest in labor-intensive assembly and manufacturing in the host country. These zones are sites where manufacturing of exports is done without tariffs. Governments have added other financial incentives to attract foreign investors and encourage economic growth. In addition to having a narrower focus than SEZs—specifically on exports—EPZs also tend to be smaller, as a single industrial park is generally sufficient for a manufacturer. EPZs also tend to be located where access to water or air transport is readily available. In many countries, EPZs are near urban centers with an adequate supply of labor and advanced infrastructure.

Tanzania initiated its EPZ program in 2002 to encourage investments in export-oriented manufacturing. Sites have been earmarked in 20 regions of the country and include 6 industrial parks as well as more than 50 single factory zones. The Tanzanian program has attracted businesses in engineering, textiles, agriculture, and mineral processing industries. EPZs also have a long tradition in Latin America. For example, many U.S. corporations have located factories in northern Mexico just outside the border in an EPZ that allows for quick export of goods back into the United States.

Incentives for companies conducting export-related business in EPZs include tax breaks and exemptions. Companies do not pay taxes on the machinery or resources that they import into the EPZ as long as the goods being manufactured are for export. This regulation helps to eliminate competition for local customers between local manufacturers and EPZs. Other incentives include support for visas, work permits, and customs documentation.

FREE TRADE ZONES The use of **free trade zones** (FTZs) has increased rapidly as countries have established them on major trade routes to provide duty-free areas for warehousing, storage, and transport of goods. While the goals of FTZs are similar to SEZs and EPZs, they tend to cover a larger geographic area. All of Hong Kong and Singapore, for instance, are free trade zones.

FTZs provide customs-related advantages and exemptions from tariffs and taxes. This enables quicker turnaround

of ships, planes, or other means of transportation engaged in international trade, which enables ports to function more easily as points along the way of a larger transportation system.

It is important not to confuse free trade zones with free trade areas. A free trade area is the region specific to two or more countries that have agreed to reduce trade barriers. A free trade zone is a special area within a country where foreign companies can import materials, manufacture goods, and export products free from the usual taxes and regulations. Free trade zones offer the same incentives and opportunities to businesses from any country.

Hong Kong is one of the most successful free trade zones. Hong Kong charges no tariffs on the import or export of goods; combined with its location and natural harbor, Hong Kong's status as an FTZ has contributed to its success as a major port city. In 2013, China added another FTZ in Shanghai; success of this initiative has led to additional FTZs in China. Other cities that are FTZs include Colon, Panama; Copenhagen, Denmark; Stockholm, Sweden; Gdansk, Poland; Los Angeles, and New York City. Across the world, these new manufacturing zones are changing trade relationships and contributing to a global economy.

GEOGRAPHIC THINKING

5. Identify three types of new manufacturing zones and what they have in common.

6. Describe three questions you would ask when deciding where to establish a special economic zone or export processing zone.

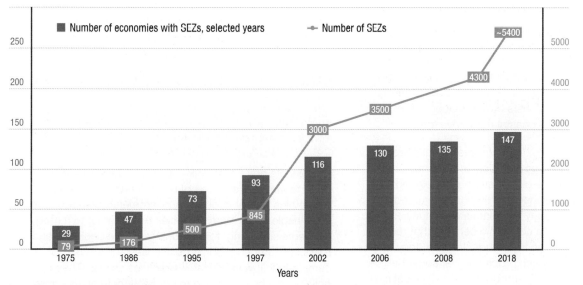

SPECIAL ECONOMIC ZONES The increase in the establishment of new SEZs globally in recent years has been rapid. ▪ Compare the total number of SEZs to the number of economies with SEZs. What conclusions can you draw from the data?

20.3 DEVELOPING A SUSTAINABLE WORLD

As the world's population grows, many people are concerned about the future availability of natural resources. With accelerated consumption, increased land use, and land cover changes come dramatic environmental degradation and a decrease in the supplies of nonrenewable resources. Are current economic development approaches sustainable?

NATURAL RESOURCES, DEVELOPMENT, AND CONSUMPTION

LEARNING OBJECTIVE
IMP-7.A Explain how sustainability principles relate to and impact industrialization and spatial development.

Whether consumed domestically as raw materials for manufacturing or sold as export goods, natural resources can contribute greatly to a country's economic development. The natural resources in oil- and mineral-rich countries like Brazil, Saudi Arabia, Canada, and India are worth trillions of dollars and contribute substantially to each country's economy. In 2018, the natural resources found in Russia alone were estimated to be worth more than $75 trillion. Russia's mining industry is one of the biggest in the world.

The depletion of natural resources, on the other hand, negatively impacts a country's economy and future productivity. Without the raw materials to create products, a country's economy could suffer. Of course, the extraction of nonrenewable resources, like oil and coal, have serious environmental and social costs.

Pollution, waste, and the loss of habitats are just some of the environmental consequences of development. The construction of roads to transport extracted products often contributes to deforestation. In some places, local workers engaged in mining operations cut down trees for fuel. Resource extraction also opens new areas to others engaged in agriculture activities, illegal logging, or the poaching of protected animals, all causing further degradation to the natural environment. Altering the land for aquaculture also has negative impacts. Shrimp farms along much of Ecuador's coasts have replaced about two-thirds of the country's coastal mangrove forests.

Resource exploration and extraction have social effects, especially on indigenous communities. In the Amazon of Ecuador and Bolivia, the oil industry has displaced indigenous peoples. Elsewhere, mining has disrupted the traditional way of life of many indigenous communities, who typically receive little of the economic benefits that result from resource extraction on their lands. Instead, they may experience devastating health problems that some believe are consequences of toxic by-products entering local rivers when oil or other resources are extracted. Leaks from oil pipelines are real risks to people and the environment.

Many believe that humans use more natural resources than the environment can sustain, and not surprisingly, the wealthiest countries are generally the largest consumers of these resources. As concerns grow about humans' ability to maintain development globally, governments, businesses, organizations, and individuals are seeking strategies that will reduce the human footprint, including ecotourism and innovative practices that cut waste. Technology is playing a significant role in efforts to conserve natural resources and ensure sustainable development that meets the needs of present populations without compromising the ability of future generations to do the same. In Singapore, technologies are being developed to help solve water shortage concerns by cleaning and filtering waste water. In addition, interest in renewable sources of energy has increased. In the United States, renewable energy grew from about 3 quadrillion BTUs (British Thermal Units) in 1950 to 11 quadrillion BTUs in 2019, when it accounted for 11 percent of the country's total energy usage.

Due to a global economy, core, peripheral, and semi-peripheral countries are all dependent on each other for natural resources and the manufacturing of products. Therefore, natural resource protection has become increasingly global in nature, but the burden of sustainability is not equitable. Peripheral countries involved in resource extraction are often more greatly impacted by the negative environmental effects and social inequalities, while core countries can better afford to undertake conservation efforts and human rights protections.

SUSTAINABLE DEVELOPMENT GOALS

LEARNING OBJECTIVE
IMP-7.A Explain how sustainability principles relate to and impact industrialization and spatial development.

Sustainable practices are key to future development in order to maintain supplies of raw materials required by the economies of every country. Governments have adopted sustainable development policies that attempt to remedy problems stemming from natural-resource depletion and mass consumption. Some businesses and industries commit to follow sustainable practices as well. These policies and practices aim to conserve natural resources and reduce environmental degradation.

CASE STUDY

REDUCING WASTE IN FISHERIES

THE ISSUE As a result of various factors, most fisheries in the world discard certain parts of the fish that they catch, resulting in waste of a potentially valuable product.

LEARNING OBJECTIVE

IMP-7.A Explain how sustainability principles relate to and impact industrialization and spatial development.

BY THE NUMBERS

1.2 MILLION METRIC TONS

Total amount of fish caught in Iceland in 2017

5 MILLION METRIC TONS

Total amount of fish caught in the United States in 2017

$655 MILLION

Potential value loss resulting from fish by-product waste in the United States

Source: FAO, Iceland Ocean Cluster

Iceland's ocean fisheries have long been a major part of its economy. Today, fisheries are utilizing more than 80 percent of the fish caught, and many leading fisheries are making it their mission to use 100 percent of the fish through sustainable methods and new business opportunities.

THE MAJORITY OF COMMERCIAL FISHING FLEETS

in the world discard the parts of a fish not intended for human consumption because they are considered to have little value. This includes the head, internal organs, and bones of the fish, known as by-products. At least 35 percent—some estimates are even higher—of the total volume of fish caught commercially in the United States is discarded. While some by-products end up in fish meal, fertilizer, and animal feed, the majority of fish waste is simply disposed of in the ocean.

In Iceland, efforts are being made to achieve 100 percent fish utilization. Icelandic authorities are working with organizations to support innovation in Iceland's seafood industry. The result has been the establishment of several successful companies in the beauty and wellness, food supplement, and medical and health product industries, which utilize enzymes found in the fish to create fish oils and proteins used in cosmetics and medical products. These companies are utilizing the parts of the fish that would otherwise be discarded to create their products and therefore increasing the value of fish by-products.

The reasons for the wide variation in fish utilization among countries' fisheries, including the United States and Iceland, is a result of a few factors. The first factor is how long fishing vessels are out at sea. Vessels that must travel greater distances to catch fish keep the fish from spoiling by freezing as much as possible on the ship. Therefore, discarding the head and organs allows more storage space for the valuable fillet. Another factor is the length of the fishing season. Icelandic fleets can fish year-round, but for many other fleets the fishing season is limited to a few months. Ships catch large amounts of fish in a short period of time, making processing the massive amount of raw fish difficult. A third factor is vertical integration, when one company manages two or more stages in the manufacturing process, leading to efficiencies that reduce the amount of fish wasted. In Iceland, companies commonly control both the catching and processing of the fish.

The effects of Iceland's efforts to increase fish utilization are proof that sustainable practices help both the economy and the environment. The increase in the use of the entire fish has led to less waste and the creation of at least 600 to 700 jobs in Iceland's by-product industry, valued at around $500 million. ∎

GEOGRAPHIC THINKING

Explain how Iceland's fish utilization efforts might impact fisheries globally.

Sustainability policies also seek to minimize negative impacts of development while still serving the needs of current communities. Renewable energy targets are often a first step. In 2005, 43 countries had renewable energy targets; by 2017, this number had escalated to 164 countries across all regions. The targets vary from one country to another. Sweden reached its 2020 target of 50 percent renewable energy in 2012 and is aiming to reach 100 percent renewable electricity by 2040. Australia also met its target for 20 percent of the electricity supply to be generated from renewables by 2020 and is determined to reach 50 percent by 2030. Brazil has set specific electricity capacity targets for biomass, wind, and hydroelectric energy.

However, in today's global environment, laws passed by one country do not ensure that natural resources are used in a sustainable way. The public and private sectors are working together to drive sustainability from a local or regional scale to a global scale. Cities have set their own goals for sustainability. For instance, the C40 group of 96 large cities across the globe has committed to fight climate change, which presents a special challenge to sustainability given the uncertainty caused by the changing climate.

In 2015, the United Nations adopted 17 Sustainable Development Goals (SDGs). The goals are intended to reduce the inequalities among countries in the core, periphery, and semi-periphery and to achieve a more sustainable future for all. The sustainability goals address global challenges related to poverty, inequality, climate, environmental degradation, prosperity, and justice. Upon adoption, the 193 members of the UN agreed that these goals would be met by 2030.

The UN's Sustainable Development Goals help measure progress in development. In many peripheral countries, limited financing for small-scale infrastructure projects impedes local development. Small-scale financing projects encouraged by the UN focus on people's basic needs, such as clean water and sanitation, transportation, and other infrastructure improvements that impact the most vulnerable people.

The implementation of SDGs varies considerably across regions and within countries. India implemented a Dedicated Freight Corridor and is building new high-capacity rail lines to increase the share of rail as the preferred mode of transport, which is projected to save more than 450 million tons of carbon dioxide in the first 30 years of operation. In Chile, meanwhile, a "connectivity subsidy program" has been implemented to create a more competitive environment for transportation providers in rural areas. The program has resulted in new water transport options in areas of Chile with extremely low population density, as well as free bus transport for children with disabilities. In the Philippines, many programs have been financed and implemented to address sustainable economic growth. For example, The Philippine Green Jobs Act of 2016 provides financial protection against job loss, in addition to skills training necessary for decent green jobs that foster sustainability and preserve the environment. Companies benefit from incentives to generate those green jobs.

UNITED NATIONS SUSTAINABLE DEVELOPMENT GOALS

GOAL 1 End poverty in all its forms everywhere.	**GOAL 2** End hunger, achieve food security and improved nutrition and promote sustainable agriculture.	**GOAL 3** Ensure healthy lives and promote well-being for all at all ages.
GOAL 4 Ensure inclusive and equitable quality education and promote lifelong learning opportunities for all.	**GOAL 5** Achieve gender equality and empower all women and girls.	**GOAL 6** Ensure availability and sustainable management of water and sanitation for all.
GOAL 7 Ensure access to affordable, reliable, sustainable and modern energy for all.	**GOAL 8** Promote sustained, inclusive and sustainable economic growth, full and productive employment and decent work for all.	**GOAL 9** Build resilient infrastructure, promote inclusive and sustainable industrialization and foster innovation.
GOAL 10 Reduce inequality within and among countries.	**GOAL 11** Make cities and human settlements inclusive, safe, resilient and sustainable.	**GOAL 12** Ensure sustainable consumption and production patterns.
GOAL 13 Take urgent action to combat climate change and its impacts.	**GOAL 14** Conserve and sustainably use the oceans, seas and marine resources for sustainable development.	**GOAL 15** Protect, restore and promote sustainable use of terrestrial ecosystems, sustainably manage forests, combat desertification, and halt and reverse land degradation and halt biodiversity loss.
GOAL 16 Promote peaceful and inclusive societies for sustainable development, provide access to justice for all and build effective, accountable and inclusive institutions at all levels.	**GOAL 17** Strengthen the means of implementation and revitalize the global partnership for sustainable development.	

SUSTAINABLE DEVELOPMENT GOALS At the center of the 2030 Agenda for Sustainable Development, which was adopted by all UN members in 2015, are 17 Sustainable Development Goals, or SDGs. The SDGs fall into the following categories: people, planet, prosperity, peace, and partnerships. They identify the core issues of sustainability while recognizing their interconnectedness. For instance, fighting poverty, inequality, and climate change all involve the construction of common goals and actions across communities, countries, and regions. ∎ Explain how goals 2, 6, and 15 are interconnected.

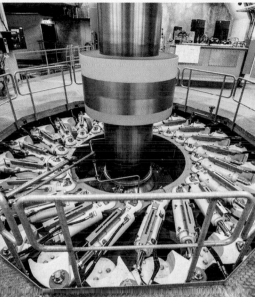

ECOTOURISM

LEARNING OBJECTIVE

IMP-7.A Explain how sustainability principles relate to and impact industrialization and spatial development.

Ecotourism has become increasingly popular as a means of environmentally friendly and sustainable economic development. The goal of ecotourism is to enable a country—often in the periphery or semi-periphery—or region threatened by industrial or other types of development to gain revenue through tourism with minimal environmental impact. Ecotourism involves travel to natural areas in ways that protect the environment and sustain the well-being of local inhabitants.

Tourism overall is an important source of income for many countries and regions, but it can come at the expense of the environment. According to a 2018 study in the journal *Nature Climate Change*, travel and tourism are responsible for 8 percent of total carbon emissions globally. Ironically, climate change threatens the pristine and unique features that draw tourists in the first place. In addition, the presence of large numbers of tourists hiking into natural areas, for instance, disrupts the ecosystem. Plants are trampled and the behaviors of the wildlife change.

PRINCIPLES OF ECOTOURISM

Ecotourism is about uniting conservation, communities, and sustainable travel. This means that those who implement, participate in, and market ecotourism activities generally adopt the following ecotourism principles, which have been adapted from The International Ecotourism Society:

- Minimize physical, social, behavioral, and psychological impacts on the local area.
- Build environmental awareness and cultural respect among visitors.
- Provide positive experiences for both visitors and hosts.
- Provide direct financial benefits for conservation.
- Generate financial benefits for both local people and private business.
- Deliver memorable experiences to visitors that help raise awareness to host countries' political, environmental, and social policies and customs.
- Design, construct, and operate low environmental impact facilities.
- Recognize the rights and spiritual beliefs of local indigenous people and work in partnership with them to create empowerment.

CRITICAL VIEWING Ecotourists who visit the Sarara Camp in the Namunyak Wildlife Conservancy in Kenya can view the mountains of the Mathews Range, come face to face with an elephant, or explore the bush led by a guide from the local Samburu community. ▮ Explain how the camp might impact the area.

Ecotourism is designed to provide a sustainable travel alternative that lessens negative impacts on the environment. Countries engaged in ecotourism advertise travel experiences to unique natural environments and enforce regulations that ecotourism lodging and recreational facilities follow to ensure that their operations have as little impact on the environment as possible. Ecolodging incorporates designs with alternative energy consumption to limit impact on the environment. Examples include Amazon tree houses for wildlife viewers on the Brazil-Peru border and tea houses for trekkers in the Himalaya of Nepal. Governments often use the revenues gained from ecotourism to fund conservation or preservation efforts.

Ecotourism also typically has an educational component. The goal is to enable tourists to learn about fragile natural environments without having a negative impact on them. People may learn about indigenous cultures, history, and issues. Ecotourism advocates hope that this understanding will encourage people and governments to take measures to protect Earth's natural environments and support the people who live within them.

Ecotourist programs are available around the world. Visitors can experience glaciers in Alaska, fjords in Norway, and rain forests in Borneo. In 2016, cruises to Antarctica permitted about 46,000 people to experience the wonders of the world's most remote continent. African safaris enable ecotourists to experience the beauty of the African wilderness and photograph the animals that live there.

Encouraging entrepreneurship and local involvement in tourism-dependent regions enhances the tourists' experience. Tourists feel more connected with the region and aware of its environmental and social issues. In Africa, the push for local involvement in tourism has contributed to gains in environmental protection and conservation. The more engaged that community members are in local tourism efforts, the more likely they are to advocate and fight for environmental protection. Monetary and educational resources from safaris encourage the appreciation and protection of fragile ecosystems and natural resources.

Despite the positive environmental and social impacts ecotourism can have, there are concerns. As ecotourism grows, many more tourists visit popular locations and can negatively impact the environment despite best efforts; and, countries may become too economically dependent on ecotourism. However, by empowering local communities with a source of income, ecotourism can help reduce poverty. The creation of protected areas in Costa Rica has helped reduce poverty by up to two-thirds in surrounding communities, in part thanks to tourism. As more people are employed in tourism-based jobs, fewer are pushed into engaging in poaching or other unsustainable or illegal activities. Ecotourism is one important way that countries are working together to achieve sustainability goals.

GEOGRAPHIC THINKING

1. Explain why pollution and environmental issues might be more difficult to address in peripheral and semi-peripheral countries than in core countries.

2. Identify which of the UN Sustainable Development Goals are most relevant to the United States and other core countries and explain why.

SUSTAINABLE ECOTOURISM

Andrés Ruzo is a geothermal scientist, conservationist, educator, host, author, and science communicator. He is best known for his work at the Boiling River of the Amazon.

LEARNING OBJECTIVE

IMP-7.A Explain how sustainability principles relate to and impact industrialization and spatial development.

In 2011, Andrés Ruzo began studying a mysterious "river that boiled" in the heart of the Amazon. This legendary river can reach temperatures of more than 200° F. But the region in which the Boiling River flows is threatened by development.

At nearly four miles long, the Boiling River is among the world's largest thermal rivers, a rare feature that requires a lot of water and the right geologic setting to keep the water flowing hot. Focused on the river, Ruzo was as concerned about uncovering its mysteries as he was protecting the Amazon from deforestation and land and water degradation. Most deforestation results from unmonitored and illegal cattle farming, logging, and land trafficking in the area. Combating these informal economic activities is challenging, especially given the proximity of the river to high-poverty areas, major population centers, and roads and waterways that facilitate easy access to the rain forest.

Ruzo established the Boiling River Project, a nonprofit organization dedicated to protecting the Boiling River area through science, responsible economic development, and local empowerment. The project supports enterprises that make the rain forest more valuable than it would be as cropland or cattle pastures. Visitors to the area learn about native medicinal plants and the traditional healing methods of local Amazonian peoples, including the Shipibo-Conibos (shown above arranging handmade crafts for sale to visitors). The project promotes responsible development like sustainable logging and ecotourism that respects the local culture and environment. Giving local inhabitants alternatives to cutting down the rain forest provides much-needed economic development for the indigenous population while protecting the valuable resources of the Amazon.

GEOGRAPHIC THINKING

Explain how the efforts of the Boiling River Project support the UN's sustainability goals. To which of the UN Sustainable Development Goals do they relate the most?

■ CHAPTER SUMMARY

Recent economic changes include increased international trade and growing interdependence among countries in the world economy.

- Supranational organizations foster greater globalization through relationships and free trade agreements, which are reorganizing the world into economic-based regions.

- Economic growth over the last century has led to deindustrialization in many core countries.

- Tariffs are used to protect domestic industry, but they have downsides. They increase the price of imported goods, which hurts consumers. In addition, tariffs sometimes lead to trade wars in which exports are taxed more heavily by other countries, increasing costs for businesses and hurting the global economy.

Global economies have become more closely connected.

- The global financial crisis of 2007–2008, the International Monetary Fund, and the World Bank demonstrate the interconnectedness of the world's financial and economic systems.

- Powerful core countries instituted an international division of labor through imperialism. Today's economic landscape has been transformed by a new international division of labor in which countries in the periphery have lower-paying jobs; core countries have decentralized; new regions and countries across the globe have developed new specializations; and the service sectors, high-tech industries, and growth poles have emerged.

- Offshore outsourcing and economic restructuring have led to economic development in peripheral countries.

- In countries outside the core, the growth of new economic activities has resulted in the creation of new manufacturing zones including special economic zones, free trade zones, and export-processing zones.

Sustainable development policies attempt to remedy problems stemming from natural resource depletion, mass consumption (the expanded use of goods), the effects of pollution and climate change, and social inequality.

- The United Nations adopted 17 Sustainable Development Goals to reduce the disparities among countries in the core, periphery, and semi-periphery.

- Sustainable development strategies include ecotourism, which is designed to generate revenue through tourism without impacting the environment.

■ KEY TERMS AND CONCEPTS

Use complete sentences to answer the questions.

1. **APPLY CONCEPTUAL VOCABULARY** Consider the terms *comparative advantage* and *complementarity*. Write a standard dictionary definition of each term. Then provide a conceptual definition—an explanation of how each term is used in the context of this chapter.

2. Explain how the interconnectedness of economic systems contributes to commodity dependence.

3. How is neoliberalism related to free trade?

4. Provide an example of deindustrialization.

5. How are Fordist systems and post-Fordist systems related?

6. Define the term *multiplier effects* in the context of offshore outsourcing.

7. Describe the negative effects of offshore outsourcing.

8. Define just-in-time delivery in relation to the manufacturing process.

9. Explain the arguments in favor of and against austerity as a way to prevent future global financial crises.

10. How does agglomeration relate to the growth pole theory?

11. Describe the international division of labor using a specific example.

12. How are the terms *special economic zones*, *free trade zones*, and *export processing zones* related?

13. Define the term *sustainable development*. Provide an example.

14. Define the term *ecotourism* and describe its goals.

■ INTERPRET CHARTS

Study the chart and then answer the following questions.

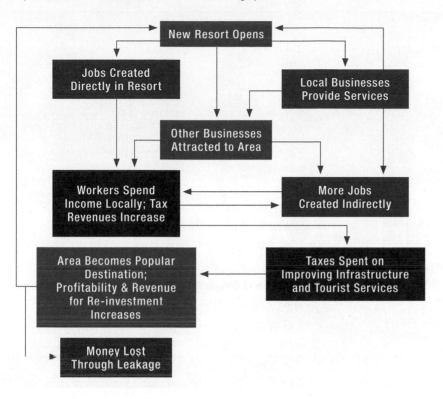

■ MULTIPLIER EFFECTS OF NEW RESORTS

15. **INTERPRET CHARTS** What are two immediate effects of establishing a new resort in an area?

16. **EXPLAIN SPATIAL RELATIONSHIPS** Explain how new resorts can attract other businesses to an area.

17. **CONNECT VISUALS & IDEAS** Leakage is the money that leaves a country's economy to purchase foreign-owned goods and services. How might an eco-friendly resort reduce leakage?

18. **PREDICT OUTCOMES** If the resort closes, how could that impact tax revenues?

19. **EXPLAIN LIMITATIONS** What does the chart not show about multiplier effects?

GEO-INQUIRY | SUSTAINABLE DEVELOPMENT IN YOUR COMMUNITY

Consider how you can use Geo-Inquiry to answer questions about sustainable development in your community. You can use the steps in the Geo-Inquiry Process below to explore how your community might be addressing 1 of the 17 Sustainable Development Goals.

ASK Start by choosing one of the SDGs and ask a Geo-Inquiry question that relates to it and your community. You might ask: *How is my community ensuring access to affordable, reliable, and sustainable energy for all?* Use the Geo-Inquiry Process to expand this question. Consider how you can link the question to action-oriented solutions, to help people who don't have access to affordable or reliable electricity or gas.

COLLECT Decide how you could gather geographic information to answer your Geo-Inquiry question. Explore local sources and federal data for information on the energy options available in your community. Consider interviewing energy providers to learn more about the

delivery and cost of energy, as well as their sustainability programs and measures taken to ensure affordability.

VISUALIZE Analyze the information you collected to draw conclusions. Organize the information and use it to create maps, charts, or other information about the energy provided in your community. Make sure to label your maps and charts so that the information is readily accessible to others, and reflects both the current state and how your proposal will improve the community.

CREATE Focus on ways to tell a Geo-Inquiry story that will describe the issue and your proposal, such as persuasive writing and providing data and other information, keeping your audience in mind. Outline or storyboard your story, then tie all of your elements together using a storytelling tool.

ACT Share your story with decision-makers. Show how your project can improve energy in your community.

ASK   COLLECT   VISUALIZE   CREATE   ACT

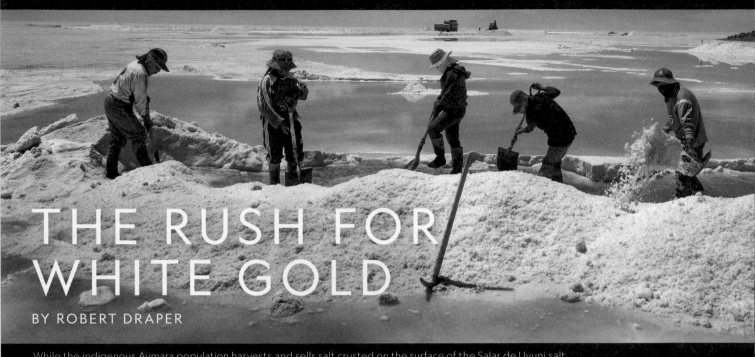

THE RUSH FOR WHITE GOLD

BY ROBERT DRAPER

While the indigenous Aymara population harvests and sells salt crusted on the surface of the Salar de Uyuni salt flat, the much more lucrative lithium is dissolved in brine found deep underground.

One morning in La Paz, Álvaro García Linera, the vice president of Bolivia, greets me outside his office. He speaks confidently about his country's natural resource. Lithium, essential to our battery-fueled world, is also the key to Bolivia's future, the vice president assures me.

WEALTH BENEATH THE SALT   Underneath the world's biggest salt flat is another wonder: one of Earth's greatest lithium deposits, perhaps 17 percent of the planet's total. By exploiting these lithium reserves, the government of Bolivia—where 40 percent of the people live in poverty—envisions a pathway out of its of misfortune.

What gold meant to earlier eras, and petroleum meant to the previous century, lithium may eclipse in the coming years. Long used in medication to treat bipolar disorders—and in items as varied as ceramics and nuclear weapons—it has emerged as an essential component for the batteries in computers, cell phones, and other electronic devices.

Though lithium-mining operations exist on every continent except Antarctica, up to three-fourths of the known lithium reserves are in the Altiplano-Puna Plateau, a 1,100-mile-long stretch of the Andes. The salt bed deposits concentrated in Chile, Argentina, and Bolivia are known as the "Lithium Triangle." Since the 1980s, Chile has produced lithium from brine, and its Salar de Atacama is now the preeminent source of the chemical in Latin America. Bolivia's lithium reserves match those of Chile's, but until recently, their potential had gone untapped.

BUILDING A LITHIUM INDUSTRY   Two years after their election, in 2008, President Evo Morales and García Linera turned their attention to the lithium reserves in the Salar de Uyuni, Bolivia's 4,000-square-mile salt flat. "We decided," said García Linera, "that we Bolivians are going to occupy the Salar, invent our own lithium extraction method, and then partner with foreign firms that can bring us a global market."

Morales confidently predicted that Bolivia would be producing lithium batteries by 2010 and electric cars by 2015. These estimates would prove to be way off. As Morales and García Linera would come to learn, lithium mining is an expensive and complicated process, requiring significant capital outlays as well as technological sophistication. Going it alone was never an option for an economically developing country like Bolivia.

Trusting nonetheless that the promise of the Salar de Uyuni's reserves would surmount any doubts, the Morales administration stated that Bolivia would have a foreign partner to assist in industrial-scale lithium production by 2013. This, too, proved to be a rash prediction. U.S. companies opted out. So did a top Korean firm. Not until 2018 did Bolivia find a partner: ACI Systems Alemania, a German firm that reportedly will invest $1.3 billion in exchange for a 49 percent stake in the venture.

The most daunting hurdle for Bolivia is a scientific one. Producing battery-grade lithium from brine involves separating out sodium chloride, potassium chloride, and magnesium chloride. This last contaminant is particularly expensive to remove. "While the ratio of magnesium in Chile is 5 to 1, in Uyuni it's 21 to 1," Bolivian chemical engineer Miguel Parra said. "So it's a much simpler operation for them. For us, separating magnesium from lithium is the biggest challenge."

I met Parra one morning at Bolivia's Llipi lithium pilot plant. Aside from a tiny pilot plant that makes batteries in the mining town of Potosí, the multimillion-dollar Llipi plant, which started producing lithium in January 2013, is all the Morales government has to show for its decade-long pursuit of lithium-fueled prosperity.

Quality control director Victor Ugarte walked me through the plant. About 20 percent of the lithium carbonate it produces is driven 190 miles to the Potosí battery plant. The rest is sold to various companies. "We started out producing about two tons per month," Ugarte told me. "We're now up to five tons." (Since then, plant officials say, they've reached 30 tons a month.)

I asked what the Llipi plant's ultimate production goal was. "Industrial level," he said, "will be 15,000 tons annually." I tried to imagine this unprepossessing little facility somehow, within the next five or so years, ratcheting up to hit that ambitious goal while maintaining 99.5 percent purity, the industry standard for battery-grade lithium.

THE SALAR'S FUTURE It's nearly impossible to assess how an industrialized version of its lithium facility will change the Salar de Uyuni. Among the greatest concerns is how much water will be required to extract the lithium. Two rivers, the Río Colorado and the Río Grande de Lípez, flow into the salt flat. Both are crucial to the local growers of quinoa, of which Bolivia is the second largest supplier. Though the Bolivian government insists that 90 percent of the water it uses will come from salt water rather than underground aquifers, some experts are skeptical that the groundwater supply will be unaffected.

And there's the still mostly unspoiled surface of the Salar itself—it's also a breeding ground for Chilean flamingos. "Our plant is located far away from these sanctuaries," García Linera said, adding, "This demonstrates our commitment to the environment."

Luís Alberto Echazú Alvarado, a vice minister of energy, said, "Our vision is this is a long-term project. So you have to mix poor and rich brine so as to exploit the whole Salar."

"So the government will always drill throughout other parts?" I asked.

"Right, right," Echazú said, nodding vigorously. "Always."

Adapted from "The Rush for White Gold," by Robert Draper, *National Geographic*, February 2019

WRITE ACROSS UNITS

Unit 7 explored industry, economic sectors, and processes that national economies develop in an interdependent world. This article takes a close look at how Bolivia is striving to exploit its most valuable resource as a way to develop its economy and improve its standard of living. Use information from the article and this unit to write a response to the following questions.

LOOKING BACK

1. What might geographers learn by conducting a regional analysis of the "Lithium Triangle"? UNIT 1

2. What effects might a developing lithium industry have on population distribution in Bolivia? UNIT 2

3. Would you expect Bolivia's cultural landscape to change if a successful lithium industry is established? Explain your answer. UNIT 3

4. In what ways do the concepts of territoriality and sovereignty come into play in Bolivia's plans for its lithium? UNIT 4

5. How do you think lithium processing will affect patterns of agriculture in Bolivia? Explain your answer. UNIT 5

6. Do you think the Salar de Uyuni might become a site for a city? What other information would help you predict whether a city will arise there? UNIT 6

7. Compare Bolivia's current situation to the Industrial Revolution. In what ways may Bolivia's development be similar to or different from countries affected by the Industrial Revolution? UNIT 7

WRITE ACROSS REGIONS & SCALES

Research a country outside of the Americas with an economy that is largely dependent on a single resource. Write an essay comparing the ways Bolivia and that country have exploited—or sought to exploit—each resource. Drawing on your research, this unit, and the article, address the following topic:

What economic patterns develop in a country with a single principal natural resource? What lessons can Bolivia learn from the other country?

THINK ABOUT

- how exploiting the resource affects all the sectors of the countries' economies

- measures of development like GDP, GNI per capita, and HDI for each country and what they indicate about each country's economic health or future

ECONOMIC SECTORS ACROSS THE GLOBE

For a long time, geographers classified economic activity into three sectors: primary, secondary, and tertiary. More recently, advanced technology and high-level leadership have been identified as sectors within the tertiary sector.

Countries in the core, periphery, and semi-periphery have distinctive Gross Domestic Product (GDP) profiles that reflect their involvement in each economic sector. Core countries tend to earn most of their money in the quaternary or quinary sectors, while peripheral countries have GDPs more weighted toward the primary sector. These charts show GDP percentages from agriculture, industry, and services in Algeria, Denmark, and Haiti.

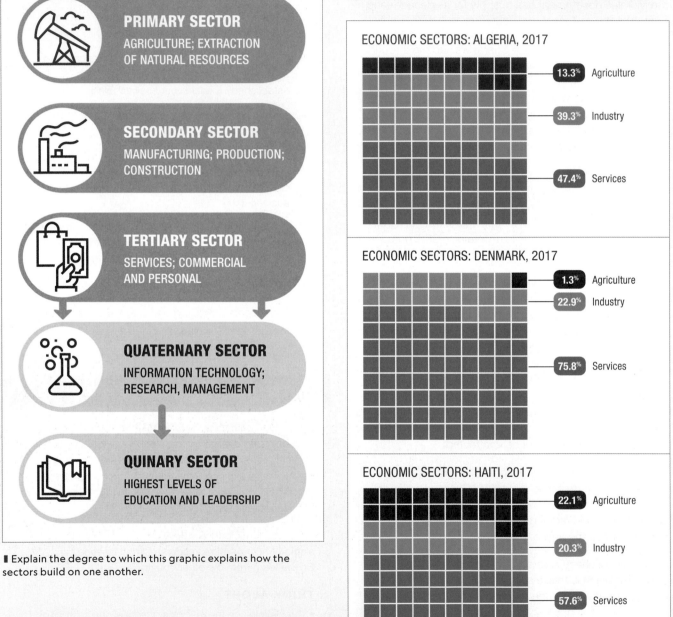

PRIMARY SECTOR
AGRICULTURE; EXTRACTION OF NATURAL RESOURCES

SECONDARY SECTOR
MANUFACTURING; PRODUCTION; CONSTRUCTION

TERTIARY SECTOR
SERVICES; COMMERCIAL AND PERSONAL

QUATERNARY SECTOR
INFORMATION TECHNOLOGY; RESEARCH, MANAGEMENT

QUINARY SECTOR
HIGHEST LEVELS OF EDUCATION AND LEADERSHIP

ECONOMIC SECTORS: ALGERIA, 2017
- 13.3% Agriculture
- 39.3% Industry
- 47.4% Services

ECONOMIC SECTORS: DENMARK, 2017
- 1.3% Agriculture
- 22.9% Industry
- 75.8% Services

ECONOMIC SECTORS: HAITI, 2017
- 22.1% Agriculture
- 20.3% Industry
- 57.6% Services

Source: CIA World Factbook

▌Explain the degree to which this graphic explains how the sectors build on one another.

▌Identify whether each country would be classified as core, peripheral, or semi-peripheral. Compare economic patterns across all three countries.

CHAPTER 18

LEAST-COST THEORY

Alfred Weber's least-cost theory takes into account several factors that influence the location of manufacturing sites, including transportation costs, agglomeration (the tendency of enterprises in the same industry to cluster in the same area), and labor costs. According to the theory, transportation is the most important element. Weber's location triangle illustrates how transportation considerations can be used to determine the ideal location for a manufacturing plant. ❚ Explain the degree to which the least-cost theory explains how manufacturing sites are chosen in the real world. Describe how factors other than transportation might alter the least-cost theory's location triangle.

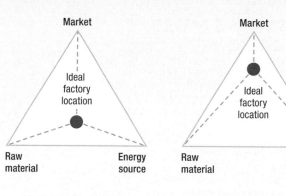

Bulk-reducing industry   Bulk-gaining industry

CHAPTER 18

BULK-GAINING AND BULK-REDUCING INDUSTRIES

Weber recognized that raw materials commonly lose or gain weight in the course of being transported from their source to the processing or manufacturing site and finally to the market. Because transporting heavier materials costs more, the ideal location for manufacturing a given product depends on whether the process causes the raw materials to gain or lose bulk. ❚ Use the infographics to explain the locations of processing plants for the soda industry and the copper industry. Consider the difference in weight between empty and full soda cans and the difference in weight between copper ore and the copper that results after other materials in the ore have been removed.

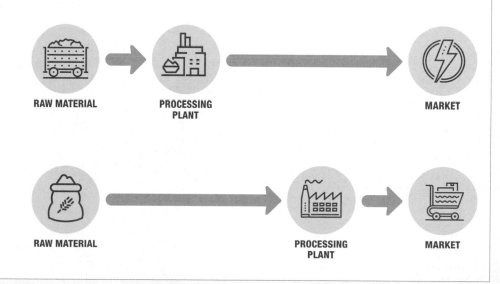

Bulk-Reducing Industry

If raw materials cost more to transport than finished goods, then processing plants will be located near the source of the raw materials.

Examples: copper smelting, furniture manufacturing

RAW MATERIAL   PROCESSING PLANT   MARKET

Bulk-Gaining Industry

If raw materials cost less to transport than finished goods, then processing plants will be located near the market.

Examples: car manufacturing, bread production, construction equipment

RAW MATERIAL   PROCESSING PLANT   MARKET

ROSTOW'S STAGES OF ECONOMIC GROWTH

Walt W. Rostow suggested that all countries could be categorized along a spectrum from traditional to modern (the social, political, economic, and technological changes that are associated with becoming industrialized). To become modern, countries needed to pass through five stages of economic growth in order.
❚ Explain the degree to which this model explains developments during and after the Industrial Revolution.

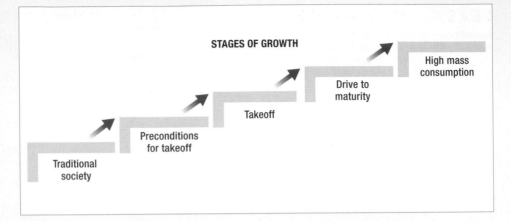

STAGES OF GROWTH

Traditional society

Preconditions for takeoff

Takeoff

Drive to maturity

High mass consumption

WALLERSTEIN'S WORLD SYSTEM THEORY

Immanuel Wallerstein's world system theory, which was introduced in Chapter 1, categorizes countries as belonging to the core, periphery, or semi-periphery and describes both the economic ties and power relationships that link the countries in a single network. ❚ Identify the patterns in the map concerning the locations of core, peripheral, and semi-peripheral countries in Africa, Europe, and Asia.

AFRICA, EUROPE, AND ASIA, 2020

Core
Semi-periphery
Periphery
Other

CHAPTER 19

DEPENDENCY THEORY

Dependency theory builds on the concepts established in world system theory to explain long-term economic inequality between core and peripheral countries. Core countries—often former colonial powers—have the means to demand low-cost raw materials and labor from peripheral countries, which in turn struggle to gather enough capital to invest in their own economies. Many peripheral and semi-peripheral countries are commodity dependent, meaning that their economies rely principally on a single commodity that they sell to more economically developed countries. Commodity dependence makes countries vulnerable to price changes for raw materials or to dropping demand for the commodities in core economies. ▌Identify and explain the patterns of commodity dependency in the bar graph and map. Identify the overall percentage of commodity-dependent countries.

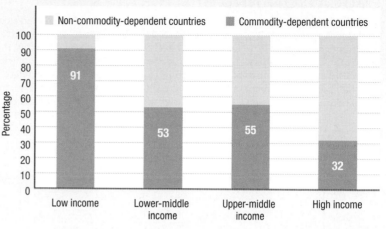

DISTRIBUTION OF COMMODITY-DEPENDENT AND NON–COMMODITY-DEPENDENT COUNTRIES WITHIN EACH INCOME GROUP, 2013–2017

Source: United Nations Conference on Trade and Development, 2019

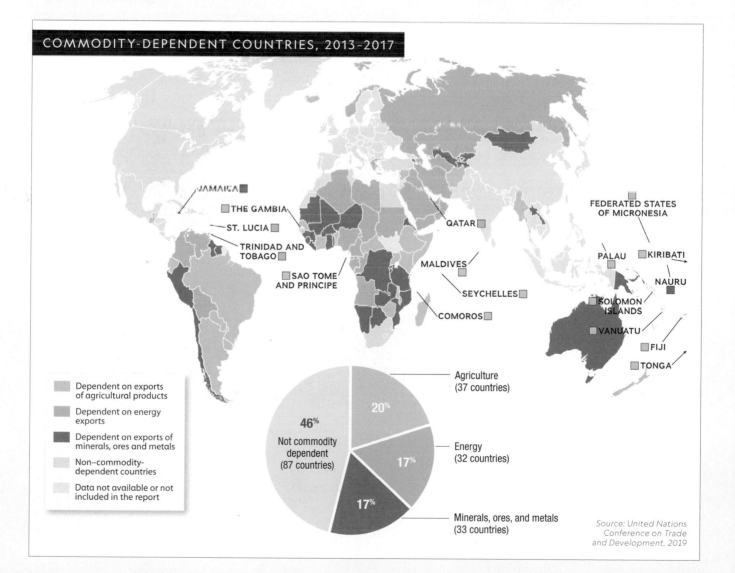

COMMODITY-DEPENDENT COUNTRIES, 2013–2017

JAMAICA
THE GAMBIA
ST. LUCIA
TRINIDAD AND TOBAGO
SAO TOME AND PRINCIPE
QATAR
MALDIVES
SEYCHELLES
COMOROS
FEDERATED STATES OF MICRONESIA
PALAU
KIRIBATI
NAURU
SOLOMON ISLANDS
VANUATU
FIJI
TONGA

Dependent on exports of agricultural products

Dependent on energy exports

Dependent on exports of minerals, ores and metals

Non–commodity-dependent countries

Data not available or not included in the report

Agriculture (37 countries) 20%

Energy (32 countries) 17%

Minerals, ores, and metals (33 countries) 17%

Not commodity dependent (87 countries) 46%

Source: United Nations Conference on Trade and Development, 2019

CHAPTER 19

GRAPHING THE CORRELATION BETWEEN EDUCATION AND BIRTH RATES

Studies have shown a correlation between levels of education for girls and a country's adolescent birth rate (ABR), or births per 1,000 females ages 15–19. This scattergram represents data from a 2015 analysis of United Nations countries. ▌Identify the patterns in the scattergram relating to ABR, education, and GDP. Select several countries, compare their GDPs and ABRs, and explain why a country's GDP might also be correlated with its ABR. For example, to compare Niger and the United States, use the data relating to their ABRs, education levels, and GDPs to consider the differences between the two countries.

THE EFFECT OF EDUCATION ON BIRTH RATES

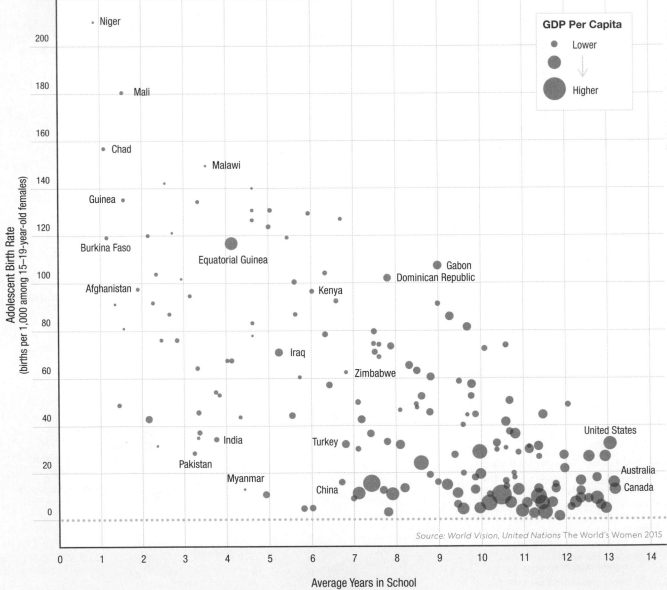

CHAPTER 20

COUNTRIES WITH THE MOST TRADE AGREEMENTS

Countries pursue trade agreements with the goal of fueling economic activity, increasing exports, and lowering costs of imported goods. In theory, trade agreements benefit all sides and boost the economies of countries in the core and periphery alike. ❚ Based on what you know about the locations of core, peripheral, and semi-peripheral countries, identify patterns in trade agreements shown on this map. (Note that the data predate Brexit, the withdrawal of the United Kingdom from the European Union in January 2020.) Explain why Europe, in general, has the largest number of trade agreements.

ACTIVE REGIONAL TRADE AGREEMENTS, 2019

Agreements made as a pre-existing group are counted individually for each country

- 11–31
- 6–10
- 1–5
- Not applicable/ no trade agreements

CHAPTER 20

WHERE YOUR CAR IS MADE

Many of the most commonly used pieces of technology in the United States—such as smartphones, computers, and cars—are manufactured using outsourced labor and materials. Automobiles, in particular, draw from a worldwide pool of parts and labor. The infographic shows the origins of parts and materials for cars manufactured in Mexico for the U.S. market by Ford Motor Company in 2017. ❚ Explain the degree to which post–Fordism (a system focused on small-scale batch production for a specialized market) and NAFTA may explain the data shown in the graphic.

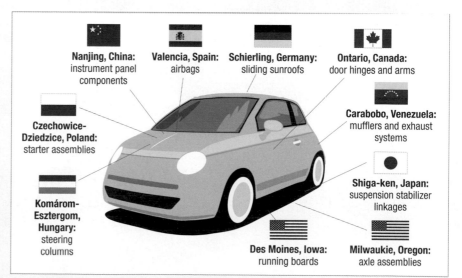

Nanjing, China: instrument panel components

Valencia, Spain: airbags

Schierling, Germany: sliding sunroofs

Ontario, Canada: door hinges and arms

Czechowice-Dziedzice, Poland: starter assemblies

Carabobo, Venezuela: mufflers and exhaust systems

Shiga-ken, Japan: suspension stabilizer linkages

Komárom-Esztergom, Hungary: steering columns

Des Moines, Iowa: running boards

Milwaukie, Oregon: axle assemblies

Source: Investopedia

COVID-19
A GLOBAL PANDEMIC

Medical staff members embrace through their personal protective equipment (PPE) in the isolation ward of a Zouping, China, hospital in January 2020.

The year 2020 may well serve as a benchmark for everyone alive today. Most will remember it as the year COVID-19— a coronavirus—spread across the world, profoundly impacting life as we know it. While the story of COVID-19 will continue to evolve, this feature serves as a snapshot of the pandemic in the spring of 2020, as the virus swept across the United States.

Your COVID-19 story depends a lot on whether you were on the front lines as a health-care or other essential worker, or doing your part on the stay-at-home front. Emergency room doctors in New Orleans, Madrid, and Rome, for example, rushed from one critically ill patient to the next. When they left the hospital, they worried about carrying the disease home to their families. Students, elderly people, and those workers confined to home faced their own challenges— feelings of social isolation, anxiety, fear, and ambiguity over when life would return to normal.

Perhaps the most surprising thing about COVID-19 was how quickly the public adapted to dramatic changes imposed on them. Overnight, they adjusted to shelter-in-place orders, the closing of schools and businesses, and restrictions on travel and public gatherings. Computers, phones, and Wi-Fi networks became a lifeline to the world as homes transformed into workplaces and classrooms, with family members competing for desk space and internet access. In the midst of the chaos, people found ways to help their neighbors and those in need. Health care workers, emergency personnel, truck drivers, grocery store employees, meatpackers, and many others in service industries continued to show up at work every day, despite the risks. Many couldn't afford not to.

As days passed, people learned to adapt to constantly changing conditions and new guidelines imposed by local and national governments and national and international organizations such as the Centers for Disease Control (CDC) and the World Health Organization (WHO). These agencies relied on data to inform their decision-making. And while it confirmed cases and death rates dropping in some locations, it suggested plateaus and increases in others. The story of COVID-19 morphed as frequently as its data.

ORIGINS OF COVID-19 The name COVID-19 is a shorthand reference to "coronavirus disease 2019," the cause of the disease (a coronavirus strain) and the year it first appeared. But when COVID-19 first emerged in early December 2019, no one knew what the disease was. Chinese health authorities reported the outbreak of a mysterious, pneumonia-like disease in the city of Wuhan to the WHO on December 31, 2019. Many of the first victims of the disease had a link to a large seafood and live animal "wet market," which suggests the virus originally spread

from animals to people. But as cases quickly spread in Wuhan, it became clear that the virus was moving from person to person through respiratory droplets expelled by those infected. It became clear that Wuhan was experiencing an epidemic, an increase in the number of cases of a disease above what is normally expected in a local area. Health officials identified the cause of the disease as a new coronavirus, one of a family of viruses common in people and in such animals as cattle, cats, and bats. This new coronavirus, named SARS-CoV2, originated in bats.

Throughout January 2020, COVID-19 began to spread explosively, not only in China but throughout the world. Travelers from Wuhan brought the disease to a number of countries, including Thailand, Japan, and the United States. China suspended all air travel in and out of Wuhan on January 23, but by March 11—over a period of less than three months—more than 118,000 cases had appeared in more than 110 countries, evidence that in a globalized world, the opportunity to contain such a contagious virus is fleeting, urgent, and often not recognized until it's too late. At that point, WHO labeled COVID-19 a pandemic.

Because COVID-19 was caused by a new virus, people lacked immunity. The medical establishment quickly put together a profile of COVID-19 that included the fact that infected people may not exhibit symptoms for 2 to 14 days, so people could infect others before they knew they were carrying the virus. In most cases, COVID-19 caused only mild illness with symptoms including fever, cough, and shortness of breath—and sometimes no symptoms at all. But in serious cases, victims developed a deadly pneumonia that often required hospitalization, including supplemental oxygen, and sometimes intensive care and the use of mechanical ventilators to save their lives. Older people and those with chronic medical conditions, such as heart disease, lung disease, obesity, and diabetes, had a higher risk of developing serious illness and were also more likely to die from the disease.

As spring 2020 turned into summer, researchers across the world worked to identify effective treatment options for COVID-19 and a vaccine that might prevent it. The earliest initial availability of vaccines was projected to be winter or spring of 2021, and companies collaborated at an unprecedented pace to meet or beat that date.

HISTORICAL PERSPECTIVE In 1918, an estimated 500 million people, or about one-third of the world's population, became infected with an influenza called the Spanish flu. It lasted until 1920 and killed between 50 and 100 million people worldwide. The disease occurred during World War I and was quickly spread by soldiers living in close quarters and then traveling throughout the world. Like COVID-19, the Spanish flu caused the shutdown of businesses and schools and overwhelmed the health-care system in many countries. However, in the United States, cities that were more aggressive in their social distancing measures tended to have lower death rates and higher employment gains throughout the pandemic. The term *social distancing* refers to purposefully maintaining physical distance between people to avoid spreading a disease. Minneapolis, for example, a city that used social distancing for a longer period of time during the Spanish flu pandemic, experienced much lower mortality rate than Pittsburgh, which observed a shorter and less strict period of social distancing. Historical data such as this has helped inform some of the public health decisions made during the COVID-19 pandemic.

A more recent pandemic—but not nearly as severe as COVID-19—was SARS, another respiratory illness caused by a coronavirus that first appeared in Asia in February of 2003. It quickly spread to 26 countries in North America, South America, Europe, and Asia, infecting about 8,000 people and killing 774. The SARS pandemic lasted only about four months, partly because the disease did not spread as readily as COVID-19. Victims of SARS were not contagious until they were very sick, and by then, most were hospitalized and kept in isolation.

EXPLOSIVE GLOBAL SPREAD The speed by which the virus spread from place to place astonished scientists. By early June 2020, COVID-19 had grown from an illness affecting a small number of people in one city in China to a disease that had stricken 7.5 million people in roughly 190 countries, killing over 420,000. How did the scale of COVID-19 escalate from a local problem to a global disaster in just a few months? Person-to-person transmission. The rise of globalization and the level of urbanization demonstrated by the growth of larger, more densely populated cities makes personal connections constant and nearly unlimited. As more people traveled internationally for business and pleasure, they came in close contact with many others, some of whom were carriers of COVID-19. And the rest is history. Or reality. Or human geography.

Without a vaccine or a cure, the only ways to slow the spread of an infectious disease are to reduce close contact between people and to increase personal hygiene. That's

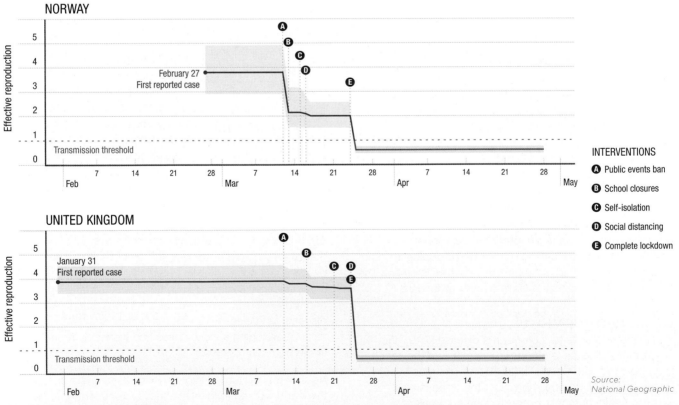

INTERVENTIONS
Ⓐ Public events ban
Ⓑ School closures
Ⓒ Self-isolation
Ⓓ Social distancing
Ⓔ Complete lockdown

Source:
National Geographic

SOCIAL MITIGATION, 2020 Like states in the U.S., European countries responded differently to the outbreak of COVID-19. Norway quickly imposed intense social mitigation steps and testing. Consequently, its transmission threshold dropped quickly and the country saw relatively low fatality rates. The UK rolled out social mitigation steps and testing more slowly and had a higher fatality rate. However, the data from both countries demonstrates the effectiveness of social mitigation practices in reducing the effective reproduction rate of COVID-19, which, if kept below 1, means the infection will spread slowly and will eventually die out.

Data from the CDC, WHO, and other sources was used to create this data dashboard, a digital tool used to track the pandemic in real time. Developed by Johns Hopkins University with the support of Esri, a pioneer in digital mapping, the dashboard displays the location and number of confirmed COVID-19 cases, deaths, and recoveries for all affected countries. The actual number of COVID-19 cases was likely much higher than the number reported for several reasons, including the fact that many infected people with mild or no symptoms were never tested.

why world health authorities advised social mitigation steps, such as social distancing, school closures, and the cancellation of public events, be taken. These measures were designed to "flatten the curve," or slow the rate at which people became infected so that hospitals would have enough beds, equipment, and health-care workers to treat patients over time. Social mitigation practices also reduce the effective reproduction rate of a disease, which means the spread of infection slows, eventually causing the disease to die out.

COMPILING & ANALYZING DATA
In a pandemic like COVID-19, public health officials around the world rely heavily on geographic data, such as the daily numbers and locations of confirmed cases. Local health departments within a country report statistics on confirmed cases to a national agency, such as the CDC in the United States. The CDC and similar agencies in other countries then share this data with the WHO. The CDC, WHO, and other national and international organizations and businesses use the data to create graphs, charts, digital maps, and other visual tools, which are then deployed to predict where the disease will appear next, how quickly the number of cases will rise, what control measures to institute, and how to allocate resources, such as testing equipment.

In fact, the importance of widespread testing emerged in the global debate about the path forward. Much of the worldwide response to the pandemic centered around the availability of testing—or lack of it—and the time needed to get test results. In the United States, a widespread shortage of COVID-19 test kits during the spring of 2020 meant that even people with clear symptoms of the disease, including health-care workers and first responders, could not always get tested. The United States lagged behind a number of countries who were able to ramp up testing much more quickly, in part because the U.S. effort was primarily left to each individual state to manage rather than directed by a coordinated process set in place by the federal government.

SOCIAL CHANGES & CHALLENGES
COVID-19 altered everyday life for most Americans, whether they contracted the disease or not. The stress of social isolation hit hard on those who live alone, the mentally ill, and hospital patients and nursing home residents who couldn't have visitors. Family members were often left to grieve for loved ones who died alone in a COVID-19 unit in a hospital. People skipped routine health examinations and delayed procedures and vaccinations to avoid doctors' offices, putting their health and the overall health of the global community at an increased risk.

The frontline heroes in this pandemic were health-care workers, who risked infection while battling the disease with limited resources and no roadmap for effectively treating the sometimes baffling symptoms of the disease. In hospitals throughout the United States, doctors and nurses lacked enough basic personal protective equipment (PPE) such as masks, gloves, and gowns. Many facilities also needed more ventilators, which were initially in short supply. As the rate of COVID-19 cases climbed, some cities lacked enough hospital beds as well as doctors and nurses. In late March 2020, New York governor Andrew Cuomo declared the state needed an additional 30,000 ventilators and 1 million more health-care workers. In other states, governors made similar pleas for ventilators and for retired health-care workers to return to work, as more and more doctors and nurses contracted the virus themselves. In response to those who promoted a focus on stabilizing the economy rather than reducing the death rate, Cuomo asserted, "My mother is not expendable and your mother is not expendable and our brothers and sisters are not expendable . . . We're not going to put a dollar figure on human life."

As the fatigue of "breaking news" set in, many people looked to the science community and to local leaders such as Governor Cuomo for the most accurate information. A few individuals emerged as straight talkers whom many people trusted to provide sound guidance. Among them

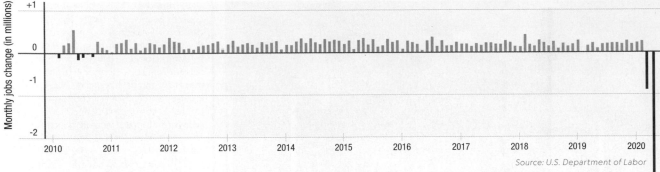

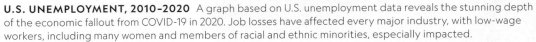

U.S. UNEMPLOYMENT, 2010–2020 A graph based on U.S. unemployment data reveals the stunning depth of the economic fallout from COVID-19 in 2020. Job losses have affected every major industry, with low-wage workers, including many women and members of racial and ethnic minorities, especially impacted.

Source: U.S. Department of Labor

were Dr. Tedros Adhanom Ghebreyesus, director general of the WHO, and Dr. Anthony Fauci, director of the U.S. National Institute of Allergy and Infectious Diseases (NIAID). In the face of the pandemic, Dr. Ghebreyesus oversaw 24-7 monitoring of disease progression and the distribution of medical resources, facilitated daily discussions with affected countries, and provided a steady stream of reliable information for an anxious world desperate for reliable and expedited information and guidance. As a public health expert, Fauci became a respected nonpartisan national spokesperson in the United States, educating the public about COVID-19, advising the president and other leaders, and testifying about the health crisis before Congress. Serving as director of NIAID since 1984 and under six presidents, Fauci had battled such infectious diseases as HIV/AIDS, West Nile Virus, and Ebola.

ECONOMIC IMPACT The economic impact of COVID-19 was staggering. From furloughs and job losses to the near shutdown of major industries such as airlines, economic uncertainty quickly sent the stock market plunging. While global connectivity made it possible for many to work from home, that wasn't possible for those in certain fields. Workers in the transportation, entertainment, fitness, food, retail, and personal care industries lost jobs in record numbers. In the United States, the April 2020 unemployment rate jumped to 14.7 percent (with some estimating closer to 20 percent)—the worst since the Great Depression. In fact, the scale and speed of the layoffs far exceeded that of the Great Recession of 2008. Many Americans worried for the first time ever about paying their rent or mortgage and not having enough money for food. In many states, food bank lines stretched for miles.

The COVID-19 pandemic disrupted the global supply chain, the established distribution of goods and services around the world designed to maximize industrial efficiency and minimize costs. With the advent of the pandemic, the global demand for medical supplies and equipment, for example, grew exponentially, with countries and states bidding against each other for goods. Companies like General Motors switched from manufacturing cars to producing ventilators for U.S. hospitals. Small businesses with access

to sewing machines and fabric pivoted from making their usual products to making cloth masks, just to stay in business. The wrenching effects of such economic changes and disruptions will play out for years to come.

To alleviate economic fallout in the United States, Congress worked in spring 2020 to produce emergency relief legislation worth $2.2 trillion, which was intended to flood the U.S. economy with money. The bill provided for payments of $1,200 to many American adults and $500 for most children. It increased unemployment benefits and created a $367 billion fund to help small businesses retain their employees. In addition, the bill set up a $500 billion lending program for businesses, cities, and states and directed $130 billion to hospitals. However, the economic stimulus immediately ran into glitches in getting relief checks out, and the allocated funding quickly ran short. While most economists and legislators recognized that more relief will be needed, it was by no means clear what form that assistance should take. At the time this piece was written, legislators were considering additional relief measures for Americans in need.

As has often been the case, a global disaster like this pandemic cast a spotlight on inequity around the world. In most countries, the cost in human life, whether from the disease itself or from the accompanying economic fallout, was nearly always greater among the poor or underserved special populations. One glaring example was the number of people who—when the guideline was to shelter at home—had no home to shelter in. Additionally, in the American West, First Nations communities lacking access to elements of basic hygiene, including running water, experienced high rates of infection and morbidity. In the United States, data revealed early on that COVID-19 was having

20.5 MILLION JOBS
LOST IN APRIL 2020

As the economic toll of COVID-19 gripped the United States in 2020, millions of Americans found themselves waiting in long lines like this one in Las Vegas, Nevada, for food and basic supplies. In cars or on foot, they pulled on masks and spent hours in queues that stretched for blocks—and sometimes miles—for donated groceries or to file for unemployment assistance.

a disproportionate impact on African American and Latinx communities. Post-pandemic, experts will analyze long-range data to determine who bore the brunt of the disease, and why.

THE NEW NORMAL? As in most crises, glimmers of hope emerged. While leaders held tense press conferences and scientists collaborated on testing methods, treatments, and vaccines, citizens found ways to inspire and support one another. Musicians serenaded empty streets to entertain lonely neighbors, and teachers and principals sought creative ways to connect with their students. Friends and families formed drive-by parades to celebrate birthdays and graduations, honor veterans, and welcome home COVID-19 survivors. Entire cities came together nightly to encourage and thank tireless essential workers. And amidst cries for racial justice and police reform in June 2020, many protesters wore face-coverings to protect themselves and others from the spread of COVID-19 as they participated in marches and rallies.

Globally, satellite images showed dramatic reductions in air pollution around COVID-19 hotspots due to the sharp decline in transportation and industrial activity. But while inspiring, these images are also a graphic reminder that, without action, the climate crisis will continue when the pandemic passes. Sustainable development strategies are still needed to correct environmental problems.

Part of our "new normal" seems to be that many questions remain unanswered. How will countries respond to the severe economic downturn? What is the right balance between protecting human health and restoring some semblance of normalcy to daily life? What kinds of long term social and cultural changes are likely to take place—and which ones should be encouraged? Will we ever shake hands again? Will we adapt our cultural practices to more safely share meals, practice our religions, and maintain our traditions? How might the pandemic impact efforts made toward sustainability and voter equity? How will cities, as key centers of global markets, adapt to address modern challenges in the aftermath of this pandemic?

Human geography teaches us that cultural ideas, practices, and innovations change or disappear over time. It also underscores the power of data. It seems like it's time to innovate, to adapt, and to let some of our old ideas and practices fade away, allowing data to be our guide.

GEOGRAPHIC THINKING

1. Identify an example of quantitative, qualitative, or geospatial data that could be used to make decisions related to COVID-19, and explain how it could be used.

2. Describe one possible cultural, geographic, or environmental result of the pandemic.

GLOSSARY

A

absolute direction *n.* the cardinal directions north, south, east, and west (page 37)

absolute distance *n.* distance that can be measured using a standard unit of length (page 37)

absolute location *n.* the exact location of an object, usually expressed in coordinates of longitude and latitude (page 8)

acculturation *n.* the process by which people within one culture adopt some of the traits of another while still retaining their own distinct culture (page 194)

adherent *n.* a person who is loyal to a belief, religion, or organization (page 171)

administer *v.* to manage the way borders are maintained and how goods and people cross them (page 250)

African city model *n.* a model of urban development depicting a city with three central business districts, growing outward in a series of concentric rings (page 437)

agglomeration *n.* the tendency of enterprises in the same industry to cluster in the same area (page 513)

agribusinesses *n.* the large-scale system that includes the production, processing, and distribution of agricultural products and equipment (page 339)

agricultural biodiversity *n.* the variety and variability of plants, animals, and microorganisms that are used directly or indirectly for food and agriculture (page 371)

agricultural density *n.* the total number of farmers per unit of arable land (page 68)

agricultural hearth *n.* an area where different groups began to domesticate plants and animals (page 324)

agricultural landscape *n.* a landscape resulting from the interactions between farming activities and a location's natural environment (page 359)

agriculture *n.* the purposeful cultivation of plants or raising of animals to produce goods for survival (page 307)

agroecosystem *n.* an ecosystem modified for agricultural use (page 359)

antecedent boundary *n.* a border established before an area becomes heavily settled (page 254)

antinatalist *adj.* describing attitudes or policies that discourage childbearing as a means of limiting population growth (page 99)

aquifer *n.* layers of sand, gravel, and rocks that contain and can release a usable amount of water (page 362)

arable land *n.* land that can be used to grow crops (page 67)

arithmetic density *n.* the total number of people per unit area of land; also called crude density (page 67)

artifact *n.* a visible object or technology that a culture creates (page 153)

assimilation *n.* a category of acculturation in which the interaction of two cultures results in one culture adopting almost all of the customs, traditions, language, and other cultural traits of the other (page 195)

asylum *n.* the right to protection in a country (page 118)

B

autonomous *adj.* having the authority to govern territories independently of the national government; for example, by having a separate currency (page 244)

bid-rent theory *n.* a theory that describes the relationships between land value, commercial location, and transportation (primarily in urban areas) using a bid-rent gradient, or slope; used to describe how land costs are determined (page 312)

biodiversity *n.* the variety of organisms living in a location (page 362)

biotechnology *n.* the science of altering living organisms, often through genetic manipulation, to create new products for specific purposes, such as crops that resist certain pests (page 371)

blockbusting *n.* a practice by real estate agents who would stir up concern that Black families would soon move into a neighborhood; the agents would convince White property owners to sell their houses at below-market prices (page 461)

boomburb *n.* a suburb that has grown rapidly into a large and sprawling city with more than 100,000 residents (page 410)

brain drain *n.* the loss of trained or educated people to the lure of work in another—often richer—country (page 135)

break-of-bulk point *n.* location where it is more economical to break raw materials into smaller units before shipping them further (page 514)

brownfield *n.* abandoned and polluted industrial site in a central city or suburb (page 476)

Buddhism *n.* the oldest universalizing religion, which arose from a hearth in northeastern India sometime between the mid-sixth and mid-fourth centuries B.C.E. and is based on the teachings of Siddhartha Gautama, called the Buddha (page 221)

bulk-gaining industry *n.* industry in which the finished goods cost more to transport than the raw materials (page 514)

bulk-reducing industry *n.* industry in which the raw materials cost more to transport than the finished goods (page 514)

C

carrying capacity *n.* the maximum population size an environment can sustain (page 69)

cartographer *n.* a person who creates maps (page 36)

cash crop *n.* a crop produced mainly to be sold and usually exported to larger markets (page 350)

census *n.* an official count of the number of people in a defined area, such as a state (page 30)

central business district (CBD) *n.* the central location where the majority of consumer services are located in a city or town because the accessibility of the location attracts these services (page 312)

central place theory *n.* a theory used to describe the spatial relationship between cities and their surrounding communities (page 414)

centrifugal force *n.* a force that divides a group of people (page 174)

centripetal force *n.* a force that unites a group of people (page 174)

chain migration *n.* type of migration in which people move to a location because others from their community have previously migrated there (page 116)

choke point *n.* a narrow, strategic passageway to another place through which it is difficult to pass (page 245)

Christianity *n.* a universalizing religion based on the teachings of Jesus Christ that began in what is now the West Bank and Israel around the beginning of the common era and has spread to all continents (page 219)

circular migration *n.* migration pattern in which migrant workers move back and forth between their country of origin and the destination country where they work temporary jobs (page 118)

circulation *n.* temporary, repetitive movements that recur on a regular basis (page 111)

climate *n.* the long-term patterns of weather in a particular area (page 64)

climate region *n.* an area that has similar climate patterns generally based on its latitude and its location on a coast or continental interior (page 310)

clustered settlement *n.* a rural settlement pattern in which residents live in close proximity to one another, with farmland and pasture land surrounding the settlement; also known as a nucleated settlement (page 315)

collectivist culture *n.* a culture in which people are expected to conform to collective responsibility within the family and to be obedient to and respectful of elder family members (page 197)

colonialism *n.* the practice of claiming and dominating overseas territories (page 245)

Columbian Exchange *n.* the exchange of goods and ideas between the Americas, Europe, and Africa that began after Christopher Columbus landed in the Americas in 1492 (page 328)

commercial agriculture *n.* an agricultural practice that focuses on producing crops and raising animals for the market for others to purchase (page 312)

commodity chain *n.* a network of people, information, processes, and resources that work together to produce, handle, and distribute a commodity or product (page 344)

commodity dependence *n.* an aspect of dependency theory that occurs when more than 60 percent of a country's exports and economic health are tied to one or two resources (page 543)

comparative advantage *n.* the relative cost advantage a country or organization has to produce certain goods or services for trade (page 547)

complementarity *n.* the mutual trade relationship that exists between two places based on the supply of raw materials and the demand for finished products or services (page 547)

concentric-zone model *n.* a model of urban development depicting a city growing outward from a central business district in a series of concentric rings (page 433)

concurrent *adj.* sharing authority (page 266)

consequent boundary *n.* a type of subsequent boundary that takes into account the differences that exist within a cultural landscape, separating groups that have distinct languages, religions, ethnicities, or other traits (page 254)

contagious diffusion *n.* the process by which an idea or cultural trait spreads rapidly among people of all social classes and levels of power (page 181)

core *n.* classification of a country or region that has wealth, higher education levels, more advanced technologies, many resources, strong militaries, and powerful allies (page 21)

cottage industry *n.* preindustrial form of manufacture in which members of families spread out through rural areas worked in their homes to make goods (page 496)

creolization *n.* the blending of two or more languages that may not include the features of either original language (page 186)

crop rotation *n.* the varying of crops from year to year to allow for the restoration of valuable nutrients and the continuing productivity of the soil (page 316)

crude birth rate (CBR) *n.* the number of births in a given year per 1,000 people in a given population (page 77)

crude death rate (CDR) *n.* the number of deaths in a given year per 1,000 people in a given population (page 78)

cultural appropriation *n.* the act of adopting elements of another culture (page 197)

cultural convergence *n.* the process by which cultures become more similar through interaction (page 189)

cultural divergence *n.* the process by which cultures become less similar due to conflicting beliefs or other barriers (page 190)

cultural hearth *n.* an area where cultural traits develop and from which cultural traits diffuse (page 179)

cultural landscape *n.* a natural landscape that has been modified by humans, reflecting their cultural beliefs and values (page 157)

cultural norm *n.* a shared standard or pattern that guides the behavior of a group of people (page 155)

cultural relativism *n.* the evaluation of a culture by its own standards (page 155)

cultural trait *n.* a shared object or cultural practice (page 153)

culture *n.* the beliefs, values, practices, behaviors, and technologies shared by a society and passed down from generation to generation (page 153)

D

debt-for-nature swap *n.* agreement between a bank and a peripheral country in which the bank forgives a portion of the country's debt in exchange for local investment in conservation measures (page 365)

de facto segregation *n.* segregation that results from residential settlement patterns rather than from prejudicial laws (page 459)

define *v.* to explicitly state in legally binding documentation such as a treaty where boundaries are located, using reference points such as natural features or lines of latitude and longitude (page 250)

deforestation *n.* loss of forested land (page 359)

deindustrialization *n.* process by which a country or area reduces industrial activity, particularly in heavy industry and manufacturing (page 549)

delimit *v.* to draw boundaries on a map, in accordance with a legal agreement (page 250)

demarcate *v.* to place physical objects such as stones, pillars, walls, or fences to indicate where a boundary exists (page 250)

demographics *n.* data about the structures and characteristics of human populations (page 77)

Demographic Transition Model (DTM) *n.* a model that represents shifts in the growth of the world's populations, based on population trends related to birth rate and death rate (page 93)

denomination *n.* a separate church organization that unites a number of local congregations (page 171)

density *n.* the number of things—people, animals, or objects—in a specific area (page 9)

dependency ratio *n.* the number of people in a dependent age group (under age 15 or age 65 and older) divided by the number of people in the working-age group (age 15 to 64), multiplied by 100 (page 74)

dependency theory *n.* a theory that describes the development challenges and limitations faced by poorer countries and the political and economic relationships poorer countries have with richer countries (page 542)

desertification *n.* a form of land degradation that occurs when soil to deteriorates to a desertlike condition (page 362)

devolution *n.* the process that occurs when the central power in a state is broken up among regional authorities within its borders (page 249)

dialect *n.* a variation of a standard language specific to a general area, with differences in pronunciation, degree of rapidity in speech, word choice, and spelling (page 170)

diffusion *n.* the process by which a cultural trait spreads from one place to another over time (page 179)

disamenity zone *n.* a high-poverty urban area in a disadvantaged location containing steep slopes, flood-prone ground, rail lines, landfills, or industry (page 435)

dispersed *adj.* spread out (page 63)

dispersed settlement *n.* a rural settlement pattern in which houses and buildings are isolated from one another, and all the homes in a settlement are distributed over a relatively large area (page 315)

distance decay *n.* a principle stating that the farther away one thing is from another, the less interaction the two things will have (pages 10, 118)

distribute *v.* to arrange within a given space (page 9)

domestication *n.* the deliberate effort to grow plants and raise animals, making plants and animals adapt to human demands and using selective breeding to develop desirable characteristics (page 324)

doubling time *n.* the number of years in which a population growing at a certain rate would double (page 87)

dual agricultural economy *n.* an economy having two agricultural sectors that have different levels of technology and different patterns of demand (page 339)

dual economies *n.* economies with two distinct distributions of economic activity across the economic sectors (page 508)

E

ecological footprint *n.* impact of a person or community on the environment, expressed as the amount of land required to sustain their use of natural resources (page 453)

ecological perspective *n.* the relationships between living things and their environments (page 7)

economic sectors *n.* collections of industries engaged in similar economic activities based on the creation of raw materials, the production of goods, the provision of services, or other activities (page 504)

economies of scale *n.* cost reductions that occur when production rises (pages 285, 339)

ecotourism *n.* a form of tourism based on the enjoyment of natural areas that minimizes the impact to the environment (page 563)

edge city *n.* a type of community located on the outskirts of a larger city with commercial centers with office space, retail complexes, and other amenities typical of an urban center (page 410)

electoral college *n.* a set of people, called electors, who are chosen to elect the president and vice president of the United States (page 269)

emigration *n.* movement away from a location (page 111)

eminent domain *n.* a government's right to take over privately owned property for public use or interest (page 468)

enclosure system *n.* system in which communal lands were replaced by farms owned by individuals, and use of the land was restricted to the owner or tenants who rented the land from the owner (page 331)

environmental determinism *n.* the idea that human behavior is strongly affected, controlled, or determined by the physical environment (page 9)

environmental injustice *n.* the ways in which communities of color and poor people are more likely to be exposed to environmental burdens such as air pollution or contaminated water; also called environmental racism (page 468)

Epidemiological Transition Model (ETM) *n.* a model that describes changes in fertility, mortality, life expectancy, and population age distribution, largely as the result of changes in causes of death (page 93)

ethnic cleansing *n.* the process by which a state attacks an ethnic group and tries to eliminate it through expulsion, imprisonment, or killing (page 278)

ethnicity *n.* the state belonging to a group of people who share common cultural characteristics (page 158)

ethnic neighborhood *n.* a cultural landscape within a community of people outside of their area of origin (page 158)

ethnic religion *n.* a religion that is closely tied with a particular ethnic group often living in a particular place (page 223)

ethnic separatism *n.* the process by which people of a particular ethnicity in a multinational state identify more strongly as members of their ethnic group than as citizens of the state (page 277)

ethnocentrism *n.* the tendency of ethnic groups to evaluate other groups according to preconceived ideas originating from their own culture (page 155)

ethnonationalism *n.* the process by which the people of a country identify as having one common ethnicity, religious belief, and language, creating a sense of pride and identity that is tied to the territory; also called ethnic nationalism (page 283)

exclusive economic zone (EEZ) *n.* an area that extends 200 nautical miles from a state's coast; a state has sole access to resources found within the waters or beneath the sea floor of its EEZ (page 256)

expansion diffusion *n.* the spread of a cultural trait outward from where it originated (page 181)

export processing zone (EPZ) *n.* an area within a country that is subject to more favorable regulations (usually including the elimination of tariffs) to encourage foreign investment and the manufacturing of goods for export (page 558)

extensive agriculture *n.* an agricultural practice with relatively few inputs and little investment in labor and capital that results in relatively low outputs (page 318)

exurb *n.* a typically fast-growing community outside of or on the edge of a metropolitan area where the residents and community are closely connected to the central city and suburbs (page 410)

GLOSSARY

F

fair trade *n.* a movement that tries to provide farmers and workers in peripheral and semi-peripheral countries with a fair price for their products by providing more equitable trading conditions (page 354)

farm subsidy *n.* a form of aid and insurance given by the federal government to certain farmers and agribusinesses (page 345)

federal state *n.* the organization of a state in which power is shared between the federal government and internal regional units (page 261)

Fertile Crescent *n.* a hearth in Southwest Asia that forms an arc from the eastern Mediterranean coast up into what is now western Turkey and then south and east along the Tigris and Euphrates rivers to western parts of modern Iran (page 324)

fertility *n.* the ability to produce children (page 77)

filtering *n.* the process of neighborhood change in which housing vacated by more affluent groups passes down the income scale to lower-income groups (page 462)

first agricultural revolution *n.* the shift from foraging for food to farming about 11,000 years ago, marking the beginning of agriculture (page 329)

flow *n.* movement of people, goods, or information that has economic, social, political, or cultural effects on societies (page 9)

food desert *n.* area where residents lack access to healthy, nutritious foods because stores selling these foods are too far away (page 380)

food insecurity *n.* the disruption of food intake or eating patterns because of poor access to food (page 377)

food security *n.* reliable access to safe and nutritious food that can support an active and healthy lifestyle (page 377)

foragers *n.* small, nomadic groups who had primarily plant-based diets and ate small animals or fish for protein (page 324)

forced migration *n.* type of migration in which people are compelled to move by economic, political, environmental, or cultural factors (page 115)

Fordism *n.* a highly organized and specialized system for industrial production that focuses on efficiency and productivity in mass production; named after Henry Ford (page 555)

formal region *n.* an area that has one or more shared traits; also called a uniform region (page 17)

formal sector *n.* businesses, enterprises, and other economic activities that have government supervision, monitoring, and protection, and are also taxed (page 522)

free trade zone (FTZ) *n.* a relatively large geographical area within a country in which businesses pay few or no tariffs on goods to encourage or facilitate its role in international trade (page 559)

friction of distance *n.* a concept that states that the longer a journey is, the more time, effort, and cost it will involve (pages 10, 115)

functional region *n.* an area organized by its function around a focal point, or the center of an interest or activity (page 17)

G

galactic city model *n.* a model of urban development depicting a city where economic activity has moved from the central business district toward loose coalitions of other urban areas and suburbs; also known as the peripheral model (page 435)

Gender Development Index (GDI) *n.* a measurement that calculates gender disparity in the three basic dimensions of human development: health, knowledge, and standard of living (page 527)

gendered space *n.* a space designed and deliberately incorporated into the landscape to accommodate gender roles (page 164)

gender identity *n.* an individual's innermost concept of self as male, female, a blend of both, or neither (page 166)

Gender Inequality Index (GII) *n.* a measurement that calculates inequality based on three categories: reproductive health, empowerment, and labor-market participation (page 527)

genetically modified organism (GMO) *n.* a plant or animal with specific characteristics obtained through the manipulation of its genetic makeup (page 332)

gentrification *n.* the renovations and improvements conforming to middle-class preferences (page 167)

geographic information systems (GIS) *n.* a computer system that allows for the collection, organization, and display of geographic data for analysis (page 31)

geometric boundary *n.* a mathematically drawn boundary that typically follows lines of latitude and longitude or is a straight-line arc between two points (page 254)

gerrymandering *n.* the dividing of legislative boundaries to give one political party an advantage in elections (page 270)

globalization *n.* the expansion of economic, cultural, and political processes on a worldwide scale (page 20)

global positioning system (GPS) *n.* a network of satellites that orbit Earth and transmit location data to receivers, enabling users to pinpoint their exact location (page 34)

global supply chain *n.* a network of people, information, processes, and resources that work together to produce, handle, and distribute goods around the world (page 350)

gravity model *n.* a model that predicts the interaction between two or more places; geographers derived the model from Newton's law of universal gravitation (page 111)

greenbelt *n.* a ring of parkland, agricultural land, or other type of open space maintained around an urban area to limit sprawl (page 457)

Green Revolution *n.* movement beginning in the 1950s and 1960s in which scientists used knowledge of genetics to develop new high-yield strains of grain crops (page 333)

Gross Domestic Product (GDP) *n.* the total value of the goods and services produced by a country's citizens and companies within the country in a year (pages 507, 521)

Gross National Income (GNI) per capita *n.* the total value of goods and services globally produced by a country in a year divided by the country's population (page 521)

Gross National Product (GNP) *n.* the total value of the goods and services produced by a country's citizens and companies both domestically and internationally (page 521)

growth pole *n.* a place of economic activity clustered around one or more high-growth industries that stimulate economic gain by capitalizing on some special asset (page 550)

guest worker *n.* a migrant who travels to a new country as temporary labor (page 117)

H

hierarchical diffusion *n.* the spread of an idea or trait from a person or place of power or authority to other people or places (page 181)

Hinduism *n.* an ethnic religion that arose a few thousand years ago in South Asia and is closely tied to India (page 223)

human development *n.* the processes involved in the improvement of people's freedoms, rights, capabilities, choices, and material conditions (page 521)

Human Development Index (HDI) *n.* a measure that determines the overall development of a country by incorporating three key dimensions of human development: life expectancy at birth, access to education measured in expected and mean years of schooling, and standard of living measured by GNI per capita (page 525)

human geography *n.* the study of the processes that have shaped how humans understand, use, and alter Earth (page 7)

human migration *n.* the permanent movement of people from one place to another (pages 65, 111)

human trafficking *n.* defined by the United Nations as "the recruitment, transportation, harboring, or receipt of persons by improper means (such as force, abduction, fraud, or coercion)" (page 120)

hybrid *n.* the product created by breeding different varieties of species to enhance the most favorable characteristics (page 339)

I

identity *n.* the ways in which humans make sense of themselves and how they wish to be viewed by others (page 157)

immigration *n.* movement to a location (page 111)

imperialism *n.* the push to create an empire by exercising force or influence to control other nations or peoples (page 247)

inclusionary zoning law *n.* law that creates affordable housing by offering incentives for developers to set aside a minimum percentage of new housing construction to be allocated for low-income renters or buyers (page 466)

industrialization *n.* the process in which the interaction of social and economic factors causes the development of industries on a wide scale (page 495)

industrial park *n.* a collection of manufacturing facilities in a particular area that is typically found in suburbs and is located close to highways to facilitate movement of raw materials and finished products (page 517)

Industrial Revolution *n.* the radical change in manufacturing methods that began in Great Britain in the mid-18th century and was marked by the shift from small-scale, hand-crafted, muscle-powered production to power-driven mass production (page 495)

industry *n.* any economic activity using machinery on a large scale to process raw materials into products (page 495)

infant mortality rate (IMR) *n.* the number of deaths of children under the age of 1 per 1,000 live births (page 79)

infill *n.* redevelopment that identifies and develops vacant parcels of land within previously built areas (page 410)

informal sector *n.* any part of a country's economy that is outside of government monitoring or regulation; sometimes called the informal economy (page 522)

infrastructure *n.* the many systems and facilities that a country needs in order to function properly (page 339)

intensive agriculture *n.* an agricultural practice in which farmers expend a great deal of effort to produce as much yield as possible from an area of land (page 314)

internally displaced person *n.* person who has been forced to flee his or her home but remains within the country's borders (page 118)

internal migration *n.* movement within a country's borders (page 115)

international division of labor *n.* a pattern of production and labor in which different countries are engaged in distinct aspects of production (page 556)

interregional migration *n.* movement from one region of the country to another (page 128)

intervening obstacle *n.* an occurrence that holds migrants back (page 117)

intervening opportunity *n.* an occurrence that causes migrants to pause their journey by choice (page 117)

intraregional migration *n.* movement within one region of the country (page 128)

irredentism *n.* attempts by a state to acquire territories in neighboring states inhabited by people of the same nation (page 243)

Islam *n.* a universalizing religion based on the teachings of Muhammad that originated in the hearth of Mecca on the Arabian Peninsula in the seventh century (page 220)

Isolate *n.* a language that is unrelated to any other known language (page 202)

J

Judaism *n.* the world's first monotheistic religion, which developed among the Hebrew people of Southwest Asia about 4,000 years ago (page 224)

just-in-time delivery *n.* a system in which goods are delivered as needed so that companies keep in inventory only what is needed for near-term production (page 555)

K

kinship links *n.* networks of relatives and friends (page 129)

L

labor-market participation (LMP) *n.* rate that measures an economy's active labor force, calculated by taking the sum of all employed workers divided by the working age population (page 529)

land degradation *n.* long-term damage to the soil's ability to support life (page 103)

landforms *n.* the natural features of Earth's surface (page 64)

land tenure *n.* the legal rights, as defined by a society, associated with owning land (page 466)

language *n.* a distinct system of communication that is the carrier of human thoughts and cultural identities (page 161)

language branch *n.* a collection of languages within a language family that share a common origin and separated from other branches in the same family several thousand years ago (page 202)

language family *n.* a group of languages that share a common ancestral language from a particular hearth, or region of origin (page 201)

language group *n.* languages within a language branch that share a common ancestor in the relatively recent past and have vocabularies with a high degree of overlap (page 203)

Latin American city model *n.* a model of urban development depicting a city with a central business district, concentric rings, and sections stricken by poverty; also known as the Griffin-Ford model (page 435)

least-cost theory *n.* industrial location theory proposed by Alfred Weber suggesting that businesses locate their facilities in a particular place because that location minimizes the costs of production (page 512)

life expectancy *n.* the average number of years a person is expected to live (page 79)

linear settlement *n.* a rural settlement pattern in which houses and buildings form in a long line that usually follows a land feature or aligns along a transportation route (page 315)

lingua franca *n.* common language used among speakers of different languages (page 186)

location *n.* the position that a point or object occupies on Earth (page 8)

M

majority-minority district *n.* an electoral district in which the majority of voters are members of an ethnic or racial minority (page 270)

map scale *n.* the relationship of the size of the map to the size of the area it represents on Earth's surface (page 38)

market gardening *n.* a type of farming that produces fruits, vegetables, and flowers and typically serves a specific market or urban area (page 317)

Mediterranean agriculture *n.* an agricultural practice that consists of growing hardy trees and shrubs and raising sheep and goats (page 311)

megacity *n.* a city with a population of more than 10 million (page 420)

mental maps *n.* internalized representations of portions of Earth's surface (page 8)

mentifact *n.* a central, enduring element of a culture that reflects its shared ideas, values, knowledge, and beliefs (page 153)

metacity *n.* a city with a population of more than 20 million (page 420)

metropolitan area *n.* a city and the surrounding areas that are influenced economically and culturally by the city (page 403)

microloan *n.* a very small short-term loan with low interest intended to help people in need (page 537)

mixed crop and livestock systems *n.* a type of farming in which both crops and livestock are raised for profit (page 317)

mixed-use development (MUD) *n.* a single planned development designed to include multiple uses, such as residential, retail, educational, recreational, industrial, and office spaces (page 453)

mixed-use zoning *n.* zoning that permits multiple land uses in the same space or structure (page 454)

mobility *n.* all types of movement from one location to another, whether temporary or permanent or over short or long distances (page 111)

model *n.* a representation of reality that presents significant features or relationships in a generalized form (page 10)

monocropping *n.* the cultivation of one or two crops that are rotated seasonally (page 316)

monoculture *n.* the agricultural system of planting one crop or raising one type of animal annually (page 316)

mortality *n.* deaths as a component of population change (page 78)

multiculturalism *n.* a situation in which different cultures live together without assimilating (page 196)

multinational state *n.* a country with various ethnicities and cultures living inside its borders (page 243)

multiple-nuclei model *n.* a model of urban development depicting a city where growth occurs around the progressive integration of multiple nodes, not around one central business district (page 433)

multiplier effect *n.* the economic effect in which a change creates a larger change, such as when a new manufacturing plant grows the economy by giving rise to more related jobs and services (page 558)

multistate nation *n.* people who share a cultural or ethnic background but live in more than one country (page 243)

N

nation *n.* a cultural entity made up of people who have forged a common identity through a shared language, religion, heritage, or ethnicity — often all four of these (page 242)

nation-state *n.* a politically organized and recognized territory composed of a group of people who consider themselves to be a nation (page 242)

neocolonialism *n.* the use of economic, political, cultural, or other pressures to control or influence other countries, especially former dependencies (page 245)

neoliberalism *n.* beliefs that favor free-market capitalism in which trade has no constraints from government (page 548)

Neo-Malthusian *adj.* describing the theory related to the idea that population growth is unsustainable and that the future population cannot be supported by Earth's resources (page 92)

net migration *n.* the difference between the number of emigrants and immigrants in a location, such as a city or a country (page 111)

New Urbanism *n.* a school of thought that promotes designing growth to limit the amount of urban sprawl and preserve nature and usable farmland (page 454)

node *n.* the focal point of a functional region (pages 17, 433)

nomadic herding *n.* a type of agriculture based on people moving their domesticated animals seasonally or as needed to allow the best grazing (page 318)

O

offshore outsourcing *n.* the condition or one or more aspects of production are moved to an organization in another country (page 556)

overpopulation *n.* a term used to describe the condition in which population growth outstrips the resources needed to support life (page 92)

P

pattern *n.* the way in which things are arranged in a particular space (page 9)

perceptual region *n.* a type of region that reflects people's feelings and attitudes about a place; also called a vernacular region (page 18)

periphery *n.* classification of a country or region that has less wealth, lower education levels, and less sophisticated technologies and also tends to have an unstable government and poor health systems (page 21)

physical geography *n.* the study of natural processes and the distribution of features in the environment, such as landforms, plants, animals, soil, and climate (page 7)

physiological density *n.* the total number of people per unit of arable land (page 67)

GLOSSARY

pilgrimage *n.* a journey to a holy place for spiritual reasons (page 161)

place *n.* a location on Earth that is distinguished by its physical and human characteristics (page 8)

placemaking *n.* a community-driven process in which people collaborate to create a place where they can live, work, play, and learn (page 168)

plantation agriculture *n.* a type of large-scale commercial farming of one particular crop grown for markets often distant from the plantation (page 317)

political geography *n.* the study of the ways in which the world is organized as a reflection of the power different groups hold over territory (page 241)

popular culture *n.* the widespread behaviors, beliefs, and practices of ordinary people in society at a given point in time (page 154)

population density *n.* the number of people occupying a unit of land (page 67)

population distribution *n.* where people live in a geographic area (page 63)

population pyramid *n.* a graph that shows the age-sex distribution of a given population (page 81)

possibilism *n.* theory of human-environment interaction that states that humans have the ability to adapt the physical environment to their needs (page 10)

post-Fordism *n.* system focused on small-scale batch production for a specialized market and flexibility that allows for a quick response to changes in the market (page 555)

postindustrial economy *n.* an economic pattern marked by predominant tertiary sector employment—with a good share of quaternary and quinary jobs (page 506)

postmodern architecture *n.* a building style that emerged as a reaction to "modern" designs, and values diversity in design (page 159)

precision agriculture *n.* a farming management concept that uses technology to apply inputs with pinpoint accuracy to specific parts of fields to maximize crop yields, reduce waste, and preserve the environment (page 373)

primary sector *n.* economic sector associated with removing or harvesting products from the earth; includes agriculture, fishing, forestry, mining or quarrying, and extracting liquids or gas (page 504)

primate city *n.* the largest city in a country, which far exceeds the next city in population size and importance (page 414)

pronatalist *adj.* describing attitudes or policies that encourage childbearing as a means of spurring population growth (page 99)

pull factor *n.* a positive cause that attracts someone to a new location (page 112)

push factor *n.* a negative cause that compels someone to leave a location (page 112)

Q

qualitative *adj.* involving data that is descriptive of a research subject and is often based on people's opinions (page 29)

quantitative *adj.* involving data that can be measured by numbers (page 29)

quaternary sector *n.* economic sector that is a subset of tertiary sector activities that require workers to process and handle information and environmental technology (page 504)

quinary sector *n.* economic sector that is a subset of the quaternary sector; involves the very top leaders in government, science, universities, nonprofits, health care, culture, and media (page 505)

quota *n.* limit on the number of immigrants allowed into the country each year (page 129)

R

range *n.* in central place theory, the distance that someone is willing to travel for a good or service (page 414)

rank-size rule *n.* explanation of size of cities within a country; states the second largest city will be one-half the size of the largest, the third largest will be one-third the size of the largest, and so on (page 413)

rate of natural increase (RNI) *n.* rate at which a population grows as the result of the difference between the crude birth rate and the crude death rate (page 87)

raw materials *n.* any metals, wood or other plant products, animal products, or other substances that are used to make intermediate or finished goods (page 495)

reapportionment *n.* the redistribution of representative seats among states based on shifts in population (page 269)

redistricting *n.* the redrawing of internal territorial and political boundaries (page 270)

redlining *n.* practice by which a financial institution such as a bank refuses to offer home loans on the basis of a neighborhood's racial or ethnic makeup (page 460)

reference map *n.* a map that focuses on the location of places (page 40)

refugee *n.* a person who is forced to leave his or her country for fear of persecution or death (page 118)

region *n.* an area of Earth's surface with certain characteristics that make it distinct yet cohesive from other areas (page 16)

regional planning *n.* planning conducted at a regional scale that seeks to coordinate the development of housing, transportation, urban infrastructure, and economic activities (page 476)

relative direction *n.* direction based on a person's perception, such as left, right, up, or down (page 37)

relative distance *n.* distance determined in relation to other places or objects (page 37)

relative location *n.* a description of where a place is in relation to other places or features (page 8)

relic *n.* a former boundary that no longer has an official function (page 255)

religion *n.* a system of spiritual beliefs that helps form cultural perceptions, attitudes, beliefs, and values (page 161)

relocation diffusion *n.* the spread of culture traits through the movement of people (page 135)

remittance *n.* money earned by an emigrant abroad and sent back to his or her home country (page 134)

remote sensing *n.* collecting or analyzing data from a location without making physical contact (page 32)

repatriate *v.* to return to one's home country (page 122)

reservoir *n.* artificial lake used to store water (page 360)

S

safe space *n.* a space of acceptance for people who are sometimes marginalized by society (page 167)

salinization *n.* the process by which water-soluble salts build up in the soil, which limits the ability of crops to absorb water (page 364)

scale *n.* the area of the world being studied (page 15)

second agricultural revolution *n.* a change in farming practices, marked by new tools and techniques, that diffused from Britain and the Low Countries starting in the early 18th century (page 331)

secondary sector *n.* economic sector associated with the production of goods from raw materials; includes manufacturing, processing, and construction (page 504)

sect *n.* a relatively small group that has separated from an established denomination (page 171)

sector model *n.* a model of urban development depicting a city with wedge-shaped sectors and divisions emanating from the central business district, generally along transit routes (page 433)

secularized *v.* focused on worldly rather than spiritual concerns (page 225)

self-determination *n.* the right of all people to choose their own political status (page 247)

semiautonomous *adj.* describing a region that is given partial authority to govern its territories independently from the national government (page 244)

semi-periphery *n.* classification of a country or region that has qualities of both core and peripheral areas and is often in the process of industrializing (page 21)

sense of place *n.* the subjective feelings and memories people associate with a geographic location (page 168)

sequent occupance *n.* the notion that successive societies leave behind their cultural imprint, a collection of evidence about human character and experiences within a geographic region, which shapes the cultural landscape (page 158)

sex ratio *n.* the proportion of males to females in a population (page 75)

shatterbelt *n.* a region where states form, join, and break up because of ongoing, sometimes violent, conflicts among parties and because they are caught between the interests of more powerful outside states (page 246)

shifting cultivation *n.* the agricultural practice of growing crops or grazing animals on a piece of land for a year or two, then abandoning that land when the nutrients have been depleted from the soil and moving to a new piece of land where the process is repeated (page 318)

Sikhism *n.* the newest universalizing religion; founded by Guru Nanak, who lived from 1469 to 1539, in the Punjab region of northwestern India (page 222)

site *n.* a place's absolute location, as well as its physical characteristics, such as the landforms, climate, and resources (page 8)

situation *n.* location of a place in relation to other places or its surrounding features (page 8)

skills gap *n.* a shortage of people trained in a particular industry (page 133)

slash and burn *n.* a method of agriculture in which existing vegetation is cut down and burned off before new seeds are sown; often used when clearing land (page 318)

slow-growth city *n.* city where planners have used smart-growth policies to decrease the rate at which the city grows outward (page 455)

smart-growth policy *n.* policy implemented to create sustainable communities by placing development in convenient locations and designing it to be more efficient and environmentally responsible (page 454)

sociofact *n.* a structure or organization of a culture that influences social behavior (page 153)

Southeast Asian city model *n.* a model of urban development depicting a city oriented around a port and lacking a formal central business district, growing outward in concentric rings and along multiple nodes (page 437)

sovereignty *n.* the right of a government to control and defend its territory and determine what happens within its borders (page 241)

space *n.* the area between two or more things (page 9)

spatial perspective *n.* geographic perspective that focuses on how people live on Earth, how they organize themselves, and why the events of human societies occur where they do (page 7)

special economic zone (SEZ) *n.* an area within a country that offers more favorable economic regulations (such as tax benefits or no tariffs) to attract foreign businesses (page 558)

squatter settlement *n.* an informal housing area beset with overcrowding and poverty that features temporary homes often made of wood scraps or metal sheeting (page 435)

stages of economic growth *n.* a model that suggests that all countries can be categorized on a spectrum from traditional to modern and that to become modern, countries need to pass through distinct stages of economic growth in succession (page 540)

state *n.* a politically organized independent territory with a government, defined borders, and a permanent population; a country (page 241)

stateless nation *n.* a people united by culture, language, history, and tradition but not possessing a state (page 244)

step migration *n.* series of smaller moves to get to the ultimate destination (page 117)

stimulus diffusion *n.* the process by which a cultural trait or idea spreads to another culture or region but is modified to adapt to the new culture (page 182)

subsequent boundary *n.* a border drawn in an area that has been settled and where cultural landscapes exist or are in the process of being established (page 254)

subsistence agriculture *n.* an agricultural practice that provides crops or livestock to feed one's family and close community using fewer mechanical resources and more people to care for the crops and livestock (pages 68, 312)

suburbanization *n.* the shifting of population away from cities into surrounding suburbs (page 377)

suburbs *n.* less densely populated residential and commercial areas surrounding a city (page 403)

superimposed boundary *n.* a border drawn over existing accepted borders by an outside or conquering force (page 254)

supranational organization *n.* an alliance of three or more states that work together in pursuit of common goals or to address an issue or challenge (page 283)

sustainability *n.* the use of Earth's land and natural resources in ways that ensure they will continue to be available in the future. (page 10)

sustainable development *n.* development that meets the needs of the present without compromising the ability of future generations to meet their own needs (page 23)

syncretism *n.* process of innovation combining different cultural features into something new (page 195)

T

tariff *n.* a tax or duty to be paid on a particular import or export (page 346)

temperate climate *n.* a climate with moderate temperatures and adequate precipitation amounts (page 64)

terracing *n.* the process of carving parts of a hill or mountainside into small, level growing plots (page 359)

territoriality *n.* the attempt to influence or control people and events by delimiting and asserting control over a geographic area; the connection of people, their culture, and their economic systems to the land (page 245)

tertiary sector *n.* economic sector that includes a host of activities that involve the transport, storage, marketing, and selling of goods or services; also called the service sector (page 504)

thematic map *n.* any map that focuses on one or more variables to show a relationship between geographic data (page 40)

theory *n.* a system of ideas intended to explain certain phenomena (page 21)

third agricultural revolution *n.* a shift to further mechanization in agriculture through the development of new technology and advances that began in the early 20th century and continues to the present day (page 332)

third place *n.* a communal space that is separate from home (first place) or work (second place) (page 167)

threshold *n.* in central place theory, the number of people needed to support a business (page 414)

time-space compression *n.* a key geographic principle that describes the ways in which modern transportation and communication technology have allowed humans to travel and communicate over long distances quicker and easier (page 10)

topography *n.* the representation of Earth's surface to show natural and man-made features, especially their relative positions and elevations (page 31)

toponym *n.* a place name (page 161)

total fertility rate (TFR) *n.* the average number of children one woman in a given country or region will have during her child-bearing years (ages 15 to 49) (page 78)

traditional architecture *n.* an established building style of different cultures, religions, and places (page 158)

traditional culture *n.* the long-established behaviors, beliefs, and practices passed down from generation to generation (page 155)

traditional zoning *n.* zoning that creates separate zones based on land-use type or economic function such as various categories of residential (low-, medium-, or high-density), commercial, or industrial (page 454)

transhumance *n.* the movement of herds between pastures at cooler, higher elevations during the summer months and lower elevations during the winter (pages 116, 318)

transnational migration *n.* international migration in which people retain strong cultural, emotional, and financial ties with their countries of origin (page 115)

transportation-oriented development *n.* the creation of dense, walkable, pedestrian-oriented, mixed-use communities centered around or located near a transit station (page 453)

U

unitary state *n.* an organization of a state in which power is concentrated in a central government (page 261)

United Nations Convention on the Law of the Sea (UNCLOS) *n.* the international agreement that established the structure of maritime boundaries (page 256)

universalizing religion *n.* a religion that tries to appeal to all humans and is open to membership by everyone (page 219)

urban area *n.* a city and its surrounding suburbs (page 403)

urban growth boundary *n.* a boundary that separates urban land uses from rural land uses by limiting how far a city can expand (page 455)

urbanization *n.* urban growth and development (page 88)

urban renewal *n.* the nationwide movement that developed in the 1950s and 1960s when U.S. cities were given massive federal grants to tear down and clear out slums as a means of rebuilding their downtowns (page 470)

urban sprawl *n.* areas of poorly planned, low-density development surrounding a city (page 409)

V

vernacular region *n.* a type of region that reflects people's feelings and attitudes about a place; also called a perceptual region (page 18)

vertical integration *n.* the combining of a company's ownership of and control over more than one stage of the production process of goods (page 344)

voluntary migration *n.* type of migration in which people make the choice to move to a new place (page 115)

von Thünen model *n.* a model that suggests that perishability of the product and transport costs to the market each factor into the location of agricultural land use and activity (page 348)

W

walkability *n.* a measure of how safe, convenient, and efficient it is to walk in an urban environment (page 453)

wetland *n.* area of land that is covered by water or saturated with water (page 362)

women's empowerment *n.* women's options and access to participate fully in the social and economic spheres of a society (page 528)

world city *n.* a city that wields political, cultural, and economic influence on a global scale (page 421)

world system theory *n.* theory describing the spatial and functional relationships between countries in the world economy; categorizes countries as part of a hierarchy consisting of the core, periphery, and semi-periphery (page 21)

Z

zone *n.* an area that exists for a specific purpose (page 431)

zone of abandonment *n.* area that has been largely deserted due to lack of jobs, declines in land value, and falling demand (page 462)

zoning *n.* the process of dividing a city or urban area into zones with which only certain land uses are permitted (page 443)

INDEX

"f" indicates figures and images
"t" indicates tables
"m" indicates maps

A

AAE. *See* African-American English
ABR. *See* adolescent birth rate
Abraham, 8.4 p. 220, 8.4 p. 224
absolute direction, 2.3 p. 37
absolute distance, 2.3 p. 37
absolute location, 1.1 p. 8
Abu Sarah, Aziz, U4 p. 238, U4 p. 239f
Abuja, Nigeria, 16.3 pp. 444–446
accountability, 16.3 p. 447
acculturation, 7.3 pp. 194–195
ACI Systems Alemania, U7 p. 568
Addario, Lynsey, 5.3 p. 126
adherents, 6.4 p. 171
Adjder oasis (Algeria), 12.2 p. 323f
administration of borders, 9.2 p. 245f
adobe, 6.2 pp. 158–159
adolescent birth rate (ABR), 19.2
    p. 528, U7 p. 574f
aerial photography, 2.2 p. 30
affordable housing, 17.2 pp. 465–466
Afghanistan
    artifacts and, U3 p. 150
    communication technology and, 11.1
        p. 278
    education and, U7 p. 492
    gender inequality and, 19.2 p. 527,
        19.3 p. 536f
    human development and, 19.1
        pp. 523–524
    hunger, conflict and, 14.3 p. 379
    photojournalism documenting life in,
        5.3 p. 126
Africa
    conservation, sustainability and, 14.1
        p. 366, 14.1 p. 366f
    cultural diffusion and, 7.2 p. 185, 7.2
        p. 186f
    Great Green Wall initiative and, 14.1
        p. 369
    Green Revolution, women and, 12.4
        p. 335
    imperialism and, 9.3 p. 249
    neocolonialism and, 9.2 p. 245
    perennialism and, U5 p. 304
African Americans. *See also* slavery
    electoral districts and, 10.2 p. 270,
        10.2 p. 272, 10.2 p. 273f
    Great Migration and, 5.4 p. 129, 5.4
        p. 129f
    housing discrimination and, 17.2
        pp. 460–462
African city model, 16.1 p. 436f, 16.1
    p. 437, U6 p. 488f
African diaspora, 7.1 p. 179, 7.1 p. 180,
    7.1 p. 184
African Union, 11.2 p. 284f, 11.2 p. 285,
    11.2 p. 286t
African-American English (AAE), 6.4
    p. 170
Africatown, Alabama, 7.1 p. 180
Afrikaans language, 7.2 p. 185
age dependency, 3.3 p. 75
Age of Exploration, U6 p. 487f
age-sex distributions, 3.4 pp. 81–82,
    3.4 p. 81f, 3.4 p. 83f, 4.4 p. 105f, U2
    p. 142f
agglomeration, 18.3 pp. 513–514, 18.3
    p. 513f, 18.3 p. 514f, U7 p. 571f
aging population, 4.4 pp. 104–107. *See
    also* dependency ratios
AGRA. *See* Alliance for a Green
    Revolution in Africa
agribusiness, 13.1 p. 339, 13.2 pp. 343–
    344, 13.2 p. 344f, 14.1 p. 368
agricultural biodiversity, 14.2
    pp. 371–372

agricultural density, 3.1 pp. 68–69, 3.1
    p. 68t
agricultural hearths, 12.3 pp. 324–326,
    12.3 p. 326m
agricultural landscapes, 14.1 p. 359
agricultural revolutions
    first, 12.4 pp. 329–331
    fourth, 12.4 p. 333
    second, 12.4 pp. 331–332, 18.1
        p. 500–501
    third, 12.4 pp. 332–334
agriculture
    in Australia, U5 p. 393f
    biodiversity and, U5 p. 397f
    census data on, 2.2 p. 30
    climate and, 12.1 pp. 309–310, U5
        p. 392f
    climate regions and, 12.1 pp. 310–311
    commercial, 12.2 p. 312, 12.2
        pp. 314–317
    commodity chains and, 13.2
        pp. 344–345
    conservation and sustainability and,
        14.1 pp. 365–366
    controversial innovations in, 14.2
        pp. 370–373
    dairying and ranching industries and,
        13.1 p. 342
    diet and, 14.2 p. 376
    diffusion of, 12.3 pp. 326–329, 12.3
        p. 327m
    economic development and, 18.2
        p. 506f
    economic forces and, 13.1
        pp. 339–340
    economic impacts of, 14.3
        pp. 381–382
    environmental alteration and, 14.1
        pp. 359–363
    environmental consequences of, 14.1
        pp. 363–364
    environmental factors and, 12.1
        pp. 307–308
    extensive, 12.2 p. 318, 12.2 p. 319
    family vs. corporate control of, 13.2
        pp. 343–344
    first revolution in, 12.4 pp. 329–331
    food choices and, 14.2 pp. 374–376
    global distribution of, 12.2 pp. 320–
        321, U5 p. 395f, U5 p. 396m
    global trade patterns and, 13.4
        pp. 353–354
    Great Migration and, 5.4 p. 129
    hardiness zones and, U5 p. 392f
    hearths of, 12.3 pp. 324–326
    human migration and, 5.1 p. 112
    infrastructure and, 13.4 pp. 351–353
    intensive, 12.2 pp. 314–317, 12.2 p. 319
    interdependence and, 13.4
        pp. 350–351
    local conversations and, U5 p. 304
    overview of, 12.1 p. 307, 12.1 p. 307m
    perennialism and, U5 p. 304
    political relationships and, 13.4 p. 353
    population change and, 4.1 p. 89
    pricing and policies and, 13.2
        pp. 345–346
    rural settlement patterns and, 12.2
        p. 315
    rural survey methods and, 12.2 p. 313
    second revolution in, 12.4 pp. 331–
        332, 18.1 pp. 500–501
    societal consequences of, 14.1 p. 368
    subsistence, 12.2 p. 312, 12.2 p. 314
    sustainable, 12.4 p. 334, C14 p. 358f,
        14.1 pp. 365–366, 14.2 pp. 370–372
    third revolution in, 12.4, pp. 332–334
    women and, 12.4 p. 335
agroecosystems, 14.1 p. 359
Ainu language, 8.2 p. 212
air, 12.1 p. 308
air pollution, 17.3 pp. 472–474
Airline Flight Routes map, 1.2 p. 17m
airline industry, 20.1 p. 548
airplanes, 18.1 p. 499
airports, 16.3 p. 444
Akinrolabu, Samuel, 17.2 p. 466
al Qaeda, 11.3 p. 288
Alabama, 1.2 p. 15m, 7.1 p. 180
Alahabad, Uttar Pradesh, India, 8.2
    p. 212
Alaska, 6.3 pp. 163–164
al-Assad, Bashar, 5.3 p. 125
Aleppo, Syria, 15.1 p. 404
Alexander the Great, 7.2 p. 185

Alexandria, Egypt, 7.2 p. 185
Algeria, 11.2 p. 285, 12.2 p. 323f, U7
    p. 570f
Ali, Hamidah, U3 p. 229
alien commercial zones, 16.1 p. 437
Allard, William, 7.3 pp. 192–193
Alliance for a Green Revolution in
    Africa (AGRA), 14.1 p. 366
alliances, 11.2 p. 283, 15.2 p. 409
Allied Forces, 11.2 p. 283
alluvial soils, 3.1 p. 64
Alonso, William, 12.2 p. 312
Altiplano-Puna Plateau (Andes
    Mountains), U7 p. 568
altitudinal zonation, 12.1 p. 308, 12.1
    p. 308f
aluminum, 13.2 p. 346
Amazon (company), 18.2 p. 505
Amazon Rain Forest, 14.1 p. 364, 14.1
    p. 364f
Amazon River, 2.4 p. 47, 14.1 p. 365
Amazon River Basin, U1 p. 57m, 20.3
    p. 560, 20.3 p. 564, 20.3 p. 565
American Community Survey, 2.2 p. 30
American flag, 11.3 p. 289
American Indians, 5.4 p. 128, 6.1
    p. 156, 6.2 p. 158, 9.2 p. 244. *See also*
    indigenous peoples
American Line Islands, U1 p. 4
AmeriCorps Urban Safety Project, 2.2
    p. 33
Amish communities, 6.3 p. 163, 17.1
    p. 456
Amsterdam, Netherlands, 16.2
    pp. 439–440, 16.3 p. 446
Amuesha people, 20.3 p. 565
Anaheim, California, 15.2 p. 410
Anatolian hearth theory, 8.2 p. 206, 8.2
    p. 208, 8.2 p. 208f
ancestral languages, 8.1 p. 201–202
Andean highland agricultural
    hearth, 12.3 p. 326m
Andes Mountain region, 6.4 p. 172, U7
    pp. 568–569
anemia, 14.3 p. 378
Angkor Wat (Cambodia), 8.3 p. 218
Angola, 19.4 p. 542
Anna Creek cattle station
    (Australia), U5 p. 393f
Annan, Kofi, 12.4 p. 333
annexation, 11.3 p. 290, U4 p. 296m
Antarctica, 20.3 p. 564
antecedent boundaries, 9.4 p. 254, U4
    p. 296m
antibiotics, 14.2 p. 372
antibullying laws, U3 p. 231m
Anti-Discrimination Center, 17.2 p. 462
antinatalist policies, 4.1 p. 89, 4.3
    p. 99–102, 4.3 p. 99f, 4.3 p. 102f
Antoniou, Anna, 10.1 p. 262
apartheid, 16.1 p. 438
apartment buildings, 16.2 p. 439
Apple (company), 18.2 p. 505, 20.2
    p. 551f–552
aquaculture, 14.2 p. 372, 14.2 p. 376
aquifers, 3.1 p. 65, 14.1 p. 360m, 14.1
    p. 362
Arab Academy of Damascus, 8.2 p. 211
Arab League. *See* League of Arab States
Arab Spring, 1.3 p. 20, 5.3 p. 125
Arabic language, 8.1 p. 201, 8.2 p. 206,
    8.2 p. 211
arable land, 3.1 p. 67–68
Aral Sea, 12.4 p. 334, 14.1 p. 360, 14.1
    p. 361f
Aralkum Desert, 14.1 p. 361f
architecture, 6.2 pp. 158–159, 6.2 p. 161
Arctic Council, 11.2 p. 285, 11.2 p. 286t
Argentina, 14.1 p. 368, 19.1 p. 524, U7
    p. 568
arithmetic density, 3.1 p. 67, 3.1 p. 68t,
    3.2 p. 72
Arkansas, 1.2 p. 15m

Arlington County, Virginia, 17.1 p. 453,
    17.1 p. 454
Armas, Carlos Castillo, 9.3 p. 247
Armenia, 6.4 p. 175
arranged marriages, 7.2 p. 190
artifacts, 6.1 p. 153, 6.3 p. 163
artificial intelligence, 18.1 p. 503
artisans, 12.4 pp. 330–331
Aryan people, 8.4 p. 224, 11.1 p. 278,
    11.3 p. 290
Asakusa Culture Tourist Information
    Center, U6 p. 482
asbestos, 4.2 p. 95
Ashoka, 8.4 p. 222
Asia Foundation, 19.3 p. 536f
Asmara, Eritrea, 15.3 p. 415f
assalamu alaikum, U3 p. 229
assembly lines, 18.1 p. 498, 18.3 p. 514,
    20.2 p. 555
assimilation, 7.3 p. 195, 7.3 p. 195f
Association of Southeast Asian
    Nations (ASEAN), 11.2 p. 283, 11.2
    p. 286t
asylum, 5.2 p. 118, 5.2 p. 121, 5.3
    pp. 122–125, 5.4 pp. 130–132
Atlanta, Georgia, 16.3 p. 444
Atlantic fall line, 15.1 p. 404, 15.1
    p. 404f, 18.1 p. 498
at-large elections, 10.2 p. 271
augmented reality, 18.1 p. 503
austerity measures, 11.2 p. 286, 20.2
    p. 554
Australia
    cattle ranching in, U5 p. 393f
    cities in, U6 p. 484f
    economic development and, 18.2
        p. 507, 18.2 p. 508f
    human development and, 19.1 p. 526f
    Sustainable Development Goals
        and, 20.3 p. 562
Austria, 20.3 p. 563f
Austronesian language family, 8.2
    pp. 209–210, 8.2 p. 210m
automation, U7 pp. 490–491f, 18.1
    p. 499
automobile manufacturing
    agglomeration and, 18.3 p. 513f, 18.3
        p. 514
    automation and, U7 pp. 490–491f
    decentralization and, 16.1 p. 434f,
        18.3 p. 512f
    Detroit, Michigan and, 15.2 p. 408,
        16.1 p. 434f, 18.3 p. 512f, 18.3
        pp. 513–514, 18.3 p. 513m
    financial crisis of 2007-2008 and, 20.2
        p. 553
    outsourcing and, U7 p. 575f
    post-Fordism and, 20.2 pp. 555–556
    relocation of, 18.3 p. 517
    Second Industrial Revolution and, 18.1
        p. 499
    urbanization and, 15.2 p. 409
autonomous regions, 9.2 p. 244
autonomous vehicles, 17.3 p. 478
autonomy, 11.3 p. 290
avocados, 13.1 p. 340, 14.2 p. 376, 14.2
    p. 376f
Aymara people, U7 p. 568
Ayodhya, 8.3 p. 218
Azerbaijan, 6.4 p. 175
azimuthal projections, 2.3 p. 38, 2.3
    p. 39m, 2.3 p. 39t
Aztecs, 7.2 p. 185, 15.1 p. 405

B

Babri Masjid (mosque), 8.3 p. 218
Baby Boom, 4.1 p. 89, 4.4 p. 107
Bach, Jaime, U3 p. 151f
Bachelet, Michelle, 19.3 p. 538f
Baku, Azerbaijan, 17.1 p. 458f
bald eagles, 11.3 p. 289
Balfour Declaration of 1917, 8.4 p. 225
Bali, 8.4 p. 224
Balkan Peninsula, 9.2 p. 246, 9.3 p. 247,
    U4 p. 296m
Baltimore, Maryland, 14.3 p. 380

Ban Tat, Vietnam, 14.1 p. 359

banana plantations, 12.2 p. 320m, 12.3 p. 328, U5 p. 395m

Bangalore, India, 15.2 p. 408

Bangkok, Thailand, 15.3 p. 414

Bangladesh
  agriculture and, 14.1 pp. 365–366
  climate and displacement from, 5.3 p. 124, U2 pp. 140–141
  imbalanced global wealth distribution and, 20.2 p. 552
  Rohingya refugees in, 5.2 pp. 118–120, 5.2 p. 120f
  textile industry and, 18.3 p. 513, 18.3 p. 517

banking industry, 20.1 p. 550, 20.2 p. 552, 20.2 p. 553

banlieues, 16.2 p. 440

bar mitzvah celebrations, 6.3 p. 166f

Barcelona, Spain, 1.1 p. 8

barley, 13.3 p. 349

Barton, Tom, U1 p. 51

basemaps, 2.3 p. 43

basic industry, 15.2 p. 409

Basij-Rasikh, Shabana, U7 p. 492, U7 p. 493f

Basque Country, Spain, 11.1 pp. 277–278

Basque language, 8.1 p. 202

Basque people, 6.4 p. 170, 6.4 p. 171f, 9.2 p. 244

bat mitzvah celebrations, 6.3 p. 166f

batteries, U7 pp. 568–569

Baxter Village (South Carolina), 17.1 p. 459

beef industry, 14.1 p. 368

beekeeping, 19.3 p. 534

Begum, Sahela, U2 p. 141

Beijing, China, 16.2 p. 441, 17.3 p. 474

Belarus, 11.3 p. 290, 11.3 p. 290f

Belgium, 11.1 p. 280, 18.1 p. 498, 19.2 p. 528

Belize, 8.2 p. 209m, 9.4 p. 249

Belo Monte Dam (Brazil), 18.2 pp. 509–511

Benetton, 20.2 p. 556

Bengali language, 8.2 p. 206

Bengaluru, India, 15.2 p. 408

Berlin Conference, 9.4 p. 249, 9.4 p. 254, 9.4 p. 254f

Berlin Wall, 5.4 p. 130, 9.4 p. 255f

Berry, John W., 7.3 p. 195

Bestor, Ted, U6 p. 482

beta-carotene, 12.4 p. 333

between-farm mixing, 12.2 p. 317

Bey, Yaslin, U3 p. 229

bicycles, U7 p. 493f, 20.1 pp. 550–551

bicycling, 16.3 p. 446, 16.3 p. 446f, 16.3 p. 449f, 17.1 p. 453

bid-rent theory, 12.2 p. 312, U5 p. 394f, 16.1 p. 431, 16.1 p. 431f, 16.2 p. 443, U6 p. 485f

Big Ears National Monument (Utah), 6.4 p. 169f

bilingual countries, 8.2 p. 213

Bill and Melinda Gates Foundation, 12.4 p. 335, 14.1 p. 366

biodigesters, 16.3 p. 445

biodiversity
  agriculture and, 14.1 p. 365
  crop diversity and, 14.2 p. 371f
  Okavango River Basin and, 1.1 p. 14
  pastoral nomadism and, 14.1 p. 362
  protecting in Earth's oceans, U1 p. 4
  threats to, U5 p. 397f

biofuels, 14.3 p. 377

biogas, 16.3 p. 445

bioluminescence, 17.3 p. 478

biotechnology, 14.2 pp. 370–372

Birmingham, Alabama, 18.1 p. 499

birth rates, U7 p. 574f. See also crude birth rate

Black Death, 4.1 p. 90, 4.2 p. 94

blight, 16.2 p. 440, 17.1 p. 459

blockbusting, 17.2 p. 400, 17.2 p. 401

blue jeans, 7.1 p. 181

bluegrass music, 7.3 p. 196

blues music, 5.5 p. 137m

boarding schools, U7 p. 492

Bodh Gaya (India), 6.4 p. 173

Bogota, Colombia, 16.3 p. 446

Boiling River Project, 20.3 p. 565

Bolivia, U3 p. 149, 9.4 p. 256, 19.2 p. 528, U7 pp. 568–569

boll weevils, 5.4 p. 129

Bollywood, 15.4 p. 422f

Bonton Farms (Dallas), 17.2 p. 469

boomburbs, 15.2 p. 410

borders. See also boundaries
  of Canadian provinces, U4 p. 296m
  conflicts over, U4 p. 298m
  Mexico-United States, 5.4 p. 131, 5.4 p. 131f, 9.2 p. 245f, 9.3 p. 249f
  overview of, U4 p. 237
  walls and, 5.4 p. 131, 5.4 p. 131f

Borlaug, Norman, 12.4 p. 333

Borneo, 9.4 p. 254

Borough Market (London), 14.2 p. 374f

Bos, Heleen, U5 p. 391

Bosco Verticale (Milan), 17.3 p. 479, 17.3 p. 479f

Boserup, Ester, 4.2 p. 92

Bosnia, 9.3 p. 247

Boston, Massachusetts, C1 p. 6f, 16.2 p. 440f, 16.2 p. 443

Boston Brahmin dialect, 6.4 p. 170

Boulder, Colorado, 17.1 p. 455, 17.1 p. 457, 17.2 p. 466

boundaries. See also borders
  defining political, 9.4 pp. 249–250
  electoral geography and, 10.2 pp. 269–273, U4 p. 299m
  imperialism, colonialism and, 9.3 p. 247, 9.3 p. 249
  importance of, 9.4 p. 257
  of metropolitan areas, 15.4 p. 425f
  political power and, 9.2 pp. 244–246
  regional planning and, 17.3 p. 476
  regions and, 1.2 p. 16, 1.2 p. 18
  sovereignty and, 9.3 p. 247
  types of, 9.4 pp. 254–257
  world political map and, 9.2 pp. 241–244

Bracero Program, 5.1 p. 113, 5.2 p. 117

Brahman, 8.4 p. 224

brain drain, 5.5 p. 135

branches, religious, 6.4 p. 171

Brando, Marlon, 7.1 p. 181

Brazil. See also specific cities
  African culture in, 7.1 p. 184
  Belo Monte Dam and, 18.2 pp. 509–511
  biotechnology and, 14.2 p. 370f, 14.2 p. 371
  ecotourism and, 20.3 p. 564
  favelas of, 17.1 p. 455, 17.2 p. 465, 17.2 p. 465f
  fires in, 14.1 p. 364, 14.1 p. 364f
  income distribution in, 19.1 pp. 521–522
  natural resources and, 20.3 p. 560
  plantation agriculture and, 12.2 p. 317
  relocation diffusion and, 7.1 p. 181f
  secondary economic sector and, 18.2 p. 505
  Sustainable Development Goals and, 20.3 p. 562
  urbanization and, 17.3 p. 472

bread, 18.3 pp. 514–516

break-of-bulk points, 18.3 p. 514

Brexit, 11.2 p. 283, 11.2 p. 287, U4 p. 300m, 13.4 p. 353

bridges, 15.1 p. 404

Britain. See Great Britain

British East India Company, 7.2 p. 185, 8.2 p. 209m, U4 p. 298m

British Honduras, 9.4 p. 249

Brooklyn Grange (New York City), 17.2 p. 469f

Brooks Mountain Range (Alaska), 6.3 pp. 163–164

Brown v. Board of Education, 10.1 p. 267

brownfields, 17.3 p. 476

brownstone apartments, 16.2 p. 443

Bruges, Belgium, 15.2 p. 408f, 15.2 p. 409

Brunei, 11.2 p. 285, 19.1 p. 523

Brussels, Belgium, 11.1 p. 280

bubonic plague, 4.1 p. 90, 4.2 p. 94

Buddha, 6.4 p. 173, 8.4 p. 221

Buddhism
  cultural landscapes and, 6.2 p. 161
  diffusion of, 7.2 p. 187, 8.3 p. 214, 8.3 p. 215f, 8.4 pp. 221–223, 8.4 p. 221f

buffalo worms, 14.3 p. 382f

buffer zones, borders as, U4 p. 237

bulk-gaining industries, 18.3 pp. 514–516, 18.3 p. 514f, 18.3 p. 516f, U7 p. 571f

bulk-reducing industries, 18.3 p. 514, 18.3 p. 514f, 18.3 p. 516f, U7 p. 571f

bullying, U3 p. 231m

Burgess, Ernest, 16.1 p. 432f. See also concentric-zone model

Burj Khalifa (Dubai), 6.2 p. 161

Burkina Faso, 14.1 p. 366f

Burney, Jennifer, 14.4 p. 383

burqa, 7.2 p. 189

Burundi, 19.1 p. 526f

bus lanes, dedicated, 16.3 p. 446

Bush, George W., U1 p. 4

business centers, 13.3 pp. 348–349, 13.3 p. 348f. See also central business districts

byproducts, 20.3 p. 561s

C

C40 group, 20.3 p. 562

cacao, 13.4 p. 350

cadastral survey system, 12.2 p. 313

CAFOs. See Concentrated Animal Feeding Operations

California Gold Rush of 1849, 7.4 p. 181

call centers, 20.2 p. 556

Cambodia, 3.1 p. 65, 8.4 p. 224, 18.3 p. 517

campesinos, U4 p. 294

Canada
  devolutionary forces and, 11.1 p. 280
  gender equity and, 19.2 p. 528
  maturity and, 19.4 p. 540
  multiculturalism and, 7.3 p. 196, 7.3 p. 197f
  natural resources and, 20.3 p. 560
  Nunavut and, 10.1 p. 268
  population distribution and, 3.2 p. 72, 3.2 p. 73f
  provinces of, U4 p. 296m
  supranationalism and, 11.2 p. 285

canals, 14.1 p. 362, 18.1 p. 497, 18.1 p. 498

Canberra, Australia, 17.3 p. 474f

Cancún, Mexico, 15.2 p. 409

Candomblé religion, 7.1 p. 184

Canon, Usama, U3 p. 228, U3 p. 229

Cape Town, South Africa, 16.1 p. 438

capital, 13.1 p. 340, 18.3 p. 512

capital cities, 15.2 p. 408

capitalism, 18.3 p. 512

carbon emissions, 14.1 p. 362. See also greenhouse gases

CARE, 12.4 p. 335

Caribbean, 14.3 p. 377

Carnival festival, 7.1 p. 184

carrying capacity, 3.2 pp. 70–71, 4.1 p. 88, 4.4 p. 103

cartograms, 2.3 p. 41m, 2.3 p. 43

cartographers, 2.3 pp. 36–37

case studies
  African Culture in Brazil, 7.1 p. 184
  Brexit, 11.2 p. 287
  Building Africa's Great Green Wall, 14.1 p. 369
  China's Population Policies, 4.3 p. 100
  Coffee Production and Consumption, 13.4 p. 355
  Damming the Xingu River, 18.2 p. 509
  Detroit—GIS Helps Find Safer Routes, 2.2 p. 33

Development of the Amazon, 18.2 p. 509
  The Development of the Grameen Bank, 19.3 p. 539
  The DMZ in Korea, 9.4 p. 251
  The Effects of Redlining in Cleveland, 17.2 pp. 462–463
  The Financial Crisis of 2007–2008, 20.2 p. 553
  Food Deserts, 14.3 p. 380
  The Fourth Industrial Revolution, 18.1 p. 503
  French or English in Quebec? 8.2 p. 213
  Fútbol—A Globalizing Force, 7.2 p. 191
  Gerrymandering and Race, 10.2 pp. 272–273
  How Shanghai Grew, 15.4 p. 423
  India—Regional Differences in Scale, 1.2 p. 19
  Informal Housing in Cape Town, 16.1 p. 438
  Irredentism in Ukraine, 11.1 p. 279
  The Kurds, 9.3 p. 248
  Land-Use Change in Beijing, 16.2 p. 441
  Migration from Central America, 5.2 p. 121
  Milan and Urban Sustainability, 17.3 p. 479
  New Orleans—Site vs. Situation, 1.1 pp. 12–13
  Political Control and Nunavut, 10.1 p. 268
  Population Distribution at the Country Scale, 3.2 pp. 72–73
  Reducing Waste in Fisheries, 20.3 p. 561
  Re-Urbanizing Liverpool, 15.2 p. 411
  Shared Sacred Sites, 8.3 p. 218
  Surviving War in Syria, 5.3 p. 125
  Tehrangeles, 6.2 p. 160
  Wisconsin's American Indian Nations, 6.1 p. 156
  Women and Africa's Green Revolution, 12.4 p. 335
  "Women-Only" Cities, 19.2 p. 531
  Zika Virus in South and North America, 4.2 p. 98

Casey, Bridget, 5.2 p. 117f

cash crops, 13.4 p. 350

Cashibo people, 20.3 p. 565

casinos, 9.2 p. 244

caste system, 8.4 p. 224

Çatalhöyük settlement, 12.4 p. 330f

Catalonia, Spain, 11.1 p. 278, U4 p. 298m

catch basins, 12.3 p. 325

Catholics, 6.4 p. 175

cattle ranching, U5 p. 393f

CBD. See central business districts

CBR. See crude birth rate

CDC. See Centers for Disease Control and Prevention

CDR. See crude death rate

CE. See circular economy

Celebration, Florida, 17.1 p. 459

Celtic languages, 8.2 p. 208

census blocks, 16.3 p. 449

Census Bureau, 16.3 pp. 448–449

census data, 2.2 p. 30, 16.3 pp. 448–449

Center for a Livable Future (CLF), 14.3 p. 380

center-pivot irrigation, 3.1 p. 66f, 14.1 p. 360

Centers for Disease Control and Prevention (CDC), 2.4 p. 44

Central American agricultural hearth, 12.3 p. 325, 12.3 p. 325f, 12.3 p. 326m

Central American Parliament, 11.2 p. 286f

central business districts (CBD)
  bid-rent theory and, 12.2 p. 312
  infrastructure and, 16.3 p. 444
  land use patterns and, U6 p. 485f
  modeling city structure and, 16.1 p. 431, 16.1 p. 431f, 16.1 p. 432f, 16.1 pp. 433–437, 16.1 p. 434f, U6 pp. 486–489f
  residential land use and, 16.2 pp. 439–440

central place theory, 15.3 pp. 414–415, 15.3 p. 414f, U6 p. 485f

centrifugal forces, 6.4 pp. 174–175, 11.3 pp. 290–291, 11.3 p. 291t, C11 p. 293, U4 p. 300m

centripetal forces, 6.4 p. 174, 11.3 pp. 288–289, 11.3 pp. 291t, C11 p. 293, U4 p. 300m

cereal crops, 13.3 pp. 348–349, 13.3 p. 348f, U5 p. 393f

Chad, 14.1 p. 367, 19.1 p. 524, 19.1 p. 526f, 19.2 p. 528

chain migration, 5.2 pp. 116–117

charcoal, 18.1 p. 496

Charles River (Boston, Massachusetts), C1 p. 6f

Charlotte, North Carolina, 2.3 p. 37m

Chávez, Hugo, 5.1 p. 113

Cheap Trains Act of 1883, 15.4 p. 426

Chicago, Illinois
concentric-zone model and, 16.1 p. 432f, 16.1 p. 433
greenbelt areas and, 17.1 p. 457
steel industry and, 18.1 p. 499
transportation systems and, 15.2 p. 407
urban parks and, C17 p. 452f
Wild Mile project and, 17.3 p. 473

Chicago River, 17.3 p. 473

Child and Youth Act, 10.1 pp. 263–264

Chile, 3.1 p. 67m, 14.2 p. 376, 14.3 p. 381, 20.3 p. 562, U7 p. 568

China. *See also specific cities*
cereal production and land use in, U5 p. 393f
complementarity and, 20.1 p. 547f
conservation, sustainability and, 14.1 p. 366
cropland in, 12.1 p. 307m
dialects and, 6.4 p. 170
drivers of migration and, 5.1 p. 112f
economic development and, 18.2 p. 505
economic zones and, 20.1 p. 550
financial crisis of 2007-2008 and, 20.2 p. 553
free trade zones and, 20.2 p. 559
human migration and, 5.1 p. 113, 5.2 p. 117
India and, U4 p. 298m
maritime boundaries and, 9.4 p. 257, 9.4 p. 257f
outsourcing and, 20.2 p. 557, 20.2 p. 557f
population change and, 4.1 p. 89, 4.1 p. 90
population distribution and, 3.1 p. 65
population policies of, 4.3 p. 99f, 4.3 p. 100
sex ratios and, 3.3 p. 76
special economic zones and, 20.2 p. 558
tariffs and, 20.1 pp. 550–551
textile industry and, 18.3 p. 517
trade war with, 13.2 p. 346, 13.4 p. 353
unitary states and, 10.1 p. 264
water resources and, 14.1 p. 362
world trade patterns and, 13.4 p. 353

Chinatown (Vancouver, British Columbia), 6.2 p. 158

Chinese Exclusion Act of 1882, 5.4 p. 130, 5.4 p. 130

chloropleth maps, 2.3 p. 43, 2.3 p. 43m

choke points, 9.2 pp. 245–246, 9.2 p. 246f, U4 p. 297m, U4 p. 297f

cholera, mapping and, 2.3 p. 37

Chou, Tracy, 19.3 p. 538f

Christaller, Walter, 15.3 p. 414

Christianity, 8.3 p. 214, 8.3 p. 215f, 8.4 pp. 219–220, 8.4 p. 220f, U3 p. 235f

Christians, Eritrea and, 11.1 p. 281

circular economy (CE), 3.1 p. 69

circular migration, 5.2 p. 118

circulation, 5.1 p. 111

cities. *See also* urbanization; *specific cities*
challenges of, 17.2 pp. 460–461
as formal regions, 1.2 p. 17
future design of, 15.3 pp. 416–419
gender opportunities and, 19.3 pp. 534–535
globalization and, 15.4 pp. 420–422
growth of, 15.1 p. 403
housing density and development in, 16.2 p. 443
infrastructure and, 16.3 pp. 444–446
interactions among, 5.1 p. 111, U2 p. 145m, 15.3 p. 412f, 15.3 p. 413, U6 p. 484f
land use patterns in, 16.1 p. 431, 16.1 p. 432f
linkage of, 15.4 p. 422
location patterns of, 15.3 pp. 412–414, 15.3 p. 413f, U6 p. 485f
modeling structure of, 16.1 p. 432f, 16.1 pp. 433–437, 16.1 p. 434f, 16.1 p. 436f, U6 p. 486f–488f
planning for sustainable, 17.1 p. 453
political organization of, 16.3 p. 447
pros and cons of urban design for, 17.1 pp. 457–459
qualitative data on, 16.3 pp. 447–448
quantitative data on, 16.3 pp. 448–449
residential land use in, 16.2 pp. 439–440
site factors and, 15.1 p. 404
situation and, 15.1 pp. 404–405
smart-growth policies and, 17.1 pp. 454–457
sprawl and, 15.2 p. 407
sustainable, 17.1 p. 453, 17.1 pp. 454–457, 17.3 pp. 472–474, 17.3 p. 476
urban renewal, gentrification and, 17.2 p. 470
women-only, 19.2 p. 531
world, 15.4 pp. 421–422, 15.4 p. 421f

Citigroup, 20.2 p. 552

citrus industry, 13.2 p. 345

Civil War (U.S.), 11.3 p. 290

clean energy, 16.3 p. 445

Cleveland, Ohio, 17.2 p. 462

climate
agricultural hearths and, 12.3 p. 325
agricultural production and, 13.1 pp. 339–340, U5 p. 392f
agriculture and, 12.1 pp. 308–311
city sites and, 15.1 p. 404
food insecurity and, 14.3 p. 377
human migration and, 5.1 p. 114
mapping indigenous knowledge of, 14.1 p. 367
population distribution and, 3.1 p. 64
urbanization and, 17.3 pp. 472–474

climate change
biodiversity and, U5 p. 397f
food insecurity and, 14.3 p. 383
Fourth Industrial Revolution and, 18.1 p. 503
human migration and, 5.1 p. 114, U2 pp. 140–141
Milan and, 17.3 p. 479
refugees and, 5.3 p. 124
slash and burn cultivation and, 12.2 p. 318
sustainable development and, 1.3 p. 23
urbanization and, 17.3 p. 474

climate migration, U2 pp. 140–141

climate refugees, 5.3 p. 124

climate regions, 12.1 p. 310m, 12.1 pp. 310–311

Clotilda (ship), 7.1 p. 180

clustered populations, 3.1 p. 63f, 12.2 p. 315, 12.2 p. 315f, 12.2 p. 321m

clustering, multiple-nuclei model and, 16.1 p. 433

coal industry
industrialization and, 18.1 p. 496, 18.1 p. 497, 18.1 p. 497m, 18.1 p. 498
least-cost theory and, 18.3 p. 514
steel industry and, 18.1 p. 499

Coca-Cola, 20.2 p. 552

cocoa, 13.4 p. 353

coffee, 13.4 p. 355, 14.2 p. 375

cognates, 8.2 p. 206

Cold War, 9.4 p. 251

collectivist cultures, 7.3 p. 197

Colombia, U4 pp. 294–295

colonialism
Christian diffusion and, 8.4 p. 219
cultural appropriation and, 7.3 p. 197
cultural diffusion and, C7 p. 178, 7.2 p. 185, 7.2 p. 186f
defined, 9.2 p. 245
global agricultural system and, 13.4 p. 353
independence movements and, 9.3 p. 249
India and, U4 p. 298m
industrialization and, 18.1 pp. 499–500
population distribution and, 3.1 p. 65
time and, 9.3 p. 247
urban development and, U6 p. 487f

Colorado River, 14.1 pp. 360–362

Columbian Exchange, 12.3 p. 328, 12.3 p. 328m, 14.2 p. 376

Columbus, Christopher, 12.3 p. 328

combines, mechanical, 12.4 p. 333, 13.1 p. 341f

commercial agriculture, 12.2 p. 312, 12.2 pp. 314–317, 12.2 p. 318, 14.1 p. 365

commercial zoning, 16.2 p. 443

commodities, 13.4 p. 350, U5 p. 395m, U7 p. 573f

commodity chains, 13.2 pp. 344–345, 13.2 pp. 344–345f

communication systems
effects of use of, 11.1 p. 282
globalization and, 1.3 p. 20m
infrastructure and, 16.3 p. 444
separatist movements and, 11.1 p. 278
urban growth and, 15.2 p. 407

communism, 18.3 p. 516

Community Supported Agriculture (CSA), 14.2 p. 375

commute times, 17.1 p. 455f, 17.1 p. 457, 17.3 p. 472

Comoros, 13.4 p. 350

comparative advantage, 20.1 p. 547

competition, land use and, 16.1 p. 431

complementarity, 20.1 pp. 547–548, 20.1 p. 547f

compulsory acquisition, 17.2 p. 468

computer manufacturing industry, 18.1 p. 499

computers, 15.2 p. 407, 18.1 p. 499, 18.2 p. 507f

Concentrated Animal Feeding Operations (CAFOs), 12.2 p. 318

concentric-zone model, 16.1 p. 432f, 16.1 p. 433, 16.1 p. 435, U6 p. 486f

Concept Plan, 10.1 p. 263

concurrent powers, 10.1 p. 266

Confederate States of America, 11.3 p. 290

confederations, 11.3 p. 289

conflicts, hunger and, 14.3 p. 379

Confucianism, 8.4 p. 223

Congressional districts, 10.2 pp. 269–270, 10.2 p. 269f

connectedness, future cities and, 15.3 p. 418

connections, data collection and, 2.2 p. 30

connectivity subsidy program, 20.3 p. 562

Connie Chambers Public Housing Project (Tucson), 17.1 pp. 456–457

consequent boundaries, 9.4 p. 254, U4 p. 296m

conservation, 14.1 pp. 365–366. *See also* sustainability

Conservation Reserve Program, 14.1 p. 365

Conservify, 2.4 p. 47

construction industry, 18.2 p. 504, 18.2 p. 504f

construction materials, 6.2 pp. 158–159

Consumer Electronics Trade Show (Las Vegas), C20 p. 546f

contagious diffusion, 7.1 p. 181, 7.1 p. 183f, U3 p. 232f

continental climates, 12.1 p. 310m, 12.1 p. 311

contraception, 4.1 p. 90, 4.2 p. 92, 4.3 p. 102

Convention on the Elimination of all Forms of Discrimination Against Women (CEDAW), 19.2 p. 531

convergence, 8.2 p. 210

Cook, James, 8.2 p. 209m

Cook County, Illinois, 17.1 p. 457

cooperatives, 13.1 p. 340, 13.4 p. 354

Copenhagen, Denmark, 16.3 p. 446f

Córdoba, Argentina, 17.3 p. 475

core countries
dependency theory and, U7 p. 573f
economic development and, 18.2 pp. 505–506
globalization, interdependence and, 20.1 pp. 547–548
world system theory and, 1.3 p. 21, 1.3 p. 22f, U7 p. 572m

core-periphery model. *See* Wallerstein's world system theory

corn
agricultural zones and, 12.1 p. 311, 12.2 p. 316, 12.2 p. 316m
formal regions and, 1.2 p. 17
origins of, 12.3 p. 325f
policies and, 13.1 p. 340
subsidies and, 14.3 p. 382

corn belt, 1.2 p. 17

corporate farms, 13.2 pp. 343–344, 13.2 p. 343f, 14.1 p. 368

Costa, Adjany, 1.1 p. 14

Costa Rica, 20.3 p. 564

Côte d'Ivoire, 13.4 p. 350

cottage industries, 18.1 p. 496

cotton crops, 5.4 p. 129, 12.4 p. 331, 12.4 p. 334, 13.4 p. 353

COVID-19 virus, 4.2 p. 95, 4.2 p. 96, 20.2 pp. 552–554, pp. R1–R5

cowboys, 7.2 p. 188

cracking districts, 10.2 pp. 270–271, 10.2 p. 270f

Crawford, James, U1 pp. 50–51

Credit Suisse, 20.2 p. 552

creolization, 7.2 p. 186, 8.2 p. 211

crime, 17.2 p. 461, 17.2 p. 465, 18.1 p. 502

Crimea, 11.1 p. 279, 11.1 p. 279m, 11.1 p. 279f, U4 p. 296m

Croatia, 9.3 p. 247, 9.4 p. 254, 11.2 p. 286

crop diversity, 14.2 pp. 371–372, 14.2 p. 371f

crop dusting, 12.4 p. 333

crop rotation, 12.2 p. 316, 12.4 p. 332, 14.1 p. 365

crops. *See* agriculture

crude (arithmetic) density, 3.1 p. 67, 3.1 p. 68t, 3.2 p. 70

crude birth rate (CBR), 3.4 pp. 77–78, 3.4 p. 78t, 4.1 p. 87

crude death rate (CDR), 3.4 pp. 78–79, 3.4 p. 78t, 4.1 p. 87

crude oil, 18.1 p. 495

cruises, 20.3 p. 564

Crusades, 8.4 p. 219, 8.4 pp. 224–225

CSA. *See* Community Supported Agriculture

Cuba, 5.5 p. 135, 5.5 p. 136f, 19.2 p. 528

Culhane, T.H., 16.3 p. 445

cultural appropriation, 7.3 p. 197

cultural change, consequences of, 7.3 pp. 194–197

cultural convergence, 7.2 pp. 189–190

cultural diffusion, 7.3 pp. 194–197, U3 p. 231f, U3 pp. 232–233f. *See also* diffusion

cultural divergence, 7.2 p. 190

cultural factors
human migration and, 5.1 p. 113, 5.5 pp. 135–137
life expectancy and, 3.4 p. 80
population change and, 4.1 p. 90
population distribution and, 3.1 p. 66

cultural hearths, C7 p. 178

cultural iceberg, 6.1 p. 153, U3 p. 230f

cultural landscapes, 6.2 pp. 157–161, 6.2 p. 162f, 6.3 p. 163, 6.4 p. 173, 17.2 p. 470

cultural norms, 6.1 p. 155

cultural relativism, 6.1 p. 155

Cultural Survival, 8.2 p. 212

cultural traits, 6.1 p. 153

culture
  defined, U3 p. 149
  dynamics of, 6.1 pp. 154–155
  ethnosphere and, 8.3 p. 217
  identity, space and, 6.3 pp. 163–167
  language and, 8.1 p. 201, 8.1 p. 202f
  museums and, U1 pp. 150–151
  overview of, 6.1 pp. 153–156
  patterns of, 6.4 pp. 168–175
  religion and, 8.3 p. 214
  urban residential land use and, 16.2 p. 440

Cupertino, California, 20.1 p. 551f

Curitiba, Brazil, 17.1 p. 454–455

customer service call centers, 20.2 p. 556

customs surcharges, 11.2 p. 285

Cyber Security Law (China), 6.1 p. 155m

cycling, U7 p. 493f, 20.1 pp. 550–551

cyclones, 12.2 p. 314

Cyprus, 10.1 p. 262, 19.1 p. 525

Czech immigrants, 6.3 p. 163

D

DACA. See Deferred Action for Childhood Arrivals

dairy industry, 13.1 p. 342, 13.3 pp. 348–349, 13.3 p. 348f

Dakar, Senegal, 15.3 p. 414

Dalai Lama, 8.3 p. 214, 8.4 p. 222

Dallas, Texas, 17.2 p. 469

Damato, Zachary, 17.3 p. 473

dams, 18.2 p. 509

Dar Al-Hijrah (Minneapolis), 6.4 p. 173

Darwin and Wolf Marine Sanctuary, U1 p. 5

data
  census, 2.2 p. 30, 16.3 pp. 448–449
  collecting, 2.1 pp. 27–28, 2.1 p. 27f, 2.2 pp. 29–30
  election, 2.2 p. 30
  interval, 16.3 p. 448
  making decisions with, 2.4 pp. 45–46
  nominal, 16.3 p. 448
  ordinal, 16.3 p. 448
  primary, 16.3 p. 448
  qualitative, 2.2 pp. 29–30, 16.3 pp. 447–448
  quantitative, 2.1 p. 29, 16.3 pp. 448–449
  ratio, 16.3 p. 448
  secondary, 16.3 p. 448
  uses of, 2.4 p. 44
  visualizing, 2.1 p. 27f, 2.1 p. 28

databases, 16.3 p. 448

Davis, Jefferson, 11.3 p. 290

Davis, Wade, 8.3 p. 217

Day of the Dead, 7.3 p. 196, 7.3 p. 196f

de Blij, Harm, 16.1 p. 437

de facto segregation, 17.1 p. 459

De León, Jason, 5.2 p. 119

dead zones, 14.1 p. 363

Dean, James, 7.1 p. 181

Dearborn, Fort, 15.2 p. 407

death penalty, 10.1 p. 267

death rate
  crude, 3.4 pp. 78–79, 3.4 p. 78t, 4.1 p. 87
  infant, 3.4 p. 79, 3.4 p. 79m, 4.1 p. 90, 18.1 p. 502, 19.1 p. 524

debt-for-nature swaps, 14.1 p. 365

decentralization, 10.1 p. 263, 10.1 p. 267, 20.2 p. 552, 20.2 p. 557

decision-making, data and, 2.4 pp. 44–46

deed restrictions, 17.2 p. 460

deeds, 17.2 p. 460

deep culture, U3 p. 230f

Deere, John, 7.1 p. 181, 12.4 p. 332

Deferred Action for Childhood Arrivals (DACA), 5.5 p. 133

deficits, 20.2 p. 554

deforestation, 12.2 p. 318, 14.1 p. 359, 14.1 p. 364, 14.1 p. 364f

deindustrialization, 18.2 pp. 506–507, 20.1 pp. 549–550

Delaware River, 16.1 p. 433

Delhi, India, 6.3 p. 164f, 6.3 p. 166, 17.2 p. 464, 17.2 p. 464m, 17.2 p. 468

Delhi-Mumbai Industrial Corridor (DMIC) Development Project, 17.2 p. 464

delimiting boundaries, 9.3 p. 249

demarcated boundaries, 9.3 p. 249

Demilitarized Zone (DMZ), U4 p. 237, 9.4 p. 250, 9.4 p. 251

Democratic Republic of Congo (DRC)
  diseases and, 4.2 p. 96
  food insecurity and, 14.3 p. 377, 14.3 p. 379
  human development and, 19.1 p. 524
  Industrial Revolution, colonialism and, 18.1 p. 500
  population composition and, 3.4 pp. 81–82, 3.4 p. 81f
  women in agriculture and, 14.4 p. 385

Demographic Transition Model (DTM), 4.2 p. 93, 4.2 p. 94f, 5.5 p. 134, U2 p. 143f, 18.1 p. 500

demographics, 3.4 p. 77, 4.4 p. 103, 5.1 p. 113. See also population change; population density; population distribution

Dengue fever, 2.3 p. 37

Denmark, 11.2 p. 285, 19.2 p. 528, U7 p. 570f

denominations, 6.4 p. 171, U3 p. 235f

density, 1.1 p. 9. See also population density

Denver, Colorado, 1.1 p. 9m, 17.3 p. 476

Department of Housing and Urban Development (HUD), 17.2 p. 469

dependency ratios, 3.3 p. 74m, 3.3 pp. 74–75, 4.4 pp. 104–107, 5.5 p. 134

dependency theory, 19.4 pp. 542–543, U7 p. 573f

deregulation, 20.1 p. 548, 20.2 p. 552

desertification, 14.1 p. 362, 14.1 p. 364, 14.1 p. 369

deserts, 12.1 p. 309

determinism, environmental, 1.1 pp. 9–10

Detroit, Michigan
  automobile manufacturing and, 15.2 p. 408, 16.1 p. 434f, 18.3 p. 512f, 18.3 pp. 513–514, 18.3 p. 513f
  decentralization and, 16.1 p. 434f, 16.1 p. 435
  geographic information systems and, 2.2 pp. 33–34
  manufacturing industry and, 18.1 p. 499
  population decline in, 15.2 p. 409, 18.3 p. 512f

Deutsche Bank, 20.2 p. 552

developed countries, 1.3 p. 21

developing countries, 1.3 p. 21, 20.2 p. 552

development, 19.1 p. 521. See also human development

devolution
  economic and social problems and, 11.1 p. 278
  ethnic separatism and, 11.1 pp. 277–278
  independence movements and, 9.4 p. 249
  overview of, 11.1 p. 277
  Philippines and, U4 p. 300m
  physical geography and, 11.1 p. 277
  responses to drivers of, 11.1 pp. 280–281

Dhaka, Bangladesh, 5.3 p. 124, U2 pp. 140–141, 17.2 p. 468

dialects, 6.4 p. 170, 8.1 p. 203, 8.1 p. 203m

diamonds, 15.1 p. 404

dietary shifts, 14.2 pp. 375–376

diffusion. See also relocation diffusion
  agricultural, 12.3 pp. 326–329, 12.3 p. 327m
  contagious, 7.1 p. 181, 7.1 p. 183f, U3 p. 232f
  cultural, 7.3 pp. 194–197, U3 p. 231f, U3 pp. 232–233f
  cultural convergence and, 7.2 pp. 189–190
  cultural divergence and, 7.2 p. 190
  expansion, 7.1 p. 181, 7.1 p. 183f, 8.2 p. 208, 8.3 p. 214
  fashion, U3 p. 233f
  hierarchical, 7.1 pp. 181–182, 7.1 p. 183f, U3 p. 232f
  historical causes of, C7 p. 178, 7.2 pp. 185–188
  of industrialization, 18.1 pp. 498–502
  mixing types of, 7.1 p. 182
  modern drivers of, 7.2 pp. 188–189
  stimulus, 7.1 p. 182, 7.1 p. 183f, U3 p. 232f, 12.3 p. 327

digital revolution, 11.1 p. 282

digitization of information, 18.1 p. 503

direction, maps and, 2.3 p. 37

disamenity zones, 16.1 p. 435, 17.2 p. 465, 17.2 p. 468, U6 p. 487f

discrimination
  devolution and, 11.1 p. 278
  housing and, 17.2 pp. 460–461, 17.2 p. 462, 17.2 p. 463m
  human migration and, 5.1 p. 113

disease. See also specific diseases
  Columbian Exchange and, 12.3 p. 328
  contagious diffusion and, 7.1 p. 181
  epidemiological transition and, 4.2 p. 95t
  genetic code and, 4.2 p. 97
  population change and, 4.1 p. 90
  population trends and, 4.2 pp. 94–96

dispersed populations, 3.1 p. 63f, 12.2 p. 315, 12.2 p. 315f, 12.2 p. 320m

displacement, U2 p. 147f, 12.4 p. 333, 17.2 p. 470

distance, 1.1 p. 10, 2.3 p. 37, U1 p. 52f, 5.2 p. 115

distance decay model, 1.1 p. 10, U1 p. 52f, 5.2 p. 118f, 7.2 p. 190, U4 p. 300m

distribution, 1.1 p. 9, 1.1 p. 9m. See also population distribution

distributors, 13.2 p. 345, 13.2 p. 345f

diversity, 10.1 p. 267. See also biodiversity

division of labor, international, 20.2 pp. 556–557, 20.2 p. 557m

DMIC Development Project, 17.2 p. 464

DMZ. See Demilitarized Zone

Dome of the Rock, U4 p. 239f

domestication, 12.3 p. 324, 12.3 p. 327m, 12.3 p. 328

dot maps, 2.3 p. 42m, 2.3 p. 43, U1 p. 56m

doubling time (DT), 4.1 pp. 87–88

Dove satellites, U1 p. 50–51

drones, 2.2 p. 34, 14.2 p. 373, U5 p. 390

droughts, 14.3 p. 377

dry climates, 12.1 p. 310, 12.1 p. 310m, 12.2 p. 314

DTM. See Demographic Transition Model

dual agricultural economies, 13.1 p. 339

dual economies, 18.2 p. 508

Dubai, United Arab Emirates, 6.2 p. 161

Ducheneaux, Kelsey, 14.4 p. 385

Dutch East India Company, 7.2 p. 185

E

Earhart, Amelia, U3 p. 151f

earthquakes, 2.4 p. 45m, 2.4 p. 46, 10.1 p. 264

East African agricultural hearth, 12.3 p. 325, 12.3 p. 326m

East African Federation, 11.3 p. 289

East Germany, 9.4 p. 255, 9.4 p. 255f

East Timor, 11.3 pp. 290–291

Eastern Europe as perceptual region, 1.2 p. 18

Eastern Orthodox Catholicism, 8.4 p. 219

Ebola, 4.2 p. 95, 4.2 p. 96, 4.2 p. 96f

Echazú Alvarado, Luís Alberto, U7 p. 569

ecolodging, 20.3 p. 564

EcoLogic, 14.1 p. 365

ecological footprints, 17.1 p. 453, 17.3 p. 472

ecological perspective, 1.1 p. 7

Economic Census, 2.2 p. 30

economic equity, 19.2 p. 527

economic sectors, 18.2 pp. 504–505, 18.2 p. 504f, 19.1 p. 522, U7 p. 570f

economic zones, 20.1 p. 550

economies and economic factors
  aging population and, 4.4 pp. 105–106
  agricultural production regions and, 13.1 pp. 339–340
  biotechnology and, 14.2 p. 372
  changes in global landscape of, 20.2 pp. 555–558
  dependency ratios and, 3.3 p. 75
  dependency theory and, U7 p. 573f
  devolution and, 11.1 p. 278
  gender roles and, 19.3 pp. 534–535
  human development and, 19.1 pp. 521–522
  human migration and, 5.1 p. 113
  impacts of globalization on, 20.2 pp. 552–554
  India and, 1.2 p. 19
  infrastructure and, 16.3 p. 444
  least-cost theory and, 18.3 pp. 512–517
  life expectancy and, 3.4 p. 80
  migrant countries of origin and, 5.5 pp. 134–135
  migrant destination countries and, 5.5 pp. 133–134
  natural resources and, 20.3 p. 560
  patterns of, 18.2 pp. 505–508
  population change and, 4.1 pp. 88–89
  population distribution and, 3.1 p. 65
  sectors of, 18.2 pp. 504–505, 18.2 p. 504f, 19.1 p. 522, U7 p. 570f
  stages of growth of, 19.4 pp. 540–541, 19.4 p. 541f, U7 p. 572f
  supranational organizations and, 11.2 p. 285, 11.2 p. 286
  urban migration and, 15.2 pp. 408–409

economies of scale, 11.2 p. 285, 13.1 p. 339, 13.1 p. 341t, 14.3 p. 381, 20.1 p. 550

ecotourism, 20.3 pp. 563–565

Ecuador, 20.3 p. 560

edge cities, 15.2 p. 410

Edicule, U3 p. 150

EDR. See elderly dependency ratio

education
  Afghanistan and, U7 p. 492
  birth rates and, U7 p. 574f
  ecotourism and, 20.3 p. 564
  empowerment and, 19.2 pp. 528–529
  gender and, 6.3 p. 165f
  gender and access to, 19.3 pp. 535–536, 19.3 p. 536f
  human development and, 19.1 p. 524
  Human Development Index and, 19.1 p. 525
  industrialization and, 18.1 p. 502
  population change and, 4.1 p. 90, 4.1 p. 91

educational attainment, 19.2 pp. 528–529

EEZ. See exclusive economic zones

efficiency, agricultural, 13.1 p. 340

Egypt
  cultural diffusion and, 7.2 p. 185
  first agricultural revolution and, 12.4 p. 331
  gendered spaces and, 6.3 p. 166
  population distribution and, 3.2 p. 72, 3.2 p. 73f
  protecting archaeological sites in, 2.2 p. 35
  soil salinization and, 14.1 p. 364

Eiffel Tower (Paris), 15.4 p. 422

El Salado, Colombia, U4 pp. 294–295

El Salvador, 5.2 p. 121

el Seed (artist), C8 p. 200

elder care industry, 4.4 p. 106

elderly dependency ratio (EDR), 4.4 p. 106m, 4.4 p. 107m

election data, 2.2 p. 30

electoral college, 10.2 p. 269

electoral geography, 10.2 pp. 269–273, U4 p. 299m

electric cars, 7.1 p. 181

electricity, 12.4 p. 333, 18.1 pp. 498–499

electronics, 18.1 p. 499, 20.2 p. 552

Elema, Ahmed, U2 p. 61f

elevation, 3.1 pp. 64–65, 12.1 p. 308, 12.1 p. 308f

elevators, cities and, 15.4 p. 427

Elkaim, Aaron Vincent, 18.2 pp. 510–511

embargoes, 11.2 p. 285

emigration, 5.1 p. 111

eminent domain, 17.2 p. 468

empowerment, 14.4 pp. 386–387, 19.2 pp. 528–529

enclosure system, 12.4 p. 331

Endangered Language Fund, 8.2 p. 212

endangered languages, 8.2 p. 212, 8.2 p. 212m

energy systems, 16.3 pp. 444–446, 17.3 p. 478. See also clean energy

English language, 8.2 p. 206, 8.2 pp. 208–209, 8.2 p. 209m, 8.2 p. 211, 8.2 p. 213

Enlightenment, 8.4 p. 225

environment
agriculture and, 12.1 pp. 307–308
human migration and, 5.1 p. 114
population change and, 4.1 p. 90
population distribution and, 3.1 pp. 63–66, 3.2 pp. 70–71, 3.2 p. 71f
population size and, 4.4 p. 103
population trends and, 4.2 p. 95

environmental determinism, 1.1 pp. 9–10

environmental injustice (racism), 17.2 pp. 468–469

environmental technology, 18.2 pp. 504–505, 18.2 p. 504f

epidemics, maps and, 2.3 p. 37

Epidemiological Transition Model (ETM), 4.2 pp. 93–96, 4.2 p. 95t, 4.4 p. 105, U2 p. 144f

EPZs. See export processing zones

equal-area projections, U1 p. 55m

equality, defined, 19.2 p. 527

equator, 12.1 p. 308, 12.1 p. 309

equity, defined, 19.2 p. 527

Erdogan, Recep Tayyip, 5.1 p. 113

Erie Canal, 15.1 p. 405

Eritrea, 11.1 p. 281

erosion, 12.2 p. 318, 14.1 p. 359

Essay on Population (Malthus), 4.2 p. 92

Estonia, 9.2 p. 242, 9.2 p. 243

Ethiopia, 9.4 p. 254, 11.1 p. 281, 19.3 p. 535

ethnic cleansing, 11.1 p. 278

ethnic neighborhoods, 6.2 p. 158

ethnic religions, 8.4 pp. 223–225

ethnic separatism, 11.1 pp. 277–278

ethnicity
devolution and, 11.1 pp. 277–278
ethnonationalism and, 11.3 p. 290
neighborhoods and, 6.3 p. 163
overview of, 6.2 p. 158
religion, language and, 6.4 p. 173–174
religion and, 6.2 p. 161, 6.4 p. 171
sense of place and, 6.4 pp. 173–174
stateless nations and, 9.3 p. 248

ethnocentrism, 6.1 p. 155

Ethnologue, 8.1 p. 201

ethnonationalism (ethnic nationalism), 11.3 p. 290

ethnosphere, 8.3 p. 217

ETM. See Epidemiological Transition Model

EU. See European Union

Euphrates River, 12.3 p. 325

Euractiv France, 14.4 p. 385

EUROGATE Container Terminal (Hamburg), C4 p. 494f

European Union (EU)
asylum in, 5.4 p. 130
austerity measures and, 20.2 p. 554
benefits of, 11.2 p. 285
Brexit and, 11.2 p. 283, 11.2 p. 287, U4 p. 300m, 13.4 p. 353
drawbacks of, 11.2 pp. 285–286
globalization and, 1.3 p. 21, 20.2 pp. 552–554
overview of, 11.2 p. 283, 20.1 p. 548, 20.1 p. 549m

Euskara language, 6.4 p. 170

Evers, Tony, 6.1 p. 156

exclusive economic zones (EEZ), 9.4 p. 256

expansion diffusion, 7.1 p. 181, 7.1 p. 183f, 8.2 p. 208, 8.3 p. 214

exploitation, world system theory and, 1.3 p. 21

export processing zones (EPZs), 20.2 p. 558–559

extensive agriculture, 12.2 p. 318, 12.2 p. 319, U5 p. 393f

exurbs, 15.2 p. 410

F

factions, 11.3 p. 291

factories, 18.1 p. 501, 20.2 p. 555

Fadel, Leila, U3 pp. 228–229

failed states, 11.3 p. 291, U4 p. 300m

Fair Housing Act of 1968, 17.2 p. 461

fair trade movement, 13.4 p. 354, 14.1 p. 365, 14.2 p. 375

fall lines, city sites and, 15.1 p. 404, 15.1 p. 404f

family farms, 13.2 pp. 343–344, 13.2 p. 343f

famine
epidemiological transition and, 4.2 p. 94, 4.2 p. 95t
human migration and, 5.2 p. 116, 5.2 p. 120
Malthus's theory of population growth and, 4.2 p. 92, U2 p. 144f
population change and, 4.1 p. 90

FAO. See Food and Agriculture Organization

FARC (Fuerzas Armadas Revolucionarias de Colombia), U4 pp. 294–295

farm aid packages, 14.3 p. 382

farm bills, 13.1 p. 340

Farm Service Agency (FSA), 14.1 p. 365

farm subsidies, 13.2 pp. 345–346, 14.3 p. 382

farming, 15.3 p. 418. See also agriculture; urban farming

farmlands, 17.3 p. 476

fashion, 7.3 p. 194, U3 p. 233f

favelas, 17.1 p. 455, 17.2 p. 465, 17.2 p. 465f

Federal Election Commission, 4.4 p. 30

federal governments, 10.1 p. 264f, 11.3 p. 291

Federal Reserve bank, 20.1 p. 550

federal states, 10.1 p. 261, 10.1 p. 263f, 10.1 pp. 264–267, 10.1 p. 264f, 10.1 p. 265f

Federal-Aid Highway Act of 1956, 17.2 p. 470

federalism, 10.1 p. 268

federations, 11.3 p. 289

feed lots, 12.2 p. 318

feedlots, 13.1 p. 342

fences, boundaries and, 9.4 p. 249, 9.4 p. 249f

Fenoglio, Maria Silvina, 17.3 p. 475

Fertile Crescent, 12.3 p. 324, 12.3 p. 325, 12.3 p. 326m

fertility, 3.4 pp. 77–78, 3.4 p. 78t, 4.1 p. 90, 4.1 p. 90m, 19.3 p. 535

fertilizer trees, U5 p. 304

fertilizers, 12.1 p. 308, 12.4 pp. 332–333, 14.1 p. 363, 14.2 p. 372

FFP. See Fund for Peace

fiber crops, 12.1 p. 307, 12.4 p. 331

FieldKit software, 2.4 p. 47

Fiesta del Gran Poder (Bolivia), U3 p. 149

Fifth Amendment of the Constitution, 17.2 p. 468

filtering, 17.2 p. 462

financial crisis of 2007-2008, 20.2 p. 553

financial services sector, 20.2 p. 552, 20.2 p. 553, 20.2 p. 557

Finland, 11.2 p. 285

firefighters, 18.1 p. 502

fires, U1 p. 57f, 11.3 p. 288, 11.3 p. 289f, 14.1 p. 364, 14.1 p. 364f, 17.3 p. 474f

firewood, 13.3 p. 349

First Nations peoples and COVID-19 R4

First Nations peoples of Canada, 10.1 p. 268

fish farms, 12.3 p. 329

fisheries, 20.3 p. 561

fishing, 15.3 p. 419

flags, 11.3 p. 289

Flame Towers (Baku), 17.1 p. 458f

flats, 16.2 p. 443

Fleming people, 11.1 p. 280

Flint, Michigan, 17.3 p. 472

flooding, 1.1 p. 12, 1.1 p. 13f

Florence (hurricane), 5.1 p. 114f

Florida, 5.5 p. 135, 5.5 p. 136f

flow, 1.1 p. 9

Folk religion, 8.3 p. 215f

food. See also agriculture
choices of, 14.2 pp. 374–376
consumption trends and, 4.2 p. 95
economic impacts of production of, 14.3 pp. 381–382
global insecurity and, 14.3 pp. 377–380
human migration and, 5.5 p. 135
Malthus's theory of population growth and, 4.2 p. 92, U2 p. 144f
trends in production of, 4.2 p. 95
wasting of, 13.2 p. 347, U5 p. 397f

Food and Agriculture Organization (FAO), 14.1 p. 365, 14.3 p. 377

food crops, 12.1 p. 307

food deserts, 14.3 p. 380, C14 p. 389, 17.2 p. 469

food insecurity, 1.2 p. 15m, 1.2 pp. 15–16, 14.3 pp. 377–380, 17.2 p. 469, 17.2 p. 469f

food security, 14.3 p. 377

food sovereignty, 14.4 p. 385

football, 7.2 p. 191

foraging, 12.3 p. 324

forced assimilation, 7.3 p. 195

forced migration, 5.2 pp. 118–120, 5.4 p. 128, U2 p. 145, U2 p. 147f

Ford, Henry, 18.3 pp. 513–514, 20.2 p. 555

Ford, Larry, 16.1 p. 435

Ford Motor Company, 18.3 p. 514, U7 p. 575f

Fordism, 20.2 p. 555

forest fires, 14.1 p. 364, 14.1 p. 364f

forest preserve districts, 17.1 p. 457

forests, 13.3 pp. 348–349, 13.3 p. 348f. See also deforestation

formal regions, 1.2 p. 17

formal sector of economy, 19.1 p. 522

fossil fuels, 18.1 p. 503, 19.1 p. 523, 19.1 p. 524f

Fourth Industrial Revolution, 18.1 p. 503

Foxconn plant, 20.1 p. 550

Frachetti, Michael, 15.1 p. 406

Fragile States Index, U4 p. 300m

fragmentation, U5 p. 397f, 16.3 p. 447

France, 4.3 p. 102, 10.1 p. 261, 14.3 p. 377, 14.4 p. 385, 18.1 p. 501

francophones, 8.2 p. 213

Frankfurt, Germany, 15.4 p. 422

free trade, 20.1 p. 548

free trade agreements, 20.1 p. 548

free trade zones (FTZs), 20.2 p. 559

Freiburg, Germany, 17.1 p. 455

French language, 8.2 p. 213

friction of distance, 1.1 p. 10, 5.2 p. 115

frost tolerant crops, 13.1 pp. 339–340

FSA. See Farm Service Agency

FTZs. See free trade zones

Fuguo Monastery (China), 6.1 p. 154f

functional regions, 1.2 p. 17m, 1.2 pp. 17–18

Fund for Peace (FFP), U4 p. 300m

funding, climate change and, 17.3 p. 474

fútbol, 7.2 p. 191

G

Gaitán, Jorge Eliécer, U4 p. 294

galactic city model, 16.1 p. 434f, 16.1 p. 435, U6 p. 487f

Gall-Peters projections, 2.3 p. 38, 2.3 p. 38m, 2.3 p. 39m, 2.3 p. 39t

GAP. See Gender in Agricultural Partnership

García Linera, Álvaro, U7 pp. 568–569

gardens, 15.3 p. 417

gas holders, 17.3 p. 477f

Gautama, Siddhartha (Buddha), 6.4 p. 173, 8.4 p. 221

GDI. See Gender Development Index

GDP. See gross domestic product

gender. See also sex ratios; women
cultural dynamics and, 6.1 p. 154
immigrants and, 5.4 p. 130
life expectancy and, 3.4 p. 80
patterns in, 6.3 p. 165, 6.3 p. 165f
population change and, 4.1 p. 91
population pyramids and, 3.4 pp. 81–82, 3.4 p. 81f
U.S workforce and, 18.2 pp. 507–508, 18.2 p. 507f

Gender Development Index (GDI), 19.2 p. 527, 19.2 p. 527f

gender disparities, 19.2 pp. 527–531

gender identity, 6.3 pp. 166–167

Gender in Agricultural Partnership (GAP), 14.4 p. 387

Gender Inequality Index (GII), 19.2 pp. 527–528

gender roles, 14.1 p. 91, 5.1 p. 113, 19.3 pp. 534–539

gendered spaces, 6.3 p. 164, 6.3 p. 166

gene transfer, 14.2 p. 372

genetic code, 4.2 p. 97

genetic engineering (GE), 14.2 p. 371

genetic modification, 14.2 p. 371

genetically-modified organisms (GMOs), U5 p. 304, U5 p. 305f, 12.4 pp. 332–333, 14.1 p. 368, 14.2 pp. 370–371

genome editing, 18.1 p. 503

gentrification, 6.3 p. 167, 17.2 p. 470, 17.2 p. 471

geographic information systems (GIS), 2.2 pp. 31–34, 2.2 p. 31f, 2.4 p. 46, 17.2 p. 468

geographic thinking
globalization, sustainability and, 1.3 pp. 20–25
human-environment interaction and, 1.1 pp. 9–10
overview of, 1.1 pp. 7–14
perspectives in, 1.1 pp. 7–9
spatial patterns in, 1.2 pp. 15–19

geography. See also physical geography
central place theory and, 15.3 p. 415
cultural divergence and, 7.2 p. 190
defined, 1.1 p. 7
electoral, 10.2 pp. 269–273, U4 p. 299m

Geography Collective, U6 p. 400
Geo-Inquiry Process
   data and tools for, 2.1 pp. 29–35
   overview of, 2.1 pp. 27–28, 2.1 p. 27f
   power of data and, 2.4 pp. 44–47
   tips for, 2.1 p. 28, 2.2 p. 30, 2.3 p. 42,
      2.4 p. 46
   understanding maps and, 2.3
      pp. 36–43
geometric boundaries, U4 p. 296m
geovisualization, 2.2 p. 32
Gerdes, Caroline, 16.3 p. 448f
German Confederation, 11.3 p. 288m,
   11.3 p. 289
Germanic branch of languages,
   8.1 p. 202, 8.1 p. 204f
Germanic languages, 8.2 p. 208
Germany
   aging population and, 4.4 p. 107
   devolution and, 11.1 p. 278
   ethnonationalism and, 11.3 p. 290
   federalism in, 10.1 p. 266
   financial crisis of 2007-2008 and, 20.2
      p. 553
   Human Development Index and, 19.1
      p. 525, 19.1 p. 526f
   immigrants and, 11.2 p. 286
   Industrial Revolution and, 18.1 p. 498
   relic boundaries in, 9.4 p. 255, 9.4
      p. 255f
   urbanization and, 18.1 p. 501
Gerry, Elbridge, 10.2 p. 270
gerrymandering, 10.2 pp. 270–271, 10.2
   p. 270f, 10.2 p. 272, 10.2 p. 273f
gers, 6.2 p. 159
GFAR See Global Forum on Agricultural
   Research
Ghana, 12.4 p. 335, 13.4 p. 350
GII. See Gender Inequality Index
GIS. See geographic information systems
Glaeser, Edward, U6 p. 482
global cities, 15.4 pp. 421–422, 15.4
   p. 421f
global food insecurity, 14.3 pp. 377–379
Global Forum on Agricultural Research
   (GFAR), 14.4 p. 387
global positioning systems (GPS), 2.2
   p. 34, 12.4 p. 333
Global Power City Index (GPCI),
   15.4 p. 421f
Global Services Location Index,
   20.2 p. 557f
global supply chains, 13.4 pp. 350–351,
   13.4 p. 355
globalization
   agricultural interdependence and, 13.4
      pp. 350–351
   bananas and, U5 p. 395m
   city linkage and, 15.4 p. 422
   city situation and, 15.1 p. 405
   Consumer Electronics Trade Show
      and, C20 p. 546f
   cultural diffusion and, 7.2 p. 188
   economic growth and, 19.4 p. 541
   economic impacts of, 20.2
      pp. 552–554
   economic landscape and, 20.2
      pp. 555–558
   government trade policies and, 20.1
      pp. 550–551
   interdependence in world economy
      and, 20.1 pp. 547–548
   manufacturing zones and, 20.2
      pp. 558–559
   overview of, 1.3 pp. 20–22
   supranational organizations and, 20.1
      pp. 548–550
   transportation, communication
      networks and, 1.3 p. 20m
   world cities and, 15.4 pp. 421–422
Glover, Jerry, U5 p. 304, U5 p. 305f
GMOs. See genetically-modified
   organisms
GNP. See gross national product
gold, 7.1 p. 181, 15.1 p. 404
Golden Temple, 8.4 p. 222
Goldman Sachs, 20.2 p. 552
González, Emma, 19.3 p. 538f
Goodall, Jane, 19.3 p. 538f
Google, 18.2 p. 505, 18.2 p. 507f

Goose Island (Chicago), 17.3 p. 473
Gorbachev, Mikhail, 11.1 p. 281
Goutte d'Or neighborhood (Paris), 6.2
   p. 158, 6.2 p. 159f
governments
   affordable housing and, 17.2 p. 466
   city organization and, 16.3 p. 447
   food production and, 14.3 pp. 381–382
   gender and participation in, 19.2
      p. 528, 19.2 p. 529f
   human migration and, 5.4 pp. 130–132
   mapping data and, 2.4 p. 46
   measuring stability of, U4 p. 300m
   population change and, 4.1 p. 89
   population policies and, 4.3 pp. 99–
      102, 4.3 p. 102f
   satisfaction with, U4 p. 299f
   trade policies and, 20.1 pp. 550–551,
      20.1 p. 551f
   urban migration and, 15.2 pp. 408–409
GPS. See global positioning systems
graduated symbols maps, 2.3 p. 41m,
   2.3 p. 43
grains, 13.3 pp. 348–349, 13.3 p. 348f
Grameen Bank, 19.3 p. 537, 19.3 p. 539
Grameen Foundation, 14.4 p. 387
grants, 20.1 p. 550
gravity model, 5.1 p. 111, U2 p. 145m,
   15.3 p. 412f, 15.3 p. 413, U6 p. 484f
Great Britain
   austerity measures and, 20.2 p. 554
   global agricultural system and, 13.4
      p. 353
   imperialism and, 9.3 p. 247
   Industrial Revolution and, 18.1
      pp. 496–498
   industrialization and, 18.1 pp. 499–500
   maturity and, 19.4 p. 540
   second agricultural revolution and,
      12.4 p. 331
Great Famine of 1845-1849, 4.1 p. 90
Great Green Wall initiative, 14.1 p. 369,
   14.1 p. 369m
Great Migration, 5.4 p. 128m, 5.4 p. 129,
   7.1 p. 179, 17.2 p. 462
Great Mosque of Djenne (Mali),
   8.3 p. 217f
Great Recession (2007-2009),
   20.2 p. 553, 20.2 p. 554, 20.2 p. 554m
Great Rift Valley (East Africa),
   U2 p. 60
Greece
   artifact preservation and,
      U3 p. 150
   austerity measures and, 20.2 p. 554
   choke points and, 9.2 p. 245
   cultural diffusion and, 7.2 p. 185
   Cyprus and, 10.1 p. 262
   supranationalism and, 11.2 p. 286
   urban location and, 15.3 p. 412
Green Belt (London), 17.1 p. 456f, 17.1
   p. 457
Green Revolution, 12.4 p. 333, 12.4
   p. 335, 14.2 p. 371, U5 p. 393f
green roofs, 15.3 p. 417, 17.3 p. 475
green streets, 17.3 p. 478
Greenbelt, Maryland, 17.1 p. 457
Greenbelt Alliance, 17.1 p. 457
greenbelt towns, defined, 17.1 p. 457
greenbelts, 15.2 p. 410f, 17.1 p. 456f,
   17.1 p. 457, 17.3 p. 476
greenhouse gases, 17.1 p. 453
greenhouses, 12.2 p. 317
Greenwich Park (London), U6 p. 401f
Griffin, Ernest, 16.1 p. 435
Griffin-Ford model, 16.1 p. 435, 16.1
   p. 436f, 16.1 p. 437f, U6 p. 487f
grills, 14.1 p. 368
gross domestic product (GDP),
   1.2 p. 19, 18.2 p. 507, 19.1 p. 521, U7
   p. 570f, U7 p. 574f
gross national income (GNI),
   19.1 p. 521, 19.1 p.522t, 19.1 p. 525,
   20.2 p. 552
gross national product (GNP),
   19.1 p. 521
groundwater, 4.2 p. 95, 14.1 p. 364
growers, 13.2 p. 343, 13.2 p. 344f
growing season, 3.1 p. 64

growth management plans,
   17.1 pp. 455–456
growth poles, 20.1 p. 550
Guatemala, 5.2 p. 121, 9.3 p. 247, 9.3
   p. 249, 19.3 p. 534
guayusa leaves, 14.1 p. 365
guerillas, U4 pp. 294–295
guerrilla geography, U6 p. 400
guest workers, 5.2 pp. 117–118
guild system, 18.1 p. 496
Guillermoprieto, Alma, U4 pp. 294–295
Gulf of Mexico dead zone,
   14.1 p. 363
Gulf Stream, 12.1 p. 309
Guttenfelder, David, 9.4 pp. 252–253,
   U6 p. 482
Guyana, 8.2 p. 209m

H

habitat loss, U5 p. 397f,
   20.3 p. 560
Haiti, U7 p. 570f
Haitian Creole, 8.2 p. 211
hajj, 6.2 p. 162f
Halloween, 7.3 p. 196
Hama-rikyu Gardens (Tokyo),
   U6 p. 483
hamburgers, 7.2 p. 188,
   20.2 p. 555f
hamlets, 15.3 p. 414
Hammond, Robert, 17.2 p. 471
Hangul language, 8.1 p. 202f
Harappan civilization, 12.3 p. 325
harbors, 15.1 p. 404
hardiness zones, U5 p. 392f
Harlem, New York City, U3 p. 229
Harris, Chauncey, 16.1 p. 433
Harris and Ullman multiple-nuclei
   model, 16.1 p. 432f, 16.1 p. 433–435,
   U6 p. 486f
Harvey (hurricane), 2.4 p. 45
Hawaiian language, 8.2 p. 212
HDI. See Human Development Index
health care, 3.4 p. 80, 4.4 p. 106, 18.1
   p. 502, 18.1 p. 502f, 19.1 p. 524
hearths, agricultural, 12.3 pp. 324–326,
   12.3 p. 326m
heavy industry, 18.1 p. 495
Hebrew language, 8.2 p. 211
Hellenistic Age, 7.2 p. 186
herbicides, 2.2 p. 30, 13.1 p. 340, 14.2
   p. 372
heritage, 17.3 p. 478
Herzegovina, 9.3 p. 247
Hiebert, Fredrik, U3 pp. 150–151, U3
   p. 151f
hierarchical diffusion, 7.1 pp. 181–182,
   7.1 p. 183f, U3 p. 232f
High Line Network, 17.2 p. 471
High Line (New York City), 17.2 p. 471
highways, 10.1 p. 266, 15.2 p. 407, 16.2
   p. 439, 17.2 p. 470
hijab, 7.2 p. 189
Himalayas, 20.3 p. 564
Hin Lad Nai, Thailand, 14.1 p. 359
Hindi language, 8.2 p. 206
Hinduism
   adherents of, 8.3 p. 215f
   as centripetal force, 11.3 p. 289
   culture and, 6.2 p. 161, 8.3 p. 214
   diffusion of, 8.3 p. 218, 8.4 pp. 223–
      224, 8.4 p. 223f
Hinton, Karliss, 7.1 p. 180f
historical factors, 3.1 p. 66
Hitler, Adolf, 11.1 p. 278, 11.3 p. 290
Hmong migration, 5.4 p. 130
HOLC. See Home Owners Loan
   Corporation
holidays, 11.3 p. 289
Holocaust, 8.4 p. 225, 11.3 p. 290
Home Owners Loan Corporation
   (HOLC), 17.2 p. 463m
homelessness, 2.4 p. 46, 2.4 p. 46m

Honduras, 5.2 p. 121
Hong Kong, 16.2 p. 442f, 20.2 p. 559
Hormuz, Strait of, 9.2 p. 246, 9.2 p. 246f
Hossain, Mohammed Kabir,
   U2 p. 141
hot dogs, 7.2 p. 188
House of Representatives,
   10.2 p. 269
housing
   affordable, 17.2 pp. 465–466
   discrimination and, 17.2 pp. 460–461,
      17.2 p. 462, 17.2 p. 463m
   urban population density and, 16.2
      pp. 439–440, 16.2 p. 443
   urbanization and, 17.2 pp. 465–466
   zoning and diversity in, 17.1
      pp. 456–457
Housing Acts (U.S.), 17.2 p. 470
Houston, Texas, 15.2 p. 408, 16.1 p. 435,
   16.2 p. 443
Hoyt, Homer, 16.1 p. 433
Hoyt sector model, 16.1 p. 432f, 16.1
   p. 433, 16.1 p. 435, U6 p. 486f
HSBC, 20.2 p. 552
Hualien County, China, 6.4 p. 170
Huangpu River, 15.4 p. 423
Huave language, 8.1 p. 202
HUD. See Department of Housing and
   Urban Development
human constructs, 1.2 p. 16
human development, 19.1 pp. 521–524
Human Development Index (HDI), 19.1
   p. 525, 19.1 p. 526f, 19.2 p. 527, 19.3
   p. 535
human geography, defined,
   1.1 p. 7
human migration
   Cleveland and, 17.2 p. 462
   climate change and, U2 pp. 140–141
   cultural and social consequences of,
      5.5 pp. 135–137
   data on, U2 p. 147f
   documenting stories of, 5.2
      pp. 119–121, 5.3 pp. 126–127, U2
      pp. 140–141
   economic consequences of, 5.5
      pp. 133–135
   economics and, 3.1 p. 65
   effects of, 5.1 pp. 110–120, 5.4 p. 128, U2
      p. 145, U2 p. 147f
   historical in U.S., 5.4 pp. 128–130
   industrialization and, 18.1 p. 501
   overview of, U2 p. 59, 5.1 p. 111
   policy drivers for, 5.4 pp. 130–132
   reasons for, 5.1 pp. 112–114, 5.1 p. 112f
   refugees, internally displaced persons
      and, 5.3 pp. 122–125
   retracing path of, U2 p. 60, U2 p. 61f
   voluntary, 5.2 pp. 115–118, 5.2 p. 120,
      U2 p. 145
human rights, 5.5 p. 133
human trafficking, 5.2 p. 120
human-environment interaction, 1.1
   pp. 9–10
humid temperate climates, 12.1 p. 310
Hungary, 4.3 p. 102, 11.2 p. 286
Huntington, Henry, 15.4 p. 424
hurricanes
   drones and, 2.2 p. 34
   Florence, 5.1 p. 114f
   Harvey, 2.4 p. 45
   human migration and, 5.1 p. 114, 5.1
      p. 114f, 5.3 p. 124f
   Katrina, 1.1 p. 12, 1.1 p. 13f, 5.1 p. 114,
      16.3 p. 448
   mapping data and, 2.4 p. 45
   Maria, 2.2 p. 34, 5.3 p. 124f
   New Orleans and, 1.1 p. 12, 1.1 p. 13f
Hutterites, 7.2 pp. 192–193
Hutu people, 9.3 p. 249
hybrid crops, 13.1 pp. 339–340
hydroelectric power, 18.2 pp. 509–511,
   20.3 p. 563f

INDEX

I

Ibrahim, Hindou Oumarou, 14.1 p. 367

ice cap climates, 12.1 p. 311

Iceland, 11.2 p. 285, 19.2 p. 528, 19.3 p. 536, 20.3 p. 561

Idai (cyclone), 12.2 p. 314

identity, 6.2 p. 157, 6.3 pp. 163–164

IDP. *See* internally displaced persons

IEA. *See* International Energy Agency

IMF. *See* International Monetary Fund

immigrants
  aging population and, 4.4 p. 107
  from Central America, 5.2 p. 121
  countries hosting, 5.2 p. 115, 5.2 p. 116m
  dialects and, 8.1 p. 203
  Liverpool and, 15.2 p. 411
  sources of, 5.3 p. 123m, 5.4 p. 132f
  supranational organizations and, 11.2 p. 286

immigration, 5.1 p. 111

Immigration and Nationality Act of 1965, 5.4 p. 130

impacts of humans, U1 p. 3

imperialism
  Christian diffusion and, 8.4 p. 219
  cultural diffusion and, C7 p. 178, 7.2 p. 185
  division of labor and, 20.2 p. 556
  independence movements and, 9.4 p. 249
  industrialization and, 18.1 pp. 499–500
  population distribution and, 3.1 p. 65
  time and, 9.3 p. 247

IMR. *See* infant mortality rate

Inca, 7.2 p. 185

incentives, 15.2 p. 409, 17.1 p. 454, 17.2 p. 466, 20.1 550

inclusionary zoning laws, 17.2 p. 466, 17.2 p. 471

income, 19.1 pp. 521–522. *See also* wages

India
  aging population and, 4.4 p. 105
  agriculture and, 14.3 p. 382, 14.4 p. 385, 14.4 p. 386
  border conflicts and, U4 p. 298m
  boundaries and, 9.4 p. 254
  Buddha and, 6.4 p. 173
  centripetal forces and, 11.3 p. 289
  cereal production and land use in, U5 p. 393f
  cropland in, 12.1 p. 307m
  diffusion and, 7.2 p. 185
  economic growth and, 19.4 p. 541
  forced sterilization and, 4.3 p. 101
  gendered spaces and, 6.3 p. 164f, 6.3 p. 166
  imperialism and, 9.3 p. 249
  megacities and, U6 p. 399
  Muslims, Hindus and, 8.3 p. 214, 8.3 p. 218
  natural resources and, 20.3 p. 560
  outsourcing and, 20.2 p. 556
  regions and, 1.2 p. 19
  Sustainable Development Goals and, 20.3 p. 562
  textile industry and, 18.3 p. 517
  urban land tenure and, 17.2 p. 468
  urbanization and, 17.3 p. 472

Indian Removal Act of 1830, 5.4 p. 128

indigenous languages, 6.4 p. 172

indigenous Muslims, U3 p. 229

indigenous peoples
  Amazon River Basin and, 20.3 p. 560, 20.3 p. 565
  Belo Monte Dam and, 18.2 pp. 509–511
  climate knowledge and, 14.1 p. 367
  fair trade movement and, 14.1 p. 365
  shifting cultivation and, 14.1 p. 359

Indigenous Peoples' Day (Wisconsin), 6.1 p. 156

Indochina Migration and Refugee Assistance Act (1975), 5.4 p. 130

Indo-European language family, 8.1 p. 201–204, 8.2 p. 206

Indo-Iranian branch of languages, 8.1 p. 205f

Indonesia, 9.4 p. 254, 11.3 p. 290–291, 17.3 p. 472, 18.3 p. 517, 20.1 p. 549

Indus River Valley, 12.3 p. 325, 12.3 p. 326m, 12.4 p. 331, 15.1 p. 403

industrial parks, 18.3 p. 517

Industrial Revolution
  city sites and, 15.1 p. 404
  first, 18.1 pp. 496–498
  fourth, 18.1 p. 503
  maturity and, 19.4 p. 540
  migration and, 5.2 p. 120
  overview of, 18.1 pp. 495–497
  population trends and, 4.1 pp. 87–88, 4.2 p. 93
  second, 18.1 pp. 498–499
  spread of, 18.1 p. 500m
  third, 18.1 p. 499
  time before, 18.1 p. 496
  transitions during, 18.2 p. 507
  urbanization and, 15.2 p. 408

industrialization
  coal deposits and, 18.1 p. 497, 18.1 p. 497m
  diffusion of, 18.1 pp. 500–502
  least-cost theory and, 18.3 pp. 512–516, 18.3 p. 514f
  localization of, 18.3 pp. 512–516
  overview of, 18.1 p. 495
  spread of, 18.1 pp. 498–500, 18.1 p. 500m
  stages of, U7 p. 572f

industry, defined, 18.1 p. 495

inequality, 10.1 p. 267, 19.2 pp. 527–528, 19.3 p. 536f, 19.4 pp. 541–543

infant mortality rate (IMR), 3.4 p. 79, 3.4 p. 79m, 4.1 p. 90, 18.1 p. 502, 19.1 p. 524

infill development, 15.2 p. 410, 16.2 p. 443

influence, world cities and, 15.4 pp. 421–422, 15.4 p. 421f

influenza activity, 2.4 p. 44, 2.4 p. 44m

informal economic sector, 19.1 p. 522–523

information technology
  fourth agricultural revolution and, 12.4 p. 333
  quaternary economic sector and, 18.2 pp. 504–505, 18.2 p. 504f, 18.2 p. 506, 18.2 p. 507f
  Third Industrial Revolution and, 18.1 p. 499

infrastructure
  agricultural production regions and, 13.1 p. 339
  census data and, 16.3 p. 449
  food insecurity and, 14.3 p. 381
  future cities and, 15.3 p. 416, 15.3 p. 418
  global agricultural system and, 13.4 p. 351–353
  importance of, 16.3 p. 444
  local, C16 p. 451
  Shanghai and, C16 p. 430f
  urbanization and, 16.3 pp. 444–446, 17.2 p. 460

inputs, intensive agriculture and, 12.2 p. 314

inquiry. See Geo-Inquiry

insects, 14.3 p. 382f, 17.3 p. 475

integration, acculturation and, 7.3 p. 195f

intensive agriculture, 12.2 pp. 314–317, 12.2 p. 319, U5 p. 393f

intensive subsistence agriculture, 12.2 p. 314, 12.2 p. 314f

interaction, theories of, 1.1 pp. 9–10. *See also* gravity model; human-environment interaction

interchangeable parts, 18.1 p. 498

interdependence, 13.4 pp. 350–351, 19.4 p. 541, 20.1 pp. 547–548

internal combustion engine, 18.1 pp. 498–499

internal migration, 5.2 p. 115, 5.4 p. 128m, 5.4 pp. 128–129

internally displaced persons (IDP), 5.2 p. 118, 5.3 pp. 122–123

international dollars, 19.1 p. 525

International Energy Agency (IEA), U4 p. 297f

International Monetary Fund (IMF), 20.1 pp. 548–549, 20.2 p. 552, 20.2 p. 554

International Union for the Conservation of Nature (IUCN), 14.1 p. 366

Internet, 7.1 p. 181, U3 p. 231f, 11.1 p. 278, 11.1 p. 282, 15.2 p. 407

internet freedom, 6.1 p. 155m

Inter-Parliamentary Union (IPU), 19.2 p. 528

interregional migration, 5.4 p. 128

Interstate Highway System, 10.1 p. 266, 16.2 p. 439, 17.2 p. 470

interval data, 16.3 p. 448

intervening obstacles, 5.2 p. 117

intervening opportunities, 5.2 p. 117

intraregional migration, 5.4 p. 128

Inuit people, 10.1 p. 268

Inupiat people, 6.3 pp. 163–164

IPU. *See* Inter-Parliamentary Union

Iran, 6.2 p. 160, 18.2 p. 505, 19.1 p. 524f

Iraq, 9.2 p. 244

Ireland
  famine and, 4.1 p. 90
  Human Development Index and, 19.1 p. 526f
  human migration and, 5.1 p. 113, 5.2 pp. 116–117, 5.2 p. 117f, 5.2 p. 120, C5 p. 139f
  religion and, 6.4 p. 175, 6.4 p. 175m

Irish Potato Famine, 15.2 p. 411

iron, 15.2 p. 409, 18.1 p. 497, 18.1 p. 499

irredentism, 9.2 p. 243, 11.1 p. 278, 11.1 p. 279

irrigation
  agricultural hearths and, 12.3 p. 325
  agriculture and, 12.1 p. 308, 14.1 p. 360m, 14.1 pp. 360–362
  first agricultural revolution and, 12.4 p. 330
  Saudi Arabia and, 3.1 p. 66f

Islam, 8.3 p. 214, 8.3 p. 216, 8.4 p. 220–223, 8.4 p. 220f, U3 pp. 228–229. *See also* Muslims

islands, 15.1 p. 404, 15.3 p. 419

isolated languages (isolates), 8.1 p. 202

isoline maps, 2.3 p. 40m, 2.3 p. 43, U1 p. 56m

Israel, U4 p. 238

Istanbul, Turkey, 16.3 p. 444

Italic-Romance branch of languages, 8.1 p. 204f

Italy, 11.3 p. 290

IUCN. *See* International Union for the Conservation of Nature

Ivory Coast, West Africa, 1.3 p. 23f

J

Jakarta, Indonesia, 17.2 p. 464, 17.3 p. 472

Japan
  economic development and, 18.2 p. 507
  financial crisis of 2007-2008 and, 20.2 p. 553
  gender roles and, 19.3 pp. 534–535
  industrialization and, 18.1 p. 500
  least-cost theory and, 18.3 p. 516, 18.3 p. 517
  life expectancy and, 3.4 p. 80
  as nation-state, 9.2 p. 243
  population composition and, 3.4 p. 81f, 4.4 p. 105f
  as unitary state, 10.1 p. 261

Japanese language, 8.2 p. 206

Japlan de Serra, Mexico, 5.5 p. 136, 5.5 p. 137

jazz, 6.2 p. 158

Jerusalem, U4 p. 238, U4 p. 239f

Jesus, 8.4 p. 219

Jim Crow laws, 5.4 p. 129

Johns Hopkins University, 14.3 p. 380, p. R3

Judaism, 6.3 p. 166f, 8.3 p. 215f, 8.4 pp. 224–225, 8.4 p. 225f

Juruna people, 18.2 p. 510–511

just-in-time delivery, 20.2 p. 555

K

Kaaba (Saudi Arabia), 6.2 p. 161, 6.2 p. 162f

Kangnido Map, 9.2 p. 241f

Kansas City, Missouri, 15.2 p. 408

Kaprun Limberg II power plant (Austria), 20.3 p. 563f

karma, 8.4 p. 224

Katrina (hurricane), 1.1 p. 12, 1.1 p. 13f, 5.1 p. 114, 16.3 p. 448

Kazakhstan, 20.1 p. 547f

Keeby, Ossa, 7.1 p. 180f

Kent Bikes, 20.1 pp. 550–551

Kenya
  boundaries and, 9.4 p. 254
  central place theory and, U6 p. 485f
  cultural dynamics and, 6.1 p. 154
  ecotourism and, 20.3 p. 564f
  extensive, intensive agriculture and, 12.2 p. 319
  food storage, transportation and, 14.3 p. 381
  gendered spaces and, 6.3 p. 164
  neocolonialism and, 9.2 p. 245
  supranationalism and, 11.2 p. 285

Khabeer, Su'ad Abdul, U3 p. 229

Khan, Sadiq, U6 p. 400

Khmer Rouge, 3.1 p. 65

Khövsgöl province, Mongolia, 12.1 p. 311f

Ki'an, China, 15.1 p. 404

Kidman cattle ranches, U5 p. 393f

Kim Il Sung, 9.4 p. 253f

Kim Jong Il, 9.4 p. 253f

Kimberley, South Africa, 15.1 p. 404

Kings Cross district (London), 17.3 p. 476, 17.3 p. 477f

kinship links, 5.4 p. 129

Kiribati, U1 p. 4

kiwi fruit, 12.3 p. 329

Koike, Yuriko, U6 p. 483

Kolivras, Korine N., 2.3 p. 37

Kongo, 8.4 p. 220

Köppen, Vladimir, 12.1 p. 310, 12.1 p. 310m

Köppen climate classifications, 12.1 p. 310, 12.1 p. 310m

Korea, U4 p. 237, 9.4 p. 250, 9.4 p. 251

Korean language, 8.2 p. 211

Kosovo, 9.2 p. 242

K-pop, 7.2 p. 188, 7.2 p. 189f

Krugliak, Amanda, 5.2 p. 119

Kuma, Kengo, U6 p. 482–483

Kurdish people, 5.1 p. 113, 5.3 p. 127f, 9.3 p. 248, 11.3 p. 291, 11.3 p. 291f

Kurdistan, 9.3 p. 248

Kurgan hearth theory, 8.2 p. 206, 8.2 p. 208, 8.2 p. 208f

Kuuk Thaayorre people, 8.1 p. 201

Kuwait, 19.1 p. 523

L

labor force, 18.3 p. 513, 18.3 pp. 516–517, 20.2 p. 552, U7 p. 571f

labor-force participation (LFP), 19.2 p. 529–530, 19.2 p. 530f

labor-market participation (LMP), 19.2 p. 529–530, 19.2 p. 530f

Lagos, Nigeria, 4.4 p. 104f, 15.4 p. 427, 17.2 p. 466, 17.2 p. 467f
  landscapes, 16.3 p. 444–446

Lancaster County, Pennsylvania, 17.1 p. 456, 17.1 p. 457, 17.3 p. 476

land cover change, 14.1 p. 364

land degradation, landscapes, 4.4 p. 103

land ownership, 12.4 p. 331, 14.4 p. 385

land readjustment, 17.2 p. 468
land tenure, 17.2 p. 466–468
Land Transport Authority (LTA), 10.1 p. 263
land use patterns, U5 p. 396f, 16.1 p. 431, 16.1 p. 432f. *See also* bid-rent theory; von Thünen model
land value, 12.2 p. 312
landforms, 3.1 pp. 64–65, 15.1 p. 404
landlocked countries, 9.4 p. 256
landscapes, 6.2 pp. 157–161, 6.2 p. 162f, 6.3 p. 163, 6.4 p. 173, 17.2 p. 470
land-use maps, 2.2 p. 30
land-use planning, 15.2 p. 409
language branches, 8.1 p. 202
language families
   Niger-Congo, U3 p. 234f
   overview of, 8.1 pp. 201–202, 8.1 pp. 204–205f
   spread and change of, 8.2 p. 206, 8.2 p. 208–210
language groups, 8.1 p. 203
languages
   acculturation and, 7.3 p. 194, 7.3 p. 194f
   Catalonia and, U4 p. 298m
   categorizing, 8.1 pp. 201–203
   cultural diffusion and, 7.2 pp. 185–188, 7.2 p. 186f, U3 p. 231f
   cultural landscapes and, 6.2 p. 161
   culture and, 8.1 p. 201, 8.1 p. 202f
   distribution of, 8.2 p. 206, 8.2 p. 207f
   ethnicity and, 6.4 pp. 173–174
   impacts of diffusion of, 8.2 pp. 210–212
   Indo-European family of, 8.1 pp. 204–205
   Niger-Congo family of, U3 p. 234f
   outsourcing and, 20.2 p. 556
   Quebec and, 8.2 p. 213, 11.1 p. 280
   sense of place and, 6.4 p. 170
   spread and change of, 8.2 p. 206, 8.2 pp. 208–210
   studying, 6.4 p. 172
Languages in Danger program, 8.2 p. 212
Laos, 5.4 p. 130
large-lot zoning, 17.1 pp. 455–456
large-scale manufacturing, 18.1 p. 495
large-scale maps, 2.3 p. 37m
LAS. *See* League of Arab States
Las Vegas, Nevada, C20 p. 546f
Lassa virus, 4.2 p. 97
Latin, 8.2 p. 200
Latin America, 20.1 p. 548
Latin American city model, 16.1 p. 435, 16.1 p. 436f, 16.1 p. 437f, U6 p. 487f
latitude, 1.1 p. 8
layers, geographic information systems and, 2.2 p. 31, 2.2 p. 31f
lead, 4.2 p. 95
League of Arab States (LAS), 11.2 p. 283, 11.2 p. 286t
League of Nations, 11.2 p. 283
least-cost theory, 18.3 pp. 512–517, 18.3 p. 514f, 18.3 p. 571f
Legislative Services Agency of Iowa, 10.2 p. 271
Lenin, Vladimir, 8.2 p. 212
Leopold II (King of Belgium), 18.1 p. 500
lettuce, 12.2 p. 323f
levees, 1.1 p. 12, 1.1 p. 13f
Levittown, New York, 17.2 p. 461f
Lewis, Charlie, 7.1 p. 180f
Lewis, Pierce, 16.1 p. 435
Lexington, Kentucky, 17.3 p. 476
LG Electronics, C20 p. 546f
LGBTQIA+ spaces, 6.3 pp. 166–167, 6.3 p. 167m, U3 p. 231m, 17.2 p. 470
Liberty Bell, 11.3 p. 289
Libya, 15.3 p. 413, 15.3 p. 413f
life expectancy
   gender and, 6.3 p. 165f
   human development and, 19.1 p. 524

Human Development Index and, 19.1 p. 525
industrialization and, 18.1 pp. 500–501, 18.1 p. 501f
overview of, 3.4 pp. 79–80
lifestyle choices, 4.2 p. 95
light industry, 18.1 p. 495
Lima, Peru, 17.3 p. 474
Line Islands, U1 p. 4
linear populations, 3.1 p. 63f, 12.2 p. 315, 12.2 p. 315f, 12.2 p. 321m
lingua franca, 7.2 p. 186, 8.2 p. 211
Lisbon, Portugal, 17.2 p. 470
literacy, 18.1 p. 502, 19.1 p. 524, 19.1 p. 525f, 19.2 p. 529
lithium, U7 pp. 568–569
Lithuania, 8.4 p. 219
Little Cuba, Miami, Florida, 5.5 p. 135, 55 p. 136f
livability, 15.2 p. 409, 17.1 p. 453, 17.3 p. 478, C17 p. 481
Liverpool, England, 15.2 p. 411, 18.1 p. 497
livestock. *See also* agriculture
   extensive agriculture and, 12.2 p. 318
   mixed systems and, 12.2 p. 314, 12.2 p. 316, 12.2 p. 317
   technology and, 12.4 p. 333
   third agricultural revolution and, 12.4 p. 334
   von Thünen model and, 13.3 pp. 348–349, 13.3 p. 348f
livestock feed crops, 12.1 p. 307
LMP. *See* labor-market participation
loans
   financial crisis of 2007-2008 and, 20.2 p. 553
   gender, agriculture and, 14.4 p. 385, 14.4 p. 387
   global economy and, 20.2 p. 552
   International Monetary Fund and, 20.1 p. 549
local food movements, 14.2 pp. 374–375, 17.2 p. 469
local power, 10.1 p. 265f, 10.1 p. 266
location, 1.1 p. 8, 18.3 pp. 512–517
locomotives, 18.1 p. 497
logging, 14.1 p. 364
logistics, 20.2 p. 555
London, England
   brownfield remediation and, 17.3 p. 476, 17.3 p. 477f
   economic growth, life expectancy and, 10.1 p. 501
   growth management and, 17.1 p. 456f, 17.1 p. 457
   growth of, 15.4 p. 426
   guerrilla geography and, U6 p. 400, U6 p. 401f
   influence of, 15.4 p. 421, 15.4 p. 422
longitude, 1.1 p. 8
long-lot survey system, 12.2 p. 313, 12.2 p. 313f, 12.2 p. 320m
looters, U3 p. 150
Los Angeles, California
   city linkage and, 15.4 p. 422
   as galactic city, 16.1 p. 435
   gentrification and, 17.2 p. 470
   growth of, 15.4 p. 424, 15.4 pp. 424–425
   residential land use and, 16.2 p. 439
Louisiana, 1.2 p.15m
Louisiana Purchase, 6.2 p. 158
LTA. *See* Land Transport Authority
lumber industry, 18.3 pp. 514-515f
Lumbini, Nepal, 6.4 p. 173
Lutheranism, 8.3 p. 216

M

Maastricht Treaty, 11.2 p. 283
Macedonia, 9.3 p. 247
machine tools, 18.1 pp. 498–499
Macron, Emmanuel, 11.3 p. 288
Madagascar, 8.2 pp. 209–210, 8.2 p. 210m, 13.4 p. 350, 13.4 p. 350f
Magdalena, Maria (Mayito), U4 pp. 294–295

Magufuli, John, 4.3 p. 101f
Mahbub, A.Q.M., U2 p. 141
maize, 12.3 p. 325f, 12.3 p. 328
majority-minority districts, 10.2 p. 270
Makoko settlement (Lagos), 17.2 p. 466, 17.2 p. 467f
Maksudov, Farhod, 15.1 p. 406
Malacca, Strait of, 9.2 pp. 245–246
Malawi, U5 p. 304, U5 p. 305f, 12.1 p. 309f, 14.4 p. 384, 19.2 p. 530f
Malaysia, C7 p. 178, 9.4 p. 254, 12.2 p. 314, 20.1 p. 549
Mali, 12.4 p. 335, 19.2 p. 528
malnutrition, 14.3 p. 378
Malthus, Thomas, 4.2 p. 92, U2 p. 144f, U5 p. 393
Malthus's theory of population growth, 4.2 p. 92, U2 p. 144f, U5 p. 393f
Mandalay, 12.2 p. 314f
Mandarin Chinese language, 6.4 p. 170, 8.2 p. 206
Mandela, Nelson, 11.3 p. 289
mangrove forests, 20.3 p. 560
Manhattan, New York, 16.2 p. 443
Manila, Philippines, 11.1 p. 277, 15.4 p. 427
manufacturing industry
   globalization and, 20.2 pp. 555–556
   industrialization and, 18.1 p. 495
   new zones of, 20.2 pp. 558–559
   scale and, 18.1 p. 496f
   secondary economic sector and, 18.2 p. 504, 18.2 p. 504f
manufacturing zones, 20.2 pp. 558–559
map scale, 2.3 pp. 37–39, U1 pp. 54–55m
MAP4DEV group, C2 p. 26f
Mapping Out a Safer Community program, 2.2 p. 33
maps. *See also* Geographic Information Systems
   distance and, 2.3 p. 37
   environmental injustice and, 17.2 p. 468
   mental, 1.1 p. 8
   overview of, 2.3 pp. 36–37
   political, 9.2 pp. 241–244
   projection types, 2.3 p. 38m, 2.3 pp. 38–39, 2.3 p. 39m
   scale on, 2.3 pp. 37–39, U1 pp. 54–55m
   types of, 2.3 pp. 40–43, U1 pp. 56–57m
marginalization, 7.3 p. 195f
Maria (hurricane), 2.2 p. 34, 5.3 p. 124f
marine west coast climate, 12.1 p. 310
maritime boundaries, 9.4 pp. 255–257, 9.4 p. 256f, 9.4 p. 257f
market gardening, 12.2 p. 314, 12.2 p. 317, 13.3 pp. 348–349, 13.3 p. 348f
Marshall, Will, U1 pp. 50–51
Maryland, 10.2 p. 271f
mass consumption, 19.4 p. 540, 19.4 p. 541f, U7 p. 572f
mass production, 18.1 pp. 498–499, 20.2 p. 555
mass transit, 16.2 p. 443, 16.3 pp. 444–446. See also transportation systems
maternal mortality rate (MMR), 19.2 p. 528
maturity, 19.4 p. 540, 19.4 p. 541f, U7 p. 572f
Maya Devi Temple (Lumbini, Nepal), 6.4 p. 173
Mbororo people, 14.1 p. 367
McCormick, Cyrus, 12.4 pp. 331–332
McDonald's, 13.2 p. 344
McGee, T.G., 16.1 p. 437
McLeod, Mary, 6.2 p. 161
measurements, 3.1 pp. 67–68, 3.1 p. 68t, 16.3 p. 448
meat consumption, 14.2 pp. 375–376, 14.3 p. 382
Mecca, 6.2 p. 161, 6.2 p. 162f
Medicare and Medicaid, 19.1 p. 522

Mediterranean agriculture, 12.1 p. 311, 12.2 p. 314, 12.2 p. 317
Mediterranean climates, 12.1 pp. 310–311
medium-scale maps, 2.3 p. 37m
megacities, U6 p. 399, 15.4 p. 420m, 15.4 pp. 420–421, 15.4 p. 421f
Mennonite communities, 17.1 p. 456
mental maps, 1.1 p. 8
mentifacts, 6.1 p. 153, 6.2 p. 161
Mercator projections, 2.3 p. 38, 2.3 p. 38m, 2.3 p. 39t, U1 p. 55m
Mercosur, 11.2 p. 286t, 20.1 p. 548
Merlion Park (Singapore), 15.4 p. 422
Mesa, Arizona, 15.2 p. 410
metacities, 15.4 p. 420
metals, 18.1 p. 495
metalworking, 12.4 pp. 330–331
metes and bounds, 12.2 p. 313
Metro (Washington D.C. subway system), 17.1 p. 453
metropolitan areas, defined, 15.1 p. 403
Metropolitan Transit Authority (MTA), 16.3 p. 447
Mexico
   automobile manufacturing and, 18.3 p. 517, U7 p. 575f
   avocados and, 14.2 p. 376
   cereal production and land use in, U5 p. 393f
   export processing zones and, 20.2 p. 559
   federalism in, 10.1 p. 266
   gender inequality and, 19.2 p. 528
   Green Revolution and, 12.4 p. 333
   human migration and, 5.1 p. 113, 5.5 p. 135, 5.5 p. 136
   state boundaries in, 10.1 p. 264f
   United States border with, 9.2 p. 245f, 9.3 p. 249, 9.3 p. 249f
   world system theory and, 10.4 p. 542
Mexico City, Mexico, 15.1 p. 405, 15.1 p. 405f, 15.3 p. 414, 16.1 p. 437f, 17.3 p. 474
Meyer, Tara, 14.4 p. 385
Miami, Florida, 5.5 p. 135, 5.5 p. 136f
microfinancing, 14.4 p. 387
microloans, 19.3 p. 537, 19.3 p. 539, 20.2 p. 552
Microsoft, 18.2 p. 505, 20.2 p. 552, 20.2 p. 556
Middle Ages, 18.1 p. 496
middle class, rise of, 10.1 p. 501
migrant workers, 15.2 p. 408
migration. *See also* human migration
   cultural diffusion and, 7.2 pp. 187–188, 7.2 p. 189
   overview of, 5.1 p. 111
   Ravenstein's laws of, 5.1 p. 111, 5.2 p. 116, 5.5 p. 135, 5.5 p. 136f, U2 p. 145
Migration period, 3.1 p. 66
Milan, Italy, 17.3 p. 479
military power, 7.2 pp. 185–186, 11.2 p. 285
Millennium Park (Chicago), C17 p. 452f
millets, 12.3 p. 328
minarets, 6.4 p. 173
Mindanao, Philippines, 11.1 p. 277
mineral particles, 12.1 p. 308
Mingzhu Roundabout (Shanghai), C16 p. 430f
miniaturization, 18.1 p. 499
minimum wage, 10.1 p. 267
mining, 18.1 p. 496
minorities, human development and, 19.1 p. 525
missionaries, 8.4 p. 219
Mississippi, 1.2 p. 15m
Mississippi River, 15.2 p. 407. *See also* New Orleans, Louisiana

mixed crop and livestock systems, 12.2 p. 314, 12.2 p. 316, 12.2 p. 317

mixed-use developments (MUDs), 17.1 p. 453

mixed-use zoning, 15.3 p. 416, 16.2 p. 443, 17.1 p. 454

MMR. *See* maternal mortality rate

mobility, migration and, 5.1 p. 111

modeling and models *See also* Wallerstein's world system theory
African city model, 16.1 p. 436f, 16.1 p. 437, U6 p. 488f
central business districts and, 16.1 p. 431f, 16.1 p. 432f, 16.1 pp. 433–437, 16.1 p. 434f, U6 pp. 486–489f
concentric-zone model, 16.1 p. 432f, 16.1 p. 433, 16.1 p. 435, U6 p. 486f
Demographic Transition Model, 4.2 p. 93, 4.2 p. 94f, 5.5 p. 134, U2 p. 143f, 18.1 p. 500
distance decay model, 1.1 p. 10, U1 p. 52f, 5.2 p. 118f, 7.2 p. 190, U4 p. 300m
Epidemiological Transition Model, 4.2 pp. 93–96, 4.2 p. 95t, 4.4 p. 105, U2 p. 144f
galactic city (peripheral) model, 16.1 p. 434f, 16.1 p. 435, U6 p. 487f
gravity model, 5.1 p. 111, U2 p. 145m, 15.3 p. 412f, 15.3 p. 413, U6 p. 484f
Griffin-Ford model, 16.1 p. 435, 16.1 p. 436f, 16.1 p. 437f, U6 p. 487f
Harris and Ullman multiple-nuclei model, 16.1 p. 432f, 16.1 pp. 433–435, U6 p. 486f
Hoyt sector model, 16.1 p. 432f, 16.1 p. 433, 16.1 p. 435, U6 p. 486f
Latin American city model, 16.1 p. 435, 16.1 p. 436f, 16.1 p. 437f, U6 p. 487f
Southeast Asian city model, 16.1 p. 436f, 16.1 p. 437, U6 p. 488f
time-space compression model, 1.1 p. 10, U1 pp. 52–53f, 7.2 p. 190, 13.3 p. 349
of urban structure, 16.1 p. 432f, 16.1 pp. 433–437, 16.1 p. 434f, 16.1 p. 436f
von Thünen model, 13.3 pp. 348–349, 13.3 p. 348f, U5 p. 394f

Modi, Narendra, 8.3 p. 218

Mongla, Bangladesh, U2 p. 141

Mongolia, 6.2 p. 159, 12.1 p. 311f, 14.1 p. 363

monocropping, 12.2 p. 316, 12.2 pp. 316–317, 13.4 p. 353, 14.1 p. 368

monoculture systems, 12.2 p. 314, 12.2 pp. 316–317

monograms, 6.3 p. 163

monopolistic measures, 11.2 p. 285

monotheism, 8.4 p. 220

moral restraint, 4.2 p. 92

Morales, Evo, U7 p. 568

Mormon Church, 8.3 p. 216

Morocco, 5.4 p. 131, 11.2 p. 285

mortality. *See also* death rate
infant, 3.4 p. 79, 3.4 p. 79m, 4.1 p. 90, 18.1 p. 502, 19.1 p. 524
maternal, 19.2 p. 528
measures of, 3.4 pp. 78–80, 3.4 p. 78t

mortgage industry, 20.2 p. 553

Mos Def, U3 p. 229

Moscow, Russia, 15.4 p. 422

mosques, 6.4 p. 173

mosquitoes, 4.2 p. 98

Motor City, 18.3 p. 514

mountains, 3.1 p. 65

Mouraria neighborhood (Lisbon), 17.2 p. 470

Mozambique, 19.2 p. 530f

MTA. *See* Metropolitan Transit Authority

MUDs. *See* mixed-use developments

Mughal empire, 8.3 p. 218

Muhammad, 8.4 p. 220

multiculturalism, 7.3 p. 196

multinational companies, 12.4 p. 333, 12.4 p. 334, 20.2 p. 552

multinational states, 9.2 pp. 243–244, 9.3 p. 248

multiple-nuclei model, 16.1 p. 432f, 16.1 pp. 433–435, U6 p. 486f

multiplier effects, 20.2 p. 558

multistate nations, 9.2 p. 243

Mumbai, India, 15.4 p. 422, 15.4 p. 422f, 16.2 p. 443

Munduruku people, 18.2 pp. 510–511

municipal governments, 16.3 p. 447

municipalities, 10.2 p. 269

museum curators, U3 pp. 150–151

music, 5.5 p. 137m

Musk, Elon, 7.1 p. 181

Muslim ban, 5.5 p. 133

Muslim Cool (Khabeer), U3 p. 229

Muslims. *See also* Islam
adherents of, 8.3 p. 215f
in America, U3 pp. 228–229
cultural diffusion and, 7.2 p. 189
cultural landscape and, 6.2 p. 161, 6.2 p. 162f, 6.4 p. 173
Eritrea and, 11.1 p. 281
ethnic cleansing and, 11.1 p. 278
spread of, 8.3 p. 218
Sudan and, 11.1 p. 281
universalizing religions and, 8.4 p. 219

Myanmar, 5.2 pp. 118–120, 5.2 p. 120f, 11.1 p. 278, 14.3 p. 379

N

NAFTA. *See* North America Free Trade Agreement

Nagorno-Karabakh region (Armenia/Azerbaijan), 6.4 p. 175

Namibia, 17.2 p. 468

Namunyak Wildlife Conservancy (Kenya), 20.3 p. 564f

Nanak, Guru, 8.4 p. 222f

nanotechnology, 18.1 p. 503

Narayanan, Sandhya, 6.4 p. 172

National Archives, 2.2 p. 30

National Capital Region (India), 17.2 p. 464, 17.2 p. 464m

National Geographic, U3 p. 150

National Geographic Explorers
Adjany Costa, 1.1 p. 14
Andrés Ruzo, 20.3 p. 565
Anna Antoniou, 10.1 p. 262
Aziz Abu Sarah, U4 pp. 238–239
Caroline Gerdes, 16.3 p. 448f
Daniel Raven-Ellison, U6 pp. 400–401
Enric Sala, U1 pp. 4–5
Fred Hiebert, U3 pp. 150–151
Hindou Oumarou Ibrahim, 14.1 p. 367
Jason De León, 5.2 p. 119
Jennifer Burney, 14.3 p. 383
Jerry Glover, U5 pp. 304–305
Lillygol Sedaghat, 3.1 p. 69
Maria Silvina Fenoglio, 17.3 p. 475
Michael Frachetti, 15.1 p. 406
Michael Wesch, 11.1 p. 282
Pardis Sabeti, 4.2 p. 97
Paul Salopek, U2 pp. 60–61
Sandhya Narayanan, 6.4 p. 172
Sarah Parcak, 2.2 p. 35
Shabana Basij-Rasikh, U7 pp. 492–493
Shah Selbe, 2.4 p. 47
T. H. Culhane, 16.3 p. 445
Tristram Stuart, 13.2 p. 347
Wade Davis, 8.3 p. 217
Zachary Damato, 17.3 p. 473

National Geographic Photographers
Aaron Vincent Elkaim, 18.2 pp. 510–511
Amy Toensing, 19.2 pp. 532–533
David Guttenfelder, 9.4 pp. 252–253
George Steinmetz, 12.2 pp. 322–323
John Stanmeyer, 12.2, p. 319f
Lynsey Addario, 5.3 pp. 126–127
William Allard, 7.2 pp. 192–193

National Park City movement, U6 p. 400, U6 p. 401f, 16.3 p. 449

National Plan for Urbanization (China), 17.3 p. 474

National Rural Water Association (NRWA), 14.1 p. 365

National Socialist German Workers' Party, 11.1 p. 278, 11.3 p. 290

nationalism, 8.4 p. 219, 10.1 p. 266

nations, overview of, 9.2 p. 242

nation-states, 9.2 pp. 242–243, 9.2 p. 243f, 9.3 p. 247

Native Americans. *See* American Indians

NATO. *See* North Atlantic Treaty Organization

natural disasters, 4.1 p. 90, 5.2 p. 118, U2 p. 147f

natural resources
city sites and, 15.1 p. 404
development and, 20.3 p. 560
Fourth Industrial Revolution and, 18.1 p. 503
population density and, 3.1 p. 67
population distribution and, 3.1 p. 65
primary economic sector and, 18.2 p. 504, 18.2 p. 504f

Navajo people, as nation, 9.2 p. 242

Naxi people, 12.2 p. 322f

Nazi Party, 11.1 p. 278, 11.3 p. 290

neighborhood maps, U3 p. 230m

neighborhoods, 1.2 p. 17, 6.3 p. 163

Neighborhoods in Bloom initiative (Richmond), 17.1 p. 459

neocolonialism, 9.2 p. 245

neoliberalism, 20.1 p. 548

Neolithic Period, 15.1 p. 403

Neolithic Revolution, 12.4 pp. 329–331

neo-Malthusian theory, 4.2 pp. 92–93, U2 p. 144f, U5 p. 393f

Nepal, 6.4 p. 173, 11.3 p. 289, 20.3 p. 564

net migration, 5.1 p. 111

Netherlands, 5.5 p. 136, 7.2 p. 185, 10.1 pp. 263–264, 13.4 p. 350, U5 pp. 390–391f

New Delhi, India, 15.4 p. 420

New England, 18.1 p. 498, 18.3 p. 517

New Orleans, Louisiana
qualitative data on, 16.3 p. 448, 16.3 p. 448f
sequent occupance and, 6.2 p. 158
site, situation and, 1.1 pp. 12–13, 1.1 p. 13f, 15.2 p. 407

New Urbanism, 17.1 pp. 454–455, 17.1 p. 457, 17.1 p. 459

New York City
High Line and, 17.2 p. 471
housing density and development in, 16.2 p. 443
as megacity, 15.4 p. 420
political organization of, 16.3 p. 447
residential land use and, 16.2 p. 439
sanitation and, 18.1 p. 502f
urban farming in, 17.2 p. 469f
urbanization and, 18.1 p. 501
as world city, 15.4 p. 421

New Zealand, 12.3 p. 329

Newark, New Jersey, 17.3 p. 472

Newcomen, Thomas, 18.1 p. 496

newly industrialized countries (NICs), 20.2 p. 556, 20.2 p. 558

Niger, 19.1 pp. 524–525, 19.1 p. 526f, 19.2 p. 528

Niger-Congo language family, U3 p. 234f

Nigeria
antinatalist policy of, 4.3 p. 101
devolutionary forces and, 11.1 pp. 280–281
hunger, conflict and, 14.3 p. 379
infrastructure, development and, 16.3 pp. 444–446
population size and distribution and, 4.4 p. 103–104, 4.4 p. 104f

Nigerian Slum and Informal Settlement Federation, 17.2 p. 466

Nike, 20.2 p. 552, 20.2 p. 556

Nile River Valley, 3.2 p. 72, 12.3 p. 325, 12.4 p. 331, 15.1 p. 403

Nobel Peace Prize, 12.4 p. 333, 19.3 p. 539

nodes, 1.2 p. 17, 1.2 p. 17m, 16.1 p. 433

Noji Gardens neighborhood (Seattle), 17.1 p. 459

Nokia, 20.2 p. 556

nomadic herding, 12.2 p. 318, 12.2 p. 319, 14.1 p. 362, 14.1 p. 366

nomads, 5.2 p. 116, 6.2 p. 159

nominal data, 16.3 p. 448

noncommunicable diseases, U2 p. 145m

nongovernmental organizations (NGOs), 14.1 p. 365, 16.3 p. 445

nonrenewable resources, 1.1 p. 10, 20.3 p. 560

Norfolk four-field crop rotation system, 12.4 p. 332, 12.4 p. 332f

Norilsk, Siberia, 3.1 p. 65

Normans, 8.2 p. 208

North America Free Trade Agreement (NAFTA), 1.3 pp. 20–21, 14.2 p. 376, 20.1 p. 548, U7 p. 575f

North Atlantic Treaty Organization (NATO), 11.2 p. 283, 11.2 p. 284m, 11.2 p. 285, 11.2 p. 286t

North Carolina, 10.2 p. 272, 10.2 p. 273f

North Central China agricultural hearth, 12.3 p. 326m

North Korea, U4 p. 237, 9.4 p. 250, 9.4 pp. 251–253

Norway, 10.1 p. 263, 11.2 p. 285, 19.1 p. 526f

Notre Dame Cathedral fire, 11.3 p. 288, 11.3 p. 289f

Novosibirsk, Russia, 15.1 p. 405

Nowakowski, Kelsey, 15.4 pp. 424–427

NRWA. *See* National Rural Water Association

Ntaiya, Kakenya, 19.3 p. 538f

nucleated settlements (clustered populations), 3.1 p. 63f, 12.2 p. 315, 12.2 p. 315f, 12.2 p. 321m

Nunavut, 10.1 p. 268

nutrition, land use and, U5 p. 396f

O

Oahu, Hawaii, C13 p. 338

OAU. *See* Organization for African Unity

Obama, Barack, U1 p. 4

obesity, 4.2 p. 95

oceans, U1 p. 4, 12.1 p. 309

offshore outsourcing, 20.2 pp. 556–558, 20.2 p. 557f

Ogallala Aquifer, 14.1 p. 360m, 14.1 p. 362

Ohio River, 15.1 p. 404

oil crops, 12.1 p. 307

oil industry
Amazon River Basin and, 20.3 p. 560
choke points and, 9.2 p. 246f, U4 p. 297m, U4 p. 297f
commodity dependence and, 19.4 p. 543
OPEC and, 20.1 p. 549

Okavango River Basin (Africa), 1.1 p. 14

Okavango Wilderness Project, 1.1 p. 14

Olympics, U6 p. 482

Omaha, Nebraska, 15.1 p. 405

Oman, 19.1 p. 523

Omran, Abdel R., 4.2 p. 93

One-Child Policy, 4.1 p. 89, 4.3 p. 99f, 4.3 p. 100

on-farm mixing, 12.2 p. 317

Ontario, Canada, 11.1 p. 278

OPEC. *See* Organization of the Petroleum Exporting Countries

open markets, neoliberalism and, 20.1 p. 548

OpenStreetMap, 2.4 p. 45

orange juice, 13.2 p. 345

oranges, 12.3 p. 328

Orbital Insight, U1 pp. 150–51

ordinal data, 16.3 p. 448

Orelius, atlas of, 2.3 p. 36m

organic farming, 12.2 p. 317, 12.2 p. 323f, 12.4 p. 334, 13.1 p. 342, 14.1 p. 368, 14.2 p. 375

organic soil matter, 12.1 p. 308

Organization for African Unity (OAU), 11.2 p. 285

Organization of the Petroleum Exporting Countries (OPEC), 20.1 p. 549, 20.1 p. 549m

ostrich farms, 12.3 p. 329

Out of Eden Walk, U2 p. 60

outsourcing, 20.2 pp. 556–558, 20.2 p. 556t, 20.2 p. 557f, U7 p. 575f

overgrazing, 14.1 p. 362, 14.1 p. 364

overpopulation, 4.2 p. 92

oxen, 12.4 p. 330, 12.4 p. 331

oysters, 14.2 p. 372

P

Pacific Alliance, 11.2 p. 286t

Pacific Electric Railway, 15.4 p. 424

Pacific Remote Islands Marine National Monument, U1 p. 4

packing districts, 10.2 pp. 270–271, 10.2 p. 270f, 10.2 p. 271f

Padania region of Italy, 11.3 p. 290

pagodas, 6.4 p. 173

Pakistan
    boundaries and, 9.4 p. 254, U4 p. 298m
    gender equity and, 19.2 p. 528
    geographic scale and, U1 p. 54m
    imperialism and, 7.2 p. 185, 9.4 p. 249

Palestine, 5.4 p. 131, 8.4 p. 219, U4 p. 238, 9.2 p. 242f, 9.2 p. 244

Pampas region (South America), 1.2 p. 16f, 1.2 p. 17

Pancras Gasworks (London), 17.3 p. 476, 17.3 p. 477f

pandemics, 20.2 pp. 552–554, pp. R1–R5

Papua New Guinea, 8.2 p. 210

paragliders, 12.2 pp. 322–323

Parcak, Sarah, 2.2 p. 35, 2.2 p. 35f

Paris, France
    centripetal forces and, 11.3 p. 288, 11.3 p. 289f
    ethnic neighborhoods and, 6.2 p. 158, 6.2 p. 159f
    population density and, 16.2 p. 439
    primate-city rule and, 15.3 p. 414
    as world city, 15.4 p. 421, 15.4 p. 422

parity, 19.2 p. 527

Park Cities, U6 p. 400, U6 p. 401f

Parra, Miguel, U7 p. 569

Partition act, U4 p. 298m

Partners in Food Solutions, 14.3 p. 381

Parveen, Almas, 14.4 p. 386

Paseo de la Reforma (Mexico City), 16.1 p. 437f

pastoral nomadism, 12.2 p. 318, 12.2 p. 319, 14.1 p. 362, 14.1 p. 366

Pathways to Empowerment program, 12.4 p. 335

patriotism, 10.1 p. 266

patterns
    cultural, 6.4 pp. 168–175
    data collection and, 2.2 p. 30
    distribution and, 1.1 p. 9, 1.1 p. 9m
    maps and, 2.3 pp. 36–37

patterns of population
    composition of population and, 3.3 pp. 74–76
    consequences of, 3.2 pp. 70–73
    distribution and, 3.1 pp. 63–69
    measuring, 3.1 pp. 67–68
    measuring growth and decline and, 3.4 pp. 77–83
    physical and environmental factors influencing, 3.1 pp. 63–66

pedestrians, 16.3 p. 446

Peltier, Autumn, 19.3 p. 538f

perceptual regions, 1.2 p. 18, 1.2 p. 18m

perenniation, U5 p. 304

peripheral countries
    agricultural interdependence and, 13.4 pp. 350–351
    dependency theory and, U7 p. 573f
    financial crisis of 2007-2008 and, 20.2 p. 553

globalization, interdependence and, 20.1 pp. 547–548
    infrastructure and, 16.3 p. 444
    rapid urbanization and, 16.1 p. 435, 17.2 p. 464
    Wallerstein's world system theory and, 18.2 p. 505
    world system theory and, 1.3 p. 21, 1.3 p. 22f, U7 p. 572m
    world trade patterns and, 13.4 pp. 353–354

peripheral model. See galactic city model

perishability, 13.3 pp. 348–349, 13.3 p. 348f

persecution, human migration and, 5.1 p. 113

perspectives, geographic, 1.1 pp. 7–9, U4 p. 296m

Peru, U3 p. 151f, 6.4 p. 172, 20.3 p. 564

pesticides
    agricultural production and, 13.1 p. 340
    effects of use of, 2.2 p. 30
    plantation agriculture and, 12.2 p. 317
    pollution from, 14.1 p. 363
    synthetic, 12.4 p. 333
    third agricultural revolution and, 12.4 pp. 332–334

Philadelphia, Pennsylvania, 15.2 p. 407, 16.1 p. 433, 16.3 p. 444

Philippine Green Jobs Act, 20.3 p. 562

Philippines. See also specific cities
    devolution and, 11.1 p. 277, U4 p. 300m
    English language diffusion and, 8.2 p. 209m, 20.2 p. 556
    outsourcing and, 20.2 p. 556
    special economic zones and, 20.2 p. 558
    Sustainable Development Goals and, 20.3 p. 562
    terracing and, 14.1 p. 360

photography, 7.2 pp. 192–193. See also National Geographic Photographer

physical footprint, 17.3 p. 472

physical geography, 1.1 p. 7, 11.1 p. 277, 16.2 p. 440

physiological density, 3.1 pp. 67–68, 3.1 p. 68t, 3.2 p. 72

Pichai, Sundar, 18.2 p. 507f

pilgrimages, 6.2 p. 161, 6.2 p. 162t

Pilgrims, 5.1 p. 113

pineapple, C13 p. 338

Pittsburgh, Pennsylvania, 15.1 p. 404, 15.2 p. 409, 10.1 p. 400

place, overview of, 1.1 p. 8

placemaking, 6.4 p. 168, 6.4 p. 168f

Planet or Plastic? initiative, 3.1 p. 69

planning
    greenbelt towns and, 17.1 p. 457
    pros and cons of, 17.1 pp. 457–459
    regional, 17.3 p. 476
    for smart buildings, 17.3 p. 478
    smart-growth policies for, 17.1 pp. 454–457
    sustainability and, 17.3 p. 476
    for sustainable cities, 17.1 p. 453

Plano, Texas, 15.2 p. 410

plant hardiness zones (USDA), U5 p. 392f

plantation agriculture, 12.2 p. 314, 12.2 p. 317

plant-based foods, 13.4 p. 354, U5 p. 396f

Pleistocene, 3.1 p. 66

plows, 7.1 p. 181, 12.4 p. 330, 12.4 p. 332

Poland, 9.2 p. 243, 18.1 p. 498

polar climates, 12.1 p. 310m, 12.1 p. 311

police forces, 18.1 p. 502

political factors
    aging population and, 4.4 pp. 106–107
    agricultural production and, 13.1 p. 340, 13.2 pp. 345–346
    city organization and, 16.3 p. 447
    human migration and, 5.1 p. 113, 5.4 pp. 130–132
    population change and, 4.1 p. 89
    population distribution and, 3.1 pp. 65–66

population trends and, 4.3 pp. 99–102, 4.3 p. 102f

political geography, 9.2 p. 241

political map of world, 9.2 pp. 241–244

political power
    boundaries and, 9.4 pp. 249–257
    colonialism, imperialism and, 9.3 pp. 247–249
    electoral geography and, 10.2 pp. 269–273
    geography and, 9.2 pp. 244–246
    sovereignty and, 9.3 p. 247
    state organization and, 10.1 pp. 261–267
    time and, 9.3 p. 247
    world political map and, 9.2 pp. 241–244

political relationships, agriculture and, 13.4 p. 353

political representation, empowerment and, 19.2 p. 528, 19.2 p. 529f

pollution
    agriculture and, 14.1 p. 363
    brownfields and, 17.3 p. 476
    environmental injustice and, 17.2 p. 468
    natural resources and, 20.3 p. 560
    urbanization and, 16.2 p. 441f, 17.3 pp. 472–474

Polynesia, 7.2 p. 190

popular culture, 6.1 pp. 154–155

population change
    consequences of, 4.4 pp. 103–107
    demographic transition model of, 4.2 p. 93, 4.2 p. 94f, U2 p. 143f
    epidemiological transition model of, 4.2 pp. 93–96, 4.2 p. 95t, U2 p. 144f
    factors influencing, 4.1 pp. 88–91
    Malthus's theory of, 4.2 pp. 92–93, 4.2 p. 92f, U2 p. 144f, U5 p. 393f
    migration and, 5.5 p. 134
    trends in, 4.1 pp. 87–88, 4.1 p. 88f
    urbanization and, 15.4 p. 420

population composition, overview of, 3.3 pp. 74–76

population density
    in Chile and Sweden, 3.1 p. 67m
    of Egypt vs. Canada, 3.2 p. 72, 3.2 p. 73f
    measuring population density, 3.1 pp. 67–68
    urban, 16.2 pp. 439–443
    urban development and, 16.2 pp. 443

population distribution
    consequences of, 3.2 pp. 70–73, 4.4 p. 103
    at country scale, 3.2 p. 72, 3.2 p. 73f
    at different scales, U1 p. 54m
    first agricultural revolution and, 12.4 p. 331
    human factors influencing, 3.1 pp. 63–66
    measuring, 3.1 pp. 67–68
    overview of, 3.1 p. 63, 3.1 p. 63f
    second agricultural revolution and, 12.4 p. 332
    urban, 16.2 pp. 439–443
    of world in 2016, 3.1 p. 64m

population pyramids, 3.4 pp. 81–82, 3.4 p. 81f, 3.4 p. 83f, 4.4 p. 105f, U2 p. 142f

Porta Nuova district (Milan), 17.3 p. 479, 17.3 p. 479f

Portland, Oregon, 17.3 p. 476

ports, 9.4 p. 256

Portuguese language, 8.2 p. 206

Posadas Sentinel (Tucson), 17.1 pp. 456–457

possibilism, 1.1 p. 10

post-Fordism, 20.2 pp. 555–556, 20.2 p. 555f, U7 p. 575f

postindustrial economies, 18.2 pp. 506–507, 18.2 p. 508f, 20.1 p. 549

postmodern architecture, 6.2 p. 159, 6.2 p. 161

Potato Famine of 1845-1849, 5.2 p. 116, 5.2 p. 120

Potosí, Bolivia, U7 p. 569

pottery, 12.4 pp. 330–331, 12.4 p. 331f

poverty, 4.2 p. 95, 17.2 p. 460, 17.2 p. 465

power, 8.2 pp. 211–212, 10.1 p. 265f. See also political power

power looms, 18.1 pp. 496–497

PPP. See purchasing power parity

PPS. See Project for Public Spaces

Prairie Freedom Movement, 11.1 p. 278

precipitation, U1 p. 56m, 15.3 p. 417

precision agriculture, 14.2 p. 373, U5 pp. 390–391

prefectures, 10.1 p. 261, 10.2 p. 269

pricing, 13.2 pp. 345–346

primary data, 16.3 p. 448

primary data sources, 2.1 p. 29, 2.2 p. 30

primary economic sector, 18.2 p. 504, 18.2 p. 504f, 18.2 p. 505, U7 p. 570f

primate-city rule, 15.3 pp. 413–414, 15.3 p. 415f

printing press, 7.2 p. 187

Pristine Seas project, U1 p. 4, U1 p. 5m

privatization, 20.1 p. 548

processed foods, 4.2 p. 95, 14.2 p. 376

processing industry, 18.2 p. 504, 18.2 p. 504f

processors, 13.2 p. 344f, 13.2 p. 345

produce, 1.1 p. 11f. See also agriculture

production lines, U7 pp. 490–491f

productivity, 12.4 p. 333

profits, 18.3 p. 512

Project for Public Spaces (PPS), 6.4 p. 168f

projection types, 2.3 p. 38m, 2.3 pp. 38–39, 2.3 p. 39m, U1 p. 55m

pronatalist policies, 4.3 pp. 99–102, 4.3 p. 102f

property rights, 6.3 p. 165m, 8.3 p. 218, 14.4 p. 385

prophets, 8.4 p. 224

prosthetics, 19.3 p. 535f

protected areas, U1 p. 5m, 15.3 p. 418, 15.3 p. 419

Protestantism, 8.3 p. 214, 8.4 p. 219

Protestants, Ireland and, 6.4 p. 175

Proto-Indo-European language, 8.2 p. 206

Providence, Rhode Island, 17.1 p. 459

provinces, 1.2 p. 17, 10.2 p. 269

proximity, 13.3 pp. 348–349

public health programs, 3.4 p. 80, 18.1 p. 502, 18.1 p. 502t

public housing developments, 17.2 p. 466

pull factors, 5.1 p. 112, 5.1 p. 112f, 15.4 p. 421

pulse crops, 13.4 p. 354

Puno region of Peru, 6.4 p. 172

purchasing power parity (PPP), 19.1 p. 525

Puritans, 5.1 p. 113

push factors, 5.1 p. 112, 5.1 p. 112f, 15.4 p. 421

Pyrenees Mountains region, 1.2 p. 17

Q

Qarakhanid people, 15.1 p. 406

Qatar, 19.1 p. 523, 19.1 p. 525

qualitative data, 2.2 pp. 29–30, 16.3 pp. 447–448

quantitative data, 2.1 p. 29, 16.3 pp. 448–449

quantum computers, 18.2 p. 507f

quaternary economic sector, 18.2 pp. 504–505, 18.2 p. 504f, 18.2 p. 506, U7 p. 570f

Quebec, Canada, 8.2 p. 213, 11.1 p. 278, 11.1 p. 280

questionnaires, 16.3 p. 448

quinary economic sector, 18.2 p. 504f, U7 p. 570f

quinceañera celebrations, 6.1 p. 153f, 7.2 p. 190

quinoa, 12.3 p. 328

quotas, 5.4 p. 129, 5.4 p. 130, 13.1 p. 340, 17.1 p. 456, 18.3 p. 516

Quran, 8.4 p. 220

INDEX

R

race and racism
  environmental, 17.2 pp. 468–469
  gerrymandering and, 10.2 p. 270, 10.2 p. 272, 10.2 p. 273f
  impact of COVID-19 and, p. R4
  wages and, 19.3 pp. 536–537

radial roads, 16.1 p. 435

railroads
  city site and, 15.1 p. 404
  city situation and, 15.1 p. 405
  global agricultural system and, 13.4 pp. 351–352
  industrialization and, 18.1 p. 498
  Liverpool and, 15.2 p. 411
  second agricultural revolution and, 12.4 p. 332
  urbanization and, 15.2 p. 407, 15.2 p. 408

Rama (Hindu god), 8.3 p. 218

Ramadan, 17.2 p. 464

ranching, 12.2 p. 318, 13.1 p. 342, 13.3 pp. 348–349, 13.3 p. 348f

random populations, 3.1 p. 63f

range, central place theory and, 15.3 p. 414–415

rank-size rule, 15.3 p. 413, U6 p. 484f

rate of natural increase (RNI), 4.1 pp. 87–88, 4.2 p. 92

ratio data, 16.3 p. 448

Raven-Ellison, Daniel, U6 p. 400, U6 p. 401f, 16.3 p. 449

Ravenstein, Ernst, 5.1 p. 111, U2 p. 145

Ravenstein's laws, 5.1 p. 111, 5.2 p. 115, 5.5 p. 135, U2 p. 145

raw materials
  dependency theory and, U7 p. 573f
  economic sectors and, 18.2 p. 504, 18.2 p. 504f
  industrialization and, 18.1 p. 495
  least-cost theory and, 18.3 pp. 514–516, 18.3 p. 514f, U7 p. 571f
  trade interdependence and, 20.1 pp. 547–548

RDP. See Reconstruction and Redevelopment Program

readjustment, 17.2 p. 468

reaper, mechanical, 12.4 pp. 331–332

reapportionment, 10.2 p. 269, 10.2 p. 269f

recessions, 20.2 pp. 552–554, 20.2 p. 554m

reconciliation, U4 p. 238

Reconstruction and Redevelopment Program (RDP), 16.1 p. 438

recreation, future cities and, 15.3 p. 418

Recuay culture, U3 p. 151f

recycling, 3.1 p. 69, 15.3 p. 416

redevelopment programs, 15.2 p. 410, 17.1 p. 459

redistricting, 10.2 pp. 270–271

redlining, 17.2 pp. 460–461, 17.2 p. 462, 17.2 p. 463m, 17.2 p. 465

reference maps, 2.3 p. 40, 2.3 p. 43

refrigerated shipping containers, 13.3 p. 349, 14.2 p. 376

refrigeration, 4.2 p. 92, 13.3 p. 349

Refugee Act (U.S.), 5.2 p. 121

Refugee Convention (1951), 5.3 p. 122

refugees. See also asylum
  forced migration and, 5.2 p. 118
  Hmong people as, 5.4 p. 130
  obstacles faced by, 5.3 pp. 122–124
  from Somalia, 5.4 p. 129
  sources of, 5.3 p. 123m, 5.4 p. 132f
  supranational organizations and, 11.2 p. 286

regional planning, 17.3 p. 476

regional units of federal governments, 10.1 p. 264f

regions, overview of, 1.2 pp. 16–18, 12 p. 16f

reincarnation, 8.4 p. 224

reindeer, 12.1 p. 311f, 12.2 p. 321m

relationships, data collection and, 2.2 p. 30

relative direction, 2.3 p. 37

relative distance, 2.3 p. 37

relative location, 1.1 p. 8

relic boundaries, 9.4 p. 255

religion
  as centrifugal force, 6.4 p. 175
  cultural diffusion and, 7.2 pp. 186–187
  cultural landscapes and, 6.2 p. 161, 6.3 p. 163
  culture and, 8.3 p. 214
  distribution patterns of, 8.3 pp. 214–216, 8.3 p. 215f, 8.3 p. 216f
  ethnic, 8.4 pp. 223–225
  influence of, U3 p. 234m
  population change and, 4.1 p. 90
  sense of place and, 6.4 pp. 171–173
  shared sacred sites and, 8.3 p. 218
  syncretism and, 7.3 pp. 195–196
  universalizing, 8.4 pp. 219–223

religious monuments, 6.3 p. 163

relocation diffusion
  agriculture and, 12.3 p. 327
  culture and, 7.1 p. 179, 7.1 p. 183f, U3 p. 233f
  industrialization and, 18.1 p. 498
  language and, 8.2 p. 208
  overview of, 5.5 p. 135
  religion and, 8.3 p. 214

remediation, 17.3 p. 476

remittances, 5.5 p. 134, 5.5 p. 136, U2 p. 146f

remote sensing, 2.2 p. 32, 15.1 p. 406

renewable energy, 19.1 p. 523, 19.1 p. 524f, 20.3 p. 560, 20.3 p. 562

renewable resources, 1.1 p. 10

renewal programs, 15.2 p. 411

rent control, 17.2 p. 466

repatriation, 5.3 p. 122

replacement levels, 3.4 p. 78

reproductive health, 19.2 p. 528

reservoirs, 14.1 p. 360

residential zoning, 16.2 p. 443

resiliency zones, 15.3 p. 418

resource curse, 19.4 p. 543

restaurants, 5.5 p. 135

retirement age, 4.4 p. 107

"Return to Village" program (Jakarta), 17.2 p. 464

revitalization programs, 15.2 p. 410, 15.2 p. 411, 17.1 p. 459

Rhine River, 18.1 p. 498

Rhode Island, 18.1 p. 498

rice, 12.1 p. 311, 12.2 p. 314, 12.4 p. 333, 14.1 p. 360

Richelieu River (Quebec), 12.2 p. 313f

Richmond, Virginia, 17.1 p. 459

Rijk Zwann company, U5 p. 391

Rio de Janeiro, Brazil, 7.1 p. 181f, 17.2 p. 465f

Rio Grande, 9.4 p. 249, 9.4 p. 249f

rivers, 3.1 p. 64, 15.1 p. 404, 15.2 p. 407, 18.2 p. 509

RNI. See rate of natural increase

Robinson projections, 2.3 p. 38, 2.3 p. 38m, 2.3 p. 39t

robotics, 18.1 p. 503

Rockefeller Foundation, 14.1 p. 366

Rohingya people, 5.2 pp. 118–120, 5.2 p. 120f, 5.3 p. 124, 11.1 p. 278

Roman Catholicism, 8.3 p. 216, 8.4 p. 219

Roman Empire, 12.3 p. 327, 15.3 p. 412

Romance branch of languages, 8.1 p. 202, 8.1 pp. 204–205f

Rome, Italy, 8.4 p. 219

Rosslyn-Ballston corridor (Virginia), 17.1 p. 453, 17.1 p. 454

Rostow, Walt W., 19.4 p. 540, U7 p. 572f

row houses, 16.2 p. 443

Royal Albert Dock (Liverpool), 15.2 p. 411

Ruhr Valley (Germany), 18.1 p. 498

ruling classes, 12.4 p. 331

rural areas
  defined, 15.1 p. 403
  empowering women in, 14.4 pp. 386–387
  gender opportunities and, 19.3 pp. 534–535
  land use patterns in, 13.3 pp. 348–349
  settlement patterns in, 12.2 p. 315
  survel methods for, 12.2 p. 313

Rural Education and Economic Development Society, 14.4 p. 386

rural-to-urban migration, 5.2 p. 117, 15.2 p. 408, 18.1 p. 501

Russia
  Crimea and, 11.1 p. 279, U4 p. 296m
  economic growth and, 19.4 p. 540
  ethnonationalism and, 11.3 p. 290
  Industrial Revolution and, 18.1 p. 498
  population composition and, 3.4 p. 81, 3.4 p. 81f
  supranationalism and, 11.2 p. 285

Russian language, 8.2 p. 206

Russians, ethnic, 9.2 p. 243

rust belt, 15.2 p. 409

Ruzo, Andrés, 20.3 p. 565

Rwanda, 4.3 p. 102, 5.1 p. 112, 9.4 p. 249, 19.2 p. 528, 19.2 p. 530f

rye, 12.3 p. 328, 13.3 p. 349

S

Saafir, Jihad, U3 p. 229

Sabbath, 8.4 p. 224

Sabeti, Pardis, 4.2 p. 97

Sack, Robert, 9.2 p. 245

sacred sites, 6.4 p. 173

SADC. See Southern African Development Community

SAE. See Southern American English

safaris, 20.3 p. 564

Safe Routes to School (SRTS) program, 2.2 p. 33

safe spaces, 6.3 p. 167

safety, urbanization and, 15.2 p. 409

Sahara desert, C2 p. 26f

Sala, Enric, U1 p. 4, U1 p. 5f

salaam, U3 p. 229

Salar de Uyuni salt flat (Bolivia), U7 pp. 568–569

salinization, 14.1 p. 364

salmon, 14.2 p. 372

salt, U7 pp. 568–569

Salopek, Paul, U2 p. 60, U2 p. 61f

Salvador, Brazil, 7.1 p. 184

Samarkand, Uzbekistan, 15.1 p. 404

samba, 7.1 p. 184

Samhain holiday, 8.4 p. 219

sampling, 16.3 p. 448

San Francisco, California, U3 p. 230m, 15.1 p. 404, 15.2 p. 408, 16.2 p. 443, 17.1 p. 457

San Jose, California, 15.2 p. 408

sanitation systems, 16.3 p. 444, 18.1 p. 502f

Santa Susana Mountains (California), 2.1 p. 29f

Santeria, 8.4 p. 220

Santería religion, 7.3 pp. 195–196

Sao Paulo, Brazil, 17.1 p. 455

Sarder, Golam Mostafa, U2 p. 140

satellites, 2.2 pp. 32–33, 2.2 p. 35, U1 pp. 50–51, 15.1 p. 406

Saudi Arabia
  agriculture and, 3.1 p. 66f
  fossil fuels and, 19.1 p. 523
  gender roles and, 19.3 p. 535
  gendered spaces and, 6.3 p. 166
  landscape of religion and, 6.2 p. 161, 6.2 p. 162f
  natural resources and, 20.3 p. 560
  "women-only" cities and, 19.2 p. 531

Sauer, Carl, 6.2 p. 158

scale
  agricultural production regions and, 13.1 p. 339
  of analysis, 1.2 p. 15–16
  economies of. See economies of scale
  globalization and, 1.3 pp. 20–22
  Malthus's theory of population growth and, 4.2 p. 92, U2 p. 144f
  manufacturing industry and, 18.1 p. 495, 18.1 p. 496f
  maps and, 2.3 pp. 37–39, U1 pp. 54–55m
  population density and, U1 p. 54m
  population pyramids and, 3.4 p. 83f
  population trends and, 4.1 p. 87
  pre-industrial manufacturing and, 18.1 p. 496
  smartphone maps and, U1 p. 55m

scallops, C14 p. 358f

Schengen Area of Europe, 9.4 p. 250

Schlinger, Robbie, U1 p. 50–51

School of Leadership, Afghanistan (SOLA), U7 p. 492, U7 p. 493f

school routes, safer, 2.2 pp. 33–34

Schuylkill River, 15.2 p. 407

science, technology, engineering, and math (STEM), 19.3 p. 535f

Scotland, 11.1 p. 280

Scottish Parliament, 11.1 p. 280

SDGs. See Sustainable Development Goals

sea boundaries. See maritime boundaries

sea level, 1.1 p. 12, 1.1 p. 13f

seafood, 20.3 p. 561

Seattle, Washington, 16.2 p. 443, 16.3 p. 449f, 17.1 p. 459, U6 p. 489m

secession, 11.3 p. 290

Second Industrial Revolution, 18.1 p. 498–499

Second Temple of Jerusalem, U4 p. 239f

secondary data, 2.1 pp. 29–30, 16.3 p. 448

secondary economic sector, 18.2 p. 504, 18.2 p. 504f, U7 p. 570f

sector model. See Hoyt sector model

sectors, economic, 18.2 pp. 504–505, 18.2 p. 504f, 19.1 p. 522, U7 p. 570f

sects, 6.4 p. 171

secularization, 8.4 p. 225

security, 15.2 p. 409

Sedaghat, Lillygol, 3.1 p. 69, 3.1 p. 69f

seed drills, 12.4 p. 331

seeds, U5 p. 391

segregation/separation, 7.2 p. 185, 7.3 p. 195f, 16.1 p. 438, 17.1 p. 459

Selbe, Shah, 2.4 p. 47, 2.4 p. 47f

self-determination, 9.3 p. 247

semiarid climates, 12.1 p. 310

semiautonomous regions, 9.2 p. 244, U4 p. 298m

semi-peripheral countries
  dependency theory and, U7 p. 573f
  economic development and, 18.2 p. 505
  financial crisis of 2007-2008 and, 20.2 p. 553
  globalization, interdependence and, 20.1 pp. 547–548
  industrialization and, 18.1 p. 500
  infrastructure and, 16.3 p. 444
  rapid urbanization and, 16.1 p. 435, 17.2 p. 464
  world system theory and, 1.3 p. 21, 1.3 p. 22f, U7 p. 572m
  world trade patterns and, 13.4 pp. 353–354

Senate, 10.2 p. 270

sense of place, 1.1 p. 8, 6.4 p. 168, 6.4 pp. 170–174

Seoul, South Korea, 16.2 p. 439

sepaade tradition, 6.1 p. 154

separation. See segregation/separation

separatism, 11.1 pp. 277–278, 11.3 p. 290

September 11 terrorist attacks, 11.2 p. 283, 11.3 p. 288

sequent occupance, 6.2 p. 158
Serbia, 9.4 p. 254, 11.2 p. 286
service (tertiary) sector, 18.2 p. 504, 18.2 p. 504f, 18.2 p. 506, 20.1 p. 549, U7 p. 570f
service industries, 18.1 p. 499
settlement patterns, 12.2 p. 315, 12.2 p. 315f
sewage, 17.3 p. 472, 18.1 p. 502
sex ratios, 3.3 pp. 75–76, 3.3 p. 76m
sex-selection, 3.3 p. 76
sexual harassment and violence, 6.3 p. 164f
sexual orientation, 6.3 pp. 166–167, 6.3 p. 167m
SEZs. See special economic zones
Shabbat, 8.4 p. 224
Shack Dwellers Federat of Namibia (SDFN), 17.2 p. 468
Shanghai, Cionhina
   growth of, 15.4 p. 423, 15.4 p. 426
   population density, environment and, 3.2 p. 71f, 17.3 p. 472
   transportation-oriented design and, C16 p. 430f, 17.1 p. 454f
Shanghai Cooperation Organization (SCO), 11.2 p. 286t
Shanghai General Sports, 20.1 pp. 550–551
Shanidar 1 (Neanderthal man), U2 p. 60
shantytowns, 16.1 p. 435, 16.1 p. 438, 17.2 pp. 464–468, 17.2 p. 467f
sharecroppers, 5.4 p. 129
sharks, U1 p. 5f
shatterbelts, 9.2 p. 246, 9.3 p. 247, 13.2U4 p. 290m
Shedd Aquarium (Chicago), 17.3 p. 473
sheep ranching, 12.2 p. 321m
shellfish farming, 14.2 p. 372
Shenzhen, China, U2 p. 59, 15.2 p. 408
Shenzhen Special Economic Zone, 20.2 p. 558
Shibuya Crossing (Tokyo), 15.4 p. 422
shifting cultivation, 12.2 p. 318, 14.1 p. 359
Shiite Muslims, 8.4 p. 221
Shinto, 8.4 p. 223
shipping, 18.3 p. 516. See also trade
shipping containers, 13.3 p. 349, C18 p. 404f
Shiroyone Senmaida rice paddies, 6.2 p. 157, 6.2 p. 157f
shivarees, 7.2 p. 193
shrimp farms, 20.3 p. 560
Siachen Glacier, U4 p. 298m
Siberia, 3.1 p. 65
Sichuan Province, China, 10.1 p. 264
Sierra Leone, 19.4 p. 543
Sikhism, 8.4 pp. 222–223
Silicon Valley (California), 15.2 p. 408
Silk Road, 7.2 p. 187, 7.2 p. 187f, 15.1 p. 404, 15.1 p. 406
Singapore
   free trade zones and, 20.2 p. 559
   population growth and, 4.3 p. 102
   postindustrial economies and, 18.2 p. 507
   Rostow's stages of economic growth and, 19.4 p. 540
   unitary states and, 10.1 p. 263
   women in agriculture and, 14.4 p. 385
   world cities and, 15.4 p. 422
single-member elections, 10.2 p. 271
Sino-Tibetan language family, 8.1 p. 202
site, 1.1 p. 8, 1.1 pp. 12–13, 1.1 p. 13f, 15.1 p. 404
Siti Khadijah market (Malaysia), C7 p. 178
situation, 1.1 p. 8, 1.1 pp. 12–13, 1.1 p. 13f, 15.1 pp. 404–405
skilled workers, 18.1 p. 495
skills gap, 5.5 pp. 133–134
sky gardens, 17.3 p. 478

skyscrapers, 16.2 p. 439
slash and burn cultivation, 12.2 p. 318, 14.1 p. 359, 14.1 p. 364
slavery
   African culture in Brazil and, 7.1 p. 184
   Civil War and, 11.3 p. 290
   cultural diffusion and, 7.1 p. 179, 7.1 p. 180
   as forced migration, 5.2 p. 120
   Great Migration and, 5.4 p. 129
   population distribution and, 3.1 p. 65
Slavic branch of languages, 8.1 p. 202
slope, 12.1 p. 308
Slovenia, 9.3 p. 247
slow-growth cities, 17.1 p. 455
slums, U2 pp. 140–141, 17.2 p. 466
small-scale maps, 2.3 p. 37m
smart buildings, 17.3 p. 478
smart-growth policies, 17.1 pp. 454–457
smartphones, U1 pp. 50–51, U1 p. 55m
smog, 16.2 p. 441f, 17.3 p. 472
soccer, 7.2 p. 191
social factors, 5.5 pp. 135–137, 11.1 p. 278, 19.1 pp. 523–524
Social Security, 4.4 p. 107, 19.1 p. 522
social services, 3.2 p. 70
social transit, 15.3 p. 417
society
   aging population and, 4.4 p. 105
   agriculture and, 14.1 p. 368
   first agricultural revolution and, 12.4 p. 330
   industrialization and, 18.1 p. 501
   population distribution and, 3.2 p. 70
   sex ratios and, 3.3 pp. 75–76
sociofacts, 6.1 p. 153, 6.1 p. 154
software engineering industry, 10.1 p. 499
SoilCares, U5 p. 391
soils
   agricultural hearths and, 12.3 p. 325
   agriculture and, 12.1 p. 308, 14.1 p. 364
   biotechnology and, 14.2 p. 372
   city sites and, 15.1 p. 404
   conservation, sustainability and, 14.1 p. 365
   population distribution and, 3.1 p. 64
   population size and, 4.4 p. 103
SOLA, U7 p. 492, U7 p. 493f
Solar C.I.T.I.E.S., 16.3 p. 445
solar walls and windows, 17.3 p. 478
Somalia
   boundaries and, 9.4 p. 254
   refugees from, 5.4 p. 129, 6.4 p. 173m, 6.4 pp. 173–174
   supranationalism and, 11.2 p. 285
   total fertility rate and, 19.1 p. 524
sorghum, 12.3 p. 328
South Africa, 11.3 p. 289, 13.1 p. 339, 15.1 p. 404, 16.1 p. 438
South Carolina, 20.1 p. 550
South China Sea, 9.4 p. 257, 9.4 p. 257f
South Korea, 8.2 p. 211, U4 p. 237, 9.4 p. 250, 9.4 p. 251, 19.2 p. 528
South Sudan, 5.3 p. 122, 11.1 p. 281, 14.3 p. 379, 19.1 p. 524, 19.1 p. 526f
Southeast Asia agricultural hearth, 12.3 p. 325, 12.3 p. 326m
Southeast Asian city model, 16.1 p. 436f, 16.1 p. 437, U6 p. 488f
Southern African Development Community (SADC), 20.1 p. 548
Southern American English (SAE), 6.4 p. 170
Southern Baptists, 8.3 p. 216
Southern Common Market (Mercosur), 11.2 p. 286t, 20.1 p. 548
Southern Line Island, U1 p. 4
South-to-North Water Diversion Project (China), 14.1 p. 362
sovereign states, 11.3 p. 291
sovereignty, 9.2 pp. 241–242, 9.3 p. 247, 9.4 p. 256, 11.2 p. 285
Soviet Union
   devolution and, 9.3 p. 249, 11.1 p. 280m, 11.1 p. 281

sovereignty and, 9.2 p. 242, 9.3 p. 247
   water resources and, 12.4 p. 334
Soy Afric, 14.3 p. 381
soybeans
   biotechnology and, 14.2 p. 370f, 14.2 p. 371
   monocropping and, 12.2 p. 316
   production of in U.S., 12.2 p. 316m
   subsidies and, 14.3 p. 382
   tariffs and, 13.2 p. 346f
space, 1.1 p. 9, 6.3 pp. 163–164
Spain
   border wall and, 5.4 p. 131
   Christianity and, 8.4 p. 219
   cultural diffusion and, 7.2 pp. 185–186
   devolution and, 11.1 pp. 277–278
   imperialism and, 9.3 p. 247
   nations, states and, U4 p. 298m
   site, situation and, 1.1 p. 8
Spanglish, 8.2 p. 210
Spanish language, 6.4 p. 172, 8.2 p. 206
spatial patterns, 1.2 pp. 15–18
spatial perspective, 1.1 p. 7
special economic zones (SEZs), 20.2 p. 558, 20.2 p. 559f
specialization, 12.2 p. 316, 13.4 pp. 350–351, 20.2 p. 556
spine roads, 16.1 p. 437f
spinning jenny, 18.1 p. 496
sponge cities, 15.3 p. 416
sprawl, urban, 14.3 p. 377, 15.2 pp. 409–410, 16.2 pp. 439–440
squatter settlements (shantytowns), 16.1 p. 435, 16.1 p. 438, 17.2 pp. 464–468, 17.2 p. 467f
Sri Lanka, 12.2 p. 317
SRTS program. See Safe Routes to School program
St. Cloud, Minnesota, 5.4 p. 129
St. Lawrence River, 15.1 p. 404
St. Paul, Minnesota, 17.3 p. 476
St. Petersburg, Russia, 8.2 pp. 211–212
stability, 4.2 p. 93
Standard English (SE), 6.4 p. 170
standardization, 17.1 p. 459
Stanmeyer, John, 12.2 p. 319f
State of the Exception exhibit, 5.2 p. 119
state power in U.S., 10.1 p. 265f, 10.1 p. 266
stateless nations, 9.2 p. 244, 9.3 p. 248
states, 1.2 p. 17, 9.2 pp. 241–242, 9.3 p. 247, 10.1 p. 261–267
Statue of Liberty, 11.3 p. 289
steam engines, 18.1 pp. 496–497
steel, 13.2 p. 346
steel industry, 15.2 p. 409, 18.1 pp. 498–499
Steinmetz, George, 12.2 p. 322–323
step migration, 5.2 p. 117, 5.4 p. 129
sterilization, forced, 4.3 p. 101
stimulus diffusion, 7.1 p. 182, 7.1 p. 183f, U3 p. 232f, 12.3 p. 327
storage, 12.4 p. 330, 14.3 p. 381
Strait of Hormuz, 9.2 p. 246, 9.2 p. 246f
Strait of Malacca, 9.2 p. 245–246
streetcar suburbs, 15.2 p. 409
Stuart, Tristram, 13.2 p. 347, 13.2 p. 347f
stunting, 14.3 p. 378
subsequent boundaries, 9.4 p. 254, U4 p. 296m
subsidies, 13.1 p. 340, 13.2 pp. 345–346, 14.3 p. 382, 17.2 p. 466, 20.3 p. 562
subsistence agriculture
   agricultural density and, 3.1 p. 68
   conservation, sustainability and, 14.1 pp. 365–366
   economic forces and, 13.1 p. 339
   environment and, 14.1 pp. 359–363
   extensive agriculture and, 12.2 p. 318
   intensive agriculture and, 12.2 p. 314
   overview of, 12.2 p. 312
subsistence whaling, 6.3 p. 164
suburbanization, 14.3 p. 377, 15.2 pp. 409–410

subways, 16.3 p. 447
succession, 16.2 p. 440
Sudan, 5.3 p. 126f, 11.1 p. 281, 14.3 p. 379
Sudetenland, Czechoslovakia, 11.1 p. 278
Sugamo neighborhood, Tokyo, Japan, U6 pp. 482–483
Sunbelt, migration to, 5.2 p. 116
Sunnah, 8.4 p. 220
Sunni Muslims, 8.4 p. 221
Superdry, 20.2 p. 556
superimposed boundaries, 9.4 p. 254, 9.4 p. 254f, U4 p. 296m
supply and demand, 13.2 p. 344, 13.2 p. 344f, 13.2 pp. 345–346
supply chains, 13.4 pp. 350–351, U5 p. 397f
supranationalism, 11.2 pp. 283–286, 11.2 p. 286t, 20.1 pp. 548–550
surface culture, U3 p. 230f
surpluses, 12.4 p. 331, 13.2 p. 347
Surprise Creek, Montana, 7.2 pp. 192–193
survey methods for rural areas, 12.2 p. 313
sustainability
   challenges to in urban areas, 17.3 p. 472–474
   economic growth and, 19.4 p. 541
   ecotourism and, 20.3 pp. 563–565
   Fourth Industrial Revolution and, 18.1 p. 503
   future cities and, 15.3 p. 416, 15.3 p. 418
   human-environment interaction and, 1.1 p. 10
   local produce and, 1.1 p. 11f
   Milan and, 17.3 p. 479
   natural resources and, 20.3 p. 660
   overview of, 1.3 p. 23
   responding to challenges of in urban areas, 17.3 p. 476
   Taiwan and, 3.1 p. 69
sustainable agriculture, 12.4 p. 334, C14 p. 358f, 14.1 pp. 365–366, 14.2 pp. 370–372
sustainable cities, 17.1 p. 453, 17.1 pp. 454–457, 17.0 pp. 470–471, 17.0 p. 476
sustainable development, 1.3 p. 23, 18.1 p. 503, 20.3 pp. 560–562
Sustainable Development Goals (SDGs), 20.3 p. 562, 20.3 p. 562t
Swahili language, 11.3 p. 289
Sweden
   aging population and, 4.4 p. 106
   economic consequences of migration and, 5.5 p. 134, 5.5 p. 134f
   population distribution in, 3.1 p. 67m, 3.1 p. 68
   supranationalism and, 11.2 p. 285
   Sustainable Development Goals and, 20.3 p. 562
   women's empowerment and, 19.2 p. 528
Switzerland, 19.1 p. 526f, 19.2 p. 528, 19.3 p. 536
symbols, 2.3 p. 41m, 11.3 p. 289
syncretism, 7.3 pp. 195–196
Syria
   gender inequality and, 19.2 p. 528
   human migration and, 5.1 p. 113, 5.3 p. 123m, 5.3 p. 125, 5.3 p. 125m, 5.3 p. 127f
   Kurdish people and, 9.3 p. 248
   population trends and, 4.1 p. 89
   pull factors and, 5.1 p. 112

T

Tahrir Square (Egypt), 6.3 p. 166
taiga, 12.1 p. 311f
Taiwan, 3.1 p. 67, 3.1 p. 69, 6.4 p. 170, 20.2 p. 552
take-off, 19.4 p. 540, 19.4 p. 541f, U7 p. 572f
Taliban, U3 p. 150, 11.1 p. 278, U7 p. 492
Tanzania, 4.3 p. 101f, 4.3 p. 102, 9.4 p. 254, 12.4 p. 335, 20.2 p. 559

Taoism, 8.4 p. 223

tariffs
agriculture and, 13.2 p. 346, 13.2 p. 346f
export processing zones and, 20.2 pp. 558–559
government trade policies and, 20.1 p. 550
least-cost theory and, 18.3 p. 516
supranationalism and, 11.2 p. 285
World Trade Organization and, 20.1 p. 549

Tashbulak (ancient city), 15.1 p. 406

Tate, Leona, 16.3 p. 448f

Taussig, Caitlyn, 14.4 p. 387f

taxes
aging population and, 4.4 pp. 105–106
agriculture and, 13.2 p. 346, 13.2 p. 346f
government trade policies and, 20.1 p. 550
informal economy and, 19.1 pp. 522–523
least-cost theory and, 18.3 p. 516
urbanization and, 15.2 p. 409, 17.2 p. 460

tea, 13.4 p. 353

tea plantations, 12.2 p. 319, 12.2 p. 321m

technology
agricultural production regions and, 13.1 p. 339–340
agriculture and, 13.1 p. 339
city sites and, 15.1 p. 404
city situation and, 15.1 p. 405
cultural diffusion and, 7.2 p. 189, 7.2 p. 190
Fourth Industrial Revolution and, 18.1 p. 503
human migration and, 5.1 p. 112
industrialization and, 18.1 p. 496
Malthus's theory of population growth and, 4.2 p. 92, U2 p. 144f
natural resource conservation and, 20.3 p. 560
population distribution and, 3.1 p. 64
population trends and, 4.1 pp. 87–88
productivity and, 12.4 p. 333
quaternary economic sector and, 18.2 pp. 504–505, 18.2 p. 504f, 18.2 p. 505f
second agricultural revolution and, 12.4 pp. 331–332
separatist movements and, 11.1 p. 278
third agricultural revolution and, 12.4 pp. 332–334
tomato production and, U5 p. 390
von Thünen model and, 13.3 p. 349

Tehrangeles neighborhood (Los Angeles), 6.2 p. 160

telecommunications industry, 15.2 p. 407, 18.1 p. 499

temperate climates, 3.1 p. 64, 12.1 p. 310m, 12.1 pp. 310–311

temperate zones, 12.1 p. 309

temperature, agriculture and, 12.1 p. 308

temporary workers, 5.5 p. 133

Tenochtitlán, 15.1 p. 405, 15.1 p. 405f

Tenth Amendment to U.S. Constitution, 10.1 p. 266

terrace farming, 12.1 p. 308, 12.1 p. 309f, 12.2 p. 314, 14.1 pp. 359–360, 14.1 p. 364

territoriality, 9.2 p. 245, 9.4 pp. 249–250

terrorist attacks, 5.5 p. 133, 11.2 p. 283, 11.3 p. 288

tertiary (service) economic sector, 18.2 p. 504, 18.2 p. 504f, 18.2 p. 506, 20.1 p. 549, U7 p. 570f

Tesla, 7.1 p. 181

test results, quantitative data and, 16.3 p. 448

Tex-Mex food, 7.2 p. 190

textile industry, 18.1 pp. 496–497, 18.1 p. 498, 18.3 p. 517

TFR. See total fertility rate (TFR)

Thailand, 14.1 p. 359, 20.1 p. 549, 20.2 p. 557

Thames River, 15.1 p. 404

thematic maps, 2.3 p. 40, 2.3 p. 43, U1 p. 57m

Theodosius, 8.4 p. 219

theories, defined, 1.3 p. 21

Thermopylae, 9.2 p. 245

Third Industrial Revolution, 18.1 p. 499

third places, 6.3 p. 167

Three Gorges Dam, 4.1 p. 91f

3-D printing, 18.1 p. 503

thresholds, 15.3 pp. 414–415

Thunberg, Greta, 19.3 p. 538f

Tibet, 14.1 p. 366

tierra caliente, 12.1 p. 308f

tierra fría, 12.1 p. 308f

tierra helada (punta), 12.1 p. 308f

tierra nevada, 12.1 p. 308f

tierra templada, 12.1 p. 308f

Tigris River, 12.3 p. 325

tilapia, 12.3 p. 329

timber, 13.3 p. 349, 18.3 p. 515

Times Square (New York City), 15.4 p. 422

time-space compression model, 1.1 p. 10, U1 pp. 52–53f, 7.2 p. 190, 13.3 p. 349

Tobler, Waldo, 1.1 p. 10

Tobler's first law of geography, 7.2 pp. 189–190

TODs. See transportation-oriented developments

Toensing, Amy, 19.2 pp. 532–533, 19.2 p. 533f

Togo, 19.2 p. 530f

Tokyo, Japan, 15.4 pp. 420–422, 16.2 pp. 439–440, U6 pp. 482–483, U6 p. 482f

tomatoes, 12.3 p. 328, U5 p. 390

tongmu, 8.2 p. 211

tool-and-die shops, 18.1 p. 499

topography, 2.2 p. 31, 12.1 p. 308, 12.2 pp. 320–321m, 15.1 p. 404

toponyms, 6.2 p. 161, 8.2 pp. 211–212, U3 p. 230m

Toronto, Ontario, Canada, 2.2 p. 31f, 15.2 p. 410, 15.2 p. 410f, 15.4 p. 422

Torres, Luis, U4 p. 295

total fertility rate (TFR), 3.4 p. 77m, 3.4 p. 78, 3.4 p. 78t, 19.1 pp. 523–524

tourism, 20.3 p. 563

Town and Country Planning Act (United Kingdom), 17.2 p. 466

townhouses, 16.2 p. 443

township and range survey system, 12.2 p. 313, 12.2 p. 313f, 12.2 p. 320m

Toyota, 18.3 p. 517

tractors, 12.4 p. 333

trade. See also fair trade movement
agricultural interdependence and, 13.4 pp. 350–351
cities and, 15.4 p. 427
city situation and, 15.1 pp. 404–405
cultural diffusion and, 7.2 pp. 186–187, 7.2 p. 187f
dietary shifts and, 14.2 p. 376
globalization, interdependence and, U5 p. 395m, 20.1 pp. 547–548
governmental policies on, 20.1 pp. 550–551
Southeast Asian city model and, 16.1 p. 436f
supranational organizations and, 12.1 pp. 548–550
worldwide agricultural, 13.4 p. 352f, 13.4 pp. 353–354

trade agreements
countries with most, U7 p. 575f
global agricultural system and, 13.4 p. 353
NAFTA, 1.3 pp. 20–21, 14.2 p. 376, 20.1 p. 548, U7 p. 575f
USMCA, 1.3 p. 21

trade barriers, 11.2 p. 285

trade not aid, 13.4. p. 354

trade routes, 15.1 p. 404

trade wars, 13.2 p. 346, 13.2 p. 346f, 13.4 p. 353

traditional architecture, 6.2 pp. 158–159

traditional culture, 6.1 p. 155

traditional society, 19.4 p. 540, 19.4 p. 541f, U7 p. 572f

traditional zoning, 17.1 p. 454

trafficking, human, 5.2 p. 120

Trail of Tears, 5.4 p. 128

Trainor, Clare, 15.4 pp. 424–427

Transcontinental Railroad, 15.1 p. 405

transhumance, 5.2 p. 116, 12.2 p. 318

transit, 16.2 p. 443, 16.3 pp. 444–446

transnational migration, 5.2 p. 115

transportation systems
agriculture and, 13.3 pp. 348–349
central place theory and, 15.3 p. 415
cities and, 15.4 p. 427
city sites and, 15.1 p. 404
designing for access to, 17.1 p. 453
food insecurity and, 14.3 p. 381
as functional regions, 1.2 p. 17m, 1.2 p. 18
future cities and, 15.3 p. 417, 15.3 p. 418
global agricultural system and, 13.4 pp. 350–352
globalization and, 1.3 p. 20m
housing density and, 16.2 p. 443
industrialization and, 18.1 pp. 499–500
infrastructure and, 16.3 pp. 444–446
least-cost theory and, 18.3 p. 513, 18.3 pp. 514–516, 18.3 p. 514f, U7 p. 571f
lumber industry and, 18.3 p. 515
mass transit, 16.2 p. 443, 16.3 pp. 444–446
municipal governments and, 16.3 p. 447
suburbanization and, 15.2 pp. 409–410
urban growth and, 15.2 p. 407, 16.2 p. 439

transportation-oriented developments (TODs), 17.1 pp. 453–454

Trans-Siberian Railroad, 15.1 p. 405

travel, supranational organizations and, 11.2 p. 285

Treat, Jason, 15.4 pp. 424–427

treaties, 9.3 p. 249, 11.2 p. 283. See also specific treaties

trickle-across theory of fashion diffusion, U3 p. 233f

trickle-down theory of fashion diffusion, U3 p. 233f

trickle-up theory of fashion diffusion, U3 p. 233f

trifectas, 10.2 p. 272

triple-decker homes, 16.2 p. 443

Tropic of Cancer, 12.1 p. 309

Tropic of Capricorn, 12.1 p. 309

tropical climates, 12.1 p. 310m, 12.1 p. 311

tropics, 12.1 p. 309

truck farming, 12.2 p. 317

Trump, Donald, 5.4 p. 131, U3 p. 228, 13.2 p. 346, 13.4 p. 353, 20.1 p. 550

Tsaatan (Dhukha) people, 12.1 p. 311f

Tuareg people, 14.1 p. 363, 14.1 p. 363f

Tucson, Arizona, 17.1 pp. 456–457

Tull, Jethro, 12.4 p. 331

tundra, 12.1 p. 311, 12.1 p. 311f

Turkey
Cyprus and, 10.1 p. 262
first agricultural revolution and, 12.4 p. 330f
guest workers and, 5.2 p. 117
human migration and, 5.1 p. 113
Kurdish people and, 9.3 p. 248, 11.3 p. 291, 11.3 p. 291f
Syria and, 5.3 p. 125

Tutsi people, 9.4 p. 249

2030 Agenda for Sustainable Development, 1.3 p. 23, 19.3 p. 538

Twin Cities region (Minnesota), 17.3 p. 476

Tysons Corner, Virginia, 15.2 p. 410

U

UAE. See United Arab Emirates

Ugarte, Victor, U7 p. 569

ugly food, 13.2 p. 347

Ukraine, 11.1 p. 279, U4 p. 296m

Ukrainian language, 8.1 p. 201

Ullman, Edward, 16.1 p. 433

Umar Al Farooq School (Kenya), C19 p. 520f

UNCLOS. See United Nations Convention on the Law of the Sea

unconscious culture, U3 p. 230f

UNESCO World Heritage Committee, 14.1 p. 366

UNHCR. See United Nations High Commission for Refugees

uniform population distribution, 3.1 p. 63f

uniform regions. See functional regions

Union Jack flag, 11.3 p. 289

unitary states, 10.1 p. 261, 10.1 pp. 263–264, 10.1 p. 263f, 10.1 p. 267

United Arab Emirates (UAE), 3.1 pp. 67–68, 6.2 p. 161

United Kingdom. See also specific countries
Brexit and, 11.2 p. 283, 11.2 p. 287, U4 p. 300m, 13.4 p. 353
devolution and, 11.1 p. 278
European Union and, 11.2 p. 286
Scotland and, 11.1 p. 280
as unitary state, 10.1 p. 261, 10.1 p. 261f
Wales ad, 11.1 p. 278

United Nations Convention on the Law of the Sea (UNCLOS), 9.4 pp. 256–257

United Nations Entity for Gender Equality and the Empowerment of Women, 5.4 p. 130

United Nations High Commission for Refugees (UNHCR), 5.3 p. 122

United Nations (UN), 1.3 p. 23, 11.2 p. 283, 11.2 p. 286t, 19.3 p. 538. See also Sustainable Development Goals

United States Agency for International Development (USAID), 4.3 p. 101f

United States-Mexico-Canada Agreement (USMCA), 1.3 p. 21, 11.2 p. 286t, 14.2 p. 376, 20.1 p. 548

universalizing religions, 8.4 pp. 219–223

unskilled workers, 18.1 p. 495

urban, defined, 15.1 p. 403

Urban Agriculture Action Team (Dallas), 17.2 p. 469

urban areas, defined, 15.1 p. 403

urban blight, 16.2 p. 440, 17.1 p. 459

urban clusters, defined, 15.1 p. 403

urban ecology, 17.3 p. 475

urban farming, 14.2 p. 374, 17.2 p. 469f

urban farms, future cities and, 15.3 p. 417

urban planning. See planning

urban renewal, 6.2 pp. 159–161, 17.2 p. 470

Urban Rivers, 17.3 p. 473

urban rooftops, 15.3 p. 417, 17.3 p. 475

urban sprawl, 14.3 p. 377, 15.2 pp. 409–410, 16.2 pp. 439–440

urban systems, location patterns of, 15.3 pp. 412–414, 15.3 p. 413f

urbanization. See also cities
biodiversity and, U5 p. 397f
challenges of, 17.2 pp. 460–461, 17.3 pp. 472–474
challenges of rapid, 17.2 pp. 464–469
cultural diffusion and, 7.2 pp. 188–189
economic development and, 18.2 p. 506
economic development, government policies and, 15.2 pp. 408–409
food insecurity and, 14.3 pp. 377–379
future cities and, 15.3 p. 417
Industrial Revolution and, 4.1 p. 88
industrialization and, 18.1 pp. 500–501
overview of, 15.1 p. 403

population growth and, 15.4 p. 420
rural-to-urban migration and, 5.2 p. 117, 15.2 p. 408
sprawl and, 15.2 pp. 409–410
sustainability and, 17.3 pp. 472–474, 17.3 p. 476
transportation and communication networks and, 15.2 p. 407

Urlanta, Guatemala, 19.3 p. 534

Uruk, 15.1 p. 403

US Census Bureau, 16.3 pp. 448–449

USDA plant hardiness zones, U5 p. 392f

USMCA. *See* United States-Mexico-Canada Agreement

Uttar Pradesh, 8.2 p. 212

Uzbekistan, 15.1 p. 404, 15.1 p. 406

V

Valley of the Gods (Utah), 6.4 p. 169f

value-added crops, 14.2 p. 375

van den Borne, Jacob, U5 p. 390

vanilla industry, 13.4 p. 350, 13.4 p. 350f

vaqueros, 7.2 p. 188

vegetable proteins, 13.4 p. 354

Venezuela, 5.1 p. 113, 19.4 p. 543

vernacular (perceptual) regions, 1.2 p. 18, 1.2 p. 18m

vertical integration, 13.2 p. 344

Vietnam
boundaries and, 9.4 p. 255
dual economies and, 18.2 p. 508
least-cost theory and, 18.3 p. 513
outsourcing and, 20.2 pp. 556–557
shifting cultivation and, 14.1 p. 359
textile industry and, 18.2 p. 517

Vietnam conflict, 5.4 p. 130, 11.2 pp. 283–285

villages, 15.3 p. 414

vineyards, 12.2 p. 321m

Virginia, 3.4 p. 83f

viruses, 4.2 p. 97, pp. R1-R5. *See also specific diseases*

visa programs, 5.5 p. 133

visas, 9.4 p. 250

vloggers, 11.1 p. 282

voluntary assimilation, 7.3 p. 195

voluntary migration, 5.2 pp. 115–118, 5.2 p. 120, U2 p. 145

von Thünen model, 13.3 pp. 348–349, 13.3 p. 348f, U5 p. 394f

Voodoo, 8.4 p. 220

voting districts, 10.2 pp. 269–273

voting rights, 18.1 p. 502

Voting Rights Act, 10.2 p. 270

W

wages, 19.3 pp. 536–537, 19.3 p. 537f

Wales, 11.1 p. 278

walkability, 17.1 p. 453

Wallerstein, Immanuel, U1 p. 53, 19.4 p. 541, U7 p. 572

Wallerstein's world system theory
colonialism, imperialism and, 18.1 p. 500
economic development, employment and, 18.2 p. 505
globalization and, 19.4 pp. 541–542, 19.4 p. 542f, U7 p. 572m
overview of, 1.3 p. 21, 1.3 p. 22f, U1 p. 53

Walloon people, 11.1 p. 280

walls, 5.4 p. 131, 5.4 p. 131f, 15.4 p. 427

Walt Disney Company, 17.1 p. 459

Wariou, Fatima, C2 p. 26f

wars, 4.1 p. 89, 4.1 p. 90, 5.3 p. 125, 14.3 p. 379. *See also specific wars*

Washington, D.C., 15.4 p. 422

Washington, D.C. Metro system, 1.2 p. 17m, 1.2 p. 18

waste, U5 p. 397f, 20.3 p. 560

water resources
agricultural hearths and, 12.3 p. 325

agriculture and, 12.1 p. 308, 12.1 p. 309, 14.1 pp. 360–362, 14.1 p. 365
biotechnology and, 14.2 p. 372
city sites and, 15.1 p. 404
future cities and, 15.3 p. 417, 15.3 p. 419
hydroelectric power and, 18.2 pp. 509–511, 20.3 p. 563f
lithium in Bolivia and, U7 p. 569
population distribution and, 3.1 p. 65
soil and, 12.1 p. 308
sustainability and, 1.3 p. 23f, 20.3 p. 560
third agricultural revolution and, 12.4 pp. 333–334
urbanization and, 17.3 p. 472, 17.3 p. 473

waterpower, 15.1 p. 404, 18.1 p. 498, 18.2 pp. 509–511, 20.3 p. 563f

waterways, 13.4 p. 350, 15.2 p. 407

Watt, James, 18.1 pp. 496–497

We Act for Environmental Justice, 17.2 p. 469

weather, 12.1 p. 308, 14.3 p. 377

weathering, 12.1 p. 308

weaving, 18.1 pp. 496–497

Weber, Alfred, 18.3 p. 512, U7 p. 571f

Wei River Valley, 15.1 p. 403

Welsh language, 8.2 p. 212

Welsh people, 11.1 p. 278

Wesch, Michael, 11.1 p. 282

West African agricultural hearth, 12.3 p. 326m

West Bank wall, 5.4 p. 131

West Germany, 9.4 p. 255, 9.4 p. 255f

Western Punjabi language, 8.2 p. 208

wetlands, 14.1 p. 362

wet-rice agriculture, 12.2 p. 314, 12.2 p. 321m

WFP. *See* World Food Programme

whaling, 6.3 p. 164

wheat, 12.4 p. 333, 13.3 p. 349

Whitney, Eli, 18.1 p. 498

Whittlesey, Derwent S., 12.2 p. 320

widowhood, 19.2 p. 532

Wild, Andy, U1 p. 61

Wild Mile project (Chicago), 17.3 p. 473

wilderness, future cities and, 15.3 p. 418

wildfires, U1 p. 57m, 17.3 p. 474f

wind, 12.1 p. 309

Wisconsin, 6.1 p. 156, 10.2 p. 272, 20.1 p. 550

women. *See also* gender
agriculture and, 14.1 p. 368, 14.4 p. 384m, 14.4 pp. 384–387
economic sectors and, 18.2 pp. 507–508, 18.2 p. 507f
empowerment of, 19.3 pp. 537–538
gender disparities and, 19.2 pp. 527–531
Green Revolution and, 12.4 p. 335
human development and, 19.1 p. 524
industrialization and, 18.1 p. 501
investing in, 19.3 p. 538
in leadership, 19.3 p. 538f
urban land tenure and, 17.2 p. 468

women's empowerment, 19.2 pp. 528–529

Woods, Lorna Gail, 7.1 p. 180f

woodworking, 12.4 pp. 330–331

wool manufacturing, 15.2 p. 409

workforce training programs, 20.1 p. 550

World Bank, 14.1 pp. 365–366, 20.2 p. 552

world cities, 15.4 pp. 421–422, 15.4 p. 421f

World Cup (Soccer), 7.2 p. 191

World Food Programme (WFP), 14.3 p. 378f

world hunger maps, 14.3 p. 378f

world system theory. *See* Wallerstein's world system theory

World Trade Center attack, 11.2 p. 283, 11.3 p. 288

World Trade Organization (WTO), 20.1 pp. 548–549, 20.1 p. 549m

World War I, 11.2 p. 283

World War II, 5.1 p. 113, 5.2 pp. 115–116, 5.3 p. 122, 9.3 p. 249, 11.2 p. 283

World Wildlife Fund (WWF), 2.2 p. 34f

WTO. *See* World Trade Organization

WWF. *See* World Wildlife Fund

X

xenophobia, 5.4 p. 130

Xingu River (Brazil), 18.2 pp. 509–511

Y

Yangtze River, 14.1 p. 362

Yangtze River Valley, 3.1 p. 65, 3.2 p. 71f, 15.4 p. 423

Yanukovych, Viktor, 11.1 p. 279

yellow vests movement, 11.3 p. 288

Yemen, 14.3 p. 379

YogaGlo app, 20.2 p. 556

Yorubans, 7.3 pp. 195–196

Yousafzai, Malala, 19.3 p. 538f

YouTube, 11.1 p. 282

Yugoslavia, 9.2 p. 246, 9.3 p. 247, 9.4 p. 254, U4 p. 296m

Yukon Territory, Canada, 11.1 p. 280

Yunus, Muhammad, 19.3 p. 539

Z

Zaatari refugee camp (Jordan), 16.3 p. 445

zakat, U3 p. 229

Zambia, 14.1 p. 365, 19.3 p. 537

Zara, 20.2 p. 556

Zenana Bagh (Delhi, India), 6.3 p. 166

zero-tolerance immigration policy, 5.5 p. 133

Zika virus, 4.2 p. 98, 4.2 p. 98m

Zimbabwe, 13.1 p. 339

Zionism, 8.4 p. 225

zones, hardiness (USDA), U5 p. 392f

zones of abandonment, 17.2 p. 462

zoning
affordable housing and, 17.2 p. 466
growth management and, 17.1 pp. 455–456
High Line and, 17.2 p. 471
housing density and, 16.2 p. 443
housing diversity and, 17.1 pp. 456–457
overview of, U6 p. 489m
smart-growth and, 17.1 p. 454
urbanization and, 15.2 p. 409
American Recovery and Reinvestment Act, 1129
American Red Cross, 395

ACKNOWLEDGEMENTS

PHOTOGRAPHIC CREDITS

Cover: Didier Marti/Getty Images. Back Cover: d3sign/Getty Images. iii (t) © Cengage Learning. (c) © Ken Martin/National Geographic Learning/Cengage Learning. (b) © Mark Thiessan/National Geographic Learning/Cengage Learning. iv (l) © National Geographic Learning/Cengage Learning. (c) © Parisa Meymand. (r) © Anita Palmer. v (row-1 L-R) Lynsey Addario, Ken Kobersteen/National Geographic Image Collection, Jen Shook, David Gill/National Geographic Image Collection. (row-2 L-R) Courtesy of Jennifer Burney, © Rachel Sussman, Mark Thiessen/National Geographic Image Collection, Courtesy of Zachary Damato, Courtesy of Wade Davis, Guillermo de Anda, Michael Wells. (row-3 L-R) Meghan Dhaliwal, © Steph Martyniuk, Courtesy of Maria Silvina Fenoglio, Esri, RANDALL SCOTT/National Geographic Image Collection, Ruben Rodriguez Perez/National Geographic Learning/Cengage Learning, James Richardson/National Geographic Image Collection. (row-4 L-R) David Guttenfelder/National Geographic Image Collection, Mark Thiessan/National Geographic Learning/Cengage Learning, RANDALL SCOTT/National Geographic Image Collection, MARK THIESSEN/National Geographic Image Collection, © freddieclaire, Brian Nehlson/National Geographic Learning, National Geographic Learning. (row-5 L-R) Courtesy of Andrés Ruzo, Chiun-Kai Shih/National Geographic Image Collection, Rebecca Hale/National Geographic Image Collection, Rebecca Hale/National Geographic Image Collection, Mark Thiessen, RANDALL SCOTT/National Geographic Image Collection, Sora Devore/National Geographic Image Collection. (row-6 L-R) RANDALL SCOTT/National Geographic Image Collection, © Richard Stanmeyer, George Steinmetz, Kat Keene Hogue/National Geographic Image Collection, Matt Moyer, © Little Leapling Photography. vi Vicki Jauron, Babylon and Beyond Photography/Getty Images. vii Photographer is my life./Getty Images. viii Giles Clarke/Getty Images. ix Chung Sung-Jun/Getty Images. x Carlton Ward/National Geographic Image Collection. xi Poras Chaudhary/The Image Bank/Getty Images. xii Bloomberg/Getty Images. 1 (l) Robert L. Booth/National Geographic Image Collection. (r) K M Asad. 2-3 Vicki Jauron, Babylon and Beyond Photography/Getty Images. 3 Paul Bruins/Getty Images. 5 (t) Enric Sala/National Geographic Image Collection. (b) National Geographic Maps. (inset) Rebecca Hale/National Geographic Image Collection. 6 ChrisBoswell/Getty Images. 8 kyoshino/Getty Images. 11 Mario Wezel/National Geographic Image Collection. 13 Vincent Laforet/The New York Times. 14 (t) Cory Richards/National Geographic Image Collection. (inset) © Rachel Sussman. 17 Martin Shields/Alamy Stock Photo. 19 Catalin Lazar/Shutterstock.com. 23 ISSOUF SANOGO/Getty Images. 26 Michael Zumstein/Agence VU/Redux. 29 trekandshoot/Alamy Stock Photo. 32 NASA Images. 33 Wayne State University | Center for Urban Studies. 34 AFP Contributor/Getty Images. 35 (t) DigitalGlobe/ScapeWare3d/Getty Images. (inset) © freddieclaire. 36 The History Collection/Alamy Stock Photo. 42 Agricultural Research Center, USDA. 47 (t) De Agostini/Universal Images Group/Alamy Stock Photo. (inset) Sora Devore/National Geographic Image Collection. 50 Craig Cutler/National Geographic Image Collection. 57 Matthew W. Chwastyk, NG Staff. 58-59 Photographer is my life./Getty Images. 59 Tim Martin/Cavan Images. 61 (t) John Stanmeyer/National Geographic Image Collection. (bl) Paul Salopek/National Geographic Image Collection. (br) Paul Salopek/National Geographic Image Collection. 62 Amos Chapple/Getty Images. 66 AP Images/Brendan Smialowski. 69 (t) Lillygol Sedaghat. (inset) RANDALL SCOTT/National Geographic Image Collection. 71 Xinhua/eyevine/Redux. 73 Nirian/Getty Images. 80 Randy Olson/National Geographic Image Collection. 82 JUNIOR D. KANNAH/Getty Images. 86 yusufozluk/iStock/Getty Images. 91 Chris De Bode/Panos Pictures/Redux. 96 AP Images/Al-hadji Kudra Maliro. 97 (t) BSIP SA/Alamy Stock Photo. (inset) Chiun-Kai Shih/National Geographic Image Collection. 99 Barry Lewis/Alamy Stock Photo. 101 Ami Vitale/National Geographic Image Collection. 104 Robin Hammond/National Geographic Image Collection. 110 REUTERS/Jorge Silva. 114 JOHNNY MILANO/The New York Times. 117 Bettmann/Getty Images. 119 (t) Richard Barnes/State of Exception. (inset) Michael Wells. 121 REUTERS/Kim Kyung-Hoon. 124 ERIC ROJAS/The New York Times. 126 (t, b) Lynsey Addario. 127 (t, b) Lynsey Addario/Reportage/Getty Images. 129 The Museum of Modern Art/Licensed by Scala/Art Resource, NY © 2019 The Jacob and Gwendolyn Knight Lawrence Foundation, Seattle/Artists Rights Society (ARS), New York. 131 GUILLERMO ARIAS/AFP/Getty Images. 133 The Washington Post/Getty Images. 136 (t) Russell Kord/Alamy Stock Photo. (c) JeffG/Alamy Stock Photo. (b) LAIF/Redux. 140 © Mahmud Hossain Opu. 148-149 Giles Clarke/Getty Images. 149 Jekaterina Sahmanova/Getty Images. 151 (t) Gabriel Scarlett/National Geographic Image Collection. (bl) BANCO CENTRAL DE RESERVA DEL PERÚ, Lima, Perú. Photo by: Kenneth Garrett. (br) Photo 12/Getty Images. 152 Alyssa Schukar/The New York Times. 153 Kirsten Luce. 154 age fotostock/Alamy Stock Photo. 156 Joe Brusky/Overpass Light Brigade. 157 Sean Pavone/Shutterstock.com. 159 ZUMA Press, Inc./Alamy Stock Photo. 160 Erin Xavier/Cengage Learning. 162 SOPA Images/Getty Images. 164 PRAKASH SINGH/Getty Images. 166 Pete Muller/National Geographic Image Collection. 169 GREG WINSTON/National Geographic Image Collection. 171 Gonzalo Azumendi/Getty Images. 172 (t) Sandhya Narayanan. (inset) MARK THIESSEN/National Geographic Image Collection. 178 El Dedeque/500px/Getty Images. 180 (tl) Sedrick Huckaby/National Geographic Image Collection. (tr) Elias Williams. (bl) Sedrick Huckaby/National Geographic Image Collection. (br) Elias Williams. 181 marchello74/Shutterstock.com. 184 Godong/Getty Images. 187 Thierry Ollivier/Getty Images News/Getty Images. 189 Kevin Winter/Getty Images. 191 Mao Siqian Xinhua/eyevine/Redux. 192 (t) Ken Kobersteen/National Geographic Image Collection. (b) William Albert Allard/National Geographic Image Collection. 193 (t, b) William Albert Allard/National Geographic Image Collection. 196 Daniel Kudish. 197 Jonny White/Alamy Stock Photo. 200 David Degner/The New York Times. 202 SIRIOH Co., LTD/Alamy Stock Photo. 211 Amos Chapple/Getty Images. 213 Graham Hughes/Canadian Press Images. 214 Dan Kitwood/Getty Images. 217 (t, inset) Courtesy of Wade Davis. 218 REUTERS/Amit Dave. 222 Hindustan Times/Getty Images. 224 GALI TIBBON/Getty Images. 228 Lynsey Addario. 236-237 Chung Sung-Jun/Getty Images. 237 Craig Ruttle/Redux. 239 (t) RICHARD NOWITZ/National Geographic Image Collection. (b) Courtesy of Aziz Abu Sarah. 240 NurPhoto/Getty Images. 241 Korea: The 'Kangnido Map' of the Eastern Hemisphere as known to the Chinese and Koreans in the 15th century, 1470 CE/Pictures From History/Bridgeman Images. 245 JR.ART.NET/Redux. 250 Kirsten Luce. 251 AP Images/Yonhap, Lim Byung-shik. 252 (t, b) David Guttenfelder/National Geographic Image Collection. 253 (t, b) David Guttenfelder/National Geographic Image Collection. 255 DC Premiumstock/Alamy Stock Photo. 260 The Washington Post/Getty Images. 262 (t) Courtesy of Anna Antoniou. (inset) Jen Shook. 268 Wayne R Bilenduke/Getty Images. 276 Dan Kitwood/Getty Images. 282 (t) Bloomberg/Getty Images. (inset) © Little Leapling Photography. 284 REUTERS/Jean Bizimana. 287 © Patrick Chappatte. 289 Stoyan Vassev/Getty Images. 290 REUTERS/Vasily Fedosenko. 291 YASIN AKGUL/Getty Images. 294 JUAN ARREDONDO/National Geographic Image Collection. 302-303 Carlton Ward/National Geographic Image Collection. 303 Dani Salva/VWPics/Redux. 305 (t) Jim Richardson/National Geographic Image Collection. (b) KEYSTONE/Christian Beutler/Redux. 306 georgeclerk/Getty Images. 309 GIANLUIGI GUERCIA/Getty Images. 311 Tuul & Bruno Morandi/Getty Images. 313 (l) Aluma Images/Stockbyte/Getty Images. (r) Dreamframer/Getty Images. 314 topten22photo/Getty Images. 315 (l) fotoVoyager/Getty Images. (c) Christian Hinkle/Shutterstock.com. (r) yorkfoto/Getty Images. 319 John Stanmeyer/National Geographic Image Collection. 322 (t,b) George Steinmetz. 323 (t, b) George Steinmetz. 330 Precision Graphics/National Geographic Learning. 331 World History Archive/Alamy Stock Photo. 334 ROMEO GACAD/Getty Images. 335 Majority World/Getty Images. 338 Tim Rue/Getty Images. 341 Blaine Harrington III/Getty Images. 342 Craig F. Walker/Getty Images. 347 (t) BRIAN FINKE/National Geographic Image Collection. (inset) Kat Keene Hogue/National Geographic Image Collection. 351 Philippe Aimar/Science Source. 358 Brian J. Skerry/National Geographic Image Collection. 361 (tl, tr) USGS. (b) Eddie Gerald/Getty Images. 363 AFP/Getty Images. 364 REUTERS/Ueslei Marcelino. 366 Karel Prinsloo/Arete/Rockefeller Foundation/AGRA. 367 (t) Jorge Fernandez/Alamy Stock Photo. (inset) RANDALL SCOTT/National Geographic Image Collection. 373 Xinhua News Agency/Getty Images. 374 Eric TSCHAEN/REA/Redux. 376 RONALDO SCHEMIDT/Getty Images. 379 © Bob Stefko Photography. 382 © Michela Dai Zovi as Bugs for Beginners, https://www.bugs4beginners.com. 383 (t) Lennart Woltering. (inset) Courtesy of Jennifer Burney. 386 © 2018 BCI/Khaula Jamil. 387 AMANDA LUCIER/The New York Times. 390 Luca Locatelli/National Geographic Image Collection. 398-399 Poras Chaudhary/The Image Bank/Getty Images. 399 Oscar Ruiz Cardeña. 401 (t) dePablo/Zurita/laif/Redux. (bl) Image by cuppyuppycake/Getty Images. (br) National Geographic Learning. 402 Chanin Wardkhian/Getty Images. 405 Konstantin Kalishko/Alamy Stock Photo. 406 (t) Michael Frachetti. (inset) ARQ Project. 408 CHRIS HILL/National Geographic Image Collection. 411 SAKhanPhotography/Getty Images. 415 Eric Lafforgue/Art in All of Us/Getty Images. 416-417 ©Jason Treat, NG Staff. Art and Source: Skidmore, Owings & Merrill (SOM). 418-419 ©Jason Treat, NG Staff. Art and Source: Skidmore, Owings & Merrill (SOM). 422 Vivek Prakash/Reuters. 423 xPacifica/National Geographic Image Collection. 424-425 CLARE TRAINOR/National Geographic Image Collection. 426-427 CLARE TRAINOR/National Geographic Image Collection. 430 Andrew Moore/National Geographic Image Collection. 434 pawel.gaul/Getty Images. 437 Orbon Alija/Getty Images. 438 RODGER BOSCH/Getty Images. 441 Kyodo News/Getty Images. 442 Abstract Aerial Art/Getty Images. 445 (t) Courtesy of T.H. Culhane. (inset) Mark Thiessen/National Geographic Image Collection. 446 Francis Dean/Getty Images. 447 View Pictures/Getty Images. 448 Ruben Rodriguez Perez/National Geographic Learning/Cengage Learning. 452 Massimo Borchi/Atlantide Phototravel/Getty Images. 454 Andrew Moore/National Geographic Image Collection. 458 Jane Sweeney/Getty Images. 461 Ewing Galloway\Uig/Shutterstock. 463 City Survey Files, compiled 1935 – 1940, ARC Identifier 720357 / MLR Number A1 39, Series from Record Group 195: Records of the Federal Home Loan Bank Board, 1933–1989. 465 Peeter Viisimaa/The Image Bank/Getty Images. 467 (t, b) Petrut Calinescu/Panos Pictures/Redux. 469 Esther Horvath. 471 Kobby Dagan/VWPics/Redux. 473 (t, b)

Courtesy of Zachary Damato. 474 Brook Mitchell/Getty Images. 475 (t, b) Courtesy of Maria Silvina Fenoglio. 477 Luca Locatelli/National Geographic Image Collection. 478 Jason Treat/National Geographic Image Collection. 479 Davide Fiammenghi/Getty Images. 482 David Guttenfelder/National Geographic Image Collection. 490-491 Bloomberg/Getty Images. 491 Marka/Getty Images. 493 (t, b) Joel van Houdt/National Geographic Image Collection. 494 TimSiegert-batcam/Getty Images. 496 (l) Damon Casarez/Redux. (r) Keith Beaty/Getty Images. 502 Department of Sanitation New York. 507 Handout/Google/Reuters. 509 (l, r) NASA Earth Observatory images by Joshua Stevens, using Landsat data from the U.S. Geological Survey. 510 (t) Steph Martyniuk. (b) Aaron Vincent Elkaim. 511 Aaron Vincent Elkaim. 512 AP Images/Paul Sancya. 517 Edward Burtynsky. 520 Lucy Young/eyevine/Redux. 523 RosalreneBetancourt 9/Alamy Stock Photo. 524 NurPhoto/Getty Images. 531 Lynsey Addario/Getty Images Reportage. 532 (t) Matt Moyer. (b) Amy Toensing/National Geographic Image Collection. 533 (t, b) Amy Toensing/National Geographic Image Collection. 535 DINA LITOVSKY/National Geographic Image Collection. 538 (tl) SALVATORE DI NOLFI/EPA-EFE/Shutterstock. (tcl) Steve Jennings/Getty Images. (tcr) Paul Morigi/Getty Images. (tr) Juan Carlos Hidalgo/EPA/Shutterstock. (bl) Jennica Stephenson/National Geographic Image Collection. (bcl) UN Photo/Manuel Elias. (bcr) ALBA VIGARAY/EPA-EFE/Shutterstock. (br) BRENDAN ESPOSITO/EPA-EFE/Shutterstock. 539 Philippe Lissac/Godong/Panos Pictures/Redux. 546 Joe Buglewicz/The New York Times. 551 Bloomberg/Getty Images. 553 Justin Sullivan/Getty Images. 555 Bloomberg/Getty Images. 561 Randy Olson/National Geographic Image Collection. 563 (l) Claudiad/Getty Images. (r) Bloomberg/Getty Images. 564 Pete McBride/National Geographic Image Collection. 565 (t) Andrés Ruzo. (inset) Sofía Ruzo. 568 CÉDRIC GERBEHAYE/National Geographic Image Collection.

R0: STR/Getty Images. R1 Alissa Eckert, MS; Dan Higgins, MAMS/CDC (Centers for Disease Control and Prevention). R3 2020 John Hopkins University. R5 Ethan Miller/Getty Images.

Unless indicated otherwise, all maps are created by Mapping Specialists and illustrations are Cengage-owned.